P9-BJV-167

PICK the RIGHT PLANT

PICK the RIGHT PLANT

By the Editors of Time-Life Books
ALEXANDRIA, VIRGINIA

Table of Contents

The Seven Principles of Plant Selection

Picking the right plant depends on making a match between what a plant needs and what you and your garden can provide. No matter how appealing a plant may look, displayed in a catalog or nursery, it will not grow well in your yard if you don't have the climate and gardening conditions it favors. Fortunately success and satisfaction are within reach for everyone who considers climate and conditions by using the seven principles of plant selection: Light, Type of Plant, Hardiness, Height, Soil and Moisture, Care, and Interest. These principles serve as a guide to picking the right plant and are fully explained on the following pages. Because your success starts with matching the light requirements of each plant to the conditions in your garden, the encyclopedia chapters that follow are organized according to the plants' preferences for sun and shade. Each entry contains information about light requirements and the other six principles. And as you read, you will find yourself increasingly sure about what plants to grow to create a beautiful, flourishing garden wherever you live.

1
Light

Select plants that thrive in your light conditions

One of the easiest and most important steps in selecting plants is knowing the amount of light each plant requires. The promise of a spectacular garden can be kept only when plants are well suited to their conditions. Light plays such a fundamental role that this book has been arranged according to the light needs of each plant.

All green plants depend on light to manufacture the food they need—the process known as photosynthesis. But all plants do not need the same amount of light to accomplish this. Some plants thrive in the bright light of uninterrupted sun, but will wither in deep shade. Many plants, such as blanket flowers and sunflowers, produce strong stems and bountiful brightly colored blossoms when grown in full sun, the environment they prefer. If grown in shade, however, these plants will have spindly stems and few, pale flowers. Other plants, such as impatiens, efficiently use small amounts of light that filter through shady trees to produce beautiful blooms and foliage, but scorch in full sun. Between these extremes are plants that do well in a range of conditions, from mostly sun to mostly shade.

To help you select the best plants for your yard, the plants in this book have been grouped into one of four categories: full sun, mostly sun, mostly shade, and full shade. Many plants will be able to grow in more than one set of conditions, but most will grow best only in one.

Amounts of Sunlight

The light preferences of plants don't change significantly over time, but the intensity of light that your yard receives varies with the time of day, weather condition, and season. Every day as the sun moves across the sky, patterns of shade and light change in your yard. Even these daily patterns change with the seasons. Watching the sun and shade patterns of your yard will help you determine the light category of each area. Once you know the light availability in your yard, select the plants that prefer those conditions.

Full Sun

Full sun is anyplace that is not shaded by permanent objects or structures, such as trees or houses. Full-sun sites occur most often on southern exposures or large, flat open areas. On a bright summer day, a full-sun spot will receive unobstructed light from dawn to dusk. The only "shade" it experiences is caused by clouds blocking the sun. Most full-sun plants use this abundant light to produce strong stems, plentiful flower buds, and thick, dark green leaves. When grown in shady locations full-sun plants often have fewer and less colorful flowers, thin, weak stems, and leaves that turn yellow and drop from lack of light.

Mostly Sun

Plants that grow in mostly sunny places have full sun for the majority of the day. Usually these places receive shade in the early morning or late afternoon from structures or nearby trees, and full sun for the remainder of the day. They are often in areas with eastern, western, and partially obstructed southern exposures. These plants can often adapt to full-sun situations, but sometimes the leaves are discolored or scorched by prolonged exposure to intense light.

Mostly Shade

These places are shaded for most of the day, but may receive some sun, either directly for short periods of time, or as dappled light filtered by a leafy canopy. Ordinarily, the sun shines directly on these sites for only a few hours, usually around midday. They are often found on eastern, western, and northern exposures. Plants that love mostly shade are efficient at photosynthesis because they must thrive where the intensity of light is from 10 percent to 25 percent of direct sunlight. To collect the energy they need these plants have leaves that are thinner and often softer than those of plants growing in direct light. Plants that like mostly shady places do not have good defenses against intense light, however, and are quickly damaged when planted in direct sunlight.

Light intensity varies from place to place and season to season within this backyard garden.

Full Shade

Plants in full shade receive only indirect light throughout the day and are often found growing in deep forests and on northern exposures. Places of full shade may exist beneath deciduous trees, where they receive some sun in the springtime but are shaded during the majority of the growing season. These plants grow slowly and need less food than other plants. Shade-loving plants are sensitive to intense light and quickly die when planted in full sun or even in mostly sunny locations. Plants included in Chapter 4 (Plants for Places with Full Shade) will thrive in the shade.

2
Type of Plant

Select the kind of plant that fits your needs

Although it is possible to have a garden made up entirely of just one plant type—perennials, for instance—most gardens incorporate several types. The best plants for your garden depend on your goals. Gardens that contain a variety of plants can be more visually appealing than a planting composed of one type. A garden brimming with blooms for cutting could include annuals, perennials, and shrubs. Spring bulbs add early-season blooms. Herbs make a garden functional as well as beautiful. Vines, ground covers, ferns, and ornamental grasses can help create a yard that is varied, attractive, and easy to care for. Trees can provide shade for your house or a windbreak.

The Seven Plant Categories

This book divides the plants into the seven major types that are described below. Specific plants within each type can be found in the following chapters, which are organized according to amounts of sunlight needed—from full sun to full shade. If, for example, you want perennials for a garden area that's mostly sunny, turn to Chapter 2 (Plants for Mostly Sunny Places) and select from the section on perennials.

Annuals

Annuals are plants that grow in the garden for only one year before they die. They include true annuals, such as ageratum and baby's-breath, which complete their entire life cycle in one growing season; biennials, such as evening primrose and Queen-Anne's-lace, which complete their life cycle in two growing seasons; and tender perennials grown as annuals, such as geranium and impatiens, which must be replanted annually in colder climates (or potted and brought indoors).

Annuals and plants grown as annuals tend to have a long blooming season, which makes them wonderful for flower gardens, especially cutting gardens. They can be planted in the wake of spring-blooming bulbs or used to fill empty spots in perennial beds and borders, and to edge walkways and paths. Use them as a bright ground cover or line your porch or doorstep with potted annuals to create a cheerful and welcoming entryway. Annuals on the whole are sun lovers, but there are some—

coleus and pansy, for instance—that do well in mostly shady places.

Annuals offer four distinct benefits: low cost, availability, ease of growing, and a range of color. They can be purchased as container-grown plants or seed, and in many cases may be self-seeding or produce seed that can be collected and resown the following year. Beginning gardeners like the instant effect of container-grown plants, but growing annuals from seed is quite easy too. Beginning and experienced gardeners alike look to annuals to add a wide range of bright color. Feel free to experiment with color and you will soon find the combinations that please you and work harmoniously in their setting.

Over most of the country, annuals generally bloom throughout the summer months. Northern gardeners often plant varieties that bloom earlier and later as well. Early bloomers, such as cornflower and sweet pea, display color as early as May and often continue throughout the season. Late-blooming annuals, such as china aster, sunflower, and annual phlox, will first flower in summer and then continue to bloom until the first frost.

Perennials

More enduring than an annual, a perennial will last through more than two seasons of growth and often much longer. Compared to annuals, perennials tend to have a shorter season of bloom, but the season may begin earlier in spring or end later in fall. The main bloom of perennials comes from late spring through summer.

Dividing perennials is a quick and economical method of increasing your stock of plants. Perennials can also be purchased from garden centers. One good mature plant can often be separated into two or three, and while the blossoms may be thin the first year, perennials grow rapidly. Many perennials are easily grown from seed. You'll need patience, though, as most of them do not come into bloom until the second season.

Pick a variety of plants for your garden to ensure an attractive setting with interest throughout the seasons.

Bulbs

For our purposes, the term *bulbs* includes true bulbs as well as rhizomes, corms, and tubers. Bulbs are a gardener's best friend. Planted at the right time and at the right depth, they're virtually guaranteed to bloom with little effort. Fortunately, it's almost impossible to plant bulbs at the wrong time, because they are usually available only when they should go into the ground. Bulbs are categorized according to their time of bloom—early spring, spring, summer, and fall. Spring bulbs, such as crocuses, daffodils, and tulips, need to be planted in late fall so the plants can make roots before the ground freezes.

All bulbous plants have periods of growth and flowering followed by a rest period known as dormancy. Bulbs are usually sold in this dormant state. Once purchased, they should be planted within a few days. Planting bulbs is relatively straightforward, but each bulb type is different and needs to be placed according to the depth and spacing it prefers. To get flowers of the same type of bulb at peak bloom simultaneously, be sure their planting holes are all the same depth. That is easy for plants like bearded iris that are placed near the surface. More care is required where bulbs need to be dug in deeply, as with summer hyacinth, which goes in 6 to 8 inches deep.

Herbs

Herbs add a little "spice" to your garden. Especially for new gardeners, herbs may be the easiest, most rewarding of all plants to grow. Not only is an herb garden attractive and fragrant but it is also useful. Herbs are grown for dyes, teas, potpourris, and medicinal purposes, but the most popular use for herbs is in cooking. Herbs may be picked and used fresh, or dried or frozen for use throughout winter.

Most herbs require very little space and aren't too fussy about soil quality. Many prefer an open, sunny spot in which to grow. Mint, chives, and parsley, however, will grow perfectly well in partial shade. Wherever you decide to plant your herbs, remember to leave easy access to them for cutting. The best spot, if you plan to use herbs for cooking, is just outside your kitchen door.

Many annual herbs, such as basil, summer savory, and borage, can be started outdoors. Coriander, cumin, anise, dill, and fennel all grow quickly and take from 2 to 3 months from sowing to harvest. All the annuals ripen in the first season. Perennial herbs, such as tarragon and rosemary, may be started indoors and harvested in the first season. Some herbs, such as caraway, do not produce seed until the second season. Be aware that certain spreading herbs such as chives, mint, horseradish, and comfrey can take over the garden. Plant these in individual pots sunk into the ground.

Vines and Ground Covers

Vines are used for ornament as well as for screening walls or objectionable views. Generally, vines can be divided into three groups depending on how they climb. Some, like Boston ivy, climb by attaching small fuzzy-stemmed roots to a support. Others, like clematis and grape, climb

by winding tendrils or leaflike appendages around the object on which they are growing. The third group, including bittersweet and wisteria, climb by twining stems. You should know in advance how each vine climbs so that a proper support can be provided, and so you can match the growth habit of the vine to the space in your garden. Some vines can also be used for ground cover.

Ground covers are attractive, low-maintenance alternatives to a lawn or flower bed. Creeping ground covers like ivy spread along the surface of the ground, forming new plants by rooting sections of their long stems into the top layer of the soil. They can be used to cover large areas beautifully. Some popular ground covers have dense foliage that prevents weeds from getting established underneath. Ground covers are also a perfect plant type for locations with less-than-ideal conditions, such as full shade, bare or rocky slopes, or wet soils. Some types of ground covers, such as partridgeberry and vinca, grow into thick ground-hugging carpets of foliage that provide a beautiful backdrop to the landscape; they are unobtrusive except when in bloom. Others such as sweet woodruff or bamboo are much taller and can function both as a ground cover and as a screen. There is also considerable variation in height among different species of the same plant. For instance, *Ardisia japonica* is a mat-forming ground cover 8 to 12 inches tall, while *A. crenata* stands shrublike at about 6 feet tall. Using a combination of different ground covers, you can form a stunning texture of varying heights and colors. Decide how you want to use ground covers and select the species carefully to match your plans.

Ferns and Ornamental Grasses

These plants offer many advantages, such as a natural, informal appearance and an attractive habitat for butterflies, birds, and other wildlife. Some species spread vigorously, while others form stately stands.

A fern is a green perennial without flowers or fruit. Its leaves are often the fern's primary interest and can be found in an array of sizes and forms. Some prefer dry, sunny places; others are at home in shady swamps. Adaptable to a wide variety of purposes and locations, ferns can be planted in exposed northern spots where flowers will not grow, along walkways, in masses; or along walls and banks. Some spread by creeping horizontally and can even be used as ground covers.

Ornamental grasses include annuals and perennials. Annual grasses are grown for their variety and color of flowers and seed heads, while perennials are grown chiefly for their feathery flowers and foliage. Annuals can be sown directly in the garden in spring or sown in flats in a greenhouse and transplanted when there is no danger of frost. While many perennial grasses can be grown from seed, it's often faster to buy established plants from a nursery or mail-order company.

Shrubs and Trees

Shrubs and trees should be a part of every permanent garden. They are beautiful in every season and provide nesting sites for birds. Selecting the right shrubs and trees for your garden is among the most important landscaping decisions you will make. Shrubs are most frequently used to give shape and background to gardens. They may be arranged to form restful or dramatic garden sanctuaries, or sheltered places for other plants. Shrubs may be used as hedges or windbreaks. Some, like heather, make ideal ground covers. There are thousands of varieties of shrubs, including the ever-popular azalea and rhododendron. Some flowering shrubs, like viburnums or some roses, display blossoms throughout the summer. Many shrubs have beautiful fall foliage. Be sure to make your selection based on hardiness, amount of sunlight, and type of soil.

The distinction between a tree and shrub is sometimes difficult to make. Generally, a shrub is a low, woody plant that has several stems instead of a single trunk. Trees are larger woody plants, most often with a single trunk. They range from small flowering plants about 10 feet tall, such as stewartia, to towering behemoths like pine and fir. They provide everything from shade to flowers and colorful bark, and add four-season interest that can last for generations. The massive size of trees offers protection from weather, such as when planted as windbreaks. Deciduous trees, which lose their leaves in fall and winter, create a varying texture of light

Lavender cotton on this bank forms an excellent slope cover and adds unusual texture to the terrain.

and shade throughout the year. Evergreen trees offer year-round shade and, depending on the variety, can add dramatic ornamental interest through the varying colors and shapes of cones and needles.

3

Hardiness

*Achieve gardening
success by knowing
what grows well
in your climate*

Hardiness is a complex subject with a simple bottom line—if a plant is to thrive it must be suited to your climate. The garden plants available today originated in scores of different climates all over the world. Your garden, wherever it may be, represents just one of those climates. Of the thousands of garden plants available, some will thrive in your garden's climate, others will just get by, and still more will perish. Picking the right plant, then, means matching the environmental conditions present in your garden to the hardiness of the plants. To make this process easier for everyone, hardiness maps have been created that depict general climate zones.

Winter Survival

Hardiness is a measure of how well a plant thrives in its growing environment as well as its resilience to changes in that environment. The factors that make up a plant's ever-changing environment include such diverse elements as soil moisture, depth of winter snow cover, summer humidity levels, and length of growing season. Even though there are dozens of variables that go into the definition of hardiness, the one most commonly used to produce hardiness maps is minimum winter temperatures: How much winter cold can a plant survive? This measure is far from perfect, but it offers a valuable index of how resilient any particular plant is. Using this idea, a hardiness map divides North America into numbered zones, with each number corresponding to an area's average minimum winter temperature range. By looking up your region on a hardiness map, it is easy to determine just which zone your garden is in.

The USDA Zone Map

The United States Department of Agriculture produces the most widely used hardiness map, which divides North America into 11 zones. The warmest of these regions, Zone 11 on the map, rarely experiences temperatures below freezing and includes tropical and subtropical climates. The coldest region, Zone 1, is north of the Arctic Circle in central Alaska and northern Canada where temperatures can plunge to 50°F below zero. This frigid region has a polar or subpolar climate. Between these extremes lie the remaining nine climate zones. Use the map on page 370 of this book to find your growing zone, then select the plants—from annuals to shrubs and trees—that will thrive where you live.

The zone range assigned to each plant in the encyclopedia chapters indicates where it will grow best. For example, the bunchberry has a hardiness range of Zones 2 to 6. This means it can survive Zone 2 winters and can also thrive as far south as Zone 6. However, it will not tolerate the climates farther south.

Hardiness and Heat

Minimum winter temperatures are not the only gauge of a plant's hardiness. Other complex factors include the length of winter and maximum summer temperatures. The adaptations that plants undergo to survive cold climates are different from those needed to thrive in hot climates. Many plants that thrive in cool northern regions need a level of winter cold for a specific number of days—a chill requirement—to grow well. These same plants may also be sensitive to summer heat and humidity.

While the USDA zone map addresses only winter hardiness, the heat and drought tolerance of plants is a subject of growing interest for gardeners. The concept of "summer hardiness" is the focus of a complementary plant-coding system and zone map being developed by the American Horticultural Society.

Backyard Hardiness

By using the USDA zone map and the hardiness range listed for each plant the process of selecting plants becomes much easier, but not quite foolproof. This is because hardiness zones are composed of a mosaic of microclimates with environments that are slightly warmer, colder, wetter, or drier than those of their neighbors. It is not unusual for a large backyard to have several microclimates. In some instances this can be frustrating, for a plant that will be perfectly happy in one location of the yard may die in another just a few feet away if pockets of cooler air collect there. For example,

A deciduous holly, 'Sunset' produces red fruit on bare branches in early winter. It has a hardiness range from Zones 3 to 9.

a cold-sensitive plant may do better on a slope than at the bottom of the slope or in a hollow where cold air naturally accumulates. Microclimates or backyard hardiness zones are especially important to consider when plants of borderline hardiness are considered for the garden. In those cases, knowledge of your backyard is important to gauge properly if a plant will thrive, and where it should be planted to ensure healthy growth. As your gardening experience grows, you will see the effects of microclimates in your area and be surprised and pleased to observe the myriad places that cold- or heat-sensitive plants have found a way to survive.

4

Height

Pick plants whose size fits your yard and garden

When planning a garden, plants should also be selected with form, shape, and growth patterns in mind. Selecting plants by mature height is a good way to assure your garden design will look great for years to come. Plant width and spread give you a good idea of how far apart to space plantings. Shape can also help you determine how much space you'll need for a particular type of plant. When in doubt, err on the side of too few plants. Crowding increases demands on the soil for water and nutrients, and can also make plants more susceptible to attack by insects and disease and induce weak, spindly growth.

Patterns of Growth

Each plant listed in this book includes a range of mature heights. As you look for plants that will flourish in your garden, be sure to note how tall each will be. Ultimately, mature height depends on the type of plant, the species and variety, and the climate or growing conditions in your area. While planning your garden, reserve the back of your flower beds or garden areas for the tallest plants, working your way down to the shortest plants to use as borders against your lawn or walkways.

Annuals

Most annuals tend to grow to heights of 2 feet or less, which makes them appropriate for the majority of flower beds and borders. Some varieties grow much taller and need to be placed at the back of the bed. Others, like edging lobelia, grow so low that they may be used along the front of walkways and borders. Annuals don't generally spread like other plant types, but they still need room to grow and fill out.

Perennials

When making your perennial selections choose a suitable shape and size of plant before considering color. After you have made your selection, plant in bold clumps and allow groups to drift into each other for best effect. Perennials grow rapidly. Once established, some will need to be divided nearly every year. It is impossible to be precise about planting distances for perennials, for some grow to about 3 feet across while others may grow to only 3 to 7 inches. As a general guideline to the number of perennials in a border, allow five plants for every 10 feet. They will appear a little thin at planting time but will soon spread and fill out. Overcrowding can distort the perennial's desired shape and reduce its flowering.

Bulbs

Bulbs come in many heights and shapes. Taller plants, like lilies and alliums, add variety to your garden. Small spring-flowering bulbs like anemones and galanthus need a shallow planting, whereas the taller tulips require a deeper planting to anchor them in the ground. Lilies, crocosmias, and cannas grow into tall, vigorous plants. Their bulbs must be planted deeper than other plants, such as irises and begonias. Generally, the taller the winter-flowering bulb, the deeper it should be planted. Some bulbs, like lilies, will spread wider with each season.

Herbs

The long-term growth pattern of herbs depends on whether they are annual or perennial. Annual herbs normally do not spread much, because they survive for only one season. Perennial herbs tend to spread as their root systems become more extensive. In your herb garden, consider a variety of heights to add visual interest. Consider too that a woody perennial herb, such as rosemary, can grow significantly taller in warmer climates.

Vines and Ground Covers

Vines and ground covers are vigorous by nature, and once growing may be hard to stop. Dutchman's-pipe can grow up to 30 feet in a season. For limited space or areas near a lawn, select plants that are easily controlled. These tend to be slower-growing varieties, such as climbing hydrangea. A ground cover, by the way, is not necessarily low to the ground, so be sure to check the height.

Ferns and Ornamental Grasses

Like vines and ground covers, ferns and ornamental grasses tend to grow and spread quickly. Ferns come in all shapes and sizes. In some ferns, rhizomes creep along just beneath the soil surface, sometimes branching, sometimes developing into a clump. If a fern clumps, its leaves go up in all directions. If it branches, it can spread over a whole hillside or meadow. When you're selecting ornamental grasses, especially perennial grasses, consider the final size

Combining plants of different heights can create spectacular vertical accent and the impression of cascading blossoms. Irises and yellow azalea highlight this perennial garden.

carefully. A mature clump of many grasses may produce a low mound of leaves in spring, followed by a 6-foot-tall spray of flowers in summer and fall.

Shrubs and Trees

Shrubs and trees vary greatly in their shapes and heights. Tree shapes can be categorized as columnar, conical, round, flat topped, or horizontal. Shrub shapes are categorized as prostrate, upright, or mounding. Heights range from less than 3 feet for dwarf shrubs to more than 100 feet for large trees. Before planting tall varieties, consider the site carefully. Mature trees can be damaged by or cause damage to utility lines, canopies of other trees, or roof overhangs. When planting a shrub or tree, be sure the site is wide enough to accommodate its eventual spread. ❧

5

Soil and Moisture

*Match plants
to your yard's
soil and moisture
conditions*

Next to sunlight, soil and water are the most important components of a successful garden. Soil anchors a plant and provides nutrients, air, and water. Some soils are too loose or shallow to be a good anchor, while others hold too much water or too few nutrients. There are three basic types of soil: sand, clay, and loam. Sandy soils are composed of coarse mineral particles that readily allow air and water to penetrate. Clay soils consist mostly of very fine mineral particles. They have better water retention than sandy soils, but tend to compact more, reducing the amount of air in the soil. Loams are the most desirable of the soil types because they include a mix of sand and clay particles that are "fluffed up" by the decomposed organic material, or humus, that holds the soil together. This combination provides the optimum levels of soil, air, and moisture for plants.

What kind of soil do you have? Try these two simple tests to determine the composition of your soil. First, firmly squeeze a handful of slightly moistened soil to form a ball and drop it from waist height onto a firm surface. If the ball flattens but does not crumble, your soil is mostly clay. If it scatters all over or won't even form a ball, the soil is mostly sand. If it breaks into particles that are pea size or smaller, the soil is a balanced loam. For the second test, dig a hole a foot deep, fill it with water, and then fill it again the next day. If all the water has not drained away within 12 hours, you have either clay soil or soil that is too compacted. The sandier your soil is, the more quickly the water will drain away.

Plant Preferences

Soil type is described in terms of moisture and drainage, fertility, and pH balance. All of the plant descriptions in this book include the plant's preferred soil type. Before you buy seed or transplants, or accept a cutting from another gardener, know what type of soil the plant prefers. Does it like moist, well-drained soil? If that's not the kind of soil you have, either choose another plant or adapt the soil you have by adding organic matter or building a raised bed.

Moisture and Drainage

Moisture is one of the most important components of soil. Drainage refers to how quickly and deeply water is absorbed and retained in the soil. Garden soils vary greatly in their ability to retain moisture. Sandy soil can be so well drained that moisture does not stay around the roots of plants long enough for proper growth. On the other hand, clay soils can hold water far too long, allowing the roots of plants to drown. The average garden needs 1 inch of water each week during the growing season, from either rainfall or the garden hose. Sandy soils, which warm up quickly in spring and dry out quickly in summer, may require more than 1 inch of water each week. Clay soils, which have properties opposite those of sand, may require less than 1 inch.

Probably the truest test for proper moisture is whether the soil 3 to 4 inches below the surface feels cool and moist (not wet) almost all the time. Soil in this condition has the proper balance of air and moisture. Soils that dry out to a greater depth between waterings are dry; those that are consistently moist just under the surface are moist. "Moist, well-drained soil" has a balance of sand, clay, and organic matter. If your soil is well drained with plentiful amounts of organic matter, you can grow a wide variety of plants.

The presence of vigorous spring-blooming azaleas like these is a telltale sign of soil pH that is slightly acid.

Acid or Alkaline

The pH of soil is a measure of how acid or alkaline the soil is. Soil pH is important because it determines the availability of nutrients for absorption by plant roots. To judge the approximate pH of your soil, look at native plants. If there are blueberries, pieris, conifers, Japanese maples, heaths, azaleas, or rhododendrons nearby, you may have acid soil. These plants require extra iron for growth, and iron dissolves better in acidic soils. If sweet clover or maiden pink dominates the meadows, you may have alkaline soil. Neutral to slightly alkaline soils are also preferred by clematis and baby's-breath.

Areas with plentiful rainfall, such as the East and Pacific Northwest, have soils that are acidic. Regions with less rainfall, such as much of the West, have mostly alkaline soils. If you want to grow a plant that requires a particular soil pH that you don't have, or if you don't know your soil pH, don't chance it. Have your soil tested or check with your county Cooperative Extension Service for the soil survey of your area.

The truth is, you can't do much about soil pH without a great deal of effort. If your soil is too acidic you can raise the pH gradually by adding lime every year. If it's too alkaline you may be able to lower your soil pH by adding organic matter or sulfur. But in the end it's easier to grow plants that like the pH balance of your soil than it is to change it. Fortunately there are plants that thrive in nearly every type of soil.

Improving Your Soil

Soil fertility is actually a combination of moisture, pH balance, and soil texture. Rich, fertile soil has abundant organic matter. Pale, sandy, chalky, or clay soils that have been derived from subsoil are poor in humus, which is decomposed organic matter. Some gardeners are fortunate enough to have beautiful loamy soil in which nearly everything flourishes. Most gardeners, though, learn to make the most out of what they have, gradually improving the soil year after year by adding compost or other organic matter. Improving your soil is an important part of making a more successful garden. The two areas where you can have the greatest impact are water retention and fertility.

Fertilizer

There are several ways to increase the fertility and moisture-holding capacity of your soil. Whatever type of soil you have, you can improve it by adding organic matter—lots of it. Experienced gardeners may have a supply of humus on hand in the form of a compost pile. New gardeners can buy commercially prepared compost or peat moss, or buy a bag of dry cow manure. In general fall is the best time to add amendments to the soil. Beds prepared in fall will be ready for planting in early spring.

Adding organic matter is easy, although physically demanding. Start with a small area and gradually increase the area you are improving. Add generous amounts of fertilizer and be sure to dig it in deeply, working it well into the soil. Then cover the spaded ground with a thick layer of leaves. Before covering, you may want to plant some spring bulbs that can be lifted out in late spring, at which time you can add new compost and plant your summer annuals.

Mulch

Another way to help soil conserve moisture is to spread mulch in layers around your plantings. Mulch keeps moisture in the soil from evaporating quickly, and it can also smother weeds. Generally, more water in the soil means a cooler soil temperature, so some gardeners use plastic mulch that retains both moisture and heat to get their transplants off to a fast start in early spring. Plastic mulch now comes in black, red, brown, and clear varieties, each with different light-screening and moisture-holding properties. Organic mulches, such as manure, act like plant food as they slowly decompose, reducing the need for fertilizing as they add nutrients to the soil. Spring is the best time to mulch, when the soil has begun to warm but is still moist.

Some plants prefer certain types of mulches, such as pine needles for rhododendrons, but generally the choice of which mulch to use is up to you. For mulching material you can use leaves, rotted cow manure, straw, grass cuttings, peat moss, old sawdust, pulverized pine bark, shredded newspaper, cocoa mulch (an aromatic mulch made from cocoa husks), salt hay (dried grass collected from sea marshes), or buckwheat hulls. In fact, any porous organic material will do well, although each mulch has its own advantages and disadvantages.

For example, rotted animal manure adds nutrients to the soil and helps to retain water, but it does not discourage weeds. Nonetheless, thoroughly rotted cow manure is excellent for mulching ornamental and fruit trees, shrubs and berry bushes, roses and asparagus, and perennial borders. These plants seem to benefit more than others from the organic material in manure. Hardwood chips act to prevent weeds and retain moisture but are largely organically inert and contribute little to enriching the soil. Pine needles are excellent for mulching rhododendrons, azaleas, evergreens, deciduous shrubs, and many native woodland plants. These plants all prefer acidic soil conditions and benefit from the acid that leaches into the soil from decomposing needles.

Peat is easily obtainable but expensive, and it must be soaked before using. Grass clippings are easy to obtain and free, although they are not a high-quality mulch. Spread in a thin layer an inch or two deep for a satisfactory temporary mulch. Straw permits excellent rain penetration but some may find it unattractive, and it may introduce weed seed into the garden. A 3-inch layer of decomposed sawdust retains moisture, smothers weeds, and has the added benefit of deterring slugs and snails. Pulverized pine bark also repels slugs and mice, which like to eat bulbs. Pine bark doesn't hold moisture as well as peat, but it's very attractive. Moistened newspapers covered with a thin layer of bark chips or other attractive mulch can be laid over beds to discourage weeds and retain moisture.

Soil Preparation

Preparing soil for planting can be the most difficult of all garden tasks—and the most important. For any plant to thrive, especially a permanent addition to the landscape such as a tree, shrub, perennial, or ground cover, it is important to dig deeply, loosening the soil and blending it with a generous measure of organic matter to lighten the soil and improve its drainage. Digging aerates the soil, and in the process covers up all weeds or spent manure. This requires driving the spade or fork almost vertically into the ground to its full depth and breaking up clumps. Do this when the ground is slightly to moderately moist, as weeds will then separate out of the clumps far more easily than if the earth is dry or overly wet.

The best time for digging is late fall, when the soil is usually moist, well aerated, and easiest to work. Turn the soil and then leave it in furrows instead of raking it flat. Frost and snow can compact smoothly raked beds, which may prevent water from percolating properly through the soil over the winter. Beds left turned into furrows over the winter will be ready for raking and planting in spring, especially if the soil is a light, sandy loam, which will not pack down. ❧

Soil preparation can be easier to manage when beds are kept to a reasonable size. To ensure best results, check your plants' requirements for fertilizer and mulch.

6

Care

*Know how much
attention each
plant needs
to grow well*

Care takes time. So the first step in selecting plants for your garden is to determine how much time you can devote to it. Garden care can be easier with a choice of plants that require minimal care. This is especially important if you have only weekend time to devote to gardening. A garden that is easy to maintain can allow you the time to develop more demanding landscaping projects as you gain experience. Choose plants that are adaptable to a wide range of climate and soil conditions, resist common pests and diseases, and require little or no staking and only infrequent dividing. Plants that can survive excess rain or drought without long-term damage are good choices. And, of course, giving plants the amount of sunlight they prefer will help them grow strong and healthy with little effort on your part.

Regular and Seasonal Care

Plant care includes both regular and seasonal care. Regular care refers to weeding, watering, and fertilizing the garden. Seasonal care includes soil preparation, spring planting, transplanting or dividing, pruning, and putting your garden to bed in fall. Some plants, such as viburnums, are easy to grow, and thrive in the garden with little attention. Other plants require more care, which may take the form of everything from pruning vigorous vines to lifting tender bulbs in fall. Every plant listed in this book includes a reference to care that can help guide you toward the best selections for your garden.

Annuals

Annuals are among the simplest of plants to grow, once you have selected the right plants for your light conditions. Plant them in spring, enjoy them all summer, and then dig them up in fall and compost.

Perennials

After planting, most perennials need a minimum of care and will bloom for years. Set perennial transplants in well-worked soil that has had some organic matter added. Apply a well-balanced fertilizer when plants begin to show growth in spring and cultivate periodically. During dry weather shallow cultivation can conserve soil moisture. Some plants, such as delphiniums, can be cut back after flowering to encourage a second bloom. In late fall, after plants have gone dormant, cut stems to about 4 inches from the ground and cover with mulch. Some perennials will need to be divided every spring, but many can go 2 to 3 years or more before showing signs of decline.

Bulbs

Once planted, most bulbs maintain themselves for years with minimal care. Permanent spring-flowering bulbs like daffodils benefit greatly from fertilizing. Apply a single dose of slow-release fertilizer at flowering time. Deadhead all bulbs after flowering to divert the plant's energy into the remaining flowers and restoration of the bulb. Many tender bulbs will need to be lifted out after the first frost, dried, and stored until they are ready to replant.

Herbs

Most herbs are not difficult to grow. They germinate readily and can be raised without any special skill. All but a few seem to thrive in a well-drained sunny location in soil that is not too rich. Picking herbs regularly and cutting back dead flowers is sometimes all the care they need. Some plants, such as chives, need to be divided and replanted every year or two.

Vines and Ground Covers

Of all the plant types, ground covers require the least maintenance. Once established, they save you the effort of weeding. Vines and many ground covers are often vigorous plants and will tend to keep spreading, so they may need to be pruned back from time to time.

Ferns and Ornamental Grasses

Ferns and ornamental grasses are easy to grow. Plant ferns in fall and cover them with a mulch of leaves that will give them protection and retain soil moisture until new rootlets have started to grow. Ornamental grasses tolerate nearly every type of soil. Once established, they need very little attention, except to keep them from spreading too fast. After the second or third year, they may be easily divided in spring or fall to prevent spreading.

Shrubs and Trees

Shrubs and trees will often look beautiful with minimal care for years. During the first year or two of growth, be

Herbs such as rosemary, basil, and sage are easy to care for. Keep them near the kitchen to pick regularly, water as needed, and they will need little additional attention.

sure to water regularly until plantings are established. After that, a shrub or tree should need no water beyond rainfall, assuming you have picked the right sort of plant for your locality. Pests and disease can affect your shrubs and trees, but they generally are less bothered than many other plants. Pruning is often advisable to remove dying branches. This redirects energy back into the healthy parts of the plant and shapes and sizes it to fit well in your garden. However, pruning is infrequent seasonal work. Shade trees do not usually need pruning beyond the initial cutting back at planting time, which is also true of many fruit trees. Purchase shrubs and trees in containers or with the roots in a ball of soil wrapped in burlap to ensure minimal damage to roots when the plant is transported and transplanted. ❦

7

Interest

Choose plants by their interesting features

Setting aside the importance of proper light, climate, and soil, most people would probably select plants based solely on "interest," which is used here to refer to flowers, fragrance, foliage, and fruit and seeds—the four Fs. These are the characteristics of plants that make them attractive and unique. While some gardeners exhibit a preference for a particular feature, most gardens incorporate a variety of features to create balance. Creating a balance that suits you involves planning your garden according to how it will be perceived or used.

To begin, examine the pathways and places where you and visitors can stop to enjoy your garden. Note the chief viewing points and natural resting places. These are the focal points where you can, with a bit of planning, present a harmonious ensemble of colors, textures, and fragrances. Decide which garden elements you want to use for any one spot and in which season those elements will be at their best. It's not necessary to feature all four Fs at every vantage point throughout the season. But if you do thoughtfully combine the four Fs, you will create a more complex sensory effect.

Making Your Selection

As you look through the plant entries and begin to make selections, you can narrow your choices by comparing interesting features.

Flowers

Some gardeners seek to highlight flowers, which are the primary appeal of annuals and perennials. Most annuals come into flower quickly after planting and have a long blooming season, brightening the garden and providing a source of color for bouquets or for dried arrangements of lasting beauty. Perennials are also loved for their flowers. Like annuals, perennial flowers and many wildflowers can be cut and dried. If you plan to do a lot of cutting, it makes sense to plant a separate cutting garden so that you do not compromise the appearance of your main garden. Flowers are also the main interest of bulbs, which include a wide selection of different colors and shapes. They are especially useful for creating short bursts of color. Tulips, for example, can provide bright color in the spring garden.

Fragrance

Fragrance adds a certain charm to a garden. Numerous annual flowers are very fragrant, including sweet alyssum, sweet peas, stock, four-o'clocks, tansy, and chrysanthemums. A few bulbs, such as hyacinths and lilies, are also grown for their rich fragrance. With annuals, perennials, and bulbs, each week of the growing year has its special scents, and with a little planning your garden can have both flowers and fragrance all season long. Lily-of-the-valley is one of the earlier—and beloved—perennial scents, followed by the many varieties of scented roses. Night bloomers, such as snow-on-the-mountain, honeysuckle, and evening stock, release their fragrances in the summer evening. Fragrant foliage is the chief interest of most herbs. Herbs with fragrant leaves include mints, thyme, rosemary, sweet marjoram, sweet basil, summer savory, balm, and chamomile. Some leaves must be pressed to release a scent, while others release it freely into the air, especially after a rain. Certain varieties of shrubs, such as the common mock orange or azalea, have extremely fragrant flowers.

Foliage

The chief appeals of foliage are texture, shape, and color. Spring and summer foliage ranges from light green to yellow-green, blue-green, and reddish purple. On some plants, foliage changes color in fall, which makes them particularly attractive and dramatic. Evergreen foliage provides a handsome appearance year round, especially when complemented by cones or berries. Silvery gray foliage offers a wonderful contrast to brilliant flowers. Vines and ground covers are appealing for their leaves, though many also produce attractive flowers and berries. Ferns and ornamental grasses, with their elongated shapes and unusual combinations of texture and color, are among the finest foliage plants. Ferns have a soft appearance, adding subtle and fine texture to the garden design. Ornamental grasses are grown for their feathery habit and the movement of bright blades of foliage in the breeze. Some grasses can be dried after picking and make impressive dried flower arrangements.

A combined planting of ornamental grasses and herbs can provide a full array of interesting features, including fragrance, flowers, fruit, and unusual foliage.

Fruit and Seeds

A few plants are grown more for fruit than foliage, such as Job's-tears, *Coix lacryma-jobi*, with its beadlike fruits. Some trees and shrubs have large, soft fruits containing many seeds, such as the pomegranate. Berrylike fruits are also found on such trees and shrubs as dogwood, mountain ash, barberry, bayberry, myrtle, black alder, boxwood, and firethorn. Some trees produce nutlike fruits like those of the oak, ironwood, and beech. Bright berries give plants color in winter, and for many types of plants, from shrubs like viburnums to trees like hemlock, the fruits and seed give the gardener an easy way to propagate more in the next season. ❦

1

Plants for Places with Full Sun

Plants that flourish in full sun are by nature a tough lot. They spend each day beneath an unrelenting sun, and instead of being burned or desiccated these plants thrive. The hardy character of many sun-loving plants makes them generally an easy group to care for. Many have not only evolved ways to protect themselves from the sun's radiation, but have become drought tolerant as well. As self-reliant as these plants can be, most of them benefit from some little luxuries. These include being grown in soil that has been amended with compost, peat moss, or other type of organic matter; a periodic, thorough watering during dry periods; and having a layer of mulch spread around their bases to help conserve soil moisture through the long, hot days of summer.

AGERATUM
Ageratum

Light: full sun

Plant type: annual

Height: 6 inches to 2 1/2 feet

Soil and Moisture: well-drained, moist

Interest: flowers, foliage

Care: easy

◀ Ageratum houstonianum 'Blue Horizon'

Ageratum has small, uniquely beautiful flowers composed of hundreds of threadlike petals that give the blossoms a fluffy, powder-puff appearance. The flowers come in a range of soft colors that accent the compact mounds of heart-shaped medium green leaves. Dwarf varieties are ideal for garden edgings. Taller forms combine well with other flowers in the middle or back of a border and add a perky touch to indoor arrangements.

Growing and care:
Sow seed indoors 6 to 8 weeks before the last spring frost. Space plants in well-worked soil 6 to 12 inches apart. Pinch early growth to promote more compact growth. Remove spent blooms to encourage continuous flower production all season long.

Selected species and varieties:
A. houstonianum bears small blue or bluish purple flowers in dense, fuzzy clusters from summer through fall; white- and pink-flowered varieties are available; 'Summer Snow' grows 6 to 8 inches tall with abundant pure white flowers from early spring to frost; 'Capri' is a heat-tolerant variety that grows to a uniform 1 foot tall, bearing bicolored flowers that are medium blue with white centers; 'Blue Horizon' grows to 2½ feet with deep blue flowers that are excellent for cutting.

AMARANTH
Amaranthus

Light: full sun

Plant type: annual

Height: 1 1/2 to 6 feet

Soil and Moisture: well-drained, moist to dry

Interest: flowers, foliage

Care: easy

◀ Amaranthus caudatus

Amaranths are large, stately plants that add a bright, bold touch to borders and gardens. The strong plants bear long-lasting, tassel-shaped flowers in shades of red and purple that hang above the richly colored leaves. Tall types are effective as accents or massed as a colorful background. Shorter varieties are show-stoppers when used in beds or containers. Flowers of all varieties are excellent additions to both fresh and dried arrangements.

Growing and care:
Amaranth seed germinates best at room temperature and can be started indoors 4 to 6 weeks prior to the last frost. In warm areas sow seed directly in the garden once soil has warmed. Thin to allow 1 to 2 feet between plants. Water frequently during dry periods.

Selected species and varieties:
A. caudatus (love-lies-bleeding) grows 3 to 5 feet tall with green or red leaves and huge, drooping tassels of red flowers that may reach 2 feet in length; 'Viridis' grows 2 to 3½ feet with light green flower tassels. *A. cruentus* (purple amaranth, prince's-feather) produces huge 12-inch leaves along erect 6-foot stems, and drooping red or purple flower spikes. *A. tricolor* 'Joseph's-coat' grows from 1½ to 5 feet tall with upper leaves marked with red and gold and lower foliage green, yellow, and brownish red.

BABY'S-BREATH
Gypsophila

Light: full sun	
Plant type: annual	
Height: 8 inches to 2 feet	
Soil and Moisture: well-drained, moist to dry	
Interest: flowers	
Care: easy	

◀ Gypsophila elegans

Baby's-breath produces airy clouds of delicate, tiny white flowers in shades of pink and rose from mid-spring to early fall. It is beautiful when used as a filler in the border, where it softens the bright colors and coarse textures of other plants. Baby's-breath is an excellent cut flower and can be used in either fresh or dried arrangements.

Growing and care:
Sow seed directly in the garden in early spring when soil is cool and moist. Thin plants to 8 to 12 inches apart. For best results fertilize and water lightly. In regions with hot summers provide some afternoon shade. Supplement acid soils with limestone. Plants are short lived, even for annuals, so make successive sowings every 2 to 3 weeks for continuous bloom. Taller varieties may need staking.

Selected species and varieties:
G. elegans has a loose, mounded habit with thin, well-branched stems bearing pairs of narrow gray-green leaves and billowy clusters of white, pink, red, or purple flowers. Each flower is ¼ to ¾ inch across.

BELLS-OF-IRELAND
Moluccella

Light: full sun	
Plant type: annual	
Height: 2 to 3 feet	
Soil and Moisture: well-drained, moist	
Interest: flowers	
Care: easy	

◀ Moluccella laevis

This native to the eastern Mediterranean region provides a lovely vertical accent to beds, borders, and cottage gardens. The plants also provide a soft background for other, more boldly colored summer flowers. Bells-of-Ireland bloom from late summer to frost and make fine additions to both fresh and dried arrangements.

Growing and care:
Start seed indoors 8 to 10 weeks prior to the last frost or direct-sow in early spring. Do not cover seed, as it needs light to germinate. Space plants 9 to 12 inches apart. Once transplanted do not disturb the roots. Fertilize monthly and water regularly. Stake if plants appear floppy. Plants often self-seed.

Selected species and varieties:
M. laevis grows to 3 feet tall and 1½ feet wide with an erect habit and 1-inch rounded, slightly serrated leaves. The rather inconspicuous, fragrant pink or white flowers are borne on upright spikes surrounded by a large but subtle white-veined, pale green calyx that resembles a bell.

BLESSED THISTLE
Silybum

Light: full sun	
Plant type: annual or biennial	
Height: 3 to 4 feet	
Soil and Moisture: well-drained, sandy, dry	
Interest: flowers, foliage	
Care: easy	

◀ Silybum marianum

The rough, spiny leaves and flowers of blessed thistle add a primitive aspect to the garden few other plants can equal. In spring the 12- to 14-inch deeply lobed, green and white basal leaves are clustered into an attractive wide-spreading rosette. In late summer strong stems rise from the rosette and are adorned with delicate, reddish purple 2-inch thistlelike flowers, each guarded by a ring of spines. Blessed thistle provides coarse texture and contrast to borders and adds a distinctly wild element to naturalistic plantings.

Growing and care:
Sow seed indoors about 8 weeks before last frost or sow directly outdoors in early spring. Space plants 2 feet apart. Once established, plants often self-seed and may become weedy. Control slugs by setting slug traps or hand picking them from plants in the evening or early morning. *Silybum* will tolerate wet conditions but is most attractive when grown in poor, dry soils.

Selected species and varieties:
S. marianum grows to 4 feet with coarse, dark green leaves mottled with white, and solitary rose or purple flowers. The soft, thin flower petals are surrounded by a collar of curved, spiny bracts.

BLUE MILKWEED
Oxypetalum

Light: full sun	
Plant type: tender perennial grown as annual	
Height: 15 inches to 3 feet	
Soil and Moisture: well-drained, fertile, moist to dry	
Interest: flowers, foliage	
Care: easy	

◀ Oxypetalum caeruleum

This elegant tender perennial from South America produces exquisite star-shaped flowers borne in delicate, graceful sprays from summer to fall. The pink flower buds open to reveal flowers of clear baby blue, which mature to rich lilac-purple. Plant blue milkweed at the edge of a border or in a patio planter or hanging basket where its stunning, long-lasting flowers can be viewed up close.

Growing and care:
Start seed indoors 6 to 8 weeks prior to the last frost, and transplant to the garden after all danger of frost has passed. Seed may also be direct sown at time of last frost. Space plants 6 to 8 inches apart. Pinch back young plants to encourage branching. If plants become infested with whitefly, which is sometimes a problem, spray with insecticidal soap once a week.

Selected species and varieties:
O. caeruleum has a weakly twining, upright habit. When grown as an annual plants reach about 1½ feet tall. In Zone 10 it may grow into a 3-foot shrub. Leaves are heart shaped and covered with downy hairs. The ½- to 1-inch flowers are borne in open clusters from summer to early fall.

BURNING BUSH
Kochia

Light:	full sun
Plant type:	annual
Height:	2 to 4 feet
Soil and Moisture:	well-drained, medium to dry
Interest:	foliage
Care:	easy

◀ Kochia scoparia
f. trichophylla

Burning bush is a fast-growing, heat-tolerant annual with lacelike, fine-textured green foliage that turns scarlet in fall. The plant's neat, symmetrical shrublike habit makes a beautiful hedge, screen, or background for flower borders. When grown in containers they are eye-catching conversation pieces.

Growing and care:

Start seed indoors in individual peat pots 6 to 8 weeks prior to the last frost or sow directly in the garden after all danger of frost has passed. Keep seed moist after planting but do not cover, as it needs light to germinate well. Plants often self-seed and may become invasive. Allow 1½ to 2 feet between plants. Plants can be sheared to maintain desired shape or size. Avoid overwatering. In windy locations, plants may require staking.

Selected species and varieties:

K. scoparia f. *trichophylla* (burning bush, summer cypress) has an erect, uniform habit with dense, feathery foliage that is light green in summer, turning bright red in fall; 'Acapulco Silver' produces variegated leaves marked with chrome-white tips.

CAPE MARIGOLD
Dimorphotheca

Light:	full sun
Plant type:	annual
Height:	12 to 16 inches
Soil and Moisture:	well-drained, fertile, dry
Interest:	flowers
Care:	easy

◀ Dimorphotheca
sinuata

The gaily colored daisylike flowers of Cape marigold add a festive touch to the front of beds and borders and lend a wonderfully cheerful air to sunny rock gardens. The plants come in a wide range of bright colors and bloom over a very long season, from late spring to early fall. The flowers open in the morning and close at night.

Growing and care:

Start seed indoors 6 to 8 weeks prior to the last frost. From Zone 9 south sow directly in the garden in winter. Space plants 6 to 9 inches apart. Do not disturb after transplanting. In regions with hot summers provide some afternoon shade. Water plants early in the day and avoid wetting foliage.

Selected species and varieties:

D. pluvialis (weather prophet) grows to 16 inches with showy 2½-inch daisylike flowers with white petal-like ray flowers surrounding yellow and violet centers. *D. sinuata* (Cape marigold) grows 12 to 15 inches with a compact, mounded habit, producing 1½-inch flower heads composed of white, yellow, pink, or orange rays around golden centers.

CASTOR BEAN
Ricinus

Light: full sun	
Plant type: tender perennial grown as annual	
Height: 8 to 10 feet	
Soil and Moisture: well-drained, moist to slightly dry	
Interest: foliage	
Care: easy	

◀ Ricinus communis 'Carmencita'

The large, glossy foliage of castor bean is an attractive, textured addition to the annual garden. It makes an excellent screen or backdrop. The small pom-pom flowers are followed by prickly husks filled with beanlike brown, speckled, very poisonous seeds. Castor bean can be an interesting addition to the garden, but must be used cautiously.

Growing and care:
Soak seed in warm water for 24 hours before planting. Sow seed indoors in peat pots 6 to 8 weeks prior to the last frost. Fertilize and water regularly for best growth. Plants grow best in hot, humid climates and can become invasive in warm regions.

Selected species and varieties:
R. communis is a shrubby plant with branches up to 10 feet tall and spreading 3 to 4 feet wide; the 1- to 3-foot star-shaped leaves emerge tinged with red and turn glossy green as they expand; clusters of red or red and green flowers appear in summer followed by prickly seedpods; 'Carmencita' produces early-blooming bright red flowers and deep greenish brown leaves.

CORN COCKLE
Agrostemma

Light: full sun	
Plant type: annual	
Height: 1 to 3 feet	
Soil and Moisture: well-drained, moist to dry	
Interest: flowers, foliage	
Care: easy	

◀ Agrostemma githago

Corn cockles are trouble-free, vigorous plants from Europe that have become naturalized throughout much of eastern North America. They provide a long season of bright blooms for sunny borders and cottage gardens, where the old-fashioned appearance of the flowers is particularly effective. The dainty, trumpet-shaped blossoms come in shades of pink, lilac, cherry red, and magenta and are excellent for cutting.

Growing and care:
Corn cockle grows best in regions with long, cool summers. Sow seed in place in late fall or early spring. Thin when seedlings are about 2 inches tall to stand 6 to 12 inches apart. Corn cockle thrives in moist or dry conditions and needs fertilizing only in the poorest soils. The plants freely self-sow and can become invasive. Dead-head spent blossoms to prevent excessive self-seeding and encourage reblooming. Water during dry periods and support plants with stakes when needed.

Selected species and varieties:
A. githago has willowy stems up to 3 feet tall and narrow leaves covered with a silvery down; each flower has five petals that sport delicate stripes or spots that seem to radiate from the center; the black seeds are plentiful but poisonous if eaten.

CREEPING ZINNIA
Sanvitalia

Light: full sun	
Plant type: annual	
Height: 4 to 6 inches	
Soil and Moisture: well-drained, sandy, medium to dry	
Interest: flowers	
Care: easy	

◀ Sanvitalia procumbens

Creeping zinnia is a low-growing annual from Mexico that produces a profuse display of small, jaunty flowers from early summer to frost. The blossoms resemble miniature sunflowers, each one only ¾ inch across. The plants make a superb edging, a show-stopping ground cover for the sunny rock garden, or an attractive hanging basket.

Growing and care:

Start seed indoors in peat pots 4 to 6 weeks prior to the last frost, or sow directly outdoors in late spring. Transplant carefully being sure not to disturb roots. Allow 6 to 9 inches between plants. Once established do not disturb plants. Soak soil thoroughly when watering. Fertilize lightly during the growing season. *Sanvitalia* thrives in hot, humid weather and tolerates extended dry periods.

Selected species and varieties:

S. procumbens grows to a height of 6 inches, with trailing stems extending 1½ feet from the crown, with compact, oval ½- to 1-inch leaves. Flowers are composed of yellow or orange rays surrounding a dark purple center and may be single, semidouble, or double; 'Gold Braid' produces double yellow blooms; 'Mandarin Orange' bears semidouble orange flowers with prominent black centers.

DAHLBERG DAISY
Dyssodia

Light: full sun	
Plant type: annual	
Height: 4 to 12 inches	
Soil and Moisture: well-drained, dry	
Interest: flowers, foliage, fragrance	
Care: easy	

◀ Dyssodia tenuiloba

Dahlberg daisy blooms from summer to fall with petite yellow flowers at the tips of 3-inch-long branches. The highly dissected foliage has a pleasant fragrance reminiscent of thyme. The medium green leaves are short and finely divided into feathery segments. This native of southern Texas and Mexico is an exquisite plant for rock gardens, sunny borders, and containers, or as edging for pathways.

Growing and care:

Sow seed indoors in late winter and plant in the garden after danger of frost has passed. Or sow directly in the garden after the last frost, spacing plants 9 to 18 inches apart. Dahlberg daisy is heat and drought tolerant and may self-sow in dry, gravelly soil.

Selected species and varieties:

D. tenuiloba [also listed as *Thymophylla tenuiloba*] (Dahlberg daisy, golden-fleece) has ½-inch flower heads with bright yellow centers and stubby yellow, gold, orange, or red petals with lighter-shaded tips and feathery, aromatic 1-inch leaves covered with very fine hairs.

DEVIL'S-CLAW
Proboscidea

Light: full sun	
Plant type: annual	
Height: 1 to 2 feet	
Soil and Moisture: well-drained, sandy, moist to dry	
Interest: flowers, fruit	
Care: easy	

◀ Proboscidea louisianica

Devil's-claw is an unusual annual that bears tubular flowers followed by very interesting fruits: fleshy 4- to 6-inch pods that split into two clawlike, curved ends as they dry. While green the pods can be pickled and eaten. The dried pods are outstanding additions to dried arrangements.

Growing and care:

Start seed indoors 6 to 8 weeks before the last frost. In Zone 8 and warmer, seed can be sown directly in the garden in midspring. Devil's-claw may self-seed and become invasive in warm climates. Space plants 6 to 12 inches apart and at least 5 feet away from other plants so that the odor of the flowers does not overpower more delicate or appealing fragrances.

Selected species and varieties:

P. louisianica (unicorn flower) grows to 2 feet with a bushy, spreading habit. The 7- to 10-inch leaves have wavy margins and are covered with sticky hairs. The unpleasantly scented flowers are colored with blends of white, yellow, pink, or purple and commonly appear right after a rain. The unique fruits appear after the blooms have faded.

EUPHORBIA
Euphorbia

Light: full sun	
Plant type: annual	
Height: 1 1/2 to 2 feet	
Soil and Moisture: well-drained, medium to dry	
Interest: flowers, foliage	
Care: easy	

◀ Euphorbia marginata

This hardy annual is native to the Great Plains and eastern Rockies and makes a wonderful addition to sunny wildflower gardens, annual beds, and perennial borders. The attractive variegated leaves and tiny white flowers of euphorbia add a beautiful, subtle touch to the garden from spring to fall. The soft stems support light green foliage generously decorated with clean white markings. The small flowers that appear above the leaves are surrounded by snow white bracts.

Growing and care:

Sow seed directly in the garden in late fall or early spring. Space plants 10 to 12 inches apart. Keep the seedbed moist from the time the seeds are sown until the plants are a few inches tall. As the plants grow they become increasingly drought tolerant. Euphorbia self-seeds so easily it may become invasive. Use gloves when handling stems to avoid contact with the sap, as it may be irritating to some people.

Selected species and varieties:

E. marginata (snow-on-the-mountain, ghostweed) has erect, stout, branched stems bearing gray-green oval leaves attractively striped and margined with white. The small late-summer flowers are surrounded by showy, pure white leaflike bracts.

EVERLASTING
Xeranthemum

Light: full sun

Plant type: annual

Height: 1½ to 2 feet

Soil and Moisture: well-drained, medium to dry

Interest: flowers

Care: easy

◄ Xeranthemum annuum

Everlasting is a longtime favorite for cutting and for dried arrangements. The daisylike purple, pink, or white flowers seem to float atop the long stems from summer to early fall, lending a cheerful air to the garden. The plants are easy to grow and do well even in poor, dry soils.

Growing and care:

In colder zones, start seed indoors in individual peat pots 6 to 8 weeks prior to the last frost. Be careful not to disturb the roots when transplanting. In warmer climates, sow seed directly in the garden in spring after all danger of frost has passed. Allow 6 to 9 inches between plants. To use in dried arrangements, cut flowers when they are fully open and hang them upside down in a dim, well-ventilated room until dry.

Selected species and varieties:

X. annuum (Immortelle) has tall, pliant stems with silvery-green leaves and crowned with bright, daisylike flowers. The delicate 1½-inch single or double blossoms are surrounded by papery bracts that are the same color as the true flowers.

GAZANIA
Gazania

Light: full sun

Plant type: tender perennial grown as annual

Height: 6 to 16 inches

Soil and Moisture: well-drained, dry

Interest: flowers, foliage

Care: easy

◄ Gazania rigens 'Fiesta Red'

This stunning tender perennial from South Africa produces large daisylike flowers from midsummer to frost. The blossoms open each morning when touched by the sun, and close at night and on overcast days. Gazanias provide brilliant color to borders and beds. They are especially suited for use in container gardens, where they brighten decks and patios all season long.

Growing and care:

Sow seed indoors in early spring to transplant to the garden after all danger of frost has passed. Space plants 1 foot apart. Do not overwater. They thrive in sunny, dry locations and tolerate wind and coastal conditions. Deadhead regularly to maintain a tidy appearance.

Selected species and varieties:

G. linearis grows to 16 inches with narrow leaves and 2¾-inch flower heads with golden rays surrounding orange-brown disks. *G. rigens* (treasure flower) grows 6 to 12 inches tall with 3-inch flower heads, borne on long stalks, in shades of orange, pink, or red; 'Chansonette' grows to 10 inches with a compact habit and flowers in a wide range of colors; 'Fiesta Red' bears flowers with burnt orange petals marked with a dark ring surrounding a yellow disk; 'Harlequin Hybrids' bear flowers in many shades with a brown zone around the central disk; 'Sunshine' has large, 4-inch-wide multicolored flowers on 8-inch stems.

GLOBE AMARANTH
Gomphrena

Light: full sun	
Plant type: annual	
Height: 8 inches to 2 feet	
Soil and Moisture: well-drained, medium to dry	
Interest: flowers	
Care: easy	

◀ Gomphrena globosa

The round, cloverlike flowers of globe amaranth add a unique look to gardens from summer to frost. A native of India, this half-hardy annual is easy to grow and imparts a cheerful, informal appearance to beds and borders as well as patio planters and window boxes. The flowers have a coarse, parchmentlike texture even when fresh, and are excellent for both fresh and dried arrangements.

Growing and care:
Start seed indoors 8 to 10 weeks before the last frost and transplant outdoors after all danger of frost has passed. Seed can also be sown directly outside in late spring after the soil has warmed. Allow 8 to 15 inches between plants. Globe amaranth grows slowly in spring but quickly once the weather warms. To use in dried arrangements, cut before the flowers are fully open and hang them upside down in an airy room until dry.

Selected species and varieties:
G. globosa produces strongly branched, erect stems and somewhat coarse, hairy leaves. The 1-inch-long globular flower heads may be pink, white, magenta, orange, or red and are borne atop the stems from summer to fall.

LATHYRUS
Lathyrus

Light: full sun	
Plant type: annual	
Height: 6 inches to 9 feet	
Soil and Moisture: well-drained, moist	
Interest: flowers, fragrance	
Care: easy	

◀ Lathyrus odoratus

Lathyrus is a hardy annual from southern Europe that has been grown in gardens for generations for its clusters of deliciously fragrant blossoms. The flowers come in many charming colors and appear over many weeks from spring to fall. Lathyrus makes an excellent trailing ground cover or an interesting hanging basket.

Growing and care:
Sow seed in 1-inch-deep drills in well-prepared soil in early spring. In the Deep South sow in fall for winter flowering. Nick seed coat or soak seed in warm water for 24 hours prior to planting for best germination. Provide climbing types with support. Mulch to keep soil cool, and provide abundant water. Remove faded blooms regularly to prolong flowering.

Selected species and varieties:
L. odoratus (sweet pea) produces fragrant spring or summer flowers up to 2 inches wide on compact 6-inch to 2½-foot-tall bushy, or 5- to 6-foot-tall twining vines. Flower colors include deep rose, blue, purple, scarlet, white, cream, salmon, pink, and bicolors; 'Bijou Mixed' is a bush type that grows to 1 foot with a full range of colors; 'Royal Family' is a vining type that comes in a wide range of colors, grows to 6 feet, and grows best in regions with hot summers.

LOVE-IN-A-MIST
Nigella

Light: full sun

Plant type: annual

Height: 1 1/2 to 2 feet

Soil and Moisture: well-drained, moist

Interest: flowers, seed heads

Care: easy

◀ Nigella damascena

Love-in-a-mist adds a delicate, fine texture to any garden or flower arrangement. The solitary wide-petaled flowers seem to float atop a leafy mist of stems and foliage throughout the summer. The blossoms mature into interesting seed capsules that are attractive additions to dried flower arrangements. The plant is native to southern Europe and North Africa.

Growing and care:
Sow seed directly in the garden in spring when soil is cool and frost is still possible. Sow every 2 weeks to extend the flowering season. Once seedlings emerge do not transplant, and cultivate carefully so roots are not disturbed. Thin to allow 6 to 10 inches between plants. Water during dry periods and fertilize lightly every few weeks. Plants often self-seed.

Selected species and varieties:
N. damascena has an erect, branching habit with delicate, threadlike leaves. Flowers are 1 to 1 1/2 inches across with blue, lavender, white, or pink notched petals. The papery 1-inch seed capsules are pale green with attractive reddish brown markings.

MENTZELIA
Mentzelia

Light: full sun

Plant type: annual or biennial

Height: 1 to 4 feet

Soil and Moisture: well-drained, moist to dry

Interest: flowers

Care: easy

◀ Mentzelia lindleyi

Mentzelias are bushy plants covered with an attractive display of star-shaped flowers from late spring until fall. The plants bear fragrant yellow or white flowers that often open in the evening and close on cloudy days. Mentzelia is used to add a soft, slightly wild look to beds and borders.

Growing and care:
North of Zone 8 sow seed directly in garden in spring after danger of frost has passed. From Zone 8 south, direct-sow in fall. Thin to allow 6 to 10 inches between plants. Keep seedlings moist, but once established keep plants on the dry side. When cultivating be careful not to disturb roots. Plants tolerate heat and drought but put on a much better floral show when regularly watered and fertilized.

Selected species and varieties:
M. decapetala (ten-petal mentzelia) is a biennial that grows 2 to 4 feet tall with 3- to 5-inch starburst-shaped flowers opening in the evening. *M. laevicaulis* (blazing-star) is a biennial that grows to 3 1/2 feet with narrow leaves and pale yellow 4-inch flowers that also open in the evening. *M. lindleyi* [also known as *Bartonia aurea*] is an annual that grows 1 to 2 1/2 feet tall with fragrant, bright yellow flowers displaying a colorful orange-red center with a prominent flush of yellow stamens.

MEXICAN SUNFLOWER
Tithonia

Light: full sun
Plant type: annual
Height: 2 to 6 feet
Soil and Moisture: well-drained, medium to dry
Interest: flowers
Care: easy

◀ Tithonia rotundifolia

Mexican sunflower is native to the hot, arid regions of Central America, where it has developed exceptional drought and heat tolerance. Its daisylike orange to red flowers and coarse-textured leaves stay perky even during the most torrid summer days. Plants are suitable for the background of borders and for cutting; they can also be used as a fast-growing summer screen.

Growing and care:
Start seed indoors 6 to 8 weeks prior to the last frost. Do not cover seed. Transplant after danger of frost has passed. Space plants 2 to 2½ feet apart. Stake plants in windy areas. Plants tolerate poor soil, heat, and drought, and usually do not need supplemental watering even during long dry periods. When cutting flowers for indoor arrangements, cut in the bud stage and sear the stem to preserve freshness.

Selected species and varieties:
T. rotundifolia has a vigorous, erect habit with large, broadly oval, velvety, serrated leaves. Flower heads consist of orange or scarlet sunflower-like petals surrounding a bright orange-yellow central disk; 'Goldfinger' grows 2 to 3 feet tall with 3-inch vivid orange blooms.

MOSS ROSE
Portulaca

Light: full sun
Plant type: annual
Height: 6 to 8 inches
Soil and Moisture: well-drained, dry
Interest: flowers, foliage
Care: easy

◀ Portulaca grandiflora 'Sundance'

Moss rose is a tough, hardworking plant that bears dozens of attractive, brightly colored flowers even in extreme summertime conditions. The creeping stems are covered with slender, succulent green leaves that serve as an excellent backdrop for the vivid flowers. *Portulaca* is a fine choice for the rock garden, an informal ground cover, or containers. The plants thrive in hot, dry sites where few other flowers would survive.

Growing and care:
Start seed indoors in peat pots 6 to 8 weeks prior to the last frost and transplant to the garden after the soil has warmed. Take care not to disturb roots. Seed can also be sown directly in the garden after danger of frost has passed. Do not cover seed. Space plants 6 to 8 inches apart. Moss rose flowers only in sunshine and blooms best in poor, dry soils and hot weather.

Selected species and varieties:
P. grandiflora produces sprawling succulent stems that bear fleshy, narrow leaves and showy bowl-shaped flowers resembling roses. Blooms come in many vivid colors including red, pink, white, yellow, orange, and magenta; 'Sundance' bears semidouble flowers in a mixture of red, orange, yellow, cream, and white.

NASTURTIUM
Tropaeolum

Light: full sun

Plant type: annual

Height: 6 inches to 8 feet

Soil and Moisture: well-drained, moist

Interest: flowers, foliage

Care: easy

◀ *Tropaeolum majus*

Nasturtium is an eye-catching annual with attractive, unusually shaped flowers and foliage. The white, yellow, orange, or red trumpet-shaped blossoms are decorated with long floral spurs. The unusual foliage has stems in the center of each shieldlike leaf. Blooms appear from summer through frost. Organically grown young flowers make a peppery addition to salads and are excellent for cutting.

Growing and care:
Nasturtiums do not transplant well and should be sown directly in the garden after the last frost. Space dwarf types 1 foot apart, climbers from 2 to 3 feet apart. Do not fertilize. Water during dry periods.

Selected species and varieties:
T. majus (common nasturtium) comes in dwarf, bushy forms, and vigorous, climbing ones; leaves are round, 2 to 7 inches across, with long stems and 2- to 3-inch showy flowers in red, yellow, white, or orange. *T. minus* (dwarf nasturtium) reaches 6 to 12 inches in height, with a bushy habit suitable for edging or massing; 'Alaska Mixed' grows 8 to 15 inches tall with variegated leaves and a wide range of flower colors. *T. peregrinum* (canary creeper, canarybird vine) is a climbing vine up to 8 feet long with pale yellow, fringed flowers and deeply lobed leaves that resemble those of a fig.

ORNAMENTAL CABBAGE
Brassica

Light: full sun

Plant type: biennial grown as annual

Height: 10 to 15 inches

Soil and Moisture: well-drained, moist

Interest: flowers, foliage

Care: easy

◀ *Brassica oleracea*

This decorative cousin of the familiar vegetable side dish is highly valued for the easy-care splash of color it provides to the fall and winter landscape. A biennial, it is grown as an annual for its brightly colored and intricately curled foliage, which grows in a flower-like rosette.

Growing and care:
For spring planting, start seed indoors 4 to 6 weeks prior to the last frost. For fall gardens, start seed 6 to 8 weeks prior to the first anticipated frost. Space plants 1½ to 2 feet apart. Plants tolerate light frost and will last all winter in Zones 8 to 10.

Selected species and varieties:
B. oleracea, Acephala Group, does not form heads but produces an open rosette of leaves that typically spreads 1 foot across. Foliage colors include lavender-blue, white, green, red, purple, pink, and assorted variegations. Color becomes brighter in cool weather; leaves of 'Cherry Sundae' are a blend of carmine and cream; 'Color Up' displays a center of red, pink, and white, surrounded by green margins; 'Peacock' series has feathery leaves in a variety of colors with notched and serrated edges.

ORNAMENTAL CORN
Zea mays

Light:	full sun
Plant type:	annual
Height:	2 to 15 feet
Soil and Moisture:	well-drained, moist, fertile
Interest:	seed heads
Care:	easy

◀ Zea mays

Corn is most often associated with vegetable gardens, yet there are many varieties that can add interesting accents to almost any bed or border. Ornamental corn provides a strong vertical aspect to the garden from spring to fall. And the decorative ears full of colorful kernels make autumn holidays even more enjoyable.

Growing and care:
Corn is a heavy feeder and grows best in well-worked soil that has been amended with organic matter prior to planting. Sow seed directly in the garden after soil warms in spring. Avoid sowing seed in cool, wet weather when the plants are more susceptible to disease. Thin plants to stand 8 to 12 inches apart. For good pollination, plant in blocks at least four rows wide with rows spaced 1½ to 2½ feet apart. Fertilize and water regularly.

Selected species and varieties:
Z. mays grows from 2 to 15 feet tall with strong, upright stalks and large, graceful lance-shaped leaves up to 2 feet long. The spreading tassels that appear atop the stalks in summer are the male flowers, while the female flowers, or ears, are found in the leaf axils; var. *rugosa* bears small, rounded ears filled with red kernels that can be used as decorations or popcorn.

OWL'S CLOVER
Orthocarpus

Light:	full sun
Plant type:	annual
Height:	4 to 15 inches
Soil and Moisture:	well-drained, medium to dry
Interest:	flowers, foliage
Care:	easy

◀ Orthocarpus purpurascens

Owl's clover is native to the southwestern United States, where it transforms desert hillsides into waves of rose, purple, and red. Individual flowers resemble snapdragons and are tipped with yellow or white on their lower lip and bracts of bright purple or crimson. These annuals are useful when massed in wildflower meadows and informal borders, where they provide a long season of color.

Growing and care:
Sow seed directly in the garden just beneath the surface as soon as the soil can be worked in early spring. Thin plants to stand 6 to 8 inches apart. Owl's clover does best in regions with long, warm summers. The plants are drought tolerant but benefit from extra water during dry periods.

Selected species and varieties:
O. purpurascens (escobita) grows from 4 to 15 inches tall with linear leaves often tinged with brown, either cut or smooth margins, and red-tipped bracts. The two-lipped rose-purple or crimson flowers are about 1 inch long and appear from early to midsummer.

PAINTED TONGUE
Salpiglossis

Light: full sun

Plant type: annual

Height: 2 to 3 feet

Soil and Moisture: well-drained, moist, fertile

Interest: flowers

Care: easy

◀ Salpiglossis sinuata 'Bolero'

The trumpet-shaped blossoms of painted tongue resemble petunias that have designs of gold etched onto the flowers. Painted tongue comes in an incredible range of colors, including red, pink, purple, blue, white, and yellow. Each blossom is marked with a contrasting inlay of rich color, most commonly gold. Plants add a cheerful, opulent accent to beds and borders, and are excellent cut flowers.

Growing and care:
Start seed indoors 6 to 8 weeks prior to the last frost or plant directly outdoors in late spring. Transplant to the garden after all danger of frost has passed. Space plants 10 to 12 inches apart. Loosen soil and amend with organic matter to increase fertility and aid drainage. Taller varieties may need staking. Water and fertilize regularly. Too much fertilizer will encourage leggy growth. Plants produce the best flower displays in areas with cool summers.

Selected species and varieties:
S. sinuata has an erect, bushy habit with narrow, 4-inch medium green leaves. Both foliage and stems are slightly hairy and sticky. Flowers are 2 to 2½ inches wide, have a soft, velvety texture, and appear in terminal clusters; 'Bolero' is 1½ to 2 feet tall with flower colors that include gold, rose, red, and blue.

PETUNIA
Petunia

Light: full sun

Plant type: annual

Height: 6 inches to 2 feet

Soil and Moisture: well-drained, moist

Interest: flowers

Care: easy

◀ Petunia x hybrida

Petunias, among the most popular of annuals, are renowned for producing a profusion of trumpet-shaped blooms in a wide variety of colors from summer to frost. The trailing or upright stems are slender, with small, pointed leaves covered with soft, sticky hairs. Dwarf varieties grow 6 to 12 inches tall, while bedding varieties can attain heights of 2 feet. Hybrid grandiflora varieties produce single ruffled or fringed flowers 4 to 6 inches across. Hybrid multiflora varieties produce smaller flowers, but in greater abundance. Petunias are effective as bedding plants, as borders, cascading over walls and banks, or as container plants.

Growing and care:
Sow seed indoors 8 to 10 weeks before the last frost or direct-sow in the garden after danger of frost has passed. Pinch back young plants to encourage a bushy form. Cut back plants if they become rangy. Remove withered flowers before they set seed to encourage further flowering. Keep soil moist and give extra water during dry periods. In areas with hot summers provide some afternoon shade.

Selected species and varieties:
P. x *hybrida* bears flowers with ruffled, fringed, or deeply veined petals in a wide range of colors; 'Blue Danube' is a double grandiflora with fringed blue petals; 'Flaming Velvet' has very deep red flowers; 'Purple Wave' has a low, trailing habit and violet-purple flowers.

PHACELIA
Phacelia

Light: full sun

Plant type: annual

Height: 6 inches to 3 feet

Soil and Moisture: well-drained, sandy, dry

Interest: flowers

Care: easy

◀ Phacelia campanularia

Phacelias are a diverse group of wildflowers with attractive blossoms in forms ranging from loose cymes of dainty bells to tightly packed spikes. Some are native to the southwestern United States, where they grow on dry, rocky desert slopes. The plants are beautiful additions to rock gardens and borders and make dynamic mass plantings.

Growing and care:
In most regions direct-sow in the garden in early spring when soil is cool. From Zone 9 south direct-sow in fall. Space plants 6 to 8 inches apart. Do not transplant. Phacelia prefers sandy, poor soils and grows well with California poppy, owl's clover, purple lupine, and golden yarrow.

Selected species and varieties:
P. campanularia (California bluebell) grows from 6 to 24 inches tall with 1-inch hairy, round or heart-shaped leaves and ¾- to 1-inch bright blue, mostly upright bell-shaped flowers borne in loose clusters. *P. tanacetifolia* (purple heliotrope) has erect, slightly hairy 1- to 3-foot-tall stems with feathery leaves and curled clusters of sweetly scented lavender flowers.

PINCUSHION FLOWER
Scabiosa

Light: full sun

Plant type: annual

Height: 1½ to 3 feet

Soil and Moisture: well-drained, moist, fertile

Interest: flowers

Care: easy

◀ Scabiosa atropurpurea

Pincushion flower is easy to grow, producing delightful dome-shaped blossoms from spring to fall. The long-lasting flowers are composed of a 1- to 2-inch mound of lacy petals beneath dozens of prominent stamens that resemble pins stuck in a pincushion. The flowers come in lavender, pink, purple, maroon, red, and white and are favorites for borders, massing, and both fresh and dried arrangements.

Growing and care:
Start seed indoors 4 to 6 weeks prior to the last frost and transplant to the garden after danger of frost has passed. Seed can also be direct sown in spring in the North, and in fall from Zone 8 south. Space plants 8 to 12 inches apart. Deadhead regularly to encourage blossoming. Supply extra water during dry periods.

Selected species and varieties:
S. atropurpurea grows 2 to 3 feet tall with slender, erect stems and showy, domed flower heads. *S. stellata* (paper moon) grows to 1½ to 2½ feet with pale blue flowers that feel papery when dry and are highly valued for dried arrangements; 'Drumstick' has pale blue flowers that fade to bronze; 'Ping-Pong' bears rounded white flowers the size of a Ping-Pong ball.

PLAINS COREOPSIS
Coreopsis

Light: full sun

Plant type: annual

Height: 2 to 3 feet

Soil and Moisture: well-drained, moist to dry

Interest: flowers

Care: easy

◀ Coreopsis tinctoria

This easy-to-grow, beautiful annual is native to the Great Plains and is a common component of wildflower mixtures. Coreopsis produces daisylike flowers that appear on supple, wiry stems throughout summer to early fall. Colors include yellow, orange, red, mahogany, and bicolors. Plant them in mixed borders and wildflower gardens, and use the fresh flowers to add a wild touch to indoor arrangements.

Growing and care:
Start seed indoors 6 to 8 weeks before the last frost or sow directly in the garden in early spring. Space plants 6 to 8 inches apart. Deadhead often to prolong flowering. Fertilize lightly for best flower production. Do not deadhead blossoms produced late in the season if self-seeding is desired.

Selected species and varieties:
C. tinctoria (calliopsis) produces pliant, many-branched stems draped with interesting lobed or dissected leaves. Flower heads may be solitary or appear in loose clusters. The blossoms have dark red or purple centers surrounded by notched and often banded ray flowers. Double-flowered and dwarf varieties are available.

PRICKLY POPPY
Argemone

Light: full sun

Plant type: annual or tender perennial grown as annual

Height: 2 to 4 feet

Soil and Moisture: well-drained, dry

Interest: flowers, foliage

Care: easy

◀ Argemone munita

The light blue-green, spiny foliage and large, showy flowers of prickly poppies make an attractive if bold statement in the garden. The sweetly fragrant white, yellow, or orange flowers have four to six crepe-paper petals surrounding a central mass of yellow stamens. The fruit of prickly poppies is composed of small, spiny capsules filled with tiny seeds. The plants are ideal for the backs of borders and beds.

Growing and care:
Prickly poppies are difficult to transplant, and grow best when sown directly in the garden after danger of frost has passed. Thin plants to 1 to 2 feet apart. Deadhead regularly to encourage blossoming. Plants grow best in poor, slightly dry soils. If spent flowers are not removed the plants often self-seed.

Selected species and varieties:
A. mexicana (Mexican poppy) is an annual with 1- to 2-foot spiny stems bearing 2- to 2½-inch yellow, golden, or orange flowers in summer above green leaves often spotted with white. *A. munita* (white prickly poppy), an annual or tender perennial, grows to 3 feet tall with many 2- to 5-inch showy white summer flowers surrounding yellow stamens and a purple stigma.

PURPLE BELL VINE
Rhodochiton

Light: full sun	
Plant type: tender perennial grown as annual	
Height: 5 to 15 feet	
Soil and Moisture: well-drained, evenly moist, fertile	
Interest: flowers, foliage	
Care: easy	

◄ Rhodochiton atrosanguineum

From summer to frost, purple bell vine bears pendent, tubular, deep violet flowers surrounded by a four-pointed calyx of bright fuchsia. Native to Mexico, where it is a perennial, the purple bell vine is grown as an annual north of Zone 9. This fast-growing vine climbs by twisting its long petioles around any nearby support. The vigorous plants are attractive when used as a seasonal cover for a fence or trellis, or when allowed to cascade from a hanging basket or patio container.

Growing and care:
Start seed indoors in individual peat pots 3 to 4 months prior to the last frost. Place several seeds in each pot, because germination may be erratic. Snip out all but the strongest seedling after plants show first true leaves. Transplant to the garden after soil has warmed, spacing plants 1 foot apart. Fertilize and water regularly. Purple bell vine grows best in hot weather.

Selected species and varieties:
R. atrosanguineum [also called *R. volubile*] grows to 15 feet in its native habitat but usually reaches 5 to 8 feet in temperate zones. Its thick-textured, heart-shaped green leaves are tipped with purple. Elongated bell-shaped flowers are about an inch in length and hang from slender stems.

SAGE
Salvia

Light: full sun	
Plant type: annual or tender perennial	
Height: 8 inches to 4 feet	
Soil and Moisture: well-drained, dry to moist, sandy	
Interest: flowers, foliage	
Care: easy	

◄ Salvia coccinea 'Lady in Red'

Hummingbirds and butterflies love a garden where sage is in bloom. There are many different types to choose from, each having soft, sometimes downy leaves, slender erect stems, and whorls of tiny hooded flowers from summer to fall. Sage is particularly effective when planted in large groups that multiply the impact of their flowers and encourage a steady stream of winged visitors.

Growing and care:
Start seed indoors in sterilized potting mix or vermiculite 6 to 8 weeks prior to the last frost. Space smaller types 1 to 1½ feet apart, larger types 2 to 3 feet apart. Pinch plants when about 6 inches high to encourage bushy growth. Sage is generally drought tolerant but needs extra watering during very dry periods. Remove faded flowers to extend bloom. Fertilize lightly during growing season.

Selected species and varieties:
S. coccinea (Texas sage) produces heart-shaped leaves on 1- to 2-foot branching stems; 'Lady in Red' has slender clusters of bright red flowers. *S. farinacea* (mealy-cup sage) grows 2 to 3 feet tall with gray-green leaves and spikes of small blue flowers; 'Silver White' grows 18 to 20 inches tall with silvery white flowers; 'Strata' reaches 16 to 24 inches with 6- to 10-inch spikes of bicolored flowers in blue and white that are useful in both fresh and dried arrangements; 'Victoria' grows to 1½ feet with

(continued)

a uniform habit and a 14-inch spread with violet-blue flowers. *S. greggii* (autumn sage) grows 2 to 4 feet tall with an erect, shrubby habit, medium green leaves, and red, pink, yellow, or white flowers that bloom from mid-summer through fall and attract hummingbirds. *S. leucantha* (Mexican bush sage) grows 2 to 4 feet with gracefully arching stems, gray-green leaves, and arching spikes of purple and white flowers in summer and fall. *S. splendens* (scarlet sage) grows to 8 to 30 inches with 2- to 4-inch bright green leaves and terminal clusters of red, pink, purple, lavender, or white flowers up to 1½ inches long; 'Blaze of Fire' grows to 12 to 14 inches with bright red blooms; 'Laser Purple' bears deep purple flowers that resist fading; 'Rodeo' grows to 10 inches with early red flowers. *S. viridis* (painted sage) grows to 1½ feet with white and blue flowers sporting showy pink to purple bracts throughout summer and fall, and is superb for fresh and dried arrangements.

SCOTCH THISTLE
Onopordum

◀ Onopordum acanthium

Light: full sun	
Plant type: annual or biennial	
Height: 6 to 9 feet	
Soil and Moisture: well-drained, light, dry	
Interest: flowers, foliage	
Care: easy	

Scotch thistle is a stately if well-armored plant bearing fuzzy, globular flower heads on tall, stiffly erect branching stems lined with spiny gray-green leaves. The foliage and unusual flowers, which look like upturned shaving brushes, add bold color and texture to the garden while supplying a strong vertical accent.

Growing and care:
Start seed indoors 6 to 8 weeks prior to the last frost, or sow directly in the garden after all danger of frost has passed. Space plants 3 feet apart. Once established they will self-seed and may become invasive. To prevent self-seeding remove entire plant from garden after flowering and toss in the compost pile. Plants can go weeks with little water or fertilizer and thrive in hot, dry locations.

Selected species and varieties:
O. acanthium (Scotch thistle, cotton thistle, silver thistle) produces stiff, downy leaves to 2 feet long, deeply lobed and scalloped into spiny segments on branching stems 6 to 9 feet tall. In late spring to summer, stems are tipped with round, prickly purple or white flowers that have flat, fuzzy tops up to 2 inches in diameter. The blossoms are often visited by butterflies.

STATICE
Limonium

Light: full sun	
Plant type: annual or biennial	
Height: 10 to 20 inches	
Soil and Moisture: well-drained, sandy, dry	
Interest: flowers	
Care: easy	

◀ Limonium sinuatum

Statice, also called sea lavender, is an essential part of any cutting garden. The plants bear clusters of brightly colored flowers surrounded by an attractive papery calyx that remains after the rest of the flower drops. This long-lasting display keeps beds, borders, and arrangements looking fresh for weeks. The flowers are easy to dry and retain their color well, making them popular additions to dried arrangements.

Growing and care:
Start seed indoors in individual peat pots 8 weeks prior to the last frost, or sow directly outdoors in midspring in warm climates. Allow 9 to 18 inches between plants. Statice thrives in drought and seaside conditions and prefers soil that is well drained and dry.

Selected species and varieties:
L. sinuatum (notchleaf statice) grows 16 to 18 inches tall with branched, winged flower stems. The papery blossoms are borne in short, one-sided clusters; colors include pink, blue, lavender, yellow, and white. *L. suworowii* [also known as *Psylliostachys suworowii*] (Russian statice) grows 10 to 20 inches tall with large basal leaves and spikes of lavender and bears green flowers from summer to frost.

STRAWFLOWER
Helichrysum

Light: full sun	
Plant type: tender perennial grown as annual	
Height: 12 to 28 inches	
Soil and Moisture: well-drained, sandy, medium to dry	
Interest: flowers	
Care: easy	

◀ Helichrysum bracteatum

This Australian native, also known as everlasting, bears attractive papery-textured flowers in shades of white, yellow, orange, salmon, red, and pink. What appear to be the flower's petals are actually colorful bracts; the true flowers arise from the center of the flower head. Dwarf types are excellent for adding color to rock gardens or the edge of the border. Taller varieties are prized as cut flowers, the brightly colored blossoms lending sparkle to dried arrangements.

Growing and care:
Start seed indoors 6 to 8 weeks prior to the last frost. In warm climates, seed can be sown directly in the garden. Space plants about 1 foot apart. Once established, plants thrive in dry soil and often self-seed. They do not perform well in areas with very high humidity. For winter arrangements, cut flowers when they are about half open and hang them upside down in an airy room to dry.

Selected species and varieties:
H. bracteatum produces narrow, coarsely toothed gray-green leaves on wiry, branching stems. Flower heads appear from midsummer to early fall and are 1 to 2½ inches across.

SUNFLOWER
Helianthus

Light: full sun	
Plant type: annual	
Height: 2 to 10 feet	
Soil and Moisture: well-drained, moist	
Interest: flowers	
Care: easy	

◀ Helianthus annuus 'Inca Jewels'

Few flowers add as much cheerfulness to the garden as sunflowers. Their large daisylike blooms appear from midsummer to frost atop strong, tall stalks. The flowers come in shades of yellow, cream, mahogany, and crimson and make a bold statement in mixed borders. A row of sunflowers makes a delightful summertime screen, and many varieties are also excellent cut flowers. In late summer and fall the ripe seeds attract many species of songbirds to the garden.

Growing and care:
Sow seed directly outdoors after the last frost. Thin seedlings to allow 1 to 2 feet between plants. Fertilize lightly every few weeks for best flower production. Plants thrive in hot, dry weather conditions but need extra water during droughts.

Selected species and varieties:
H. annuus (common sunflower) has an erect habit and pleasingly coarse texture, producing sturdy stems, broad leaves, and large flowers; 'Inca Jewels' has a branching habit with yellow-tipped orange rays; 'Italian White' has multiple stems to 4 feet and 4-inch cream-colored flowers with a brown center; 'Sunbeam' grows 5 feet tall with 5-inch pollenless flowers ideal for cutting; 'Teddy Bear' produces single and double yellow flowers on 2-foot plants.

SWAN RIVER DAISY
Brachycome

Light: full sun	
Plant type: annual	
Height: 9 to 14 inches	
Soil and Moisture: well-drained, moist, fertile	
Interest: flowers	
Care: easy	

◀ Brachycome iberidifolia

Swan River daisies produce tidy mounds of well-branched, feathery foliage smothered all season long with an abundance of small, dainty, daisylike flowers in enchanting shades of blue, lavender, and violet. They are excellent additions to beds and borders, where they add a soft, colorful accent, but are most popular when allowed to cascade over the edges of patio containers or hanging baskets.

Growing and care:
Start seed indoors 6 to 8 weeks before the last spring frost or sow directly in the garden after the soil has warmed. Thin seedlings to 6 to 12 inches apart. For continuous flowering do not allow soil to dry out. In areas with hot summers provide some afternoon shade. Fertilize lightly but regularly from spring to frost. In regions with cool summers sow every month for continuous bloom.

Selected species and varieties:
B. iberidifolia grows to 1 foot with a compact, mounding habit. The delicate, fernlike gray-green leaves are 3 inches long and are borne on slender stems. Flowers are asterlike and come in white, lavender, pink, rose, and blue.

TAHOKA DAISY
Machaeranthera

Light: full sun

Plant type: annual

Height: 6 to 12 inches

Soil and Moisture: well-drained, sandy, medium to dry

Interest: flowers

Care: moderate

◀ Machaeranthera tanacetifolia

Tahoka daisy is a free-flowering plant with abundant dainty, asterlike blossoms from late spring to frost. Native to the sunny, open spaces from southern Canada through the Great Plains, this low-spreading annual wildflower is a charming addition to borders and cutting gardens. The flowers are excellent for use in fresh floral arrangements.

Growing and care:
Start seed indoors 6 to 8 weeks before last frost or direct-sow in the garden in early spring when soil is still cool. Do not cover, as seeds need light to germinate. Space plants 9 to 12 inches apart. In areas with hot summers provide some afternoon shade. Tahoka daisy grows best in sandy soil where summers are cool.

Selected species and varieties:
M. tanacetifolia has clusters of 2-inch, thin-petaled lavender flowers with yellow centers, on 6- to 12-inch-tall stems densely covered with deeply cut, pointed foliage. Native to the Great Plains from Alberta south to northern Mexico. Plants readily self-seed.

TASSEL FLOWER
Emilia

Light: full sun

Plant type: annual

Height: 1 1/2 to 2 feet

Soil and Moisture: well-drained, light, dry

Interest: flowers

Care: easy

◀ Emilia javanica

Tassel flower is a lovely, informal plant with attractive, brilliantly colored flowers and a relaxed growth habit. The blossoms appear all season long and look like small brushes that have been dipped in red, orange, or yellow paint. Plant tassel flower among other annuals in a border or in a wildflower meadow. The flowers can be cut for both fresh and dried arrangements.

Growing and care:
Start seed indoors in peat pots 6 to 8 weeks prior to the last frost for earliest bloom. Do not disturb roots after transplanting. Sow outdoors 2 to 3 weeks before last frost. From Zone 8 south sow seed in fall. Space plants 6 to 9 inches apart. Plants often produce more flowers if slightly crowded. Tassel flower thrives in coastal conditions and prefers well-drained, dry soils.

Selected species and varieties:
E. javanica [also known as *E. coccinea* and *Cacalia coccinea*] develops a mounded, 6-inch-high clump of oblong leaves. Erect stems are topped with 1-inch clusters of dainty flowers in shades of red, orange, and yellow.

THORN APPLE
Datura

Light: full sun	
Plant type: annual	
Height: 2 to 6 feet	
Soil and Moisture: well-drained, medium	
Interest: flowers	
Care: easy	

◄ Datura inoxia

Thorn apple has thick, woody stems, large leaves, and huge trumpet-shaped flowers during summer. These fast-growing plants are excellent when grown in large containers for the deck or patio, or to add a tropical flavor to borders. The large leaves are pungently aromatic, while the night-blooming flowers are often pleasantly scented. Many species of *Datura* are poisonous and should be used in the garden with care. They should always be placed well away from children and pets.

Growing and care:
Start seed indoors 8 to 12 weeks prior to moving outdoors to warmed soil. From Zone 9 south, seed may be direct sown in the garden after danger of frost has passed. Space plants 1½ to 2 feet apart or grow a single plant in a large container. Provide shelter from wind. *D. inoxia* sometimes becomes a short-lived perennial in Zones 9 and 10. Elsewhere, it often self-sows.

Selected species and varieties:
D. inoxia (thorn apple, angel's-trumpet) commonly grows to 3 feet but may reach twice that height with 10-inch leaves and pendent pink, white, or lavender flowers 8 inches long and 5 inches wide. *D. metel* (Hindu datura) grows 3 to 6 feet tall with 8-inch leaves and 7-inch white, yellow-, or purple-tinged flowers.

TIDY-TIPS
Layia

Light: full sun	
Plant type: annual	
Height: 6 inches to 2 feet	
Soil and Moisture: well-drained, moist, sandy	
Interest: flowers	
Care: easy	

◄ Layia platyglossa

Tidy-tips is native to California, where it is a prized wildflower. The plants have slender, pliant stems and gray-green leaves decorated with abundant sun-yellow flowers. Its common name refers to the showy white-tipped ray petals that surround the brilliant golden disk. *Layia* is beautiful in borders, rock gardens, and wildflower meadows. The flowers are excellent for fresh arrangements.

Growing and care:
Start seed indoors 6 to 8 weeks prior to the last frost, or sow outdoors in early spring. In Zone 9 and warmer, seed can be sown in fall. Space plants 9 to 12 inches apart, and provide abundant moisture to seedlings. Once plants are established, they are quite drought tolerant. Remove flowers as they fade to prolong blooming period.

Selected species and varieties:
L. platyglossa has a neat habit and coarsely toothed gray-green leaves covered with dense hairs. The single, bright yellow daisylike flowers appear from spring to early summer. *Layia* is a popular ingredient in wildflower mixes.

TOADFLAX
Linaria

Light: full sun	
Plant type: annual	
Height: 10 to 18 inches	
Soil and Moisture: well-drained, moist	
Interest: flowers	
Care: easy	

◀ Linaria maroccana
'Fairy Bouquet'

This popular, hardy annual from Morocco has erect stems, slender lanced-shaped leaves, and stiff spikes of colorful flowers that resemble little snapdragons. Its dainty bicolored flowers come in a rainbow of colors and are at home in mixed borders and rock gardens. Cut flowers make nice additions to indoor arrangements.

Growing and care:
Sow seed directly in the garden 2 to 3 weeks before the last frost. Thin seedlings to stand 6 inches apart. Provide extra water during dry periods. Plants do best in regions with warm summer days and cool nights. In areas with hot summers provide afternoon shade and water frequently. Plants often reseed.

Selected species and varieties:
L. maroccana (Moroccan toadflax) has an erect, bushy habit with narrow, light green leaves and slender spikes of ½-inch flowers in shades of pink, purple, yellow, and white, usually with a contrasting throat; 'Fairy Bouquet' grows to 10 inches and bears flowers in shades of pink, rose, coppery orange, purple, white, and pale yellow, all with a deeper yellow throat. It is suitable for an edging or a window box.

TWINSPUR
Diascia

Light: full sun	
Plant type: annual	
Height: 8 to 12 inches	
Soil and Moisture: well-drained, moist, fertile	
Interest: flowers	
Care: easy	

◀ Diascia barberae
'Ruby Fields'

Twinspur is an elegant plant with slender, pliant stems bearing loose spikes of shell pink flowers from summer to fall. Each blossom has a pair of gently curving floral spurs at its back. The plants add a graceful touch to the front of beds or borders and are interesting additions to rock gardens. Twinspur also makes a charming container plant, suitable for window boxes and hanging baskets.

Growing and care:
Start seed indoors 6 to 8 weeks prior to the last frost. Transplant to the garden after the soil has warmed, spacing plants 8 inches apart. Plants can also be seeded directly in the garden in early spring. Pinch young plants to encourage bushiness. Cut back plants after flowering to encourage rebloom. In regions with hot summers provide some shade in midafternoon.

Selected species and varieties:
D. barberae has a mounding habit with slender stems bearing loose clusters of rosy pink flowers from early summer to early fall; 'Pink Queen' grows to 1 foot and bears 6-inch clusters of yellow-throated pastel pink flowers; 'Ruby Fields' produces deep-rose-colored flowers over an exceptionally long period.

VERBENA
Verbena

Light: full sun

Plant type: annual or tender perennial grown as annual

Height: 6 inches to 4 feet

Soil and Moisture: well-drained, moist, fertile

Interest: flowers

Care: easy

◀ Verbena bonariensis

Throughout the season verbena bears clusters of small, vividly colored flowers that are irresistible to butterflies. The plants make excellent annual ground covers or fillers for empty spots in the garden. Smaller forms look great in containers, while taller types add an airy touch to summer bouquets.

Growing and care:
Start seed indoors 8 to 10 weeks prior to the last frost and transplant outdoors after all danger of frost has passed. Allow 1 foot between plants of garden verbena and 2 feet between Brazilian verbenas. Pinch tips from young plants to encourage branching. Plants are drought tolerant but produce more abundant flowers when watered regularly.

Selected species and varieties:
V. bonariensis (Brazilian verbena) grows to 4 feet tall with slender, branching stems and fragrant, rosy violet flower clusters that seem to float above the wrinkled, toothed leaves. *V. x hybrida* (garden verbena) grows 6 to 12 inches tall and twice as wide, with wrinkled leaves and small pink, red, blue, purple, or white flowers arranged in rounded 2-inch heads; 'Peaches and Cream' bears flowers in shades of apricot, orange, yellow, and cream; 'Silver Ann' has bright pink blossoms that fade to watercolor shades of pink and white.

VIPER'S BUGLOSS
Echium

Light: full sun

Plant type: biennial grown as annual

Height: 1 to 10 feet

Soil and Moisture: well-drained, light, dry to moist

Interest: flowers, foliage

Care: easy

◀ Echium candicans

Viper's bugloss is a bold addition to borders or rock gardens. These tropical natives are particularly striking in flower, when large, bottlebrush-shaped spikes of blossoms loom high above the silvery gray foliage. The plants do especially well in sunny, dry locations where the soil is poor.

Growing and care:
Start seed indoors in peat pots 6 to 8 weeks before the last frost. Sow outdoors as soon as soil can be worked in spring. From Zone 9 south sow seed in fall. Space plants 1 to 1½ feet apart. Transplant carefully and do not disturb established plants. Viper's bugloss often self-seeds and can become invasive. It will grow in wet or dry soils but does best in dry locations.

Selected species and varieties:
E. candicans (pride-of-Madeira) grows 3 to 6 feet tall with narrow gray-green leaves covered with silvery hairs, and erect 20-inch clusters of white or purple ½-inch flowers held well above the leaves. *E. lycopsis* (viper's bugloss) grows 1 to 3 feet tall with a bushy habit; flowers are blue, lavender, purple, pink, or white and appear on dense 10-inch spikes. *E. wildpretii* (tower-of-jewels) grows to an eye-catching 10 feet, with pale red blooms.

WALLFLOWER
Cheiranthus

Light: full sun
Plant type: tender perennial grown as annual
Height: 6 to 24 inches
Soil and Moisture: well-drained, moist, fertile
Interest: flowers, fragrance
Care: easy

◀ Cheiranthus cheiri 'Bowles' Mauve'

Wallflowers are vigorous, bushy plants that bear abundant clusters of richly fragrant 1-inch flowers in a rainbow of colors including shades of yellow, orange, red, and purple. Dwarf varieties are perfect for rock gardens or filling in gaps of stone walls. Taller types are a must for informal borders and cottage gardens.

Growing and care:
Sow seed outdoors in spring or fall for bloom the following season. Early-flowering varieties can be started indoors in midwinter, hardened in a cold frame, and transplanted to the garden as soon as the soil can be worked in spring. Space plants about 1 foot apart. Pinch plants to encourage bushiness. Give extra water during dry periods. Wallflowers thrive in cool climates and do well in coastal and mountainous areas such as the Pacific Northwest.

Selected species and varieties:
C. cheiri [also listed as *Erysimum cheiri*] (English wallflower) has a low, erect habit; dwarf varieties grow to 6 to 9 inches, while tall varieties may reach 2 feet. Early-flowering strains often bloom their first year from seed if started early enough, but most varieties are treated as biennials; 'Bowles' Mauve' produces large clusters of deep pink flowers.

WALLFLOWER
Erysimum

Light: full sun
Plant type: biennial grown as annual
Height: 9 inches to 2 feet
Soil and Moisture: well-drained, light, dry
Interest: flowers, fragrance
Care: easy

◀ Erysimum x perofskianum

The sweet, spicy fragrance of wallflower is just as charming as the vivid flowers it comes from. From spring to early summer the plants are covered with open clusters of yellow or orange blossoms that perk up rock gardens, window boxes, or borders.

Growing and care:
In areas with mild winters, sow seed outdoors in fall; elsewhere, sow in early spring as soon as soil can be worked. Thin plants to stand 6 inches apart. Remove spent flowers regularly to encourage increased flowering. Plants often self-seed if old flowers are not removed. Grows well in dry, neutral soils.

Selected species and varieties:
E. x *perofskianum* (fairy wallflower) produces a rosette of narrow 3-inch leaves and erect 9- to 24-inch flower stems crowded with yellow, orange, or red-orange blossoms. Each flower is ½ inch long and is composed of four petals and four sepals. *E.* 'Blood Red' bears fragrant, magenta flowers; 'Cloth of Gold' has large, fragrant golden yellow blossoms; 'Eastern Queen' bears salmon-colored flowers.

YELLOW AGERATUM
Lonas

Light: full sun	
Plant type: annual	
Height: 10 to 18 inches	
Soil and Moisture: well-drained, light, moist	
Interest: flowers	
Care: easy	

◀ *Lonas annua*

This charming native of Italy and northwestern Africa has deep green, feathery leaves beneath showy clusters of yellow flowers that resemble miniature powder puffs. The everlasting blossoms appear all season long and are excellent for both fresh and dried arrangements. Yellow ageratum is a sure bet to add zip to sunny informal borders and cutting gardens.

Growing and care:
Start seed indoors 6 to 8 weeks prior to the last frost or sow directly in the garden when danger of frost has passed. Thin seedlings to 8 to 12 inches apart. Deadhead regularly to encourage flowering. Plants thrive in light, infertile soil and do well in seaside conditions. To use for winter arrangements, cut flowers when they reach full color, tie in bunches and hang them upside down in an airy room until dry.

Selected species and varieties:
L. annua (African daisy) is a vigorous grower with an open, rounded habit. It sports fine-textured, deeply divided leaves along erect, branched stems, and 1- to 2-inch clusters of tiny yellow flowers.

ZINNIA
Zinnia

Light: full sun	
Plant type: annual	
Height: 8 inches to 3 feet	
Soil and Moisture: well-drained, moist, fertile	
Interest: flowers	
Care: easy	

◀ *Zinnia angustifolia*

Zinnias brighten the border with vividly colored pompom or daisylike blooms composed of petal-like ray flowers surrounding a center of yellow or green. Colors range from riotous yellows, oranges, and reds to shades of pastel pink, rose, salmon, cream, maroon, and purple. Zinnias bloom from summer through frost and are best planted in large groups, used as edgings, or set in a mixed border. Low, spreading types are at home in window boxes and patio planters, while taller forms are excellent for fresh summer arrangements.

Growing and care:
Zinnias are among the easiest annuals to grow. Start seed indoors 6 weeks prior to the last frost, or sow directly outdoors after all danger of frost has passed. Keep soil moist but do not overwater young plants. Space seedlings 6 to 12 inches apart and pinch young plants to encourage bushiness. Remove spent blooms to keep plants attractive and to encourage flowering. Zinnias thrive in hot weather but benefit from regular watering.

Selected species and varieties:
Z. angustifolia (narrowleaf zinnia) has a compact, spreading habit, growing from 8 to 16 inches in height with narrow, pointed leaves and 1-inch-wide single orange flowers from summer to fall; 'White Star' bears abundant 2-inch flowers with snow white petals around orange-yellow centers.

AFRICAN DAISY
Osteospermum

Light: full sun	
Plant type: perennial	
Hardiness: Zones 9-10	
Height: 6 to 12 inches	
Soil and Moisture: well-drained, fertile, moist to dry	
Interest: flowers	
Care: moderate	

◀ Osteospermum fruticosum

African daisy is a truly stunning flowering perennial for warm zones. The eye-catching flowers have round centers surrounded by long, graceful, nearly translucent white to pinkish petals. It has a trailing habit and spreads rapidly to create a dense mat. Flowers bloom most heavily in late winter and early spring, and intermittently throughout the rest of the year. It makes a lovely show in containers or behind stone walls, where it can spill over in graceful cascades.

Growing and care:
Sow seed directly in the garden in early spring or late fall. Plant thickly, for germination of seed is erratic. Because the stems root as they grow along the ground, African daisy spreads easily and quickly over large areas. It thrives in full sun and, once established, tolerates drought. Cut back old plants occasionally to encourage branching and to prevent stems from becoming straggly. Water early in the day so leaves can dry off. Cut back stems after flowering.

Selected species and varieties:
O. fruticosum grows 6 to 12 inches tall and 3 feet wide with oval, 1- to 2-inch-long leaves and 2-inch-wide flowers with lavender petals around a purple center; 'African Queen' bears very attractive deep purple flowers; 'Hybrid White' is more upright in habit with enchanting pure white flowers.

BABY'S-BREATH
Gypsophila

Light: full sun	
Plant type: perennial	
Hardiness: Zones 4-9	
Height: 3 to 4 feet	
Soil and Moisture: well-drained, slightly alkaline, moist	
Interest: flowers, foliage	
Care: easy	

◀ Gypsophila repens 'Rosea'

Perennial baby's-breath resembles the annual types with the bonus that it comes back to the garden year after year. Baby's-breath bears airy clouds of tiny, single or multipetaled flowers on open-branched stems above fine-textured foliage. The plants are well suited for the middle of the border and are a must for the cutting garden. Dwarf forms make charming additions to rock gardens, especially when allowed to cascade over stone walls.

Growing and care:
Start seed indoors in peat pots 8 to 10 weeks before the last frost. Space dwarf forms 1 to 1½ feet apart and larger types 3 feet apart. Established plants are difficult to divide or transplant. Keep soil evenly moist while plants are actively growing. Use wire frames to support larger plants.

Selected species and varieties:
G. paniculata (perennial baby's-breath) has airy clusters of white flowers on stems to 4 feet tall; 'Bristol Fairy' has double white flowers; 'Perfecta' is similar to 'Bristol Fairy', with larger flowers; 'Pink Fairy' has pink double flowers on 1½-foot stems. *G. repens* (creeping baby's-breath) is a low-growing dwarf type with trailing stems 6 to 8 inches long; 'Rosea' has pale pink flowers.

BALSAMROOT
Balsamorhiza

◀ Balsamorhiza sagittata

Light: full sun	
Plant type: perennial	
Hardiness: Zones 4-10	
Height: 2 to 2 ½ feet	
Soil and Moisture: sandy, moderately dry	
Interest: flowers	
Care: easy	

A perennial native to the mountain grasslands and prairies of the American West, balsamroot has all the jaunty brightness of sunflowers on shorter, more compact stems. The vivid yellow blossoms appear in spring to early summer and look even more brilliant against the plant's broad, dark green leaves. Balsamroot is a novel and beautiful addition to borders or specialty gardens, or naturalized in upland wildflower meadows.

Growing and care:
Balsamroot thrives in full sun and deep, well-drained, sandy soil. The plants appreciate regular soakings and fertilizing but also do well if left on their own. Propagate from seed sown in fall where you want the plants to grow. Balsamroot generally requires 2 years of growth to reach flowering size. The plants produce a very long, woody taproot and transplanting should be avoided.

Selected species and varieties:
B. sagittata (balsamroot, Oregon sunflower) has a low clump of arrow- or heart-shaped, dark green leaves covered with silvery hairs and measuring up to 6 inches wide and 12 inches long; they may be undivided or deeply divided into fernlike segments; flower stems up to 32 inches tall bear a single 2½- to 4-inch flower with deep yellow petals surrounding a golden yellow center.

BASKET-OF-GOLD
Aurinia

◀ Aurinia saxatilis

Light: full sun	
Plant type: perennial	
Hardiness: Zones 3-10	
Height: 6 to 12 inches	
Soil and Moisture: well-drained, dry	
Interest: flowers	
Care: easy	

Basket-of-gold bears masses of tiny golden yellow flowers in early to midspring atop thick, compact mats of silvery gray foliage. The plants are excellent for rock gardens and borders, or when allowed to cascade over rocks and walls. The flowers of this easy-to-grow plant look like golden versions of their close relative sweet alyssum *(Lobularia maritima),* but basket-of-gold has cleft leaves that are slightly long.

Growing and care:
Basket-of-gold has been a popular plant for generations, in part because it thrives in a wide variety of conditions. It spreads quickly and reliably produces a profusion of flowers every spring. After the flowers have faded, shear the top of the plant back by one-third to encourage rebloom. Old, woody plants bloom less abundantly and should be replaced. Propagate by division in early spring or sow seed (except double-flowered varieties) in summer for bloom the following year. Do not cover seed, as light is needed for germination. Space plants 9 to 12 inches apart.

Selected species and varieties:
A. saxatilis (also listed as *Alyssum saxatile*) has mounds of 10-inch stems bearing 3-inch lance-shaped leaves covered with smooth, silvery hairs and dense clusters of yellow flowers; 'Citrina' has pale yellow flowers; 'Plena' has deep yellow double flowers; Zones 3-7.

BLACKFOOT DAISY
Melampodium

Light: full sun	
Plant type: perennial	
Hardiness: Zones 4-9	
Height: 6 to 12 inches	
Soil and Moisture: well-drained, sandy, dry	
Interest: flowers	
Care: easy	

◀ Melampodium leucanthum

Blackfoot daisy is an easy-to-grow, low-maintenance plant that is as beautiful as it is tough. The plant is native to the dry desert slopes, mesas, and high plains of the Southwest, where it has developed extreme tolerance to drought. Blackfoot daisy's deep taproot efficiently gleans moisture from the soil but also makes it difficult to transplant once established. This low-growing evergreen perennial naturally forms neat mounds that require no shaping, making it a good selection for rock gardens. It can also be massed on a sunny, sandy bank for attractive erosion control.

Growing and care:
Sow seed directly in the garden once soil has warmed. Thin plants to stand 12 to 16 inches apart. Keep soil moist until seedlings are about 4 inches tall. Fertilizing is not needed. Cut back plants in fall. Blackfoot daisy naturalizes quickly and often self-seeds.

Selected species and varieties:
M. leucanthum bears abundant solitary 1-inch white daisylike flowers with yellow centers borne on slender stalks throughout spring and summer. Gray-green leaves form a neat evergreen mound 6 to 12 inches tall and up to 16 inches wide.

BLANKET FLOWER
Gaillardia

Light: full sun	
Plant type: perennial	
Hardiness: Zones 3-8	
Height: 1 to 3 feet	
Soil and Moisture: well-drained, moist to dry	
Interest: flowers	
Care: easy	

◀ Gaillardia x grandiflora 'Goblin'

Blanket flower is an easy-to-grow perennial with cheerful, very brightly colored, daisylike flowers from early summer to frost. The flowers that bloom provide vivid color to borders, rock gardens, and wildflower meadows. Blanket flower also makes an excellent cut flower.

Growing and care:
Start seed indoors 6 to 8 weeks before the last frost. Do not cover, as seed needs light to germinate. Transplant to the garden when soil has warmed. Space plants 1½ feet apart. Blanket flower tolerates hot, dry locations, poor soil, and seaside conditions, but puts on a more vibrant show when grown in bright sun. The plants are susceptible to root rot in wet soils and very well-drained conditions are required for best growth.

Selected species and varieties:
G. x *grandiflora* has 3-inch daisylike yellow ray flowers surrounding a yellow or purplish red central disk on stems up to 3 feet tall with large, hairy, gray-green leaves; 'Goblin' bears bright red flowers edged with yellow on stems to 1 foot; 'Monarch Strain' produces flowers in varying vivid combinations of red and yellow on 2½-foot stems.

BOLTONIA
Boltonia

Light: full sun

Plant type: perennial

Hardiness: Zones 4-8

Height: 3 to 5 feet

Soil and Moisture: well-drained, dry to moist

Interest: flowers

Care: easy

◀ Boltonia asteroides
var. latisquama

Clouds of asterlike flowers atop the tall, branching stems of boltonia add an airy accent to island beds, borders, and meadows from midsummer through early fall. Boltonia's gray-green, willowlike, 5-inch leaves contrast nicely with the abundant white, pink, or lavender flowers. The plants are native to the eastern and midwestern United States, where they grow in gravelly, sandy soil along roadsides, stream banks, and waste places.

Growing and care:
Plant seed directly in the garden in spring when soil is cool. Space taller varieties 3 to 5 feet apart, and smaller varieties 1 to 2 feet apart. Propagate species by seed or division, and cultivars by division in early spring or late fall. Pinch tops in late spring to encourage bushy, compact growth. The tallest varieties may need staking. Plants often self-seed and can become invasive if not controlled.

Selected species and varieties:
B. asteroides (white boltonia) grows 3 to 5 feet tall with 1-inch daisylike flowers; var. *latisquama* (violet boltonia) has 1½-inch purple to pink flowers; 'Nana' bears white flowers on 1- to 2-foot stems; 'Pink Beauty' has pale pink blossoms in late summer on 4- to 5-foot stems, and delicate, dusky green, mildew-resistant foliage.

CALIFORNIA FUCHSIA
Zauschneria

Light: full sun

Plant type: perennial

Hardiness: Zones 9-10

Height: 6 inches to 2 feet

Soil and Moisture: well-drained, moist to dry

Interest: flowers, foliage

Care: easy

◀ Zauschneria californica

California fuchsias are shrubby perennials with lance-shaped dull green leaves and 2- to 3-inch-long tubular flowers of intense scarlet. They spread rapidly by rhizomes to form broad mats that make fine ground covers. The plants can be grown in borders or specialty gardens, where the brilliant flowers draw hummingbirds and butterflies from summer to fall.

Growing and care:
Sow seed directly in the garden in spring after soil warms. Do not cover seed, as light is necessary for germination. Thin seedlings to stand 14 to 18 inches apart. Pinch young plants to induce branching. California fuchsia prefers well-drained, dry, slightly alkaline soil. Propagate by seed, fall cuttings, or root divisions in early spring.

Selected species and varieties:
Z. californica is a broad shrubby perennial with much-branched stems 6 to 24 inches in height and woolly gray-green foliage; trumpet-shaped, brilliant scarlet flowers 2½ inches long bloom from late summer through fall; ssp. *latifolia* [also called *Epilobium canum* ssp. *latifolium*] (hummingbird trumpet) is a compact shrubby plant up to 2 feet tall with trumpet-shaped scarlet flowers from early summer through fall.

CALIFORNIA TREE POPPY
Romneya

Light: full sun

Plant type: perennial

Hardiness: Zones 7-10

Height: 4 to 8 feet

Soil and Moisture: well-drained, dry

Interest: flowers, fragrance

Care: difficult

◀ Romneya coulteri

California tree poppies are large, shrubby perennials that bear extraordinarily beautiful flowers in summer to early fall. The fragrant blossoms are 3 to 6 inches in diameter with a mounded center of pincushion stamens surrounded by wide, paper-thin, delicately ruffled white petals. Though short lived, the flowers are striking in fresh floral arrangements. To keep cut flowers fresh longer, sear the ends of the stems with a flame to seal in their milky sap.

Growing and care:
California poppies grow well only in regions with hot, dry summers followed by cool, moist winters. They are very difficult to grow in areas with pronounced humidity. Space California tree poppies 3 to 4 feet apart in sites where their wide-spreading, invasive roots will not present a problem. They grow best in Zones 8 and 9 but will survive in Zone 7 given a heavy winter mulch. Cut stems back to 6 inches in fall.

Selected species and varieties:
R. coulteri bears icy white flowers with nearly translucent, ruffled petals throughout summer on branching 8-foot stems with gray-green leaves in clumps 3 feet wide.

CANDYTUFT
Iberis

Light: full sun

Plant type: perennial

Hardiness: Zones 4-8

Height: 6 to 12 inches

Soil and Moisture: well-drained, fertile, moist

Interest: flowers, foliage

Care: easy

◀ Iberis sempervirens 'Snow Mantle'

The glossy, dark green leaves of candytuft provide a perfect background for the clusters of pure white flowers that cover the plant in spring. Candytuft is very effective when planted in the front of the perennial border, as an edging along a walkway, or allowed to cascade over a stone wall or sprawl across a rock garden.

Growing and care:
Plant candytuft in well-worked soil that has been generously amended with compost or peat moss. Space plants 12 to 15 inches apart. Keep soil evenly moist for best flowering. After blossoms have faded cut plants back 2 to 3 inches to encourage rebloom. Mulch around plants to keep soil moist and roots cool.

Selected species and varieties:
I. sempervirens produces 1-foot-tall mounds of linear, 1-inch-long evergreen leaves on semiwoody stems, and dense clusters of very showy white flowers; 'Snowflake' grows 10 inches high with 2- to 3-inch flower clusters; 'Snow Mantle' is 8 inches high with a dense, compact habit and pure white flowers.

CHICKWEED
Cerastium

Light: full sun

Plant type: perennial

Hardiness: Zones 3-7

Height: 6 to 12 inches

Soil and Moisture: well-drained, sandy, dry

Interest: flowers, foliage

Care: easy

◀ Cerastium
tomentosum

Snow-in-summer is a robust creeping plant with small, usually silvery green leaves that nearly disappear beneath the mounds of starry white flowers. These vigorous plants make excellent ground covers for dry, sandy sites and can be used as accents near steps and walkways or in rock gardens, although they may crowd other plants. Snow-in-summer is often used to control erosion on sunny slopes where its masses of frosty white flowers lend coolness to the hottest summer day.

Growing and care:
Propagate by division in fall. Space divided clumps 1 to 1½ feet apart. Snow-in-summer grows well without regular watering or fertilizing. Once established, these plants often naturalize, becoming self-sustaining members of the garden. Divide them regularly to control their spread.

Selected species and varieties:
C. alpinum (alpine chickweed) has tight clusters of small, white, late-spring flowers atop spreading 6-inch mounds of tiny, oval gray leaves. *C. arvense* (starry grass-wort) produces 1-inch oval leaves beneath 1-foot clusters of star-shaped, white, spring flowers; 'Compactum' has a spreading habit and pure white flowers nestled in a mat of 2- to 3-inch foliage. *C. tomentosum* (snow-in-summer) has 6- to 9-inch prostrate stems bearing narrow, 1-inch, lance-shaped woolly whitish green leaves and small spring to summer flowers; Zones 4-7.

CONEFLOWER
Rudbeckia

Light: full sun

Plant type: perennial

Hardiness: Zones 4-9

Height: 1 to 7 feet

Soil and Moisture: well-drained, moist to dry

Interest: flowers, foliage

Care: easy

◀ Rudbeckia hirta
'Goldilocks'

Coneflowers are prolific bloomers from early summer to frost and are the backbone of many perennial gardens. These natives of North American grasslands and meadows have daisylike flower heads with intense yellow rays that contrast to their centers of deep brown. Coneflowers have large, hairy leaves and stiff stems. They are excellent in sunny borders, mixed with clumps of ornamental grasses, or naturalized in meadows.

Growing and care:
Space plants 1½ to 2 feet apart. *R. hirta* grows as an annual, biennial, or short-lived perennial, and should be propagated by seed. Its flowering season can be prolonged by sowing seed at biweekly intervals. Other species of coneflowers can be propagated by seed or division in early spring.

Selected species and varieties:
R. fulgida (orange coneflower, black-eyed Susan) is a 1- to 3-foot perennial that produces 3- to 5-inch yellow-orange flowers with dark, domed centers from early summer through fall. *R. hirta* (black-eyed Susan) is a 1- to 3-foot short-lived perennial with 2-inch petals surrounding conical centers in late summer; 'Gloriosa Daisy' is yellow with a mahogany center; 'Goldilocks' has brilliant yellow semidouble flowers.

COREOPSIS
Coreopsis

Light: full sun	
Plant type: perennial	
Hardiness: Zones 4-9	
Height: 6 inches to 3 feet	
Soil and Moisture: well-drained, fertile, moist	
Interest: flowers, foliage	
Care: easy	

◀ Coreopsis grandiflora

Coreopsis is easy to grow and famous for its reliable displays of intense, sunny yellow flowers and dainty, dark green foliage. The plants bloom for many weeks in summer and are eye-catching additions to borders, rock gardens, or naturalistic plantings. Coreopsis is excellent for cutting.

Growing and care:
Sow seed indoors 6 to 8 weeks before the last frost. In areas with mild winters direct-sow in the garden in fall. Space plants 6 to 12 inches apart. Water during dry periods and fertilize lightly in spring. Excessive fertilizer or dry soil can inhibit flowering. Remove spent flowers to extend bloom time. Grow coreopsis where it is sheltered from winds. Divide plants after flowering in northern areas, and in fall in southern regions.

Selected species and varieties:
C. grandiflora has yellow or orange single, semidouble, and double flowers 1 to 1½ inches across, blooming from early to late summer on 1- to 2-foot stems. *C. lanceolata* (lance coreopsis) 'Goldfink' is a 10- to 12-inch-tall dwarf with yellow flowers 1½ to 2½ inches across that blooms prolifically from summer to fall. *C. verticillata* (threadleaf coreopsis) bears golden yellow flowers from late spring to late summer; 'Zagreb' is 1½ feet tall with bright yellow flowers; 'Moonbeam' grows to 2 feet tall with abundant lemon yellow flowers.

COYOTE MINT
Monardella

Light: full sun	
Plant type: perennial	
Hardiness: Zones 6-10	
Height: 4 to 24 inches	
Soil and Moisture: well-drained, dry	
Interest: flowers, foliage, fragrance	
Care: easy	

◀ Monardella odoratissima

Coyote mints have round, ragged clusters of thin-petaled flowers that resemble more casual versions of bee balm. These informal plants have strong, flexible stems and aromatic, minty blue-green leaves. Coyote mints are often used in sunny, dry rock gardens, especially in the American Southwest, where they are native. Like those of their bee balm cousins, the blossoms of coyote mints are very attractive to butterflies and hummingbirds.

Growing and care:
Sow seed directly in the garden in spring after soil has warmed, or start indoors 6 to 8 weeks before the last frost. Space plants 10 to 12 inches apart. Water regularly until seedlings are a few inches high. Once established the plants are very drought tolerant and need supplemental water only during extended dry periods. Overwatering leads to weak growth and less aromatic foliage. Divide plants after they go dormant in fall.

Selected species and varieties:
M. macrantha (hummingbird mint, scarlet coyote mint) grows 4 to 12 inches tall with glossy green foliage and tubular bright red flowers in showy, round terminal clusters in summer; Zones 8-10. *M. odoratissima* (coyote mint, mountain mint) bears flowers ranging from nearly white to bright blue-purple in 2-inch clusters; the stems form large mats about 1 foot tall with fragrant leaves.

CRAMBE
Crambe

Light: full sun

Plant type: perennial

Hardiness: Zones 5-9

Height: 2 to 6 feet

Soil and Moisture: well-drained, fertile, slightly alkaline

Interest: flowers, foliage, fragrance

Care: moderate

◀ Crambe cordifolia

Crambe is a very large shrubby perennial with huge, billowy clouds of tiny white blossoms in late spring to early summer. In form these airy plants resemble baby's-breath but are much larger. Mingled among the fragrant gossamer flowers are masses of wrinkled gray-green leaves. Crambe is a good choice for the back of the border or as a filler in large specialty gardens. When grown in wildflower meadows the plants nicely complement daisies, asters, and boltonias.

Growing and care:
Crambe does not transplant well and seed should be sown directly in the garden in early spring or in fall soon after ripening. Thin plants to stand 2 to 3 feet apart. Plants grown from seed usually require about 3 growing seasons to reach flowering size. Crambe is attractive to a number of insect pests and should receive regular sprayings of insecticidal soap. Stake plants if they seem floppy, and prune to ground level in fall.

Selected species and varieties:
C. cordifolia (colewort) produces broad leafy mounds up to 4 feet across crowned by an equally wide froth of icy white flowers on stalks to 6 feet tall. *C. maritima* (sea kale) produces 2-foot-wide mounds of attractive blue-green leaves with a powdery coating topped by a billow of tiny white flowers on stalks up to 3 feet tall.

DELPHINIUM
Delphinium

Light: full sun

Plant type: perennial

Hardiness: Zones 3-7

Height: 2 to 8 feet

Soil and Moisture: well-drained, fertile, moist

Interest: flowers

Care: moderate

◀ Delphinium 'Blue Fountains'

Delphiniums are stately, majestic plants that give any perennial border or specialty garden a touch of class. The plants bear enormous showy spikes packed with scores of 2-inch flowers on upright stalks above clumps of finely cut, lobed leaves. The various colors of the spurred flowers are stunning shades of royal blue, lavender, rose, and white. Many of the flowers also have a ruffled, contrastingly colored center called a bee.

Growing and care:
Start seed indoors 8 to 10 weeks before planting out or sow directly in the garden in early spring or fall. The plants do best in areas with cool summers and are grown as annuals where summers are hot. Space plants 1 to 2 feet apart in soil enriched with organic mater. Water and fertilize regularly throughout the growing season. Cut back flower stalks after flowering to encourage rebloom in late summer. Tall varieties should be staked.

Selected species and varieties:
D. x *belladonna* (belladonna delphinium) produces porcelain blue or white flowers on delicate, branching 3- to 4-foot-tall stems. *D.* 'Blue Fountains' is a dwarf delphinium 2½ to 3 feet tall with flowers in enchanting shades of blue. *D. elatum* 'Pacific Hybrids' has spires of intensely colored blue, violet, lavender, pink, or white mostly double flowers on stalks 4 to 6 feet tall.

FALSE SUNFLOWER
Heliopsis

Light: full sun	
Plant type: perennial	
Hardiness: Zones 4-9	
Height: 3 to 5 feet	
Soil and Moisture: well-drained, fertile, moist	
Interest: flowers	
Care: easy	

◀ Heliopsis helianthoides

False sunflower bears bright flowers in shades of yellow and gold, each blossom with single or double rows of petals surrounding prominent centers. The tall, strongly upright stems and perky flowers are good for adding colorful accents to the back of the border but are best when allowed to naturalize and spread in wildflower meadows. False sunflowers make excellent cut flowers.

Growing and care:
Start seed indoors 8 to 10 weeks before the last spring frost or sow directly in the garden in early spring or fall. Space plants 2 feet apart and stake taller forms. Water plants during extended dry periods. Divide clumps every 3 to 4 years in spring.

Selected species and varieties:
H. helianthoides var. *scabra* bears single, semidouble, or double flowers 2 to 3 inches across on plants 3 to 5 feet tall; 'Golden Plume' grows double yellow flowers; 'Incomparabilis', semidouble yellow flowers with dark centers; 'Karat', large single yellow flowers; 'Summer Sun', semidouble golden yellow flowers.

FIREWEED
Epilobium

Light: full sun	
Plant type: perennial	
Hardiness: Zones 2-9	
Height: 4 inches to 7 feet	
Soil and Moisture: well-drained, moist	
Interest: flowers	
Care: easy	

◀ Epilobium angustifolium

Fireweeds are vigorous, strongly upright plants with strong, pliant stems, coarse medium green leaves, and bright conical spikes of lilac, ruby, pink, or white flowers in summer. The plants are easy to grow and are good choices for informal borders, clearings, meadows, open slopes, or the wet areas along streams, ponds, and marshes. Fireweeds are so vigorous that they can quickly colonize wide areas, a trait that should be considered before planting.

Growing and care:
Fireweed does not transplant well and seed should be sown directly in the garden in fall. Small seedlings can be transplanted for a few weeks following germination. Space plants 1 to 2 feet apart. Fireweed grows best where summers are cool.

Selected species and varieties:
E. angustifolium (fireweed, willow herb) produces clumps of reddish stems 3 to 7 feet tall with elongated, willowlike leaves 3 to 8 inches long. Spikes of lilac-purple, rose, or occasionally white flowers appear atop the stems throughout summer over much of Canada and the United States. *E. latifolium* (dwarf fireweed), found from Alaska south through the mountain states, grows 4 to 16 inches tall with clusters of large magenta-pink flowers and bluish green leaves.

FLAX LILY
Phormium

Light:	full sun
Plant type:	perennial
Hardiness:	Zones 9-10
Height:	7 to 15 feet
Soil and Moisture:	well-drained, moist
Interest:	flowers, foliage
Care:	easy

◀ Phormium tenax

Flax lily bears dramatic fans of very long spear-shaped evergreen leaves, sometimes split at their ends or edged with red. The sharp appearance of the leaves coupled with their vibrant color makes the plant perfect for adding a bold statement to the landscape. In summer an impressively tall stem emerges from the foliage, bearing dull red 2-inch flowers. Use flax lily like yucca—as a specimen, at the back of informal borders, or as a screen.

Growing and care:
Flax lily thrives in evenly moist soil enriched with rotted manure or compost. Space plants from 1 foot apart for small types to 3 feet apart for large varieties. Provide extra water during hot, dry periods. Flax lily can be propagated from seed, but division in spring is preferred. Plants tolerate seaside conditions and pollution.

Selected species and varieties:
P. tenax (New Zealand flax) has large swordlike leathery leaves 3 to 10 feet tall with flower stalks to 10 feet; 'Atropurpureum' produces large leaves of rich purple; 'Bronze' has long, deep red-brown leaves; 'Maori Sunrise' bears large bronze leaves striped with pink and cream; 'Tiny Tim' is a semidwarf cultivar with yellow-striped bronze leaves; 'Variegatum' has creamy white striping on long green leaves.

GAURA
Gaura

Light:	full sun
Plant type:	perennial
Hardiness:	Zones 5-9
Height:	2 to 5 feet
Soil and Moisture:	well-drained, sandy, medium to dry
Interest:	flowers
Care:	easy

◀ Gaura lindheimeri

Gauras were once rarely seen in gardens but in recent years have become very popular. The plants produce abundant pale pink tubular flowers from summer to fall above neat, airy mounds of lance-shaped leaves. The unique blossoms, which have four spatula-shaped white petals and long red stamens, are beautiful when viewed close up. In addition to their beauty gauras are also tough plants well suited for use in coastal gardens, natural meadows, or informal borders.

Growing and care:
Sow seed indoors in late winter for planting out after danger of frost has passed, or direct-sow in the garden in spring when soil is still cool. Space plants 2 to 4 feet apart. Fertilize lightly and provide extra water only during hot, dry periods to prevent plants from going dormant before flowering. Seedlings will grow to flowering-size plants the first season. Gaura can also be propagated from softwood cuttings in summer or by dividing plants in fall.

Selected species and varieties:
G. lindheimeri (white gaura) has loose panicles of white tubular flowers touched with pale pink and fading to coral, in late summer to fall, on lanky 2- to 5-foot stems with lance-shaped 3½-inch leaves and spreading clumps of carrotlike taproots; 'Corre's Gold' has white flowers on 2-foot stems and green leaves edged with gold; 'Siskiyou Pink' has maroon buds and pink blossoms.

GLOBE MALLOW
Sphaeralcea

Light:	full sun
Plant type:	perennial
Hardiness:	Zones 3-10
Height:	2 to 3 feet
Soil and Moisture:	well-drained, sandy, dry
Interest:	flowers
Care:	easy

◄ Sphaeralcea coccinea

Globe mallows are easy-to-grow, drought-resistant perennials that thrive in regions with dry, sandy soils and hot summers. They bear brightly colored cupped flowers in shades of apricot, orange, red, and violet that resemble hollyhocks. Globe mallows are an excellent choice for sunny, dry rock gardens or informal borders.

Growing and care:
Globe mallows do not transplant well and seed should be planted directly in the garden in fall as soon as seed is ripe. Thin plants to stand 1½ to 2 feet apart. Once established do not disturb. Globe mallows are very drought tolerant but, when supplied with even moisture, grow quite large with more abundant flowers. Allow plants to self-seed for years of attractive blooms.

Selected species and varieties:
S. ambigua (desert mallow) has 3-foot stems bearing wandlike clusters of apricot-orange flowers up to 2 inches across in spring; Zones 6-10. *S. coccinea* (scarlet globe mallow) grows to 3 feet tall with orange-pink flowers surrounded by red bracts in spring, summer, or fall, and hairy gray-green leaves. *S. munroana* (Munro's globe mallow) produces 2- to 3-foot-tall spikes of numerous bright pink to deep apricot flowers and gray-green foliage. *S. parvifolia* is 2 to 3 feet tall with clusters of orange-red flowers and whitish gray leaves from spring to summer.

GLOBE THISTLE
Echinops

Light:	full sun
Plant type:	perennial
Hardiness:	Zones 3-8
Height:	6 inches to 8 feet
Soil and Moisture:	well-drained, moist to dry
Interest:	flowers, foliage
Care:	easy

◄ Echinops ritro 'Veitch's Blue'

Globe thistles have bold, slightly wild-looking foliage that contrasts nicely to the refined look of their ornate, spherical, summer-blooming flowers. The stiff, upright stalks are lined with thick, hairy, deeply lobed leaves bearing attractive if intimidating metallic blue spines at their tips, and topped with soft blue to white flowers that bloom for 2 months. Globe thistles are excellent for attracting butterflies and honeybees to the garden, and make beautiful and unusual additions to dried flower arrangements. Use globe thistle in borders as an informal accent or as a background to rock gardens.

Growing and care:
Globe thistles thrive in heat and drought, but in hot regions they produce more intensely colored flowers when given some afternoon shade. Space plants 1½ to 2 feet apart. Propagate by division in early spring. Globe thistle can be propagated from seed but plants produced in this way are often inferior to their parents in form and flower color. Wear leather gloves when handling these plants to protect hands from the spiny leaves.

Selected species and varieties:
E. ritro (small globe thistle) has blue-violet or deep blue flowers, rarely white, in 2-inch spheres on 2- to 5-foot white, woolly stems, and 8-inch glossy, dark green leaves with white undersides; 'Veitch's Blue' has lapis blue flowers on strong 3- to 4-foot stems.

GOAT'S RUE
Tephrosia

Light: full sun	
Plant type: perennial	
Hardiness: Zones 5-10	
Height: 1 to 2 feet	
Soil and Moisture: well-drained, sandy, dry	
Interest: flowers, foliage	
Care: easy to moderate	

◀ Tephrosia virginiana

Goat's rue is a perennial wildflower with complex pealike blossoms in vivid, contrasting bicolors of red and white or yellow and purple. The plants are easy to grow and quite tolerant of dry, hot conditions. When goat's rue is not in flower the delicate, finely cut compound leaves and 1- to 2-inch silky seedpods give the plants a soft textured appearance. Goat's rue is excellent for specialty gardens, wildflower meadows, or informal borders. The seeds attract ground birds such as quail and grouse.

Growing and care:
Plant goat's rue seed directly in the garden in fall or spring after the soil has warmed. Thin plants to stand 1 foot apart. Water regularly until seedlings are about 4 inches tall. For best growth inoculate soil with the appropriate nitrogen-fixing bacteria. Plants can be allowed to self-sow or can be divided in fall.

Selected species and varieties:
T. virginiana grows 1 to 2 feet tall with compact clusters of ¾-inch flowers composed of yellowish to white upper petals and purple to pinkish red lower petals from late spring to early summer. The foliage forms a mound of attractive, silvery, pinnately compound leaves with eight to 15 pairs of small leaflets covered with silky white hairs. In late summer to fall small, silky seedpods decorate the plant.

GOLDEN ASTER
Chrysopsis

Light: full sun	
Plant type: perennial	
Hardiness: Zones 4-10	
Height: 6 inches to 5 feet	
Soil and Moisture: well-drained, sandy, medium to dry	
Interest: flowers	
Care: easy	

◀ Chrysopsis mariana

The perennial golden asters are tough, vigorous plants that punctuate the landscape with long-lasting clusters of bright, daisylike blossoms. They are especially useful at the back of informal borders or naturalized in wet areas along ponds and streams or on dry hillsides and fields. They do best if planted with care and then left to their own devices.

Growing and care:
Grass-leaved and golden aster are easy to grow on sunny, dry sites but may do poorly in rich, fertile soil. Propagate by seed sown in fall or early spring while soil is cool. Thin plants to stand 2 to 3 feet apart. Plants may be divided every 3 to 4 years in spring.

Selected species and varieties:
C. graminifolia [also called *Pityopsis graminifolia*] (grass-leaved golden aster) has 1-foot grasslike leaves and clusters of bright yellow flowers on 2½-foot stems, and makes a good evergreen ground cover; Zones 5-10. *C. mariana* (Maryland golden aster) grows 1½ to 2½ feet tall with showy clusters of flowers on sturdy stems; Zones 4-9. *C. villosa* can grow from as little as 6 inches to as much as 5 feet in height, with flowers near the tips of stems that may be upright or trailing; Zones 4-9.

HENS AND CHICKS
Echeveria

Light: full sun	
Plant type: perennial	
Hardiness: Zones 9-10	
Height: 3 inches to 3 feet	
Soil and Moisture: well-drained, dry	
Interest: flowers, foliage	
Care: easy	

◄ Echeveria agavoides

Hens and chicks are easy-to-grow perennials that provide a wonderfully interesting and attractive accent to rock gardens. The plants are known for their colorful, succulent leaves that grow in compact rosettes. Bell-shaped, nodding flowers develop on slender stems in summer that rise well above the foliage. Hens and chicks thrive in warm, hot climates, where they spread reliably with very little care.

Growing and care:
Plant hens and chicks in dry, sandy soil. Water regularly for a few weeks until the plants have become established. Hens and chicks thrive in warm locations and are quite tolerant of drought and coastal conditions. Propagate from offsets anytime by cutting the "chick" from the mother plant and setting it directly in the garden, or potting it in a container to grow as a houseplant.

Selected species and varieties:
E. agavoides has 6- to 8-inch rosettes of bright green leaves with reddish margins, topped in summer by red and yellow flowers. *E. crenulata* bears loose rosettes of pale green leaves with wavy margins growing up to 1 foot long and covered with white powder, and red to orange flowers on stems up to 3 feet tall. *E.* x *imbricata* has 4- to 6-inch rosettes of gray-green leaves and delicate stems of orange, red, and yellow flowers, and develops many offsets around the base.

HOLLYHOCK
Alcea

Light: full sun	
Plant type: perennial or biennial	
Hardiness: Zones 2-9	
Height: 2 to 9 feet	
Soil and Moisture: well-drained, fertile	
Interest: flowers	
Care: moderate	

◄ Alcea rosea

The eye-catching, bell-shaped flowers of hollyhock are borne on sturdy, erect, wandlike stems. The lower flowers open first, and new blossoms appear from midsummer to early fall, with approximately 1½ to 2 feet of the stem covered with blooms throughout the season. This old-fashioned favorite provides both height and a long season of color for the back of a mixed border. It is also a good choice for growing along a fence or wall. While technically a biennial, hollyhock will last for several years under favorable conditions in cooler areas.

Growing and care:
Plant seed indoors in winter for spring transplanting. Some varieties will bloom their first summer. Seed sown outdoors in late summer will bloom the following year. Space plants 1 to 1½ feet apart in neutral to slightly alkaline soil. In windy locations they may require staking. When blossoms fade, remove the entire flower stalk to encourage the plant to behave as a perennial. Once established, hollyhocks will self-sow.

Selected species and varieties:
A. rosea has 5- to 9-foot-tall stems bearing 2- to 4-inch single or double flowers in colors that include white, pink, red, and yellow above a clump of hairy, coarse leaves 6 to 8 inches long; 'Chater's Double' grows 6 to 8 feet tall, producing peony-shaped flowers in shades of white, scarlet, pink, and yellow from early to midsummer.

KNAUTIA
Knautia

Light: full sun	
Plant type: perennial	
Hardiness: Zones 6-10	
Height: 2 to 4 feet	
Soil and Moisture: well-drained, sandy, dry to moist	
Interest: flowers	
Care: easy	

◀ Knautia macedonica

Knautias are less common than their relatives the pincushion flowers, but are just as attractive. The lilac or deep red blossoms accented with white pinlike stamens are neatly arranged in rounded, dome-shaped clusters that appear from late spring to fall. The informal flowers are held on long, wiry stems and seem to float in the air. Knautias are good as fillers at the backs of borders, or for interplanting with ornamental grasses in naturalized gardens.

Growing and care:
Knautia arvensis performs best in slightly alkaline, gravelly soil, while *K. macedonica* prefers sandy loams. Mulch plants in Zones 6 and 7 in fall. Propagate knautias by seed in spring, or by division or transplanting of self-sown seedlings in fall.

Selected species and varieties:
K. arvensis (blue-buttons, field scabious) has 2- to 4-foot stems with pairs of narrowly oval, highly dissected leaves and nearly globular 1-inch lilac or white flowers with pink anthers from midsummer to frost. *K. macedonica* [also listed as *Scabiosa macedonica* or *Scabiosa rumelica*] grows 1½ to 2½ feet tall with slender, curved stems, lyre-shaped pale green leaves, and 1¼-inch rounded, dark purple, red, or maroon summer flowers. *K. tatarica* is a biennial that grows to 6 feet tall with 10-inch toothed, oblong-elliptic leaves and 1½-inch bright yellow flowers.

LAMB'S EARS
Stachys

Light: full sun	
Plant type: perennial	
Hardiness: Zones 4-8	
Height: 8 to 18 inches	
Soil and Moisture: well-drained, fertile, moist to dry	
Interest: flowers, foliage	
Care: easy	

◀ Stachys byzantina
'Silver Carpet'

There are few plants that people love to touch more than lamb's ears. The plant produces thick mats of woolly, wonderfully velvety leaves that are so soft they were used as bandages during colonial times. In summer slender stems bearing loose spikes of pinkish flowers rise from the clumps of low-growing foliage. Lamb's ears make wonderful additions to specialty gardens, edges, or the front of borders.

Growing and care:
Plant lamb's ears in soil that is sandy and amended with organic matter. Sow seed indoors 8 to 10 weeks before last frost. Space plants 1 to 1½ feet apart. Remove dead leaves in late fall or early spring before new growth begins. Lamb's ears often self-sow, and volunteer seedlings can be transplanted easily in early spring. Divide established plants every 3 to 4 years.

Selected species and varieties:
S. byzantina (lamb's ears, woolly betony) forms dense 8-inch-high mats of soft, 6-inch-long velvety gray-green leaves and woolly, pinkish flower spikes up to 1½ feet tall in summer; 'Silver Carpet' is a flowerless cultivar with beautiful chrome-gray, furry leaves. *S. macrantha* (big betony) has stems to 1½ feet, tipped with whorls of purple summer flowers above heart-shaped, rippled green leaves.

LAVENDER COTTON
Santolina

Light: full sun	
Plant type: perennial	
Hardiness: Zones 6-8	
Height: 1½ to 2 feet	
Soil and Moisture: well-drained, medium to dry	
Interest: flowers, foliage	
Care: easy	

◀ Santolina
chamaecyparissus

Lavender cotton forms an attractive, spreading clump of pewter gray aromatic leaves, with slender stems topped by tiny yellow flowers that resemble miniature buttons. Lavender cotton is a hardworking, tough plant that not only thrives in dry, hot locations but even grows well near the ocean, where it is daily doused with salt spray. The foliage makes an attractive edging for a bed or walkway, or can be used as an accent in rock gardens. It also makes a beautiful, low hedge around herb or kitchen gardens.

Growing and care:
Space plants 1½ to 2 feet apart. Prune after flowering to promote dense growth, or shear anytime for a formal, low hedge. Lavender cotton prefers dry soils of low fertility and becomes unattractive and straggly in moist, fertile soils. Avoid excess moisture, especially in winter. Propagate from seed or from stem cuttings taken in early summer.

Selected species and varieties:
S. chamaecyparissus produces cushionlike mounds of evergreen foliage up to 2 feet tall with equal or greater spread. Leaves are silvery gray-green, ½ to 1½ inches long. In summer yellow flowers are held above the leaves. *S. virens* has green, tooth-edged leaves in dense 1½-foot clumps bearing solitary yellow flowers in summer.

LEOPARD'S-BANE
Doronicum

Light: full sun	
Plant type: perennial	
Hardiness: Zones 4-8	
Height: 1 to 2 feet	
Soil and Moisture: well-drained, fertile, moist	
Interest: flowers, foliage	
Care: moderate	

◀ Doronicum cordatum

Leopard's-bane is a sophisticated spring-blooming perennial, native to the steppes of Asia, with clear yellow, daisylike flowers and dark green heart-shaped leaves. These short-lived perennials grow best in cool, evenly moist soils and are bright additions to borders and fresh floral arrangements.

Growing and care:
Start seed indoors 8 to 10 weeks before planting out in spring. Do not cover, as seed needs light to germinate. Space plants 1 to 2 feet apart. In areas with cool summers plant in full sun. In regions with warmer summers provide plants with partial shade. Foliage dies back and plants go dormant after flowers bloom in spring. Mulch to keep roots and soil cool. Propagate from seed or by division every 2 to 3 years.

Selected species and varieties:
D. cordatum produces lemon yellow flowers 2 to 3 inches across on 1- to 2-foot stems above mounds of deep green leaves; 'Miss Mason' has a compact, mounding habit with long-lasting foliage; 'Spring Beauty' bears double-petaled yellow flowers.

MACLEAYA
Macleaya

Light: full sun

Plant type: perennial

Hardiness: Zones 3-8

Height: 6 to 10 feet

Soil and Moisture: well-drained, moist, fertile

Interest: flowers, foliage

Care: easy

◀ Macleaya cordata

Macleaya is a very large perennial with massive, irregularly rounded clumps of wavy, deeply lobed leaves. The small pink or white flowers are displayed in misty sprays atop very tall, upright stems in summer. The plants make a wonderful substitute for shrubs, and can be used at the back of a border, as a temporary screen, or beneath eaves where falling winter ice would damage woody shrubs.

Growing and care:
Macleaya grows best in moist soil well amended with rotted manure or compost. Plant volunteer seedlings, divisions, or container-grown plants in the garden in spring after soil has warmed, spacing plants 3 to 4 feet apart. Provide extra water during dry periods. If soil dries out the plants may go dormant earlier than normal. Propagate by division in spring, or by transplanting plantlets that develop along the roots.

Selected species and varieties:
M. cordata (plume poppy) bears creamy or pink ½-inch flowers on 6- to 10-foot-tall stems above 8- to 10-inch-wide, wavy-edged gray-green leaves. The plant is very vigorous and can spread rapidly.

MILKWEED
Asclepias

Light: full sun

Plant type: perennial

Hardiness: Zones 3-9

Height: 1 to 3 feet

Soil and Moisture: well-drained, sandy, moist to dry

Interest: flowers

Care: easy

◀ Asclepias tuberosa

In summer, milkweed's thick, stiff stems lined with willowy deep green leaves are tipped with broad, domed clusters of tiny nectar-rich flowers attractive to bees and butterflies. The flowers are long lasting in arrangements. The boat-shaped pods produced by some species burst open in fall to release tiny seeds that float through the air on downy tufts of silky hair. Milkweed's stems and leaves are thought to be poisonous to animals. The dried roots have been used in herbal medicines.

Growing and care:
Propagate milkweeds from seed or root cuttings in spring or fall, spacing plants 1 foot apart. Because of their long taproots, milkweeds are not easily propagated by division and should not be transplanted once established. Mature plants often self-sow. For long-lasting arrangements of milkweed cut for fresh use, sear the stems. To dry pods, cut before the seeds are released and hang until dry.

Selected species and varieties:
A. tuberosa (butterfly weed) has deep orange flower clusters throughout summer on thick stems filled with milky sap and lined with narrow, 4-inch-long leaves. *A. syriaca* (common milkweed) bears round clusters of richly fragrant, pinkish maroon flowers and interesting greenish seedpods that turn silvery brown when dried.

MULLEIN
Verbascum

Light: full sun	
Plant type: biennial, perennial	
Hardiness: Zones 4-9	
Height: 3 to 6 feet	
Soil and Moisture: well-drained, dry	
Interest: flowers, foliage	
Care: easy	

◀ Verbascum chaixii 'Album'

Mulleins are sturdy, stately plants with rosettes of coarse, sometimes velvety leaves and tall, sturdy spikes of beautiful, long-lasting summer flowers. These versatile plants are easy to grow and add a strong vertical element to the rear of a border, specialty gardens, or when naturalized in wildflower meadows.

Growing and care:
Start seed indoors 6 to 8 weeks before last frost or direct-sow in the garden in early spring when soil is cool. Space mulleins 1 to 2 feet apart. Plants tolerate and even thrive in dry conditions. Do not disturb established plantings. Cut back flower stalks in late summer or early fall.

Selected species and varieties:
V. bombyciferum (silver mullein), a biennial, bears attractive rosettes of oval leaves covered with silvery, silky hairs and 4- to 6-foot spikes of sulfur yellow flowers in summer; Zones 5-9. *V. chaixii* (Chaix mullein) produces ½- to 1-inch-wide yellow flowers with fuzzy purple stamens creating a prominent eye; 'Album' has white flowers and gray foliage. *V.* x 'Cotswold Queen' grows to 4 feet tall and 1 to 2 feet wide with apricot flowers; 'Pink Domino' grows 3 to 4 feet tall with deep pink flowers.

PHLOX
Phlox

Light: full sun	
Plant type: perennial	
Hardiness: Zones 3-9	
Height: ½ to 4 feet	
Soil and Moisture: well-drained, moist	
Interest: flowers, foliage, fragrance	
Care: moderate	

◀ Phlox paniculata 'Starfire'

Phlox produces clusters of dainty, brightly colored five-petaled flowers in spring, summer, or fall. The flowers often sport a conspicuous eye that adds to their attractiveness. Species of phlox vary widely in their heights, habits, uses, and cultural requirements but they all produce exquisite flowers.

Growing and care:
Plant low-growing phlox 1 to 1½ feet apart, tall species 2 feet apart. Phlox prefers full sun with ample moisture and regular fertilization. Allow space between plants for good air circulation to discourage mildew. Set phlox in a sheltered location away from strong breezes. Promote dense growth and prolong the flowering season by cutting plants back after flowering. Propagate by division or from cuttings.

Selected species and varieties:
P. maculata (wild sweet William) grows to 3 feet with fragrant, conical, summer to fall flower clusters; 'Alpha' has rosy pink flowers with darker centers. *P. paniculata* (garden phlox) has 4-foot stems tipped with very fragrant flower clusters to 8 inches wide in summer and fall; 'David' is a mildew-resistant selection that bears huge white flower clusters on 3- to 4-foot stems; 'Starfire' has large clusters of brilliant cherry red flowers in late summer; Zones 3-8.

PINCUSHION FLOWER
Scabiosa

Light:	full sun
Plant type:	perennial
Hardiness:	Zones 4-9
Height:	1½ to 2 feet
Soil and Moisture:	well-drained, fertile, moist
Interest:	flowers
Care:	easy

◀ Scabiosa caucasica 'Clive Greaves'

Pincushion flowers are some of the workhorses of the garden, providing beautiful, long-lasting summertime flowers with very little care. The plants produce abundant lilac, blue-violet, or white blooms up to 3 inches across with prominent stamens resembling a dome of pinheads surrounded by a ruffle of petals. Pincushion flower is excellent for the middle of the border or for cutting gardens. The blossoms make stunning fresh arrangements.

Growing and care:
Start seed indoors 8 to 10 weeks before last frost or direct-sow in the garden in early spring. Space pincushion flowers 1½ to 2 feet apart. Remove faded flowers for continuous bloom. Cut plants back to ground level after flowering is completed. Divide clumps every 2 to 4 years to rejuvenate plants.

Selected species and varieties:
S. caucasica (pincushion flower, Caucasian scabiosa) has pinkish blue 3-inch flowers on long, pliant stems from summer to fall; 'Clive Greaves' has lavender-blue flowers touched with white in the center; 'Fama' bears deep blue petals encircling silver centers on 1½-foot stems. *S. columbaria* 'Butterfly Blue' is a prolific compact form with small, beautiful flowers that resemble butterflies on 15-inch slender stems.

POPPY MALLOW
Callirhoe

Light:	full sun
Plant type:	perennial
Hardiness:	Zones 3-10
Height:	6 inches to 3 feet
Soil and Moisture:	well-drained, sandy, dry
Interest:	flowers
Care:	easy

◀ Callirhoe involucrata

Poppy mallow is a care-free flower for the wild meadow, field, rock garden, or other naturalistic planting. These long-blooming, drought-tolerant perennials are native to the open woods and dry plains over much of the central United States. In spring to summer the showy, ruby-colored cup-shaped flowers appear on very slender, nearly invisible stems.

Growing and care:
Before sowing seed scarify seed coat by scratching it with a nail file. Sow seed in flats in early spring. After the plants have gone dormant at the end of the first growing season transplant to the garden, spacing plants 1½ to 2 feet apart. Poppy mallows develop a thick taproot and should not be transplanted once established. Extend flower season by deadheading spent flowers.

Selected species and varieties:
C. involucrata (purple poppy mallow, winecups) is a trailing plant that grows 6 to 12 inches tall and 2 to 3 feet wide with attractive, deeply lobed hairy leaves, and 2-inch magenta flowers with a white spot at the base of the petals in spring and summer, opening during the day and closing in the evening; Zones 4-8. *C. papaver* (poppy mallow) has prostrate stems as much as 10 feet in length and solitary 2- to 3-inch magenta flowers; Zones 5-8.

PURPLE CONEFLOWER
Echinacea

Light: full sun

Plant type: perennial

Hardiness: Zones 3-8

Height: 2 to 4 feet

Soil and Moisture: well-drained, moist to dry, fertile

Interest: flowers

Care: easy

◀ Echinacea purpurea

Purple coneflowers are robust natives of the prairies and open spaces of the eastern United States. These hardy perennials combine beauty with tough character, making them invaluable additions to borders, massed in beds or herb gardens, or naturalized in wildflower meadows. Their very large, daisylike flowers have softly drooping pink to purple petals surrounding spiny, conical centers that glow purple, orange, or bronze depending on how the sunlight strikes them. Coneflowers blossom from early summer to fall, and make excellent cut flowers.

Growing and care:
Purple coneflowers grow best in full sun, but in hot climates the flower color is more intense if the plants are grown in light shade. Propagate in spring by division or by transplanting self-sown seedlings. Seed can also be sown directly in the garden in spring while soil is still cool. Space plants 2 feet apart. Wear gloves if collecting the prickly seeds, and gently tap the seed heads with a hammer to extract them.

Selected species and varieties:
E. purpurea has pink, purple, or white flowers 2 to 4 inches across in summer and fall on strong 2- to 4-foot stems, and broad, pointed, tooth-edged leaves; 'Magnus' has brilliant rosy pink flowers; 'White Swan' has snow white flowers; Zones 5-8.

PUSSY-TOES
Antennaria

Light: full sun

Plant type: perennial

Hardiness: Zones 3-8

Height: 2 to 16 inches

Soil and Moisture: well-drained, dry to moist

Interest: flowers, foliage

Care: easy

◀ Antennaria rosea

Pussy-toes are easy-to-grow perennial wildflowers that form velvety soft carpets of fuzzy, gray-green leaves generously sprinkled with delicate tubular flowers from spring to summer. The tidy flowers can be red, pink, or white and are held on silvery stems. Pussy-toes are excellent as ground covers in open, sunny places, for rock gardens, or when used to frame steppingstones and garden paths. The vigorous plants naturalize quickly and can also be used for erosion control in dry areas where few other plants would thrive.

Growing and care:
Sow seed indoors in late winter or early spring or direct-sow in the garden in spring while soil is still cool. Space plants 12 inches apart. Fertilize lightly and water regularly until plants are established. Alpine everlasting prefers moist, well-drained soil; the other two species grow best in dry conditions. Under ideal conditions *Antennaria* may become invasive. Divide plants every 2 to 3 years in late summer or fall.

Selected species and varieties:
A. alpina (alpine everlasting) is native to the western mountains and has hairy leaves and white summer flowers on 4-inch stems; Zones 4-8. *A. rosea,* native to western states, has soft gray leaves that form a 2- to 3-inch mat and bears clusters of six to 10 small, light pink flowers on 10-inch stalks in spring; Zones 3-7.

RED-HOT POKER
Kniphofia

Light: full sun

Plant type: perennial

Hardiness: Zones 5-9

Height: 2 to 4 feet

Soil and Moisture: well-drained, moist

Interest: flowers, foliage

Care: easy

◀ Kniphofia uvaria

Red-hot pokers are some of the most brilliantly colored perennials available. The plants produce long, cylindrical flower clusters in bold shades of orange or yellow on thick stems that gracefully arc over clumps of narrow, sword-shaped leaves. Red-hot pokers produce a succession of flower spikes from summer to early fall. Spectacular as specimens, they add unique color and texture to beds and borders.

Growing and care:
Plant red-hot pokers 1½ to 2 feet apart in sunny locations sheltered from the wind. Remove flower stalks after blossoms have faded. In late fall cut back foliage and cover with salt hay or other light mulch. Propagate by seed or division in early spring. Seedlings and offsets may require several years to reach flowering size.

Selected species and varieties:
K. uvaria has narrow, rough-textured leaves, and produces many 1- to 2-inch individual blossoms forming a 6- to 10-inch bottlebrush-shaped flower cluster atop 2- to 4-foot stems. *K.* 'Little Maid' has pastel yellow flowers that fade to antique white; 'Primrose Beauty' produces light yellow flowers; 'White Fairy' is a dwarf with creamy white flowers in midsummer.

ROCK CRESS
Arabis

Light: full sun

Plant type: perennial

Hardiness: Zones 3-7

Height: 6 to 12 inches

Soil and Moisture: well-drained, moist to dry

Interest: flowers, foliage, fragrance

Care: easy

◀ Arabis caucasica

Rock cress is a durable, low-growing plant that produces carpets of snow white, fragrant flowers in spring. When not in bloom the small, attractive green leaves fill in the spaces in rock gardens or low borders.

Growing and care:
Rock cress is easily grown, but humid weather and standing water will cause rot. Prune after flowering to keep the plants compact. In regions with hot summers set plants where they will receive some afternoon shade. Propagate from seed sown in spring or divide clumps every 3 to 4 years in fall. Do not disturb established plantings.

Selected species and varieties:
A. alpina 'Flore Pleno' has small, white, fragrant double-petaled flowers in spring. *A. caucasica* 'Rosabella' is a low-growing, compact, 5-inch-tall plant with rosy pink flowers; 'Snow Cap' is a creeping form with plentiful pure white single flowers. *A. procurrens* is a low-growing plant with a spreading habit bearing sprays of white flowers above mats of glossy evergreen leaves.

RUSSIAN SAGE
Perovskia

Light: full sun	
Plant type: perennial	
Hardiness: Zones 5-8	
Height: 2 to 3 feet	
Soil and Moisture: well-drained, dry to moist	
Interest: flowers, foliage, fragrance	
Care: easy	

◀ Perovskia atriplicifolia

Russian sage is a low, shrubby perennial bearing long clusters of small, soft, slightly hairy blue-violet flowers from late summer to early fall. It forms somewhat woody clumps with fine-textured, aromatic, gray-green foliage. The leaves have a warm, sagelike fragrance when bruised. Russian sage is a hardworking, easy-care perennial that is most effective when massed in mixed borders with ornamental grasses.

Growing and care:
Plant Russian sages 2 to 3 feet apart and lightly fertilize in spring. To promote bushy form and promote better flowering, cut woody stems back in spring before new growth begins. Propagate by cuttings taken in spring or summer.

Selected species and varieties:
P. atriplicifolia (Russian sage, azure sage) has tiny, lavender-blue, two-lipped summer to fall flowers on 1-foot spikes, and 1½-inch downy, toothed, finely divided gray leaves on woody stems; 'Blue Mist' has pale blue flowers in summer; 'Filagran' has fine-textured foliage and blue flowers from summer to fall; 'Longin' has erect 3-foot stems and blue flowers. *P. scrophulariifolia* produces 2- to 3-foot stems with oval leaves and sprays of light blue flowers from late spring to early summer.

SAGE
Salvia

Light: full sun	
Plant type: perennial	
Hardiness: Zones 4-10	
Height: 1 to 8 feet	
Soil and Moisture: well-drained, moist to dry	
Interest: flowers, foliage, fragrance	
Care: easy	

◀ Salvia leucantha

Sages are classic garden plants that have spikes or whorls of hooded, two-lipped flowers at the tips of their branched stems, and pairs of aromatic leaves that clasp or are attached by petioles to their square stems, while the larger shrubby species are well suited to shrub borders and filling spaces in gardens south of Zone 7.

Growing and care:
Sages tolerate drought well but grow poorly in sites that are wet in winter. Space smaller varieties 1½ feet apart, larger ones 2 to 3 feet apart. Deadheading stimulates rebloom. Prune old stems in fall or early winter. Provide tender perennials with mulch over winter in regions colder than Zone 8. Propagate by division in spring or fall, or by softwood cuttings in summer.

Selected species and varieties:
S. leucantha (Mexican bush sage, white sage) is a 3- to 4-foot, very drought-resistant shrubby perennial with white, woolly leaves and long, open clusters of pink flowers, and is excellent for xeriscaping; Zones 7-10. *S. x superba* (violet sage) is a 1½- to 3-foot perennial with dense whorls of violet to dark blue-violet flowers above narrow, medium green leaves from late spring to early summer; Zones 5-8.

SEA HOLLY
Eryngium

Light: full sun	
Plant type: perennial	
Hardiness: Zones 4-9	
Height: 1 to 6 feet	
Soil and Moisture: well-drained, sandy, dry	
Interest: flowers, foliage	
Care: easy	

◀ Eryngium bourgatii

Sea holly is an intriguingly interesting-looking plant with spiny collars of pewter-purple bracts surrounding the conical, bluish white flower heads. The long-lasting summer-blooming flowers rise on stiff stalks above crisp, leathery, often wavy leaves with deeply cut, spiny margins. Sea holly adds an unusual, coarse texture to specialty gardens or the back of borders.

Growing and care:
Sow seed on soil surface in flats in spring. Cover with plastic and refrigerate for 3 weeks. Place flats outdoors in a shady place until seedlings appear. Transplant to the garden, spacing plants 1 to 1½ feet apart. Water during extended periods of dry, hot weather. Sea holly requires little care once established and self-seeds readily.

Selected species and varieties:
E. alpinum (bluetop sea holly) bears frilled bracts and rounded flower heads on 1- to 2-foot-tall plants. *E. bourgatii* (Mediterranean sea holly) has narrow, pointed bracts and wavy, gray-green leaves with prominent white veins on plants to 2 feet. *E. giganteum* (stout sea holly) produces wide bracts similar in size to silvery holly leaves on plants 4 to 6 feet tall. *E. planum* (flat-leaved eryngium) has steel blue flower heads with blue-green bracts on plants to 3 feet. *E. yuccifolium* (rattlesnake master) is covered with narrow, drooping gray-green leaves with spiny edges on 4-foot stalks.

SEA LAVENDER
Limonium

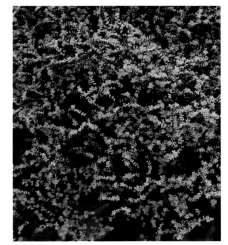

Light: full sun	
Plant type: perennial	
Hardiness: Zones 4-9	
Height: 18 to 30 inches	
Soil and Moisture: well-drained, sandy, dry	
Interest: flowers	
Care: easy	

◀ Limonium latifolium

Sea lavender is prized for the abundant sprays of small, lacy flowers that seem to smother the pliant stems from spring to fall. Beneath the flowers are dense clumps of glossy, forest green leaves that are handsome all by themselves. Sea lavender's casual form adds informal beauty to borders and cutting gardens and is a must for fresh and dried arrangements.

Growing and care:
Start seed indoors 6 to 8 weeks before last frost or direct-sow in the garden in early spring when the soil is still cool. Space plants 1½ feet apart. Sea lavender thrives in dry conditions and does very well in coastal gardens. Extremely fertile soils produce weak branches that require staking. Do not disturb established plantings. Cut plants back to the ground in fall after flowering is completed.

Selected species and varieties:
L. latifolium has branching flower stems that carry panicles of airy, rounded lavender-blue blossoms above a tuft of leathery, oblong evergreen leaves; 'Blue Cloud' produces soft, light blue flowers; 'Violetta' bears enchanting sprays of deep violet blossoms.

SENNA
Chamaecrista

Light: full sun	
Plant type: perennial	
Hardiness: Zones 4-10	
Height: 1 to 4 feet	
Soil and Moisture: well-drained, sandy, wet to dry	
Interest: flowers	
Care: easy	

◀ Chamaecrista
fasciculata

Senna is an unusual perennial with a shrubby habit that makes it look like a miniature tree. The branching stems are upright, stiff, and covered with ferny compound leaves. In summer the plants bear small, bright yellow pealike flowers. This native wildflower doesn't appeal to everyone, but those who like it, love it. Senna is excellent in naturalized plantings, where it adds color when most other flowers have gone by. It is also an excellent choice for difficult sites where the soil is too wet or dry for other plants.

Growing and care:
Before sowing scratch seed with a file and soak in warm water for 24 hours. Plant indoors 2 months before planting out or sow directly in the garden in fall or spring. Space plants 2 to 3 feet apart. For best growth inoculate soil with nitrogen-fixing bacteria and water, and fertilize regularly until plants are established. Plants can be divided every 3 to 4 years in spring.

Selected species and varieties:
C. marilandica [also classified as *Senna marilandica* and *Cassia marilandica*] (wild senna) is a semiwoody perennial with branching stems to 4 feet, bold yellow flower clusters, and finely divided leaves.

SMARTWEED
Polygonum

Light: full sun	
Plant type: perennial	
Hardiness: Zones 3-9	
Height: 1/2 to 3 feet	
Soil and Moisture: well-drained, fertile, moist to wet	
Interest: flowers, foliage	
Care: easy	

◀ Polygonum bistorta
'Superbum'

The genus *Polygonum* contains many hardy perennials, some with large, primroselike dark green leaves and cylindrical clusters of rose or pink flowers borne high above the foliage on strong stems. These versatile plants add color to bog and wildflower gardens as well as along garden paths or the front of the border.

Growing and care:
Space plants 1 foot apart. In areas with cool summers plant in full sun. In regions with hot summers provide some afternoon shade. Water well during dry periods. Propagate by division in spring. Cut back plants to about ground level in fall.

Selected species and varieties:
P. affine (Himalayan fleeceflower) produces spikes of rose pink flowers 6 to 9 inches tall above dark green leaves turning bronze in fall; 'Superbum' produces crimson flowers; Zones 4-9. *P. bistorta* (snakeweed) bears pink flowers like bottlebrushes on 2-foot stems above striking clumps of 4- to 6-inch-long wavy green leaves with a white midrib; 'Superbum' grows to 3 feet with dense spikes of rose pink flowers.

SNEEZEWEED
Helenium

Light: full sun	
Plant type: perennial	
Hardiness: Zones 3-10	
Height: 2 to 6 feet	
Soil and Moisture: well-drained, moist to wet	
Interest: flowers, foliage	
Care: easy	

◀ Helenium autumnale 'Brilliant'

Free-flowering sneezeweeds provide masses of vividly colored daisylike flowers from late spring through early fall, when most perennials have long since stopped flowering. The fiery yellow, orange, or red fan-shaped petals surround a prominent, burnt red center, and sit atop the 2- to 6-foot-tall stems and above the attractive, willowy foliage. Sneezeweeds are native to streamsides and wet meadows in much of the United States, and are stunning when naturalized in wildflower gardens or planted in large groups in borders.

Growing and care:
Sneezeweeds are virtually pest-free as well as being heat and drought tolerant, making them low maintenance as well as attractive. Plant in either spring or fall, spacing plants 1½ to 2 feet apart. Pinch stems in spring to promote bushy growth and more flowers, and fertilize lightly. For best flower production keep soil moist during growing season. Cut back plants in fall. Propagate by division of clumps every 3 to 4 years.

Selected species and varieties:
H. autumnale (yellow star) has 2-inch flaring, slightly reflexed yellow petals surrounding a raised yellow disk on branched stems up to 6 feet; 'Brilliant' has bright red-orange flowers that fade to lighter watercolor shades on 3-foot stems; 'Butterpat' produces light yellow petals surrounding a bronze disk.

SPURGE
Euphorbia

Light: full sun	
Plant type: perennial	
Hardiness: Zones 3-10	
Height: 6 inches to 3 feet	
Soil and Moisture: well-drained, dry	
Interest: flowers, foliage	
Care: easy	

◀ Euphorbia griffithii 'Fireglow'

Spurge is a diverse group of easy-to-grow plants bearing small clusters of flowers surrounded by colorful bracts. The foliage of many species turns from medium green in summer to intense shades of red in fall. The plants make wonderful additions to borders or specialty gardens.

Growing and care:
Sow seed in peat pots 6 to 8 weeks before the last frost. Space plants 1 to 2 feet apart. Once established do not transplant. Spurge thrives in soils that are infertile and dry. If grown in moist, fertile locations growth may become rangy and unattractive. Use gloves when handling plants, as they exude a milky sap that can cause skin irritation in some people.

Selected species and varieties:
E. corollata (flowering spurge) grows 1 to 3 feet tall, with slender green leaves that turn red in fall. In mid- to late summer it bears clusters of flowers resembling baby's-breath. *E. epithymoides* (cushion spurge) forms a neat, symmetrical, 1- to 1½-foot mound of green leaves that turn dark red in fall. In spring it produces small green flowers surrounded by showy, chartreuse-yellow bracts; Zones 4-8. *E. griffithii* 'Fireglow' has well-branched, 3-foot upright stems topped with umbels of fiery red flowers; Zones 4-9.

STOKES' ASTER
Stokesia

Light: full sun	
Plant type: perennial	
Hardiness: Zones 5-9	
Height: 1 to 1½ feet	
Soil and Moisture: well-drained, moist, fertile	
Interest: flowers	
Care: easy	

◀ Stokesia laevis
'Blue Danube'

The large, very showy, fringed flowers of Stokes' aster are held on strong stalks rising from neat rosettes of glossy green, straplike, leathery leaves. The flowers, which come in soft pastel shades of purple, blue, lilac, pink, and white, contrast nicely to the shiny dark green leaves. Stokes' aster is an excellent choice for the perennial border and adds a refined touch to fresh summertime bouquets.

Growing and care:
Space Stokes' asters 1½ feet apart. Mulch with straw to protect plants over winter in colder climates. Plants are prone to disease when grown in wet soils. The species may be propagated from seed or by division in spring. Propagate cultivars by division in spring. Cut plants back after flowering is complete.

Selected species and varieties:
S. laevis bears solitary flower heads 2 to 5 inches across, blooming over a 4-week season in summer; 'Blue Danube' has 5-inch clear blue flowers; 'Blue Moon' bears lilac flowers; 'Klaus Jelitto' has 4-inch deep blue blossoms; 'Silver Moon' blooms white.

STONECROP
Sedum

Light: full sun	
Plant type: perennial	
Hardiness: Zones 3-10	
Height: 1 to 2 feet	
Soil and Moisture: well-drained, dry to moist	
Interest: flowers, foliage	
Care: easy	

◀ Sedum spectabile

Stonecrops have thick, succulent stems topped by dense clusters of five-petaled star-shaped flowers. The plants add color and texture in perennial borders and rock gardens, and the leaves often are covered with a white, waxy bloom or tinged with copper or bronze. *Sedums* can be massed as a succulent ground cover that attracts numerous species of butterflies to its summer and fall flowers.

Growing and care:
Sedums are heat and drought tolerant, and spread slowly. Space plants 1½ to 2 feet apart. Propagate species by seed or division in spring, and all cultivars by division in early spring or by stem cuttings in late spring through summer. Fertilize lightly in spring. Wet conditions can lead to fungal and bacterial diseases. Cut back plants in fall once flowering is completed.

Selected species and varieties:
S. spectabile (showy stonecrop) produces round clumps of 1½- to 2-foot stems lined with 3-inch fleshy, rounded blue-green leaves and topped by flat clusters of white or pink flowers from summer to frost; 'Brilliant' has deep rose red flowers. *S. telephium* (orpine, live-forever) grows 1 to 2 feet tall with oblong, toothed leaves and rounded clusters of pink, red, or sometimes white flowers in late summer; *S.* x 'Vera Jameson' has coppery purple leaves and dusty pink or magenta flowers in early fall.

SUNDROPS
Oenothera

Light: full sun	
Plant type: perennial	
Hardiness: Zones 4-8	
Height: 6 inches to 2 feet	
Soil and Moisture: well-drained, fertile, moist	
Interest: flowers	
Care: easy	

◀ Oenothera fruticosa

Sundrops produce perhaps the most intensely yellow flowers of any perennial. The showy, four-petaled, saucer-shaped blossoms open atop gracefully pliant stems and are stunning when planted in masses or as bright focal points in the middle of borders.

Growing and care:

Plant sundrops in well-worked soil that has been amended with compost or rotted manure. Space small species 8 inches apart and large ones 18 inches apart. Provide extra water during dry periods. Cut back plants 2 to 3 inches after flowering. From Zone 6 north divide plants in spring. From Zone 7 south divide in fall.

Selected species and varieties:

O. fruticosa (sundrops) is a prolific bearer of 1- to 2-inch bright yellow flower clusters atop 1½- to 2-foot stems. *O. macrocarpa* [also classified as *O. missouriensis*] (Ozark sundrops) has large 5-inch yellow flowers on 6- to 12-inch plants. *O. speciosa* (evening primrose) bears showy white or pink blossoms on spreading, 6- to 18-inch-tall stems. *O. tetragona* [also called *O. fruticosa* ssp. *glauca*] produces abundant red-tinged buds that open to bright yellow flowers.

SUNFLOWER
Helianthus

Light: full sun	
Plant type: perennial	
Hardiness: Zones 4-9	
Height: 3 to 7 feet	
Soil and Moisture: well-drained, fertile, moist	
Interest: flowers	
Care: easy	

◀ Helianthus x multi-florus 'Flore Pleno'

The large, cheerful yellow blossoms of sunflowers brighten the garden even on gloomy days. Sunflowers bear large, yellow, single or double blossoms from summer to fall on strong, erect stems lined with medium green, coarse-textured leaves. They add zip to the back of the border or when naturalized in wildflower meadows. Sunflowers are excellent for cutting. The ripe seeds attract many species of songbirds to the garden in fall.

Growing and care:

Sow seed directly in the garden after danger of frost has passed. Thin plants to stand 1 foot apart for dwarf forms and 3 feet apart for larger types. Pinch young plants to encourage branching and increased flowering. Water regularly during the growing season and fertilize lightly once a month.

Selected species and varieties:

H. angustifolius (swamp sunflower) bears flowers 2 to 3 inches across with dark brown to purple centers on stems to 7 feet tall. *H.* x *multiflorus* (many-flowered sunflower) grows blooms 3 to 5 inches wide, often with overlapping petals; 'Flore Pleno' has double flowers on 4-foot stems; 'Lodden Gold' bears deep yellow double flowers on 5-foot stems; 'Morning Sun' has golden yellow flowers on 5- to 6-foot stems.

THRIFT
Armeria

Light: full sun	
Plant type: perennial	
Hardiness: Zones 3-8	
Height: 6 inches to 2 feet	
Soil and Moisture: well-drained, moist to dry	
Interest: flowers, foliage	
Care: moderate	

◀ Armeria maritima 'Laucheana'

Thrifts have adorable round clusters of small, brightly colored flowers held high above tufted mounds of narrow, needle-shaped leaves. The plants make excellent additions to rock gardens, serve as edging around borders, or can be massed in formal gardens. They do not do well in hot, humid areas but are extremely tolerant of seaside locations.

Growing and care:
Soak seed in warm water for 8 to 10 hours before planting. Direct-sow in the garden in early spring when soil is cool. Space plants 6 to 12 inches apart. Replace clumps when center begins to die back. Provide extra water during dry periods and mulch with straw or pine needles in winter.

Selected species and varieties:
A. alliacea [also called *A. plantaginea*] (plantain thrift) has 1¾-inch rosy pink or white flower clusters on 2-foot stems; 'Bee's Ruby' bears intense ruby red flower clusters. *A. maritima* (common thrift) has white to deep carmine pink flowers on 1-foot stems; 'Alba' is a dwarf with white flowers on 5-inch stems; 'Bloodstone' has brilliant, bright red flowers on 9-inch stems; 'Laucheana' has dark green foliage and bright pink flowers.

VERBENA
Verbena

Light: full sun	
Plant type: perennial	
Hardiness: Zones 8-10	
Height: ½ to 4 feet	
Soil and Moisture: well-drained, fertile, dry to moist	
Interest: flowers, foliage, fragrance	
Care: easy	

◀ Verbena rigida

Verbenas are rugged plants that provide week after week of flowers in vivid whites, reds, purples, and blues. Their small, five-petaled, tubular flowers are often highly fragrant and borne in rounded or domed clusters on wiry stems. Butterflies and hummingbirds are drawn to the blossoms. Verbenas are versatile plants that fit well into many areas of the garden. They add color and form to mixed beds and borders, and accent rock gardens.

Growing and care:
Once established, these plants thrive in hot, dry sites, are low maintenance, and are excellent in naturalistic plantings. They grow more vigorously and produce more flowers if given additional water during dry spells. Pinch young plants to encourage branching and increase flowering. Propagate by seed sown in spring, spacing plants 1 foot apart, or take cuttings in late summer, root them, and overwinter indoors for planting the following spring. Verbenas are short-lived perennials that will self-sow in warm climates, and are grown as annuals in northern regions.

Selected species and varieties:
V. rigida [also listed as *V. venosa*] grows 1 to 2 feet tall and 2 feet wide with erect, branching stems and dense clusters of deep purple flowers from summer through fall, and narrow, medium green 2- to 3-inch leaves mostly at the bases of the stems; Zones 8-10.

WILD BUCKWHEAT
Eriogonum

Light: full sun	
Plant type: perennial	
Hardiness: Zones 3-10	
Height: 3 inches to 3 feet	
Soil and Moisture: well-drained, gravelly, dry	
Interest: flowers	
Care: moderate	

◀ Eriogonum
compositum

Wild buckwheat is an informal, rather wild-looking plant with tall, sturdy stems capped with white, red, or sulfur yellow blossoms in spring, summer, or fall. The plants grow best in hot, dry conditions and are most popular in California and other areas of the far West. Wild buckwheat is exceptionally attractive to bees and is often planted near vegetable gardens or orchards to aid pollination.

Growing and care:
Sow wild buckwheat in gravelly soils in spring. Water well until seed germinates. The plants often self-sow and naturalize freely. The low-growing sulfur buckwheat is the easiest species to grow, as it does not need gravelly soil to do well.

Selected species and varieties:
E. compositum (northern buckwheat) bears 1- to 4-inch clusters of white or yellow flowers on 8- to 18-inch stalks in late spring to summer, and forms a cushiony mat of oval to heart-shaped leaves that are green above and white and fuzzy below; Zones 4-7. *E. umbellatum* var. *subalpinum* (sulfur buckwheat) has 2- to 4-inch rounded clusters of creamy yellow summer flowers on 3-inch stems; Zones 3-8. *E. wrightii* (Wright buckwheat) is shrubby, growing 2 to 3 feet tall with gray leaves, and clusters of white flowers in summer and fall that turn reddish orange in cool weather; Zones 6-10.

WILD INDIGO
Baptisia

Light: full sun	
Plant type: perennial	
Hardiness: Zones 3-9	
Height: 3 to 4 feet	
Soil and Moisture: well-drained, dry, sandy	
Interest: flowers	
Care: moderate to easy	

◀ Baptisia australis

Wild indigo is often considered a workhorse of the perennial garden with a tough, hardy character ably balanced by delicate compound leaves and porcelain blue or ice white pealike flowers from midspring to early summer. The tall stems and blue-green leaves provide an excellent background to borders or when massed in wildflower meadows. The flowers are followed by attractive, dark-colored seedpods that are often dried and used in arrangements.

Growing and care:
Soak seed in warm water for 24 hours before planting. Direct-sow in the garden in fall or in spring after danger of frost has passed. Space plants 2 to 3 feet apart. Wild indigo takes 1 to 2 years to become fully established. Cultivate carefully so roots are not disturbed. Do not transplant. Tall selections may require staking.

Selected species and varieties:
B. alba grows to 3 feet tall with upright clusters of white flowers sometimes tinged with purple; Zones 5-8. *B. australis* has erect stems reaching 4 feet tall with attractive compound leaves and pealike indigo blue flowers in long, terminal racemes, good for cutting.

WORMWOOD
Artemisia

Light: full sun	
Plant type: perennial	
Hardiness: Zones 5-8	
Height: 3 feet	
Soil and Moisture: well-drained, dry	
Interest: foliage, fragrance	
Care: easy	

◀ Artemisia x 'Powis Castle'

Wormwood is wonderfully easy to grow, with distinctive silvery gray foliage that is strongly aromatic. Forms range from woody evergreen perennials 4 to 5 feet high to soft, feathery mounds scarcely 6 inches tall. The larger types are perfect for the back of the border, while the smaller forms shine in rock gardens or as edgings. The pewter-gray color of the leaves allows *Artemisia* to blend especially well with blue, lavender, and pink flowers, and softens plants with coarse textures.

Growing and care:
Start seed indoors 10 to 12 weeks before the last frost or direct-sow in the garden in fall. Space smaller forms including 'Silver Mound' 1 foot apart and larger types, such as 'Powis Castle', 2 to 3 feet apart. *Artemisia* grows best in sunny, warm, dry sites with excellent air circulation. In humid locations some types are prone to fungal diseases. Cut back in late fall or early spring to keep plants shapely and reduce chance of disease.

Selected species and varieties:
A. x 'Powis Castle' forms an airy, 4-foot-wide mound of lacy, finely divided, steel gray to silvery leaves up to 4 inches long on woolly stems; Zones 6-8. *A. schmidtiana* 'Silver Mound' produces a low, 8-inch-high mound of very airy, fernlike, chrome-gray foliage; Zones 3-7. *A. stellerana* forms a compact carpet of deeply lobed, bluish silver leaves on 1-foot stems; Zones 3-7.

YARROW
Achillea

Light: full sun	
Plant type: perennial	
Hardiness: Zones 4-8	
Height: 6 inches to 4 feet	
Soil and Moisture: well-drained, dry	
Interest: flowers	
Care: easy	

◀ Achillea 'Coronation Gold'

Yarrow bears large, vividly colored, flat-topped flower clusters atop strong stems covered with lacy gray-green leaves. The plants provide exquisite form and color to borders and rock gardens and may flower from early to late summer, depending on the variety. The plants are also excellent for fresh and dried arrangements.

Growing and care:
Sow seed indoors 8 to 10 weeks before last frost. Do not cover seed. Space plants 1 to 2 feet apart. Once plants are established, propagate by dividing clumps in spring or fall every 3 to 4 years. Cut plants back to ground level after first few frosts in fall. Some tall forms may need support. Provide extra water during dry periods.

Selected species and varieties:
A. 'Coronation Gold' is a hybrid with 3-inch, deep yellow flower clusters on 3-foot stems. *A. filipendulina* (fernleaf yarrow) bears bright yellow flower clusters up to 5 inches across; 'Gold Plate' has 6-inch yellow flower heads on 4-foot stems. *A.* x *lewisii* 'King Edward' has small yellow flowers on 4-inch stalks. *A. millefolium* (common yarrow) bears 2-inch white flowers, with cultivars blooming in shades from pink to red.

AMARYLLIS
Hippeastrum

Light: full sun	
Plant type: bulb	
Hardiness: Zones 9-10	
Height: 1 to 2 feet	
Soil and Moisture: well-drained, moist, sandy	
Interest: flowers	
Care: easy to moderate	

◀ Hippeastrum 'Bold Leader'

The only word fit to describe an amaryllis in flower is "spectacular." Amaryllis bears enormous, vividly colored flowers up to 8 inches across atop stout, very sturdy stems. In warm regions the flowers brighten sunny borders. In northern areas the plants are potted in containers and forced into flower during the winter months.

Growing and care:
Outdoors in Zone 10, plant in fall or spring, setting bulbs 6 inches deep and 1 foot apart in well-worked soil rich in rotted manure or compost. Indoors, plant the bulb with its top third exposed in a pot 2 inches wider than the width of the bulb anytime from late fall through winter. Keep soil around bulb barely moist until growth starts. After flowering, remove flower stalk and provide regular watering and fertilizing until foliage dies back in late summer or fall. Allow soil to dry out and repot bulb into fresh potting soil with a high organic matter content. Propagate by separating offsets while plant is dormant.

Selected species and varieties:
H. 'Apple Blossom' is cherry pink flushed white; 'Bold Leader' is signal red; 'Double Record' has double white flowers veined and tipped red; 'Lady Jane', deep salmon-orange double flowers; 'Picotee', white petals rimmed red; 'Red Lion', velvety red flowers.

AUTUMN DAFFODIL
Sternbergia

Light: full sun	
Plant type: bulb	
Hardiness: Zones 6-10	
Height: 6 to 12 inches	
Soil and Moisture: well-drained, sandy, dry	
Interest: flowers, foliage	
Care: easy	

◀ Sternbergia lutea

Autumn daffodil is a bright, charming addition to any fall garden. The small, egg-shaped flower buds open to reveal clear yellow, shimmering, waxy flowers reminiscent of crocuses. The blossoms appear on slender stems shorter than the grassy foliage. Use autumn daffodils in sunny, dry rock gardens, or any hot, dry location. The plants can also be forced indoors to provide color during dreary winter months.

Growing and care:
Plant autumn daffodils in summer, setting bulbs 4 inches deep and 4 to 6 inches apart. In Zone 6 mulch with straw or pine needles to provide winter protection. North of Zone 6, grow as annuals or in bulb pans, placing five or six bulbs 2 inches deep in each 6-inch pan. Autumn daffodils can be propagated by removing the small bulb offsets from larger clumps after plants have finished flowering.

Selected species and varieties:
S. lutea bears 1½- to 2-inch cup-shaped golden yellow blossoms on sturdy 4-inch stems above upright clusters of thin, glossy green, 6- to 12-inch leaves.

AZTEC LILY
Sprekelia

Light: full sun

Plant type: bulb

Hardiness: Zones 9-10

Height: 1 foot

Soil and Moisture: well-drained, fertile, dry to moist

Interest: flowers, foliage

Care: moderate

◀ Sprekelia formosissima

Aztec lily produces spectacular orchidlike flowers with six long, velvety petals. The three upper petals curve gracefully, like a bird in flight, while the lower ones form a colorful trumpet accented by the long, yellow-tipped stamens. The solitary flowers are borne on leafless stems before narrow, straplike leaves appear. In warm zones, Aztec lily can be grown in the border. Elsewhere, it is grown as an annual or container plant.

Growing and care:
From Zone 9 south, plant Aztec lilies in any season, setting bulbs 3 to 4 inches deep and 8 to 12 inches apart. The bulbs sprout quickly and will bloom in about 6 weeks. From Zone 8 north, plant the bulbs outdoors in spring and lift in fall, drying and storing the bulbs like gladiolus. Indoors, plant with half the bulb above the soil surface, allowing one bulb per 4-inch pot or three bulbs per 6-inch pot. Propagate by removing bulblets that develop around the base of mature bulbs.

Selected species and varieties:
S. formosissima (Aztec lily, Jacobean lily, St. James's lily, orchid amaryllis) has 1-foot-long, lance-shaped green leaves and very showy, 4- to 6-inch, deep red-orange or deep crimson flowers with long, graceful petals and bright yellow stamens.

BELLADONNA LILY
Amaryllis

Light: full sun

Plant type: bulb

Hardiness: Zones 9-10

Height: 1 to 2 feet

Soil and Moisture: well-drained, moist

Interest: flowers

Care: moderate

◀ Amaryllis belladonna

In late summer the splendid blossoms of belladonna lily provide a pleasant surprise when they rise from what seems like barren ground. The straplike foliage, which appears in early to late spring, disappears in summer a few weeks before the bold clusters of six to 12 sweetly scented, flowery trumpets seem to appear from nowhere. Force belladonna lilies indoors as houseplants or use as border plantings in Zones 9 and 10.

Growing and care:
Pot in containers in late winter with the neck of the bulb at the soil surface, or set bulbs outdoors 4 to 6 inches deep and 1 foot apart in spring when soil has warmed. Water well from the time foliage appears until the leaves turn brown and disappear. When the flower stalk emerges resume watering and fertilize regularly until all flowers have faded. If planted in sheltered, warm spots and mulched heavily, belladonna lilies have survived as far north as Zone 5. Propagate from seed, planting the fleshy seeds as soon as they appear after flowers fade, or by removing bulblets from parent bulbs. Caution: Belladonna lily bulbs are poisonous and must be kept out of the reach of children.

Selected species and varieties:
A. belladonna has 3-inch white, pale pink, or rose blossoms on 1- to 2-foot-tall stems in late summer; 'Cape Town' has deep rose red flowers.

BELLEVALIA
Bellevalia

Light:	full sun
Plant type:	bulb
Hardiness:	Zones 6-10
Height:	6 to 18 inches
Soil and Moisture:	well-drained, fertile, moist
Interest:	flowers
Care:	easy

◀ Bellevalia pycnantha

Bellevalia at first glance looks like grape hyacinth that has had too much fertilizer. The conical flower clusters hold 20 to 30 small flower bells that open from bottom to top. The single, fleshy stalk rises from a clump of thick, glossy green, straplike leaves. After the flowers fade they are replaced by blue-black seeds in fall. Use bellevalia anywhere hyacinth would be at home—in borders, rock gardens, or where it may naturalize.

Growing and care:
Plant bellevalias in fall, setting bulbs 3 inches deep and 3 inches apart. Bulbs tolerate both wet spring conditions and summer drought. Propagate by removing and replanting the small bulblets that develop at the base of parent bulbs in fall. For container growing, plant three to five bulbs in a 6-inch pot filled with potting soil. Moisten well and place pot in a cool, shaded place while roots develop. When leaves and shoots emerge place on a sunny window sill in a warm room.

Selected species and varieties:
B. pycnantha has downward-facing clusters of flat, blue-black flowers with yellow edges that slowly unfold in spring on 1-foot-tall stalks above 12-inch-long, semisucculent leaves. *B. romana* [also called *Hyacinthus romanus*] has grayish blue clustered flower buds that open into dull white, ¼-inch flowers sometimes tinged with violet, brown, or green on 6- to 18-inch stalks in spring.

BLAZING STAR
Tritonia

Light:	full sun
Plant type:	bulb
Hardiness:	Zones 7-10
Height:	1½ feet
Soil and Moisture:	well-drained, moist
Interest:	flowers
Care:	moderate

◀ Tritonia crocata

Blazing star is often confused with montbretia, but is actually more closely related to freesia. The very attractive flowers are arranged along one side of an arching flower spike and shaped like small bowls of pointed petals. The flower stems rise from small fans of narrow, pointed leaves. Blazing star provides stunning color in beds, borders, or rock gardens, and is a long-lasting cut flower.

Growing and care:
From Zone 7 south, plant bulbs in fall, setting corms 3 to 4 inches deep and 6 inches apart. From Zone 6 north, plant bulbs in spring. Fertilize in spring and keep soil evenly moist during growing season. As leaves begin to yellow allow soil to dry out. In northern areas lift corms in fall and dry in a cool, dark place for a few days. Cut off foliage and store in a cool, dry place over winter. Propagate from seed or by removing the small cormels growing around mature corms.

Selected species and varieties:
T. crocata has long, sword-shaped leaves and 2-inch-wide flowers on 1½-foot-tall stems in a wide range of colors including salmon, white, pink, and red.

BUGLE LILY
Watsonia

Light: full sun	
Plant type: bulb	
Hardiness: Zones 8-10	
Height: 1 1/2 to 4 feet	
Soil and Moisture: well-drained, moist	
Interest: flowers, foliage	
Care: moderate	

◀ Watsonia 'Pink Opal'

Bugle lily's simple, funnel-shaped flowers appear at the tips of the tall, slightly arching stems. The soft texture of the blossoms contrasts to the sharp-looking clumps of narrow, sword-shaped leaves. The spikes of blossoms, which open from bottom to top, are similar to those of the gladiolus but are daintier and less formal. Bugle lilies will slowly form clumps in gardens in warm climates. Elsewhere, they can be grown as annuals or lifted in fall and stored like gladiolus. They make very attractive, long-lasting cut flowers.

Growing and care:
From Zone 8 south, plant bugle lily corms directly in the garden 3 inches deep and 6 to 9 inches apart in fall for spring flowering. From Zone 7 north, plant in the garden in spring for summer blooms, then lift in fall after foliage withers. Dry bulbs in a cool, dark place for a few days, then trim off leaves a few inches above top of bulb. Store over winter in a cool, dry basement or shed. Propagate from seed, although seedlings can be difficult to transplant, or by removing cormels.

Selected species and varieties:
W. hybrids bear 2- to 3-inch flowers in pastel shades; 'Bright Eyes' is powder pink; 'Dazzle', soft orange with a purple throat; 'Humilis' has pink flowers on 1 1/2-foot dwarf stems; 'Mrs. Bullard's White' is pure white; 'Pink Opal', bright pink; 'Rubra', dusty reddish purple.

BUTTERCUP
Ranunculus

Light: full sun	
Plant type: bulb	
Hardiness: Zones 9-10	
Height: 10 to 18 inches	
Soil and Moisture: well-drained, sandy, moist	
Interest: flowers	
Care: moderate	

◀ Ranunculus asiaticus

These are not the little buttercups of fields and pastures but spectacular relatives. Buttercups produce very formal flowers in a wide range of colors composed of dozens of richly colored petals arranged in roselike swirls. Each tuber may produce five or six dozen flowers up to four at a time throughout the season on stems lined with lacy green leaflets. Buttercups can be used in borders and rock gardens where the weather is warm, or grown indoors in containers for early-spring flowering.

Growing and care:
Plant Persian buttercups in fall, soaking the tubers overnight then setting them in the soil with the claws down and the tops 1 1/2 inches deep. Space tubers 8 inches apart. For plants set outdoors good drainage is essential to avoid rotting of the tubers. As tubers go dormant in summer, stop watering and allow soil to dry out. North of Zone 9, treat plants as annuals, setting them out in spring and lifting them in fall for winter storage. Propagate from seed or by dividing tubers.

Selected species and varieties:
R. asiaticus 'Tecolote Giants' (Persian buttercup) produces gorgeous flowers up to 5 inches across in pastel shades of pink, rose, yellow, tangerine, and white, with bi- and tricolors.

CALLA LILY
Zantedeschia

Light: full sun	
Plant type: bulb	
Hardiness: Zones 9-10	
Height: 2 to 3 feet	
Soil and Moisture: well-drained, moist to wet	
Interest: flowers, foliage	
Care: moderate	

◄ Zantedeschia aethiopica

Calla lily's gracefully curved and sculpted flowers have a cool, formal elegance few other blooms can match. Petal-like spathes curl into elongated trumpets with a flared lip pulled to a point. The waxy spathe folds around a colorful, sometimes fragrant, fingerlike spadix bearing the true flowers, which are tiny and inconspicuous. Up to 12 or more blossoms open at the same time amid broad, stalked, arrow-shaped, wavy-edged leaves that are often attractively flecked and spotted with white. In warm zones, calla lilies are eye-catching specimens for beds or borders and will naturalize where conditions suit them. Elsewhere they are grown as annuals or as potted plants for patio or indoor use. Callas are prized as cut flowers.

Growing and care:
Outdoors in Zones 9 and 10, plant calla lilies in spring or fall, setting rhizomes 1 to 4 inches deep and spacing them 1 to 2 feet apart. Calla lilies tolerate boggy conditions and can be grown with their roots in water at the edges of ponds. North of Zone 9, start them indoors in early spring and transplant them outside after all danger of frost has passed for blooming in summer. Lift rhizomes in fall after foliage withers and store for winter. For pot culture, set growing tips of rhizomes at soil level and allow one root per 6-inch pot. Callas bloom about 2 months after planting. Golden calla lily can be propagated from seed. Propagate all calla lilies by dividing their rhizomes in spring or fall.

Selected species and varieties:
Z. aethiopica (common calla, giant white calla, arum lily, trumpet lily) bears fragrant, snowy white flowers 10 inches long on 2-foot plants; 'Perle Von Stuttgart' is somewhat smaller than the species, with abundant blossoms. *Z. albomaculata* (spotted calla, black-throated calla) has 5-inch white flowers with purple throats on 2-foot plants. *Z. elliottiana* (golden calla, yellow calla) produces 6-inch golden yellow flowers, tinged greenish yellow on the outside, on 2½-foot plants. *Z. rehmannii* (red calla, pink calla) has 3-inch pink flowers on 1½- to 2-foot plants. *Z.* 'Black-Eyed Beauty' produces creamy white blossoms veined green, with a black throat or eye rimming the spadix; 'Black Magic' is yellow with a black eye; 'Cameo', salmon; 'Harvest Moon' is yellow with a red eye; 'Pink Persuasion', purple-pink; 'Solfatare' is a creamy pale yellow with a black eye.

CANNA
Canna

Light: full sun	
Plant type: bulb	
Hardiness: Zones 8-10	
Height: 2 to 10 feet	
Soil and Moisture: well-drained, fertile, moist to wet	
Interest: flowers, foliage	
Care: moderate	

◀ Canna x generalis 'The President'

Cannas have stately spikes of flashy, colorful flowers and bold foliage that add a carnival atmosphere to any garden. Underground rhizomes produce clumps of 8- to 24-inch-long, glossy deep green leaves on fleshy stems. The impressive 4- to 5-inch flowers have three true petals and several petal-like stamens, and are borne on stiff stems above the foliage. These tropical plants are used as lush summer to fall bedding plants and are stunning when massed in large groups.

Growing and care:
Plant after all danger of frost has passed in thoroughly warmed soil rich in organic matter. North of Zone 8, cut back tops to 6 inches after flowering is completed. In fall lift rhizomes after first killing frost, and store them in a cool place in barely moist peat moss. Leave rhizomes in the ground over winter in Zones 8 to 10, but provide them with a protective mulch of straw or pine needles. Propagate by dividing rhizomes in spring.

Selected species and varieties:
C. x *generalis* [also listed as *C.* x *hybrida*] comes in 4- to 6-foot standard varieties, 2- to 3-foot dwarfs, and 7- to 10-foot giants; 'Mohawk' has orange blossoms; 'Panache' is ivory and rose; 'Pfitzer's Primrose Black Knight' has deep blood-red flowers; 'The President' has deep green leaves and bright red flowers.

CAPE COWSLIP
Lachenalia

Light: full sun	
Plant type: bulb	
Hardiness: Zones 9-10	
Height: 6 to 12 inches	
Soil and Moisture: well-drained, sandy, moist	
Interest: flowers	
Care: moderate	

◀ Lachenalia aloides

Cape cowslips bear long spikes of drooping, uniquely shaped tubular flowers that look like brightly colored peanuts. The waxy, inch-long blossoms are often tinged and tipped in multiple colors, and contrast nicely with the fleshy purple and green leaves. Cape cowslips are eye-catching plants in rock gardens where winters are warm, and are grown as container specimens elsewhere. They make long-lasting cut flowers.

Growing and care:
In Zones 9 and 10, plant Cape cowslips outdoors in fall, setting bulbs 1 inch deep and 2 inches apart in sandy soil amended with some organic matter. Indoors, set five or six bulbs 1 inch deep in a 6-inch pot. Propagate by removing the bulblets that grow alongside mature bulbs or, for *L. bulbiferum,* potting the small bulbils that develop in the leaf joints of the plant.

Selected species and varieties:
L. aloides (tricolored Cape cowslip) bears flowers with yellow petals tinged green and touched with red; 'Aurea' blooms bright yellow-orange; 'Pearsonii' has golden yellow blossoms with maroon tips. *L. bulbiferum* (nodding Cape cowslip) has coral pink to red flowers, tipped with green and purple.

CORN LILY
Ixia

Light: full sun

Plant type: bulb

Hardiness: Zones 8-10

Height: 1½ to 2 feet

Soil and Moisture: well-drained, sandy, fertile, moist

Interest: flowers

Care: moderate

◀ Ixia viridiflora

Corn lilies are reliable warm-weather bulbs that produce clusters of cup- or star-shaped, gaily colored flowers at the tips of wandlike stems rising from clumps of sparse, grassy leaves. In warm, dry climates, their multicolored blossoms can be used to decorate beds or borders. Elsewhere, grow them in containers for winter or spring indoor color.

Growing and care:
In Zones 8 to 10, plant outdoors in late fall, setting corms 3 inches deep and 6 inches apart. North of Zone 8, plant them in late spring or early summer after the soil has warmed. After plants have finished flowering allow soil to stay dry over summer. Lift corms in fall and store over winter. Indoors, plant five or six corms 1 inch deep in 6-inch pots in fall for winter to spring bloom. Propagate by removing cormels growing around mature bulbs.

Selected species and varieties:
I. hybrids produce flower bells in shades of white, yellow, orange, pink, red, or blue; 'Bluebird' has violet petals streaked purple outside and white inside and a black throat; 'Marquette' has purple-tipped yellow blossoms. *I. maculata* has foot-long, narrow, slightly ribbed leaves and softly colored yellow, orange, or white flowers accented with a gold or orange throat; Zones 9-10. *I. viridiflora* (green ixia) has 1-inch pale green flowers with black throats and black anthers at the tips of their stamens.

CRIMSON FLAG
Schizostylis

Light: full sun

Plant type: bulb

Hardiness: Zones 6-10

Height: 1 to 2 feet

Soil and Moisture: moist to wet, fertile

Interest: flowers, foliage

Care: moderate

◀ Schizostylis coccinea 'Mrs. Hegarty'

Crimson flag is a beautiful flower, with satiny, pointed petals embracing a cluster of curled stamens. The multiple blossoms are borne on a slender stem above a clump of narrow, sometimes evergreen, leaves. In warm climates, crimson flag may produce sparse flowers in spring and summer and a full burst of fall bloom. Crimson flag thrives in bog gardens or along streams and ponds. In colder areas, grow crimson flag indoors in containers. It produces excellent cut flowers.

Growing and care:
Plant crimson flag outdoors in spring or fall, setting roots 2 inches deep and 9 to 12 inches apart. For containers, set plants outdoors in spring after the threat of frost has passed, then pot them to bring indoors for fall to winter bloom. The plants can then be stored and planted again the following spring. Propagate by division in spring or fall, although disturbed roots may take a year or more to resume flowering.

Selected species and varieties:
S. coccinea (river lily) produces 1- to 2-inch-wide crimson flowers on slender stems above green, grasslike leaves; 'Major' has flowers slightly larger than the species; 'Mrs. Hegarty' produces blossoms colored a pale rose pink.

DAHLIA
Dahlia

Light: full sun	
Plant type: bulb	
Hardiness: Zones 9-10	
Height: 1 to 8 feet	
Soil and Moisture: well-drained, moist, fertile	
Interest: flowers	
Care: moderate	

◄ Dahlia tamjoh

Dahlias reliably brighten the flower border over a long season of bloom with highly diverse blossoms varying from flat-faced, single-petaled types to those with round, dense mounds of petals. Dahlia sizes are as variable as petal forms, with some flowers only a few inches across and others the diameter of a dinner plate. The centers of dahlia blossoms are composed of small, tightly packed disk flowers surrounded by one or more rows of broad, petal-like ray flowers. Colors vary widely, and some dahlias are bicolored or variegated, with petals tipped, streaked, or backed with contrasting color. The types with smaller flowers are easier to work into a bed or border design. Regardless of their size, all dahlias make long-lasting cut flowers.

Growing and care:
Plant dahlia tubers in spring, in well-worked soil amended with compost or other organic matter. Place taller cultivars in a hole 6 to 8 inches deep and cover with 2 to 3 inches of soil. Space the holes 3 to 4 feet apart. Plant tubers of shorter cultivars 2 to 3 inches deep and 1 to 2 feet apart. When transplanting potted seedlings, position them 2 inches deeper than the depth of their pot. Stake all but dwarfs, pompoms, and miniatures. For long-lasting cut flowers, pick dahlias when outdoor temperatures are cool, and stand cut stems in hot water (100° to 160°F) in a cool, shaded location for several hours before arranging. Propagate dahlias from seed started indoors in very early spring to flower that season, from stem cuttings, or by dividing tubers in spring.

Selected species and varieties:
Single dahlias have one or two rows of flat petals surrounding a flat central disk; 'Bambino White' is a dwarf cultivar with 1-inch flowers on 14-inch bushes. *Anemone-flowered dahlias* have a central disk obscured by a fluffy ball of short, tubular petals and rimmed by one or more rows of longer flat petals; 'Siemen Doorenbosch' has flat lavender petals surrounding a creamy central pincushion on 20-inch plants. *Collarette dahlias* have central disks surrounded by a collar of short, often ruffled or cupped petals, backed by a second collar of broader, flat petals; 'Jack O'Lantern' has an inner collar streaked yellow and orange, and deep orange outer petals on 4-foot plants; 'Mickey' has a yellow inner collar backed by deep red outer ray flowers on 3-foot bushes. *Ball dahlias* have cupped, double petals crowded into round domes; 'Nijinsky' has purple flowers on 4-foot stems; 'Rothsay Superb' has red blooms on 3-foot plants. *Pompom dahlias* produce small, round balls of tightly curled petals; 'Amber Queen' has golden to bronze flowers on 4-foot stems; 'Chick-a-dee' has wine red blossoms touched with pink. *Cactus dahlias* have straight or twisted petals rolled like quills; 'Brookside Cheri' has salmon pink petals tinged with gold on 4-foot plants; 'Juanita' bears ruby red flowers on 4-foot stems. *Semi-cactus dahlias* have flat, slightly curling petals with less than half their length rolled into tubes; 'Amanda Jarvis' has rose colored flowers on 3-foot plants; 'Bella Bimba' bears apricot pink flowers on 4-foot plants. *Chrysanthemum dahlias* have double rows of petals all curving inward and hiding the flower's central disk. *Waterlily dahlias* bear short petals clasped tightly over the central disk surounded by several rows of broad, flat petals; 'Lauren Michelle' has rosy-lavender petals with purple underneath on 4-foot plants; 'Gerry Hoek' bears shell pink flowers.

DELICATE LILY
Chlidanthus

Light: full sun	
Plant type: bulb	
Hardiness: Zones 9-10	
Height: 8 to 10 inches	
Soil and Moisture: well-drained, sandy, moist	
Interest: flowers, foliage	
Care: moderate	

◀ Chlidanthus fragrans

Everyone should grow delicate lily at least once. This summer-blooming native of tropical South America bears large, daffodil yellow flowers sweetly scented with a lemony perfume. The funnel-shaped flowers appear in clusters, each having six pointed petals layered like overlapping triangles at the tips of the slender stalks. Narrow gray-green leaves appear after the flowers. Delicate lilies slowly naturalize in Zones 9 and 10, where they lend a graceful element to beds and borders or cutting and specialty gardens. North of Zone 9, delicate lilies are grown as indoor container plants.

Growing and care:
In Zones 9 and 10, plant outdoors in spring, setting bulbs 2 inches deep and 6 to 8 inches apart in loose soil amended with organic matter. North of Zone 8, plant bulbs in spring and lift in fall before the first frost. Store in a cool, dry place over winter. In containers, allow one bulb per 6-inch pot, setting bulb tops at the soil line. Remove bulbs in fall, dry and store. In spring repot in fresh potting soil. Propagate by removing and replanting small bulblets from the base of larger bulbs.

Selected species and varieties:
C. fragrans (perfumed fairy lily) is native to the Andes Mountains and bears loose clusters of three or four yellow blossoms up to 3 inches across and clumps of green, daffodil-like leaves in summer.

DICHELOSTEMMA
Dichelostemma

Light: full sun	
Plant type: bulb	
Hardiness: Zones 5-7	
Height: 1 1/2 to 3 feet	
Soil and Moisture: well-drained, sandy, moist to dry	
Interest: flowers	
Care: moderate	

◀ Dichelostemma congestum

Dichelostemma grows wild across far western North America from central Washington to southern California. The attractive, bluish purple 1-inch-wide flowers are borne in loose clusters atop slender stems and above the sparse, grassy green leaves. The plants thrive in dry grasslands and chaparral, where they blossom each spring. In the garden, dichelostemmas prefer long periods of dry weather interspersed with soaking rains. They are excellent planted in large groups or naturalized in wildflower meadows. The flowers are also useful in fresh floral arrangements.

Growing and care:
Plant dichelostemma corms in fall, setting them 3½ to 5 inches deep and 3 inches apart. The plants thrive in hot, dry weather, especially in summer after they have flowered. In areas with wet summers, dig corms after foliage fades and replant in fall. Protect bulbs in northern zones with a layer of mulch applied in fall. In pots, plant four or five bulbs per 6-inch container. Propagate by removing the small cormels that develop alongside mature bulbs for planting in fall.

Selected species and varieties:
D. congestum bears clusters of trumpet-shaped, pale blue-violet flowers decorated with long, split stamens on 1- to 3-foot stems. *D. pulchellum* has 2-foot stems topped with clusters of purple or white flowers in spring.

FRITILLARY
Fritillaria

Light: full sun	
Plant type: bulb	
Hardiness: Zones 3-8	
Height: 6 inches to 2½ feet	
Soil and Moisture: well-drained, sandy, moist	
Interest: flowers, foliage	
Care: moderate	

◄ Fritillaria imperialis

Fritillaries are a wonderfully diverse group of plants that range from the bold, imposing crown-imperial with a garland of garish blossoms on stout stalks, to the small, dainty woodland species with single, modest flowers on slender stems. Fritillaries produce nodding flower bells in unusual colors and patterns in a variety of forms, providing a variety of ways for gardeners to accent their spring gardens. The flowers have prominent, colorful stamens and are often striped, speckled, or checkered in a wide range of watercolor hues. Touching the petals sometimes produces a small "tear" from reservoirs of nectar at the base of each petal. The often glossy leaves are highly variable, sometimes appearing in whorls extending halfway up the flower stalk, sometimes alternating from one side of the stem to the other along its length, and occasionally growing in a tuft at the base of the stem. Mass fritillaries in wildflower gardens, rock gardens, or perennial borders where other plants will fill in when their foliage dies down in early summer.

Growing and care:

Plant fritillaries in late summer or fall, setting large bulbs 4 inches deep and 1 foot apart and smaller bulbs 2 inches deep and 8 inches apart. Bulbs may take a year to become established in new locations before they flower. Most fritillaries like full sun and very well-drained soil, but *F. meleagris* and *F. pallidiflora* prefer some light shade and moist soil. For all fritillaries, avoid sites with cold, wet soils, and reduce watering once foliage dies back. Both *F. imperialis* 'Rubra Maxima' and *F. persica* are endangered in the wild and should be purchased only from reputable growers selling stock propagated by themselves or other growers. The musky, faintly skunklike odor of crown-imperial is said to repel rodents. Propagate by removing and replanting bulb offsets in late summer or early fall. Plants started from offsets will reach flowering size in 3 to 4 years.

Selected species and varieties:

F. imperialis (crown-imperial) has bold 2½-foot stalks, the lower half lined with whorls of glossy, pointed leaves, the tip crowned by a tuft of shorter leaves with a ring of large 2-inch flower bells with dangling yellow stamens below it; 'Maxima Lutea' is lemon yellow; 'Rubra Maxima', dark red; Zones 4-7. *F. meleagris* (snake's-head fritillary, checkered lily, guinea-hen tulip, leper lily) bears 1½-inch flower bells checkered dark maroon and white on 8- to 10-inch stems; 'Alba' is pure white. *F. michailovskyi* produces up to five deep purplish red and yellow flower bells with their tips flipped daintily outward on 4- to 8-inch stems; Zones 5-8. *F. pallidiflora* has up to a dozen 1- to 1½-inch pale yellow and green flower bells flecked with brown and red, borne in the upper leaf joints along arching 1½-foot stems. *F. persica* has up to 30 velvety purple blossoms lining 2½-foot stems; 'Adiyaman' yields inch-wide plum flowers; Zones 4-8. *F. pudica* (yellow fritillary, yellow bell) bears ¾-inch yellow-orange flowers tinged purple in clusters of three on 9-inch stems; Zones 4-8. *F. purdyi* 'Tinkerbell' has six or seven dainty white flower bells striped rusty brown on the outside and spotted red inside on 6-inch stems above a low rosette of 6-inch leaves; Zones 5-8. *F. uva-vulpis* produces solitary purplish gray flower bells edged in yellow on 1- to 1½-foot stems. *F. verticillata* has 1¼-inch cup-shaped pale yellow blossoms flecked with green outside and spotted purple inside lining 2-foot stems, the tips of the upper leaves elongating into tendrils; Zones 6-8.

GLADIOLUS
Gladiolus

Light: full sun	
Plant type: bulb	
Hardiness: Zones 7-10	
Height: 1 to 7 feet	
Soil and Moisture: well-drained, fertile, moist	
Interest: flowers	
Care: moderate	

◀ Gladiolus communis ssp. byzantinus

Gladiolus is one of the most beautiful of garden flowers, producing very showy spikes of 1½- to 5½-inch flowers above ornamental fans of stiff, sword-shaped leaves. The closely spaced flowers open from bottom to top on alternate sides of the upright flower stems. The abundant, sometimes fragrant flowers open one at a time to provide a long-lasting display that looks fresh for up to several weeks. Tall gladiolus are striking when massed in large groups or planted at the back of a border. Shorter species liven up rock gardens or mixed borders and look charming planted alongside late-blooming daffodils. Gladiolus are long-lasting cut flowers and turn ho-hum floral arrangements into flamboyant bouquets.

Growing and care:
Work well-rotted manure or other organic matter deeply into the soil a year before planting. North of Zone 8, plant hardy gladiolus in fall, tender ones in spring. Set large corms 4 to 6 inches deep and 6 to 9 inches apart, smaller ones 3 to 4 inches deep and 4 to 6 inches apart. Provide ample water while growing and blooming. North of Zone 8, tender gladiolus should be dug in fall for replanting in spring. Early-blooming hybrids flower 90 days after planting, midseason varieties in 110 days, and late-midseason ones in 120 days. To avoid fungus problems, do not plant gladiolus in the same location from year to year. Pick for cut flowers as the first bloom begins to open, leaving four or five leaves in place to feed the corm. Propagate by removing the cormels that develop around mature mother corms in fall.

Selected species and varieties:
G. callianthus [formerly classified as *Acidanthera bicolor*] 'Murielae' yields fragrant, 2- to 3-inch white flowers with purple throats on 2-foot stems in summer. *G. carneus* (painted lady) produces white, cream, mauve, or pink blossoms flecked purple on 2-foot stems, blooming spring to summer; Zones 9-10. *G.* x *colvillei* (Coronado hybrid) has 2-inch scarlet flowers blotched yellow on branching 2-foot stems in spring. *G. communis* ssp. *byzantinus* (Byzantine gladiolus) has white-streaked burgundy flowers on 2-foot stems in spring to summer; Zones 5-10. *G.* hybrids have ruffled, waved, crimped, or frilled flowers in shades of white, yellow, red, purple, blue, or green, sometimes bicolored or multicolored, on stems to 7 feet in summer through fall; 'Nova Lux' is pure velvety yellow; 'Red Bird', flaming red; 'Priscilla', white-feathered pink with a yellow throat; 'Royal Blush' has deep rose red petals edged in white; 'White Knight' is pure white; tender. *G. nanus* [also classified as *Babiana nana*] is a spring- to summer-blooming dwarf plant 1 to 2 feet tall; 'Amanda Mahy' is salmon with violet splotches; 'Desire', cream; 'Guernsey Glory' has pink to purple petals with red edges and cream blotches; 'Impressive' is pinkish white splotched deep rose; 'Prins Claus', ivory with purple spotting.

GLORY-OF-THE-SUN
Leucocoryne

Light:	full sun
Plant type:	bulb
Hardiness:	Zones 9-10
Height:	10 to 12 inches
Soil and Moisture:	well-drained, moist to dry
Interest:	flowers, fragrance
Care:	moderate

◀ Leucocoryne ixioides

Glory-of-the-sun is an uncommon plant that bears small clusters of fragrant, uncommonly attractive star-shaped flowers. The pure white or lapis blue flowers are sparingly produced on slender stems above clumps of foot-long grassy leaves. Glory-of-the-sun thrives in warm, seasonally dry climates such as southern California's, where it adds a dainty accent to rock gardens or borders. Elsewhere the plants are grown in containers and appreciated indoors. Glory-of-the-sun makes an excellent, long-lasting cut flower.

Growing and care:
Outdoors, plant glory-of-the-sun in early to midfall, setting bulbs 4 to 6 inches deep and 6 to 8 inches apart. Water well while plants are actively growing but keep bulbs dry after foliage withers in early summer. Indoors, set bulbs in pots 1 inch deep, allowing two or three bulbs per 6-inch pot. Propagate from seed or from offsets that develop at the base of mature bulbs.

Selected species and varieties:
L. ixioides has up to a half-dozen white to sky blue blossoms ½ inch long and ¾ inch across on stems up to 1 foot tall, and narrow, 10- to 12-inch leaves.

HABRANTHUS
Habranthus

Light:	full sun
Plant type:	bulb
Hardiness:	Zones 9-10
Height:	9 to 12 inches
Soil and Moisture:	well-drained, moist
Interest:	flowers, foliage
Care:	moderate

◀ Habranthus robustus

Habranthus are relatives of amaryllis, and add a soft, lilylike accent to warm-climate rock gardens and flower beds. Each plant produces a single, slender, 12-inch stem bearing two or three blossoms composed of six pointed, delicately recurved petals surrounding a group of prominent stamens. The attractive tuft of dark, glossy green foliage seems to cradle the flower stem. The upright or slightly pendent blossoms of habranthus are beautiful but do not last long. In northern regions the plants are frequently grown indoors in containers.

Growing and care:
From Zone 9 south, plant habranthus outdoors anytime, setting bulbs 4 to 5 inches deep and 6 inches apart in well-worked, evenly moist soil. Water and fertilize regularly while plant is actively growing. Indoors, plant bulbs singly in 6-inch pots in spring for summer blooms. Propagate from seed or from the small bulblets that develop at the base of mature bulbs.

Selected species and varieties:
H. brachyandrus [formerly *Hippeastrum brachyandrum*] has 3-inch flowers edged in light pink with deep burgundy throats on 1-foot stems. *H. robustus* bears slightly pendent, 1-inch rosy pink to red flowers with lime green throats on 9- to 12-inch stems.

HARDY GLOXINIA
Incarvillea

Light: full sun	
Plant type: bulb	
Hardiness: Zones 5-7	
Height: 1 to 2 feet	
Soil and Moisture: well-drained, moist	
Interest: flowers, foliage	
Care: moderate	

◀ Incarvillea delavayi

Hardy gloxinias bear ornate, funnel-shaped flowers with fused, flaring petals in complex shades of pink, rose, and cream. The blossoms line the tips of leafless stems that rise above a graceful clump of ferny foliage. Hardy gloxinias are great for adding splashes of color to rock gardens or sunny borders.

Growing and care:
Plant hardy gloxinias in spring, setting tubers 3 to 4 inches deep and 15 inches apart. Keep soil moist throughout the growing season and fertilize regularly. In northern areas mulch plants in fall with straw or pine needles. Plants grown from seed will reach blooming size in 3 years. Hardy gloxinia can also be propagated by division but plants will produce more flower buds if left undisturbed.

Selected species and varieties:
I. compacta has abundant purple flowers 2½ inches long and 1½ inches across on 1-foot stems above 8-inch dark green leaves; 'Bee's Pink' has white to pink flowers. *I. delavayi* bears 3-inch purplish pink flower trumpets with yellow throats on 2-foot stems above 10-inch leaves.

HERMODACTYLUS
Hermodactylus

Light: full sun	
Plant type: bulb	
Hardiness: Zones 6-9	
Height: 1½ feet	
Soil and Moisture: well-drained, fertile, moist	
Interest: flowers, foliage	
Care: moderate	

◀ Hermodactylus tuberosus

The very unusual flowers of hermodactylus look like a cross between a daylily and an iris. The solitary blossoms are richly colored with contrasting shades of green, yellow, and purple and emit a subtle, rosy fragrance. Beneath the flowers are square, blue-green leaves shaped like upright swords. Hermodactylus are very showy in rock gardens or sunny borders, where they will slowly grow into large colonies. They can also be grown in containers. The plant is still uncommon in the United States but has been popular in Europe for many years.

Growing and care:
Plant tubers 3 inches deep and 6 to 8 inches apart in well-worked, neutral to slightly alkaline soil in late summer or fall. After flowering, the main tuber produces fingerlike offsets before dying. The offsets then bloom the following year. In regions with mild winters hermodactylus will naturalize. Repot container-grown specimens annually after plants go dormant in late summer or fall. Separate offsets from old tubers and replant in fresh potting mix.

Selected species and varieties:
H. tuberosus (snake's-head iris, widow iris) has 2-inch vase-shaped flowers with delicate, lime green, ruffled inner petals enclosed in broad, yellow-green outer petals tipped with dark purple, rising from 1½-foot-tall squared, leafy stems.

HYACINTH
Hyacinthus

Light: full sun	
Plant type: bulb	
Hardiness: Zones 3-7	
Height: 4 to 12 inches	
Soil and Moisture: well-drained, fertile, moist	
Interest: flowers	
Care: easy	

◀ Hyacinthus orientalis 'Blue Jacket'

With their heady fragrance and richly colored blossoms, hyacinths have long been regarded as a classic plant for the spring border. The plants have stiff, narrow, slightly glossy leaves and short, stout stems packed with star-shaped flowers from mid- to late spring. The tips of the petals curve backward gracefully, giving the dense clusters a frilly appearance, an effect that is heightened when flowers are shaded in two tones of the same color. Hyacinths come in many different types, ranging from double-flowered cultivars with whorls of petals to multiflora varieties that produce several flower stems decorated with loose, open flower clusters. Hyacinths make excellent companions to other spring-flowering bulbs in sunny beds and borders. When forced indoors in containers the flowers emit a floral fragrance that can perfume an entire room for weeks.

Growing and care:

Outdoors, plant bulbs in fall, setting them 4 to 6 inches deep and 6 to 8 inches apart in rich soil well amended with compost or well-rotted manure. Indoors, allow four or five bulbs per 6-inch pot. Plant indoor bulbs in fall as well. Prechilled bulbs will bloom earlier than ordinary bulbs. Keep newly potted, previously unchilled bulbs in a dark location below 50°F for about 12 weeks or until roots fill the pot and bulbs show 2 inches of leaf growth.

Then move the pots into filtered sunlight at a temperature no higher than 65°F. If using special hyacinth vases, suspend the bulb above (but not touching) the water and treat the same as potted bulbs. 'Anne Marie' and 'Blue Jacket' are particularly good cultivars for forcing, providing more reliable flowering than other types. Hyacinths are difficult to propagate but sometimes form offsets alongside mature bulbs. Plants propagated from offsets can reach blooming size in about 6 years.

Selected species and varieties:

H. orientalis (Dutch hyacinth, common hyacinth, garden hyacinth) has clusters of star-shaped blossoms in an array of colors above foot-long leaves; 'Anne Marie' is pastel pink aging to salmon; 'Blue Giant' has large, pastel blue clusters; 'Blue Jacket' is deep purple with paler petal edges; 'Blue Magic', purple-blue with a white throat; 'Carnegie', elegant pure white; 'City of Harlem', pastel lemon yellow; 'Delft Blue', porcelain blue with paler edges; 'French Roman Blue' is a multiflora cultivar with blue blooms; 'Gipsy Queen', yellow-tinged clear orange; 'Hollyhock' has flowers with double red petals on 4-inch stalks; 'Jan Bos' is clear candy-apple red on slender spikes; 'Lady Derby', rosy pink; 'Lord Balfour' has loose clusters of rose-purple blossoms; 'Oranje Boven' is salmon; 'Peter Stuyvesant', deep purple-blue; 'Pink Pearl', deep luminescent pink; 'Snow White' is a white multiflora variety; 'Violet Pearl' is lilac-rose aging to silver.

IRIS
Iris

Light: full sun	
Plant type: bulb	
Hardiness: Zones 5-9	
Height: 4 inches to 5 feet	
Soil and Moisture: well-drained, moist to dry	
Interest: flowers, foliage	
Care: moderate	

◀ Iris ensata

Irises blossom in a rainbow of colors in spring and summer on zigzag stems rising above clumps of flat, sword-shaped foliage that remains attractive long after the flowers fade. Each flower is composed of three dropping petal-like sepals called falls, three erect petals called standards, and three narrow, petal-like styles. Some spread from rhizomes, while others grow from bulbs. Irises can be used in borders or rock gardens, or naturalized in woodland settings. Many irises are quite fragrant, and those with long stalks make good cut flowers. With more than 200 species and countless varieties, there is a type of iris to fit any garden anywhere.

Growing and care:

Plant irises in summer in the North and in fall in the South, spacing smaller types 1 foot apart and taller varieties 1½ feet apart. Dig a hole and refill until the top of the mound of soil is at ground level. Place rhizomes on mound and spread roots. Finish filling the hole and gently tamp the soil. Bearded iris should have the top half of the rhizomes above soil level while Siberian iris should have the rhizome completely buried beneath the soil surface. *I. pseudacorus* prefers wet meadows or the shallow edges of ponds. Siberian, Louisiana, and Japanese irises need constant moisture and thrive in soil high in organic matter. Propagate rhizomatous irises after flowering by first trimming foliage to a 6-inch fan with a sharp, clean knife. Cut the rhizome cleanly into sections, being sure each piece has several buds and a quantity of healthy roots.

Selected species and varieties:

I. bearded hybrids bear 3- to 5-inch white to purple flowers with yellow beards on 2- to 3-foot stems, and clumps of light green leaves in summer; 'Austrian Sky' has sky blue flowers with navy blue falls; 'Broadway' has golden standards and white falls; 'Vanity' has light pink flowers splashed with white. *I. cristata* (crested iris, dwarf crested iris) grows from small, spreading rhizomes that produce grassy 6-inch leaves and 2-inch white or blue-violet flowers crested in yellow or white in midspring on 4-inch stems; 'Shenandoah Sky' has pale blue flowers; 'Summer Storm' has dark blue blossoms. *I. ensata* [also listed as *I. kaempferi*] (Japanese iris) has graceful, stiff 2-foot leaves with beardless 3- to 6-inch flowers in many different colors on 4-foot stalks in summer; 'August Emperor' has giant, deep red flowers in late summer; 'Pink Triumph' bears 8-inch deep pink, double-petaled flowers. *I. pallida* 'Variegata' grows 3 feet tall with fragrant lavender-blue flowers in early spring and lovely foliage all summer. *I. pseudacorus* (yellow flag, yellow iris) has 2-inch bright yellow, beardless flowers from late spring to early summer on 4- to 5-foot stems, spreading vigorously from rhizomes. *I. reticulata* (reticulated iris) has 8- to 10-inch-tall stems rising from bulbs in late winter bearing blue to red-purple flowers in early spring; 'Harmony' has 6-inch brilliant blue flowers. *I. sibirica* (Siberian iris) produces 2- to 4-foot clumps of leaves with 3- to 5-inch beardless, late-spring flowers in many colors including violet, blue, white, and red, on 3-foot stems, growing from rhizomes; 'Eric the Red' has dark red flowers; 'Periwinkle' has powder blue flowers; 'Super Ego' has robust 3-foot stems and striking 5-inch pale blue petals boldly etched with navy blue. *I. versicolor* (blue flag) has 2- to 3-foot-tall clumps of graceful, lance-shaped leaves and strong stalks bearing several showy violet-blue flowers in summer; 'Rosea' has pink flowers; Zones 3-6.

MARIPOSA LILY
Calochortus

Light: full sun	
Plant type: bulb	
Hardiness: Zones 6-10	
Height: 8 inches to 2 feet	
Soil and Moisture: well-drained, sandy, moist to dry	
Interest: flowers	
Care: moderate	

◄ Calochortus venustus

These eye-catching native wildflowers of the American West are stunning additions to naturalistic plantings, rock gardens, and fresh floral arrangements. The teacup-shaped flowers come in many colors depending on the species, including white, pink, yellow, lilac, and purple. The blossoms appear from the leaf axils or atop the erect stems that rise from a small clump of shiny, fleshy, narrow leaves, and are usually stained with darker tones along the flower's throat.

Growing and care:
Purchase only nursery-grown bulbs. Plant mariposa lilies in fall, setting the bulbs 2 to 4 inches deep and 8 to 10 inches apart. Keep soil dry while bulbs are dormant from late summer to winter, and evenly moist while plants are actively growing from late winter to summer. In areas with wet summer and fall seasons, lift bulbs in late summer, store in a cool, dry place, and replant in fall. Propagate from seed or by removing and replanting bulblets growing alongside mature bulbs in summer after plants are dormant.

Selected species and varieties:
C. clavatus has charming yellow blossoms borne on 2-foot-tall stems in summer. *C. venustus* (white mariposa) bears 2-inch white, yellow, purple, or red flowers with throats splotched in darker shades or contrasting colors on 8-inch to 2-foot stems.

MONTBRETIA
Crocosmia

Light: full sun	
Plant type: bulb	
Hardiness: Zones 5-9	
Height: 2 to 4 feet	
Soil and Moisture: well-drained, moist	
Interest: flowers, foliage	
Care: moderate	

◄ Crocosmia 'Lucifer'

Montbretias produce dozens of small, vibrantly colored flowers in summer that seem to float above masses of long, sword-shaped leaves. They make excellent container plants in northern regions, and naturalize where winters are mild, forming thick beds that are striking when in bloom. Montbretias are excellent plants for sunny borders and for moist areas near streams, ponds, or lakes.

Growing and care:
Plant montbretia corms in spring, setting them 3 to 5 inches deep and 6 to 8 inches apart. Fertilize in spring with a well-balanced fertilizer. Protect from frost with mulch applied in early winter, or lift corms in fall and store at 50°F for spring planting. Propagate montbretias by replanting small cormels that develop at the base of mature corms, or from seed sown as soon as it ripens in fall.

Selected species and varieties:
C. x *crocosmiiflora* produces horizontal sprays 2 to 4 feet long in red, orange, yellow, maroon, or bicolors, with large-flowered types bearing 1½- to 3-inch blossoms and leaves ½ to 1 inch wide and 2 to 3 feet long; 'Aurantiaca' has deep orange flowers; 'Venus' has peach-yellow flowers; Zones 6-9. *C.* 'Citronella' has yellow flowers with maroon markings in the center; 'Lucifer' bears fiery red blossoms on 3-foot stems.

NECTAROSCORDUM
Nectaroscordum

Light: full sun	
Plant type: bulb	
Hardiness: Zones 6-10	
Height: 4 feet	
Soil and Moisture: well-drained, moist	
Interest: flowers	
Care: easy	

◀ Nectaroscordum siculum

Nectaroscordum is one of the most attractive members of the onion family. The plants bear large, loose clusters of pendent, flowery bells atop 4-foot stems. While in flower the blossoms are pendulous but become more erect as the seedpods form. The long, straplike leaves are bright green and emit an oniony odor when bruised. Nectaroscordum adds a strong upright presence to borders or sunny wildflower gardens, where it slowly spreads into larger clumps. The dried seedpods are very attractive in arrangements.

Growing and care:

Plant nectaroscordum in fall, setting bulbs 2 inches deep and 1½ feet apart. They bloom best when clumps are undisturbed, and they often freely self-sow. Keep soil moist while plants are actively growing. Fertilize lightly in spring. Plants grown from seed will reach flowering size in 2 years. Clumps can also be divided in fall after leaves wither.

Selected species and varieties:

N. siculum (Sicilian honey garlic) has clusters of ½-inch-wide flowers composed of six rounded petals, overlapping at their bases and flared open at their tips, each dull buff petal tinged green to purple-green with a darker purple stripe down its center.

NERINE
Nerine

Light: full sun	
Plant type: bulb	
Hardiness: Zones 9-10	
Height: 8 inches to 2 feet	
Soil and Moisture: well-drained, sandy, dry to moist	
Interest: flowers, foliage	
Care: moderate	

◀ Nerine bowdenii

Nerines bear large clusters of star-shaped flowers with prominent stamens that resemble giant honeysuckle blossoms. The flowers appear on leafless stems in fall, followed by narrow, strap-shaped, glossy leaves from late winter to early spring. In warmer zones nerines make bold additions to beds or borders. Elsewhere they make excellent container plants for portable autumn color. Nerine is good for cutting and adds an unforgettable, exotic touch to arrangements.

Growing and care:

Plant nerine bulbs in late summer, setting them 8 inches apart with the upper half of the bulb above the soil surface. In northern areas, grow in containers and bring plants indoors after they flower in fall. When the foliage turns brown in spring, stop watering and keep bulbs dry until late summer. Propagate from seed or by removing bulb offsets.

Selected species and varieties:

N. bowdenii has 9-inch open clusters of lively, rose pink flowers on 2-foot-tall stems that appear with the leaves; 'Pink Triumph' produces blossoms of shockingly iridescent pink. *N. sarniensis* (Guernsey lily) bears 10-inch clusters of icy white to dark scarlet flowers on 1½-foot stems; 'Cherry Ripe' has rosy red blossoms; 'Early Snow' produces flowers of pure white; 'Radiant Queen' has rosy pink flowers; 'Salmon Supreme' bears light pink blossoms.

PANCRATIUM
Pancratium

Light: full sun	
Plant type: bulb	
Hardiness: Zones 9-10	
Height: 1 to 2 feet	
Soil and Moisture: well-drained, sandy, dry	
Interest: flowers, fragrance	
Care: moderate	

◀ Pancratium maritimum

Pancratium produces clusters of clear white, extremely fragrant, exotic flowers reminiscent of frilled daffodils. The blossoms are borne on sturdy stems above a nest of gray-green sword-shaped leaves. Where climates are reliably frost-free they are a sophisticated addition to borders and rock gardens. North of Zone 9, plant them in containers for patio display or indoor use.

Growing and care:
Plant pancratium bulbs where they can remain undisturbed for several years, setting them 3 inches deep and 10 to 12 inches apart. Set one large bulb per 1-foot pot to allow room for bulb offsets to develop. Plant so the tip of the bulb is level with the soil surface. Repotting or division may reduce flowering the following season. Propagate by carefully removing the offsets from around the fragile, mature bulbs.

Selected species and varieties:
P. maritimum (sea daffodil, sea lily) has 3-inch flaring, snow white flowers with a deeply toothed, trumpet-shaped corona surrounded by six narrow, pointed petals in clusters at the tip of each stem.

PEACOCK FLOWER
Tigridia

Light: full sun	
Plant type: bulb	
Hardiness: Zones 7-10	
Height: 1 to 2 feet	
Soil and Moisture: well-drained, fertile, moist	
Interest: flowers, foliage	
Care: moderate	

◀ Tigridia pavonia

Peacock flower's unique blossoms are composed of three large outer petals forming a broad triangle enfolding three gaily spotted inner petals united to form a deep cup. The blossoms appear singly on erect stems rising from stiff fans of swordlike leaves. Each flower lasts only a day, but the corms produce a succession of blossoms over 6 to 8 weeks. The vivid tones of peacock flowers are stunning when massed in borders and beds. In southern regions the plants often naturalize.

Growing and care:
Plant peacock flowers in spring, setting corms 3 to 4 inches deep and 6 to 9 inches apart. Provide a protective winter mulch in Zone 7. North of Zone 7, plant bulbs in spring and lift in fall. Allow plants to dry for a few days and snip off foliage 2 to 3 inches above the bulb. Store over winter in a cool, dark place. Plants grown from seed will bloom the first year. Peacock flower can also be propagated from the small cormels that develop at the base of mature corms.

Selected species and varieties:
T. pavonia (peacock flower, tiger flower) bears 3- to 6-inch white, yellow, orange, purple, or pink flowers with conspicuously spotted and mottled centers; 'Alba' has white outer petals; 'Aurea' is yellow; 'Rosea', rosy pink.

POLIANTHES
Polianthes

Light: full sun	
Plant type: bulb	
Hardiness: Zones 9-10	
Height: 2 to 4 feet	
Soil and Moisture: well-drained, moist	
Interest: flowers, foliage, fragrance	
Care: moderate	

◀ Polianthes tuberosa 'The Pearl'

Polianthes is one of the most intensely fragrant flowers around. The long, curving buds open above grassy, gray-green leaves into clusters of waxy flowers with a rich, sweet, jasminelike fragrance. Each bud forms a narrow trumpet whose petal ends depict a tiny, succulent star. In warm regions use polianthes outdoors in beds and borders. In cooler regions use containers indoors; a single blossom can perfume an entire room. As cut flowers, they last as long as 2 weeks.

Growing and care:

Plant outdoors in spring, setting the tubers 3 inches deep and 6 inches apart. Mature tubers bloom then die, leaving behind many small offsets that reach blooming size in 1 or 2 years. North of Zone 9, start tubers indoors 4 to 6 weeks before night temperatures reach 60°F, and lift for winter storage. For potted plants, allow one tuber per 6-inch pot, setting bulbs 1 inch deep. Propagate by removing offsets that develop around mature tubers.

Selected species and varieties:

P. tuberosa (tuberose) bears very fragrant 2½-inch-long white flowers above 1- to 1½-inch rich green leaves; 'The Pearl' has double-petaled, richly fragrant blossoms on 2-foot stems; 'Single Mexican' produces single flowers on 3- to 4-foot stems.

RED-HOT POKER
Veltheimia

Light: full sun	
Plant type: bulb	
Hardiness: Zone 10	
Height: 15 to 20 inches	
Soil and Moisture: well-drained, sandy, moist to dry	
Interest: flowers	
Care: moderate	

◀ Veltheimia bracteata

Red-hot poker bears oval clusters of up to 50 pink or white blossoms. The attractive flower spikes open from bottom to top into long, drooping funnels with curled lips. Clusters are carried on sturdy stems above attractive rosettes of glossy green leaves with wavy edges. Both leaves and stems are attractively mottled. Use red-hot poker outdoors in warm climates, and as a container plant for the patio or deck in cooler regions.

Growing and care:

Outdoors in Zone 10 plant red-hot poker bulbs 1 inch deep and 6 to 10 inches apart in fall. In pots, group several of the 6-inch bulbs together in large bulb pans for best effect. Plant them 4 to 6 inches apart with the top third of the bulb exposed, and allow bulbs to dry off during summer dormancy. Propagate by removing bulb offsets after foliage withers.

Selected species and varieties:

V. bracteata has 2-inch pink-red or pink-purple blossoms with green- and white-flecked lips above foliage and stems marbled green and purple. *V. capensis* has long, lance-shaped leaves and 1-foot-tall stems topped with pale pink flowers; 'Rosalba' has white flowers lightly spotted with pink.

RHODOHYPOXIS
Rhodohypoxis

Light: full sun
Plant type: bulb
Hardiness: Zones 6-10
Height: 3 to 4 inches
Soil and Moisture: well-drained, sandy, dry
Interest: flowers
Care: moderate

◀ Rhodohypoxis baurii

Rhodohypoxis are perky summertime plants with tufts of 3-inch, stiff, grassy leaves covered with downy hairs in spring, followed by dainty, flat-faced blossoms that appear throughout the season. Each blossom sits atop a slender stem, with each plant producing several stems at a time. Rhodohypoxis are excellent planted among paving stones and will naturalize in rock gardens or borders. They can also be grown as container specimens.

Growing and care:
Plant rhodohypoxis in fall, setting rhizomes 1 to 2 inches deep and 2 to 3 inches apart. Protect plants with mulch in winter in Zones 5 and 6. North of Zone 5, plant rhodohypoxis in spring and lift in fall after foliage has turned brown. Dry and store like gladiolus. To grow as a container plant, set four or five rhizomes in a 6-inch bulb pan. Propagate by division of roots in spring before the leaves appear.

Selected species and varieties:
R. baurii (red star) has low-growing, 3- to 4-inch-high stems bearing 1- to 1½-inch white, pink, rose, or red flowers with petals crowded closely together at the center, obscuring the stamens and dainty clusters of grasslike green leaves.

SANDERSONIA
Sandersonia

Light: full sun
Plant type: bulb
Hardiness: Zones 9-10
Height: 2 to 3 feet
Soil and Moisture: well-drained, sandy, dry
Interest: flowers
Care: moderate

◀ Sandersonia
aurantiaca

Children love the chubby little lantern-shaped blossoms of sandersonia. The petals fuse into tiny, balloon-shaped flowers that dangle from thin stalks growing in the upper leaf joints along semierect, climbing stems. Soft green, narrow, pointed leaves line the stems, sometimes tapering into threadlike tendrils. Sandersonia not only is enchanting to children but will impress adults as well when planted along fences or walls, or grown in containers as patio specimens. Sandersonia also makes an excellent cut flower.

Growing and care:
Plant sandersonia in spring, after danger of frost has passed, carefully setting the brittle tubers 4 inches deep and 8 to 12 inches apart. North of Zone 9, lift tubers in fall and store over winter in a cool, dry place. The plants can also be grown outdoors in containers during summer and brought indoors during the colder months. Plants propagated from seed will bloom in about 2 years. Established plantings can be divided in spring.

Selected species and varieties:
S. aurantiaca (Chinese-lantern lily, Christmas-bells) has 1-inch lantern-shaped golden orange blossoms hanging from 2- to 3-foot-tall stems covered with narrow green leaves.

SAUROMATUM
Sauromatum

Light:	full sun
Plant type:	bulb
Hardiness:	Zone 10
Height:	1 to 2 feet
Soil and Moisture:	well-drained, moist to wet
Interest:	flowers, foliage
Care:	moderate

◀ Sauromatum venosum

Sauromatum is a plant for wet places, where the colorful spathe and feathery foliage add a distinctive, tropical touch to water gardens. The tiny, inconspicuous true flowers are carried on a pencil-shaped spadix that emerges from an exotically shaped and colored hood or spathe. The pointed, curled spathe rises from the thick, bottle-shaped stem. The blossoms look pretty but smell awful. After the spathe withers, a finely divided leaf resembling a miniature palm tree appears. Sauromatums are great for warm-climate bog gardens or in containers as specimen plants.

Growing and care:
In Zone 10 where the air is humid and temperatures remain above 68° F, the tubers can be set in a saucer of water on a sunny window sill, where they will grow without soil. For a more conventional garden, plant them outdoors, setting tubers 4 to 6 inches deep and 1 foot apart. North of Zone 10, grow them as container plants, with the tubers set 2 inches deep in pots.

Selected species and varieties:
S. venosum [formerly *S. guttatum*] (voodoo lily, monarch-of-the-East, red calla) produces a 12- to 20-inch-tall spathe mottled and flecked purple, brown, green, and yellow, followed by 20- to 24-inch palmlike foliage.

SCARBOROUGH LILY
Vallota

Light:	full sun
Plant type:	bulb
Hardiness:	Zone 10
Height:	3 feet
Soil and Moisture:	well-drained, sandy, fertile, dry to moist
Interest:	flowers, foliage
Care:	moderate

◀ Vallota speciosa

Scarborough lily (also called *Cyrtanthus*) bears whorls of vividly colored amaryllis-like blossoms with star-like pointed petals forming deep trumpets around long, prominent stamens. Clusters of up to 10 flowers are borne atop sturdy stems above clumps of straplike evergreen leaves. *Vallota* can be used in beds and borders in very warm regions. In cooler climates it makes an excellent container plant.

Growing and care:
In frost-free climates plant outdoors in early spring, setting bulb tips at the soil line and spacing them 15 to 18 inches apart. For pot culture, plant one bulb in a 6-inch pot, leaving the top half of the bulb above the soil line. Bulbs potted in spring will bloom in fall. Keep soil moist during winter dormancy. Repot bulbs every 5 to 6 years. Propagate at repotting time by removing the small bulblets that grow around the base of mature bulbs.

Selected species and varieties:
V. speciosa [also called *Cyrtanthus elatus*] bears 3-inch-wide deep scarlet, sometimes pink or white, flower funnels above attractive, deep green, glossy leaves.

SEA ONION
Urginea

Light: full sun	
Plant type: bulb	
Hardiness: Zones 8-10	
Height: 3 to 5 feet	
Soil and Moisture: well-drained, sandy, dry	
Interest: flowers	
Care: easy	

◀ Urginea maritima

Sea onion is an interesting addition to warm-climate gardens and has long been a favorite houseplant in northern regions. The plants produce long spikes of up to 100 tiny flowers at the tips of erect, tall stems that are often bent or twisted by the weight of the blossoms. The flower stalks appear in advance of a rosette of shiny, fleshy, narrow green leaves. In warm, dry areas of the Southwest these plants are perfect for the backs of beds and borders. Elsewhere, enjoy them as indoor potted specimens.

Growing and care:
Plant sea onions in summer with the upper portion of the bulb out of the soil, spacing bulbs 1 to 1½ feet apart. The bulb juice is irritating, and all parts of the plant are poisonous. In cool regions pot bulbs in containers in summer. Grow outdoors until a week or so before the first frost, when they should be brought indoors for winter. Propagate by removing bulb offsets in summer.

Selected species and varieties:
U. maritima has 1½-foot spikes of ½-inch white, yellow, or pink blossoms that open from bottom to top on 3- to 5-foot-tall upright stems. After flowering, 10 to 20 dark green, straplike leaves emerge from the top of the bulb.

SIBERIAN LILY
Ixiolirion

Light: full sun	
Plant type: bulb	
Hardiness: Zones 7-10	
Height: 1 foot	
Soil and Moisture: well-drained, moist to dry	
Interest: flowers	
Care: moderate	

◀ Ixiolirion tataricum

Siberian lilies are small plants that put on a dynamic floral display, each tiny bulb producing a large cluster of lilylike flowers with gracefully curved petals and prominent yellow stamens. The flowers cluster atop slender, pliant stems lined with narrow, grassy leaves. They will slowly naturalize in rock gardens where summers are hot and dry, and can be grown as annuals or container plants in northern zones. Siberian lilies make excellent cut flowers.

Growing and care:
In Zones 7 to 9, plant Siberian lilies outdoors in fall, and from Zone 6 north, in spring after danger of frost has passed. Set bulbs 3 to 4 inches deep and 2 to 6 inches apart in well-worked, moist soil. In Zone 7 provide winter mulch; in more northern areas lift bulbs in fall and store over winter. For container growing, plant five or six bulbs in a 6-inch pot in spring. Keep soil moist and cool for several weeks while roots develop, then grow in full sun until blossoming is completed.

Selected species and varieties:
I. tataricum bears up to 15 clear blue to lilac, slightly fragrant 2-inch flowers with narrow petals on 1-foot stems in spring.

TRITELEIA
Triteleia

Light: full sun	
Plant type: bulb	
Hardiness: Zones 7-10	
Height: 1½ to 2½ feet	
Soil and Moisture: well-drained, sandy, dry	
Interest: flowers, foliage	
Care: moderate	

◀ Triteleia laxa

Triteleias are good looking if uncommon plants that produce loose clusters of dainty, starlike flowers on tall stems above sparse clumps of glossy green leaves. They make good cut flowers and are charming when naturalized in sunny beds, borders, or rock gardens.

Growing and care:
Plant triteleias in fall, setting corms 3 inches deep and 2 to 3 inches apart. They grow best where summers are completely dry, as in the western portions of Zones 8 to 10. Elsewhere, lift corms after foliage withers to dry for summer, and replant in fall. Provide a protective winter mulch in Zone 7. Propagate from seed to bloom in 2 years or by removing and replanting small cormels that develop around mature bulbs.

Selected species and varieties:
T. hyacinthina (wild hyacinth) has 1- to 2-foot-tall stems of flat-topped clusters of up to 30 ½-inch white, blue, or lilac star-shaped flowers in late spring to summer. *T. laxa* (grass nut, triplet lily) bears loose, open spheres of 1¾-inch blue to violet, sometimes white, flowers on 2½-foot stems in spring; 'Queen Fabiola' has dense spheres of pale blue blossoms.

TULIP
Tulipa

Light: full sun	
Plant type: bulb	
Hardiness: Zones 3-8	
Height: 8 inches to 1½ feet	
Soil and Moisture: well-drained, fertile, moist	
Interest: flowers	
Care: moderate	

◀ Tulipa 'Easter Fire'

Tulips are available in almost every color but blue, and often are splashed with a second hue. They spring forth as single flowers or in clusters from clumps of fleshy, wavy-edged leaves, providing accents in borders and rock gardens, or naturalized in meadows. They come in many forms, including Darwins, with softly curved, cup-shaped petals; peony-flowered, with blossoms crowded with wavy petals; and species types, with open, starry flowers.

Growing and care:
Plant tulip bulbs in late fall in a warm, sunny location at a depth equal to three times their diameter. They can withstand crowding with no ill effects—even five bulbs per square foot. Species tulips can provide years of beautiful blossoms, but the flower production of even well-tended hybrids declines after the second or third year.

Selected species and varieties:
T. fosteriana grows 1½ feet tall with very large spring flowers and leaves often streaked or mottled with darker colors; 'Red Emperor' is an old favorite with brilliant red flowers edged with yellow. *T.* hybrids comprise 15 divisions, including single early, double early, Darwins, single late, lily-flowered, fringed, multiflowering, parrot, and double late, flowering from early spring to early summer.

ALOE
Aloe

Light: full sun

Plant type: tender perennial

Hardiness: Zone 10

Height: 2 to 3 feet

Soil and Moisture: well-drained, sandy, moist to dry

Interest: foliage

Care: easy

◀ Aloe vera

Aloes are easy-to-grow succulent plants, some of which have a well-deserved reputation for soothing burns and skin irritations. The plants produce rosettes of fleshy, pointed, medium green leaves mottled with splashes of pale white. Where aloe can be grown outdoors, plants produce a slender flower stalk in summer, but those grown as houseplants seldom bloom. Studies have proved that when applied to the skin, the thick, clear sap relieves the pain of burns and scrapes.

Growing and care:
Grow aloes from the small offsets produced by mature plants, removing 1-inch offsets for potted plants or 6- to 8-inch offsets for outdoor specimens. Allow offsets to harden 2 days before replanting outdoors or potting in a 50:50 mixture of compost and sand. Water aloes infrequently. To use the gel-like sap, split leaves lengthwise and rub the cut surface on the skin; fresh sap is best, as stored sap loses its healing properties.

Selected species and varieties:
A. vera [also classified as *A. barbadensis*] (medicinal aloe, Barbados aloe, unguentine cactus) has mottled gray-green leaves up to 3 feet long and 3- to 4-foot-tall flower stalks with dense clusters of 1-inch yellow to orange or red flowers.

ARNICA
Arnica

Light: full sun

Plant type: perennial

Hardiness: Zones 6-9

Height: 6 inches to 2 feet

Soil and Moisture: well-drained, sandy, moist

Interest: flowers, foliage

Care: easy

◀ Arnica montana

The small, golden, asterlike summer flowers of arnica have a casual, dainty appearance and are held above rosettes of narrow, aromatic leaves. Arnica once figured prominently in herbal medicine but is now regarded as toxic when taken internally and is legally restricted in some countries. Arnica preparations for external use, however, are important homeopathic remedies, and ointments made from its flowers are used in Europe for sprains and bruises, though they may cause dermatitis in some.

Growing and care:
Sow arnica seeds in fall or divide mature plants in spring, setting divisions 6 to 8 inches apart. Arnica does not do well in hot, humid sites or where winters are wet. Flower stems become leggy and floppy in rich soils. For an aromatic muscle liniment, pick flowers when fully open, heat equal parts of flowers and oil or lard, then strain and cool.

Selected species and varieties:
A. montana (leopard's-bane) bears tufts of 2- to 5-inch-long blunt-tipped, finely toothed leaves and golden yellow 3-inch flowers composed of narrow petals surrounding a buttonlike center.

BALM-OF-GILEAD
Cedronella

Light: full sun

Plant type: tender perennial grown as annual

Hardiness: Zone 10

Height: 3 to 5 feet

Soil and Moisture: well-drained, fertile, moist

Interest: flowers, foliage

Care: moderate

◀ Cedronella canariensis

Balm-of-Gilead's aromatic leaves lend an earthy air to the garden and impart a warm, woodsy smell with a hint of citrus to potpourri. The pointed, oval leaves line square stems tipped with tufts of small tubular flowers from summer through fall. In frost-free gardens, train it against trellises or walls or grow it in patio containers where its fragrance can be enjoyed. Elsewhere, it grows well as a houseplant. The fresh leaves make a delightful tea when blended with other herbs. The dried leaves and flower buds are wonderful in sachets and potpourris.

Growing and care:
Sow balm-of-Gilead seed or plant divisions of mature plants in spring, spacing transplants or thinning seedlings to stand 1½ feet apart. Prune in early spring and again in fall after flowering to encourage branching and bushiness. Pick leaves just before flowers open, or use leaves from pruned branches. Dry the leaves and buds in a single layer in a shady, well-ventilated area.

Selected species and varieties:
C. canariensis (balm-of-Gilead, canary balm) has toothed leaves up to 4 inches long and dense spikes of pink to lilac flowers on upright, square stems.

BASIL
Ocimum

Light: full sun

Plant type: annual

Height: 6 inches to 3 feet

Soil and Moisture: well-drained, fertile, moist

Interest: foliage

Care: easy

◀ Ocimum 'African Blue'

Basil is one of the most valued culinary herbs, with pointed, oval, slightly up-curved leaves richly fragrant with the aromas of cinnamon, clove, anise, lemon, rose, orange, thyme, mint, or camphor. The plants not only add a classic touch to hundreds of recipes, but contribute spicy fragrance to the garden as well. All species do well in containers, and most are ideal for window sill gardens throughout winter. Whorls of tiny flowers grow in spikes at the tips of stems from summer through fall. Add fresh or dried basil leaves to salads, sauces, soups, and vegetable dishes or steep them for tea. Use flowers as an edible garnish or in herbal bouquets. Add dried basil to herbal potpourri.

Growing and care:
Sow basil indoors 8 to 12 weeks before the last frost or outdoors where it is to grow, spacing or thinning plants to 1 to 2 feet apart. Basil can be sown in pots for indoor culture year round. It can also be propagated from cuttings, which remain true to type. Basil needs soils 50°F or warmer to thrive. Provide mulch to keep roots from drying out and to keep leaves clean. Leaves are best picked before flowers appear; to delay flowering and encourage bushiness, pinch stems back to four sets of leaves as flower buds form. Avoid wetting the leaves of basil, as mold forms quickly on damp leaves. Preserve by blending fresh leaves into olive oil and refrigerating the

BASIL
(continued)

oil or freezing it in small batches. Whole leaves can be layered in olive oil to preserve them, frozen flat on trays after first brushing both sides with olive oil, or layered in white vinegar; the leaves of purple bush basil give vinegar a burgundy tint. Basil can be difficult to dry successfully; lay the leaves in a single layer on trays between layers of paper towels to keep them from turning black.

Selected species and varieties:
O. 'African Blue' has resinous leaves tinged with purple-green on 3-foot stems tipped with purple flower spikes, and is valued as a border specimen and for fresh flowers. *O. basilicum* (common basil, sweet basil) produces bushy, 8- to 24-inch plants prized by cooks and ideal for garden edging, with fragrant 2- to 3-inch leaves lining stems tipped with white flowers; 'Anise' has purple-tinged licorice-scented leaves and pink flowers; 'Cinnamon' has cinnamon-scented leaves especially good in tea; 'Dark Opal' has deep purple leaves and pink flowers; 'Minimum' (bush basil, Greek basil) is a 6- to 12-inch dwarf with ½-inch leaves that is ideal indoors; 'Minimum Purpurascens' (purple bush basil) has small purple leaves on 1-foot plants; 'Purple Ruffles' has purple-black leaves whose edges are curled and frilled and is excellent in pots. *O. sanctum* [also classified as *O. tenuiflorum*] (holy basil, clove basil, sri tulsi) bears clove-scented 1½-inch leaves and branching spikes of tiny white flowers on stems 1½ to 2 feet tall, primarily used in landscaping.

CALAMINT
Calamintha

◀ Calamintha nepeta

Light: full sun	
Plant type: perennial	
Hardiness: Zones 5-9	
Height: 1 to 2 feet	
Soil and Moisture: well-drained, moist to dry	
Interest: flowers, foliage, fragrance	
Care: easy	

Calamints are members of the mint family with attractive, aromatic leaves and decorative flowers. The vigorous, upright plants often are used to add an airy touch to walkway edges, where their fragrant foliage emits a pungent, minty aroma when brushed by passersby. In summer the plants are sprinkled with clusters of white, pink, or violet flowers that last until fall.

Growing and care:
Calamints are heat and drought tolerant. Plant them in spring, spacing them about 1 foot apart, and mulch. Calamints spread rapidly by underground stolons or self-sown seed. Cut back the foliage after plants have finished flowering in fall, and mulch with pine boughs in areas north of Zone 6.

Selected species and varieties:
C. grandiflora [formerly listed as *Satureja grandiflora*] (greater calamint) grows 1 to 1½ feet tall with 2-inch coarsely toothed, oval leaves, and small clusters of 1-inch pink flowers in summer; 'Variegata' has the same bright pink flowers as the species but has attractive light green foliage mottled with golden splotches. *C. nepeta* [formerly listed as *Satureja calamintha*, and sometimes listed as *C. nepetoides*] grows 1 to 2 feet tall with hairy, finely toothed leaves and ½-inch white or lilac flowers.

CHAMOMILE
Anthemis

Light:	full sun
Plant type:	perennial
Hardiness:	Zones 3-8
Height:	2 to 3 feet
Soil and Moisture:	well-drained, dry
Interest:	flowers, foliage
Care:	easy

◀ Anthemis tinctoria

Chamomile has daisylike blossoms resembling yellow buttons 2 to 3 inches across and scattered over mounds of sweetly scented, silvery green foliage. The blossoms appear from early summer through fall and range from a clear, sunny yellow to pale sunset orange. The plants are excellent choices for low borders, specialty gardens, or when grown beside stone walls or fences.

Growing and care:
Start seed indoors 8 to 10 weeks before last frost or direct-sow in early spring when soil is still cool. Do not cover, as seeds need light to germinate. Space plants 10 to 18 inches apart. Remove spent flowers for continuous bloom over several months. Propagate by division every 2 years, from seed, or from stem cuttings in spring. *Anthemis* can become infested with powdery mildew during hot, humid weather and should be grown in a breezy, open location.

Selected species and varieties:
A. sancti-johannis (St. John's chamomile) bears 2-inch bright orange flowers on evergreen shrubs; Zones 5-8. *A. tinctoria* (golden marguerite) has 2-inch upturned, gold-yellow flowers above finely cut, aromatic foliage; 'Kelwayi' has bright yellow flowers; 'Moonlight', pale yellow; 'E. C. Buxton', creamy white.

CHICORY
Cichorium

Light:	full sun
Plant type:	perennial
Hardiness:	Zones 3-10
Height:	1 to 5 feet
Soil and Moisture:	well-drained, moist to dry
Interest:	flowers
Care:	easy

◀ Cichorium intybus

Chicory is an informal, charming plant with loose mounds of coarsely toothed leaves and plentiful azure blue, sometimes pink or white flowers from summer to fall. Common chicory forms conical heads of young leaves called chicons. While it can be grown for ornament in a wildflower garden, chicory is most useful in the kitchen. Steam or braise young seedlings and roots. Toss bitter young leaves into salads. Roast and grind the young caramel-flavored roots to blend with coffee. Cultivars can be forced to produce blanched chicons ideal for salads or braising. Dried flowers add color to potpourri.

Growing and care:
Sow chicory seed in spring and thin to 1½ feet. Chicory self-sows freely. The flowers open in the morning and close in the late afternoon and on cloudy days. To roast, lift year-old roots in spring, slice and dry at 350°F. For blanched chicons, lift roots their first fall, cut back all but 1 inch of foliage, and shorten root 1 inch; bury in moist, sandy compost and keep in total darkness at 50°F for 4 weeks.

Selected species and varieties:
C. intybus (common chicory, witloof, barbe-de-capuchin, succory) bears beautiful, daisylike, 1- to 1½-inch sky blue, white, or pink flowers in summer to fall on freely branched, open stems with dark green leaves.

CINNAMON
Cinnamomum

Light:	full sun
Plant type:	tree
Hardiness:	Zone 10
Height:	30 to 50 feet
Soil and Moisture:	well-drained, fertile, moist
Interest:	foliage, bark
Care:	moderate

◀ Cinnamomum zeylanicum

Cinnamon and camphor are best known for their fragrant bark and aromatic leaves but the plants make beautiful specimens as well. Both trees have very attractive, glossy evergreen leaves that are tinged with red, pink, or bronze when young. Use either species as a specimen tree, as their vigorous roots crowd out other plants. Alternately, pot them for indoor enjoyment. Use camphor tree's foliage in potpourri or moth-repellent sachets. When cut and dried, the inner bark of cinnamon curls into sticks or quills, which can be used whole or powdered to flavor teas, baked goods, and fruit dishes, and to scent potpourri.

Growing and care:
Sow camphor tree or cinnamon seed in spring, or root softwood cuttings in spring or summer. Plants are susceptible to root diseases if planted in heavy, wet locations. Pinch and prune potted specimens to maintain a height of 6 to 8 feet.

Selected species and varieties:
C. camphora (camphor tree) grows slowly to 50 feet and half as wide or wider with 3- to 6-inch, pungently aromatic oval leaves and yellow-green spring to summer flowers. *C. zeylanicum* (cinnamon, Ceylon cinnamon) grows to 30 feet and half as wide with russet brown, papery outer bark, leathery 7-inch leaves, and clusters of yellowish white summer flowers.

DILL
Anethum

Light:	full sun
Plant type:	annual
Height:	3 to 4 feet
Soil and Moisture:	well-drained, fertile, moist
Interest:	foliage, seeds
Care:	moderate

◀ Anethum graveolens

The tall, softly scented stems and leaves of dill have been part of the herb garden for centuries. The aromatic, feathery leaves and flat, open clusters of yellow summer flowers add delicate texture to garden beds and kitchen and herb gardens. In winter, dill makes a fine addition to window sill gardens. The ferny, delicate leaves of this very versatile herb are used to flavor fish, egg, meat, and vegetable dishes. The immature flower heads add tang to cucumber pickles, and the flat, ribbed seeds add a warm flavor to breads and sauces.

Growing and care:
Sow dill seed in the garden every 2 to 3 weeks from early spring to summer. Thin seedlings to stand 8 to 10 inches apart. Plants often need staking and should not be planted in breezy locations. Do not plant near fennel. Snip leaves and immature flower heads as needed. Harvest seed heads just before they turn brown, and place in paper bags until seeds loosen and fall. For best flavor preserve leaves by freezing whole stems or drying in a microwave oven or refrigerator; air-dried dill has weak flavor.

Selected species and varieties:
A. graveolens has soft 3- to 4-foot stems lined with fine, aromatic, threadlike foliage; 'Bouquet' is a compact cultivar producing abundant crops of leaves and few flowers; 'Mammoth' is fast growing with large blue-green leaves.

EUCALYPTUS
Eucalyptus

Light: full sun	
Plant type: tree	
Hardiness: Zones 9-10	
Height: 60 to 100 feet	
Soil and Moisture: well-drained, fertile, moist	
Interest: foliage, bark	
Care: moderate	

◀ *Eucalyptus citriodora*

Eucalyptus is best known for its penetratingly aromatic lemon-camphor-scented evergreen leaves, but the smooth bark on the bare, branching trunks is stunningly beautiful in the landscape. The tree grows rapidly outdoors, quickly draping the yard in shade. The plants can also be grown as container specimens for patios and city gardens. Use dried leaves in potpourri, and the dried branches or seed capsules in arrangements. The oil derived from the leaves, roots, and bark is often used as a respiratory aid.

Growing and care:
Sow eucalyptus seed in spring or fall in soil generously amended with compost or rotted manure. Choose planting sites carefully, as roots secrete toxins that inhibit the growth of nearby plants. Once established, trees grow 10 to 15 feet per year. Prune in spring to contain size and develop sturdier trunks.

Selected species and varieties:
E. citriodora (lemon-scented gum) has white, sometimes pink to red bark on trees up to 160 feet tall and spreading half as wide, with 3- to 7-inch golden green, narrow leaves and clusters of tiny white winter blooms followed by ⅜-inch seed capsules.

FENNEL
Foeniculum

Light: full sun	
Plant type: tender perennial	
Hardiness: Zones 9-10	
Height: 4 to 6 feet	
Soil and Moisture: well-drained, fertile, moist	
Interest: foliage, seeds	
Care: easy	

◀ *Foeniculum vulgare*

Fennel is a tall, boldly graceful herb with erect, succulent stems and abundant feathery, aromatic foliage. From summer to fall, pale yellow flowers form atop the stems, followed by seed heads in late summer and fall. The stems, leaves, and seeds all taste of anise. Leaves complement seafood or garnish salads. Add seeds to baked goods, chew to freshen breath, or sprout for use in salads.

Growing and care:
Fennel, though a tender perennial, is usually grown as an annual. Sow seeds successively from spring through summer for a continuous supply of leaves and stems. Left to form seed, fennel readily self-sows in fall for a spring harvest. Snip leaves anytime and use them fresh or frozen; they lose flavor when dried. Collect seed heads as they turn from yellow-green to brown, and store in a paper bag until the seeds drop. Store in airtight containers.

Selected species and varieties:
F. vulgare (fennel, sweet anise) has upright, branching stems to 6 feet with soft, needlelike foliage and pale yellow flowers in summer; 'Purpurascens' (copper fennel) has pink, copper, or bronze young foliage.

GERMAN CHAMOMILE
Matricaria

Light: full sun	
Plant type: annual	
Height: 2 to 3 feet	
Soil and Moisture: well-drained, moist to dry	
Interest: flowers, foliage	
Care: easy	

◄ Matricaria recutita

German chamomile is a delightfully pleasant herb with ferny green foliage and daisylike, honey-scented flowers from late spring to early summer. The soft foliage is excellent as a filler in the herb garden. The flowers can be brewed alone or with other herbs to make a soothing, relaxing tea with a fruity, floral aroma.

Growing and care:
Sow German chamomile in early spring while the soil is cool. Do not cover, as the seed needs light to germinate. Thin or transplant seedlings to stand 8 to 10 inches apart. Fertilize when plants are coming into flower and keep soil evenly moist. Pinch back young plants to encourage bushier growth. Harvest flowers on a dry, sunny day that is not overly warm. Dry flowers in the microwave oven or the refrigerator. Store in an airtight container.

Selected species and varieties:
M. recutita (German chamomile, sweet false chamomile, wild chamomile) produces airy clumps of fine-textured, ferny leaves and inch-wide daisylike flowers with yellow centers fringed with small, slightly drooping white petals.

GOOSEFOOT
Chenopodium

Light: full sun	
Plant type: annual	
Height: 2 to 5 feet	
Soil and Moisture: well-drained, fertile, moist	
Interest: foliage	
Care: easy	

◄ Chenopodium
ambrosioides

Goosefoot can be planted in two varieties—epazote and ambrosia—that add beauty to the garden and zest to the house. Epazote's leaves are prized for flavoring beans, corn, and fish in Central American cuisines. They should be used sparingly, however, as the plant's oils are a potent, sometimes toxic vermifuge and insecticide. Ambrosia's fragrant foliage and plumy flower spikes are valued in both fresh and dried arrangements; leaves and seeds can be used to spice up potpourri.

Growing and care:
Sow seed in spring or fall, and thin seedlings to stand 1 foot apart. Pinch plants to keep them bushy. Both epazote and ambrosia self-sow freely and can become invasive weeds. Use epazote leaves either fresh or dried for cooking. For dried arrangements, hang ambrosia in a shady, well-ventilated area or stand stems in vases without water.

Selected species and varieties:
C. ambrosioides (epazote) has spreading clumps of woody stems to 5 feet tall, lined with broad, toothed, oval leaves and with finely lacy leaves. *C. botrys* (ambrosia) has lobed ½- to 4-inch leaves that are deep green above and red below, and airy sprays of tiny yellow-green summer flowers without petals along arching 2-foot stems.

HOREHOUND
Marrubium

Light:	full sun
Plant type:	perennial
Hardiness:	Zones 4-9
Height:	1½ to 2 feet
Soil and Moisture:	well-drained, dry
Interest:	flowers, foliage
Care:	moderate

◀ Marrubium vulgare

There is no middle ground with horehound: Either you like the distinctive, aromatic flavor of the leaves, or you don't. Horehound's deeply puckered, woolly, very fragrant gray-green leaves add texture and soft color to the edges of herb gardens or the middle of borders. The small white flowers attract bees. Use the branching foliage as a filler in fresh or dried bouquets. Steep the fresh or dried leaves, which taste slightly of thyme and menthol, for a soothing tea, or add seeds to cool drinks for flavor. Horehound is a staple for cough remedies in herbal medicine.

Growing and care:
Sow horehound seed in spring in light, sandy soil, thinning seedlings to stand 1 foot apart. Horehound can also be grown from divisions in spring and from stem cuttings taken in summer. If allowed to go to seed, horehound self-sows freely. Prune before or after flowering to keep edgings or container plants compact. Dry the leaves in a single layer and store in airtight containers.

Selected species and varieties:
M. vulgare (common horehound, white horehound) has pairs of 2-inch heart-shaped leaves with deeply scalloped edges along square stems, and whorls of tiny white spring to summer flowers.

LAVENDER
Lavandula

Light:	full sun
Plant type:	perennial
Hardiness:	Zones 5-10
Height:	1 to 3 feet
Soil and Moisture:	well-drained, moist
Interest:	flowers, foliage, fragrance
Care:	moderate

◀ Lavandula dentata

Lavender's clean, invigorating fragrance and beautiful form have made it one of the best loved of all herbs. The fragrant purple flowers blossom in late spring to summer above pairs of metallic gray-green leaves that line erect, square stems. Plants form shrubby cushions of soft foliage that can be clipped into a low hedge. They can also add an informal accent to edgings, borders, and rock or herb gardens.

Growing and care:
Plant lavenders in spring, spacing them 1 to 1½ feet apart in well-worked soil. Cut back to 8 inches to encourage a bushy form. Lavenders can be propagated from cuttings made in late spring or early fall, or by divisions made in early spring.

Selected species and varieties:
L. angustifolia ssp. *angustifolia* [also listed as *L. officinalis*] (English lavender, true lavender) produces 3- to 4-inch whorls of ¼-inch flowers atop 2- to 3-foot stems with 1- to 2-inch aromatic leaves; 'Fragrance' has particularly pungent flowers; 'Hidcote' is a tightly compact dwarf with deep purple flowers and silvery foliage on 20-inch stems; 'Munstead Dwarf' is more spreading and only 1 foot tall. *L. dentata* (French lavender) has dense, woolly gray foliage at the base of 1- to 3-foot shrubby stems, topped by 1½-inch clusters of slightly fragrant lavender-blue flowers; Zones 8-9.

LEMON, ORANGE
Citrus

Light: full sun	
Plant type: shrub, tree	
Hardiness: Zones 9-10	
Height: 8 to 30 feet	
Soil and Moisture: well-drained, fertile, moist to dry	
Interest: flowers, foliage, fruit	
Care: moderate	

◀ Citrus aurantium

Few plants combine beauty and utility as well as citrus. The trees have a lovely, formal appearance with dense, glossy, evergreen foliage plentifully sprinkled with pure white, intensely fragrant flowers, and colorful, juicy fruits. Citruses can be massed into barrier hedges, grown as specimen trees, or planted in containers for patio and deck gardens. Use Seville oranges for piquant marmalade or dry their peels for potpourri. Add lemon slices to tea, or squeeze the juice for cool drinks. Grate lemon or orange peels for flavoring, or dry them for potpourri.

Growing and care:
Sow lemon seed in spring or propagate from softwood cuttings in summer. Choose sites protected from wind and frost. Plants thrive in well-drained soil that has been amended with sand as well as organic matter. Provide mulch around base of plant to conserve soil moisture. Grow potted citruses in containers 1½ feet in diameter or larger. Prune branches as needed to keep plant in shape, and prune roots whenever tree is repotted.

Selected species and varieties:
C. aurantium (bitter orange) reaches up to 30 feet tall and 30 feet wide with bright orange fruits. *C. limon* (lemon) 'Eureka' is a nearly thornless spreading tree that grows to 20 feet tall; 'Meyer' is a cold-resistant 8- to 12-foot-tall dwarf with sweet yellow fruits; 'Ponderosa' has large, grapefruit-size yellow fruits.

LEMON VERBENA
Aloysia

Light: full sun	
Plant type: tender perennial	
Hardiness: Zones 9-10	
Height: 2 to 8 feet	
Soil and Moisture: well-drained, moist to dry	
Interest: flowers, foliage, fragrance	
Care: easy	

◀ Aloysia triphylla

Lemon verbena has an uncommonly sweet fragrance. The aromatic citrus scent of the long, lance-shaped leaves, perfumes the garden from spring through fall. In summer slender spikes of lilac or white flowers add a gentle accent. Where lemon verbena can be grown outdoors, it is often pinched and pruned as an espalier or standard to give it special shape. The young, fresh leaves are used to add a fruity zip to cold drinks, salads, and fish or poultry dishes. Steep fresh or dried leaves for tea. Dried leaves retain their fragrance for several years in potpourri.

Growing and care:
Sow lemon verbena seed directly in the garden 3 feet apart in spring after danger of frost has passed. In Zones 9 and 10, cut stems to 6 to 12 inches in fall and provide protective winter mulch. Potted plants drop their leaves in winter and do best if moved outdoors during warmer months. Propagate lemon verbena from seed or from cuttings taken in summer.

Selected species and varieties:
A. triphylla (lemon verbena, cidron, limonetto) has whorls of lance-shaped, strongly lemon-scented leaves along open, sprawling branches growing 6 to 8 feet tall in warm climates and 2 to 4 feet tall as an indoor potted plant. Loose clusters of tiny white to lilac flowers appear on thin, upright stems in late summer.

MADDER
Rubia

Light: full sun

Plant type: perennial

Hardiness: Zones 6-10

Height: 10 inches to 3 feet

Soil and Moisture: well-drained, fertile, moist

Interest: roots

Care: moderate

◀ Rubia tinctorum

Madder's jointed, prickly stems ramble along the ground or climb weakly over other plants. Leathery leaves grow in whorls at each joint, and in summer and fall a light froth of tiny, pale flowers blooms among the foliage. Madder forms mats of pencil-thick, red-fleshed roots up to 3 feet long, which yield red dye valued by textile craftspeople or, with various mordants, shades of pink, lilac, brown, orange, or black.

Growing and care:

Sow seed while ripe in fall, divide plants anytime between spring and fall, or start new plants from cuttings. Plants root wherever joints touch the ground. Provide supports to control madder's spread and give plants structure. Dig roots of plants that are at least 3 years old in fall.

Selected species and varieties:

R. tinctorum has 2-inch oblong, pointed leaves in whorls of four to eight and $\frac{1}{10}$-inch pale yellow or white open flower bells in airy clusters on plants 3 years old or older, followed by $\frac{1}{8}$-inch reddish brown fruits, which turn black.

MARJORAM
Origanum

Light: full sun

Plant type: perennial

Hardiness: Zones 5-10

Height: 6 inches to 2 feet

Soil and Moisture: well-drained, fertile, moist to dry

Interest: flowers, foliage

Care: easy

◀ Origanum majorana

Mounds of small, fragrantly spicy oval leaves and branching clusters of tiny, appealing flowers are the hallmarks of this classic culinary herb. The plants can be used as border edgings or ground covers and are essential to the well-stocked herb or kitchen garden. The aromatic leaves can be snipped and added to flavor meat, vegetable, cheese, and fish dishes. The dried leaves and flowers are used in herbal teas or added to potpourri. Tender perennial species are grown as annuals in cooler climates or potted in containers and enjoyed both indoors and out.

Growing and care:

Sow marjoram seed or plant divisions in spring or fall, spacing or thinning plants to 1 to $1\frac{1}{2}$ feet apart. Give golden-leaved cultivars light afternoon shade to prevent leaf scorch. Pinch stems to promote bushiness and delay flowering. Cut perennial marjorams back to two-thirds of their height before winter to promote bushier growth the following season. *O. vulgare* can be invasive. Indoors, pot up divisions or sow seed in pots. Propagate marjorams from seed, from early-summer stem cuttings, or by division in spring or fall. For best flavor, harvest leaves just as flower buds begin to open. Mash leaves in oil to preserve them, layer with vinegar, or freeze. Dry leaves or flowers in the microwave or refrigerator, or in an airy, well-ventilated area.

MARJORAM
(continued)

Selected species and varieties:

O. dictamnus (dittany-of-Crete) has tiny, woolly white leaves and loose, nodding clusters of tiny pink summer to fall flowers on sprawling 1-foot-high plants that are ideal in rock gardens or hanging baskets; Zones 8-9. *O. majorana* (sweet marjoram) has spicy 1¼-inch leaves, an essential seasoning in Greek cuisine and more intensely flavored than those of *O. vulgare,* along 2-foot stems tipped with white to pink flowers; Zones 9-10. *O. x majoricum* (hardy marjoram, Italian oregano) is a hybrid similar to sweet marjoram but slightly hardier; Zones 7-10. *O. onites* (Greek oregano, pot marjoram) bears very mildly thyme-flavored medium-green leaves used in bouquets garnis or laid across charcoal to flavor grilled foods, and mauve to white flowers from summer to fall on 2-foot plants; Zones 8-10. *O. vulgare* (oregano, pot marjoram, wild marjoram, organy) has mildly pepper-thyme-flavored green leaves on sprawling 2-foot stems. It is not the same plant used in commercial dried oregano, but is used for flavoring and valued in landscaping for its branching clusters of white to red-purple summer flowers; Zones 5-9; 'Aureum' has golden leaves; Zones 6-9; 'Aureum Crispum' has round, wrinkled, ½-inch golden leaves on 1-foot plants; Zones 7-9; 'Nanum' is an 8-inch dwarf with purple flowers; Zones 6-9; 'White Anniversary' has green leaves edged in white on 6- to 10-inch plants ideal for edging or containers; Zones 8-9.

MARSH MALLOW
Althaea

◄ Althaea officinalis

Light: full sun	
Plant type: perennial	
Hardiness: Zones 3-9	
Height: 4 to 5 feet	
Soil and Moisture: well-drained, fertile, moist	
Interest: flowers, foliage	
Care: easy	

Marsh mallows are old-fashioned plants with tall, upright spikes of showy flowers that give any planting the ambiance of an English cottage garden. The plants create colorful border backdrops and temporary screens in marshy, wet garden sites or moist upland soils. The tender young leaves and the cup-shaped flowers growing from the leaf axils can be tossed in salads, as can the nutlike seeds contained in the plant's ring-shaped fruits, called cheeses. Steam leaves or fry roots after softening by boiling and serve as a side dish. Roots release a thick mucilage after long soaking, which was once an essential ingredient in the original marsh-mallow confection and is sometimes used in herbal medicine.

Growing and care:

Sow seed in spring or divide in spring or fall, setting plants 2 feet apart. Keep marsh mallow's woody taproot constantly moist. Pick leaves and flowers just as the blossoms reach their peak. Dig roots of mature 2-year-old plants in fall, remove rootlets, peel bark, and dry whole or in slices.

Selected species and varieties:

A. officinalis (marsh mallow, white mallow) has clumps of stiffly erect 4- to 5-foot-tall stems lined with velvety triangular leaves and showy pink or white summer flowers.

MEXICAN OREGANO
Lippia

Light: full sun	
Plant type: shrub	
Hardiness: Zones 9-10	
Height: 3 to 6 feet	
Soil and Moisture: well-drained, fertile, moist to dry	
Interest: flowers, foliage	
Care: moderate	

◀ Lippia graveolens

Mexican oregano has spicy, wrinkled leaves that add a bold accent to tomato and other vegetable dishes as well as seafood, cheese dishes, and chili. Add them to salads and dressings, or steep them with other herbs for teas. In frost-free areas, Mexican oregano can be grown as a specimen plant or pruned into a hedge. Elsewhere, grow it as a container plant to move indoors for the winter.

Growing and care:
Sow Mexican oregano seed anytime, or start new plants from softwood cuttings taken anytime. Keep soil moist until seedlings are a few inches high, then allow to grow in moderately dry conditions. Remove deadwood in spring and prune severely to keep the vigorous shrubs from becoming gangly. Pinch to promote branching and bushiness. Container-grown plants should be pruned annually and root pruned when repotted. Pick leaves anytime for fresh use, or dry and store in an airtight container.

Selected species and varieties:
L. graveolens [also called *Poliomintha longiflora*] produces pointed, oval, 1- to 2½-inch downy leaves and tiny yellow to white winter to spring flowers growing where leaves meet stems on vigorous, spreading branches.

MULLEIN
Verbascum

Light: full sun	
Plant type: biennial	
Hardiness: Zones 3-10	
Height: 4 to 6 feet	
Soil and Moisture: well-drained, sandy, dry	
Interest: flowers, foliage	
Care: easy	

◀ Verbascum thapsus

Mullein is an easy-to-grow perennial with two very different personalities. From afar the plant is bold and imposing with strong, starkly upright stems and large leaves. Viewed more closely mullein reveals its velvety soft foliage and delicate, pastel yellow blossoms. Mullein is a biennial that forms a broad rosette of gray-green velvety leaves its first year, followed by dramatic, tall flower spikes the second. Woolly leaves clasp each thick stalk, crowded at its tip with large green buds that open into small flowers with prominent stamens. Yellow spiders or moths commonly seek out the blossoms as camouflaged refuges. Great mullein is one of the few gray-leaved plants that tolerate heat and humidity, making it a back-of-the-border specimen. Dry the honey-scented flowers for potpourri.

Growing and care:
Sow great mullein seed in fall or spring and space seedlings 2 to 2½ feet apart. Plants die after flowering but reseed themselves freely if flowers remain on plants. Once established the plants are very drought and heat tolerant and need no fertilizing.

Selected species and varieties:
V. thapsus (great mullein, common mullein, flannel plant, Aaron's rod) has thick, woolly leaves 6 to 18 inches long and spreading 3 feet wide, and ¾- to 1-inch-wide yellow flowers with orange stamens.

MUSTARD
Brassica

Light: full sun

Plant type: annual

Height: 3 to 4 feet

Soil and Moisture: well-drained, moist to dry

Interest: flowers, foliage, seeds

Care: easy

◄ Brassica juncea

Mustard is a prolific herb that produces peppery foliage that adds zest to salads. The medium green oval leaves can also be boiled or sautéed as a side dish. The four-petaled yellow summer flowers are followed by small pods filled with tiny round seeds that give pickles and curries a zippy flavor. They can also be ground and mixed with vinegar for a tasty condiment. Mustard can be grown in pots indoors for a continuous supply of young salad greens in winter.

Growing and care:
Sow mustard seed ¼ inch deep in spring in rows 1½ feet apart and thin plants to stand 8 inches apart. Use the thinnings in salads; young leaves are ready for salad picking in 8 to 10 days. Mustard self-sows freely for future crops. Harvest pods as they begin to brown, and finish drying them in paper bags to collect the ripening seed. Brown mustard develops its hottest flavor when ground seeds are mixed with cold, water-based liquids.

Selected species and varieties:
B. juncea (brown mustard, Chinese mustard, Indian mustard, mustard cabbage, mustard greens) has leaves 6 to 12 inches long with open, branching clusters of pale yellow flowers followed by 1½-inch beaked pods filled with dark reddish brown seeds.

ORACH
Atriplex

Light: full sun

Plant type: annual

Height: 2 to 6 feet

Soil and Moisture: well-drained, moist to dry

Interest: foliage

Care: moderate

◄ Atriplex hortensis 'Rubra'

Garden orach is a large, upright plant with huge, imposing, arrowhead-shaped leaves that have a unique, rough beauty. The plants are best used planted close together to make a seasonal screen or background. The greenish burgundy leaves add color and a slightly salty tang to salads. Leaves and young shoots can be boiled like spinach. Use the colorful foliage as a filler in fresh arrangements.

Growing and care:
Sow orach seed indoors 6 weeks before planting out or direct-sow in early spring. Thin plants to stand 8 to 12 inches apart. If started indoors transplant seedlings when small. Do not disturb plants once established. Orach will tolerate both saline soils and dry conditions but produces the most succulent leaves when kept constantly moist. Successive sowings every 2 weeks ensure a continuous supply of young salad leaves. Pinch out flower heads to encourage greater leaf production. Orach self-sows freely and can become invasive. Dip stem ends in boiling water to seal them before using in arrangements.

Selected species and varieties:
A. hortensis (orach, mountain spinach) has smooth, deep green leaves with a port wine tinge and branching clusters of tiny yellow-green flowers tinged red in summer on stems to 6 feet; 'Rubra' (purple orach) has deep burgundy red leaves and stems.

PEPPER
Capsicum

Light: full sun

Plant type: annual

Height: 1 to 3 feet

Soil and Moisture: well-drained, fertile, moist

Interest: fruit

Care: moderate

◀ Capsicum frutescens 'Tabasco'

Peppers are much more versatile than many people imagine and are used in herbal remedies and as ornamental plants, as well as being a tasty vegetable. Some varieties produce hundreds of small, colorful fruits from summer through fall, held above low clumps of narrow, dark green oval leaves. Use them as border edgings, massed in beds, or in patio containers as well as in kitchen and herb gardens. Chop the fiery fruits into salsas, chutneys, marinades, vinegars, salad dressings, and baked goods. The peppers become spicier when dried.

Growing and care:

Start peppers indoors 8 to 10 weeks before the last frost and transplant to the garden when soil temperature reaches 65°F or more. Set plants 1½ feet apart and mulch from midsummer on to prevent drying out. Peppers thrive in hot conditions. Harvest by cutting stems above the fruit. To dry, string on a line or pull entire plants and hang in a cool, dark place.

Selected species and varieties:

C. annuum var. *annuum* 'Jalapeno' (chili pepper) bears narrow, conical 2½- to 4-inch-long fruits ripening from green to red. *C. chinense* 'Habañero' (papaya chili) bears extremely hot, bell-shaped 1- to 2-inch fruits ripening from green to yellow-orange. *C. frutescens* 'Tabasco' (tabasco pepper) has small, upright green fruits ripening to red with a zesty, slightly smoky flavor.

POT MARIGOLD
Calendula

Light: full sun

Plant type: annual

Height: 1 to 2 feet

Soil and Moisture: well-drained, moist to dry

Interest: flowers

Care: easy

◀ Calendula officinalis

Pot marigold got its common name from its marigold-like flowers that were routinely tossed into cooking pots to add saffron color to recipes. The long-lasting blooms are flattened, with broad ray petals in shades of orange, yellow, or cream from spring to frost. Their bright colors and long season of bloom make them valuable for use in borders, mixed beds, herb gardens, and containers. Use the fresh, slightly salty-tasting flower petals in salads, soups, sandwiches, and pâtés. Dried and ground, the petals add saffron color to puddings and rice dishes.

Growing and care:

Start seed indoors 6 to 8 weeks prior to the last frost. Transplant into loosened soil amended with some organic matter once soil has warmed. In areas with mild winters it can be sown directly outdoors in fall or early spring. Space plants 1 to 1½ feet apart. Deadhead to increase flowering. Calendulas thrive in cool conditions and tolerate poor soils if they have adequate water.

Selected species and varieties:

C. officinalis has a neat, mounding habit and grows 1 to 2 feet tall with a similar spread. Leaves are 2 to 6 inches long, blue-green, and aromatic. The solitary 2½- to 4½-inch flower heads close at night; 'Bon-Bon' grows 1 feet tall with a compact, early-blooming habit and a mixture of flower colors.

ROCKET
Eruca

Light: full sun	
Plant type: annual	
Height: 2 to 3 feet	
Soil and Moisture: well-drained, fertile, moist	
Interest: flowers, foliage	
Care: easy	

◀ Eruca vesicaria ssp. sativa

Rocket's tangy young leaves add biting zest to mixed green salads. This easy-to-grow plant is an essential ingredient in mesclun blends of salad greens, and can also be chopped and added to sauces or steamed as a spicy side dish. The whitish pink, violet-veined flowers have a slightly milder flavor than the leaves and are added to late-summer salads.

Growing and care:
Sow rocket directly in the garden in early spring while the soil is still cool. Make successive sowings every 2 weeks through early summer. Thin plants to stand 6 to 8 inches apart. Leaves are ready to pick 6 to 8 weeks after sowing. Plants develop their best flavor when they grow quickly in cool, evenly moist soil. Older leaves or those grown in dry ground during hot weather become strong and bitter.

Selected species and varieties:
E. vesicaria ssp. *sativa* (arugula, rocket, Italian cress, roquette) bears rounded or arrowhead-shaped mustard-like leaves, coarsely toothed along their midrib, with delicate, purple-veined, creamy late-summer to fall flowers followed by slender, upright seedpods.

ROMAN CHAMOMILE
Chamaemelum

Light: full sun	
Plant type: perennial	
Hardiness: Zones 4-8	
Height: 1 to 6 inches	
Soil and Moisture: well-drained, moist to dry	
Interest: flowers, foliage	
Care: easy	

◀ Chamaemelum nobile

Roman chamomile is one of the most popular herbs grown, with feathery, intensely aromatic leaves that release a soothing, fruity scent when crushed. The plants spread quickly into dense mats ideal as informal ground covers or as fillers among walkway stones and rock gardens. Dry the leaves for potpourri. The flowers that bloom from late spring through early fall can be dried and steeped for a relaxing tea.

Growing and care:
Sow Roman chamomile seed in spring or fall or plant divisions in spring. The species self-seeds freely, but cultivars only come true from division. To make a chamomile lawn, space plants 4 to 6 inches apart and allow to spread before mowing. Harvest flowers as petals begin to fade, and dry on screens in a shady, well-ventilated area. Store in a sealed container away from bright light.

Selected species and varieties:
C. nobile [formerly classified as *Anthemis nobilis*] (Roman chamomile, garden chamomile) produces very attractive, lacy, bright green leaves and dainty 1-inch white daisylike flowers with golden yellow centers; 'Flore Pleno' has double-petaled cream flowers on plants 6 inches high spreading 1½ feet wide; 'Treneague' is a nonflowering cultivar that grows 1 to 2 inches tall and 1½ feet wide.

ROSE
Rosa

Light: full sun

Plant type: shrub

Hardiness: Zones 3-10

Height: 10 feet

Soil and Moisture: well-drained, moist

Interest: flowers, fruit

Care: easy to moderate

◀ Rosa canina

Besides using roses in arrangements, try adding the petals to salads or crystallizing them as a garnish. Dry the buds and petals for potpourri. Use the fruit, or hips, for tea or jam. Herbs for the teapot make soothing beverages, and the steeped hips of *Rosa canina* provide a healthy dose of vitamin C.

Growing and care:
Sow fresh rose seed, root hardwood cuttings, or plant commercial rootstock in fall. Mulch to conserve moisture. Prune dead or damaged wood in late winter, avoiding the previous season's growth, on which this season's flowers grow.

Selected species and varieties:
R. canina (dog rose, brier rose) has 10-foot canes with white or pink 2-inch blooms and ¾-inch hips; Zones 4-9. *R. damascena* (damask rose) bears very fragrant 3-inch blooms on 6-foot canes; 'Autumn Damask' is a double pink; 'Madame Hardy', a double white; Zones 5-9. *R. gallica* (French rose) has 2- to 3-inch blooms on 3- to 4-foot plants; 'Officinalis' (apothecary rose) is a semidouble deep pink; 'Versicolor' (rosa mundi) is a semidouble pink- or red-striped white, red, or pink; Zones 4-10. *R. rugosa* (Japanese rose) produces crimson 3½-inch blossoms and 1-inch hips; 'Alba' is white; 'Rubra', burgundy red; Zones 3-8.

RUE
Ruta

Light: full sun

Plant type: perennial

Hardiness: Zones 5-9

Height: 1 to 3 feet

Soil and Moisture: well-drained, moist

Interest: flowers, foliage

Care: easy

◀ Ruta graveolens

Common rue forms delicate clumps of lacy, aromatic blue-green foliage that adds a soft, surreal quality to beds and borders. For several weeks in summer, frilly, spidery flowers bloom from pliant stems held high above the foliage. The inflated lobed seed capsules that appear in late summer and fall can be gathered and dried for use in dried arrangements. Once used in herbal medicine, rue is now considered poisonous. Sensitive individuals develop a blistering dermatitis after touching the leaves. Wear gloves when handling the plants.

Growing and care:
Start rue seed indoors 8 to 10 weeks before the last frost; sow outdoors once soil has warmed. Divide mature plants in spring or fall. *R. graveolens* 'Variegata' comes true from seed, but 'Jackman's Blue' must be grown from cuttings or divisions. Wearing gloves, prune back hard to force new growth and to keep plants compact.

Selected species and varieties:
R. graveolens (common rue) has upright stems lined with oblong leaflets and ½-inch yellow flowers in loose, open clusters; 'Jackman's Blue' is a compact, nonflowering cultivar with waxy blue foliage; 'Variegata' has leaves splashed with cream.

SAFFLOWER
Carthamus

Light:	full sun
Plant type:	annual
Height:	1 to 3 feet
Soil and Moisture:	well-drained, moist to dry
Interest:	flowers
Care:	moderate

◀ Carthamus tinctorius

Safflower bears attractive yellow flowers in summer that add color to annual gardens and also are a wonderfully economical substitute for saffron. The plants produce stiff, upright stems lined with spiny leaves and thistlelike summer flowers surrounded by a cuff of spiny bracts. The blossoms make excellent cut flowers. When in full bloom the blossoms are gathered and dried, the petals ground and used to season sauces, soups, and other dishes calling for saffron.

Growing and care:
Sow safflower seed in spring and thin seedlings to stand 6 inches apart. Safflower does not transplant well. Young plants should be protected from rabbits, which find them a tasty nibble. Safflowers grow best under dry conditions and are subject to disease in rainy or humid areas. Cut and dry the mature flowers, storing in airtight containers until ready to use.

Selected species and varieties:
C. tinctorius (safflower, saffron thistle, false saffron, bastard saffron) bears yellow to yellow-orange tousled flowers nestled in a collar of thistlelike bracts up to 1 inch across followed by white seeds.

SAGE
Salvia

Light:	full sun
Plant type:	annual, biennial, perennial, shrub
Hardiness:	Zones 4-10
Height:	1 to 8 feet
Soil and Moisture:	well-drained, moist to dry
Interest:	flowers, foliage
Care:	easy

◀ Salvia officinalis 'Purpurea'

Sages are some of the most important garden herbs, with distinct gray-green leaves and pronounced veins. Sage brings both interesting texture and an aroma reminiscent of pine or rosemary to the border or kitchen garden. The leaves vary in different species from rounded, lance-shaped forms to oval types with pointed tips. In addition to the fragrant, spicy foliage, sage produces long flower spikes covered with white, lilac, pink, red, or purple blossoms. Sages are useful as edgings or when mixed throughout the border. Many are indispensable ingredients of herb and kitchen gardens and can be grown as container plants to perk up a winter window sill. Those suitable only for mild winter climates are often grown as half-hardy annuals in cooler zones.

Growing and care:
Sow sage seed in spring or set divisions out in spring or fall, spacing them 1½ to 2 feet apart. Avoid hot, humid locations or those with too rich soils. Provide a protective winter mulch in cooler climates. Prune sage heavily in spring to remove winter-killed stems and encourage bushy growth. Prune lightly after plants have finished flowering. Perennial sages are short lived as perennials go and should be replaced every 4 or 5 years. Propagate by division or by rooting 4-inch stem cuttings taken in summer to plant in fall. Seedlings or rooted cuttings take 2 years to reach maturity for picking. Fresh leaves can be

(continued)

harvested anytime but are most flavorful when grown in moist soil in full sun and gathered just as the flower blossoms begin to open. Dry leaves slowly to prevent a musty odor, laying them in a single layer on a screen or cloth; refrigerate or freeze the dried leaves, as the aromatic oils dissipate easily. To make an infusion for an aftershave or a hair rinse, steep leaves in boiling water, cool to room temperature, strain, and bottle. Refrigerate unused portion.

Selected species and varieties:
S. clevelandii (blue sage) is an evergreen shrub with wrinkled 1-inch leaves on downy stems 2 to 3 feet tall tipped with violet or white spring to summer flowers; Zones 9-10. *S. coccinea* (Texas sage, scarlet sage) is a perennial or subshrub grown as an annual, with 2-inch heart-shaped leaves having wavy, indented edges on 3-foot stems tipped with branched spikes of red or white summer flowers that are valued in landscaping. *S. dorisiana* (fruit-scented sage) is an evergreen perennial with sweetly scented, velvety oval leaves 4 inches wide and up to 7 inches long on stems to 4 feet tall tipped with 6-inch spikes of 2-inch magenta to pink flowers in fall and winter; Zones 10-11. *S. elegans* (pineapple sage) is an evergreen perennial with fruit-scented, red-edged 3½-inch oval leaves lining 3- to 4-foot red stems tipped with red to pink 8-inch late-summer flower spikes used in cold drinks and fruit salads; Zones 8-10. *S. fruticosa* (Greek sage) is an evergreen shrub to 4½ feet with lavender-scented leaves and loose, 8-inch clusters of mauve to pink spring to summer flowers; Zones 8-9. *S. lavandulifolia* (Spanish sage, narrow-leaved sage) is a spreading evergreen shrub 12 to 20 inches tall with 1-inch white woolly leaves having a piny lavender aroma and red-violet summer flowers; Zones 7-9. *S. officinalis* (common sage, garden sage) is an evergreen shrub in mild climates, with 2-inch velvety leaves on branching 2- to 3-foot stems tipped with edible violet to purple flower spikes in summer; 'Purpurea' has aromatic purple leaves.

SALAD BURNET
Poterium

◀ Poterium sanguisorba

Light: full sun	
Plant type: perennial	
Hardiness: Zones 3-9	
Height: 1 to 3 feet	
Soil and Moisture: well-drained, moist	
Interest: flowers, foliage	
Care: easy	

Salad burnet is a tasty addition to perennial borders or kitchen and herb gardens, with mounds of delicate blue-green foliage and tall stalks of thimble-shaped clusters of tiny summer flowers. The young leaves have a distinct, slightly nutty, cucumber flavor and add an unusual accent to salads, coleslaw, soups, and vegetables and brighten up cool summer drinks. Preserve the leaves in vinegar as a base for flavorful salad dressings.

Growing and care:
Sow burnet seed in spring or fall or divide young plants before taproots become well established. Space plants 8 to 12 inches apart. Established plants self-sow freely. Burnet is evergreen in milder climates; elsewhere, shear old foliage to the ground in late fall or early spring. Leaves are most flavorful when picked in early spring or late fall and when plants are grown in soil amended with well-rotted manure or compost.

Selected species and varieties:
P. sanguisorba [also classified as *Sanguisorba minor*] (burnet, garden burnet, salad burnet) produces ¾-inch oval leaflets with deeply scalloped edges paired along the flexible leafstalks that grow to 1 foot, and dense ½-inch heads of minute greenish flowers tinged pink on stems to 3 feet.

SAVORY
Satureja

Light: full sun	
Plant type: annual, perennial	
Hardiness: Zones 4-10	
Height: 2 to 18 inches	
Soil and Moisture: well-drained, dry	
Interest: flowers, foliage, fragrance	
Care: easy	

◀ *Satureja montana*

While most familiar in the herb garden, savories have distinctive gray-green foliage and masses of delicate, subtle-hued flowers that make them deserving of use in rock gardens and borders or as edging. The leaves are highly aromatic and frequently used as a culinary herb for their peppery flavor. Members of the mint family, they have square stems that bear clusters of two-lipped flowers that are highly attractive to bees.

Growing and care:
Savories can be grown in ordinary garden conditions as long as the soil is not soggy. Propagate by seed sown indoors in early spring. Do not cover seed, as light is needed for germination.

Selected species and varieties:
S. hortensis (summer savory) is a 1- to 1½-foot shrubby, branching annual with narrow, 1-inch-long, finely hairy leaves and ¼- to ⅓-inch lavender, pink, or white two-lipped flowers in small clusters at the base of the top pairs of leaves from midsummer to frost. *S. montana* (winter savory) is a 9- to 15-inch woody species with narrow, ¾-inch shiny evergreen leaves and tiny lavender or white flowers dotted with purple spots in spikes at the end of branch tips from summer to early fall; 'Prostrate White' has white flowers atop a 3- to 6-inch-tall creeping mat of glossy leaves.

SESAME
Sesamum

Light: full sun	
Plant type: tender perennial	
Hardiness: Zone 10	
Height: 1½ to 3 feet	
Soil and Moisture: well-drained, moist	
Interest: flowers, seeds	
Care: moderate	

◀ *Sesamum indicum*

Sesame is an exotic herb originally from Asia and Africa with delicate, lightly colored bell-shaped flowers and distinctive, very tasty seeds. The plants are naturalized along the Gulf Coast, where each summer and fall the upright, pointed, oval capsules yield small tan seeds prized for their oil and nutty flavor. The seeds are used whole in candies and baked goods, such as hamburger buns and bagels, and to add a unique taste to vegetable dishes and salads. They can also be ground into dips, spreads, and sauces or pressed for cooking oil.

Growing and care:
Sow sesame seed directly in the garden ¼ inch deep once nighttime low temperatures climb to 60°F, or start indoors 6 to 8 weeks before last frost. Space plants 6 to 8 inches apart. Plants need at least 120 days of hot weather to set seed. Harvest just as oldest pods begin to dry, cutting stems off at ground level. Hang plants upside down within a paper bag until pods dry and release the seeds. Each plant produces approximately 1 tablespoon of dried seeds.

Selected species and varieties:
S. indicum (sesame, benne) has square, sticky stems lined with oval, pointed 3- to 5-inch leaves and 1-inch white flowers lightly tinged with pink, yellow, or red accents.

THYME
Thymus

Light: full sun

Plant type: perennial

Hardiness: Zones 4-9

Height: 1 to 1½ feet

Soil and Moisture: well-drained, moist to dry

Interest: flowers, foliage

Care: easy

◀ Thymus x citriodorus 'Aureus'

Thyme is another classic herb with very slender stems, densely packed small green leaves bursting with a warm, spicy aroma, and countless tiny bundles of gaily colored summer blossoms. The many varieties range from ground-hugging types to mounding perennials to billowy low-growing shrubs. They are excellent for adding fine texture and soft color to borders, rock gardens, and garden paths. Shrubby species can be grown as specimens or low hedges while creeping types quickly fill niches among rocks or between paving stones. Thyme is also easy to grow in containers on window sills. The plentiful white, pink, or rose red blossoms are attractive to bees. Fresh or dried, the tiny ¼- to ½-inch, narrow, green to gray-green, sometimes variegated leaves are used as a basic ingredient in bouquets garnis and fines herbes and are used to make tea. Both leaves and flowers are used in potpourris and toiletries. Herbalists use thyme as an insect repellent, medicinal plant, household disinfectant, and preservative.

Growing and care:
Start seed indoors by sowing thickly in pots 6 to 8 weeks before the last frost, then set 4- to 6-inch seedlings out in clumps. Space transplants 1 to 2 feet apart in well-worked, sandy soil with some organic matter and bone meal blended in. Start thyme for a window sill garden from seed, or pot divisions in late summer to bring in-doors in late fall. To shape plants and encourage branching, prune hard in early spring before flowering or lightly after blooms appear. Remove shoots with solid green leaves from variegated cultivars. Leaves are most fragrant when picked from plants grown in full sun and in bloom. Add leaves to meat dishes, stuffings, pâtés, salad dressings, vegetable dishes, herb butter, vinegars, and mayonnaise. To dry, hang bundles of branches upside down in a shady, warm, well-ventilated location for a few days, then crumble or strip fresh leaves from stems and dry on screens; store in airtight containers for use in cooking or sachets. An infusion of thyme made by boiling fresh leaves and flowers in water, then straining the liquid, creates a soothing facial rinse; add rosemary to the infusion for a hair rinse. To propagate thyme, root softwood cuttings taken in late spring or early summer or divide mature plants in early spring or late summer.

Selected species and varieties:
T. caespititius [formerly classified as *T. azoricus*] (tufted thyme, Azores thyme) is a subshrub forming 6-inch-high mats of twiggy branches lined with sticky, resinous leaves and tipped with white, pink, or lilac flowers; 'Aureus' has deep yellow-green leaves and pink flowers; Zones 8-9. *T. capitatus* (conehead thyme) produces upright, bushy plants 10 inches tall and as wide with gray leaves and pink flowers crowded into cone-shaped tufts at the tips of branches; Zone 9. *T. cilicicus* (Cilician thyme) has deep green lemon-scented leaves and clusters of pale mauve to lilac blossoms on 6-inch stems; Zones 6-8. *T.* x *citriodorus* (lemon thyme) forms a shrubby carpet up to 2 feet wide of foot-tall branches with tiny lemon-scented leaves; 'Aureus' (golden lemon thyme) has gold-edged leaves; 'Silver Queen' has leaves marbled cream and silvery gray; Zones 5-9. *T. herba-barona* (caraway thyme) is a fast-growing subshrub forming mats 4 inches tall and 2 feet across with leaf flavors reminiscent of caraway, nutmeg, or lemon, and loose clusters of rose flowers; Zones 4-8.

TOBACCO
Nicotiana

Light:	full sun
Plant type:	annual
Height:	2 to 4 feet
Soil and Moisture:	well-drained, fertile, moist
Interest:	flowers, foliage
Care:	easy

◀ Nicotiana rustica

Indian tobacco's bold leaves, sturdy stems, and hundreds of summer to fall flowers create a dramatic background for beds and borders. Plants contain nicotine, a natural insecticide that is poisonous if taken internally or absorbed through the skin. Dry and powder the leaves for an insecticidal dust effective against both root- and leaf-chewing insects.

Growing and care:
Sow Indian tobacco seed outdoors in warm soil or start indoors 6 to 8 weeks before the last frost. Do not cover, as seeds need light to germinate. Space seedlings 1½ to 2 feet apart. Harvest wearing protective rubber gloves, picking leaves individually as they begin to yellow. Hang to dry, then crumble, remove stems, and store in airtight containers. Wearing protective clothing and equipment, grind the dried leaves to a powder and dust on plants at least 1 month before harvest.

Selected species and varieties:
N. rustica (wild tobacco) has large, pointed oval leaves 4 to 8 inches long and half as wide, covered with sticky hairs and hundreds of ½-inch yellow-green flowers atop sturdy 2- to 4-foot-tall stems.

WOAD
Isatis

Light:	full sun
Plant type:	perennial
Hardiness:	Zones 4-8
Height:	2 to 4 feet
Soil and Moisture:	well-drained, fertile, moist
Interest:	flowers, foliage
Care:	easy

◀ Isatis tinctoria

Before the discovery of indigo, weavers used fermented leaves of dyer's woad to produce blue hues. Now dyer's woad is enjoyed as a specimen or border backdrop, where the clouds of tiny yellow spring flowers produced on 2-year-old plants contrast attractively to the blue-green foliage. Dangling fiddle-shaped black seeds decorate the plants in fall. Dry the flowers to add color to potpourri.

Growing and care:
Sow dyer's woad in late summer for flowering the following year. Space plants 6 inches apart in deep, loosened soil, well amended with compost or rotted manure, to accommodate the plant's long taproots. Pick flowers just after opening and dry on screens in a well-ventilated area. Woad self-sows freely and looks charming naturalized in a wildflower meadow.

Selected species and varieties:
I. tinctoria (dyer's woad, asp-of-Jerusalem) produces rosettes of oval leaves the first year, followed the second year by tall flowering stalks tipped with large, airy clusters of ¼-inch four-petaled yellow flowers on sprawling to erect stems lined with narrow leaves.

BUGLEWEED
Ajuga

Light: full sun	
Plant type: perennial	
Hardiness: Zones 3-9	
Height: 3 to 9 inches	
Soil and Moisture: well-drained, moist to dry, fertile, acidic	
Interest: foliage, flowers	
Care: easy	

◀ Ajuga reptans 'Burgundy Glow'

Bugleweed is a vigorous and reliable ground cover in sun or bright shade and is very useful under trees where grass is difficult to grow. Its colorful foliage is effective year round, and is available in shades of green, purple, and bronze, as well as variegated hues. It makes an excellent choice for the foreground of a shrub border or rock garden. The tiny, two-lipped blue, white, pink or purple flowers appear along short, erect spikes from spring to early summer. The leaves produce their best color in full sun.

Growing and care:
Carpet bugle thrives in poor soil. Space plants 6 inches apart for best growth. This species spreads rapidly by stolons and chokes out weeds; however, it may become invasive in the garden. If planted near a lawn, carpet bugle will encroach upon the grass, but it does not withstand heavy foot traffic. Propagate by division. Plants should be divided in spring or fall when they become crowded, to promote air circulation and prevent crown rot.

Selected species and varieties:
A. reptans (carpet bugle) grows to 9 inches tall with oblong leaves that form a basal clump, and violet-blue flowers appearing on an erect spike in spring; 'Alba' bears white blooms; 'Bronze Beauty' produces waxy bronze-purple leaves and blue flowers; 'Burgundy Glow' has white, green, and dark pink variegated leaves and blue flowers.

CALABASH GOURD
Lagenaria

Light: full sun	
Plant type: annual	
Height: 10 to 30 feet	
Soil and Moisture: well-drained, fertile, moist	
Interest: fruit, flowers, fragrance	
Care: easy	

◀ Lagenaria siceraria

The large, fragrant white flowers and strange-shaped fruit of calabash gourd make these very vigorous vines the conversation piece of any garden. The strong stems can grow up to 30 feet in one season, making them ideal as a temporary ground cover or screen. In the fall the fruit can be harvested and, depending upon its shape, be used for containers, bird feeders, or autumn decorations.

Growing and care:
Start seed indoors in peat pots 6 to 8 weeks prior to the last frost. In areas with long growing seasons, seed can be planted directly in the garden after the last frost and when soil is warm. Space plants 2 feet apart, and provide a sturdy support for climbing. Harvest fruits before the first hard frost, and dry in an airy room.

Selected species and varieties:
L. siceraria produces a hairy stem with branched tendrils and broad 6- to 12-inch leaves. The 5-inch white flowers open in the evening or on overcast days, and are sweetly fragrant. The fruit ranges from 3 to 36 inches in length and may be rounded or flattened, coiled, bottle shaped, or dumbbell shaped.

CROSS VINE
Bignonia

Light:	full sun
Plant type:	woody vine
Hardiness:	Zones 6-9
Height:	30 to 50 feet
Soil and Moisture:	well-drained, moist
Interest:	flowers, foliage
Care:	easy

◀ Bignonia capreolata

A vigorous, rapidly growing plant, cross vine is graced in spring with clusters of large, trumpet-shaped flowers that are dark orange on the outside and yellow-orange on the inside. In summer slender, 4- to 6-inch flattened fruit appears that turns from green to brown. Cross vine's attractive, 2- to 6-inch dark green compound leaves are borne in pairs along with clasping tendrils by which the vine attaches itself to supports. Where winters are mild, the foliage turns reddish purple in fall. Cross vine is a wonderful addition to naturalistic plantings, where their blossoms attract hummingbirds in summer.

Growing and care:
Cross vine is easy to grow and thrives in all soils excluding those that are excessively wet or dry. In Zone 6 cross vine dies back to the ground each winter, but sends up vigorous new shoots in spring. In warmer regions prune to help restrain growth and keep tidy. Propagate by seed or cuttings.

Selected species and varieties:
B. capreolata (cross vine, trumpet flower) grows 30 to 50 feet with lustrous, thinly spaced, dark green, semievergreen to evergreen leaves and orange-red, mocha-scented flowers in clusters of two to five; 'Atrosanguinea' has narrower, dark purple-red flowers tinted with brown or sometimes orange-red, and long, narrow leaves.

CUP-AND-SAUCER VINE
Cobaea

Light:	full sun
Plant type:	tender perennial grown as annual
Hardiness:	Zones 9-10
Height:	10 to 25 feet
Soil and Moisture:	well-drained, moist to dry
Interest:	flowers
Care:	easy

◀ Cobaea scandens

This extremely vigorous, sturdy vine from Mexico has showy, velvet blue, cup-shaped flowers with masses of tendril-like stamens surrounded by an attractive green saucer-shaped calyx. This tender perennial is usually grown as an annual and can reach 25 feet in a single season. In Zones 9 and 10, where the plants are perennial, they can reach up to 40 feet. Cup-and-saucer vine is very useful for providing quick cover for a fence, a wall, an arbor, or a trellis.

Growing and care:
Start seed indoors in individual peat pots 6 weeks prior to the last frost, first nicking the hard seed coat, and barely covering the seed. Transplant outdoors in late spring to a warm, sunny site in soil well amended with organic matter. Space plants 1 to 2 feet apart, and provide abundant water. Pinch tips from young plants to encourage branching. Provide a trellis or staking for support as the plant grows.

Selected species and varieties:
C. scandens climbs easily on any support, using tendrils to cling to its anchor itself. Each leaf is divided into two or three pairs of oblong leaflets. Flowers are green at first, turning deep violet or rose-purple as they mature; 'Alba' bears flowers in a pale shade of greenish white.

GOURD
Cucurbita

Light: full sun

Plant type: annual, tender perennial

Hardiness: Zones 9-10

Height: 5 to 12 feet

Soil and Moisture: well-drained, sandy, moist to dry

Interest: flowers

Care: easy

◀ Cucurbita pepo var. ovifera

Plant these tropical squash and pumpkin vines on a trellis, a fence, or an arbor, and watch how quickly they will cover it with their lush foliage. In late summer and fall the brightly colored ornamental fruit can be harvested and used for fall holiday decorations.

Growing and care:

Sow seed directly in the garden after the last frost, allowing 9 to 12 inches between plants. Or start indoors in individual peat pots 4 weeks before the last frost. Plants thrive in warm weather and grow best when given some support for climbing. Water regularly from sowing until fruit set.

Selected species and varieties:

C. ficifolia (Malabar gourd, fig-leaf gourd) is a perennial in Zones 9 to 10 and is grown as an annual elsewhere. It climbs to 12 feet, producing smooth, rounded, white-striped green fruit up to 1 foot long. *C. maxima* (Hubbard squash) is an 8-foot annual vine bearing edible rounded or oblong furrowed fruit; the variety 'Turbaniformis' (Turk's-cap squash, Turban squash) produces 6- to 7-inch orange, white, and green fruit that looks as if it is made of two separate parts. Annual *C. pepo* var. *ovifera* (pumpkin gourd) grows to 5 to 12 feet and produces small fruit in a wide range of shapes and colors.

HEATH
Erica

Light: full sun

Plant type: shrub

Hardiness: Zones 6-9

Height: to 16 inches

Soil and Moisture: well-drained, sandy, rich, acidic, moist

Interest: flowers, foliage

Care: moderate

◀ Erica carnea 'Winter Beauty'

Spring heath produces a mass of colorful flower spikes from winter to spring above an airy, spreading evergreen carpet of bright green needlelike foliage. The plants create a festive, holiday mood and are excellent in rock gardens and flower beds, or when planted in masses to cover a sunny slope or as an edging along a path.

Growing and care:

Plant in very well-drained sandy loam amended with peat moss or acidic leaf mold. Heath does not grow well in heavy clay. Mulch to conserve moisture for the shallow roots, and water during dry periods. Spring heath needs acid soil. Prune after flowering to encourage compactness. Heaths are slightly more difficult to grow than heathers, and thrive in areas with long, cool summers, mild winters, and plentiful, frequent rains.

Selected species and varieties:

E. carnea (spring heath, snow heather) has slender, prostrate branches up to 16 inches high and spreading 2 to 6 feet wide bearing bell-shaped flowers of white, pink, rose, red, or purple in nodding clusters; 'Springwood Pink' grows 6 to 8 inches high with clear pink flowers; 'Springwood White', 6 to 8 inches high with pure white flowers and bronze new growth; 'Winter Beauty', to 5 inches high with a profusion of dark pink flowers.

HEATHER
Calluna

Light: full sun	
Plant type: shrub	
Hardiness: Zones 4-7	
Height: 2 feet	
Soil and Moisture: well-drained, moist, acidic, rich	
Interest: flowers, foliage	
Care: moderate	

◄ Calluna vulgaris 'Corbett's Red'

Scotch heather produces a wavy sea of deep green, scalelike evergreen leaves that are smothered with hundreds of tiny pink or white flowers in midsummer. These beautiful plants make stunning ground covers and add an artistic dimension to rock gardens.

Growing and care:
Scotch heather must be grown in a slightly acid, sandy soil rich in organic matter. Good drainage is critical to its proper growth. Plant in full sun for best flowering and protect from drying winds. Mulch to conserve moisture, and water during dry spells. Prune faded flowers and stem tips to reduce legginess.

Selected species and varieties:
C. vulgaris (Scotch heather) grows up to 2 feet, spreading 2 feet or more, and bearing purplish pink flower clusters up to 1 foot long until fall; 'County Wicklow' is one of the best double-flowered varieties, with dark green foliage and pink, fully double flowers in summer; 'Else Frye' has double white summer flowers and reaches 1½ feet; 'H. E. Beale' grows 2 feet high with silvery pink flowers in late summer to fall; 'Mrs. Ronald Gray' is 4 inches high with reddish flowers in summer; 'Robert Chapman' has pale green foliage turning shades of orange and red in fall and winter, with rose-purple flowers in late summer.

HYACINTH BEAN
Dolichos

Light: full sun	
Plant type: annual	
Height: 10 to 20 feet	
Soil and Moisture: well-drained, moist, fertile	
Interest: flowers, foliage, fruit	
Care: easy	

◄ Dolichos lablab

This lush, tropical twining vine produces abundant pink, purple, or white pealike flowers in loose spikes from late spring to fall. The flowers are followed by vivid red to purple seedpods. The attractive, dark green compound leaves are veined in deep purple and rise from rose-violet-colored stems. The seeds are edible and are an important food source in many parts of the world. As an ornamental, hyacinth bean is one of the more beautiful annual vines and provides a colorful screen or covering for a fence, an arbor, or a trellis.

Growing and care:
Start seed indoors in peat pots 4 to 6 weeks prior to the last frost, or sow directly in the garden after the soil has warmed. Soak seed in warm water for 24 hours before planting. Space plants 1 to 2 feet apart and provide support for climbing. Hyacinth bean thrives in warm weather.

Selected species and varieties:
D. lablab climbs to 20 feet in one season by twining stems. Leaves are composed of three heart-shaped leaflets, each 3 to 6 inches long. The loosely clustered flowers stand out against the deeply colored leaves. Colorful pods are 1 to 3 inches long.

JASMINE
Jasminum

Light: full sun

Plant type: perennial, shrub

Hardiness: Zones 6-10

Height: 3 to 15 feet

Soil and Moisture: well-drained, moist to dry

Interest: flowers, foliage, fragrance

Care: moderate

◀ Jasminum mesnyi

A perfect solution for sunny slopes with poor soil, jasmine forms a wide-spreading mound of arching stems that bear bright yellow trumpetlike flowers and triplets of dark green leaflets. Branches root wherever they contact the soil and can soon cover a large area. Jasmine can also be trained to climb a support, where it may reach 15 feet. In winter, the naked green stems are effective, especially when allowed to trail over a wall.

Growing and care:
Jasmine is easy to transplant and spreads quickly. Water regularly until plantings are established and during extended dry periods. Cut back almost to the ground every 3 to 5 years to restore vigor. Propagate by cuttings taken in summer.

Selected species and varieties:
J. mesnyi (primrose jasmine, Japanese jasmine, yellow jasmine) is an evergreen shrub reaching 5 to 6 feet high with yellow flowers up to 1¾ inches wide, often semi-double to double, from early spring sporadically to midsummer, and leaflets 1 to 3 inches long; Zones 8-9. *J. nudiflorum* (winter jasmine) bears 1-inch-wide single yellow flowers that bloom erratically on warm days in winter before 1-inch leaflets appear, the thicket of arching vines reaching 3 to 4 feet high and 4 to 7 feet wide or up to 15 feet if trained to a support; 'Aureum' has dark green leaves marked with irregular patches of yellow.

JUNIPER
Juniperus

Light: full sun

Plant type: shrub

Hardiness: Zones 2-9

Height: 6 inches to 60 feet

Soil and Moisture: well-drained, moist to dry

Interest: foliage

Care: easy

◀ Juniperus conferta

Junipers are a very diverse group of woody shrubs that include some of the best ground covers available. Their scalelike evergreen foliage ranges in color from green to silvery blue to yellow. The cold temperatures and winds in winter often turn the foliage from green to shades of greenish purple. Female plants produce small blue berries that are strongly aromatic when crushed.

Growing and care:
Junipers are easy-to-grow shrubs that require no fertilizer and little supplemental watering under normal conditions. Most junipers tolerate drought and pollution. Shore junipers grow well in seaside gardens. Savin and Chinese junipers accept limestone soils. Plant container-grown or balled-and-burlapped specimens in spring, summer, or fall, watering regularly until plants become established. Prune winter damage in spring.

Selected species and varieties:
J. chinensis (Chinese juniper) comes in many forms, from narrow, conical trees 50 to 60 feet high with green to bluish to gray-green foliage, to thick ground covers; Zones 3-9; 'Arctic' is a hardy, spreading variety with blue-green needles, and stems reaching 1½ feet in height and 6 feet across; 'Blue Cloud' is a large, spreading ground cover type with attractive, steel blue-green foliage; 'Pfitzeriana Glauca' has bluish foliage becoming purplish blue in winter, normally 5 feet high by 10 feet

JUNIPER
(continued)

wide but often larger; 'San Jose' is a creeping variety that reaches just over a foot tall and spreads up to 8 feet wide; 'Sea Spray' has blue-green foliage and a vigorous, spreading habit reaching 1 foot tall and 6 feet wide. *J. conferta* (shore juniper) is a shrub spreading 6 to 9 feet and 1 to 1½ feet high with soft, needlelike bluish green foliage in summer turning bronzy or yellow-green in winter; Zones 6-9; 'Boulevard' has a very low-growing habit and deep green foliage. *J. horizontalis* (creeping juniper, creeping savin) grows 1 to 2 feet high by 4 to 8 feet wide, with trailing branches bearing glaucous green, blue-green, or blue plumelike foliage turning plum purple in winter; Zones 3-9; 'Bar Harbor', discovered along the coast of Maine, has a creeping habit, reaching less than 1 foot high with a spread of 8 feet, and is very tolerant of coastal conditions; 'Wiltonii' (blue rug juniper) forms a flat mat less than 6 inches high, spreading up to 8 feet, with grayish blue foliage. *J. procumbens* [sometimes classified as *J. chinensis* var. *procumbens*] (Japanese garden juniper) grows 1 to 2 feet high and 10 to 15 feet wide, with bluish green to gray-green foliage; 'Nana', a dwarf of the species, forms a low, rounded, compact mat 6 to 12 inches high and spreading up to 12 feet, with overlapping branches of bluish green foliage turning purplish in winter. *J. sabina* (savin) is a vase-shaped shrub 4 to 6 feet high by 5 to 10 feet wide, with dark green foliage turning a drab green tinged with yellow in winter; 'Broadmoor' grows 2 to 3 feet high with a 10-foot spread, bearing soft gray-green foliage in short, upright sprays; Zones 4-9.

MOONFLOWER
Ipomoea

◄ Ipomoea alba

Light: full sun

Plant type: tender perennial

Hardiness: Zone 10

Height: 15 to 20 feet

Soil and Moisture: well-drained, sandy, moist

Interest: flowers, fragrance

Care: easy

Moonflowers are night-blooming vines with large, fragrant, pure white blossoms in mesmerizing hues of moonlight white. The strong, easy-to-grow plants can reach to 20 feet in a season and quickly cover fences, trellises, and arbors with large, heart-shaped leaves and showy blossoms. Moonflowers are excellent for hanging baskets and are popular in summer moon gardens.

Growing and care:
Amend heavy soils with sand, and add only a modest amount of organic matter; too rich soil will produce lush foliage but few flowers. Plant seed 1 to 1½ feet apart in a sunny location after all danger of frost has passed, or start indoors in individual pots 4 to 6 weeks before the last frost date. Germination takes 5 to 7 days but can occur more quickly if the seeds are nicked with a nail file or soaked in water for 2 days before planting. Transplant gently, being careful not to disturb the roots. Pinch plants once when they begin to climb.

Selected species and varieties:
I. alba [also listed as *Calonyction aculeatum*] is a semi-woody tender perennial vine that quickly climbs to 20 feet, with shiny, bright green leaves up to 8 inches long and white, trumpet-shaped, very fragrant flowers up to 6 inches long and wide, opening after sundown and closing before noon the next day, blooming from midsummer to frost.

PASSIONFLOWER
Passiflora

Light: full sun

Plant type: perennial vine

Hardiness: Zones 6-10

Height: 15 to 25 feet

Soil and Moisture: well-drained, moist

Interest: flowers, foliage, fruit

Care: easy

◀ Passiflora incarnata

Passionflowers bear complex, spectacular blossoms in shades of blue, white, and greenish yellow along trailing vines covered with dark green, sometimes evergreen leaves. These vigorous plants are perfect for seaside plantings, or when allowed to freely ramble over fences and trellises. Passionflower also grows well in containers, where the plants add class to patio gardens in summer and elegance indoors in winter.

Growing and care:
Grow passionflowers in well-drained soil that has been well amended with rotted manure or compost. Their vigorous growth requires the sturdy support of a wall or trellis. Pinch vines regularly to increase bushiness. Propagate by seed or cuttings, or separate suckers from the base of established plants.

Selected species and varieties:
P. incarnata (passionflower, maypop) reaches to 25 feet with white to lavender flowers 2 to 3 inches across followed by large apricot-colored fruit. The 4- to 6-inch leaves have three lobes and are dark green above and whitish below. *P. lutea* grows to 15 feet with greenish yellow flowers and purple-black fruit. Its leaves turn yellow in fall.

SCARLET RUNNER BEAN
Phaseolus

Light: full sun

Plant type: tender perennial grown as annual

Hardiness: Zone 10

Height: 6 to 10 feet

Soil and Moisture: well-drained, moist, fertile

Interest: flowers, fruit

Care: easy

◀ Phaseolus coccineus

Scarlet runner bean is a fast-growing, low-maintenance plant that adds color to the garden and food to the table. This twining tender perennial is grown as an annual and produces abundant dark green leaves that are a perfect foil for its brilliant scarlet flowers. The vine quickly covers trellises, fences, and outdoor railings, creating a dense and dramatic backdrop. Use scarlet runner bean in the back of the border, in specialty gardens, or to add color to the vegetable patch, where the brilliant flowers will attract hummingbirds all season long.

Growing and care:
Start seed indoors 4 weeks before planting out or sow directly in the garden after the last frost. Set seed in 1-inch-deep drills with eye facing down. Inoculate soil with nitrogen-fixing bacteria for best growth. Water regularly until seedlings are a few inches high. Thin to allow 2 to 4 inches between plants. Provide support for climbing.

Selected species and varieties:
P. coccineus produces twining stems with 5-inch dark green leaves composed of three leaflets. Bright red, pealike flowers appear in large clusters from early to midsummer, followed by flat 4- to 12-inch pods filled with black-and-red-mottled seeds. Both flowers and beans are edible.

SUN ROSE
Helianthemum

Light:	full sun
Plant type:	shrubby perennial
Hardiness:	Zones 5-7
Height:	6 to 12 inches
Soil and Moisture:	well-drained, alkaline, dry
Interest:	flowers
Care:	difficult

◀ Helianthemum nummularium

Sun roses provide a colorful, cheerful cover for dry, sunny slopes and brighten rock gardens with their beautiful flowers from late spring to early summer. The blossoms resemble wild roses with crepe-paper petals and are freely sprinkled atop the low-growing evergreen foliage. Varieties come in yellow, orange, red, rose, pink, apricot, salmon, peach, white, and bicolors, and in double-flowered forms.

Growing and care:
Sun roses prefer dry, poor, gravelly or sandy soils and do not grow well in fertile soils. Good drainage is essential, as plants will not tolerate wet conditions, especially in winter. Prune in early spring to encourage dense growth, and prune again after flowering to get a flush of bloom in late summer. Protect with mulch over winter. Propagate by division in spring or by soft stem cuttings.

Selected species and varieties:
H. nummularium (yellow sun rose) forms a sprawling mound, 1 to 2 feet wide, with trailing stems that bear grayish green leaves 1 to 2 inches long with silvery undersides and 1-inch-wide flowers with broad petals and prominent stamens.

WISTERIA
Wisteria

Light:	full sun
Plant type:	woody vine
Hardiness:	Zones 4-9
Height:	10 to 30 feet
Soil and Moisture:	well-drained, moist
Interest:	flowers, foliage
Care:	moderate

◀ Wisteria sinensis

Wisteria is one of the most popular garden vines, with long panicles of lavender, white, or pinkish lilac, softly fragrant flowers. These elegant plants are sure to stir images of romantic springtime places or nostalgic memories of Grandma's. The lovely, twining vines are picturesque additions to patios, porches, or sturdy arbors, where the bright green foliage provides dense summertime shade.

Growing and care:
Amend soil with organic matter and add lime if soil is very acid. Prune roots before planting. Water regularly during dry periods and fertilize with a high-phosphorus, high-potassium, low-nitrogen fertilizer to promote flowering. Only grow wisteria on very strong supports.

Selected species and varieties:
W. floribunda (Japanese wisteria) twines clockwise, bearing small, slightly fragrant, violet, white, or violet-blue flowers in clusters 9 to 20 inches long in early to midspring just before the leaves emerge; 'Alba' bears snow white flowers in 11-inch-long, fragrant clusters; 'Rosea' produces long 1½-foot panicles of very fragrant lilac-rose flowers in spring. *W. sinensis* (Chinese wisteria) twines counterclockwise and produces blue-violet flowers, not as fragrant as those of Japanese wisteria, borne in dense, 6- to 12-inch-long clusters in mid- to late spring; cultivars include white, dark purple, double varieties; Zones 5-8.

BLUESTEM
Andropogon

Light: full sun	
Plant type: ornamental grass	
Hardiness: Zones 4-9	
Height: 2 to 8 feet	
Soil and Moisture: well-drained, moist to dry	
Interest: foliage	
Care: easy	

◀ Andropogon gerardii

Bluestems are perennial bunch grasses native to the prairies, open woods, fields, and lowlands over much of the United States. Unlike many other ornamental grasses that produce large displays, bluestem's small clumps add a subtle touch to rock gardens and wildflower meadows. The narrow leaves are blue-green in spring and summer and turn tan-copper or maroon in fall.

Growing and care:
Big bluestem grows best in a sandy loam and withstands periodic flooding and clay soil. Bushy bluestem prefers a site that stays evenly moist. Cut bunches nearly to ground level in late winter or early spring before new growth begins. Propagate by seed sown directly in the garden in spring or by division in spring or fall.

Selected species and varieties:
A. gerardii (big bluestem, turkeyfoot) produces upright clumps 4 to 8 feet tall with purplish late-summer flowers in branched clusters resembling a turkey's foot, and leaves that are blue-green in summer and maroon to tan in fall. *A. glomeratus* (bushy bluestem) has clumps 2 to 5 feet tall with silvery green to pinkish flowers in bold, feathery racemes surrounded by salmon sheaths in fall followed by fluffy white seed heads. Leaves and stems turn a coppery bronze after frost and remain attractive through winter; Zones 6-9.

DROPSEED
Sporobolus

Light: full sun	
Plant type: ornamental grass	
Hardiness: Zones 3-8	
Height: 2 feet	
Soil and Moisture: well-drained, sandy, dry	
Interest: flowers, foliage	
Care: easy	

◀ Sporobolus heterolepis

Dropseed is a truly charming ornamental grass with fountainlike sprays of fine-textured, gracefully arching stems and leaves. Native to the prairies of the central United States and Canada, this perennial grass is ideal for small and large meadow gardens, herbaceous borders, and as a ground cover for dry, sunny sites. In autumn the leaves and seed heads turn a metallic tan color that persists through winter, making this plant valuable every season of the year.

Growing and care:
Northern prairie dropseed grows best in dry, sandy soil and full sun, but in areas with very hot, dry summers the plants benefit from a little afternoon shade. Sow seed directly in the garden in either fall or spring. Plants require about 3 years to reach their mature size. Divide every 2 to 3 years, though the thick roots make this task more difficult than it looks.

Selected species and varieties:
S. heterolepis (northern prairie dropseed) has narrow, rich green leaves 20 inches long in a clump 2 feet tall and 3 feet wide, and loose clusters of dark green flowers that bloom in summer and fall. The entire plant, including the seed heads, turns an attractive tan-bronze in fall.

EULALIA
Miscanthus

Light: full sun	
Plant type: ornamental grass	
Hardiness: Zones 5-9	
Height: 5 to 8 feet	
Soil and Moisture: well-drained, moist	
Interest: flowers, foliage	
Care: easy	

◀ Miscanthus sinensis 'Zebrinus'

These tall, fine-textured grasses with their long, narrow, arching leaves and feathery fan-shaped plumes of fall flowers make striking specimens or screens and are some of the most popular ornamental garden grasses. They are easy to grow and add multiseason interest to borders and mass plantings.

Growing and care:
Eulalia grows well in any ordinary garden soil with adequate moisture and grows best with little or no fertilizing. Excessive nitrogen in the soil produces weak stems that flop over. Cut clumps to within 2 to 6 inches of the ground in late winter. Propagate by division in spring.

Selected species and varieties:
M. sinensis (Japanese silver grass, Chinese silver grass) has upright clumps 6 to 8 feet tall and 3 feet wide or more, consisting of leaves 3 to 4 feet long and ⅜ inch wide, with pale pink to reddish flower clusters 8 inches long blooming in fall and lasting nearly all winter; 'Gracillimus' (maiden grass) has 5- to 8-foot-tall clumps and narrower leaves than the species, with a prominent white midvein; 'Morning Light' has light green leaves with silvery white margins and midrib; 'Zebrinus' (zebra grass) has distinctive yellow bands across the leaves, and pinkish brown flower clusters.

FOUNTAIN GRASS
Pennisetum

Light: full sun	
Plant type: ornamental grass	
Hardiness: Zones 5-10	
Height: 2 to 4 feet	
Soil and Moisture: well-drained, fertile, moist	
Interest: flowers, foliage	
Care: easy	

◀ P. alopecuroides 'Hameln'

Fountain grass produces stunning clumps of arching leaves and sweeping sprays of bottlebrush flower heads borne on thin, arching stems in summer and fall. The plants are extremely versatile with a fluid, sinuous form that complements rock gardens, mixed borders, and water gardens, and are spectacular massed in large plantings in meadows or wildflower gardens.

Growing and care:
Set plants 2 feet apart. In spring, cut to within 6 inches of the ground before new growth begins. Divide every 5 to 10 years to prevent the center from falling open. *P. setaceum* self-sows readily and is often grown as an annual in regions north of Zone 5.

Selected species and varieties:
P. alopecuroides (Chinese fountain grass, swamp foxtail grass) has clumps of light green foliage 3 to 4 feet high, with nodding, reddish brown flowers 6 inches long; 'Hameln' is a semidwarf form growing to 2 feet; 'National Arboretum' grows to 2 feet with a dark brown inflorescence; Zones 7-9. *P. setaceum* grows 2 to 3 feet tall, with narrow leaves and pinkish spikes 1 foot long; Zones 8-10; 'Rubrum' (purple-leaved fountain grass) has rose-colored foliage and rosy to dark red spikes.

GRAMA
Bouteloua

Light: full sun

Plant type: ornamental grass

Hardiness: Zones 3-10

Height: 1 to 2 feet

Soil and Moisture: well-drained, moist to dry

Interest: flowers, foliage

Care: easy

◀ Bouteloua
curtipendula

These clump-forming drought-tolerant grasses are found in prairies, open woodlands, and on rocky slopes throughout much of the United States. Their tough, hardy nature makes them very useful in wildflower meadows or used as accents in specialty gardens where the tall, slender flower spikes add an informal, wild look. When planted in mass and mowed, the plants produce a good grassy cover for dry areas.

Growing and care:

For best growth grama grasses require full sun and a well-drained, moist soil, but do very well in dry conditions. The plants require almost no care and are well suited for low-maintenance gardens. To propagate, collect seed in fall and sow immediately in well-worked soil. Seed can also be stratified over winter and sown in spring. Divide clumps every 4 years in early spring or fall when plants are dormant.

Selected species and varieties:

B. curtipendula (sideoats grama, mesquite grass) has wiry clumps 1 to 2 feet tall and small flowers arranged in numerous spikelets with downward-pointing tips along one side of each flower stem in summer; in fall the seed heads bleach to a tan color and foliage often turns red or purple. *B. gracilis* (blue grama) grows 1 to 1½ feet tall with narrow, fine-textured foliage forming a dense sod when mowed.

LITTLE BLUESTEM
Schizachyrium

Light: full sun

Plant type: ornamental grass

Hardiness: Zones 3-10

Height: 2 to 3 feet

Soil and Moisture: well-drained, moist to dry

Interest: foliage, seed heads

Care: easy

◀ S. scoparium

Little bluestem is a cute, casual ornamental grass native to the prairies, rocky slopes, open woodlands, and fields from eastern Canada to the Gulf of Mexico and west to Idaho. In spring and summer the plants have upright, pliant blue-green stems and leaves that turn soft shades of tan to mahogany in fall through winter. Little bluestem is lovely massed as a ground cover, used in a meadow garden, or planted singly in a perennial border. Its flowers and seed heads are attractive in arrangements.

Growing and care:

Little bluestem is adaptable and easy to grow, thriving in most soils, moist or dry, including those of low fertility. It does not, however, tolerate wet conditions. Cut plants nearly to the ground in early spring before new growth begins. Propagate by seed or by dividing plants in spring or fall before new growth begins.

Selected species and varieties:

S. scoparium (little bluestem, prairie beard grass) has narrow blue-green foliage in an upright clump, most often about 3 feet tall and to 8 inches in diameter. In fall the foliage turns shades of khaki to burgundy brown. Loose clusters of tiny flowers on 2½-inch spikes open from late summer to fall and are followed by soft, shiny white seed heads.

PANIC GRASS
Panicum

Light: full sun	
Plant type: ornamental grass	
Hardiness: Zones 5-9	
Height: 3 to 6 feet	
Soil and Moisture: well-drained, moist	
Interest: flowers, foliage	
Care: easy	

◀ Panicum virgatum 'Heavy Metal'

Panic grass is a large, erect grass that is attractive nearly all year round and is easy to care for as well. The plants produce tall, branching stalks up to 6 feet high topped with airy feathers of tiny buff-colored flowers above 3-foot-high clumps of arching, colored leaves in fall. The distinctive seed heads that follow remain attractive through winter. *Panicum* is widely used as a specimen or filler for large borders. It is very effective when interplanted with other ornamental grasses in mass displays. Brooms have long been made from the stiff, dried stalks.

Growing and care:
Switch grass grows most vigorously in evenly moist soil but will tolerate much drier conditions, even drought, and doesn't mind the sea spray of coastal locations. Cut it back nearly to ground level in early spring, before new growth begins. Propagate by division every 2 to 3 years in spring in the North and in fall in southern regions. Sow seed directly in the garden in spring after last frost.

Selected species and varieties:
P. virgatum (switch grass) has loose, open flower clusters above green leaves that turn yellow and red in fall and fade to brown in winter; 'Haense Herms' has red foliage from summer to fall and grayish seed heads on 3- to 3½-foot stalks; 'Heavy Metal' bears 3- to 4-foot flower stalks above stiff, deep blue leaves that turn yellow in fall.

RABBIT-TAIL GRASS
Lagurus

Light: full sun	
Plant type: annual	
Height: 6 to 18 inches	
Soil and Moisture: well-drained, light, moist to dry	
Interest: foliage, seed heads	
Care: easy	

◀ Lagurus ovatus

The long, furry seed heads of rabbit-tail grass resemble the cottony puff of a rabbit's tail. This neat, good-looking ornamental grass produces a low mound of slender leaves and pliant stalks topped with creamy white, silky seed heads that add soft texture to the late-summer and autumn garden and are very attractive in dried arrangements. Rabbit-tail grass is good for borders, specialty gardens, or when planted in drifts in wildflower meadows. The dwarf varieties are great for rock gardens.

Growing and care:
Start seed indoors 8 weeks prior to the last frost or sow directly outdoors as soon as the soil can be worked. Allow 6 to 12 inches between plants. Water well while seedlings establish themselves and during dry periods. Rabbit-tail grass tolerates heat very well and freely self-seeds, especially in areas of the western states.

Selected species and varieties:
L. ovatus produces narrow, hairy leaves and distinctive seed heads that are fuzzy and light green, turning creamy white as they mature. At 1½ to 2½ inches long, they resemble a rabbit's tail, hence the common name; 'Nanus' is a dwarf variety that grows to 6 inches.

REED GRASS
Calamagrostis

Light: full sun

Plant type: ornamental grass

Hardiness: Zones 5-9

Height: 5 to 7 feet

Soil and Moisture: well-drained to heavy, wet to dry

Interest: flowers, foliage

Care: easy

◀ C. acutiflora 'Stricta'

One of the most adaptable of ornamental grasses, reed grass produces dense, picturesque clumps of narrow, arching leaves and feathery flower plumes on tall, upright stems. One of the first ornamental grasses to bloom, reed grass is a fine multiseason specimen, singly or in groups, for perennial beds, borders, or streamside plantings. It also blends well with rocks and walls and provides interesting wintertime contrast to dark green, broad-leaved evergreens.

Growing and care:
Plant container-grown plants 3 feet apart in spring or fall. Reed grass is remarkable for being able to thrive just about anywhere and grows equally well in heavy, wet soils and in poor, dry ones. Little attention is required. Cut the clump to within 6 inches of the ground before new growth begins in spring. Propagate by division in spring.

Selected species and varieties:
C. acutiflora 'Stricta' has attractive 2-foot-wide clumps of matte green leaves ½ inch wide that arch below 4-foot shafts bearing 15-inch-long flower panicles in early summer. The pinkish green summer foliage turns tan in summer, and golden brown throughout winter.

VETIVER
Vetiveria

Light: full sun

Plant type: ornamental grass

Hardiness: Zones 9-10

Height: 6 to 9 feet

Soil and Moisture: well-drained, moist to wet

Interest: flowers, foliage

Care: easy

◀ Vetiveria zizanioides

Vetiver forms fountains of narrow, rough-edged leaves with blades that are bent to look as if they are blowing in the breeze. Its deep, fibrous roots hold soil very well, making it useful for erosion control of sunny slopes and stream banks. Flowers are flat, plumed spikes on tall stems above the leaf clumps. The fragrant roots have a woodsy, resinous scent with violet overtones and can be dried to scent sachets. In the Far East, roots are woven into mats, screens, and baskets whose fragrance is renewed by dampening to scent rooms. Vetiver also yields an oil prized in expensive perfumes, soaps, and cosmetics.

Growing and care:
Vetiver grows best from divisions. Space plants 2 to 3 feet apart. The complex roots form dense sods that choke out weeds. Harvest roots and renew plants by lifting and dividing every 3 to 4 years. Scrub the roots and spread on racks or screens to dry slowly. Use dried roots as weaving material or crumble for potpourri and sachets.

Selected species and varieties:
V. zizanioides (vetiver, khus-khus) produces leaves ⅓ inch wide and up to 3 feet long with foot-long flowering spikes on stalks to 9 feet.

ACACIA
Acacia

Light:	full sun
Plant type:	tree
Hardiness:	Zones 9-10
Height:	20 to 60 feet
Soil and Moisture:	well-drained, moist to dry, acidic
Interest:	flowers, foliage
Care:	moderate

◀ Acacia dealbata

Acacias thrive in dry, tropical climate. In the United States they are grown in southern California and Arizona, where they provide some of the earliest flowers of the season. Typically, each flower is composed of a mass of stamens that form a dense cluster. Though not long lived, these trees are remarkably fast growers and may reach 30 feet in only 5 years.

Growing and care:
Acacias require warm climates and, once established, tolerate both drought and seaside conditions. They are easy to care for and are virtually pest- and disease-free. Their rapid growth, however, results in weak wood that is subject to wind damage. Plant container-grown specimens and stake them until roots are well established. Prune young plants to desired shape at anytime. Propagate by seed or cuttings.

Selected species and varieties:
A. baileyana (cootamundra wattle) grows 20 to 40 feet tall with a wide canopy of fernlike leaves, and tiny yellow flowers in winter; Zone 10; 'Purpurea' (purple-leaf acacia) has young foliage tinged with burgundy. *A. dealbata* (silver wattle) grows 30 to 60 feet tall with silvery green, doubly pinnate leaves, silvery bark, and extremely fragrant yellow flowers, and is less drought tolerant than cootamundra wattle.

'AMERICAN PILLAR' ROSE
Rosa

Light:	full sun
Plant type:	shrub
Hardiness:	Zones 5-9
Height:	10 to 20 feet
Soil and Moisture:	well-drained, fertile, moist
Interest:	flowers, fruit
Care:	easy to moderate

◀ Rosa
'American Pillar'

The climbing rose 'American Pillar' has been one of the most beautiful garden roses for nearly a century. The plants bear huge clusters of bright, carmine red flowers accented with a white eye. This vigorous plant reaches 15 to 20 feet tall with dark green, leathery leaves on thorny canes and is virtually disease- and pest-free. Use 'American Pillar' on trellises or train it into trees for an unforgettable effect.

Growing and care:
Plant 'American Pillar' in well-worked, fertile soil that has been amended with some organic matter. The plant prefers full sun but will tolerate some very light shade. Fertilize in early spring and again after flowering. Prune trained specimens to shape in summer. Remove older canes in fall. Mulch around plants with compost in spring and fall.

Selected species and varieties:
R. setigera (prairie rose) is another 'American Pillar' parent with thorny, reddish canes with rough-textured green leaves and single, pink flowers with a pale white eye on canes reaching 10 to 15 feet; Zones 4-9. *R. wichuraiana* (memorial rose) is a parent of 'American Pillar' and a vigorous grower with dark green foliage on canes reaching 15 feet and clusters of pure white flowers.

BALD CYPRESS
Taxodium

Light: full sun	
Plant type: tree	
Hardiness: Zones 4-9	
Height: 50 to 70 feet or more	
Soil and Moisture: moderately well-drained to heavy, wet to moist	
Interest: foliage, bark	
Care: easy	

◀ Taxodium distichum

Bald cypresses are strong, dramatic-looking trees that are most often envisioned draped with Spanish moss in a southern swamp. While these stately trees grow well in wet sites, they also thrive in deep, moist upland soils as far north as New England. Bald cypress has soft, sage green needlelike foliage that turns burnt orange in fall. In wet areas the shaggy, reddish brown main trunk is flanked by narrow root projections called knees that absorb oxygen for the tree. In fall the graceful branches hold 1-inch-round, greenish purple, fragrant cones. Use bald cypress as a dramatic, fine-textured vertical accent in the garden, or plant in groups along the edge of a pond.

Growing and care:
Plant in deep, well-worked soil amended with generous amounts of compost or rotted manure. The plants are very strong and resist strong winds and winter storm damage. Once established they are care-free with no pest or disease problems.

Selected species and varieties:
T. distichum (common bald cypress) produces new foliage that opens bright yellow-green in graceful sprays amid short, ascending branches on a slender pyramid 50 to more than 70 feet high by 20 to 30 feet wide; 'Shawnee Brave' has a narrow, almost conical habit reaching 75 feet tall and nearly 20 feet in width.

BANKSIAE (LADY BANKS ROSE)
Rosa

Light: full sun	
Plant type: shrub	
Hardiness: Zones 8-10	
Height: 12 to 25 feet	
Soil and Moisture: well-drained, moist	
Interest: flowers, fragrance	
Care: easy	

◀ Rosa banksiae 'Lady Banks'

Lady Banks rose is a free-flowering, vigorous grower bearing abundant double white flowers for up to 6 weeks in spring. While in bloom the plant seems smothered in sweetly fragrant blossoms. Each flower is less than 1 inch across, pure white, and extremely fragrant with the scent of violets. Leaves are long, light green, and shiny, and the canes are nearly thornless. Lady Banks rose looks beautiful scrambling up a tree, wall, or trellis.

Growing and care:
Plant Lady Banks rose in loosened soil amended with a little organic matter. Provide support for the fast-growing canes. Once established the plants need little care and are not troubled by insects or disease. Prune as needed to control growth or shape plant.

Selected species and varieties:
R. banksiae var. *lutea* (yellow Lady Banks rose) bears small, fully double yellow flowers with no fragrance along vigorous, 20-foot-tall canes in spring; 'Fortuniana' produces fragrant, double, large white blossoms on 20-foot-tall canes covered with abundant, glossy green foliage.

BARBERRY
Berberis

Light: full sun

Plant type: shrub

Hardiness: Zones 4-8

Height: 1½ to 8 feet

Soil and Moisture: well-drained, moist to dry

Interest: foliage, fruit

Care: easy

◄ Berberis x gladwynensis 'William Penn'

Barberries are neat, tidy shrubs with dense foliage and brightly colored fruit. All are more or less thorny, making them perfect for barrier hedges. Deciduous forms exhibit bright fall foliage and colorful berries that persist through winter. Barberries are useful as hedges, barriers, foundation plants, or specimens. Varieties with red or yellow leaves provide dramatic contrast in green landscapes and work especially well in combination with low-growing junipers.

Growing and care:
Barberries are easy to grow and require very little care. Plant container-grown specimens anytime in spring, summer, or fall. Water well until plants are established. Evergreen barberries grow best in moist, slightly acid soil in sites that are protected from drying winds and strong sun. Deciduous barberries adapt to almost any soil and are tolerant of drought and urban pollution. They show their best fall color in full sun. The red and yellow forms revert to green in shade. Pruning is usually not necessary.

Selected species and varieties:
B. buxifolia var. *nana* (dwarf Magellan barberry) has spiny leaves up to 1 inch long on an evergreen shrub 1½ feet tall and 2 feet wide, usually bearing orange-yellow flowers and purple berries; hardy to Zone 5. *B.* x *gladwynensis* 'William Penn' is a mounded evergreen 4 feet high and wide, with showy flowers and lustrous dark green foliage that turns bronze in winter; hardy to Zone 6, but deciduous north of Zone 8. *B. julianae* (wintergreen barberry) is an evergreen mound with an upright habit, 6 to 8 feet high and wide, with often light-colored stems bearing spines up to 1 inch long and narrow, spiny leaves 2 to 3 inches long that may turn bronze or dark reddish in color in winter, profuse bloom in spring, and ⅓-inch bluish black berries that may linger into fall; hardy to Zone 5. *B. thunbergii* (Japanese barberry) is a multibranched deciduous shrub, 3 to 6 feet tall and 4 to 7 feet wide, producing bright green leaves that appear early to hide small flower clusters and turn orange, red, and reddish purple in fall as ⅓-inch bright red berries form; 'Aurea' grows 3 to 4 feet tall, with vivid yellow leaves in the growing season but relatively few flowers and fruit; var. *atropurpurea* 'Crimson Pygmy' (sometimes referred to as 'Little Gem', 'Little Beauty', 'Little Favorite', or 'Atropurpurea Nana') has maroon to purplish red summer foliage and grows to 2 feet tall and 3 feet wide; 'Rose Glow' reaches 5 to 6 feet tall and produces foliage opening rosy pink with splotches of darker red-purple changing later to solid red-purple; 'Kobold' is 2 feet tall with very rich, dark green boxwoodlike leaves and a formal, round habit that needs no pruning; 'Vermillion' grows to 3 feet with dense green leaves turning brilliant red in fall.

'BLANC DOUBLE DE COUBERT'
Rosa

Light: full sun

Plant type: shrub

Hardiness: Zones 3-10

Height: 4 to 6 feet

Soil and Moisture: well-drained, moist

Interest: flowers, fragrance

Care: easy

◀ Rosa 'Blanc double de Coubert'

The rose 'Blanc double de Coubert' is very hardy and easy to grow, with beautiful, intensely fragrant, linen white double flowers in spring with rebloom in fall. The plant belongs to the hybrid rugosa group and has long, gracefully arching canes forming a mounded shrub 3 to 4 feet high. The leaves are deep forest green in summer turning russet yellow in fall. When the foliage drops the canes are covered with large, orange-red hips that persist into winter. 'Blanc double de Coubert' is one of the best specimen roses but also blends nicely into mixed borders and herb gardens. The petals can be dried and used in potpourri.

Growing and care:
Plant in loosened soil, spacing plants 3 to 4 feet apart. Prune like rugosa roses, removing about one-third of the cane in late winter to shape plant. 'Blanc double de Coubert' can be used almost everywhere: in seaside gardens, as city plantings, or on dry, sandy hillsides. The plants are virtually pest- and disease-free, although Japanese beetles sometimes are attracted to the flowers.

Selected species and varieties:
'Frau Dagmar Hartopp' is a hybrid rugosa type with a dense, compact form reaching 3 feet tall and 3 feet wide with nearly everblooming blush pink single blossoms and misty yellow stamens, dark green leaves, and bright red hips in fall.

BLUEBERRY
Vaccinium

Light: full sun

Plant type: shrub

Hardiness: Zones 2-8

Height: 1/2 to 12 feet

Soil and Moisture: well-drained, moist, acidic

Interest: flowers, foliage, fruit

Care: moderate

◀ Vaccinium corymbosum

Blueberries are well known as providers of some of the tastiest fruit around, yet they also add delicate white flowers in spring and vibrant, intensely colored foliage in fall. Blueberries are available in a range of heights, from ground cover types to upright shrubs, and grow well in poor soils as well as rich ones. They are useful mixed into perennial borders or naturalized in sunny wildflower meadows.

Growing and care:
Plant blueberries in moist, well-drained soil with a pH of 4.5 to 5.5. Add generous amounts of organic matter prior to planting. Mulch to preserve moisture around highbush types. Lowbush forms are drought tolerant once established. Prune after fruiting to encourage better fruit set.

Selected species and varieties:
V. angustifolium (lowbush blueberry) grows 6 to 24 inches tall with a low, spreading habit. Leaves are small, blue-green in summer, turning bright red in fall; flowers are white with reddish tinge. Fruit is delicious, pale blue to blue-black with tart, wild taste; Zones 2-6. *V. corymbosum* (highbush blueberry) reaches 6 to 12 feet tall with multiple stems and a rounded, upright habit. Leaves are blue-green in summer, turning red, orange, yellow, and bronze in fall. Flowers are white, urn shaped, 1/2 inch long; fruit is a sweet, blue-black berry; Zones 3-8.

BROOM
Cytisus

Light: full sun	
Plant type: shrub	
Hardiness: Zones 5-10	
Height: 6 inches to 5 feet	
Soil and Moisture: well-drained, moist to dry	
Interest: flowers, foliage, fragrance	
Care: moderate	

◀ Cytisus x kewensis

Broom is a fast-growing, reliable shrub that brightens the spring border with its masses of pealike, often fragrant flowers. Small simple or trifoliate leaves line arching stems that remain green all year, providing welcome interest during winter months. Broom's spreading habit and minimal requirements make it ideal for stabilizing the soil of a sunny hillside or dry bank. Low-growing types are useful in rock gardens or borders.

Growing and care:
Plant in early spring in well-worked soil. Broom is adaptable to seaside conditions, but does poorly in damp locations. Prune flowering stems by two-thirds immediately after flowering. Do not cut back stems more than a year old, because they will not resprout. Propagate by cuttings or by layering in spring.

Selected species and varieties:
C. x *kewensis* (Kew broom) grows 6 inches tall, spreading to form a mat of green stems up to 6 feet across, with pale yellow spring flowers and small, hairy leaves; excellent for the rock garden; Zones 6-10. *C.* x *praecox* (Warminster broom) grows 3 to 6 feet tall with a similar spread and graceful, slender, cascading stems that produce lemon yellow blooms in early spring; 'Albus' is a slightly smaller shrub with white flowers; 'Luteus' is a dwarf variety with darker yellow blooms.

BUSH CLOVER
Lespedeza

Light: full sun	
Plant type: shrub	
Hardiness: Zones 4-8	
Height: 3 to 10 feet	
Soil and Moisture: well-drained, sandy, dry	
Interest: flowers	
Care: easy	

◀ Lespedeza thunbergii 'White Fountain'

Bush clovers are vigorous deciduous shrubs valued for their late-season flowers that appear from midsummer to fall. The small rose-purple blossoms are borne on 5- to 6-inch-long clusters that hang from the thin, pendulous branches. These easy-care plants are not troubled by pests or disease, making them good for borders or interplanted with spring-flowering shrubs.

Growing and care:
Well-drained soils are essential. Avoid fertilizers. Prune stems to the ground in early spring before growth begins. New stems will reach 3 to 4 feet by flowering time. Propagate by seed or stem cuttings.

Selected species and varieties:
L. bicolor (shrub bush clover) reaches 6 to 10 feet, with trifoliate leaves along arching stems, and rosy purple flowers in 2- to 5-inch-long clusters arising from the current season's growth from mid- to late summer. *L. thunbergii* [also listed as *L. sieboldii*] (purple bush clover) grows to 6 feet tall and 10 feet wide with slender arching stems that become weighted down by the 8-inch-long dark purple flower clusters from late summer to early fall; 'White Fountain' has white flowers; Zones 5-8.

BUTTERFLY BUSH
Buddleia

Light: full sun	
Plant type: shrub	
Hardiness: Zones 5-9	
Height: 4 to 20 feet	
Soil and Moisture: well-drained, moist, fertile	
Interest: flowers, fragrance	
Care: easy	

◀ Buddleia alternifolia

Butterfly bushes have long, arching stems covered with long, conical clusters of tiny, exceptionally fragrant summer flowers in shades of white, red, pink, lavender, or purple. Butterflies find the blossoms irresistible, sometimes completely covering the flower heads with their slowly beating wings on warm days. The willow-shaped leaves are dark green above and slightly hairy beneath. These shrubs are superb as specimens or massed as background in a shrub border.

Growing and care:
Butterfly bushes are vigorous, pest-free plants. Prune flower heads after blossoms fade to prolong the flowering season. Prune *B. davidii* in early spring before growth begins. In regions north of Zone 6 it dies back to the ground and resprouts in the spring. Prune *B. alternifolia* immediately after flowering in summer.

Selected species and varieties:
B. alternifolia (fountain butterfly bush) reaches 8 to 15 feet with 4-inch dull, dark green leaves that are gray on the underside, and long, drooping clusters of soft purple flowers. *B. davidii* (summer lilac, orange-eye butterfly bush) grows to 10 feet with 10-inch leaves that are white underneath, and 8- to 18-inch clusters of orange-throated flowers in a wide array of colors; var. *magnifica* has dark blue-purple blossoms with a bright orange eye; 'Peace' has ivory flowers.

CAPE FUCHSIA
Phygelius

Light: full sun	
Plant type: shrub	
Hardiness: Zones 7-10	
Height: 2 to 6 feet	
Soil and Moisture: well-drained, moist	
Interest: flowers	
Care: easy	

◀ Phygelius aequalis
'Yellow Trumpet'

Cape fuchsias have dramatic clusters of dangling, colorful, five-lobed tubular flowers and pairs of dark green, triangular to lance-shaped leaves that are most dense toward the base of the stems. These woody-based perennials will grow as small shrubs where winters are mild. In colder regions the plants die back to the ground in winter and resprout in spring. Cape fuchsias are excellent container plants that add summer color to patio and deck gardens. The plants also attract hummingbirds.

Growing and care:
The long flower clusters of cape fuchsias need to be sheltered from strong breezes. In Zones 7 and 8 the entire plant should be protected from cold winter winds as well. They benefit from additional water and fertilizer. Prune old stems and winter-damaged shoots in very early spring. Propagate by seed or softwood cuttings made in late autumn or spring.

Selected species and varieties:
P. aequalis grows 3 to 4 feet tall with dense, cylindrical clusters of 2-inch brown, red, or dusky pink late-summer flowers; 'Yellow Trumpet' has a dense, bushy habit and creamy yellow flowers. *P.* x *rectus* grows 3 to 4 feet tall with pendulous clusters of light red summer to fall flowers and lance-shaped, slightly toothed leaves; 'Devil's Tears' has deep red flowers with a yellow throat.

'CÉCILE BRUNNER' ROSE
Rosa

Light: full sun	
Plant type: shrub	
Hardiness: Zones 4-9	
Height: 1 to 3 feet	
Soil and Moisture: well-drained, fertile, moist	
Interest: flowers, fragrance	
Care: moderate	

◀ Rosa 'Cécile Brunner'

One of the most popular polyantha roses, 'Cécile Brunner' has abundant clusters of richly scented double flowers from late spring to fall. The plants are small, reaching from 2 to 3 feet tall with dainty spiraled buds and small, rich pink flowers. The slender canes have few thorns and are lightly covered with glossy, dark green leaves. 'Cécile Brunner' is well suited for mixed borders and is an excellent source of cut flowers.

Growing and care:
Plant in a bright, sunny place in soil that has been well amended with compost or rotted manure. Top-dress annually with compost. Prune in spring as buds are breaking, removing the top one-third of the canes. Fertilize after pruning and again after first flush of blooms has faded.

Selected species and varieties:
R. 'Climbing Cécile Brunner' is a very vigorous, rambling rose reaching to 20 feet with light pink, fragrant flowers in late spring; 'Baby Cécile Brunner' is a miniature rose with small 1-foot-tall stems and light pink blossoms; 'Baby Betsy McCall' grows 6 to 10 inches high with dark green, leathery foliage and very small, double, fragrant pink blossoms; 'Perle d'Or' grows 3 feet tall with clusters of fragrant, yellow-pink double blossoms.

'CHICAGO PEACE' ROSE
Rosa

Light: full sun	
Plant type: shrub	
Hardiness: Zones 5-9	
Height: 4 to 5 feet	
Soil and Moisture: well-drained, fertile, moist	
Interest: flowers, fragrance	
Care: moderate	

◀ Rosa 'Chicago Peace'

The hybrid tea rose 'Chicago Peace' has been a favorite of gardeners since the early 1960s. It is related to the famous 'Peace' rose and bears stunning, fragrant double blossoms, each with slightly curved petals colored rose pink at the edges and blending to golden yellow at the base. The plants are upright and vigorous with good disease resistance. Plant 'Chicago Peace' as a specimen or mingled with other roses and shrubs in an informal border. The flowers are excellent for cutting.

Growing and care:
Plant 'Chicago Peace' in a sunny location in well-worked soil generously amended with compost or other organic matter. Prune bushes lightly in spring, removing only dead or damaged branches. Do not cut back healthy canes. Fertilize in spring as buds begin to swell and again when flowering begins. Mulch in fall in Zones 5 and 6.

Selected species and varieties:
R. 'Climbing Peace' bears abundant, golden double blossoms in spring and fall on vigorous, 10-foot-tall canes. R. 'Peace' grows from 3 to 4 feet tall with moderately vigorous upright canes, dark, glossy green foliage, and classic golden yellow, fragrant double blossoms. The plants are susceptible to black spot and mildew in warm, humid regions.

CORK TREE
Phellodendron

Light: full sun

Plant type: tree

Hardiness: Zones 3-8

Height: 30 to 45 feet

Soil and Moisture: well-drained, moist to dry

Interest: bark

Care: easy

◀ Phellodendron
   amurense

Cork tree is valued for its very ornamental, deeply ridged and furrowed gray-brown corky bark, which cloaks the wide-spreading horizontal main branches of mature trees. Lustrous green compound leaves, like those of black walnut, cast a light shade and sometimes turn yellow in autumn before dropping. Small yellowish green flowers bloom in late spring, followed by small clusters of black berries in late fall on female trees. Both flowers and fruit have a turpentine-like odor when they are bruised.

Growing and care:
Cork tree is easy to transplant and has moderate tolerance for drought and pollution. In hot conditions it can defoliate, sometimes completely. For best growth plant in soil freely amended with compost or rotted manure and water regularly. Mulch around root zone to keep soil cool and moist.

Selected species and varieties:
P. amurense (Amur cork tree) reaches 30 to 45 feet with an equal or greater spread, with orange-yellow stems bearing glossy dark green leaflets to 4 inches long, and corky bark developing in old age. *P. chinense* (Chinese cork tree) grows 30 feet tall, with dark yellow-green leaflets to 5 inches long on red-brown stems; hardy to Zone 5.

CRAB APPLE
Malus

Light: full sun

Plant type: shrub, tree

Hardiness: Zones 2-8

Height: 6 to 50 feet

Soil and Moisture: well-drained, moist, acidic

Interest: flowers, fruit, fragrance

Care: moderate

◀ Malus floribunda

Crab apples are very popular ornamental shrubs and trees that bear clusters of white to red, usually fragrant spring blossoms before the leaves appear. Small green, yellow, or red applelike fruit is produced in summer and often persists into fall. Crab apples are excellent specimen trees and make good additions to shrub borders. The flowers attract bees in spring and the fruit brings songbirds to the garden in fall.

Growing and care:
Plant in spring or fall in well-worked soil amended with compost or rotted manure. Water regularly during the first growing season. Prune crab apples each year immediately after flowering to maintain shape, and remove suckers. Feed in spring with a balanced fertilizer, and mulch with compost.

Selected species and varieties:
M. floribunda (Japanese flowering crab apple) is a rounded, 15- to 25-foot tree with pink to red buds opening to white or pink fragrant flowers, followed by red or yellow fruit; Zones 5-8. *M. sargentii* (Sargent crab apple) is a spreading, densely branched, 6- to 8-foot-tall shrub with clusters of red buds opening to ½-inch to 1-inch highly fragrant white flowers, and bright red ¼-inch fruit; 'Callaway' grows 15 to 20 feet tall with a rounded canopy and abundant snow white flowers in spring.

CRAPE MYRTLE
Lagerstroemia

Light: full sun	
Plant type: shrub, tree	
Hardiness: Zones 7-9	
Height: 7 to 25 feet	
Soil and Moisture: well-drained, moist	
Interest: flowers, bark	
Care: easy	

◀ Lagerstroemia indica 'Seminole'

Crape myrtle is a reliable, easy-to-grow plant that also looks fantastic in flower. The large clusters of crinkly pink, white, rose, or purple flowers blossom in late summer at a time when little else may be in bloom. In fall, the summer's dark green leaves turn into a painter's palette of red, orange, and yellow. The light gray bark exfoliates as it ages, revealing shades of gray and brown. Crape myrtle is often grown as a specimen or grouped into large screens.

Growing and care:
Plant into well-worked soil generously amended with compost or rotted manure. Prune hard in fall to encourage increased flowering and restrain the plant's vigorous growth. In northern areas crape myrtle is grown as an herbaceous perennial that dies to the ground each winter. Mulch around plant to keep soil moist and reduce heaving.

Selected species and varieties:
L. indica (common crape myrtle) is a fast-growing multistemmed shrub or tree 15 to 25 feet tall, with flower clusters 6 to 8 inches long; 'Natchez' reaches 20 feet tall and wide, with cinnamon brown exfoliating bark and white flower clusters 6 to 12 inches long from early summer to fall, when glossy dark green leaves turn orange and red; 'Seminole' bears medium pink flowers for 6 to 8 weeks beginning in midsummer on a 7- to 8-foot shrub.

CYPRESS
Cupressus

Light: full sun	
Plant type: tree	
Hardiness: Zones 7-9	
Height: 30 to 40 feet	
Soil and Moisture: well-drained, moist to dry	
Interest: foliage	
Care: easy	

◀ Cupressus sempervirens

These graceful, fine-textured trees make handsome specimens, screens, or windbreaks, and add a stately elegance to their surroundings. Their aromatic foliage consists of scalelike leaves closely pressed on braided-cord stems. Reddish brown exfoliating bark becomes dark brown and furrowed with age. Attractive cones with shieldlike scales are 1 inch across.

Growing and care:
Best suited to the West and the Southwest, cypress enjoys mild to hot, dry climates and needs no supplemental water once established. Soil must be perfectly drained, as the trees do poorly in wet soils. Cypress transplants best from container-grown plants, and is generally insect- and disease-free.

Selected species and varieties:
C. glabra [sometimes labeled by nurseries as *C. arizonica,* which is actually a separate species] (smooth-barked Arizona cypress) grows to a dense, bushy pyramid 30 to 40 feet tall and 15 to 20 feet wide with soft green, gray-green, or blue-green foliage. *C. sempervirens* (Italian cypress, Mediterranean cypress) produces a slender column 30 or more feet tall, with horizontal branches and dark green foliage; cultivars include bright green, gold, and blue forms.

DESERT WILLOW
Chilopsis

Light: full sun
Plant type: shrub, tree
Hardiness: Zones 8-10
Height: 10 to 25 feet
Soil and Moisture: well-drained, sandy, dry
Interest: flowers, foliage
Care: easy

◀ Chilopsis linearis

Desert willow is a great ornamental shrub or tree for hot, arid areas. The showy, trumpet-shaped, fragrant spring flowers resembling snapdragons bloom in clusters at the tips of desert willow's branches in spring and often sporadically until fall. Its open, branching, and willowlike leaves, evergreen in milder climates, lend an airy appearance. A heavy crop of thin, foot-long pods persists through winter. Desert willow can be trained into a graceful specimen for dry gardens.

Growing and care:
Native to arid lands of the Southwest, desert willow enjoys light soil that is very well drained. Prune to develop a tree form or to eliminate shagginess. Transplant container-grown plants in spring or late fall and water until the roots establish themselves.

Selected species and varieties:
C. linearis (desert catalpa, flowering willow) is a shrubby tree 10 to 25 feet tall and 10 to 15 feet wide, with interestingly twisted branches bearing narrow 6- to 12-inch-long leaves and fragrant lilac, rosy pink, purple, or white flowers with curled lobes and white or yellow markings.

'DORTMUND' ROSE
Rosa

Light: full sun
Plant type: shrub
Hardiness: Zones 4-10
Height: 7 to 15 feet
Soil and Moisture: well-drained, moist
Interest: flowers, fruit
Care: easy

◀ Rosa kordesii
'Dortmund'

The variety 'Dortmund' is a spectacular climbing rose with rafts of vivid scarlet single blossoms in spring. This *kordesii* hybrid is a very hardy, easy-to-care-for plant with vigorous, thorny canes reaching to 15 feet and attractive glossy green foliage. Each blossom has broad red petals surrounding a white center marked with a tuft of yellow stamens and has a light fragrance. Use 'Dortmund' against a wall or fence for a show-stopping spring display or plant in a rock garden and allow the canes to cascade.

Growing and care:
Plant in well-worked soil that has been lightly amended with organic matter. Fertilize in early spring and again after flowers fade in spring. With vigorous deadheading, blooming continues throughout the growing season. If spent blooms are allowed to remain, flowering ceases and bright orange hips develop.

Selected species and varieties:
R. 'Hamburger Phoenix' is similar in habit to 'Dortmund' but has fragrant, double, bright red flowers in large clusters followed by orange-red hips in late summer and fall; 'Raymond Chenault' has strong 12-foot-tall canes and stunning single red flowers in huge clusters in spring and again in late summer.

ESCALLONIA
Escallonia

Light: full sun	
Plant type: shrub	
Hardiness: Zones 8-10	
Height: 3 to 5 feet	
Soil and Moisture: well-drained, dry to moist	
Interest: flowers, foliage, fragrance	
Care: easy	

◀ E. x langleyensis 'Apple Blossom'

Escallonia is a very attractive, warm-climate shrub that forms an informal mound of glossy, often fragrant evergreen foliage. The pink, white, or red funnel-shaped flowers are arranged in small clusters and bloom profusely over a long season. Escallonia thrives in coastal locations and needs little pruning. It is a good choice for informal hedges or screens.

Growing and care:
Plant escallonia in a loose, well-drained soil that has been amended with some compost or other organic matter. It is tolerant of soils with some salts but does not like high alkalinity. Water well when transplanting. Once established the plants are moderately drought tolerant but should be given extra water during extended dry periods. Do not locate plantings in windy areas.

Selected species and varieties:
E. x *langleyensis* 'Apple Blossom' is a dense, sprawling shrub 3 to 5 feet high, with arching branches bearing large leaves and pink buds opening to pinkish white flowers throughout the warm months. *E.* 'Pride of Donard' has a dense, broad-spreading habit with rosy pink flowers throughout the year in mild climates. *E. rubra* 'C. F. Ball' (red escallonia) is one of the best varieties, with a compact, upright habit reaching 5 feet high. Excellent for hedging, the plant bears very glossy leaves and bright red flowers.

FALSE CYPRESS
Chamaecyparis

Light: full sun	
Plant type: shrub, tree	
Hardiness: Zones 4-8	
Height: 4 to 75 feet	
Soil and Moisture: well-drained, fertile, moist	
Interest: foliage	
Care: easy	

◀ Chamaecyparis obtusa

False cypresses are a diverse group of evergreens that contain some of the most ornamental conifers in the world. The plants range from slow-growing dwarf forms that resemble bonsai to tall, graceful, soft-textured trees. False cypresses have fan-shaped sprays of dark green to golden yellow foliage and beautiful shapes that accent formal gardens, wildflower meadows, and all styles of plantings in between.

Growing and care:
Plant in loosened soil generously amended with organic matter. Transplant container-grown specimens in spring or fall and water well until established. Mulch around base of tree with pine needles or bark chips to retain moisture and keep soil cool. False cypress grows well in many regions and thrives in areas with moist, cool summers and mild winters. Locations with hot, humid summers or heavy soils are not appropriate. The plants should not be placed in windy locations.

Selected species and varieties:
C. obtusa (hinoki false cypress, hinoki cypress) produces a dark green, slender pyramid growing 50 to 75 feet tall; 'Crippsii' forms a broad pyramid with drooping golden yellow branch tips; 'Gracilis' grows 6 to 10 feet tall with a narrow conical form; 'Nana Gracilis' is 4 to 6 feet tall and 3 to 4 feet wide with very dark green foliage arranged in slightly curved sprays.

FIR
Abies

Light: full sun	
Plant type: tree	
Hardiness: Zones 3-7	
Height: 30 to 50 feet	
Soil and Moisture: well-drained, moist	
Interest: foliage	
Care: easy	

◀ Abies concolor

White fir is a majestic tree of mountains and northern forests with soft, gray-green evergreen needles, maroon-purple cones, and a stately pyramidal form. The upper branches are upright in habit; the middle and lower are horizontal to descending. The trees bear flat, wonderfully aromatic needles that yield a homey, slightly resinous fragrance. Greenish or purplish upright cones, up to 6 inches long, mature to a brown hue and fall apart when ripe. White fir is excellent as a specimen plant, or used as a thick, soft-textured screen.

Growing and care:
Plant white fir in deep, sandy or gravelly loams, well amended with organic matter. The plants need little attention and withstand drought, heat, and cold well. Mulch well with shredded bark, woodchips, or leaves.

Selected species and varieties:
A. concolor (white fir, Colorado fir) grows 30 to 50 feet high (but reaches 100 feet under ideal conditions) by 15 to 30 feet wide, with a central trunk and whorled branches, and produces bluish green, grayish green, or silvery blue needles up to 2½ inches long; 'Compacta' is a densely branched dwarf usually 3 feet high, with 1½-inch blue needles, acquiring an attractively irregular form as it matures; 'Violacea' has silvery blue-green needles resembling blue spruce.

FIRETHORN
Pyracantha

Light: full sun	
Plant type: shrub	
Hardiness: Zones 6-9	
Height: 2 to 16 feet	
Soil and Moisture: well-drained, moist	
Interest: flowers, foliage, fruit	
Care: moderate	

◀ Pyracantha coccinea 'Mohave'

Firethorn is as vibrant as its name, with shiny, dark brown branches, plentiful ½-inch thorns, and dark, glossy evergreen or semievergreen leaves. In spring clusters of tiny white flowers are followed by bright, fire red or orange berries that persist through fall. Firethorn adds sparkle to informal hedges, and dresses up walls and trellises when trained into espaliers.

Growing and care:
Plant container-grown specimens in spring or fall in well-worked soil amended with compost or rotted manure. Firethorn grows best in evenly moist soil but is tolerant of dry, summer conditions. Once established, plants should not be moved.

Selected species and varieties:
P. coccinea (scarlet firethorn) has 1- to 1½-inch oval leaves and red-orange fall berries; 'Apache' bears bright red berries on compact, evergreen shrubs to 5 feet tall and 5 feet wide; 'Mohave' is a cold-hardy, disease-resistant, evergreen shrub with heavy crops of berries growing to 12 feet tall and as wide; 'Navajo' has red-orange fruit on dense, 6-foot-round mounds of branches; 'Teton' grows narrow columns of branches 16 feet tall and half as wide with yellow-orange berries.

FLOWERING QUINCE
Chaenomeles

Light:	full sun
Plant type:	shrub
Hardiness:	Zones 4-8
Height:	3 to 10 feet
Soil and Moisture:	well-drained, moist to dry, acidic
Interest:	flowers, fruit
Care:	moderate

◀ Chaenomeles speciosa 'Texas Scarlet'

Flowering quince is an old-fashioned plant that has never lost its popularity. A thorny, rounded, spreading shrub, flowering quince puts on a sparkling spring show when a profusion of showy flowers in a wide range of colors appears before the leaves. The small, yellowish green quincelike fruits that ripen in fall make unforgettable jams and jellies. Budded stems can be used for late-winter arrangements.

Growing and care:
Plant container-grown flowering quince in well-worked soil amended with some organic matter in spring or fall. Prune each spring to remove dead or broken branches and restore shape. Some leaves usually drop in the summer but long periods of wet weather can exaggerate this tendency.

Selected species and varieties:
C. speciosa (common flowering quince, Japanese quince) reaches 6 to 10 feet tall with equal or greater width, usually with red or scarlet but sometimes pink or white flowers and lustrous dark green leaves that open bronzy red; 'Cameo' produces peachy pink double flowers in early spring; 'Jet Trail' has contrail white flowers; 'Nivalis' bears pure white flowers; 'Texas Scarlet' produces profuse tomato red flowers on an attractive, spreading 3- to 5-foot plant.

FORSYTHIA
Forsythia

Light:	full sun
Plant type:	shrub
Hardiness:	Zones 4-9
Height:	4 to 10 feet
Soil and Moisture:	well-drained, moist
Interest:	flowers
Care:	moderate

◀ Forsythia x intermedia

Forsythia is the traditional harbinger of spring, gracing gardens with vibrant yellow flowers about the time the crocus blossoms open. The plants are a standard in shrub borders, masses, and banks, where the fountain-like sprays of yellow blooms are a welcome relief from winter gloom. The budded twigs can be snipped in late winter and easily forced indoors for early floral bouquets.

Growing and care:
Forsythia is easy to transplant from containers, balled and burlapped, or even bareroot, in early spring. Plant in well-worked soil generously amended with organic matter. Water during dry periods. The plants are often hardy into Zone 3 but the flower buds often hardy only to Zone 5.

Selected species and varieties:
F. x *intermedia* (border forsythia) grows 12 feet wide with upright, arching canes that bear 1- to 1½-inch pale to deep yellow flowers and dark green leaves 3 to 5 inches long turning dull olive purple in fall; 'Spectabilis' bears a profusion of richly hued, bright yellow flowers at the stem axils and is easily the showiest-blooming cultivar. *F. suspensa* var. *sieboldii* (weeping forsythia) has an arching habit with long, trailing branches with fewer flowers than border forsythia; 'Northern Sun' is a hardy variety that reliably flowers as far north as Zone 4 with bright, sunny yellow flowers on stems reaching 10 feet.

GOLDEN-RAIN TREE
Koelreuteria

Light:	full sun
Plant type:	tree
Hardiness:	Zones 5-9
Height:	30 to 40 feet
Soil and Moisture:	well-drained, moist
Interest:	flowers, foliage
Care:	easy

◀ K. paniculata
'September'

Adelightful small tree to shade a garden bench, walkway, or patio, golden-rain tree produces arching, wide-spreading branches and airy sprays of yellow flowers in early to midsummer. The dense canopy consists of abundant, large compound leaves that are medium bright green, changing to yellow before dropping in fall. Golden-rain tree adds a tasteful touch to any garden and is useful as a specimen or planted to shade a gazebo or quiet retreat.

Growing and care:
Golden-rain tree is easy to care for and tolerates a wide variety of conditions, including drought. It grows best—about 1½ feet per year—in soil well amended with compost or rotted manure. Provide shelter from wind and prune broken or dead branches in spring.

Selected species and varieties:
K. paniculata (golden-rain tree, varnish tree) has a rounded crown with a spread equal to or greater than its height, bearing 6- to 18-inch-long leaves composed of seven to 15 toothed and lobed leaflets 1 to 3 inches long, purplish red when opening, and flower clusters 12 to 15 inches long and wide; 'September' flowers in late summer and is less hardy than the species; Zones 6-9.

HAWTHORN
Crataegus

Light:	full sun
Plant type:	shrub, tree
Hardiness:	Zones 4-7
Height:	20 to 35 feet
Soil and Moisture:	well-drained, moist
Interest:	flowers, fruit
Care:	moderate

◀ Crataegus viridis
'Winter King'

Hawthorns are neat, small trees or large shrubs that produce flowers in spring, beautifully colored leaves in fall, and attractive fruit through winter. The plants have round crowns of finely toothed leaves and a delicate texture, making them very useful as specimen trees or in a shrub border. The green foliage turns reddish purple in fall. The dainty clusters of small white flowers yield to bright red berries in late summer that persist through winter, if the birds don't get them first. The plants are tolerant of urban conditions and their long thorns make them great for barrier hedges.

Growing and care:
Plant hawthorns in loose, well-worked soil amended with organic matter. The thorns make pruning or shearing difficult, so allow room for the tree or shrub's mature spread. Remove broken or dead branches in spring and prune lightly to shape if desired. Water during dry periods and fertilize in spring just before flowering.

Selected species and varieties:
C. phaenopyrum (Washington hawthorn) is a multiple-stemmed shrub or tree growing to 30 feet with foliage that turns scarlet in fall, and clusters of white flowers in spring. *C. viridis* 'Winter King' (green hawthorn) is a round to vase-shaped tree reaching to 35 feet with lustrous green foliage turning purple or red in fall, and 1-inch bright red fruit from fall through winter.

HONEY LOCUST
Gleditsia

Light: full sun	
Plant type: tree	
Hardiness: Zones 3-9	
Height: 30 to 70 feet	
Soil and Moisture: well-drained, moist to dry	
Interest: foliage	
Care: easy	

◀ Gleditsia triacanthos var. inermis

Honey locust has become one of the most popular shade trees chiefly because it combines beauty with unmatched versatility. The trees develop a wide-spreading canopy of arching branches and bright green ferny foliage, creating light to dappled shade beneath. Small fragrant flowers in late spring are followed by 12- to 18-inch reddish brown to brown strap-shaped pods, usually viewed as a nuisance. In fall the leaves turn golden yellow before falling.

Growing and care:
Honey locusts grow best in moist, rich loam but tolerate acid and alkaline soils, drought, and salt. The trees transplant well and should be set in loosened soil amended with some organic matter. Under average conditions the trees are very vigorous, growing up to 2 feet per year. Recently some serious insect and disease problems have been noted.

Selected species and varieties:
G. triacanthos var. inermis (thornless honey locust, sweet locust) is highly variable in size, from 30 to 70 feet tall and equally wide ranging in spread, with a short trunk and an open crown bearing doubly compound leaves with oblong leaflets 1/3 to 1 1/2 inches long and greenish yellow flowers; 'Imperial' [also called 'Impcole'] is a seedless version that grows to 35 feet high; Zones 4-7.

INDIAN HAWTHORN
Raphiolepis

Light: full sun	
Plant type: shrub	
Hardiness: Zones 9-10	
Height: 3 to 5 feet	
Soil and Moisture: well-drained, moist	
Interest: flowers, foliage, fragrance	
Care: moderate	

◀ Raphiolepis indica

Indian hawthorn is a dense, glossy-leaved evergreen shrub generously decorated with loose, showy clusters of apple-blossom-like fragrant flowers in early spring. The pink or white flowers yield to purplish to blue-black berries that ripen in fall and linger though winter. This slow-growing, sturdy shrub is often used in low hedges and borders or as background for a flower bed. It also makes a good container plant for the patio or deck.

Growing and care:
Pinch the tips of growing branches to encourage a bushy habit and prune to shape if plant becomes leggy. Water regularly and provide extra moisture during dry periods. Once established, Indian hawthorn withstands drought and is tolerant of salt and seaside conditions.

Selected species and varieties:
R. indica forms a 3- to 5-foot-wide dense mound of 2- to 3-inch-long dark green lance-shaped leaves with toothy margins clustered at the ends of the branches, sometimes turning a dull purplish green in winter, and 1/2-inch-wide fragrant white flowers blushed with pink toward the center with red stamens; 'White Enchantress' is a dwarf form with single white flowers.

'JOHN CABOT' ROSE
Rosa

Light: full sun	
Plant type: shrub	
Hardiness: Zones 3-10	
Height: 4 to 10 feet	
Soil and Moisture: well-drained, fertile, moist	
Interest: flowers, fragrance	
Care: easy	

◀ Rosa kordesii 'John Cabot'

This beautiful, versatile, easy-to-care-for rose is just about perfect. 'John Cabot' is one of the Canadian Explorer series and bears satin red, nicely fragrant double flowers on strong, gently arching 6-foot canes covered with dark green glossy foliage. The plants are disease-free and will grow just about anywhere. 'John Cabot' looks beautiful when trained along a fence or over a trellis and is outstanding when planted near plants with blue flowers or gray foliage.

Growing and care:

Plant 'John Cabot' in well-worked soil that has been amended with organic matter. The plants are slow to establish and should be regularly watered for the first 2 growing seasons. Prune out dead or damaged canes in late winter or early spring. Deadhead faded flowers as they occur. 'John Cabot' is not troubled by disease or insects and is virtually trouble-free.

Selected species and varieties:

R. kordesii 'Henry Kelsey' resembles 'Don Juan' but is much hardier, with dark, velvet red double blossoms marked with yellow stamens on strong 8-foot canes; 'William Baffin' is nearly as perfect a plant as 'John Cabot', with abundant sprays of strawberry pink blossoms from spring to fall on arching 8- to 10-foot canes.

LANTANA
Lantana

Light: full sun	
Plant type: shrub	
Hardiness: Zones 9-10	
Height: 1 to 6 feet	
Soil and Moisture: well-drained, moist	
Interest: flowers, foliage, fragrance	
Care: moderate	

◀ Lantana montevidensis

The abundant flowers of lantana are arranged in perky little bouquets that can't help but brighten the garden. The blossoms appear from spring through summer in pastel shades of white, pink, yellow, and lavender at the tips of somewhat stiff stems lined with cool green, pungently aromatic foliage. Lantanas are beautiful accents for rock gardens or when allowed to flow over stone walls. In the North they are often planted in containers, used in patio or deck displays, and brought indoors for the winter. The flowers are very attractive to hummingbirds and butterflies.

Growing and care:

Start seed 6 to 8 weeks before planting out. Space plants 1½ feet apart. They can be trained to standards, and are easily dug and potted in fall for indoor winter flowering. Pinch young plants to encourage branching. The plants sometimes suffer from infestations of whitefly or spider mites.

Selected species and varieties:

L. camara (yellow sage) is a 2- to 6-foot shrub with dark, hairy leaves and flat-topped clusters of tiny flowers that start yellow and turn orange-red; 'Confetti' bears white, pink, and red flowers all on the same plant. *L. montevidensis* [also listed as *L. sellowiana*] (weeping lantana) grows to 2½ feet with a mounding habit, dark green leaves, and flat-topped clusters of tiny yellow flowers.

LEYLAND CYPRESS
x Cupressocyparis

Light: full sun

Plant type: tree

Hardiness: Zones 6-10

Height: 60 to 70 feet

Soil and Moisture: well-drained, moist to dry

Interest: foliage

Care: easy

◀ x Cupressocyparis leylandii 'Silver Dust'

A dense, towering, very vigorous columnar or pyramidal tree, Leyland cypress is a hybrid of *Cupressus* and *Chamaecyparis.* It produces some of the fastest-growing and finest-textured screen or hedge plants available. The fanlike arrangement of bluish green scalelike needles appears soft and feathery. In addition to its versatile use in the landscape, Leyland cypress is also a very popular Christmas tree in the South.

Growing and care:
Leyland cypress grows best in moist, well-drained, moderately fertile loams but grows very well in almost any soil. Provide protection from drying winter winds. It is best transplanted from container-grown plants. Leyland cypress is virtually pest- and disease-free and is resistant to salt spray and cold damage.

Selected species and varieties:
x *C. leylandii* (Leyland cypress) is a cross between *Cupressus macrocarpa* (Monterey cypress) and *Chamaecyparis nootkatensis* (Alaska cedar) that grows 3 feet a year or more to 70 feet tall and usually 10 to 18 feet wide, with reddish brown scaly bark; cultivars include silvery green, variegated, and golden yellow forms; 'Silver Dust' has creamy white markings on green foliage.

LILAC
Syringa

Light: full sun

Plant type: shrub, tree

Hardiness: Zones 3-8

Height: 4 to 15 feet

Soil and Moisture: well-drained, moist

Interest: flowers, foliage, fragrance

Care: moderate

◀ Syringa vulgaris 'Sarah Sands'

L ilacs are sturdy, elegantly old-fashioned favorites with dense, grapelike clusters of fragrant single or double flowers in shades of white, lavender, and red in late spring. The pairs of pointed, oval dark green leaves add medium foliage texture to the garden after the flowers have faded. Lilacs make attractive specimens or informal hedges, and add a nostalgic ambiance to mixed-shrub borders.

Growing and care:
Lilacs grow best in loamy soil, and benefit from annual additions of compost and extra moisture during dry spells. Prune older stems with reduced flower production immediately after flowering, and deadhead faded flowers as well. Lilacs often suffer from powdery mildew on their leaves during summer, so plant them where they will receive good air circulation.

Selected species and varieties:
S. vulgaris is an erect, spreading, 8- to 15-foot shrub with 2- to 5-inch leaves concentrated near the top of the crown, and 4- to 8-inch clusters of extremely fragrant flowers in colors ranging from classic lilac to white and shades of blue, purple, or red; 'Albert F. Holden' is bicolored; 'Blue Boy' is heat tolerant and has blue flowers; 'Edith Cavell' has double white flowers; 'Sarah Sands' has purple flowers; Zones 3-7.

LOQUAT
Eriobotrya

Light:	full sun
Plant type:	shrub, tree
Hardiness:	Zones 8-10
Height:	15 to 25 feet
Soil and Moisture:	well-drained, moist
Interest:	foliage, fruit, fragrance
Care:	easy

◀ Eriobotrya japonica

Loquat is a gorgeous shrub or tree with lustrous, large evergreen leaves and deliciously fragrant wintertime flowers. In very warm regions the plants bear quantities of tasty yellow fruit. Loquats are often used as street trees or specimens, or are trained as espalier and grown as container plants for more northern patio gardens. Tucked among the coarsely textured leaves are stiff panicles of fragrant, but not showy, woolly flowers in fall or winter, and by late spring edible yellow-orange fruits decorate the plant.

Growing and care:
Loquat is easy to grow. Plant in well-worked soil amended with organic matter, and water well until established. Loquats will adapt to slightly alkaline soil and weather droughts reliably once established. Provide protection from wind. Feed only lightly. Rampant new growth is subject to fire blight.

Selected species and varieties:
E. japonica (Chinese loquat, Japanese plum, Japanese medlar) is a tree or rounded multistemmed shrub 15 to 25 feet tall and wide, with supple branches bearing heavily veined 6- to 12-inch-long toothy leaves that are deep green above and a rust color on the undersides, with five-petaled, dull white ½-inch-wide flowers borne in 6-inch clusters and covered with brown fuzz. In the southern half of its range, it bears 2-inch pear-shaped fruit.

'LOUISE ODIER' ROSE
Rosa

Light:	full sun
Plant type:	shrub rose
Hardiness:	Zones 5-9
Height:	4½ to 6 feet
Soil and Moisture:	well-drained, fertile, moist
Interest:	flowers, fragrance
Care:	moderate

◀ Rosa 'Louise Odier'

The very large, richly fragrant blossoms of 'Louise Odier' roses are wonderful additions to the flower garden. The plants are vigorous growers with strongly upright canes reaching 5 feet tall. In midseason and again in fall the bushes bear large, 3- to 4-inch-wide, very double rose pink blossoms that are enchantingly fragrant. 'Louise Odier' is excellent for the shrub or rose border and makes a good companion for perennial flowers.

Growing and care:
Plant 'Louise Odier' in well-worked soil generously amended with compost or other organic matter. Prune in late winter or early spring, cutting canes back by one-third and removing any dead or damaged stems. Fertilize lightly in spring and again as flower buds begin to open. The plants are susceptible to black spot.

Selected species and varieties:
R. 'Madame Isaac Pereire' is a bourbon rose with vigorous 6-foot very thorny canes and glossy green leaves. In midseason the bushes are covered with large, fully double, intensely fragrant deep pink flowers.

'NEARLY WILD' ROSE
Rosa

Light: full sun	
Plant type: shrub	
Hardiness: Zones 4-10	
Height: 2 to 4 feet	
Soil and Moisture: well-drained, fertile, moist	
Interest: flowers, fragrance	
Care: moderate	

◀ Rosa 'Nearly Wild'

The small, tapered buds of 'Nearly Wild' open to rose pink blooms that have five petals and are very fragrant. The flowers occur prolifically along the length of each stem. The main flowering season is spring, but some blooms appear through summer. Plants are very hardy, compact, and bushy, often wider than tall. This rose is very effective when planted in masses on sunny banks. Placed in front of taller shrubs, it provides good foreground color, and it makes a fine container specimen.

Growing and care:
Space plants 2½ to 3 feet apart in soil that has been amended with organic matter. Prune hard in late fall and remove all fallen leaves and twigs from around base of plant. Fertilize after blooming in spring and water regularly. Mulch with bark chips in spring and fall. 'Nearly Wild' tolerates slightly alkaline soil and is very hardy.

Selected species and varieties:
R. 'Dr. W. van Fleet' is a parent of 'Nearly Wild' and bears pointed buds opening to reveal large, double pink, very fragrant flowers. Foliage is glossy dark green with long canes easily trained to trellises or fences; 'Leuchtstern', the other parent of 'Nearly Wild', produces single, deep rose pink blossoms in small clusters atop 8- to 10-foot-tall canes.

OLEASTER
Elaeagnus

Light: full sun	
Plant type: tree	
Hardiness: Zones 2-9	
Height: 10 to 20 feet	
Soil and Moisture: well-drained, moist to dry	
Interest: flowers, foliage, fragrance	
Care: easy	

◀ Elaeagnus angustifolia

Oleasters are valued as landscape plants for difficult sites because they are extremely adaptable. Their silvery gray foliage contrasts well with that of green-leaved plants. The small but very fragrant flowers attract bees and butterflies in late spring to early summer, and the fall fruit brings a wide variety of birds to the garden. Oleasters are excellent as a windbreak, hedge, or accent in a shrub border, or naturalized in a wildflower meadow. They are frequently planted along roadsides to provide food and shelter for wildlife.

Growing and care:
Oleasters adapt to a wide range of soil types but perform best in a light, sandy loam. They tolerate wind, drought, alkaline soil, and seaside conditions. They transplant easily, grow rapidly, and, although pruning is not necessarily required, they respond well to shearing. For use as a hedge, plant shrubs 3 to 5 feet apart.

Selected species and varieties:
E. angustifolia (Russian olive) is usually a 12- to 15-foot-tall shrub with equal or greater spread, but may grow to 20 feet as a single-trunk tree. Its inconspicuous but very fragrant flowers are followed in late summer and fall by ½-inch yellow fruit coated with silvery scales, and 1½- to 3-inch gray to silvery green leaves that provide dramatic color contrast in the garden.

PEAR
Pyrus

Light:	full sun
Plant type:	tree
Hardiness:	Zones 5-8
Height:	30 to 40 feet
Soil and Moisture:	well-drained, moist to dry
Interest:	flowers, foliage
Care:	moderate

◀ Pyrus calleryana
'Chanticleer'

Callery pears are picturesque, very showy trees that burst with abundant white flowers in early spring. Their lustrous dark green leaves form a dense, symmetrical canopy until midfall, when they turn shades of sunset red and wine purple. The small rounded fruit persists for many weeks and is enjoyed by many species of birds. Use callery pears as an accent in gardens, planted in masses as screens, or as an easy-care shade tree.

Growing and care:
Callery pears adapt to almost any well-drained soil and tolerate drought and pollution better than most flowering trees. If pruning is needed it should be done in late winter while tree is still dormant. They tend to lose their tight form after 20 years or so, due to many branches arising close together on the trunk. 'Chanticleer' has stronger crotches than other cultivars, is less subject to snow and ice damage, and shows good resistance to fire blight. Transplant in spring or fall when plants are not leafed out.

Selected species and varieties:
P. calleryana 'Chanticleer' (callery pear) grows 35 feet high to 16 feet wide in 15 years, with a pyramidal crown narrower than some other cultivars in this species, bearing ⅓-inch-wide flowers in profuse 3-inch clusters and rounded oval leaves to 3½ inches long.

PERSIAN PARROTIA
Parrotia

Light:	full sun
Plant type:	small tree
Hardiness:	Zones 4-8
Height:	20 to 40 feet
Soil and Moisture:	well-drained, moist
Interest:	foliage, bark
Care:	easy

◀ Parrotia persica

Parrotia is one of the best small trees for the yard and garden. The trunk and branches grow in a distinctive, very attractive form with brownish bark that exfoliates as it ages, revealing underbark in shades of green, gray, and brown. Tiny, inconspicuous flowers with red stamens blossom along the younger branches before the leaves emerge in spring. The oval leaves have a red tint when unfolding that cools into green, then brightens into yellows, reds, and oranges in fall. It is virtually pest-free and tolerates even city conditions. As a specimen tree, few can compare.

Growing and care:
Plant Persian parrotia in well-worked, slightly acidic soil that has been generously amended with organic matter. Leave space for its mature spread, as these trees grow best if left undisturbed once established. Plants are drought tolerant but should receive extra water during long periods of dry weather.

Selected species and varieties:
P. persica grows to 30 feet tall with a spread as wide or wider and with 3- to 4-inch-long lustrous green leaves in brilliant shades of yellow and orange, turning rosy pink and scarlet in fall.

PINE
Pinus

Light: full sun

Plant type: tree

Hardiness: Zones 2-10

Height: 6 to 100 feet or more

Soil and Moisture: well-drained to heavy, wet to dry

Interest: foliage, fruit

Care: easy

◀ Pinus strobus

Simply stated, there is a pine for nearly every garden or yard. This diverse genus of needle-leaved evergreens includes picturesque and stately trees, low-growing, spreading forms, and unique dwarf specimens.

Growing and care:

Pines often develop a deep taproot and should be transplanted only when young. The area around the root zone should be mulched with pine needles yearly to retain soil acidity. Bristlecone pine does well in poor, dry soils but suffers in drying winds or pollution. Shore pine grows naturally in boggy areas. Japanese red pine prefers well-drained, slightly acid soil. Afghanistan pine and pinyon thrive in desert conditions; the former also tolerates salt spray. Mountain pine needs moist, deep loam. Austrian pine tolerates alkaline soils, moderate drought, salt, and urban pollution but grows best where moisture is assured. White pine grows best in moist loams but is also found in dry, shallow soils and wet bogs; it is intolerant of air pollutants, salt, and highly alkaline soil. Japanese black pine thrives in moist loams but is tolerant of sand and salt.

Selected species and varieties:

P. aristata (bristlecone pine) is a very slow grower, some examples of which are, at more than 4,000 years old, the oldest living things on earth. It grows 8 to 20 feet tall with bluish white to dark green needles; Zones 4-7.

P. contorta var. *contorta* (shore pine) is a 25- to 30-foot-tall tree with twisted trunk and branches; hardy to Zone 7. *P. densiflora* 'Umbraculifera' (Japanese red pine) has an upright, spreading habit, with an umbrella-like crown. It grows to 9 feet tall or more, with exfoliating orange bark and bright to dark green needles; Zones 3-7. *P. edulis* [also classified as *P. cembroides* var. *edulis*] (pinyon, nut pine) is slow growing, 10 to 20 feet tall, with horizontal branches, an often flat crown, and dark green needles; hardy to Zone 5. *P. eldarica* (Afghanistan pine) is fast growing, 30 to 80 feet tall, with dark green needles to 6 inches long; hardy to Zone 7. *P. mugo* (mountain pine, mugo pine) forms a broad pyramid to 20 feet tall or a low, broad, bushy shrub, with usually medium green foliage; Zones 2-7. *P. nigra* (Austrian pine) has a pyramidal shape broadening over time to a flat top with heavy, spreading branches, 50 to 60 feet tall by 20 to 40 feet wide, with dark green needles; Zones 4-7. *P. palustris* (longleaf pine, southern yellow pine, pitch pine) is a sparsely branched tree, 55 to 90 feet tall, bearing needles to 9 inches long on mature trees, and 10-inch cones; Zones 7-10. *P. strobus* (white pine) is a low-branched tree growing 50 to more than 100 feet tall and half as wide. It is pyramidal when young but becomes broad crowned with age, producing a dense growth of bluish green needles; 'Pendula' is a weeping form with long, drooping branches; 'UConn' grows to 20 feet with a thick-branching, heavily needled conical form that stays dense with no pruning; Zones 3-8. *P. thunbergiana* (Japanese black pine) forms an irregular pyramid usually 20 to 40 feet tall, with sometimes drooping, wide-spreading branches bearing dark green, crowded, twisted needles 2½ to 7 inches long, and 1½- to 2½-inch cones; Zones 5-7.

PISTACHIO
Pistacia

Light: full sun	
Plant type: tree	
Hardiness: Zones 6-9	
Height: 30 to 35 feet	
Soil and Moisture: well-drained, moist to dry	
Interest: foliage, fruit	
Care: easy	

◀ Pistacia chinensis

One of the best deciduous trees for fall foliage in the South, Chinese pistache has lustrous dark green compound leaves that turn a brilliant orange to orange-red even in hot, arid conditions. Tiny clusters of inedible fruits turn from red and to robin's-egg blue when mature. Use Chinese pistache for shade, or along sidewalks and garden paths.

Growing and care:
Chinese pistache grows best in moist, well-drained soil, where it may achieve 2 to 3 feet per year, but it tolerates other soil types and drought. Young trees sometimes go through a gangly stage and should be pruned to a single leader. Once corrective pruning is done, Chinese pistache usually needs little other special attention and is disease- and insect-free.

Selected species and varieties:
P. chinensis (Chinese pistache) grows 30 to 35 feet high with an equal spread. It is rather awkward in youth but eventually oval to rounded, bearing 10 to 12 leaflets, 2 to 4 inches long per leaf, and inconspicuous male and female flowers on separate trees.

ROCK ROSE
Cistus

Light: full sun	
Plant type: shrub	
Hardiness: Zones 8-10	
Height: 3 to 5 feet	
Soil and Moisture: well-drained, dry	
Interest: flowers, foliage	
Care: easy	

◀ Cistus x purpureus

Rock roses have an eye-catching beauty that provides a memorable accent to the garden. The flowers are stunning, with roselike petals colored in warm shades of red, pink, and white usually marked with darker spots near the golden centers. In addition to their beauty, rock roses are versatile, tough shrubs that grow equally well in coastal gardens and desert plantings. They are useful in rock gardens or mixed borders, massed, or as a ground cover on banks. The leaves of rock rose are nicely fragrant and resist burning, making the plant a top choice for landscapes near areas prone to fire.

Growing and care:
Rock roses grow well in poor, dry soil and accept heat, ocean spray, and alkaline or even slightly acid soils. They are most often grown along the West Coast. Transplant container-grown plants in spring or late fall. Water until established.

Selected species and varieties:
C. x *hybridus* (white rock rose) bears 1½-inch-wide white flowers with yellow centers in late spring and crinkly gray-green leaves to 2 inches long on a shrub 3 to 5 feet high and wide, sometimes spreading 6 to 8 feet. *C.* x *purpureus* (orchid rock rose) is a compact shrub 4 feet tall and wide, with wrinkled dark green leaves 1 to 2 inches long, and 3-inch-wide reddish purple flowers in early to midsummer, each petal with a red blotch at its base.

RUGOSA ROSE
Rosa

Light: full sun	
Plant type: shrub	
Hardiness: Zones 3-8	
Height: 4 to 6 feet	
Soil and Moisture: well-drained, moist to dry	
Interest: flowers, fragrance	
Care: easy	

◀ Rosa rugosa 'Alba'

Rugosa roses are very reliable, easy-to-grow roses that are as hardy as they are beautiful. The plants bear large, single, softly fragrant rose pink blossoms nearly continually from late spring to fall. Rugosa roses have an informal, mounding habit with gently arching, prickly canes and dark green, slightly wrinkled leaves that turn bronze in autumn. The plants are well known for producing very large, scarlet-colored hips that persist into winter. Rugosa roses naturalize readily and are excellent for wildflower meadows, seaside plantings, or city environments.

Growing and care:
Plant rugosa roses in a bright, sunny spot in loosened well-drained soil. The plants thrive in hot, dry locations and need little care once established. They do poorly in wet sites or heavy soil. Prune canes back by one-third in winter. Rugosa roses are virtually pest- and disease-free.

Selected species and varieties:
R. rugosa 'Alba' bears beautiful, pure white single flowers from spring to fall on spreading 4-foot canes. The dark green leaves yellow in fall; 'Rubra' bears magenta-purple flowers continuously from spring to fall and red hips in autumn.

'SEA FOAM' ROSE
Rosa

Light: full sun	
Plant type: shrub	
Hardiness: Zones 4-9	
Height: 2 to 3 feet	
Soil and Moisture: well-drained, moist to moderately dry	
Interest: flowers	
Care: easy	

◀ Rosa 'Sea Foam'

Easy to care for, 'Sea Foam' splashes forth a seemingly endless supply of double, snow white flowers from summer to fall. The vigorous canes have a low-growing, spreading habit, reaching about 3 feet high and twice as wide with small, dark, glossy leaves. 'Sea Foam' is stunning when planted in masses over slopes or in wildflower meadows, and is well suited for use as a low hedge or specimen plant. The blossoms make good cut flowers for summer floral arrangements.

Growing and care:
Plant 'Sea Foam' in well-worked soil that has been amended with some organic matter. For mass plantings or hedges set plants 3 to 4 feet apart. Fertilize in early spring and again after first flush of flowers have faded. Provide extra water during dry periods. Prune old or crowded canes every 2 to 3 years.

Selected species and varieties:
R. 'Fiona' has a low, mounding habit with double, nearly ever-blooming rich red flowers; 'Two Sisters' forms dense thickets of glossy green leaves and arching canes reaching to 4 feet high and 6 feet wide with double pink flowers that fade to antique white.

SERVICEBERRY
Amelanchier

Light: full sun	
Plant type: shrub, tree	
Hardiness: Zones 4-9	
Height: 2 to 40 feet	
Soil and Moisture: well-drained, moist to dry	
Interest: flowers, foliage, fruit	
Care: easy	

◀ Amelanchier alnifolia

Serviceberries have billowy clusters of dainty five-petaled small white blooms in early spring followed in summer by small red to black tasty fruit. The oval leaves emerge purplish green in spring, turn green in summer, and finally change to dramatic shades of yellow, apricot, and red in fall. The plant's delicate form and light gray bark add interest to the winter garden. Serviceberries can be grown as specimen trees or used to great effect in sunny wildflower meadows.

Growing and care:

Serviceberries are easy-to-grow plants that thrive everywhere from stream banks to open woodlands and along rocky mountain cliffs. In the garden they tolerate a wide range of moisture conditions, although a well-drained, evenly moist soil is best. Propagate serviceberries by seed. Stoloniferous types can also be propagated by root cuttings or by separating offshoots.

Selected species and varieties:

A. alnifolia is a 3- to 6-foot-tall shrub that spreads by stolons to form colonies, with white midspring flowers and small black fruit; Zones 5-8. *A. arborea* (downy serviceberry) is 20 to 30 feet tall with pendulous 2- to 4-inch flower clusters in midspring, small red fruit that turns dark purple, and gray-green leaves that turn orange to deep red in fall.

SWEETBRIAR ROSE
Rosa

Light: full sun	
Plant type: shrub	
Hardiness: Zones 4-8	
Height: 4 to 14 feet	
Soil and Moisture: well-drained, moist	
Interest: flowers, fragrance, fruit	
Care: easy	

◀ Rosa eglanteria

Sweetbriar is a very popular species rose that has been grown in gardens for more than 400 years. The single blush pink flowers are sweetly fragrant while the dark, glossy green leaves have an aroma all their own, filling the garden with a fruity aroma when bruised. In fall the long canes are decorated with bright red hips. This large, vigorous rose has a rambling, shrubby habit and looks beautiful when naturalized in wildflower meadows or planted as an informal barrier hedge.

Growing and care:

Plant sweetbriar in loosened soil in either spring or fall. For hedges set plants about 4 feet apart. Prune to control growth or to shape plants. Every 2 to 4 years remove older canes at ground level to invigorate plants. Sweetbriar is rarely troubled by insects or diseases.

Selected species and varieties:

R. eglanteria 'Amy Robsart' bears deep pink, fragrant semidouble blossoms in spring and bright red hips in late summer to fall; 'Greenmantle' has stunning vivid scarlet single flowers in spring; 'Manning's Blush' produces abundant whitish pink, fragrant double flowers in spring on compact 4-foot-tall plants with apple-scented dark green leaves.

SWEET GUM
Liquidambar

Light: full sun	
Plant type: tree	
Hardiness: Zones 5-9	
Height: 60 to 120 feet	
Soil and Moisture: well-drained, moist to wet	
Interest: foliage	
Care: easy	

◀ Liquidambar styraciflua

The sweet gum is a neatly conical, very stately tree with star-shaped medium green leaves that turn lovely shades of yellow, purple, and scarlet and linger late into fall. The bark is deeply furrowed and resembles cork. The small, spiny globe-shaped fruits drop in late fall to early spring, which adds adventure to late-season walks in the grass. Its name is derived from its fragrant, gummy sap, used in making perfume.

Growing and care:
Sweet gum is native to rich, moist bottom lands but grows well in a wide variety of soil types. The roots need plenty of room to develop and the tree can get quite large. Plant in spring in soil amended with peat moss or leaf mold. Sweet gum usually takes 2 to 5 years to become established, during which time it should be watered regularly.

Selected species and varieties:
L. styraciflua (American sweet gum, red gum, bilsted) has a narrow pyramidal habit when young, maturing into a semirounded crown with a spread two-thirds that height. The branches are edged with corky wings and bear glossy, rich, medium green leaves 4 to 7½ inches long and wide, with five to seven finely serrated, pointed lobes; 'Aurora' has leaves marked with golden yellow variegation in summer, turning vivid orange and red in fall.

'TOUCH OF CLASS' ROSE
Rosa

Light: full sun	
Plant type: shrub rose	
Hardiness: Zones 5-9	
Height: 4 to 5 feet	
Soil and Moisture: well-drained, moist, fertile	
Interest: flowers	
Care: moderate	

◀ Rosa 'Touch of Class'

This hybrid tea rose produces spiraled orange buds that take on a coral and cream shading as they open, eventually evolving to pink. Flowers are 4½ to 5½ inches across and double, but have little or no fragrance. They are borne singly on long stems, making them good candidates for long-lasting indoor arrangements. The dark green, semiglossy foliage provides an attractive contrast to the showy blooms, although the leaves are prone to mildew. Tall and upright, the 'Touch of Class' is well suited to beds and borders, and flowers over a lengthy season.

Growing and care:
Plant 'Touch of Class' in sunny, well-drained sites. Work in organic matter and fertilize after pruning and again after first bloom. Prune in late winter or early spring to remove damaged canes and disease spores. Add a layer of compost each year. Deadhead spent blooms to encourage more blooming. Mulch to suppress weeds and, in Zone 5, to protect roots in winter.

Selected species and varieties:
R. 'Queen Elizabeth' is an ever-blooming rose with large, clear pink double flowers in attractive sprays on upright 6-foot-tall canes.

TREE PEONY
Paeonia

Light: full sun	
Plant type: shrub	
Hardiness: Zones 3-8	
Height: 4 to 5 feet	
Soil and Moisture: well-drained, fertile, moist	
Interest: flowers, fragrance	
Care: difficult	

◀ Paeonia suffruticosa

In the world of gardening the tree peony is in a class by itself. Native to eastern Asia, these regal, mounded, multibranched shrubs bear huge 6-inch-wide flowers of incredible beauty. The showy springtime blossoms may be single, semidouble, or double, and they come in shades of white, pink, red, or yellow. Tree peonies are not easy to grow and require patience and careful tending.

Growing and care:
Plant tree peonies in midfall in well-worked, near neutral soil generously amended with compost. Provide afternoon shade in the South. Water regularly, especially during dry periods. Prune out old and diseased wood, being careful to disinfect the pruning shears to avoid transmission of diseases. Fertilize in spring before and after flowering with a well-balanced fertilizer. Avoid using animal manures on tree peonies. Mulch around base of plant to keep roots cool and retain soil moisture. Stake blossoming branches to avoid breakage.

Selected species and varieties:
P. suffruticosa bears 6- to 10-inch-wide midspring flowers from white to pink to deep red and yellow with crinkled, satiny petals often bearing a red blotch at their bases. Large, deeply lobed medium green leaves turn yellowish green in fall on 4- to 5-foot woody stems; 'Souvenir de Maxine' bears very large, fully double golden yellow blossoms marked with red in spring.

TULIP TREE
Liriodendron

Light: full sun	
Plant type: tree	
Hardiness: Zones 4-9	
Height: 70 to 100 feet	
Soil and Moisture: well-drained to heavy, moist	
Interest: flowers, foliage	
Care: easy	

◀ Liriodendron tulipifera

Tulip trees are very attractive, vigorous trees that grow into towering giants up to 100 feet tall. The plants have a neat columnar to oval shape with distinctive, hand-shaped, bright green foliage that turns golden yellow in fall. In mid- to late spring, tuliplike greenish white flowers with a deep orange blotch at the base of the petals appear high on the tree after the foliage unfurls. Conelike clusters of winged fruit persist into winter.

Growing and care:
Plant tulip trees in moist, deep loam with plenty of room to grow. They prefer slightly acid soils but will tolerate neutral to slightly alkaline ones. In some regions the trees are prone to damage from ice and snow. In ideal conditions tulip trees may grow 2½ to 3 feet per year.

Selected species and varieties:
L. tulipifera (yellow poplar, tulip magnolia, tulip poplar, whitewood) is fast growing with a spread of 35 to 50 feet and the potential of topping 100 feet tall. It is pyramidal when young, bearing lobed leaves up to 8 inches wide and long that open early in spring, and cup-shaped yellow-green, white, and orange flowers 2½ inches wide with six petals, borne singly at or near branch tips.

'TUSCANY' ROSE
Rosa

Light: full sun	
Plant type: shrub	
Hardiness: Zones 4-10	
Height: 3 to 4 feet	
Soil and Moisture: well-drained, fertile, moist	
Interest: flowers, fragrance	
Care: easy	

◀ Rosa 'Tuscany'

A high-quality rose, 'Tuscany' is recognizable for its velvet red, richly fragrant semidouble petals surrounding a golden yellow splash of stamens in the center. The vigorous plants have a tidy, rounded form with slightly arching 2- to 3-foot canes covered with dark green leaves. The blossoms are produced abundantly for a few weeks in spring with no repeat in fall. 'Tuscany' is ideal for small borders or when used in kitchen or herb gardens.

Growing and care:
Plant in loosened soil that has been well amended with compost or rotted manure. Fertilize in early spring when growth begins and again after flowering season has passed. Prune to shape while plant is dormant, and remove older canes every other year. Black spot sometimes occurs on the leaves in humid weather but is seldom a serious problem.

Selected species and varieties:
R. 'Superb Tuscan' [also called 'Tuscany Superb'] produces large, well-formed, loosely double burgundy red flowers with yellow centers in late spring on vigorous canes reaching 3 to 4 feet high.

VIRGINIA ROSE
Rosa

Light: full sun	
Plant type: shrub	
Hardiness: Zones 3-7	
Height: 3 to 5 feet	
Soil and Moisture: well-drained, moist	
Interest: flowers, foliage, fruit	
Care: moderate	

◀ Rosa virginiana

Virginia rose is a graceful, hardy rose that is easy to care for, providing the garden with beautiful flowers, bright fall foliage, and colorful, tasty fruit. The plants burst into bloom in late spring to early summer, the long, arching canes sprinkled with single, rose pink flowers. In fall the leaves turn a brilliant scarlet-orange and the stems carry the plump, red rose hips well into winter. Virginia rose is excellent in wildflower meadows or when combined with perennials in beds and borders.

Growing and care:
Plant Virginia rose in well-drained soil generously amended with compost or rotted manure. Allow plants to develop long, arching canes in open areas, or prune canes to fit in smaller spaces. Cut back older plants to the ground to encourage new growth. Virginia rose tolerates salt spray and sandy soils.

Selected species and varieties:
R. carolina (pasture rose) is similar to Virginia rose, with vigorous 6-foot-tall canes, medium green leaves, and single pink flowers in late spring or early summer followed by red fruits; var. alba bears white flowers; var. plena has double pink blossoms; Zones 4-9.

YELLOWWOOD
Cladrastis

Light: full sun

Plant type: tree

Hardiness: Zones 4-8

Height: 30 to 50 feet

Soil and Moisture: well-drained, moist

Interest: flowers, foliage, bark

Care: moderate

◀ Cladrastis kentukea

An excellent deciduous shade tree for small landscapes, yellowwood produces long, hanging panicles of fragrant white flowers in mid- to late spring and a broad canopy of bright green foliage that turns a warm yellow in fall. The open, delicate branches grow in a zigzag pattern, creating a light, airy form. In winter the smooth gray bark contrasts well to the white snow. The color of the interior wood, which is a rich yellow, gives the tree its name.

Growing and care:

Although it occurs naturally in rich, limestone soils, American yellowwood adapts to a wide range of soil types, from acid to alkaline, and is remarkably pest-free. Once established, it is drought tolerant. Prune only in summer, to prevent heavy sap bleeding. Cable branches that develop weak crotches.

Selected species and varieties:

C. kentukea [formerly called *C. lutea*] (American yellowwood, Kentucky yellowwood, virgilia) has a low-branching habit with a rounded crown 40 to 55 feet wide, producing 3- to 4-inch-long compound leaves opening bright yellowish green before darkening slightly later, with flower clusters up to 14 inches long, and thin brown seedpods 4 to 5 inches long in fall.

ZELKOVA
Zelkova

Light: full sun

Plant type: tree

Hardiness: Zones 5-8

Height: 50 to 80 feet

Soil and Moisture: well-drained, moist

Interest: foliage

Care: easy

◀ Zelkova serrata

Japanese zelkova is an elegant tree with a symmetrical, vase-shaped habit similar to that of an elm, but with no disease problems. This easy-care plant has smooth gray bark on young trees that exfoliates in mature specimens. The rough-textured, toothed dark green leaves turn a warm russet yellow in fall. This tree, with its noble form, is perfect as a shade or specimen tree and even looks great in winter when the garden is full of snow.

Growing and care:

Japanese zelkova grows best in deep, moist, fertile soil. Plant in spring or fall and water regularly during the first growing season. Mulch to conserve soil moisture, and provide extra water during extended dry periods. Once established, the tree tolerates wind, drought, and pollution and is resistant to storm damage.

Selected species and varieties:

Z. serrata (Japanese zelkova, saw-leaf zelkova) reaches 50 to 80 feet high and wide, with ascending branches bearing 2- to 5-inch-long pointed oval leaves that are somewhat rough with prominent veins, and bark that is smooth, gray, and beechlike in youth, eventually flaking to expose patches of orange; 'Green Vase' is a vigorous, extremely fast-growing tree 60 to 70 feet tall with arching branches bearing orange-brown to bronze-red fall foliage.

2

Plants for Mostly Sunny Places

Plants that prefer mostly sunny places are sunbathers that like a brief, shady break sometime during the day. Usually this respite is best for the plants if it comes in the early afternoon, when the sun is most intense and the air is at its hottest. An hour or two of shade at this time gives the plants an opportunity to cool down and begin to replenish some of the moisture lost to the atmosphere during the first part of the day. A light watering just as the plants enter the shade is helpful, as is a layer of mulch spread over the soil surface to keep the roots cool throughout the hot summer months. The bright sun not only steals precious moisture from leaves but often fades the vivid colors of many flowers, turning sharp, bold colors to watercolor pastels. A shady siesta can often help keep the flower border more colorful for longer periods of time. Look for mostly sunny places on the southeast and southwest corners of structures or shrub borders.

BABY-BLUE-EYES
Nemophila

Light:	mostly sun
Plant type:	annual
Height:	6 to 10 inches
Soil and Moisture:	well-drained, moist
Interest:	flowers
Care:	moderate

◀ Nemophila menziesii

Baby-blue-eyes are dainty, cool-weather plants with tidy mounds of dark green leaves dotted with 1-inch-wide lapis blue flowers with white centers. These beautiful wildflowers make good edgings, rock garden specimens, and companions for spring-flowering bulbs. They are also attractive when planted so that their trailing stems spill over the edge of a wall.

Growing and care:
Sow seed directly in the garden in early spring, thinning the seedlings to stand 6 inches apart. Enrich the soil with organic matter and provide abundant moisture. Mulch around plants to keep soil cool. Plants thrive in areas with cool summers and will self-seed under favorable conditions. Baby-blue-eyes can die during periods of hot, humid weather.

Selected species and varieties:
N. menziesii produces trailing stems to form a mounding plant, usually about 6 inches tall and 12 inches across, with deeply cut light green leaves. Flowers are tubular, 1 to 1½ inches across, and sky blue in color with white centers; 'Pennie Black' has deep purple ¾-inch blooms edged with silvery white.

BISHOP'S FLOWER
Ammi

Light:	mostly sun
Plant type:	annual
Height:	2 to 3 feet
Soil and Moisture:	well-drained, fertile, moist
Interest:	flowers
Care:	easy

◀ Ammi majus

The delicate flower heads of bishop's flower resemble Queen-Anne's-lace in appearance, but the plant is far more manageable in the garden. Originally from Eurasia, it has naturalized in many parts of North America. It is well suited to flower borders, where it provides fine-textured contrast with coarser and more colorful plants. It can be sprinkled among annuals and perennials or planted in drifts. The flowers are highly valued for indoor arrangements; wear gloves when cutting as sap can irritate skin.

Growing and care:
Start seed about 6 weeks indoors—or 2 weeks outdoors—before the last frost. Thin or transplant to allow 6 to 12 inches between plants. Plants transplant easily at nearly any stage and, once established, are free flowering. They thrive in cooler regions but may be stressed by high temperatures and humidity.

Selected species and varieties:
A. majus develops thin, well-branched stems up to 3 feet tall with sharply serrated leaves. In summer, stems are topped with 5- to 6-inch umbels, each containing numerous delicate white flowers that tremble with the slightest wind or touch.

BUTTERFLY FLOWER
Schizanthus

Light: mostly sun

Plant type: annual

Height: 1 to 4 feet

Soil and Moisture: well-drained, moist, fertile

Interest: flowers

Care: difficult

◀ Schizanthus pinnatus

Butterfly flower is a truly beautiful plant, with exotic flowers resembling orchids. Borne in loose clusters, the two-tone flowers, which come in many colors, are pleasantly displayed against fernlike foliage. They are useful in beds or containers and are excellent for cutting.

Growing and care:

Start seed indoors 8 weeks before the last frost. In Zones 9 and 10 seed may be sown outdoors in spring. Space plants 1 to 1½ feet apart. Pinch plants when about 3 inches tall and again when 6 inches high to encourage branching. Water regularly, keeping leaves and flowers dry. Set stakes for tall varieties in the ground while plants are small. Dwarf forms make excellent edging plants.

Selected species and varieties:

S. pinnatus grows to 4 feet with light green, finely cut leaves and 1½-inch flowers produced in open clusters from early summer to early fall. Flowers have a tropical appearance, and colors include pink, rose, salmon, vivid red, lavender, violet, and cream. Each displays contrasting markings on the throat.

CALIFORNIA POPPY
Eschscholzia

Light: mostly sun

Plant type: annual, tender perennial

Height: 4 inches to 2 feet

Soil and Moisture: well-drained, dry

Interest: flowers

Care: easy

◀ Eschscholzia californica

California poppies are popular garden plants with gaily colored, broad-petaled flowers on long, graceful stalks. The brilliant flowers open during the day and close at night and in cloudy weather. California poppies are effective for massing in beds and borders, and thrive in wildflower meadows.

Growing and care:

California poppies are difficult to transplant. Sow seed directly in the garden in early spring. Thin plants to stand 6 inches apart. Plants do well in sunny or mostly sunny conditions and in dry soil but flower best when watered regularly. Once established, plants self-seed freely. Though they tolerate most soil, they prefer a poor, sandy one.

Selected species and varieties:

E. caespitosa (tufted California poppy, pastel poppy) is an annual with pale yellow flowers on 4- to 12-inch stalks above finely cut basal foliage. *E. californica* is a 1- to 2-foot tender perennial from Zone 8 south but is grown as an annual elsewhere, with 1- to 3-inch yellow or orange flowers from spring to fall and feathery blue-green foliage; 'Aurantiaca' is an old variety with rich orange single blooms; 'Monarch Mixed' bears single and semidouble flowers in yellow, orange, red, and pink; 'Orange King' bears translucent orange flowers.

CAMPION
Silene

Light: mostly sun

Plant type: annual, biennial

Height: 6 inches to 2 feet

Soil and Moisture: well-drained, moist to dry

Interest: flowers

Care: easy

◀ Silene coeli-rosa

Robust and easy to grow, campion provides an abundance of cheerful summer flowers for borders and beds. Low-growing types are well suited to rock gardens or for use as edgings, and taller types are attractive when cut for fresh arrangements. The blossoms are white, pink, lavender, or violet with a deep-colored contrasting eye in the center and notched petals.

Growing and care:
Sow seed directly outdoors in early spring as soon as the soil can be worked. Established plants often self-seed. Allow 8 inches between plants. They perform best in well-drained, sunny locations but will tolerate light shade.

Selected species and varieties:
S. armeria (sweet William catchfly) grows 1 to 1½ feet tall with blue-gray leaves and 3-inch clusters of pink or red flowers. It is often included in wildflower mixes and is suitable for naturalizing. *S. coeli-rosa* [also known as *Lychnis coeli-rosa* and *Viscaria coeli-rosa*] usually grows to about 1 foot with narrow, pointed leaves and blue, lavender, pink, or white flowers that often sport a contrasting eye; each single, saucer-shaped flower is 1 inch across. *S. pendula* (drooping catchfly) grows 6 to 16 inches tall with a compact habit, hairy medium green leaves, and loose clusters of pale pink flowers.

CANDYTUFT
Iberis

Light: mostly sun

Plant type: annual

Height: 6 inches to 1½ feet

Soil and Moisture: well-drained, moist

Interest: flowers, fragrance

Care: easy

◀ Iberis umbellata

These European wildflowers are easy to grow and free flowering with abundant clusters of tiny four-petaled flowers above dark green leaves. Candytuft flowers throughout the summer and is very effective in rock gardens and borders, as an edging, or in a planter. Set the plants where their fragrance can be appreciated.

Growing and care:
Sow seed in the garden in fall or as soon as soil can be worked in the spring, thinning to allow 6 to 9 inches between seedlings. Make successive sowings to extend the flowering season. Cut back lightly after bloom if flowering stops in summer. Plants thrive in city conditions.

Selected species and varieties:
I. amara (rocket candytuft) grows 1 to 1½ feet tall with fragrant white flowers in cone-shaped spikes that can be cut for fresh arrangements. *I. odorata* (fragrant candytuft) grows 6 to 12 inches with flat clusters of white flowers. *I. umbellata* (globe candytuft) grows 8 to 16 inches with clusters of pink, red, lilac, or violet flowers that are not fragrant.

CELOSIA
Celosia

Light: mostly sun

Plant type: annual

Height: 6 inches to 2 feet

Soil and Moisture: well-drained, moist to dry

Interest: flowers, foliage

Care: easy

◀ Celosia cristata 'Pink Tassels'

These vibrant annuals sport bold, crested or plumed flowers that are extremely long lasting, making them ideal for bedding and cutting for both fresh and dried arrangements. They are easy to grow and are perfect for filling empty places in perennial borders.

Growing and care:
Start seed indoors 4 to 6 weeks before transplanting to the garden after all danger of frost has passed. In warm areas, sow directly outside once soil has warmed. Space plants 6 to 18 inches apart. Celosias thrive in warm weather and some afternoon shade. For use in winter arrangements, cut flowers at their peak and hang them upside down to dry.

Selected species and varieties:
C. cristata displays a range of heights and flower types. Leaves may be green, purple, or variegated. Flowers appear from midsummer to fall and are usually deep shades of red, orange, yellow, or gold. The species is divided according to flower type: Childsii group (crested cockscomb) produces crested or convoluted flower heads that resemble lumps of coral. Plumosa group (feather amaranth) bears feathery 6- to 12-inch flower heads. Spicata group bears flowers in slender spikes; 'Pink Tassels' bears long, pale pink spikes with bright pink tips.

CHRYSANTHEMUM
Chrysanthemum

Light: mostly sun

Plant type: annual

Height: 1 to 3 feet

Soil and Moisture: well-drained, moist

Interest: flowers

Care: moderate

◀ Chrysanthemum coronarium 'Primrose Gem'

Annual chrysanthemums are vigorous plants with dark green, deeply lobed foliage and an abundant supply of summer and fall daisylike flowers. Chrysanthemums are perfect as edging plants or tucked into beds and borders. They are also cheerful and dependable cut flowers.

Growing and care:
These plants are easily grown from seed planted directly in the garden as soon as soil can be worked in spring. Thin plants to stand 1 to 1½ feet apart. Pinch seedlings to encourage bushy growth. Once established they will self-seed.

Selected species and varieties:
C. carinatum (tricolor chrysanthemum) grows 2 to 3 feet tall with dark green toothed leaves. It derives its common name from its 2½-inch flower heads that are white with a yellow band surrounding a purple or chocolate brown central disk; 'Court Jesters' produces red, pink, orange, yellow, maroon, and white flowers with red or orange bands. *C. coronarium* (crown daisy, garland chrysanthemum) grows 1 to 2½ feet tall with coarsely cut leaves and yellow and white flowers, 1 to 2 inches across, which may be single, semidouble, or double; 'Primrose Gem' bears semidouble soft yellow blooms with darker yellow centers.

CIGAR PLANT
Cuphea

Light:	mostly sun
Plant type:	tender perennial grown as annual
Height:	8 inches to 3 feet
Soil and Moisture:	well-drained, moist
Interest:	flowers, foliage
Care:	easy

◄ Cuphea ignea

These eye-catching plants bear abundant, shiny green foliage richly decorated with brilliant scarlet flowers from summer to frost. Cigar plant's mounded habit is excellent for rock gardens or mixed with perennials in beds and borders. From Zone 9 south, the plants are winter hardy and can reach 3 feet tall in a few seasons. In cooler areas grow cigar plant as an annual or plant in containers for summer use on patios and overwinter indoors as a houseplant.

Growing and care:
Start seed indoors in midwinter. Do not cover seed, as it needs light to germinate properly. Transplant to the garden after soil has warmed. Allow 1 to 1½ feet between plants. They adapt to any well-drained soil and thrive in warm weather.

Selected species and varieties:
C. ignea (Mexican cigar plant, firecracker plant) grows to 1 foot with an equal spread and narrow dark green leaves. Its scarlet tubular flowers are 1 inch long with a black and white tip. *C. llavea* 'Bunny Ears Mixed' grows to 1½ feet with a neat, uniform habit and bright red flowers with two protruding stamens bearded with violet hairs. *C. x purpurea* grows to 1½ feet with hairy 3-inch leaves. Its bright rose red flowers are tinged with purple and borne in terminal clusters.

COSMOS
Cosmos

Light:	mostly sun
Plant type:	annual
Height:	3 to 6 feet
Soil and Moisture:	well-drained, moist to dry
Interest:	flowers
Care:	easy

◄ Cosmos bipinnatus 'Sonata'

Cosmos enlivens the summer and fall garden with long-lasting displays of brightly colored daisylike flowers on loose clumps of slender, pliant stems. The cheerful flowers accent graceful masses of feathery-textured foliage. The smaller varieties can be used as edging plants or fillers in borders; taller ones are effective as backdrops or transition plants.

Growing and care:
Cosmos produces abundant flowers in poor soil. Taller varieties may need staking, and should be planted in sites protected from summer winds. They are easily propagated from seed sown ¼ inch deep after all danger of frost has passed. Plant seedlings 1 to 1½ feet apart.

Selected species and varieties:
C. bipinnatus is an annual with 4- to 6-foot stems bearing 3- to 4-inch pink, white, or red flowers from summer to frost with yellow centers; 'Daydream' has bright pink flowers with dark red centers; 'Sonata' has pink, white, or red blossoms on 2-foot stems. *C. sulphureus* (yellow cosmos) is an annual bearing 2- to 3-inch yellow, orange, gold, or red flowers in early summer on 3- to 6-foot stems; 'Goldcrest' has a sturdy, compact form with bright golden flowers, and is more robust and wind resistant than other species.

DUSTY-MILLER
Senecio

Light: mostly sun	
Plant type: tender perennial grown as annual	
Height: 6 inches to 2 ½ feet	
Soil and Moisture: well-drained, medium to dry	
Interest: foliage	
Care: easy to moderate	

◄ Senecio cineraria

Dusty-miller has soft, woolly white to silvery gray leaves that combine well with brightly colored flowers in borders and beds. Native to the Mediterranean region, dusty-miller is perennial from Zone 9 south but is grown as an annual elsewhere. It makes an attractive edging, rock garden specimen, or container plant, and is stunning when interplanted with salmon-flowered begonias.

Growing and care:

Start seed indoors 8 to 10 weeks prior to the last frost. Do not cover the seed, as light is necessary for germination. Transplant outdoors when all danger of frost has passed, spacing plants 10 inches apart. Avoid soils that are too fertile. Overwatering will result in weak growth and susceptibility to disease. Plants tolerate drought.

Selected species and varieties:

S. cineraria (dusty-miller, silver groundsel) has a rounded, branched habit. Leaves are thick, up to 8 inches long, and deeply cut into rounded lobes; they are covered with dense woolly hairs, giving the foliage a felt-like texture. Flowers are yellow or cream, appearing in small terminal clusters in late summer, but are best removed to encourage foliage growth.

EDGING LOBELIA
Lobelia

Light: mostly sun	
Plant type: tender perennial grown as annual	
Height: 4 to 8 inches	
Soil and Moisture: well-drained, moist, fertile	
Interest: flowers	
Care: easy	

◄ Lobelia erinus

Edging lobelia is an easy-to-grow plant with abundant clusters of intensely colored flowers from spring to fall. The plants produce very neat, tidy mounds of dark green foliage that are perfect for edging walkways, beds, or borders. The bright flowers range from an intense sapphire blue to softer shades of violet and white. Edging lobelia is also excellent for container growing, including window boxes and hanging baskets.

Growing and care:

Plant edging lobelias in spring, spacing plants 4 inches apart. The plants respond well to periodic additions of organic mulch and compost. The best flower colors result when they are grown in a mostly sunny place with shade during the hottest time of the day. Cut back *L. erinus* after its first flowering to encourage reblooming.

Selected species and varieties:

L. erinus (edging lobelia, trailing lobelia) is a tender perennial producing mounds of 4- to 8-inch stems with blue or white ½-inch flowers from summer to frost and thin, ½-inch leaves; 'Cambridge Blue' has light green foliage and light blue flowers; 'Crystal Palace' has dark blue flowers.

EVENING PRIMROSE
Oenothera

Light:	mostly sun
Plant type:	biennial
Height:	2 to 8 feet
Soil and Moisture:	well-drained, moist to dry
Interest:	flowers
Care:	easy

◀ Oenothera biennis

Among this genus of mostly perennial plants are a few hardy biennials that are often grown as annuals. Evening primrose sports vivid to pastel yellow blooms from early summer to midfall, opening in the evening atop tall, erect stems. The plants are easy to grow and are well suited for massing at the rear of a border or for use in a wildflower garden.

Growing and care:

Start seed indoors 8 to 12 weeks prior to the last frost, or outdoors in early spring. Where winters are mild, seed can be sown outdoors in fall. Space plants 1 foot apart. Once established, plants will often self-seed, and may become invasive if not confined. They thrive in warm weather and tolerate poor soil.

Selected species and varieties:

O. biennis produces a clump of coarse basal leaves from which a stout, erect flower stem rises. Stems may reach 6 feet and bear 1- to 2-inch flowers that open pale yellow and turn gold. *O. erythrosepala* [also called *O. glaziovinia*] grows 2 to 8 feet tall with yellow flowers that turn orange or red; 'Tina James' grows 3 to 4 feet with showy yellow flowers that burst open in 1 to 2 minutes and are pleasantly fragrant.

FLOWERING TOBACCO
Nicotiana

Light:	mostly sun
Plant type:	annual, tender perennial grown as annual
Height:	1 to 6 feet
Soil and Moisture:	well-drained, moist, fertile
Interest:	flowers, fragrance
Care:	easy

◀ Nicotiana alata

The blossoms of many flowering tobaccos open in late afternoon and fill the evening with a heavy, sweet perfume. Erect stems arise from coarse clumps of large, sticky leaves and are topped by loose clusters of long, tubular flowers that are pollinated by honeybees, hummingbirds, and nocturnal moths. Flowering tobacco makes an excellent border filler or specimen for the back of beds.

Growing and care:

Propagate flowering tobaccos by seed, sowing seed indoors 6 to 8 weeks before the last frost. Seed needs light to germinate, so sprinkle on top of the soil, moisten, and cover the container with plastic wrap. Space transplants 1 foot apart. Remove dead flowers before they set seed to encourage further blooming.

Selected species and varieties:

N. alata (jasmine tobacco, flowering tobacco) produces 1- to 4-foot clumps bearing 2- to 4-inch flowers from spring to fall above 4- to 10-inch leaves; 'Daylight Sensation' has flowers in shades of lilac, white, purple, and rose that open at dawn; 'Fragrant Cloud' has heavily scented snow white blossoms that open in the evening; 'Lime Green' has bright yellow-green flowers from summer to fall on 1½-foot stems; 'Nikki' series produces bushy, 1½- to 2-foot plants with flowers in a range of colors that includes shades of pink, red, white, and yellow.

GERANIUM
Pelargonium

Light: mostly sun

Plant type: tender perennial grown as annual

Height: 10 inches to 6 feet

Soil and Moisture: well-drained, moist

Interest: flowers, foliage

Care: easy

◀ Pelargonium x hortorum

These easy-to-grow tender perennials are some of the most popular bedding plants grown. They have a shrubby habit with showy, often heavily zoned leaves and clusters of vividly colored flowers from spring to frost. Geraniums will bloom their first year when grown from seed. Their reliable and long-lasting flowers are useful in beds and borders and are especially suited to container growing, providing nonstop color for hanging baskets and window boxes.

Growing and care:
Start seed indoors 10 to 12 weeks prior to the last frost. Geraniums can also be started indoors from cuttings taken from overwintered plants. Transplant outdoors after danger of frost has passed, spacing plants 8 to 15 inches apart. Geraniums prefer cool climates and may die out during the heat of the summer in southern zones. Water during dry periods. Remove faded flowers to encourage continuous flowering. Geraniums can be dug up and potted in fall for growing indoors during winter.

Selected species and varieties:
P. x *hortorum* (zonal geranium) has a rounded habit and grows from 10 inches to 6 feet tall. It produces rounded, pale to medium green leaves with scalloped edges, usually marked with a brown or maroon horseshoe-shaped zone, and single, semidouble, or double flowers in dense, long-stemmed, 5-inch clusters in many colors.

GODETIA
Clarkia

Light: mostly sun

Plant type: annual

Height: 1 to 3 feet

Soil and Moisture: well-drained, dry

Interest: flowers

Care: easy

◀Clarkia amoena

Godetias are free-flowering wildflowers from the coastal ranges of the western United States. The flowers resemble a wild rose with broad, richly colored petals surrounding a light-colored center. They are named after the explorer William Clark, who collected their seed during the Lewis and Clark expedition. *C. amoena* and *C. purpurea* are also listed under the genus *Godetia*.

Growing and care:
Sow seed outdoors in fall where winters are mild, and elsewhere in spring as soon as the soil can be worked. Sow fairly heavily, since crowding will encourage flowering. Plants perform best where nights are cool.

Selected species and varieties:
C. amoena (farewell-to-spring, satin flower) grows 1 to 3 feet tall. Throughout summer, 2- to 4-inch cup-shaped flowers appear in the axils of the upper leaves. Its four petals are pink to lavender with a bright red or pink splash at the base; the four sepals are red. *C. concinna* (red-ribbons) grows 1 to 2 feet tall and bears rose-purple flowers with deeply cut fan-shaped petals in late spring and early summer. *C. purpurea* grows to 3 feet tall with 1-inch flowers in shades of purple, lavender, red, and pink, often with a dark eye.

HELIOTROPE
Heliotropium

Light: mostly sun

Plant type: tender perennial grown as annual

Height: 1 to 3 feet

Soil and Moisture: well-drained, moist, fertile

Interest: flowers, fragrance

Care: moderate

◀ Heliotropium
arborescens 'Marine'

Heliotrope is an old-fashioned plant with sprays of small white, lilac, or burgundy-violet flowers that emit an enchantingly rich vanilla fragrance. The plants have dark green leaves and a bushy habit that make them welcome additions to mixed borders. They are ideal container plants, and flowers can be cut for fresh arrangements. Heliotropes can also be trained into standards for a more formal Victorian look.

Growing and care:
Start seed indoors 10 to 12 weeks prior to the last frost, or buy young plants in spring. Plants can also be started from cuttings. Do not transplant to the garden until soil has warmed, as plants are very frost sensitive. Allow 1 foot between plants and keep them well watered.

Selected species and varieties:
H. arborescens (cherry pie) grows 1 to 3 feet in the garden, though plants grown in a greenhouse or in their native range may reach 6 feet. Foliage is dark green and wrinkled. Five-petaled flowers are ¼ inch across, occurring in clusters as large as a foot across; 'Marine', a compact variety reaching 2 feet, has large, deep purple flowers and is excellent for bedding, although it lacks intense fragrance.

HONESTY
Lunaria

Light: mostly sun to part shade

Plant type: biennial

Height: 2 to 3 feet

Soil and Moisture: well-drained, moist to dry

Interest: fruit

Care: easy

◀ Lunaria annua

This old-fashioned biennial is native to southern Europe. It is grown primarily for its fruit, a flat, oval, silvery seedpod. Plants are best suited to the cutting garden, an informal border, or a wildflower meadow. Their papery seedpods are highly valued for dried arrangements.

Growing and care:
Lunaria can be grown as an annual or a biennial. For flowers and seedpods the first year, sow seed outdoors in very early spring, or plant in midsummer to early fall for flowers and seedpods the following year. Once established plants will reseed through Zone 4. Space plants 8 to 12 inches apart. They tolerate wet and dry conditions and are not fussy about soil quality, as long as they are well drained. They grow well in mostly sun or partial shade.

Selected species and varieties:
L. annua (silver-dollar, bolbonac) has an erect habit with broad, coarsely toothed leaves and fragrant pink or purple flowers, each with four petals, borne in terminal clusters in late spring. Flowers are followed by the seedpods, which fall apart, revealing a thin, silvery white disk, 1 to 2 inches across, to which the seeds cling; 'Alba' produces white flowers well displayed when grown against a dark background.

HOUND'S TONGUE
Cynoglossum

Light: mostly sun	
Plant type: biennial	
Height: 1½ to 2 feet	
Soil and Moisture: well-drained, moist to dry	
Interest: flowers	
Care: easy	

◀ Cynoglossum amabile

Hound's tongue has an open, casual habit with slender, slightly droopy stems and clusters of tiny clear blue flowers throughout summer and into fall. The blossoms are reminiscent of forget-me-nots, and put on a fine show in borders or beds. Hound's tongue is excellent for massing and fresh flower arrangements.

Growing and care:
Though biennial, *C. amabile* usually flowers the first year from seed, especially if started indoors in late winter or early spring. Plant seedlings in garden after last frost, spacing plants 9 to 12 inches apart. It thrives in a wide range of soils and will often self-seed. When cutting for arrangements, immediately submerge the stems three-quarters of their length in water to prevent flowers from collapsing.

Selected species and varieties:
C. amabile (Chinese forget-me-not) has an irregular to rounded habit with a clump of erect stems with somewhat coarse leaves. Each stem is topped with an arching cluster of light blue blossoms. Individual flowers are ¼ inch across and have five petals. Pink- and white-flowered forms are also available.

LARKSPUR
Consolida

Light: mostly sun to part shade	
Plant type: annual	
Height: 1 to 4 feet	
Soil and Moisture: well-drained, fertile, moist	
Interest: flowers	
Care: easy	

◀ Consolida ambigua

This native of southern Europe produces tall, pliant spikes of stately blue, lilac, pink, red, white, and violet flowers that accent the garden for weeks in summer. The soft-textured, lacy foliage provides an excellent foil for the pastel flowers, which are a graceful accent to the back of the border. Larkspur is regarded as a fine cut flower for fresh floral arrangements.

Growing and care:
Start seed indoors in peat pots 6 to 8 weeks prior to the last frost. Seed can be sown directly outdoors in fall from Zone 7 south, and in early spring elsewhere. Space plants to stand 8 to 15 inches apart. Tall varieties often require staking. Plants thrive in cool conditions and light shade. Keep soil evenly moist throughout the growing season.

Selected species and varieties:
C. ambigua (rocket larkspur) produces lacy, deeply cut leaves. Spurred flowers in many pastel shades are borne in dense, graceful spikes throughout the summer; 'Imperial Blue Bell' grows to 4 feet with double blue flowers; 'Imperial White King' is similar with double white flowers.

MARIGOLD
Tagetes

Light: mostly sun

Plant type: annual, tender perennial grown as annual

Height: 6 inches to 3 feet

Soil and Moisture: well-drained, moist

Interest: flowers, foliage

Care: easy

◀ Tagetes erecta 'Primrose Lady'

Marigolds are among the most popular bedding plants in the United States. They are easy to grow, provide a reliable display, and are available in a wide range of heights. Their flowers typically range from pale yellow to bright orange and burgundy and are produced nonstop from early summer to frost in many varieties. Some species are grown for their fernlike foliage, which is often quite aromatic. Marigolds are suited to many uses, depending on their size: They can be placed in the background of a border, used as an edging, or massed in a bed. They are suitable for cutting for fresh arrangements and can be effectively grown in patio planters and window boxes. Despite some of their common names, marigolds are native to Mexico and Central and South America.

Growing and care:

Start seed indoors 6 to 8 weeks prior to the last frost, or sow directly outdoors 2 weeks before that date. Space plants 6 to 18 inches apart, depending on the variety, and pinch the seedlings to promote bushiness. Marigolds thrive in a moist, well-drained soil but tolerate dry conditions. Remove dead blossoms to encourage continuous flowering. Avoid overwatering.

Selected species and varieties:

T. erecta (American marigold, African marigold, Aztec marigold) has an erect to rounded habit and a wide range of heights, categorized as dwarf (10 to 14 inches), medium (15 to 20 inches), or tall (to 3 feet). Flower heads are solitary, single to double, and 2 to 5 inches across; 'Primrose Lady' is 15 to 18 inches with a compact habit and double yellow carnation-like flowers. *T. filifolia* (Irish lace), grown primarily for its finely divided fernlike foliage, is 6 to 12 inches tall and wide and produces small white blooms in late summer. *T. lucida* (Mexican tarragon, sweet-scented marigold) grows 2 to 2½ feet tall with dark green tarragon-scented leaves and small, single yellow flowers in clusters. It may be perennial in warm climates. *T. patula* (French marigold, sweet mace) grows 6 to 18 inches tall with a neat, rounded habit and deeply serrated bright green leaves. Flower heads are solitary, up to 2½ inches across, and may be single or double; double flowers often display a crest of raised petals at their center. Colors include yellow, orange, maroon, and bicolors. *T. tenuifolia* (dwarf marigold, signet marigold) grows 6 to 12 inches tall with compact mounds of fernlike foliage and single yellow or orange 1-inch flowers that are so profuse they almost completely cover the leaves. It is excellent for edgings and window boxes.

MIGNONETTE
Reseda

Light:	mostly sun
Plant type:	annual
Height:	6 inches to 1 1/2 feet
Soil and Moisture:	well-drained, moist to dry, fertile
Interest:	flowers
Care:	moderate

◄ Reseda odorata

Mignonette is a casual, open-growing annual with veils of soft-textured, grassy green foliage and conical clusters of wonderfully fragrant white or yellow summer to fall flowers. The star-shaped flowers are creamy white to greenish yellow with bright orange stamens and are excellent planted at the edge of a border or in a patio planter or window box, where their free-flowing fragrance can be most appreciated. Flowers are long lasting and excellent for cutting.

Growing and care:
Plants are difficult to transplant, so sow seed directly in the garden in early spring. Do not cover seed, as it requires light to germinate. A second sowing a month later will extend the flowering season. In Zones 9 and 10 seed can be planted in fall for flowering in late winter or spring. Thin seedlings to stand 6 to 12 inches apart. Water and mulch to keep soil evenly moist and cool.

Selected species and varieties:
R. odorata develops thick stems and small oval leaves. Flowers are 1/3 inch across with four to seven fringed petals. Although not extremely showy, the flowers are so fragrant as to be well worth growing.

NAVELWORT
Omphalodes

Light:	mostly sun
Plant type:	annual
Height:	6 to 12 inches
Soil and Moisture:	well-drained, moist
Interest:	flowers, foliage
Care:	easy

◄ Omphalodes linifolia

This dainty little annual from Spain and Portugal produces loose one-sided spikes of white flowers sprinkled among rafts of compact silvery gray leaves. Appearing from summer to fall, the flowers are slightly fragrant and well suited for use in fresh floral arrangements. Plants are effectively used in rock gardens and are quite decorative when planted along a stone wall.

Growing and care:
Start seed indoors 4 to 6 weeks prior to the last frost, or sow directly outdoors in midspring. Allow 4 to 6 inches between plants. They prefer a somewhat acid soil rich in organic matter. Water plants during dry periods. Mulch with peat moss or pine needles after planting to keep roots cool. Navelwort often self-seeds. Cut back plants after flowering to encourage rebloom.

Selected species and varieties:
O. linifolia produces narrow gray-green lance-shaped leaves and sprays of 1/2-inch-wide five-petaled flowers. Each petal displays a prominent vein running from its tip to its base, giving it a starlike appearance. Seeds resemble navels.

NEMESIA
Nemesia

Light: mostly sun
Plant type: annual
Height: 9 inches to 2 feet
Soil and Moisture: well-drained, moist
Interest: flowers
Care: easy

◀ Nemesia strumosa 'Carnival Mixed'

These brightly colored annuals from South Africa bear pouched, orchidlike flowers from early summer to fall, and are perfect for massing in beds and borders or for growing in containers in areas where summers are cool. They also make effective edgings and provide an attractive cover for the yellowing foliage of spring bulbs.

Growing and care:
Start seed indoors 4 to 6 weeks prior to the last frost in a sterilized medium such as vermiculite. Transplant to the garden after danger of frost has passed in soil well amended with organic matter. Allow 6 inches between plants. Plants require a long, cool growing season to perform well and benefit from some afternoon shade. Pinch young plants to encourage bushiness, and provide water during dry periods.

Selected species and varieties:
N. strumosa has an attractive, bushy, mounded habit with narrow, bright green toothed leaves and spurred five-lobed flowers in clusters 4 inches long. Flower colors include yellow, white, red, purple, orange, pink, and bicolors; 'Carnival Mixed' is a dwarf variety that grows to 9 inches with brightly colored flowers.

PERIWINKLE
Catharanthus

Light: mostly sun
Plant type: tender perennial grown as annual
Height: 3 inches to 1½ feet
Soil and Moisture: well-drained, moist
Interest: flowers, foliage
Care: easy

◀ Catharanthus roseus

Periwinkle provides charming, star-shaped flowers in a range of pastel shades from summer to fall. The flowers resemble those of *Vinca*. Available in both creeping and upright varieties, periwinkle can be used as a summer ground cover or in mass plantings, annual borders, or containers. It is stunning when grown in hanging baskets.

Growing and care:
Start seed indoors 10 to 12 weeks prior to the last frost for late-spring transplanting to the garden. Set plants 1 to 2 feet apart. Plants can also be started from cuttings. They thrive in warm, humid conditions and are perennial in Zones 9 and 10.

Selected species and varieties:
C. roseus [sometimes listed as *Vinca rosea*] (Madagascar periwinkle) produces glossy oblong leaves 1 to 3 inches long. Creeping varieties grow 3 inches tall, spreading 1½ to 2 feet across. Erect strains grow 8 to 18 inches tall. Flowers are 1½ inches wide and cover the plant throughout the summer; colors range from shades of pink or mauve to white; 'Parasol' produces large 1½- to 2-inch white flowers with pink eyes on 1- to 1½-foot plants; 'Tropicana' grows to 1 foot and produces flowers in several shades of pink, from pale blush to deep rose, with contrasting eyes.

PHLOX
Phlox

Light: mostly sun

Plant type: annual

Height: 6 to 20 inches

Soil and Moisture: well-drained, moist to dry

Interest: flowers

Care: moderate

◀ Phlox drummondii
'Palona Rose with Eye'

This native Texas wildflower bears profuse blossoms of white, pink, red, purple, yellow, and bicolors over a long season on low, spreading plants. Annual phlox are versatile—useful as edgings, in rock gardens, massed in beds, and in containers. Flowers are also good for cutting.

Growing and care:

Start seed indoors 8 weeks prior to the last frost. In Zone 8 and warmer, seed should be sown in fall. Space plants 6 to 12 inches apart. Remove spent flowers to extend bloom, and provide water when dry. If flowering declines in midsummer cut back plants to encourage new bud set. The plants are ideal for sandy soil.

Selected species and varieties:

P. drummondii (annual phlox, Drummond phlox) grows to 20 inches with a spreading, mounded habit, hairy leaves and stems, and five-lobed flowers that are 1 inch across; 'Palona Rose with Eye' is compact, 6 to 8 inches tall, and has rose flowers with contrasting white eyes; 'Petticoat' series are compact 6-inch plants that come in a mix of colors with good drought and heat tolerance; 'Twinkle' series are 8 inches tall with small, early star-shaped flowers in mixed colors.

PINK
Dianthus

Light: mostly to full sun

Plant type: annual, biennial, tender perennial

Height: 4 inches to 2 1/2 feet

Soil and Moisture: well-drained, moist

Interest: flowers, foliage

Care: easy

◀ Dianthus chinensis
'Telestar Picotee'

Pinks are perky flowers with a tidy habit, forming mats of grassy foliage with white, pink, red, and bicolored flowers with fringed or "pinked" petals. Low-growing types make delightful edgings or rock garden or container specimens, while taller selections are useful in the foreground or middle of a border, and as cut flowers.

Growing and care:

Sow sweet William seed outdoors in late spring for flowers the following year. Start seed of China pink indoors 6 to 8 weeks prior to the last frost for transplanting to the garden in midspring. Space plants 8 to 18 inches apart. Sweet William grows best in mostly sunny locations but will tolerate some shade. China pink prefers mostly sun but does well in full sun also.

Selected species and varieties:

D. barbatus (sweet William) is a biennial that self-seeds freely. Dwarf varieties grow 4 to 10 inches tall, while tall varieties may reach 2 feet. Flowers are borne in dense, flat-topped clusters from late spring to early summer. *D. chinensis* (China pink, rainbow pink) is an annual, biennial, or short-lived perennial that grows 6 to 30 inches tall with a dense, mounded habit; 1- to 2-inch flowers, often fragrant, are borne singly or in loose clusters from early summer to fall; 'Telestar Picotee' has a compact habit with deep pink flowers fringed with white.

POPPY
Papaver

Light: mostly sun	
Plant type: annual, tender perennial grown as annual	
Height: 1 to 4 feet	
Soil and Moisture: well-drained, moist to dry	
Interest: flowers	
Care: easy	

◀ Papaver nudicaule

Poppy's broad, showy petals surround prominent centers above clumps of coarse, hairy, deeply lobed leaves in spring. The brightly colored flowers are extremely delicate in appearance, with a transluscent, tissuelike quality. Flowers may be single, with four overlapping petals, or double, with many petals forming a rounded bloom. They are borne on solitary stems, and are suitable for mixed borders and good for cutting.

Growing and care:
Annual species are so difficult to transplant that they are best sown in place. *Papaver* seed is very small and can be mixed with sand for easier handling. *P. rhoeas* does best in full shade to mostly sun. Thin plants to stand about 1 foot apart. *P. somniferum* likes mostly sun and can be thinned to stand 4 to 8 inches apart. Double-flowered varieties of *P. somniferum* often require staking. Poppies will often self-seed. Deadhead plants to prolong flowering season. For use in indoor arrangements, cut the flowers as the buds straighten on their nodding stems but before the flowers actually open.

Selected species and varieties:
P. nudicaule (Iceland poppy, Arctic poppy) produces a fernlike clump of 6-inch lobed gray-green leaves from which 18-inch leafless flower stems rise from spring to early summer. Flowers are fragrant, 2 to 4 inches across, and saucer shaped in a range of colors including white yellow, orange, salmon, and scarlet. *P. rhoeas* (corn poppy, Flanders poppy, Shirley poppy, field poppy) grows to 3 feet with wiry, branching stems and pale green deeply lobed leaves. Flowers may be single or double, and are borne from late spring to early summer in colors of red, purple, pink, and white; 'Fairy Wings' produces flowers in soft shades of blue, lilac, dusty pink, and white with faint blue margins; 'Mother of Pearl' bears flowers in shades of blue, lavender, pink, gray, white, and peach, and the flowers may be solid or speckled. *P. somniferum* (opium poppy) grows 3 to 4 feet tall with large white, red, pink, or mauve flowers that appear throughout summer and are often double or fringed; 'Alba' bears white blooms; 'Pink Chiffon' produces double bright pink flowers; 'White Cloud' bears large, double white blooms on sturdy stems.

QUEEN-ANNE'S-LACE
Daucus

Light: mostly sun	
Plant type: biennial	
Height: 3 to 4 feet	
Soil and Moisture: well-drained, moist to dry	
Interest: flowers	
Care: easy	

◄ Daucus carota var. carota

Queen-Anne's-lace is a weedy plant to the unimaginative, and a hardy, very graceful addition to the garden to others. The plant produces large, flat umbels of intricate, lacy white flowers atop strong, pliant stems from summer to fall. The plant's beautiful flowers and ferny foliage make it a nice filler in a sunny border. It naturalizes easily in wildflower meadows, attracting butterflies and bees. Flowers are valued for both fresh and dried arrangements.

Growing and care:
Sow seed outdoors in late spring for flowers the following year. Once established, plants will vigorously self-seed. To prevent unwanted plants, remove flowers before seeds mature. Plants are easy to grow and thrive in nearly any well-drained soil.

Selected species and varieties:
D. carota var. *carota* (Queen-Anne's-lace, Queen's-lace, wild carrot) produces a prominent rosette of fernlike leaves in early spring, from which grows a 3- to 4-foot branched flowering stem. Each branch is topped by a 3- to 4-inch umbel of tiny white flowers.

ROSE MALLOW
Hibiscus

Light: mostly sun	
Plant type: tender perennial	
Height: 1½ to 8 feet	
Soil and Moisture: well-drained, moist	
Interest: flowers, foliage	
Care: easy to moderate	

◄ Hibiscus acetosella

Rose mallows are a diverse group of tender perennials with distinctive ornamental foliage and showy, funnel-shaped exotic flowers. The plants lend a tropical ambiance to beds, borders, and specialty gardens. Plant rose mallows individually as specimens or in groups for a fast-growing, informal summer hedge. Tall types are effective as a background for mixed borders or as the centerpiece of an island bed. Shorter forms are useful for fronting shrub borders or planting in the foreground of annual beds. Both large and small types are excellent choices for patio containers.

Growing and care:
Start seed of *H. acetosella* indoors about 8 weeks prior to the last frost and transplant outdoors after all danger of frost has passed. Space *H. acetosella* 12 to 14 inches apart. Because *H. trionum* is difficult to transplant, seed should be sown directly in the garden after all danger of frost has passed, allowing 1 foot between plants. Plants tolerate heat as long as abundant moisture is supplied.

Selected species and varieties:
H. acetosella hails from Africa and is grown primarily for its attractive foliage. Purple flowers form so late in the season in most areas that they fail to open before frost. The plant grows to 5 feet tall, with glossy red leaves and stems. Leaves may be either smooth in outline or deeply lobed. This plant makes a bold accent mixed with other

ROSE MALLOW
(continued)

annuals, or a stunning summer hedge; the variety 'Red Shield' produces burgundy leaves with a metallic sheen that resemble maple leaves in shape. *H. moscheutos* (common rose mallow, swamp rose mallow, wild cotton) grows 3 to 8 feet tall with a shrubby habit. It is native to marshlands of the eastern United States and can be grown as a perennial in Zone 7 and south but is often grown as a half-hardy annual. The large gray-green leaves provide a soft foil for the huge white, pink, rose, or red summer flowers that are often 8 inches across; *'Southern Belle'* grows 4 to 6 feet tall with red, pink, or white flowers with a distinct red eye, up to 10 inches across. *H. trionum* (flower-of-an-hour) grows 1½ to 3 feet with a bushy habit and dark green three- to five-lobed leaves. Flowers are 2 inches across and are creamy yellow with a deep maroon throat. Though flowers are short lived, they appear in abundance from midsummer to late fall.

SNAPDRAGON
Antirrhinum

◀ Antirrhinum majus

Light: mostly sun	
Plant type: tender perennial grown as annual	
Height: 6 inches to 4 feet	
Soil and Moisture: well-drained, moist, fertile	
Interest: flowers	
Care: easy	

Snapdragons are easy-to-grow plants with distinctive, brightly colored flowers that have been grown since ancient times. Their lasting popularity is easy to understand given their wide range of heights and flower colors and their long season of bloom. Short varieties add color to rock gardens and edgings, while taller types are well suited to the middle and rear of mixed borders. They are outstanding flowers for fresh arrangements.

Growing and care:
Though snapdragons are technically tender perennials, they are commonly grown as annuals except in the Deep South. Sow seed indoors 8 to 10 weeks prior to the last frost. Do not cover seed, which needs light to germinate. Space smaller varieties 6 inches apart, taller types 1½ feet apart in soil amended with compost. Pinch young plants to promote bushiness, and deadhead to encourage continuous flowering. Taller types may need staking.

Selected species and varieties:
A. majus bears terminal clusters of flowers, each with five lobes, divided into an upper and lower lip; varieties are classified by height: dwarf, 6 to 9 inches; intermediate, 1 to 2 feet; and tall, 2 to 4 feet; 'Madame Butterfly' grows to 3 feet with wide flaring blossoms in a range of colors; 'Pink Rocket' grows 2 to 3 feet tall with pink blooms; 'White Sonnet' reaches 22 inches and has white flowers.

SPIDER FLOWER
Cleome

Light: mostly sun

Plant type: annual

Height: 3 to 4 feet

Soil and Moisture: well-drained, moist

Interest: flowers, seedpods

Care: easy

◀ Cleome hasslerana 'Helen Campbell'

Spider flowers bear enormous clusters of 1-inch flowers atop tall, graceful stems continuously from summer until frost. Pink, lavender, or white flower petals surround 2- to 3-inch-long stamens that protrude from the center, creating a spiderlike effect further enhanced by the slender, conspicuous seedpods that follow the flowers. *Cleome* makes a graceful summer hedge, accent, or border plant.

Growing and care:
Start seed indoors 4 to 6 weeks prior to the last frost, or plant directly in the garden in early spring. Plants often self-seed. Space plants about 2 feet apart. Spider flower thrives in warm weather and responds well to abundant moisture.

Selected species and varieties:
C. hasslerana [also known as *C. spinosa*] has an erect habit with dark green palmately compound leaves and airy, ball-shaped flower heads. Although flowers are short lived, new ones are produced continuously at the top of the stem; 'Cherry Queen' bears rose red flowers; 'Helen Campbell' has white blooms; 'Pink Queen' bears clear pink blossoms; the flowers of 'Violet Queen' are purple, and leaves display a purple tint at their edges.

STOCK
Matthiola

Light: mostly sun

Plant type: annual, biennial

Height: 1 to 2 ½ feet

Soil and Moisture: well-drained, moist, fertile

Interest: flowers

Care: moderate

◀ Matthiola incana

The abundant blossoms of stock perfume a garden throughout summer. Plant them in beds, window boxes, or patio containers where their fragrance can be appreciated. Flowers add a dainty appearance and sweet scent to fresh indoor arrangements.

Growing and care:
Start seed indoors 6 to 8 weeks prior to the last frost, or sow directly in the garden in early spring. Space plants to stand 6 to 12 inches apart; they tolerate crowding. Plants thrive in cool weather and may stop flowering when temperatures rise. *M. bicornis* will tolerate poorer soil and drier conditions than will *M. incana*.

Selected species and varieties:
M. bicornis [also known as *M. longipetala* ssp. *bicornis*] (night-scented stock, evening stock, perfume plant) has a bushy habit and grows 1 to 1½ feet tall. It bears single ¾-inch flowers in shades of lilac and pink that open at night from mid- to late summer and are extremely fragrant. *M. incana* (common stock, gillyflower) grows 1 to 2½ feet with gray-green oblong leaves and terminal clusters of 1-inch-long flowers that may be single or double and bear a spicy fragrance; colors include pink, purple, white, and blue.

SWEET ALYSSUM
Lobularia

Light: mostly sun	
Plant type: tender perennial grown as annual	
Height: 3 to 6 inches	
Soil and Moisture: well-drained, moist	
Interest: flowers, fragrance	
Care: easy	

◀ Lobularia maritima

Sweet alyssum produces robust mounds of narrow, lance-shaped gray-green leaves that are usually hidden beneath masses of petite, fragrant four-petaled flowers from spring to frost. Long a favorite for beds, borders, rock gardens, and containers and as a cover for the withering foliage of spring bulbs, it is usually grown as an annual except in warmer climates.

Growing and care:

Propagate from seed sown indoors 6 to 8 weeks before the last frost, or outdoors after danger of frost has passed. Thin seedlings to 6 inches apart. Young plants will spread quickly and flower rapidly if kept moist and cool with light afternoon shade. Periodic shearing of old blossoms during summer will stimulate further flowering. In warm climates they will self-sow.

Selected species and varieties:

L. maritima [also listed as *Alyssum maritimum*] grows 3 to 6 inches tall with white, pink, or violet flowers; 'Little Dorrit' has a greater abundance of more densely packed clusters of white flowers and a more compact form than many other sweet alyssums; 'Pastel Carpet' has flowers with a variety of pastel shades and white centers; 'Royal Carpet' has violet-purple flowers; 'Tiny Tim' is 3 inches tall with white flowers.

THISTLE
Cirsium

Light: mostly sun	
Plant type: biennial	
Height: 1½ to 2½ feet	
Soil and Moisture: well-drained, moist to dry	
Interest: flowers, foliage	
Care: easy	

◀ Cirsium japonicum

Thistle is a coarse-textured plant with bold, dark green spiny leaves and solitary rose or magenta flowers that are as soft as velvet. The abundant leaves and upright stems provide a dramatic foil for the intensely colored flowers. Thistle adds a dynamic element to the mixed border or wildflower meadow. The blossoms attract butterflies, and are also beautiful in floral arrangements.

Growing and care:

Sow seed directly in the garden as soon as soil can be worked in spring for late-summer flowers. Once established, plants will self-seed. Space plants 1 to 2 feet apart. They are adaptable to a wide range of soils as long as drainage is good.

Selected species and varieties:

C. japonicum (rose thistle) produces an erect, branched stem with deeply lobed 4-inch leaves. The leaves are deep green with spiny edges and often display silvery veins. Flower heads top each stem in summer. The buds are covered with silvery overlapping scales, and the opened flower heads are 1 to 2 inches across. Each head consists of a mass of tiny tubular flowers.

TREE MALLOW
Lavatera

◀ Lavatera trimestris

Light: mostly sun	
Plant type: annual	
Height: 2 to 6 feet	
Soil and Moisture: well-drained, moist	
Interest: flowers	
Care: easy	

Native to the Mediterranean region, tree mallow is a hardy annual with a bushy habit and cup-shaped summer flowers that resemble hollyhocks. Their long blooming season makes these plants a good choice for the mixed border. They are also useful as a summer hedge, and flowers can be cut for fresh arrangements.

Growing and care:
Sow seed outdoors in midspring, thinning to allow plants to stand 1½ to 2 feet apart. Young plants require abundant water and should be mulched. Once established, plants are drought resistant. Deadhead to prolong flowering.

Selected species and varieties:
L. trimestris produces pale green rounded leaves on branched stems that may reach 6 feet, although most varieties are between 2 and 3 feet; both leaves and stems are hairy. Solitary 2½- to 4-inch flowers, each with five wide petals, are borne in great numbers throughout the summer. Colors include shades of pink, red, and white; 'Mont Blanc' grows only 2 feet tall and bears pure white flowers; 'Silver Cup' also grows to 2 feet, bearing salmon-pink flowers with darker veins.

TULIP GENTIAN
Eustoma

◀ Eustoma grandiflorum 'Lion Mixed'

Light: mostly sun	
Plant type: biennial	
Height: 2 to 3 feet	
Soil and Moisture: well-drained, moist	
Interest: flowers, foliage	
Care: difficult	

This native American Great Plains wildflower produces waxy blue-green leaves on a thick stem with intricate, very beautiful upturned flowers. Though exacting in their requirements, the grace these plants lend to the garden make the effort well worthwhile. When grown properly they are exquisite border or container plants and make superb cut flowers, lasting up to 2 weeks.

Growing and care:
Start seed indoors in peat pots about 3 months prior to the last frost. Do not cover seed, as light is needed for proper germination. Keep soil moist and temperatures about 70°F. Transplant to the garden when about 6 inches tall, planting seedlings very carefully. Space plants 6 to 10 inches apart. Water only enough to keep soil evenly moist but not too wet. Do not allow blossoms to get wet. Gentians are slow growers and need a long growing season to perform well.

Selected species and varieties:
E. grandiflorum [also known as *Lisianthus russellianus*] (prairie gentian) has an erect habit with sturdy stems and 3-inch oblong leaves. Flowers may be single or double; they are 2 inches wide and usually purple, although pink, blue, and white varieties are available; 'Lion Mixed' is a double-flowered strain with colors from white to deep purple.

AEONIUM
Aeonium

Light:	mostly sun
Plant type:	perennial
Hardiness:	Zones 9-10
Height:	1 to 3 feet
Soil and Moisture:	well-drained, moist to dry
Interest:	flowers, foliage
Care:	moderate

◀ Aeonium arboreum 'Schwartzkopf'

Aeoniums bear colorful fleshy leaves in attractive rosettes on succulent stems that provide a desertlike ambiance to borders, containers, and rock gardens. The flowers develop in terminal pyramidal clusters in striking shades of yellow. The plants are prized in areas of the Southwest, where the warm, dry climate allows these decorative perennials to thrive.

Growing and care:
Aeoniums thrive in California coastal conditions, where their soil and light needs are best met. Site the plants where they will receive a little afternoon shade during the hottest portion of the day. Aeoniums make good container plants for patio gardens but should be brought indoors before frost.

Selected species and varieties:
A. arboreum 'Schwartzkopf' grows 2 to 3 feet tall with an upright shrubby habit and golden yellow flowers with dark, shiny purple-black leaves appearing in 6- to 8-inch rosettes on branched stems. *A. tabuliforme* reaches 1 foot tall with pale yellow flowers and succulent leaves forming saucer-shaped stemless rosettes 3 to 10 inches across.

ALUMROOT
Heuchera

Light:	mostly sun
Plant type:	perennial
Hardiness:	Zones 3-8
Height:	1 to 2 ½ feet
Soil and Moisture:	well-drained, moist, fertile
Interest:	flowers, foliage
Care:	easy to moderate

◀ Heuchera micrantha 'Palace Purple'

Alumroot produces handsome mounds of deeply colored lobed leaves and delicate, gracefully arching stems of small flowers. The spring and summer bell-shaped blossoms are gentle shades of white or pink, or bold hues of red. Some types sport rich ruby red leaves that accent rock gardens, edgings, and perennial beds.

Growing and care:
Plant alumroot in well-worked soil generously amended with rotted manure or compost. Water well at planting and regularly over the growing season. Mulch in areas with hot summers. As stems become woody, the plant falls open in the center. Divide every 3 to 4 years after flowering or in fall.

Selected species and varieties:
H. x *brizoides* bears red, pink, or white blooms on 1- to 2½-inch stems and dark green leaves; 'Pluie de Feu' ('Rain of Fire') grows to 1½ feet tall with red flowers. *H. micrantha* 'Palace Purple' (small-flowered alumroot) bears 15- to 18-inch-high mounds of wrinkled leaves that are deep purple-red in spring and fall, fading to purplish bronze-green in hot weather, bearing pinkish white flowers; it is grown primarily for its foliage. *H. sanguinea* (coral bells) grows 1 to 1½ feet tall with dark green leaves and pink, white, or red flowers among the hybrids; Bressingham Hybrids have rose-colored flowers.

ANEMONE
Anemone

Light:	mostly sun
Plant Type:	perennial
Hardiness:	Zones 2-9
Height:	6 inches to 4 feet
Soil and Moisture:	well-drained, dry
Interest:	flowers
Care:	easy

◀ Anemone pulsatilla

This diverse genus carries sprightly 1- to 3-inch-wide flowers with single or double rows of petals shaped like shallow cups surrounding prominent stamens and pistils. The flowers are held on branched stems above mounds of handsome deeply cut foliage. Many species brighten the garden during periods when few other plants with similar flowers are in bloom. Native to North America, anemone species can be found in moist woodlands, meadows, and dry prairies.

Growing and care:

Plant small anemones 1 foot apart, taller varieties 2 feet apart. The latter may require staking. Meadow anemone prefers a moist, sandy soil and needs frequent division to prevent overcrowding. Pasqueflowers need full sun and a neutral to alkaline soil in a cool location. Snowdrops windflowers prefer moist soil; grapeleaf anemones tolerate dry conditions. Protect all anemones from afternoon sun and do not allow to dry out completely. Propagate cultivars of Japanese anemone by root cuttings or division, others from seed. Divide Japanese and grapeleaf anemones in spring every 3 years to maintain robustness. Other species grow slowly and division is rarely needed.

Selected species and varieties:

A. canadensis (meadow anemone) grows 1 to 2 feet tall with deeply lobed basal leaves and 1½-inch white flowers with golden centers on leafy flower stems in late spring; Zones 2-6. *A. caroliniana* (Carolina anemone) grows 6 to 12 inches tall with numerous 1½-inch white flowers with yellow centers in spring; Zones 6-8. *A.* x *hybrida* (Japanese anemone) bears white or pink flowers with a silky sheen on their undersides above dark green foliage from late summer to midfall; Zones 6-8; 'Alba' grows 2 to 3 feet tall with large clear white flowers; 'Honorine Jobert' has white flowers with yellow centers on 3-foot stems; 'Prince Henry' has deep rose flowers on 3-foot stems; 'Queen Charlotte' has full, semidouble pink flowers; 'September Charm' has single-petaled silvery pink flowers; 'September Sprite' has single pink flowers on 15-inch stems. *A. magellanica* bears cream-colored flowers from late spring through summer atop 1½-foot stems; Zones 2-8. *A. multifida* (early thimbleweed) produces loose clumps of silky-haired stems up to 20 inches tall with deeply divided leaves on long stalks; sepals of the ⅜-inch flowers that appear from late spring to summer are usually yellowish white but occasionally bright red; Zones 3-9. *A. pulsatilla* [also classified as *Pulsatilla vulgaris*] (pasqueflower) is known by its 2-inch-wide blue or purple bell-shaped spring flowers on 1-foot stems above hairy leaves; Zones 5-8. *A. sylvestris* 'Snowdrops' (snowdrops windflower) stands 1 to 1½ feet tall with light green foliage topped by dainty, fragrant 2-inch spring flowers. *A. vitifolia* 'Robustissima' (grapeleaf anemone) features branching clusters of pink flowers from late summer to fall on 1- to 3-foot stalks; it is an invasive variety good for naturalizing; Zones 3-8.

ASTER
Aster

Light:	mostly sun
Plant type:	perennial
Hardiness:	Zones 3-9
Height:	6 inches to 8 feet
Soil and Moisture:	well-drained, dry, fertile
Interest:	flowers
Care:	easy

◄ Aster novae-angliae 'Harrington's Pink'

Asters are a large group of versatile, hardy plants prized for their large, showy, daisylike flowers that appear over weeks and even months. The blossoms are distinctive and delicate with very slender ray flowers surrounding a small button-shaped disk. Asters brighten the late summer and fall garden with a rainbow of whites, light blues, pinks, purples, and lavender. The plants are perfect for beds, borders, and rock gardens or planted in large groups in meadows and fields.

Growing and care:

Plant asters in an open, airy location with good air circulation to lessen the risk of powdery mildew. Water plants in the early morning when possible and avoid wetting leaves. Space dwarf asters 1 foot apart, taller ones 2 to 3 feet apart, and thin out young plants to improve air circulation. Taller varieties may require staking. Prompt deadheading encourages a second flowering in early-summer bloomers. *A.* x *frikartii* grown in Zone 5 or colder must be mulched over the winter and should not be cut back or divided in fall; otherwise, divide asters in early spring or fall every 2 years or so when a plant's center begins to die out. Asters can also be propagated by stem cuttings in spring and early summer. Cultivars seldom grow true from seed.

Selected species and varieties:

A. alpinus is a low-growing species forming 6- to 12-inch-high clumps topped by violet-blue 1- to 3-inch flowers with yellow centers; 'Dark Beauty' produces deep blue flowers; 'Goliath' grows a few inches taller than the species, with pale blue flowers; 'Happy End' has semidouble lavender flowers. *A.* x *frikartii* (Frikart's aster) produces 2- to 3-foot-tall plants topped by fragrant 2½-inch lavender-blue flowers with yellow centers blooming in summer and lasting 2 months or longer; 'Monch' has profuse blue-mauve flowers and is resistant to mildew. *A. novae-angliae* (New England aster) grows 2 to 5 feet tall with 4- to 5-inch leaves and 2-inch violet-purple flowers with bright golden disks; it is less important than its many cultivars, most of which are quite tall and require staking; 'Alma Potschke' has vivid rose-colored blossoms from late summer to fall; 'Harrington's Pink' grows to 4 feet tall with large salmon-pink flowers in fall; 'Purple Dome' is a dwarf variety growing 1½ feet tall and spreading 3 feet wide, with profuse deep purple fall flowers. *A. novi-belgii* (New York aster, Michaelmas daisy) cultivars range from 10 to 48 inches tall and bloom in white, pink, red, blue, and purple-violet from late summer through fall; 'Eventide' has violet-blue semidouble flowers on 3-foot stems; 'Professor Kippenburg' is compact and bushy, 12 to 15 inches tall with lavender-blue flowers; 'Royal Ruby' is a compact cultivar with large crimson fall flowers; 'Winston S. Churchill' grows violet-red flowers on 2-foot stems.

BALLOON FLOWER
Platycodon

Light: mostly sun	
Plant type: perennial	
Hardiness: Zones 4-9	
Height: 1 to 3 feet	
Soil and Moisture: well-drained, moist	
Interest: flowers	
Care: easy	

◀ Platycodon
grandiflorus

Balloon flowers have inflated buds that form 2- to 3-inch-wide cup-shaped blossoms with pointed translucent petals that add a uniquely beautiful touch to summer gardens. Flowers are usually blue, but cultivars with white or pink blossoms are also available. The branched 2- to 3-foot-tall shoots have 3-inch toothed oval leaves. Taller varieties may need staking. Balloon flowers are excellent for massing and borders, while dwarf cultivars can be used in rock gardens. Taller varieties make good cut flowers.

Growing and care:
Balloon flowers grow well in mostly sun, where they get enough light to thrive and enough shade to preserve the soft flower color. Propagate by seed or division in early spring or late autumn. Since shoots are late to emerge in spring, mark the locations of plants during the summer so plants are not damaged when soil is cultivated the following spring. Space plants 1½ feet apart. It usually takes 2 years for seedlings to reach flowering size.

Selected species and varieties:
P. grandiflorus (balloon flower, Japanese bellflower) sprouts deep blue flowers on slender 2- to 3-foot stems above neat clumps of blue-green leaves from mid- to late summer; 'Album' has white flowers; 'Shell Pink' and 'Mother-of-Pearl' have pale pink flowers; 'Sentimental Blue' has bright blue flowers on 15-inch stems.

BEAR'S-BREECH
Acanthus

Light: mostly sun	
Plant type: perennial	
Hardiness: Zones 7-10	
Height: 3 to 4 feet	
Soil and Moisture: well-drained, moist	
Interest: flowers, foliage	
Care: easy to moderate	

◀ Acanthus
spinosissimus

Bear's-breech is valued for its bold sculptural effects, with spreading clumps of broad, deeply lobed shiny leaves up to 2 feet long and stiff spikes of tubular flowers borne well above the foliage in summer. The plants provide a strong vertical accent to the back of the border and look very appealing in natural plantings. The flowers and seed heads are effective in arrangements.

Growing and care:
Bear's-breech thrives in sunny places where a little afternoon shade tempers the heat of summer days. Plant 3 feet apart, and propagate by seed or by division in early spring or fall after the plant has bloomed at least 3 years. Tolerant of moderate drought, bear's-breech abhors wet winter soil. Once established, this plant is difficult to remove from a site, as bits of fleshy roots inadvertently left behind easily grow into new plants.

Selected species and varieties:
A. spinosissimus (spiny bear's-breech) produces dense flower spikes, usually mauve but sometimes white, on 3- to 4-foot stalks overarching, deeply cut thistlelike leaves.

BEE BALM
Monarda

Light: mostly sun

Plant type: perennial

Hardiness: Zones 4-9

Height: 3 feet

Soil and Moisture: well-drained, moist

Interest: flowers, foliage, fragrance

Care: easy to moderate

◀ Monarda didyma
'Cambridge Scarlet'

Bee balms have round clusters of purple, lilac, red, pink, or white two-lipped tubular flowers arranged in moplike tufts at the tops of tall leafy stems. Their lance-shaped leaves are aromatic when crushed, and are used to make refreshing teas. Bee balms are members of the mint family and are excellent for planting in beds and borders or naturalizing in woodland plantings.

Growing and care:
Plant in spring or fall. Space plants 1½ to 2 feet apart. Prune withering flower heads to prolong the flowering season. Propagate by seed or division every few years in early spring, or from early-summer cuttings. Bee balms need good air circulation so they do not get mildew. Water during hot, dry periods.

Selected species and varieties:
M. didyma (bee balm, Oswego tea) bears 1- to 2-inch scarlet flowers in rounded 2- to 3-inch-wide clusters from late spring to late summer on 3- to 4-foot stems; 'Cambridge Scarlet' is wine red; 'Croftway Pink' is rosy pink; 'Granite Pink' is a dwarf with pink flowers; 'Mahogany' has dark red flowers; 'Marshall's Delight' is mildew resistant and bears large pink flowers over a longer season; 'Salmonea' has salmon-pink flowers; 'Snow Queen' has icy white blossoms. *M. fistulosa* (wild bergamot) produces 2- to 4-inch pompom-like clusters of lilac to pink flowers from mid- to late summer.

BLUE-EYED GRASS
Sisyrinchium

Light: mostly sun

Plant type: perennial

Hardiness: Zones 3-10

Height: 3 inches to 1½ feet

Soil and Moisture: well-drained, moist to dry

Interest: flowers, foliage

Care: moderate

◀ Sisyrinchium bellum

Dainty-looking blue-eyed grass bears starry six-petaled flowers and clumps of narrow leaves that add subtle beauty to the garden. It is a member of the iris family, and its flowers, which appear in spring and early summer, may be blue, reddish purple, or white. Its grasslike foliage is attractive in spring even when the plant is not in bloom. Blue-eyed grass looks especially good planted in drifts in the dappled shade of deciduous trees, among other wildflowers in a meadow garden, or with alpine plants in rock gardens.

Growing and care:
S. angustifolium needs poor to average, evenly moist soil; it tends to be short lived if allowed to dry out. *S. bellum* needs soil that is moist in spring and dry in summer. Grow blue-eyed grass from seed; plants also often self-sow. Plant in late winter or early spring about 6 to 12 inches apart, setting crowns about ½ inch deep. Divide every other year in spring or fall.

Selected species and varieties:
S. angustifolium (narrow-leaved blue-eyed grass) bears ½-inch-wide light blue flowers with a star-shaped yellow eye on twisted stalks that rise above the 1- to 1½-foot foliage clump from spring to summer. *S. bellum* (California blue-eyed grass) grows 3 to 18 inches high with large numbers of blue, violet, or white spring flowers that have yellow centers and 4- to 20-inch-long leaves.

BRUNNERA
Brunnera

Light: mostly sun to mostly shade	
Plant type: perennial	
Hardiness: Zones 4-8	
Height: 1 to 2 feet	
Soil and Moisture: well-drained, moist	
Interest: flowers, foliage	
Care: easy	

◀ Brunnera macrophylla

Brunnera is native to the Caucasus, where its mounds of lightly wrinkled heart-shaped leaves grow beneath groves of spruce and on grassy hillsides. In early spring the plants produce masses of showy, small blue flowers that resemble forget-me-nots. The foliage enlarges after the plants flower, and remains attractive throughout fall. These are excellent plants for borders or rock gardens, and put on an unforgettable springtime show when naturalized with forget-me-nots and daffodils in woodland gardens or meadows.

Growing and care:
Space plants 1 foot apart and mulch to keep roots cool and soil moist. Fertilize lightly after flowers have faded. Propagate by division in spring or fall, or by transplanting self-sown seedlings. This also rejuvenates older clumps. Brunnera does best in mostly sun and also does well in partial shade.

Selected species and varieties:
B. macrophylla [also listed as *Anchusa myosotidiflora*] (Siberian bugloss) bears loosely branched flower clusters on 1- to 1½-foot stems above rough-textured clumps of heart-shaped leaves with fuzzy petioles; 'Hadspen Cream' has sky blue flowers and light green leaves edged with white.

BUGLOSS
Anchusa

Light: mostly sun	
Plant type: perennial	
Hardiness: Zones 3-8	
Height: 3 to 5 feet	
Soil and Moisture: well-drained, moist	
Interest: flowers	
Care: easy	

◀ Anchusa azurea

Bugloss has a loose habit with clusters of small, lapis blue trumpetlike flowers above hairy, tongue-shaped leaves. The eye-catching blossoms persist a month or more and add an airy, vibrant splash to beds, borders, and wildflower gardens.

Growing and care:
Plant 1½ to 3 feet apart in spring or fall. Water plants regularly and fertilize in spring as plants begin active growth. Tall varieties may require staking, especially in breezy locations. Cutting plants to the ground after flowers fade forces a second show of blossoms in late summer or fall and prevents foliage from becoming lank. Provide good drainage, as standing moisture will rot roots in winter. Propagate by division every 2 to 3 years or from root cuttings.

Selected species and varieties:
A. azurea (Italian bugloss) has bright blue ¾-inch flowers that bloom abundantly on 3- to 5-foot stems; 'Little John' is a dwarf cultivar growing to 1½ feet with deep blue flowers and hairy dark green leaves; 'Loddon Royalist' grows 3 feet tall with royal blue flowers and an open habit.

BURNET
Sanguisorba

Light: mostly sun	
Plant type: perennial	
Hardiness: Zones 3-8	
Height: 2 ½ to 6 feet	
Soil and Moisture: well-drained, moist	
Interest: flowers, foliage	
Care: easy	

◀ Sanguisorba
canadensis

Burnets have spikes of white flowers resembling a bottlebrush on wandlike stems that add a coarse, bold aspect to gardens. The buds at the base of the flower spike open first, forming a wave of white moving upward from summer to midfall. The tall stems rise above the very attractive, toothed compound leaves. Native to low meadows and bogs in eastern North America, burnets are an excellent choice for perennial beds, natural gardens, and waterside plantings. They form spreading clumps over time.

Growing and care:
Burnets adapt to most conditions as long as the soil does not dry out completely. Taller varieties may need staking, so avoid adding extra fertilizer or plants may become even lankier than under ordinary conditions. Space plants 1½ to 2 feet apart. Propagate by division in early spring, or by seed sown in damp soil in fall or spring.

Selected species and varieties:
S. canadensis (Canadian burnet, American burnet) grows 3 to 6 feet tall with upright leafy-stemmed clumps and 6- to 8-inch-long flower spikes in summer made up of individual flowers, each having a four-lobed petal-like calyx and long white stamens but no petals. Its attractive compound leaves have seven to 15 oblong leaflets with sharply toothed edges.

CAMPION
Lychnis

Light: mostly sun	
Plant type: perennial	
Hardiness: Zones 4-9	
Height: 1 to 3 feet	
Soil and Moisture: well-drained, moist	
Interest: flowers, foliage	
Care: easy	

◀ Lychnis chalcedonica

Catchfly produces distinctive cross-shaped flowers of intense fiery scarlet. The brilliantly colored spring or summer blooms are set off by handsome dark green foliage. Catchfly is most impressive when planted in small groupings, where it provides a splash of intense color in a perennial border or bed. It is also effective massed as an accent in natural plantings such as wildflower meadows. The flowers of taller varieties are excellent for indoor arrangements.

Growing and care:
Catchfly thrives in mostly sunny places with a few hours of bright shade during hot summer days. Poorly drained soil results in short-lived plants; otherwise, the genus has very few pest or disease problems. Space plants 1 to 1½ feet apart. Propagate by seed in spring or by division in spring or fall.

Selected species and varieties:
L. x *arkwrightii* (Arkwright campion) is a bushy plant 12 to 15 inches tall with dark bronze foliage and bright orange-red summer flowers. *L. chalcedonica* (Maltese cross) produces 2- to 3-foot erect stems bearing pointed, clasping leaves and dense 3- to 4-inch terminal clusters of scarlet flowers, each blossom shaped like a small cross. *L. coronaria* (mullein pink, rose campion) has a spreading habit, woolly silvery white leaves, and 1-inch-wide magenta-pink flowers in late spring; Zones 5-9.

CATMINT
Nepeta

Light: mostly sun	
Plant type: perennial	
Hardiness: Zones 3-9	
Height: 1 to 3 feet	
Soil and Moisture: well-drained, moist	
Interest: flowers, foliage, fragrance	
Care: easy	

◀ Nepeta x faassenii

Catmints have fragrant, soft, dusty green heart-shaped leaves and square stems topped by spikes of tiny white or blue flowers. The plants are easy to grow and very durable, with flower spikes appearing nearly all summer long. Catmints are excellent as ground covers, in rock or herb gardens, or as edgings in informal plantings.

Growing and care:
Plant catmints in spring, spacing them 1 to 1½ feet apart. Shear plants after flowering to encourage rebloom. Fertilize lightly in spring when growth begins. To propagate, take softwood cuttings in summer from non-flowering shoots and stick directly in moist sand away from direct sunlight.

Selected species and varieties:
N. cataria (catnip) spreads in 2-foot clumps on pliant stems covered with gray-green leaves and topped with spikes of white and violet flowers; 'Citriodora' has tart lemon-scented leaves. *N. x faassenii* (blue catmint) produces 1½- to 2-foot mounds of silvery gray leaves and lavender-blue sterile flowers from spring to summer; 'Dropmore' has upright stems with lavender flowers; 'Six Hills Giant' is robust, very hardy, and grows to 3 feet tall with large sprays of deep blue flowers; 'Superba' has spreading branches covered with gray-green leaves and abundant dark blue flowers; Zones 4-9.

CHECKERMALLOW
Sidalcea

Light: mostly sun	
Plant type: perennial	
Hardiness: Zones 4-10	
Height: 2 to 4 feet	
Soil and Moisture: well-drained, wet to dry	
Interest: flowers	
Care: moderate	

◀ Sidalcea malviflora

Checkermallows are perky, hardworking wildflowers from the western United States. The plants bear showy pink or purple flowers resembling small holly-hocks and provide a colorful vertical accent in mixed herbaceous borders or meadow plantings.

Growing and care:
S. malviflora prefers soil that is moist in winter and well drained to dry in summer. It is an ideal choice for coastal gardens. *S. neomexicana* grows best in moist, well-drained to wet soils. Remove faded flowers or cut back spent flower stems to prolong blooming. Cut stems to ground in fall. Tall varieties may need staking, especially in breezy locations. Propagate by seed sown directly in the garden after last frost, or by division in fall.

Selected species and varieties:
S. malviflora (checkermallow, checkerbloom) grows up to 4 feet tall with pink or purple flowers on erect stems in spring and summer and dark green lobed leaves; the flowers open in the morning and close up in the evening; Zones 5-10. *S. neomexicana* (prairie mallow) grows up to 3 feet tall with mauve flowers in spring and early summer on pliant stems with dark green leaves; Zones 4-10.

CHRYSANTHEMUM
Chrysanthemum

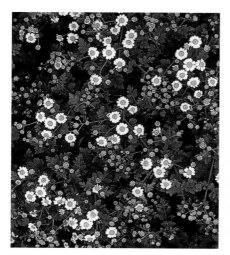

Light: mostly sun	
Plant type: perennial	
Hardiness: Zones 3-9	
Height: 6 inches to 3 feet	
Soil and Moisture: well-drained, moist, fertile	
Interest: flowers, foliage	
Care: easy to moderate	

◀ Chrysanthemum
parthenium

Chrysanthemums are the backbone of many fall gardens, with the varied forms reliably providing a long-lasting display both in the garden and cut for fresh arrangements. These hardworking plants bloom throughout summer and into fall. Their mounds of attractively lobed foliage blend well with other border plantings, or they can be massed for effect.

Growing and care:
Space chrysanthemums 1 to 2 feet apart in soil enriched with organic matter. Water plants during dry periods of the growing season but do not allow them to stay wet over winter or to become overcrowded. Provide a winter mulch. Divide in spring.

Selected species and varieties:
C. coccineum [also listed as *Tanacetum coccineum*] (painted daisy) has wiry 2- to 3-foot stems lined with fine-textured ferny leaves supporting 2- to 3-inch, usually single, red, pink, or white flowers with yellow centers from late spring to early summer; 'Helen' has pink double blooms; Zones 3-7. *C. parthenium* (feverfew) grows 1 to 3 feet tall, producing prolific white flower buttons with yellow centers in clusters from midsummer to fall above aromatic fernlike foliage; Zones 4-9. *C.* x *superbum* (Shasta daisy) bears white flowers with yellow centers 3 to 6 inches across on 2½-foot stems; 'Alaska' bears large, single white flowers on 2-foot stems.

CINQUEFOIL
Potentilla

Light: mostly sun	
Plant type: perennial	
Hardiness: Zones 2-7	
Height: 1 to 4 feet	
Soil and Moisture: well-drained, moist to dry	
Interest: flowers, foliage	
Care: easy	

◀ Potentilla nepalensis
'Miss Wilmott'

Cinquefoils are very hardy, easy-to-grow perennials with cheerful yellow, white, or rose flowers and attractive silvery green compound leaves. The plants range from ground-hugging dwarf types that resemble yellow-flowered strawberries to loosely branched, more upright forms with an open, airy appearance. Cinquefoil is a tasteful addition to the mixed border and rock garden, and offers special charm when naturalized in wildflower gardens and meadows.

Growing and care:
Cinquefoils grow almost anywhere but perform best in moist, well-drained soil that has some organic matter. Provide extra water during dry times. Mulch lightly in spring and fall with compost. Propagate by dividing established plants in spring every 3 to 4 years or by sowing seed in spring while soil is still cool.

Selected species and varieties:
P. nepalensis (Nepal cinquefoil) is a sprawling perennial 1½ feet tall with weak stems bearing serrated leaves in a star-shaped pattern and 1-inch-wide cup-shaped flowers in a range of colors from late spring to summer, hardy to Zone 5; 'Miss Wilmott' grows to 1 foot high and has cherry pink flowers. *P. tridentata* is a low-growing sub-alpine plant with three-part compound leaves that turn red in fall, and small white flowers in summer.

CULVER'S ROOT
Veronicastrum

Light: mostly sun to mostly shade

Plant type: perennial

Hardiness: Zones 3-8

Height: 2 to 6 feet

Soil and Moisture: well-drained, fertile, moist

Interest: flowers, foliage

Care: easy to moderate

◀ Veronicastrum virginicum

Culver's root is a perennial found on stream banks and moist prairies of the eastern United States. It produces showy erect clusters of narrow flower spikes atop tall stems from mid- to late summer, making it a valuable performer at the back of a herbaceous border.

Growing and care:
V. virginicum is easy to grow in full sun or light shade in moist, well-drained soil. Plants also do well in shady places. Plant in well-worked soil generously amended with compost or rotted manure. The upright, strong stems require no staking. Propagate by seed, cuttings, or root division.

Selected species and varieties:
V. virginicum [also listed as *Veronica virginica*] (Culver's root, bowman's-root) has strong unbranched stems up to 6 feet tall with white or pale blue flowers in spikes up to 9 inches long arranged in candelabra-like clusters at the tops of stems. The sharply toothed 6-inch leaves fan out horizontally from the stem in symmetrical whorls; the cultivar 'Roseum' has pale pink blossoms.

DAYLILY
Hemerocallis

Light: mostly sun

Plant type: perennial

Hardiness: Zones 3-10

Height: 1 to 6 feet

Soil and Moisture: well-drained, moist

Interest: flowers, foliage, fragrance

Care: easy

◀ Hemerocallis 'Stella d'Oro'

Daylilies are old-fashioned favorites that are easy to care for. The original 15 species have yielded more than 26,000 varieties with flowers in every color except blue. So many cultivars and hybrids allow you to create beds and borders graced with daylily flowers from late spring to fall. The flowers are borne on stems that often are twice as tall as the mounds of foliage. Each flower lasts from 1 to 2 days, but the numerous buds keep daylilies blooming for many weeks.

Growing and care:
Plant daylily crowns 1 inch below the soil surface, 1½ to 2 feet apart for smaller types and 2 to 3 feet apart for taller ones, in spring, summer, or fall. Provide organic mulch to conserve water and prevent frost heaving where winters are cold, and afternoon shade where summers are hot and dry. A light application of fertilizer in spring is helpful. Rejuvenate established plants by dividing clumps every 3 to 6 years in early spring, or after flowering in late summer or fall.

Selected species and varieties:
H. fulva 'Europa' (orange daylily, tawny daylily) is a vigorous, growing 4-foot-tall cultivar with clusters of six to 12 tawny orange 4- to 5-inch flowers in midsummer. *H.* 'Stella d'Oro' is a nearly ever-blooming miniature hybrid with slightly ruffled 2½-inch orange-throated canary yellow flowers.

EVERLASTING
Anaphalis

Light: mostly sun
Plant type: perennial
Hardiness: Zones 3-9
Height: 1 to 3 feet
Soil and Moisture: well-drained, moist to medium
Interest: flowers, foliage
Care: easy

◀ Anaphalis margaritacea

Everlastings are vigorous, woolly plants that add contrast to borders and rock gardens from summer through fall. Narrow, elongated white leaves clasp the stems. The small, tight, globular summer flowers often are cut before they are fully open, to be dried and used in flower arrangements. In addition to their ornamental qualities, everlastings repel some insects harmful to garden plants and also attract butterflies.

Growing and care:
Everlastings do well in nutrient-poor sandy soil. They need no additional fertilizers and, once established, are quite drought resistant. They spread freely by underground stems called rhizomes, and form large clumps in just a few years. Separate rhizomes in early spring and plant ½ inch deep; or propagate from fresh seed sown in the fall, planting ⅛ inch deep; or start in flats and transplant seedlings 1½ feet apart.

Selected species and varieties:
A. margaritacea (pearly everlasting, silverleaf) is native to the North Temperate Region, including North America. Its ¼- to ½-inch pearly white flower heads with burnt yellow centers that appear in late summer on 8- to 24-inch stems, and narrow 4- to 8-inch green leaves often so densely covered with hairs that they appear to have a silvery cast.

FALSE LUPINE
Thermopsis

Light: mostly sun
Plant type: perennial
Hardiness: Zones 3-9
Height: 1½ to 5 feet
Soil and Moisture: well-drained, moist to dry, fertile
Interest: flowers, foliage
Care: easy to moderate

◀ Thermopsis montana

False lupines are strong, handsome plants with stout stems and spikes of vivid yellow flowers from spring to summer. These hardy perennials are native to open woodlands, meadows, and stony flats, where they have evolved a tolerance to heat and drought. False lupines combine well with ornamental grasses in a mixed perennial border and are excellent when naturalized in a meadow.

Growing and care:
Grow *T. montana* in a well-drained sandy soil and *T. villosa* in a humus-rich soil. The plants flower best with extra water during dry periods. Propagate *T. montana* by seed and *T. villosa* by seed or division.

Selected species and varieties:
T. montana (golden pea) is a western native with slender branched stems to 32 inches tall bearing dense 4- to 12-inch clusters of bright yellow flowers in spring, followed by velvety pods; Zones 3-8. *T. villosa* (bush pea) is native to the Appalachian Mountains and grows 3 to 5 feet tall with dark green foliage and deep yellow flowers in dense clusters up to a foot long from spring to summer, followed by hairy pods; Zones 4-9.

FLAX
Linum

Light: mostly sun	
Plant type: perennial	
Hardiness: Zones 5-9	
Height: 1 to 2 feet	
Soil and Moisture: well-drained, sandy, moist to dry	
Interest: flowers	
Care: easy	

◀ Linum perenne

The delicate, softly colored blossoms of flax decorate the open, branching stems with abundant porcelain blue, golden yellow, or linen white flowers from spring to summer. The fine-textured, deep green foliage provides a light aspect to borders and rock gardens. Though blossoms last only a day, new buds open continuously for 6 weeks or more.

Growing and care:

Direct-sow in the garden in spring in northern regions and in fall from Zone 8 south. Thin plants to stand 6 inches apart for smaller types and to 1½ feet apart for larger forms. Cut the stems back in spring to encourage branching, and snip stems to ground level in fall. Do not transplant, as flax does not like being disturbed. The plants are short lived and best propagated by seed.

Selected species and varieties:

L. flavum (golden flax) bears bright yellow flowers on stems 1 to 1½ feet tall. *L. perenne* (perennial flax) has abundant sky blue, saucer-shaped flowers on stems up to 2 feet tall; 'Diamant White' has abundant white blossoms on 1- to 1½-foot stems.

FLEABANE
Erigeron

Light: mostly sun	
Plant type: perennial	
Hardiness: Zones 3-8	
Height: 6 inches to 2 feet	
Soil and Moisture: well-drained, moist to dry	
Interest: flowers	
Care: easy	

◀ Erigeron speciosus 'Pink Jewel'

Fleabane's asterlike blossoms grow singly or in branched clusters with a fringe of slender ray flowers surrounding a yellow center. Flowers sit atop graceful leafy stems that rise from basal rosettes of fuzzy swordlike or oval leaves. Fleabane is an easy-to-grow, vigorous plant that brings the distinctiveness of asters to the spring and early-summer garden. The plants are excellent in borders or displayed in natural plantings.

Growing and care:

Plant fleabane 1½ feet apart in soil amended with some organic matter. Water during dry, hot periods to extend flowering season. Propagate by transplanting self-sown seedlings or by division in spring.

Selected species and varieties:

E. pulchellus (poor Robin's plantain) bears pink, lavender, or white flowers 1½ inches across on plants up to 2 feet tall. *E. speciosus* (Oregon fleabane), the most popular species in the genus, bears purple flowers 1 to 2 inches across on stems to 2½ feet; 'Azure Fairy' has semidouble lavender flowers; 'Double Beauty', double blue-violet flowers; 'Foerster's Liebling', deep pink semidouble flowers; 'Pink Jewel', single lavender-pink flowers; 'Sincerity', single lavender flowers.

FOUR-O'CLOCK
Mirabilis

Light:	mostly sun
Plant type:	perennial
Hardiness:	Zones 5-10
Height:	1½ to 3 feet
Soil and Moisture:	well-drained, dry
Interest:	flowers
Care:	easy

◀ Mirabilis multiflora

Among the many types of four-o'clocks are several wildflowers native to dry areas of the western United States. These hardy perennials are easy to grow and quickly spread over slopes and rocky areas, stabilizing the soil and reducing erosion. The brightly colored tubular flowers open in the afternoon and close the following morning. Wild four-o'clocks are lovely massed as a ground cover or trailing over a wall.

Growing and care:
Four-o'clocks are low-maintenance plants that are also long lived and very drought tolerant. Supplemental watering during dry periods will extend the season of bloom. Propagate by seed or by dividing roots in fall.

Selected species and varieties:
M. froebelii (wild four-o'clock, wishbone plant) bears numerous clusters of 1½- to 2¼-inch-long deep rose pink to reddish purple flowers at the ends of multibranched stems up to 3 feet; Zones 7-10. *M. multiflora* (wild four-o'clock) grows up to 1½ feet with magenta tubular flowers about 2 inches long and dark green leaves.

GAS PLANT
Dictamnus

Light:	mostly sun
Plant type:	perennial
Hardiness:	Zones 3-9
Height:	2 to 3 feet
Soil and Moisture:	well-drained, moist
Interest:	flowers, foliage, fragrance
Care:	moderate

◀ Dictamnus albus 'Purpureus'

Gas plant offers open, decorative mounds of lemon-scented glossy foliage crowned in late spring to early summer with tall flower spikes of white, pink, rose or purple blossoms. The flowers are excellent in fresh bouquets. In late summer star-shaped seed capsules appear that add interest to dried arrangements. Gas plant is a nice addition to borders and informal plantings.

Growing and care:
Sow gas plant seed outdoors in spring or fall in soil generously amended with organic matter. Thin plants to stand 2 to 3 feet apart. Do not disturb or transplant. Mulch in spring and fall. Cut back stems to ground level in fall, especially in warm regions. Propagate from seed, as dividing plants is rarely successful.

Selected species and varieties:
D. albus (gas plant, fraxinella, white dittany) features leathery oval leaflets with finely toothed edges in mounds to 3 feet high and as wide with spikes of 1-inch white flowers on erect stems; 'Purpureus' has mauve-purple blossoms veined deeper purple; 'Ruber' bears rose pink flowers.

GEUM
Geum

Light:	mostly sun
Plant type:	perennial
Hardiness:	Zones 5-8
Height:	6 inches to 2½ feet
Soil and Moisture:	well-drained, moist, fertile
Interest:	flowers, foliage
Care:	moderate

◀ Geum x borisii

Geums produce open, attractive flowers in single or double blooms. The flowers, which resemble wild roses in some types and buttercups in others, have satiny or ruffled petals surrounding frilly centers that grow singly on slender stems; they make excellent cut flowers. The bright green hairy leaves, which are lobed and frilled at their edges, form attractive mounds of foliage ideal for the front of a border or for the rock garden.

Growing and care:
Space geums 1 to 1½ feet apart in soil enriched with organic matter. They grow best in moist but well-drained sites in cooler climates and will not survive wet winter soil. Mulch around plants to keep soil moist and cool. Site geums in locations that receive some shade during the hottest portion of the day. Water regularly during hot, dry periods. Mulch in fall north of Zone 7. Keep geums robust by dividing every 3 to 4 years in late summer. Direct-sow seed in early spring while soil is still cool.

Selected species and varieties:
G. x *borisii* produces orange-scarlet flowers on 1-foot plants. *G. coccineum* (scarlet avens) bears early-summer-blooming ½-inch bright orange flowers that ride above bright green, toothed leaves on 1-foot-tall stems; 'Red Wings' has semidouble scarlet flowers atop 2-foot stems. *G.* 'Georgenberg' bears drooping orange flowers on 10- to 12-inch stems.

GLOBEFLOWER
Trollius

Light:	mostly sun
Plant type:	perennial
Hardiness:	Zones 4-10
Height:	1½ to 5 feet
Soil and Moisture:	well-drained, moist
Interest:	flowers, foliage
Care:	easy

◀ Trollius ledebourii 'Golden Queen'

Globeflower is a bright addition to any garden, with vivid 2- to 4-inch golden yellow blossoms on graceful stems. The flowers consist of waxy, curved petals forming dense balls that provide a long-lasting display in perennial borders, rock gardens, or wildflower meadows.

Growing and care:
Space globeflowers 1½ feet apart in soil containing generous amounts of organic matter. Mulch around base of plants during warm, dry periods and water regularly. Propagate from seed or by division in fall every 4 years. Globeflower is long lived but does not like to be disturbed once established.

Selected species and varieties:
T. x *cultorum* (hybrid globeflower) bears yellow to orange flowers. *T. europaeus* (common globeflower) has lemon yellow flowers on stems up to 2 feet tall with dark green lobed leaves; 'Superbus' has light yellow flowers in spring and often again in late summer or fall. *T. ledebourii* (Ledebour globeflower) has bright orange flowers on graceful 3-foot stems; 'Golden Queen' has golden orange blossoms.

GOAT'S RUE
Galega

Light: mostly sun	
Plant type: perennial	
Hardiness: Zones 4-10	
Height: 1½ to 5 feet	
Soil and Moisture: well-drained, moist	
Interest: flowers, foliage	
Care: easy	

◄ Galega officinalis

Goat's rues are rambling members of the bean family with upright clusters of white, lavender, or violet-blue pealike flowers in summer on erect stems. Their bold, featherlike compound leaves have oval leaflets and form dense mounds that completely cover the ground. A robust growth habit makes them useful at the back of borders or naturalized in wildflower gardens. Goat's rues make good cut flowers.

Growing and care:

Goat's rues thrive in locations with plentiful afternoon shade, especially in regions with hot summers. Plant in spring or fall 2 inches deep and 1 to 2 feet apart, and mulch lightly. Propagate in early spring from seed sown where plants are desired, or by dividing root crowns.

Selected species and varieties:

G. officinalis bears sprays of white, lilac, pink, or lavender flowers on 2- to 5-foot stems from summer to early fall, and five to eight narrow, blue-green leaflets with pointed tips; 'Carnea' has rosy pink flowers that contrast beautifully with its blue-green leaves; 'Lady Wilson' has fine, slender spikes of lilac-blue flowers. *G. orientalis* is a more compact species with 1½-foot stems spreading to 2 feet, and violet flowers tinged with blue in early summer; Zones 6-10.

GROUNDSEL
Senecio

Light: mostly sun	
Plant type: perennial	
Hardiness: Zones 4-10	
Height: 1 to 5 feet	
Soil and Moisture: well-drained, moist to dry	
Interest: flowers	
Care: moderate	

◄ Senecio aureus

Groundsels are vigorous perennials that quickly ramble over meadows and open woodlands, creating masses of bright golden yellow flowers from midspring to fall. The plants are easy to grow and maintain, and the daisylike flowers are cheerful additions to natural plantings and informal gardens.

Growing and care:

Plant groundsel in spring or fall in loose, sandy soil amended with some organic matter. Water regularly for a few weeks after planting. Propagate by seed, division, or cuttings.

Selected species and varieties:

S. aureus (golden groundsel, golden ragwort) grows 1 to 3 feet tall with clusters of deep golden yellow flowers in late spring and summer above the heart-shaped dark green basal foliage. It spreads rapidly by horizontal off-shoots to form attractive colonies; native to eastern North America; Zones 4-8. *S. douglasii* (shrubby senecio) is a shrubby perennial up to 5 feet tall with bright yellow flowers in summer and fall and fuzzy greenish white foliage; native to California; Zones 6-10.

INULA
Inula

Light: mostly sun	
Plant type: perennial	
Hardiness: Zones 4-9	
Height: 6 to 12 inches	
Soil and Moisture: well-drained, moist	
Interest: flowers	
Care: easy	

◀ Inula ensifolia

Inula produces cheerful, bright yellow daisylike flowers that enliven summer gardens. The blossoms have slender ray petals surrounding a yellow center, making each flower look like a child's drawing of the sun. Inula is excellent in mixed borders and sprinkled through wildflower gardens and meadows.

Growing and care:
Sow seed indoors 6 to 8 weeks before last frost, or direct-sow in garden in early spring while soil is cool. Plant seedlings 1 foot apart for smaller types and 1½ to 2 feet apart for larger forms. Water regularly during growing season; mulch in spring and again in fall. Cut plants back in fall. Divide every 3 years.

Selected species and varieties:
I. acaulis (stemless inula) has single yellow flowers borne on 6-inch stems in midsummer, over tufts of spatulate leaves. *I. ensifolia* (swordleaf inula) forms dense, rounded clumps 1 foot tall and wide of wiry erect stems lined with narrow 4-inch pointed leaves and tipped with 1- to 2-inch yellow flowers. The blooms last 2 to 3 weeks in warmer zones, up to 6 weeks in cooler areas.

IRONWEED
Vernonia

Light: mostly sun	
Plant type: perennial	
Hardiness: Zones 4-9	
Height: 4 to 8 feet	
Soil and Moisture: well-drained, moist to wet	
Interest: flowers	
Care: easy	

◀ Vernonia
    noveboracensis

Ironweeds are tall, vigorous perennials native to moist meadows and prairies in the eastern half of the United States. Their loosely branched terminal clusters of purple flowers are effective in the back of a wildflower border or in a meadow garden.

Growing and care:
Ironweeds thrive in rich to average moist soil. *V. altissima* grows equally well in marshes and other wet sites. *V. noveboracensis* will tolerate wet soil. Ironweeds have sturdy stems that rarely require staking. Propagate by seed, cuttings, or division.

Selected species and varieties:
V. altissima (tall ironweed) grows 5 to 8 feet tall with ½-inch reddish purple flower heads in clusters of 30 to 40 from late summer through midautumn. The lance-shaped dark green leaves are up to 1 foot long; native from New York south to Louisiana and west to Nebraska. *V. noveboracensis* (New York ironweed) grows 4 to 6 feet tall with clusters of as many as 50 frilly purple flower heads in late summer; native to southern New England, the mid-Atlantic states, and the Southeast; Zones 5-8.

JACOB'S-LADDER
Polemonium

Light: mostly sun

Plant type: perennial

Hardiness: Zones 2-9

Height: 4 inches to 3 feet

Soil and Moisture: well-drained, moist, fertile

Interest: flowers, foliage

Care: easy

◀ Polemonium viscosum

Jacob's-ladder is native to meadows, open woodlands, and stream banks. Its dark green compound leaves provide an attractive foil for its upward-facing cup-shaped flowers.

Growing and care:
P. viscosum grows in full sun and well-drained rocky soil. The other species prefer partial shade and moist soil; for *P. reptans,* provide ample organic matter. Propagate by seed or division in spring.

Selected species and varieties:
P. carneum (royal polemonium) grows 1 to 2 feet tall with clusters of purple, pink, or salmon flowers 1½ inches across from spring through summer; California and Oregon; Zones 7-9. *P. occidentale* [also called *P. caeruleum* ssp. *amygdalinum*] (western polemonium) grows to 3 feet with clusters of pale blue summer flowers; Alaska to Colorado; Zones 3-9. *P. reptans* (creeping polemonium) reaches to 2 feet with large clusters of blue or pink flowers from spring to summer; eastern United States. *P. viscosum* (sky pilot) grows 4 to 20 inches tall with light blue or white flower clusters in spring and summer; western mountains; Zones 3-7.

JUPITER'S-BEARD
Centranthus

Light: mostly sun

Plant type: perennial

Hardiness: Zones 4-9

Height: 1 to 3 feet

Soil and Moisture: well-drained, fertile, moist

Interest: flowers

Care: easy

◀ Centranthus ruber

Jupiter's-beard is a robust, vigorous plant with strong upright stems amid dense, round flower clusters in summer. The lance-shaped bluish green leaves accent the handsome wine red flowers. Jupiter's-beard is a good choice for the back of the border or planted in masses in woodland gardens. The plants are also popular cut flowers in fresh floral arrangements.

Growing and care:
Plant Jupiter's-beard in well-worked soil with plentiful organic matter and a pH near neutral. Space plants 1 to 1½ feet apart. Fertile soil results in larger growth. Cut back stems after flowering is completed to encourage rebloom. Trim to ground level in fall. Propagate by transplanting self-sown seedlings. Established plantings do not transplant well and should not be disturbed.

Selected species and varieties:
C. ruber forms bushy plants to 3 feet tall with fragrant ½-inch spurred flowers in rounded terminal clusters above paired blue-green leaves; 'Albus' has white flowers; 'Atrococcineus', deep red flowers; 'Coccineus', scarlet flowers.

LILY-OF-THE-NILE
Agapanthus

Light: mostly sun
Plant type: perennial
Hardiness: Zones 8-10
Height: 3 to 5 feet
Soil and Moisture: well-drained, moist
Interest: flowers, foliage
Care: easy

◀ Agapanthus africanus

Lily-of-the-Nile is an easy-to-grow plant with long, narrow, glossy green leaves and stout stems bearing open clusters of lilac-blue blossoms in summer. The plants are gorgeous when planted in masses or in borders in warm regions. In colder areas lily-of-the-Nile is a reliable container plant that graces the deck or patio in summer and the living room in winter.

Growing and care:

Plant *Agapanthus* 2 feet apart and water well during the growing season. In containers set plants in rich soil well amended with organic matter. Plants tolerate dryness while dormant in winter. Do not repot too often, as plants bloom best when slightly potbound. Cut stems back after flowering. Propagate by dividing every 4 to 5 years in spring.

Selected species and varieties:

A. africanus bears up to 30 eye-catching deep blue blossoms on 3-foot stems; leaves are 4 to 10 inches long. *A. orientalis* grows 5 feet tall with up to 100 blue flowers in each cluster; 'Albidus' has white flowers; the leaves of 'Variegatus' are striped white.

LOOSESTRIFE
Lysimachia

Light: mostly sun
Plant type: perennial
Hardiness: Zones 4-8
Height: 2 inches to 3 feet
Soil and Moisture: well-drained, fertile, moist
Interest: flowers, foliage
Care: easy

◀ L. nummularia 'Buttercup'

Loosestrifes have neat, very attractive blossoms that add a warm, pleasant touch to gardens. Flowers bloom singly or in small spikes amid attractive foliage. Loosestrife is native to moist prairies and stream banks, and can be planted near a garden pond or at the edge of a moist woodland, where its flowers present a fine summer display. However, in moist soil it may spread too rapidly and take over the garden. Gooseneck loosestrife flowers are excellent for fresh arrangements.

Growing and care:

Space plants 1 to 2 feet apart in well-worked soil amended with some organic matter. Loosestrife will need frequent division in spring or fall to contain its growth if planted in a border. Propagate by seed or division in spring.

Selected species and varieties:

L. clethroides (gooseneck loosestrife) grows to 3 feet tall with an erect habit, rich green leaves that turn bronze to yellow in fall, and 3- to 6-inch-long gracefully arching white flower spikes from mid- to late summer that resemble a goose's neck. *L. nummularia* (creeping Jenny) is a 2- to 4-inch creeper with yellow flowers in late spring; 'Buttercup' has intense sunny yellow flowers atop dark green leaves. *L. punctata* (yellow loosestrife) grows 1½ to 2½ feet tall with lemon yellow summer blooms.

LUPINE
Lupinus

Light: mostly sun	
Plant type: perennial	
Hardiness: Zones 4-6	
Height: 1½ to 4 feet	
Soil and Moisture: well-drained, moist	
Interest: flowers, foliage	
Care: moderate	

◀ Lupinus 'Russell Hybrids'

Lupines bear stout, elongated spikes of small, densely packed butterfly-shaped flowers in a wide array of bright colors. The long-lasting blossoms cover the tips of stiff stalks lined with whorls of narrow leaves that dramatically embellish the flower border. Lupines are most effective massed into large groups in meadows or wildflower gardens, or mixed into the perennial border.

Growing and care:
Plant lupines in acidic soil enriched with rotted manure or compost. Space plants 1½ to 2 feet apart. Provide a little afternoon shade and water regularly. Mulch plants in spring to keep roots cool. Plants may require staking. Propagate from seed or from root cuttings taken with a small piece of crown in early spring.

Selected species and varieties:
L. 'Russell Hybrids' is a large group of plants to 4 feet tall with showy 1½- to 2-foot-long summer-blooming flower spires that open from the bottom up in a multitude of colors and combinations; dwarf strains 1½ feet tall include 'Little Lulu' and 'Minarette'.

MALLOW
Hibiscus

Light: mostly sun	
Plant type: perennial	
Hardiness: Zones 5-9	
Height: 3 to 8 feet	
Soil and Moisture: well-drained, moist to wet	
Interest: flowers	
Care: easy	

◀ Hibiscus coccineus

Mallows thrive in wet meadows and along the banks of streams and ponds, lending color and form to these moist areas. The plants bear white, pink, rose, or purple bell-shaped flowers in summer on tall, pliant stems reaching to 8 feet high. Mallows grow well in the moist soils of perennial beds as well as accenting natural plantings near water.

Growing and care:
Plant mallows in a moist spot where they will receive some high-afternoon shade. Allow plenty of room between plants, which may spread to 5 feet in width. The plants are vigorous, and once established need little attention. Propagate by seed or early-summer cuttings.

Selected species and varieties:
H. coccineus (wild red mallow) grows 4 to 7 feet tall with blue-green leaves and scarlet flowers 6 inches across; Zones 7-9. H. grandiflorus (great rose mallow) grows up to 6 feet tall and bears pale pink to purplish rose flowers, sometimes with crimson centers. H. lasiocarpus (woolly mallow) grows 3 to 5 feet tall with terminal clusters of 5- to 8-inch pink or white flowers that sometimes have purple centers. H. moscheutos (swamp rose mallow, wild cotton) grows 3 to 8 feet tall with a shrubby habit gray-green leaves, and white, pink, or rose flowers 8 inches across, often with red or purple centers; Zones 6-9.

MARSHALLIA
Marshallia

Light: mostly sun

Plant type: perennial

Hardiness: Zones 5-9

Height: 8 inches to 2 feet

Soil and Moisture: well-drained, moist to dry, sandy

Interest: flowers

Care: easy

◀ Marshallia grandiflora

Marshallia is a clump-forming perennial with buttonlike flowers and a tidy form, making them suitable for planting at the front of a mixed border, along a garden walk, or among stones in a rock garden, terrace, or in a moist meadow. These beautiful wildflowers bear rounded clusters of small rose pink flowers from spring to summer on graceful, slender 1- to 2-foot stems.

Growing and care:

Marshallias grow well in either moist or dry soils as long as drainage is excellent. Plant in spring or fall in soil well amended with rotted manure or compost. In areas that stay wet, dig the planting hole twice as deep as needed and fill halfway with peastone. Propagate by seed or division.

Selected species and varieties:

M. caespitosa (Barbara's buttons) bears ball-shaped clusters of dainty, fragrant white flowers on leafless stalks 8 to 18 inches tall above a rosette of narrow leaves. *M. grandiflora* (large-flowered marshallia) has large, densely packed balls of rose pink flowers with purple stamens on 1- to 2-foot stalks above a dense rosette of glossy dark green oval leaves.

MEADOW BEAUTY
Rhexia

Light: mostly sun

Plant type: perennial

Hardiness: Zones 4-9

Height: 1 to 2 feet

Soil and Moisture: well-drained to heavy, wet to moist

Interest: flowers

Care: easy

◀ Rhexia mariana

Meadow beauties are dainty perennials that bear small, distinctive pinkish flowers from early to late summer. The plants thrive in boggy soils and are native to wetlands and moist meadows in the eastern United States. The individual blossoms are uniquely shaped with pink to white slightly reflexed petals highlighted by slender central filaments that look like the protruding legs of a wayward insect. Meadow beauties are excellent for wet sites and water gardens.

Growing and care:

Meadow beauties thrive in boggy soil or in rich, sandy garden soil as long as moisture is abundant. They prefer full sun but tolerate light shade. *Rhexia* spreads by rhizomes to form colonies. Propagate by seed or by dividing the rhizomes.

Selected species and varieties:

R. mariana (Maryland meadow beauty) grows to 2 feet with loose clusters of white, pink, or pale rose flowers 2 inches across with bright yellow stamens. *R. virginica* (Virginia meadow beauty) grows 1 to 2 feet in height with deep magenta petaled flowers 1½ inches across with golden yellow stamens and bright green foliage; Zones 5-9.

MEADOWSWEET
Filipendula

Light: mostly sun	
Plant type: perennial	
Hardiness: Zones 3-8	
Height: 1 to 8 feet	
Soil and Moisture: well-drained, moist	
Interest: flowers, foliage	
Care: easy to moderate	

◀ Filipendula rubra 'Venusta'

Meadowsweets have long-lasting feathery plumes of midsummer flowers that rise above thick clumps of reddish green compound leaves. These tall, stately plants are especially striking when massed at the back of borders, or naturalized in meadows or fields.

Growing and care:
Meadowsweets benefit from additions of compost and organic mulch in spring. Plant in spring or fall, spacing plants 1 to 2 feet apart. Add a thin layer of mulch again in fall. Divide clumps every 3 to 4 years in spring by cutting the rhizome that connects the main clump to the new shoots. Plant the divisions about 2 inches deep. Cut foliage to the ground in late summer or early fall when the leaves begin to turn brown.

Selected species and varieties:
F. palmata bears large clusters of small pink flowers fading to snowy white on 2- to 3-foot stems with dark green leaves with pale undersides; 'Rubra' has dark red flowers. *F. rubra* (queen-of-the-prairie) has clusters of very ornamental pink flowers on sturdy 4- to 8-foot stems; 'Venusta' has plumes of rosy pink flowers on 6-foot stems. *F. ulmaria* (queen-of-the-meadow) bears creamy white flower clusters in summer on 3- to 6-foot stems bearing large compound leaves; 'Variegata' has leaves marked with a prominent yellow stripe.

PEONY
Paeonia

Light: mostly sun	
Plant type: perennial	
Hardiness: Zones 3-8	
Height: 1½ to 3 feet	
Soil and Moisture: well-drained, moist, fertile	
Interest: flowers	
Care: easy to moderate	

◀ Paeonia lactiflora

Peonies are classic garden plants renowned for their large, regal blossoms and attractive mounds of deeply cut foliage. Stately and dramatic in the garden, peonies are also stunning in bouquets. This large, diverse group of plants is classified by form. Single-flowered peonies have a single row of five or more petals surrounding a center of bright yellow stamens. Japanese and anemone peonies have a single row of petals surrounding modified stamens that resemble finely cut petals. Semidouble peonies have several rows of petals surrounding conspicuous stamens. Double-flowered peonies have multiple rows of petals crowded into ruffly hemispheres. Peonies add a touch of class to borders and specialty gardens and make exceptional displays when planted as a low hedge or edging or grouped in a mass display.

Growing and care:
Plant peonies 3 feet apart in soil containing some organic matter other than manure. Set the buds (eyes) 2 inches below the soil surface; setting them deeper delays flowering and reduces vigor. Fertilize lightly in spring as leaves are emerging and again after blossoms have faded. Cut back stems to ground level in fall. Propagate by dividing clumps into sections containing three to five eyes each in late summer or early fall every 10 years.

(continued)

Selected species and varieties:

P. lactiflora (garden or Chinese peony) bears white, pink, or red flowers on 3-foot stems. *P. mlokosewitschii* (Caucasian peony) has very early-blooming, 2-inch single lemon yellow flowers on 2-foot-tall stems with soft gray-green foliage. *P. officinalis* (common peony) comes in hundreds of varieties with 3- to 6-inch blooms in various forms and colors ranging from red to light pink to white on 2-foot stems. *P. tenuifolia* (fern-leaf peony) bears single deep red flowers and finely divided fernlike leaves on 1½- to 2-foot stems; 'Flore Pleno' has double flowers. Hundreds of peony hybrids are available: 'Lobata' (red-pink), 'Krinkled White' and 'Lotus Bloom' (pink) are outstanding singles; 'Isani-Gidui' (white) and 'Nippon Beauty' (dark red) are lovely Japanese types; 'Gay Paree' (pink with white-blush center) grows anemone-type blossoms; semidouble varieties include 'Lowell Thomas' (deep red) and 'Ludovica' (salmon-pink); among the double-flowered varieties 'Festiva Maxima' (white with red marking), 'Karl Rosenfeld' (deep red), 'Mons. Jules Elie' (early pink), 'Nick Shaylor' (blush pink), and 'Red Charm' (deep true red, early blooming) are all exceptional.

PICKERELWEED
Pontederia

◀ Pontederia cordata

Light:	mostly sun
Plant type:	perennial
Hardiness:	Zones 4-9
Height:	1 to 4 feet
Soil and Moisture:	wet to water-covered
Interest:	flowers, foliage
Care:	easy

Pickerelweed is an aquatic perennial that grows wild in shallow freshwater ponds, streams, and marshes in the eastern half of the United States. Its vivid lavender flowers, long blooming season, and attractive dark green foliage make it a good choice for bog and water gardens or naturalized along the banks of ponds, lakes, or slow-moving streams.

Growing and care:

Pickerelweed will grow in wet boggy soil, but it performs best when its roots are completely covered by several inches of water. When setting out new plants, use stones or pebbles to hold them in place until their roots are established. In the case of a small garden pool, plant pickerelweed in a large pot or shallow wooden flat. Propagate by division in summer.

Selected species and varieties:

P. cordata has spikes of pastel blue-purple funnel-shaped flowers held 1 to 2 feet above the water's surface on sturdy stems from early summer through fall. Dark green heart-shaped leaves up to 10 inches long and 6 inches wide rise 2 to 4 feet above the surface on long stems.

PITCHER PLANT
Sarracenia

Light: mostly sun	
Plant type: perennial	
Hardiness: Zones 2-10	
Height: 8 inches to 4 feet	
Soil and Moisture: organic, wet	
Interest: flowers, foliage	
Care: moderate	

◀ Sarracenia leucophylla

Excellent for bog gardens, pitcher plants are valued for their striking upright trumpets of tightly furled leaves as well as for their handsome umbrella-shaped chocolate-colored flowers borne on tall leafless stems. Insects trapped in the water-filled trumpets are slowly dissolved by acids released by the plants, and the freed nutrients are then absorbed by the plants—a little gruesome, but effective. Pitcher plants thrive in peaty wet soils.

Growing and care:
Pitcher plants thrive in wet sandy soil or peat bogs and require constant moisture. Propagate by seed sown immediately after collection or by division.

Selected species and varieties:
S. flava (yellow pitcher plant, trumpet pitcher plant) bears a trumpets of yellowish green red-veined leaves up to 4 feet tall and drooping yellow flowers up to 4 inches across; Zones 6-7. *S. leucophylla* (crimson pitcher plant) bears a red-veined trumpets 2 to 4 feet tall and dark red flowers 3 to 4 inches across; Zones 8-10. *S. purpurea* (northern pitcher plant) has a bronze-green trumpets 8 to 18 inches tall and solitary 2-inch maroon-purple flowers.

PLUMBAGO
Ceratostigma

Light: mostly sun	
Plant type: perennial	
Hardiness: Zones 5-10	
Height: 8 to 12 inches	
Soil and Moisture: well-drained, moist	
Interest: flowers, foliage	
Care: easy	

◀ Ceratostigma plumbaginoides

Plumbago's brilliant blue 1-inch-long slightly flattened flowers are borne in profusion on reddish stems from late summer to frost. The plant makes an effective, fast-spreading semievergreen ground cover or low shrubby perennial. Its glossy green oval leaves turn bronzy red in fall.

Growing and care:
Divide plants every 4 years in spring, spacing them 1 to 2 feet apart in soil amended with peat moss and compost. Mulch young plants in late spring, and water regularly. In Zones 5 and 6, cover with pine boughs in winter. Plumbago benefits from yearly additions of compost and light fertilizing in spring.

Selected species and varieties:
C. plumbaginoides (dwarf plumbago) has intensely blue, five-lobed tubular ½-inch flowers in dense clusters above tufts of 3-inch-long glossy semievergreen leaves on 8- to 12-inch zigzag stems that turn bronzy red in winter in cold regions. *C. willmottianum* (Chinese plumbago) bears 4-foot multibranched woody stems with vibrant blue flowers from late summer to fall, and bright green leaves that turn red in late fall; Zones 8-10.

POPPY
Papaver

Light: mostly to full sun

Plant type: perennial

Hardiness: Zones 3-9

Height: 1 to 4 feet

Soil and Moisture: well-drained, moist

Interest: flowers

Care: moderate to difficult

◄ Papaver orientale

Stately plants, poppies have large, brilliantly colored silky-textured blossoms that are mesmerizing in the garden. The flowers are held at the ends of strong wiry stems above finely cut hairy leaves. Poppies add vivid accents to borders and specialty gardens, where their bold presence is impossible to overlook.

Growing and care:

Poppies grow well in mostly sun or full sun as long as the soil is kept moist. Space poppies 1½ feet apart. Water regularly during the growing season but do not fertilize. Once established the plants should not be disturbed. If plants must be moved, transplant carefully when fully dormant. Propagate Oriental poppies, which are tough, long-lived plants, from seed or from root cuttings. Grow Iceland poppies from seed to flower in their first year; sow in late summer in the North and in fall in southern climates.

Selected species and varieties:

P. nudicaule (Iceland poppy) bears fragrant flowers up to 3 inches across on 1- to 2-foot stems. *P. orientale* (Oriental poppy) has blossoms up to 8 inches across composed of tissue-thin petals on wiry stems rising from mounds of coarse, hairy leaves; 'Beauty of Livermore' has deep red petals spotted black at the base; 'Glowing Embers' has orange-red ruffled petals; 'Mrs. Perry', clear pink flowers; 'Princess Victoria Louise', bright salmon-pink flowers.

PRAIRIE CONEFLOWER
Ratibida

Light: mostly to full sun

Plant type: perennial

Hardiness: Zones 3-9

Height: 2 to 5 feet

Soil and Moisture: well-drained, moist to dry

Interest: flowers

Care: easy

◄ Ratibida columnifera

Prairie coneflowers are sturdy, tough perennials with brightly colored daisylike summer flowers in shades of yellow and red that add a civilized yet wild touch to gardens and landscapes. The tall, pliant stems rise from a rosette of hairy green leaves and sport long-lasting flowers that look as good in a vase on the dining room table as in a perennial border.

Growing and care:

Coneflowers thrive in well-drained soil that has some organic matter. They do well in sun or mostly sun, and once established the plants are very drought tolerant and flower well even during hot, dry summers. Coneflowers often self-sow freely; they should be controlled in beds and borders, but allowed to spread in natural plantings. Propagate by seed.

Selected species and varieties:

R. columnifera (Mexican hat) has branching stems 1½ to 3 feet tall bearing daisylike flowers with drooping yellow, red, or bicolored notched petals surrounding an elongated purplish brown cylindrical cone that rises as much as 2 inches above the petals; it is native to prairies and waste areas from the central United States to British Columbia. *R. pinnata* (gray-headed coneflower) grows 3 to 5 feet tall with long-stalked flowers composed of yellow petals surrounding a grayish brown cone; Zones 3-8.

ROSINWEED
Silphium

Light:	mostly to full sun
Plant type:	perennial
Hardiness:	Zones 3-9
Height:	2 to 12 feet
Soil and Moisture:	well-drained, moist
Interest:	flowers, foliage
Care:	easy

◀ Silphium perfoliatum

Rosinweeds are handsome plants native to prairies and woodland openings of eastern and central North America, with small, pure yellow sunflower-like heads from summer to fall held far above clumps of interesting foliage. Their bold foliage accents the backs of borders. Interplant with ornamental grasses, or naturalize in meadows. The lower leaves of *S. laciniatum* point north and south to avoid the heat of the noonday sun, giving the plant its common name of compass plant.

Growing and care:
Rosinweeds require a lot of space to grow, so plant them 1 to 2 feet apart in sites where they will not dwarf other plants. Propagate by seed, since the roots of these plants can be massive. Seeds require several months of chilling at 40°F before germinating, and benefit from having their hard coats nicked with a sharp knife before being planted $1/3$ to $1/2$ inch deep. It takes 2 to 3 years for seedlings to reach flowering size. Plants do well in sun or mostly sun.

Selected species and varieties:
S. laciniatum (compass plant) has 3- to 12-foot rough stems with 1- to 2-foot deeply pointed leaves and showy clusters of 5-inch flower heads. *S. perfoliatum* (cup plant) has 3- to 8-foot hairy stems clasping pairs of 6- to 12-inch leaves joined at the base to form a cup, and small clusters of 3-inch flowers.

SANDWORT
Arenaria

Light:	mostly to full sun
Plant type:	perennial
Hardiness:	Zones 5-9
Height:	2 inches to $1 1/2$ feet
Soil and Moisture:	well-drained, moist to dry
Interest:	flowers, foliage
Care:	easy

◀ Arenaria montana

Sandwort is one of the easiest perennials to grow, quickly forming mats of small, feathery evergreen foliage liberally sprinkled with tiny white flowers in spring. This low, spreading perennial is ideal for growing in wall crevices and between pavers. Sandwort is so vigorous it can easily become a weed in beds and borders if not confined.

Growing and care:
Sow seed indoors 6 to 8 weeks before last frost or directly in the garden in early spring when soil is workable but cool. Do not cover seed, as light is needed for germination. Plant sandworts 6 to 12 inches apart. Water well during dry spells in the growing season and fertilize lightly for fastest growth and abundant flowering. Sandwort does well in sun or mostly sun. Propagate by division in late summer or early fall.

Selected species and varieties:
A. montana has trailing stems up to 1 foot long topped by 1-inch white flowers with yellow centers. *A. verna* (Irish moss) has narrow mosslike leaves and very small star-shaped white flowers in dainty 2-inch clumps that withstand heavy foot traffic.

SPEEDWELL
Veronica

Light:	mostly to full sun
Plant type:	perennial
Hardiness:	Zones 4-8
Height:	1 to 2 feet
Soil and Moisture:	well-drained, moist
Interest:	flowers, foliage
Care:	easy

◀ Veronica spicata
'Rosea'

Speedwells form bold upright clumps of spreading stems lined with narrow soft-textured leaves and tipped with spikes of tiny flowers densely packed into tapered conical spires from spring to summer. They fit well into rock gardens and are a good choice for edging, as a filler, or for naturalizing in shady informal gardens.

Growing and care:
Space plants 1 to 2 feet apart. Speedwells will flower best in full sun where moisture is abundant. Deadhead withering flower spikes to encourage an extended season of bloom. Propagate by seed, cuttings, or by division in spring or fall. Taller types may need support. Plants do well in mostly sun to full sun.

Selected species and varieties:
V. austriaca ssp. *teucrium* (Austrian speedwell) grows to 2 feet tall with ½-inch deep blue flowers from late spring to early summer and deeply cut leaves; 'Crater Lake Blue' has many flower spikes crowded in early summer with large, brilliant blue blossoms above compact mounds of dark green foliage. *V. incana* (silver speedwell, woolly speedwell) grows 1 foot tall with pale lilac-blue flowers in early summer and 6-inch-tall mats of woolly, silvery gray foliage. *V. spicata* (spike speedwell) is 1½ feet tall with lavender-blue to pink flowers from late spring to midsummer; 'Rosea' has tall spikes of rose red flowers.

TANSY
Tanacetum

Light:	mostly to full sun
Plant type:	perennial
Hardiness:	Zones 3-9
Height:	2 to 5 feet
Soil and Moisture:	well-drained, moist to dry
Interest:	flowers, foliage
Care:	easy

◀ Tanacetum vulgare

Tansy has been grown in American gardens since colonial times, when it was planted near the entrances of homes to repel insects. Its aromatic fernlike foliage provides lush contrast to colorful flowering plants grown nearby. Clusters of golden yellow button-shaped flowers appear in late summer and brighten the backs of borders. Tansy leaves can be used in fresh or dried arrangements, and frequently are used in potpourris.

Growing and care:
Tansy grows particularly well in a moist loamy soil. Because it is aggressive and somewhat invasive, poorer soil may be desirable; otherwise, its growth may need to be restricted by planting it in a bottomless container. Plants may require staking, especially in windy locations. Tansy also self-sows, but this can be avoided by removing flowers as they develop. Space plants 1 to 2 feet apart. Tansy grows well in mostly sun or full sun.

Selected species and varieties:
T. vulgare has 2- to 5-foot-tall stems with pungently scented, deeply cut 4-inch-wide lacy leaves each and clusters of ¼-inch petal-less flowers appearing from mid- to late summer, followed by flat-topped seed heads that persist throughout winter; var. *crispum* (fernleaf tansy) grows 2 to 3 feet tall, produces lush, wavy, rich green leaves that are more finely dissected than the species, and is valued for indoor arrangements.

TRANSVAAL DAISY
Gerbera

Light:	mostly sun
Plant type:	perennial
Hardiness:	Zones 8-10
Height:	1 to 1½ feet
Soil and Moisture:	well-drained, moderately moist
Interest:	flowers
Care:	moderate to difficult

◀ Gerbera jamesonii

Transvaal daisies produce spectacular 4-inch daisylike flowers on stout, sturdy stems, providing a fine display in the garden, in containers, or as cut flowers for indoor arrangements. Although they are hardy only to Zone 8, in cooler areas they can be planted as annuals or dug up in fall and planted in containers to grow indoors as houseplants. The blossoms come in a wide range of clear pastel shades that complement most other colors.

Growing and care:
Plant Transvaal daisies in soil that has been amended with organic matter. The plants are very susceptible to disease in soil that is kept too moist, but are not tolerant of dry conditions, either. Water deeply, allowing soil to dry before watering again. For massing, space plants 2 feet apart. Protect plants over winter in Zone 8 with a nonmatting mulch.

Selected species and varieties:
G. jamesonii has deeply lobed gray-green leaves 5 to 10 inches long growing in the form of a basal rosette, erect flower stems 1 to 1½ feet tall, and flowers 2 to 4 inches across with strap-shaped petals in yellow, salmon, cream, pink, rose, or red.

VERBENA
Verbena

Light:	mostly sun
Plant type:	perennial
Hardiness:	Zones 3-10
Height:	8 inches to 5 feet
Soil and Moisture:	well-drained, fertile, moist to dry
Interest:	flowers, foliage
Care:	easy

◀ Verbena stricta

The perennial verbenas are native to meadows, prairies, and open woods. They feature small brightly colored flowers arranged in terminal spiked clusters of white, lavender, rose, or purple. The leaves of *Verbena stricta* have a soft gray-green appearance underneath the plant's downy cover. The flowers of this species grow in 6-inch-long slender purple spikes that bloom from June to September.

Growing and care:
Plant verbena in spring in well-worked soil that has some organic matter. Once established the plants are drought tolerant and thrive in sunny locations. Fertilize in spring and prune lightly after flowering. Propagate by seed.

Selected species and varieties:
V. canadensis (rose verbena) produces fragrant ¾-inch pink flowers in rounded clusters in summer and fall on a mat of creeping stems 8 to 12 inches tall and 3 feet across; native from the Southeast to Colorado; Zones 6-10. *V. hastata* (blue verbena) reaches heights of 2 to 5 feet with spikes of blue-purple flowers in late spring and summer; widely found in moist sites in the United States and Canada; Zones 4-10. *V. stricta* (woolly verbena, hoary vervain) matures at 1 to 4 feet tall with dense 1-foot spikes of blue to violet flowers in summer and fall and large woolly leaves; it is found from Ontario south to Texas and west to Idaho.

WATER LILY
Nymphaea

Light: mostly to full sun

Plant type: perennial

Hardiness: Zones 2-10

Height: 2 to 4 inches above water

Soil and Moisture: shallow water

Interest: flowers, foliage

Care: moderate

◀ Nymphaea odorata

The sweetly scented, sophisticated flowers of these hardy aquatic perennials grace ponds, lakes, and slow-moving streams over much of the eastern and central United States. The blossoms, each of which lasts for about 3 days, float upright on the surface of the water, surrounded by a sea of dark green lily pads. The lotus-shaped flowers close at night and on cloudy days.

Growing and care:
Plant water lily rhizomes 3 to 4 inches deep in pots or shallow wooden flats containing clayey soil and cover the soil surface with 2 inches of fine gravel. Submerge the containers in up to 4 feet of water. In far northern regions remove the containers from the water in fall and store indoors in a cool location over winter. Propagate by dividing the rhizomes. Grows well in mostly sun or full sun.

Selected species and varieties:
N. odorata (water lily, pond lily) bears white or pink flowers 3 to 5 inches across with numerous gold stamens from mid- to late summer. Flat 4- to 12-inch leaves are glossy green on the upper surface, reddish below, and float on the surface of the water.

ZINNIA
Zinnia

Light: mostly to full sun

Plant type: perennial

Hardiness: Zones 4-10

Height: 6 to 8 inches

Soil and Moisture: well-drained, medium to dry

Interest: flowers

Care: easy

◀ Zinnia grandiflora

Most gardeners are familiar only with annual zinnias. The two perennial species described here are native to the central and southwestern United States, where they are commonly found along roadsides and on dry slopes. Both of these wildflowers bloom profusely for months and are attractive in rock gardens and on dry banks, where they help control erosion.

Growing and care:
Perennial zinnias require average, well-drained, medium to dry soil and are very tolerant of drought and heat. Zinnias grow well in mostly sun to full sun. Fertilize lightly just before flower buds appear. Sow seed directly in the garden after danger of frost has passed, or in fall. Young plants can also be divided in spring.

Selected species and varieties:
Z. acerosa (dwarf white zinnia) is a multibranched, shrubby plant 6 inches tall with ¾-inch white flowers with yellow centers and narrow, silvery leaves less than an inch long; Zones 8-10. *Z. grandiflora* (little golden zinnia, prairie zinnia, Rocky Mountain zinnia) has 1½-inch yellow flowers with red or green centers on an 8-inch mound of needlelike, nearly evergreen foliage.

ALPINE HYACINTH
Brimeura

Light:	mostly sun
Plant type:	bulb
Hardiness:	Zones 4-10
Height:	6 to 12 inches
Soil and Moisture:	well-drained, moist
Interest:	flowers
Care:	easy

◀ Brimeura amethystina

Alpine hyacinths are easy-to-grow spring flowers with glossy clumps of narrow leaves and showy spikes of nodding blue flower bells. The plants resemble *Hyacinthus* in shape and form but bloom later in spring. These dainty plants easily naturalize in most soils and climates, making great additions to borders, rock gardens, or wildflower meadows. The bulbs can also be planted in containers and forced indoors to brighten up late-winter days.

Growing and care:
Plant alpine hyacinths in fall, setting bulbs 1 to 2 inches deep and 4 to 5 inches apart. Fertilize at planting time with an organic fertilizer and again as flower shoots are emerging. These small bulbs make the best show when planted close together and left to multiply on their own. Save bulbs forced as potted plants to set out in the garden in fall. Propagate by removing and replanting the small bulblets that form alongside parent bulbs.

Selected species and varieties:
B. amethystina [formerly *Hyacinthus amethystinus* and *Scilla amethystina*] bears up to 15 tiny ½-inch blue bells lining one side of the stalks in spring; 'Alba' yields pure white flower bells.

AUTUMN CROCUS
Colchicum

Light:	mostly sun
Plant type:	bulb
Hardiness:	Zones 4-9
Height:	8 to 12 inches
Soil and Moisture:	well-drained, fertile, moist
Interest:	flowers
Care:	easy

◀ Colchicum speciosum

Autumn crocus is a lovely fall plant with several leafless stems topped with showy pink, purple, or red flowers. The strap-shaped foliage appears in late winter or early spring, and disappears in late summer a few weeks before the cupped, star-shaped flowers appear. Autumn crocus is excellent for naturalizing in meadows or as an addition to borders or rock gardens. The bulbs can also be planted in containers and forced indoors.

Growing and care:
Plant in summer, setting corms 3 to 4 inches deep and 6 to 9 inches apart in loose soil. *C. autumnale* thrives in mostly sunny spots with evenly moist soil. Propagate from cormlets that form at the base of mature corms. If the plant is naturalized in a meadow or field, be careful not to mow while foliage or flowers remain above ground.

Selected species and varieties:
C. autumnale bears 4-inch white, pink, or purple flowers on 8-inch stems; 'Alboplenum' has pure white double flowers; 'Plenum' has lilac-pink double flowers. *C. speciosum* (showy autumn crocus) has 4- to 8-inch rose to purple flowers with white throats on 8- to 12-inch stems; 'Atrorubens' has dark red flowers; 'Waterlily' has large, bright pink double-petaled flowers on 10-inch stems, and makes an excellent cut flower.

BLACKBERRY LILY
Belamcanda

Light:	mostly sun
Plant type:	bulb
Hardiness:	Zones 5-10
Height:	1 to 4 feet
Soil and Moisture:	well-drained, moist
Interest:	flowers, fruit
Care:	easy

◀ Belamcanda chinensis

Blackberry lilies carry cheerful sprays of flat, star-shaped flowers with narrow, pointed petals on zigzag-branching flower stalks above fans of swordlike leaves. Each flower lasts only a day, but new blossoms open over several weeks. Flowers are followed by attractive seedpods that burst open to reveal shiny, black, berrylike seeds. Use blackberry lilies in the midground of a sunny border or as cut flowers. Dried seedpods decorate the winter garden and can be used in dried arrangements.

Growing and care:
Plant blackberry lilies in spring or fall, setting rhizomes 1 inch deep and 6 to 8 inches apart. They grow best in moist, fertile soil well amended with organic matter. Plants grown in dry soil are shorter with slightly smaller flowers. Propagate by division in spring or fall. Blackberry lilies often self-sow, producing flowers in 2 years.

Selected species and varieties:
B. chinensis has 2-inch orange flowers with pointed, curving petals spotted with red on 2- to 4-foot stalks. *B. flabellata* bears light yellow flowers.

BLOOD LILY
Haemanthus

Light:	mostly sun
Plant type:	bulb
Hardiness:	Zones 9-10
Height:	1 to 1½ feet
Soil and Moisture:	well-drained, moist
Interest:	flowers, fragrance
Care:	moderate

◀ Haemanthus katherinae

Blood lilies give the garden an infusion of summer color with starburst blossoms collected into airy clumps. The clusters of tubular flowers are decorated with colorful protruding stamens cradled within broad, petal-like bracts atop stout, leafless stems. In warm regions the plants add an interesting accent to borders. In cooler areas blood lilies are excellent container plants that brighten patios and decks.

Growing and care:
Plant blood lilies 6 to 8 inches apart outdoors or in pots, with the tip of the bulb at the soil surface. Start potted lilies in spring, then lift and dry the bulbs before storing over winter. Propagate from seed or from bulb offsets.

Selected species and varieties:
H. albiflos 'White Paintbrush' has 2-inch flower clusters with yellow-orange stamens within greenish white bracts on 1- to 1½-inch stems. *H. coccineus* (Cape tulip) has 3-inch clusters of 1-inch flowers with golden stamens within red bracts on 1-foot stems. *H. katherinae* [also known as *Scadoxus multiflorus* ssp. *katherinae*] (Catherine-wheel) produces more than 200 small 2½-inch pink-red flowers in 9-inch globes on 1½-foot stems. *H. multiflorus* (salmon blood lily) bears up to 200 inch-long coral red flowers with spiky stamens in 3- to 6-inch spheres on 1½-foot stems.

BULBOCODIUM
Bulbocodium

Light:	mostly sun
Plant type:	bulb
Hardiness:	Zones 3-10
Height:	4 inches
Soil and Moisture:	well-drained, sandy, moist
Interest:	flowers
Care:	easy

◀ Bulbocodium vernum

One of the earliest flowers to brighten the spring garden, bulbocodium sends up delicate sprays of rose-violet blossoms that open into upright trumpets of narrow, ribbonlike petals. The narrow, grassy leaves appear after the flowers bloom. The plant will naturalize in a border, rock garden, or wildflower meadow, providing years of care-free beauty.

Growing and care:
Plant in late summer or fall, spacing corms 3 to 4 inches apart and setting them 3 inches deep in well-worked soil amended with organic matter. Locations that provide moisture in spring when bulbs are blooming and foliage is maturing but are slightly dry in summer are ideal. Propagate after the grassy leaves die back in early summer by removing and replanting the small cormels that grow at the base of each corm every 3 to 4 years.

Selected species and varieties:
B. vernum (spring meadow saffron) bears one to three 2- to 3-inch-wide rose-violet flower trumpets on short stalks in early spring before grasslike glossy leaves appear.

CAMASS
Camassia

Light:	mostly sun
Plant type:	bulb
Hardiness:	Zones 5-8
Height:	1 to 3 feet
Soil and Moisture:	well-drained, moist
Interest:	flowers, fragrance
Care:	moderate

◀ Camassia quamash

Camass is a striking wildflower of open woods, wet meadows, and prairies, with fragrant velvet purple, white, or lilac flowers from spring to early summer. The plants produce loose clusters of star-shaped flowers on upright stalks beneath clumps of erect lance-shaped leaves. Camass is especially handsome planted in drifts in a woodland border or meadow.

Growing and care:
Grow camass in a moist, well-drained soil that has had some organic matter added to it. Fertilize established plantings in spring as growth begins. Water regularly while plants are actively growing but allow soil to dry out after plants go dormant. Propagate from seed or offsets.

Selected species and varieties:
C. quamash (common camass, quamash) is a western species with bright green grasslike leaves and 1- to 3-foot flower stalks bearing dozens of star-shaped flowers in white and shades from light blue to deep blue or lavender-blue. *C. scilloides* (wild hyacinth, eastern camass), native to the central and southern United States, produces a clump of leaves up to 16 inches long, and the leafless 6- to 24-inch stems bearing loose clusters of fragrant white, blue, or lavender-blue flowers.

CRINODONNA
x Crinodonna

Light: mostly sun

Plant type: bulb

Hardiness: Zones 9-10

Height: 2 to 3 feet

Soil and Moisture: well-drained, moist

Interest: flowers, fragrance

Care: moderate

◀ x Crinodonna corsii

Crinodonna bears enchanting pastel pink and white flowers that perfume the garden with a rich fragrance in late summer and fall. The dense heads of oval, pointed flower buds open into large funnels with gracefully curving stamens and prominent anthers to add color and interest. The fragrant flowers unfold at the tips of sturdy, erect flower stalks. Each stalk rises from a clump of arching, narrow evergreen leaves that remain attractive year round. Crinodonnas can be grown as border specimens in frost-free areas but bloom best as root-bound container plants.

Growing and care:

Outdoors, plant crinodonna bulbs at the soil line in well-worked soil, spacing them 8 to 12 inches apart. Indoors, plant one 4-inch bulb per 6- to 8-inch pot. Bulbs should be left undisturbed for several years, as they bloom best when roots are crowded. Propagate by removing offsets, which grow at the base of larger bulbs.

Selected species and varieties:

x *C. corsii* [also called x *Amarcrinum memoria-corsii*] bears 4- to 5-inch-wide pink flowers accented with blush white edges on graceful 3-foot-tall stalks in late summer and early fall.

CROCUS
Crocus

Light: mostly sun

Plant type: bulb

Hardiness: Zones 3-8

Height: 2 to 8 inches

Soil and Moisture: well-drained, moist

Interest: flowers, fragrance

Care: easy

◀ Crocus chrysanthus 'Cream Beauty'

Crocuses are one of the best-loved spring bulbs, with abundant, cheerful flowers in a rainbow of perky colors. Crocus flowers hug the ground on short stems from late winter through midspring. There are also fall-blooming species, not to be confused with the flowers commonly known as autumn crocus, which are actually *Colchicum*. Narrow, grassy crocus leaves are sometimes attractively banded down their centers in gray-green or white and may appear before, at the same time as, or after several flowers rise from each small corm. They last several weeks before dying back. Some are fragrant. Each flower has six wide petals that open into a deep, oval cup shape, then relax into a round, open bowl. Crocuses are available in a broad range of hues, and are often striped, streaked, or tinged with more than one color. Prominent yellow or orange stigmas decorate the center of each blossom. Mass crocuses for best effect in beds, borders, and rock gardens. They naturalize easily and are often planted as edgings and allowed to ramble in lawns. Force them for indoor winter display.

Growing and care:

Plant corms 3 to 4 inches deep and 4 to 5 inches apart in groups. They are not fussy about soil, but good drainage is essential. Space more closely in pots for forcing, allowing six to eight corms per 6-inch pot or shallow bulb pan, and setting the corms 1 inch deep. Hold potted

CROCUS
(continued)

corms at 40°F until roots form, then bring indoors at 65°F for flowering. After forcing, allow foliage to die back, then plant corms out in the garden for reflowering the following spring. To plant crocuses in lawns, cut and lift small patches of grass, place the corms, then replace the sod. Plant spring-flowering varieties from September to November, fall-flowering ones no later than August. Where crocuses have established themselves in lawns, avoid mowing in spring until the foliage of spring-flowering crocuses dies back; in fall, postpone mowing once the buds of fall-blooming species have broken through the ground until their flowers fade and foliage withers. Propagate by lifting and dividing crowded clumps after foliage dies back, or by removing and replanting the smaller cormels that develop alongside mature corms.

Selected species and varieties:

C. chrysanthus (snow crocus) bears late-winter flowers on 4-inch stems before the 1-foot leaves appear; 'Blue Bird' has blooms that are blue-violet outside, creamy inside; 'Blue Pearl', petals that are lavender outside touched with bronze at their base, white inside blending to a yellow throat; 'Cream Beauty' has long-lasting creamy yellow flowers; 'Snow Bunting' has white flowers with lilac streaking and yellow throats; Zones 4-8. *C. speciosus* produces light blue fall flowers with darker blue veining and prominent orange stigmas on 3- to 6-inch stems; 'Artabir' grows fragrant light blue flowers with conspicuous veining; 'Cassiope', lavender-blue blooms with creamy yellow throats; 'Conqueror', clear blue flowers; var. *aitchisonii* has pale lilac flowers veined with deeper lilac, the largest of all crocus blossoms; Zones 5-8. *C. vernus* (Dutch crocus, common crocus) bears large flowers on stems to 8 inches tall, appearing at the same time as leaves in late winter to spring; 'Flower Record' is deep purple; 'Jeanne d'Arc', white; 'Paulus Potter', shiny reddish purple; 'Remembrance', bluish purple.

FREESIA
Freesia

Light:	mostly sun
Plant type:	bulb
Hardiness:	Zones 9-10
Height:	1 to 2 feet
Soil and Moisture:	well-drained, sandy, moist
Interest:	flowers, fragrance
Care:	moderate

◀ Freesia 'Ballerina'

Of all the alluring fragrances in the world, none is quite like the perfume of freesias. These lovely flowers have a unique, ethereal aroma that is faint and intense at the same time. Freesias have crowded fans of flaring tubular flowers held at right angles to branched, arching stems that rise from clumps of 6-inch sword-shaped leaves, which persist after flowers fade. The flowers open in sequence along each upright cluster for a long period of bloom. In warm zones, grow freesias in borders or rock gardens. Elsewhere, pot them for houseplants or greenhouse specimens.

Growing and care:

Plant freesias outdoors in fall or winter in Zones 9 and 10, setting corms 2 inches deep and 2 to 4 inches apart. Provide support for their weak stems. Indoors, pot six to eight corms per 6-inch bulb pan or 10 to 12 per 8-inch pan, setting corms barely below the surface. Water and feed freesias while growing and blooming, then withhold water after foliage fades to induce dormancy. Remove corms from pots and store in a cool, dark place.

Selected species and varieties:

F. x *hybrids* produces 2-inch flowers on stems 1½ to 2 feet tall; 'Ballerina' produces large white flowers touched with yellow at the throat; 'Diana', double white flowers; 'Fantasy', cream-colored double petals; 'Riande' is yellow-gold; 'Royal Gold', golden yellow.

GLORIOSA LILY
Gloriosa

Light:	mostly sun
Plant type:	bulb
Hardiness:	Zone 10
Height:	6 to 12 feet
Soil and Moisture:	well-drained, fertile, moist
Interest:	flowers
Care:	moderate

◀ Gloriosa superba 'Rothschildiana'

Gloriosa lilies produce wonderfully exotic flowers that add a tropical ambiance wherever they blossom. The flowers have narrow, strongly reflexed, fiery petals with wavy or crimped edges that expose a spray of prominent stamens. The tips of the slender 4- to 6-inch-long leaves elongate into clasping tendrils to enable the plant to cling to fences or trellises at the back of a border. In northern zones, plant gloriosa lilies outdoors as annuals or grow them indoors as container plants. They make excellent cut flowers.

Growing and care:

In Zone 10, plant gloriosa lilies anytime, laying tubers on their sides 4 inches deep and 8 to 12 inches apart. North of Zone 10, plant in spring and lift in fall for winter storage. Indoors, pot tubers 1 to 2 inches deep in midwinter for blooms from late summer through fall. Propagate from seed or by dividing tubers.

Selected species and varieties:

G. superba (Malabar gloriosa lily, crisped glory lily) has twisted yellow petals tipped with red, aging to dark red; 'Africana' has orange petals edged in yellow; 'Rothschildiana', wavy reddish purple petals edged in yellow.

GLORY-OF-THE-SNOW
Chionodoxa

Light:	mostly sun
Plant type:	bulb
Hardiness:	Zones 4-9
Height:	4 to 10 inches
Soil and Moisture:	well-drained, moist
Interest:	flowers
Care:	easy

◀ Chionodoxa luciliae 'Pink Giant'

Glory-of-the-snow is one of the hardiest bulbs and, as a bonus, is one of the earliest flowers to appear in spring, often before snows have completely melted. The small clusters of white to pink flowery stars with narrow, gracefully curved petals are held above the grassy leaves on short stems. Glory-of-the-snow naturalizes easily in rock or wildflower gardens to create carpets of color beneath taller spring bulbs or deciduous shrubs. Once established the plants are pest- and disease-free and provide years of beauty with little effort. Glory-of-the-snow can also be planted in containers and forced for indoor winter bloom.

Growing and care:

Plant glory-of-the-snow in masses for best effect, setting bulbs 3 inches deep and 3 inches apart. For forcing, allow 12 to 18 bulbs per 8-inch bulb pan. Propagate from seed or by removing and replanting bulblets growing alongside older bulbs.

Selected species and varieties:

C. luciliae has clusters of three or more 1-inch blue flowers with centers suffused with white on 4-inch stems; 'Alba' grows pure white; 'Pink Giant' produces bright pink flowers on 3- to 6-inch stems; 'Rosea' is pink. *C. sardensis* bears deep blue flowers on stems to 6 inches.

IPHEION
Ipheion

Light: mostly sun	
Plant type: bulb	
Hardiness: Zones 5-10	
Height: 1 to 1½ feet	
Soil and Moisture: well-drained, moist	
Interest: flowers, fragrance	
Care: moderate	

◀ Ipheion uniflorum

Ipheion bears subtle, softly colored flowers from a maze of grasslike leaves in spring. The flowers have tiny, triangle-shaped pointed petals surrounding a cluster of bright orange stamens. The blossoms have a faint mint scent, while the foliage gives off an onion odor when bruised. The leaves appear in fall, and persist through winter and spring until the bulbs go dormant in summer. Plant ipheion in woodland or rock gardens, in meadows, or among paving stones, where it will rapidly naturalize. It can also be forced indoors for mid-winter bloom.

Growing and care:
Plant ipheion in late summer or fall, setting bulbs 3 inches deep and 3 to 6 inches apart in well-worked soil. Provide winter mulch in Zones 5 and 6. Pot bulbs 1 inch deep for forcing. Propagate by dividing clumps of bulb offsets.

Selected species and varieties:
I. uniflorum [formerly *Brodiaea uniflora* and *Triteleia uniflora*] (spring starflower) has 1-inch white flowers tinged with blue; 'Rolf Fiedler' has deep electric blue blossoms; 'Wisley Blue' bears light blue flowers with a white center.

LILY
Lilium

Light: mostly sun	
Plant type: bulb	
Hardiness: Zones 4-8	
Height: 2 to 8 feet	
Soil and Moisture: well-drained, fertile, moist	
Interest: flowers, fragrance	
Care: easy to moderate	

◀ Lilium columbianum

Few garden flowers can compare with the majesty of lilies. These aristocratic plants have been prized for centuries for their beauty, form, and fragrance. There are many diverse types of lilies to choose from, yet each maintains a stately presence that is enchanting. Lilies offer a wide range of colors and color combinations. They bloom either singly or in clusters, at the tips of stiff, erect stems lined with short, grassy leaves. Up to 50 often highly fragrant flowers may appear on a single stem. The wide range of choices allows fanciers to plant lilies for continuous bloom throughout the summer. Lilies are excellent for borders. Many types naturalize quickly and look stunning in meadows or large rock gardens. Lilies can also be grown in patio containers, forced for indoor bloom, or used as long-lasting cut flowers.

Growing and care:
Plant lilies in spring or fall in well-worked, well-drained soil that has some organic matter. If grown in beds and borders the soil around the bulbs should be mulched to keep it cool. The plants also thrive when set among sun-tolerant ferns and ground covers. Space bulbs 4 to 6 inches apart. Fertilize plants in spring as plants emerge from the soil. Keep soil moist but not wet during dry periods. Propagate lilies by removing and replanting the small bulblets that grow along the underground stem.

(continued)

Selected species and varieties:

Asiatic hybrids: Early summer flowering compact lilies usually 2 to 4 feet tall with 4- to 6-inch flowers, borne singly or in clusters; Zones 4-8; 'Connecticut King' bears abundant sunny yellow flowers on 30-inch stems; 'Dreamland' has upright deep golden yellow flowers on strong 30-inch stems; 'Marseille' bears elegant satin white flowers touched with a brush of rose near the base of the petals; 'Scarlet Emperor' has rich red, upward-facing flowers on 30-inch stems; 'Sorbet' has white blossoms edged with burgundy-pink on 40-inch stems. *Oriental hybrids*: Mid- to late-summer-blooming garden favorites from 2 to 8 feet tall bearing trumpet-shaped, flat-faced, or bowl-shaped flowers up to 12 inches across or trusses of smaller turban-shaped flowers; Zones 4-8; 'Arena' bears upward-facing white flowers with a solid yellow streak along the center of each petal on 3-foot stems; 'Belle Epoque' has large, outward-facing blossoms of the softest blush pink on 4-foot stems; 'Gold Band' has very large, fragrant white flowers freckled with red on 3-foot stems; 'Muscadet' bears stunning flat-faced flowers of linen white, freckled and streaked with blush pink on 30-inch stems; 'Tompouce' has rose-pink petals with a center stripe of lemon-yellow on 30-inch stems. Species lilies: *L. canadense* (Canada lily) has down-facing yellow to reddish orange blossoms in summer on 4-foot-tall stems; Zones 4-8 *L. columbianum* (Columbia lily, Oregon lily) has nodding yellow to reddish flowers with maroon spots and gently recurved petals; Zones 6-8. *L. martagon* (Martagon lily) bears abundant rose-purple flowers spotted with dark violet in summer on 6-foot stems; Zones 4-8. *L. pumilum* (coral lily) has abundant vivid red, nodding flowers with sharply recurved petals in summer on 2-foot stems; Zones 4-8. *Trumpet Hybrids* have trumpet, star-burst, or bowl-shaped flowers in summer atop strong 3- to 6-foot stems; Zones 4-8; 'Bright Star' has white flowers marked with a golden yellow, star-shaped eye.

ONION
Allium

Light: mostly sun	
Plant type: bulb	
Hardiness: Zones 3-9	
Height: 9 inches to 5 feet	
Soil and Moisture: well-drained, sandy, moist	
Interest: flowers, foliage, fragrance	
Care: easy	

◀ Allium giganteum

Though *Allium* are related to edible onions, these spectacular plants bear little resemblance to their culinary cousins. Their showy 2- to 12-inch-wide flower clusters are dynamite in the garden. The dense, spherical flower heads are composed of hundreds of tiny blooms packed tightly together. Most species flower in late spring and early summer. Many species smell faintly like onion or garlic when the leaves or stems are cut or bruised, but a few bear sweetly fragrant flowers. Mass small or medium *Allium* for striking displays and site larger ones as stately accents. *Allium* are durable, very attractive cut flowers. Rodents that like to dine on other flowering bulbs usually find *Allium* bulbs unappealing.

Growing and care:

Plant ornamental onions in the fall in northern zones, in spring or fall in warmer areas. They grow rapidly in spring, produce blooms, and then die back to the ground. Because their foliage must be allowed to wither naturally, site *Alliums* where other plants will hide the dying leaves. Even those species that tolerate partial shade need full sun for part of the day. *A. cernuum* prefers humus-rich soil and thrives in dry or moist conditions in full sun or partial shade; divide clumps about every 3 years. *A. aflatunense, A. christophii,* and *A. giganteum* require full sun. Since its flower stalk is so tall, *A. giganteum* should not be planted in windy sites. *A. moly*

ONION
(continued)

prefers a sunny, well-drained site. *A. aflatunense, A. cernuum, A. karataviense,* and *A. moly* are suitable for naturalizing. *Allium* may be left undisturbed in the garden for years until the presence of fewer blooms signals that bulbs are overcrowded. Remove flower stems after flowering. Protect bulbs with winter mulch north of Zone 5. Propagate by separating and replanting tiny bulblets after the foliage dies back, by planting the bulblets that appear amid flower clusters, or by sowing seed.

Selected species and varieties:
A. aflatunense (ornamental onion) produces deep purple, perfectly rounded 4-inch globes composed of densely clustered tiny star-shaped flowers appearing in late spring to midsummer on 2- to 4-foot stalks above 4-inch-wide leaves; Zones 4-8. *A. cernuum* (nodding wild onion) has loose clusters of 30 to 40 delicate pink or white flowers that dangle atop 8- to 18-inch stems in late spring above rosettes of grassy 10-inch leaves; it is most effectively planted in groups; 'Early Dwarf' grows 6 to 8 inches tall, forming neat clumps and producing deep lavender blooms with protruding stamens; Zones 3-8. *A. christophii* (stars-of-Persia) bears the largest flowers of the genus, appearing in late spring and early summer in spherical clusters 8 to 12 inches across, composed of many star-shaped amethyst blue flowers, each ½ inch wide, held above three to seven leaves on a sturdy 1½- to 2-foot stalk; Zones 4-8. *A. giganteum* (giant ornamental onion, giant garlic) has the tallest flower stalks of the genus, with 5- to 6-inch spherical clusters of deep purple to lilac-pink flowers borne in early summer atop 3- to 5-foot scapes that rise from stiff, gray-green basal leaves 2 inches wide and up to 30 inches long. They provide a stately accent for the rear of a border or center of an island bed, and are best planted in groups of three to five. Cut flowers may last up to 3 weeks; Zones 5-8. *A. moly* (lily leek, golden onion) has clusters of vivid yellow ¾- to 1-inch-wide star-shaped blooms appearing in mid- to late spring on 8- to 12-inch stems above a clump of 12-inch basal leaves; 'Jeannine' bears long-lasting 2- to 3-inch flowers on 1-foot stems above blue-green leaves.

ORNITHOGALUM
Ornithogalum

◀ Ornithogalum nutans

Light: mostly sun	
Plant type: bulb	
Hardiness: Zones 5-10	
Height: 6 inches to 2 feet	
Soil and Moisture: well-drained, moist	
Interest: flowers, fragrance	
Care: moderate	

Ornithogalum bears star-shaped, often fragrant flowers in spring or summer with a distinctive tight "eye" of pistils at their centers. The attractive blossoms are most often white with a green stripe down the outside of each petal, though some types have yellow to orange petals. The flowers are carried in large clusters that are sometimes pendent but more often are facing upward in flat-topped bouquets above neat clumps of shimmering green, ribbonlike leaves. Ornithogalum looks beautiful naturalized in borders, beds, and rock gardens, or grown indoors as a potted plant.

Growing and care:
Outdoors, plant ornithogalum bulbs 4 inches deep and 2 to 5 inches apart in well-worked soil amended with rotted manure or compost. Keep soil evenly moist throughout growing season. North of Zone 8, treat tender species as annuals, lifting bulbs in fall for replanting in spring, or grow as container plants. Indoors, pot five or six bulbs 1 inch deep in a 6-inch pot. Propagate from seed sown in spring or by dividing bulbs and offsets in fall.

Selected species and varieties:
O. nutans (nodding star-of-Bethlehem) has fragrant, greenish white 2-inch flowers nodding along one side of 1- to 1½-inch stems from late spring to early summer; Zones 5-9.

PERSIAN VIOLET
Cyclamen

Light:	mostly sun
Plant type:	bulb
Hardiness:	Zones 6-9
Height:	3 to 12 inches
Soil and Moisture:	well-drained, fertile, moist
Interest:	flowers, fragrance
Care:	moderate

◀ Cyclamen hederifolium

Persian violet has distinctive, sometimes fragrant flowers with strongly reflexed petals swept back from a prominent center or eye. The petals are sometimes twisted, double, ruffled, shredded, or ridged, giving the delicate inch-long blossoms the appearance of exotic butterflies or fiery shooting stars. Each flower rises on a slender stem from a clump of long-lasting kidney- or heart-shaped leaves that are sometimes marbled green and gray above or reddish underneath. Allow hardy Persian violets to naturalize in wildflower gardens, rock gardens, and shady borders, where they often grow into low ground covers.

Growing and care:
Plant Persian violet's flat, cormlike tubers in summer or fall, setting them ½ inch deep and 4 to 6 inches apart. Provide an annual top dressing of leaf mold. Propagate from seed to reach blooming size in 3 years or by transplanting the self-sown seedlings in summer or fall.

Selected species and varieties:
C. hederifolium [also called *C. neapolitanum*] (baby cyclamen) has pink or white, sometimes fragrant flowers with a crimson eye on 3- to 6-inch stems above marbled leaves with toothed edges in winter.

PINEAPPLE LILY
Eucomis

Light:	mostly sun
Plant type:	bulb
Hardiness:	Zones 8-10
Height:	1 to 2 feet
Soil and Moisture:	well-drained, sandy, moist
Interest:	flowers, foliage
Care:	moderate

◀ Eucomis bicolor

Pineapple lilies are novel plants with dense bottle-brush spikes of tiny white starry flowers topped by a crowning tuft of leaflike bracts. The sturdy spikes rise from glossy rosettes of strap-shaped leaves in summer. Pineapple lilies blend well into borders, and when grown in containers are the conversation pieces of patio and deck gardens. They make long-lasting cut flowers.

Growing and care:
Plant outdoors in fall, setting bulbs 5 to 6 inches deep and 1 foot apart. Mulch plantings in Zone 8. North of Zone 8, grow pineapple lilies as container plants, setting bulbs just below the surface and allowing three to five bulbs per 1-foot pot. Propagate by removing bulb offsets that develop at the base of mature bulbs, or from seed to flower in 5 years.

Selected species and varieties:
E. autumnalis has spikes of ¾-inch greenish white flowers fading to yellow-green on 1- to 2-foot stems. *E. bicolor* bears greenish white flowers edged with purple on 2-foot stems. *E. comosa* (pineapple flower) has ½-inch greenish white, sometimes pinkish blossoms with purple throats on 2-foot stems.

PUSCHKINIA
Puschkinia

Light: mostly sun	
Plant type: bulb	
Hardiness: Zones 3-8	
Height: 4 to 6 inches	
Soil and Moisture: well-drained, moist	
Interest: flowers, fragrance	
Care: moderate	

◀ Puschkinia scilloides var. libanotica 'Alba'

Puschkinia is a charming plant with profuse, softly colored flowers above rafts of glossy green leaves in spring. The slender wandlike stems hold oval buds that open into loose clusters of tiny flower bells that metamorphose into little, gently nodding stars. Puschkinia is a vigorous, easy-to-grow plant that naturalizes quickly, making it a sure bet for borders, edgings, rock gardens, or wildflower meadows.

Growing and care:
Plant bulbs in fall, setting them 2 inches deep and 6 inches apart in well-worked soil that has had some organic matter added to it. After flowering, top-dress with a light covering of compost or rotted manure. Group bulbs in small colonies for best effect. They bloom best when left undisturbed. Propagate by removing the small bulblets that grow alongside mature bulbs.

Selected species and varieties:
P. scilloides var. *libanotica* (striped squill) bears ½-inch bluish white flowers delicately striped with porcelain blue above 6-inch shiny green leaves in spring; 'Alba' has pure white flowers above dark green leaves in spring.

SPIDER LILY
Hymenocallis

Light: mostly sun	
Plant type: bulb	
Hardiness: Zones 6-10	
Height: 1 ½ to 2 ½ feet	
Soil and Moisture: well-drained, wet to moist	
Interest: flowers	
Care: moderate	

◀ Hymenocallis caroliniana

Spider lilies add a dreamlike, ethereal atmosphere to the garden, with large, fragile-looking blossoms above deep green foliage. The large, fragrant white flowers are composed of six long grasslike petals surrounding a funnel-shaped cup. Spider lilies are excellent for wet meadows and bog gardens, or when planted along the shores of streams, ponds, and water gardens.

Growing and care:
Plant *H. caroliniana* bulbs 5 inches deep in loose soil high in organic matter and moisture. North of Zone 6 the bulbs can be planted in spring and lifted and brought indoors in fall for winter storage. Propagate by seed or division of bulb offsets.

Selected species and varieties:
H. caroliniana [also listed as *H. occidentalis*] is native to the southeastern and south-central United States. It grows 1½ to 2½ feet tall with a basal clump of shiny, light green strap-shaped leaves up to 17 inches long. White flowers 7 inches across are borne atop leafless stalks in clusters of up to six. Flowers appear in spring in the South and in summer in cooler regions.

SUMMER HYACINTH
Galtonia

Light:	mostly sun
Plant type:	bulb
Hardiness:	Zones 6-10
Height:	2 to 4 feet
Soil and Moisture:	well-drained, sandy, fertile, moist
Interest:	flowers, fragrance
Care:	moderate

◀ Galtonia candicans

Summer hyacinth produces bold spires of fragrant, nodding, snow white flowers accented by dark stamens from summer to fall. The blossoms are loosely arranged on stout stems above clumps of fleshy, narrow straplike leaves. Plant tall varieties at the back of flower borders, where they add late-season interest. Summer hyacinth naturalizes slowly into large clumps that provide years of enjoyment.

Growing and care:
Plant summer hyacinths in spring or fall, placing bulbs 6 inches deep and 1½ to 2 feet apart. Mulch bulbs in northern zones with 2 inches of leaf mold or compost in winter. North of Zone 6, lift bulbs in fall, allow to dry several hours, then remove tops and store for replanting the following spring. Propagate from seed to bloom in several years or by removing and replanting the few bulblets that may develop alongside mature bulbs.

Selected species and varieties:
G. candicans (giant summer hyacinth) has 2-inch fragrant white blossoms tinged with green on erect stalks to 4 feet tall in late summer. *G. viridiflora* has greenish flowers on 2- to 3-foot stalks above broad leaves in late summer to fall.

WILD HYACINTH
Brodiaea

Light:	mostly sun
Plant type:	bulb
Hardiness:	Zones 9-10
Height:	4 inches to 3 feet
Soil and Moisture:	heavy, moist to dry
Interest:	flowers
Care:	easy to moderate

◀ Brodiaea elegans

Wild hyacinths are loose, airy plants with brightly colored pink to violet flowers from spring to summer. These hardy wildflowers are native to the grasslands and plains in the West, where they have developed a tolerance for drought. *Brodiaea* have grasslike foliage and terminal clusters of ½- to 1½-inch tubular flowers on wiry stems. After flowering the plants go dormant, so place them where the foliage of other plants will fill in the space they leave. For best effect use wild hyacinths in groups of 12 or more in a perennial border, in a rock garden, or naturalized in meadows.

Growing and care:
B. elegans thrives in mostly sunny spots with poorly drained, heavy soils ranging from dry to moist. *B. pulchella* prefers mostly sunny places with poor, dry soils. Propagate by seed or offsets. Seedlings take 3 to 4 years to flower.

Selected species and varieties:
B. elegans (harvest brodiaea) has mounds of foliage up to 16 inches tall and violet to purple flowers that open in late spring to early summer on erect stems of about the same height as the foliage. *B. pulchella* [also called *Dichelostemma pulchellum*] (wild hyacinth) bears pinkish violet flowers in spring on stalks 2 to 3 feet tall.

AMERICAN PENNYROYAL
Hedeoma

Light:	mostly sun
Plant type:	annual
Height:	4 to 12 inches
Soil and Moisture:	well-drained, fertile, moist, sandy
Interest:	foliage
Care:	moderate

◄ Hedeoma pulegioides

With aromatic mint-scented leaves growing along erect branching stems, American pennyroyal has been a popular plant for herb gardens for many years. The plant develops into low, bushy mounds with tiny flower clusters appearing where the leaves meet the stems from summer through fall. Use American pennyroyal as an edging, ground cover, or filler plant in informal borders. Sow it into lawns for fragrance, or allow it to trail gracefully over the edges of hanging baskets. Add dried leaves and stems to herbal potpourri; they are widely used as an herbal repellent for fleas and weevils. Although it figures in herbal medicine, its oil can be toxic.

Growing and care:

Start American pennyroyal seed indoors 6 weeks before the last frost or sow directly outdoors in early spring. Seed-grown plants take 2 years to reach flowering, but plants self-sow freely and seedlings transplant easily. To dry, pick stems while they are in flower and hang.

Selected species and varieties:

H. pulegioides (American pennyroyal, mock pennyroyal) has 1½-inch hairy oval leaves along square stems to 1 foot tall, and ¼-inch blue to lavender flowers.

ANGELICA
Angelica

Light:	mostly sun
Plant type:	biennial, perennial
Hardiness:	Zones 3-9
Height:	3 to 8 feet
Soil and Moisture:	well-drained, fertile, moist
Interest:	flowers, foliage, seed heads
Care:	easy

◄ Angelica gigas

Tall columns of coarse-textured, licorice-scented leaves make angelica a bold border specimen or backdrop. In their second year, plants produce broad, flat clusters of tiny summer flowers followed by dramatic, rounded seed heads. Fresh angelica leaves are used to flavor acidic fruits such as rhubarb. The stems are steamed as a vegetable or candied for a garnish, and the seeds add sweet zest to pastries. The dried aromatic leaves can be used to scent potpourri. Angelica can cause dermatitis and should be eaten sparingly, as some herbalists believe it may be carcinogenic. Do not attempt to collect angelica in the wild, as it closely resembles poisonous water hemlock.

Growing and care:

Sow very fresh angelica seed in the garden in spring or fall. Remove flower stalks to prolong the life of the plants. Angelica self-sows readily; transplant seedlings before taproots become established.

Selected species and varieties:

A. archangelica (archangel, wild parsnip) grows to 8 feet tall with 6-inch-wide clusters of greenish white flowers. *A. gigas* reaches 6 feet with 8-inch clusters of burgundy flowers.

BORAGE
Borago

Light: mostly sun
Plant type: annual
Height: 2 to 3 feet
Soil and Moisture: well-drained, moist
Interest: flowers, foliage
Care: easy

◀ Borago officinalis

Borage is native to Europe and makes an attractive addition to flower or herb gardens, fresh flower arrangements, and summer salads. Both leaves and flowers are edible, with a refreshing cucumber-like flavor, and can be used to garnish salads or fruit cups. The plant has a somewhat sprawling habit that is best suited to an informal garden, where its soft-textured leaves and sky blue flowers add a cool, gentle touch.

Growing and care:
Sow seed directly in the garden at monthly intervals beginning 2 to 3 weeks prior to the last frost for continuous summer bloom. Allow 1 to 1½ feet between plants. Once established, plants will self-seed. Where summers are very hot, afternoon shade is recommended. Borage tolerates drought.

Selected species and varieties:
B. officinalis (talewort, cool-tankard) is a hardy annual with a rounded sprawling habit, bristly gray-green foliage, and succulent stems. Flowers are arranged in drooping clusters. Each is ¾ inch across and star shaped, with five petals. Though usually clear blue, they are sometimes light purple. Flower buds are covered with fine hairs.

CARAWAY
Carum

Light: mostly sun
Plant type: biennial grown as annual
Height: 2 feet
Soil and Moisture: well-drained, fertile, moist
Interest: flowers, foliage, seeds
Care: easy

◀ Carum carvi

Caraway is a delightful as well as useful addition to the herb garden, with feathery, aromatic carrotlike leaves and flavorful seeds. In late spring or early summer the plants send up branching flower stalks tipped with flat clusters of tiny white flowers followed by tasty seeds. Chop the leaves, which have a parsley-dill flavor, into salads, and cook the roots like carrots or parsnips. Use the anise-flavored seeds in breads and cakes, add them to meat, cabbage, and apple dishes, or crystallize them in sugar for an after-dinner candy to sweeten the breath and settle the stomach.

Growing and care:
Sow caraway in the garden in spring or fall and thin seedlings to stand 8 inches apart; once established, it self-sows. Snip leaves at anytime. Harvest seeds as flower clusters turn brown but before the seed capsules shatter. Hang to dry over a tray or cloth, and store the seeds in airtight containers. Dig 2-year-old roots to serve as a side dish.

Selected species and varieties:
C. carvi has ferny leaves up to 10 inches long and white flowers followed by ¼-inch dark brown seeds.

CHERVIL
Anthriscus

Light: mostly sun	
Plant type: annual	
Height: 1 to 2 feet	
Soil and Moisture: well-drained, moist	
Interest: flowers, foliage	
Care: easy	

◀ Anthriscus cerefolium

One of the fines herbes of French cuisine, chervil's finely divided leaves resemble parsley with a hint of warm anise flavor. Chervil is an ideal outdoor container plant. Chop fresh chervil into fish, vegetable, egg, and meat dishes. Use flower stalks in fresh or dried arrangements, and add dried leaves to herbal potpourri.

Growing and care:
Sow chervil seed in the garden for harvestable leaves in 6 to 8 weeks. Make successive sowings for a continuous supply of fresh leaves; seed sown in fall produces a spring crop. Remove flowers to encourage greater leaf production; alternately, allow plants to go to seed and self-sow, producing both early- and late-summer crops. Pick leaves before flowers appear, starting when plants reach 4 inches in height, and preserve by freezing alone or mixed with butter. Flavor fades when leaves are dried. Hang flower stalks to dry for use in winter bouquets.

Selected species and varieties:
A. cerefolium (chervil, salad chervil) produces 1- to 2-foot mounds of lacy bright green leaves topped by small, open clusters of tiny white flowers in summer.

COMFREY
Symphytum

Light: mostly sun	
Plant type: perennial	
Hardiness: Zones 3-9	
Height: 3 to 5 feet	
Soil and Moisture: well-drained, fertile, moist	
Interest: flowers, foliage	
Care: easy	

◀ Symphytum officinale

Comfrey forms bold clumps of coarse, hairy oval leaves useful as a backdrop in large borders or meadow gardens. From spring through fall, drooping clusters of funnel-shaped flowers are held on upright stems. Rich in nutrients, comfrey once figured prominently in herbal medicine but is now a suspected carcinogen and is recommended only for external use. Add dried and crumbled leaves to a bath as a skin softener. Steep leaves for liquid fertilizer, or add to the compost heap.

Growing and care:
Grow comfrey from root cuttings containing a growing tip, setting these divisions 6 to 8 inches deep and 2 to 3 feet apart. Choose sites carefully, as comfrey is difficult to eradicate once established. To control its spread, grow in large containers removed from other garden sites.

Selected species and varieties:
S. officinale (common comfrey) has deep green, rough-textured 10- to 20-inch basal leaves and ½-inch blue, white, purple, or rose tubular flowers. *S.* x *uplandicum* (Russian comfrey) is free flowering with blue or purple blossoms; 'Variegatum' has leaves marbled cream and green.

CORIANDER
Coriandrum

Light: mostly sun	
Plant type: annual	
Height: 1 to 3 feet	
Soil and Moisture: well-drained, fertile, moist	
Interest: foliage, seeds	
Care: easy	

◀ Coriandrum sativum

Coriander's pungent young leaves, commonly known as cilantro or Chinese parsley, are a staple in East Asian, Mexican, and Indian cuisines. With a hint of citrus, the round, ribbed seeds are used whole or ground in baked goods, curries, chutneys, and vegetable dishes. Add them to potpourri for a lingering lemon fragrance. The unpleasant odor of immature fruits earned coriander the nickname stinkplant; the characteristic agreeable fruity aroma develops as they ripen. Chop coriander roots into curries or steam them as a nutty vegetable.

Growing and care:
Sow coriander seed in spring and thin seedlings to stand 8 inches apart. Use fresh immature leaves for best flavor; cilantro loses flavor if dried. Collect mature seed heads and dry them in a paper bag to catch seeds. Dig roots in fall.

Selected species and varieties:
C. sativum has leaves that grow in small, scalloped fans resembling parsley when young, older leaves look ferny and threadlike, with flat, loose clusters of tiny white to mauve summer flowers; 'Long Standing' is a slow-to-bolt cultivar.

GERMANDER
Teucrium

Light: mostly sun	
Plant type: shrub	
Hardiness: Zones 5-9	
Height: 6 to 15 inches	
Soil and Moisture: well-drained, moist	
Interest: flowers, foliage	
Care: easy to moderate	

◀ Teucrium chamaedrys

Wall germander's spreading mounds of shiny evergreen foliage are covered from early to midsummer with spikes of small purple-pink flowers that add a perky cheerfulness to many types of gardens. Allow a specimen to spread in a rock or herb garden, or plant closely and clip into a low hedge resembling a miniature boxwood. The scalloped oval leaves release a faintly garlicky odor when bruised. Weave branches into dried wreaths. Wall germander once figured in herbal medicine but has fallen out of use.

Growing and care:
Grow wall germander from seed, from spring cuttings, or by division, setting plants 1 foot apart. Prune to shape in spring and deadhead to encourage bushiness. Provide protection from drying winter winds.

Selected species and varieties:
T. chamaedrys (wall germander) has square stems that trail then turn up to stand 10 to 15 inches high, lined with pairs of oval- to wedge-shaped ¼- to 1-inch leaves and tipped with whorls of ¾-inch white-dotted purple-pink flowers; 'Prostratum' has stems 6 to 8 inches tall spreading to 3 feet and pink flowers; 'Variegatum' has green leaves splotched white, cream, or yellow.

GIANT HYSSOP
Agastache

Light: mostly sun	
Plant type: perennial	
Hardiness: Zones 4-9	
Height: 2 to 5 feet	
Soil and Moisture: well-drained, moist	
Interest: flowers, foliage, fragrance	
Care: easy	

◀ Agastache barberi 'Tutti-Frutti'

Giant hyssop is a bold addition to any garden, with clumps of erect stems lined with fragrant leaves and tipped with spikes of colorful flowers. The nectar-filled summer flowers are edible and make a delightful nibble. The blossoms also attract bees and butterflies and dry well for everlasting arrangements. Scatter the leaves in salads or infuse them for teas.

Growing and care:
Start giant hyssop seed indoors 10 to 12 weeks before the last frost, and set seedlings out 1½ inches apart to bloom the first year. Plant in soil that has been amended with some organic matter and water regularly during the growing season. Established plantings self-sow, or you can propagate by division in spring or fall every 3 to 5 years. Hang flowers upside down in bunches to dry.

Selected species and varieties:
A. barberi bears red-purple flowers with a long season of bloom on stems to 2 feet tall; 'Firebird' has coppery orange blooms; 'Tutti-Frutti' bears raspberry pink to purple flavorful flowers; Zones 6-9. *A. foeniculum* (anise hyssop, blue giant hyssop, anise mint, licorice mint) has licorice-scented leaves and purple-blue flowers on 3-foot stems; 'Alba' has white blossoms. *A. rugosa* (Korean anise hyssop) bears wrinkly mint-scented leaves and small purple flower spikes on 5-foot stems; Zones 5-9.

HOP
Humulus

Light: mostly sun	
Plant type: perennial	
Hardiness: Zones 3-8	
Height: 10 to 25 feet	
Soil and Moisture: well-drained, fertile, moist	
Interest: flowers, foliage	
Care: easy	

◀ Humulus lupulus 'Aureus'

Hops are twining deciduous vines with coarse foliage like that of grapevines. They quickly clamber over trellises to form dense, textured screens. In summer female and male flowers appear on separate plants. Weave lengths of hopvine into garlands or wreaths for drying. Stuff dried female flowers, used as a bitter flavoring for beer, into herbal pillows to promote sleep. Blanch young leaves to remove bitterness and add to soups or sauces. Cook young side shoots like asparagus.

Growing and care:
Because female plants are more desirable than male ones and the gender of plants grown from seed is unknown for 3 years, it is best to grow hops from tip cuttings taken from female plants, divide their roots, or remove their rooted suckers in spring. Space plants 1½ to 3 feet apart. Cut hops to the ground at season's end.

Selected species and varieties:
H. lupulus (common hop, European hop, bine) has heart-shaped lobed leaves up to 6 inches across and female plants with paired yellow-green flowers ripening to papery scales layered in puffy cones; 'Aureus' has golden green leaves.

HORSERADISH
Armoracia

Light: mostly sun	
Plant type: perennial	
Hardiness: Zones 3-10	
Height: 2 to 4 feet	
Soil and Moisture: well-drained, moist to wet	
Interest: roots	
Care: easy	

◀ Armoracia rusticana

The pungent bite of fresh horseradish root grated into vinegar, cream, or mayonnaise for sauces and dressings is reason enough to grow this spicy herb. In spring, clumps of oblong leaves with ruffled, wrinkled edges grow from horseradish's fleshy taproot, followed by clusters of tiny white summer flowers. Chop fresh young leaves and toss in salads. Horseradish was used as a medicinal plant before it became popular as a condiment, and its dried leaves yield a yellow dye.

Growing and care:
Plant pieces of mature root at least 6 inches long in spring or fall. Set root pieces 3 to 4 inches deep and 1 to 2 feet apart in soil to which some organic matter has been added. Dig roots in fall and store in dry sand; slice and dry for later grinding, or grate into white vinegar to preserve. Horseradish can be invasive if not confined, as new plants grow from any root pieces left in the garden.

Selected species and varieties:
A. rusticana (horseradish, red cole) has thick, branching white-fleshed roots a foot long or longer with leaves to 2 feet and flower stalks to 4 feet; 'Variegata' has leaves streaked white.

HYSSOP
Hyssopus

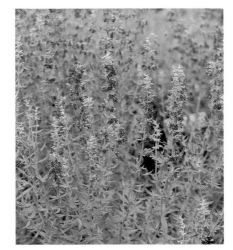

Light: mostly sun	
Plant type: perennial	
Hardiness: Zones 3-8	
Height: 1 1/2 to 3 feet	
Soil and Moisture: well-drained, moist to dry	
Interest: flowers, foliage	
Care: easy	

◀ Hyssopus officinalis

Hyssop's square stems are lined with narrow camphor-scented leaves and tipped with thick spikes of slightly flaring tubular flowers. The blue or white blossoms make attractive additions to herb gardens and attract bees, butterflies, and hummingbirds. Grow hyssops as bushy specimens or plant them closely for low hedges. Add the flowers to salads; or use the sage-like leaves to flavor poultry or stuffings. Use dried flowers and leaves in herbal teas or potpourri.

Growing and care:
Hyssop grows from seed to bloom in 2 years. Plants propagated from rooted cuttings or divisions taken in spring or fall will bloom in 1 season. Remove spent flowers to prolong bloom. Prune mature plants to the ground in spring. Shear into formal hedges for knot gardens or for use as edgings in formal gardens. Hyssop is sometimes evergreen in milder climates.

Selected species and varieties:
H. officinalis (common hyssop, European hyssop) has willowlike 3/4- to 1 1/4-inch leaves and 1/2-inch blue-violet flowers on plants to 3 feet; ssp. *aristatus* (rock hyssop) produces fine leaves on 1 1/2- to 2-foot plants; 'Albus' [also called 'Alba'] (white hyssop) has white flowers.

INDIAN BORAGE
Plectranthus

Light: mostly sun	
Plant type: annual	
Height: 1 to 3 feet	
Soil and Moisture: well-drained, fertile, moist	
Interest: foliage	
Care: easy to moderate	

◀ Plectranthus amboinicus 'Variegata'

The succulent, spicy leaves of Indian borage have a flavor reminiscent of a combination of thyme, oregano, and savory. In tropical areas where these herbs fail to thrive, cooks grow Indian borage as an attractive, tasty substitute. The plants are often allowed to ramble through the garden, forming an attractive ground cover, and in cooler areas are grown in containers. The leaves trail attractively from hanging baskets that are often hung just outside the kitchen door where the plants are always in easy reach. Use fresh leaves to complement beans, meats, and other strong-flavored dishes.

Growing and care:
Start Indian borage from tip cuttings or divisions in spring or summer. Plants stop growing at temperatures below 50°F and are quickly killed by even light frost. Pinch tips to keep plants bushy and contain their spread. Cut leggy plants back in spring. Feed potted plants monthly.

Selected species and varieties:
P. amboinicus (Indian borage, Spanish thyme, French thyme, soup mint, Mexican mint, Indian mint, country borage) has round gray-green leaves up to 4 inches across in pairs along thick stems, and whorls of tiny mintlike blue summer flowers in spikes up to 16 inches long; 'Variegata' has gray-green leaves edged in cream.

JOB'S-TEARS
Coix

Light: mostly sun	
Plant type: annual	
Height: 3 to 4 feet	
Soil and Moisture: well-drained, moist to wet	
Interest: flowers, foliage, seed heads	
Care: easy	

◀ Coix lacryma-jobi

Job's-tears produces long, narrow leaves clasping tall, jointed stems that create a lacy vertical accent as a border backdrop or temporary screen. When grown in containers the plants add a bold presence to patios and decks. In summer, arching flower spikes rise like froth above the foliage, and female flowers, enclosed in hard oval husks, hang decoratively in strings like dripping tears. Children enjoy stringing the small beads into bracelets and necklaces. Dry the stems for everlasting arrangements.

Growing and care:
Sow Job's-tears in spring when soil warms to 68°F; in colder climates, start seed indoors 2 to 3 months before last frost. Transplant or move established plants in spring or fall. Keep soil constantly moist while plants are growing. To dry, pick stems before seeds dry and shatter.

Selected species and varieties:
C. lacryma-jobi has leaves 2 feet long and 1½ inches wide on stems to 4 feet tipped with spiky flower clusters, male at the end, female at the base, encased in hard green husks that turn pearly white, gray, or iridescent violet as they ripen.

LAUREL
Laurus

Light: mostly sun

Plant type: shrub, tree

Hardiness: Zones 8-10

Height: 4 to 40 feet

Soil and Moisture: well-drained, moist

Interest: foliage

Care: easy to moderate

◀ Laurus nobilis

Laurel is an attractive evergreen plant with a handsome treelike form and aromatic leaves that emit a warm, spicy fragrance when crushed. In warm climates, bay laurel grows as a multistemmed shrub or tree to 40 feet. In northern areas the plant is frequently grown in containers, where it often reaches 4 to 6 feet tall. The glossy, leathery, aromatic leaves are prized by cooks and essential in bouquets garnis. Add leaves to potpourri, or dry branches for bouquets or wreaths.

Growing and care:
If planting outdoors choose a site protected from winds. To grow as standards, train plants to a single stem and prune frequently, rubbing off any new growth that appears along the trunk. Bring plants indoors before frost. Bay laurel can be propagated from seed or from hardwood cuttings but grows very slowly. Dry the leaves in a single layer in a warm, dark place; weigh down with a board to dry them flat. Store in airtight containers.

Selected species and varieties:
L. nobilis (bay laurel, bay, bay tree, true laurel) bears narrow 2- to 4-inch gray-green oval leaves; 'Angustifolia' (willow-leaved bay) has extremely narrow leaves; 'Aurea' has tapered golden yellow leaves.

LEMON BALM
Melissa

Light: mostly sun

Plant type: perennial

Hardiness: Zones 4-9

Height: 1 to 2 feet

Soil and Moisture: well-drained, moist

Interest: foliage, fragrance

Care: easy

◀ Melissa officinalis 'All Gold'

Lemon balm is a delightful herb with highly aromatic, citruslike foliage. The plant's fresh leaves are medium green and toothed, resembling mint, and add a lemony tang to salads, poultry or fish dishes, marinades, beverages, and vinegar. Dried leaves and stems are a potpourri ingredient.

Growing and care:
Sow lemon balm seed indoors about 8 weeks before planting out. Do not cover, as the seed needs light to germinate. Space plants 1 to 2 feet apart in well-worked soil that has had some organic matter added to it. Plant 'All Gold' in light shade to prevent leaf scorch, and shear 'Aurea' to prevent flower formation and greening of leaves. Lemon balm self-sows readily. Mature plants can also be divided in early spring. Contain the creeping roots by planting in bottomless pots at least 10 inches deep. Dry the leaves on screens.

Selected species and varieties:
M. officinalis (lemon balm, bee balm, sweet balm) bears 1- to 3-inch pointed oval leaves puckered by deep veins, and whorls of ½-inch white to yellow flowers in summer and fall; 'All Gold' has golden yellow foliage; 'Aurea' has green-veined yellow leaves.

LICORICE
Glycyrrhiza

Light: mostly sun	
Plant type: perennial	
Hardiness: Zones 5-9	
Height: 3 feet	
Soil and Moisture: well-drained, fertile, moist	
Interest: flowers, roots	
Care: moderate	

◀ Glycyrrhiza glabra

Licorice is a flavor that brings back fond memories of childhood. The herb that yields the flavoring spreads in broad clumps of erect branching stems lined with long leaves composed of paired 1- to 2-inch sticky yellow-green leaflets. In summer short flower spikes appear in leaf axils. The branching taproot contains glycyrrhizin, a compound 50 times sweeter than sugar and a source of the food flavoring. Dry root pieces to chew, or boil dried roots to extract the flavoring. Caution: Some people are severely allergic to glycyrrhizin.

Growing and care:
Licorice grows very slowly from seed. More often, it is grown from division of the crowns, rooted suckers, or root cuttings at least 6 inches long with two or three eyes. Space plants 1½ feet apart. Wait at least 3 years before harvesting roots; root pieces left behind will sprout the next year. Dry the roots in a shady location for up to 6 months and store in a cool location in airtight containers.

Selected species and varieties:
G. glabra bears yellow-green leaflets and white to blue, sometimes violet, ½-inch flowers resembling tiny sweet peas on plants growing from a 4-foot or longer taproot branching into tangled mats.

LOVAGE
Levisticum

Light: mostly sun	
Plant type: perennial	
Hardiness: Zones 3-8	
Height: 3 to 6 feet	
Soil and Moisture: well-drained, fertile, moist	
Interest: foliage	
Care: easy to moderate	

◀ Levisticum officinale

Lovage is a vigorous herb with towering clumps of greenish red stalks covered with divided leaflets resembling flat parsley. The plants are excellent grown in borders as well as the herb garden. Lovage's hollow stems, wedge-shaped leaves, thick roots, and ridged seeds all share an intense celery flavor and aroma. Chop leaves and stems or grate roots to garnish salads or flavor soups, potatoes, poultry, and other dishes. Steam stems as a side dish. Toss seeds into stuffings, dressings, and baked goods. Steep leaves for herbal tea.

Growing and care:
Sow lovage seed in fall or divide roots in spring or fall, spacing plants 2 feet apart. Top-dress annually with compost or aged manure and keep well watered during dry spells. Harvest leaves two or three times a season. Deadhead to encourage greater leaf production, or allow flowers to ripen for seed. Dry leaves in bundles, or blanch and freeze.

Selected species and varieties:
L. officinale has deep green leaflets with toothed edges on branching stems to 6 feet topped with a flat cluster of tiny yellow-green spring to summer flowers.

MINT
Mentha

Light: mostly sun

Plant type: perennial

Hardiness: Zones 3-10

Height: 1 inch to 4 feet

Soil and Moisture: well-drained, moist

Interest: flowers, foliage, fragrance

Care: easy

◄ Mentha aquatica var. crispa

Mints are the backbone of many herb gardens, with richly colored, very aromatic foliage. These vigorous plants are very easy to grow and quickly spread into low mounds of attractive leaves. Tiny white, pink, lilac, purple, or blue summer flowers appear in spiky tufts at stem tips or in whorls where leaves join stems. Mints thrive in containers and can be potted for indoor use. Low-growing species make good ground covers for potted shrubs and quickly fill niches among paving stones; mow sturdy species into an aromatic carpet. Cooks prize the hundreds of mint varieties, which vary greatly in leaf shape, size, and fragrance. Fresh leaves are the most intensely flavored, but mint can also be frozen or dried. Use sprigs of fresh mint to flavor iced drinks and accent vegetable dishes. Mint sauces and jellies are a traditional accompaniment for meats; mint syrups dress up desserts; and crystallized mint leaves make an edible garnish. Steep fresh or dried leaves in boiling water for tea, or allow the infusion to cool into a refreshing facial splash. Add to bathwater for an aromatic soak. Mix dried leaves into herbal potpourri. Mints are a traditional herbal remedy, especially as a breath freshener and digestive aid.

Growing and care:

Plant divisions or rooted cuttings in spring or fall, setting them 8 to 12 inches apart. Provide apple mint with a protective winter mulch in colder zones. Restrain mint's aggressive spread by spading deeply around plants at least once annually or, more reliably, by confining plants in bottomless plastic or clay containers sunk with their rims projecting at least 2 inches above the soil and their sides at least 10 inches deep; pull out any stems that fall to the ground and root outside this barrier. Mints can also be restrained by growing them in patio containers. Established beds of peppermint, apple mint, and spearmint tolerate mowing. The leaves are most flavorful when cut before flowers appear; shear plants when buds first form to yield about 2 cups of leaves per plant, and continue to pinch or shear at 10-day intervals to prolong fresh leaf production. Dry the leaves flat on screens, or hang stems in bunches in a warm, well-ventilated area to dry, then rub the leaves from the stems. Crystallize leaves for garnishes by simmering gently in a heavy sugar syrup.

Selected species and varieties:

M. aquatica (water mint) bears heart-shaped 2-inch leaves on 1- to 2-foot stems; var. *crispa* (curly mint) has decoratively frilled leaf edges; Zones 5-10. *M.* x *gracilis* (gingermint) has shiny red-tinged leaves and stems, and is popular in Southeast Asian cuisine; Zones 3-9. *M.* x *piperita* (peppermint) characteristically bears 1- to 2-foot purple stems lined with intensely menthol-flavored deep green leaves yielding commercially important peppermint oil; var. *citrata* (orange bergamot) has a lemon fragrance and flavor; other varieties have aromatic overtones ranging from citrus to floral to chocolate; Zones 5-9. *M. spicata* (spearmint) produces wrinkled, pointed oval leaves 2 inches long with a sweet taste and fragrance lining 1- to 3-foot stems; Zones 3-9. *M. suaveolens* (apple mint, woolly mint) has hairy, wrinkled 2-inch leaves with a distinctly fruity aroma on 1- to 3-foot stems; 'Variegata' (pineapple mint, variegated apple mint) has creamy leaf edges and a pineapple scent; Zones 5-9.

MYRTLE
Myrtus

Light:	mostly sun
Plant type:	shrub
Hardiness:	Zones 7-10
Height:	5 to 20 feet
Soil and Moisture:	well-drained, moist
Interest:	flowers, foliage
Care:	easy to moderate

◀ Myrtus communis
'Variegata'

Myrtle's lustrous evergreen leaves, tiny flower buds, and white flowers with puffs of golden stamens share a spicy orange scent that has made the plant a favorite in wedding bouquets for generations. The plant has a mounding, upright habit ideal for massing into hedges. In colder areas myrtle is often grown as a container plant to accent patios in summer, and is then brought indoors over the winter. Weave fresh branches into wreaths. Toss fresh, peeled buds into salads. Use leaves and berries to flavor meats. Add dried flowers and leaves to potpourri.

Growing and care:
Start myrtle from seed sown in spring or from half-ripe cuttings taken in summer; plant in sites protected from drying winds. Myrtle will grow in light shade but prefers full sun. It tolerates severe pruning to maintain its size in containers.

Selected species and varieties:
M. communis (sweet myrtle, Greek myrtle) bears pairs of glossy 2-inch pointed oval leaves and creamy white ¾-inch flowers followed by blue-black berries; 'Flore Pleno' has doubled petals; 'Microphylla' is a dwarf ideal for containers; 'Variegata' has leaves marbled gray-green and cream.

PARSLEY
Petroselinum

Light:	mostly sun
Plant type:	biennial
Hardiness:	Zones 6-9
Height:	1 to 2 feet
Soil and Moisture:	well-drained, fertile, moist
Interest:	foliage
Care:	easy

◀ Petroselinum crispum
var. neapolitanum

Whether bundled into a classic bouquet garni or chopped for use in sauces, eggs, vegetables, stuffings, or herb butters, parsley's classic deep green curly or flat leaves are as appealing to the eye as they are to the palate. The vitamin-rich sprigs freshen breath, and cooks around the world consider this herb a staple of the kitchen. The flatleaf types are more strongly flavored than curly varieties. Parsley is a biennial usually grown as an annual in the herb garden, as an edging plant, or in containers indoors or out.

Growing and care:
Soak parsley seed overnight before sowing to speed germination. Sow seed ¼ inch deep in soil warmed to at least 50°F. Thin seedlings to stand 4 to 6 inches apart. Begin harvesting leaves when plants are about 6 inches tall. Dry Italian parsley in the shade, oven, or microwave oven. Chop curly parsley and freeze in ice cubes for best flavor.

Selected species and varieties:
P. crispum var. *crispum* (curly parsley, French parsley) has highly frilled leaves on plants 1 to 1½ feet tall; var. *neapolitanum* (Italian parsley, flatleaf parsley) has flat, deeply lobed celery-like leaves on plants to 2 feet.

PATCHOULI
Pogostemon

Light:	mostly sun
Plant type:	perennial
Hardiness:	Zone 10
Height:	3 to 4 feet
Soil and Moisture:	well-drained, fertile, moist
Interest:	foliage, fragrance
Care:	moderate

◀ Pogostemon cablin

Patchouli's hairy triangular leaves contain a minty, cedar-scented oil valued in the making of perfume. Dried leaves gradually develop the scent and retain it for long periods in potpourri. In tropical gardens, patchouli forms mounds of fragrant foliage; elsewhere it is grown in containers to bring indoors when frost threatens.

Growing and care:
Patchouli rarely sets seed. Start new plants from tip cuttings or divisions in fall or spring. Outdoors where patchouli is not hardy, start tip cuttings to overwinter and treat plants as annuals, or grow in containers to move indoors. Feed potted plants weekly during spring and summer. Young leaves develop the best fragrance. Pinch plants two or three times each year to harvest young leaves and keep plants bushy. Dry leaves in a shady, well-ventilated area.

Selected species and varieties:
P. cablin [also classified as *P. patchouli*] has lightly scalloped leaves up to 5 inches long and half as wide in pairs along square stems tipped with 5- to 6-inch spikes of violet-tinged white flowers with violet filaments in fall.

PERILLA
Perilla

Light:	mostly sun
Plant type:	annual
Height:	1 to 3 feet
Soil and Moisture:	well-drained, sandy, moist
Interest:	foliage
Care:	easy to moderate

◀ Perilla frutescens 'Atropurpurea'

The foliage of perilla adds color and fragrance to the herb garden or border, with mounds of wrinkled, aromatic burgundy leaves that contrast nicely when used as a filler among gray or white foliage. The leaves and seeds have a fragrance and flavor that blend mint and cinnamon, and yield an oil 2,000 times sweeter than sugar. Perilla is a staple in Japanese cuisine, where it is used fresh or pickled to garnish sushi and flavor bean curd. Spikes of flower buds are batter-fried for tempura. Leaves are used to color vinegar and fruit preserves. Add the dried seed heads to herbal wreaths.

Growing and care:
Sow perilla seed in spring, and thin seedlings to stand 1 foot apart. Harvest leaves anytime; gather flowers for tempura just as buds begin to form. Harvesting flower buds also encourages bushier growth. Allowed to produce mature seed, the plants self-sow readily.

Selected species and varieties:
P. frutescens 'Atropurpurea' (black nettle) has pairs of wrinkled oval leaves up to 5 inches long on square stems tipped with spikes of tiny white summer flowers in whorls, followed by brown nutlets.

PYCNANTHEMUM
Pycnanthemum

Light:	mostly sun
Plant type:	perennial
Hardiness:	Zones 4-8
Height:	2 to 3 feet
Soil and Moisture:	well-drained, moist
Interest:	flowers, foliage, fragrance
Care:	easy

◀ Pycnanthemum
virginianum

Apleasingly sharp, peppery aroma fills the garden wherever pycnanthemum grows. The stout, square stems of this vigorous, mounding perennial herb are lined with whorls of very narrow aromatic leaves. In summer tufts of flowers appear at the tips of the stems and attract bees and butterflies to the garden. The plant is excellent in the herb garden or naturalized in wildflower meadows. As intensely flavored as it is fragrant, pycnanthemum is an excellent culinary substitute for true mint. Dry the dense flower heads for arrangements, or add dried leaves and flowers to potpourri.

Growing and care:
Pycnanthemum is easy to grow from cuttings or divisions of mature plants. Set plants out in spring or fall, spacing them 8 to 12 inches apart. Restrain their spread by spading around plants annually or by planting them in bottomless tubs and removing branches that root outside this barrier.

Selected species and varieties:
P. virginianum (Virginia mountain mint, wild basil, prairie hyssop) has smooth or slightly toothed, pointed, very narrow 1- to 1½-inch aromatic leaves and tiny white to lilac flowers in very dense, flat heads in summer.

SCENTED GERANIUM
Pelargonium

Light:	mostly sun
Plant type:	annual, perennial, or shrub
Hardiness:	Zone 10
Height:	1 to 6 feet
Soil and Moisture:	well-drained, fertile, moist
Interest:	foliage, fragrance
Care:	easy

◀ P. capitatum

Scented geraniums are a diverse group of plants, with more scents than a spice rack. When brushed or rubbed, the foliage emits a citrusy, floral, minty, or resinous perfume, depending on the species or cultivar. The kidney-shaped or broad triangular leaves are wrinkled, lobed, frilled, or filigreed to add texture to a border. Loose, open clusters of small white, pink, mauve, or lilac flowers on branching stalks add color in spring or summer. Outdoors year round where they can be protected from frost, taller species grow as border specimens or background shrubs or can be pruned into standards; sprawling types can be used as ground covers or trained against trellises. Elsewhere, scented geraniums are treated like summer bedding plants or grown in containers or hanging baskets; they also do well year round as houseplants. Use fresh leaves of citrus-, floral-, or mint-scented geraniums in teas and to flavor baked goods, jam, jelly, vinegar, syrup, or sugar; use resinous leaves to flavor pâté and sausage. Toss flowers into salads for color. Add dried leaves to floral or herbal potpourri. Infuse leaves in warm water for an aromatic, mildly astringent facial splash.

Growing and care:
Sow seed indoors 10 to 12 weeks before the last frost. While all scented geraniums do best in mostly sunny spots, lemon geranium, apple geranium, and peppermint geranium will tolerate a bit more shade. Too-rich soil

(continued)

tends to minimize fragrance. Remove faded flowers to encourage further blooming. In containers, scented geraniums do best when slightly potbound; repot only into the next larger size pot. Indoors, provide daytime temperatures of 65° to 70°F, about 10° cooler at night, with at least 5 hours of direct sunlight daily. Keep potted plants from becoming leggy by pruning them hard after blooming or in very early spring, then feeding with any complete houseplant fertilizer. To propagate scented geraniums, cut a branch tip at least 3 inches long just below a leaf node, dip into rooting hormone, and place in clean, moist sand to root; transplant into potting soil after 2 weeks. Pick scented geranium leaves for drying anytime and lay in a single layer on screens in a shady location.

Selected species and varieties:

P. capitatum (wild rose geranium, rose-scented geranium) is a spreading plant 1 to 2 feet tall and up to 5 feet wide with crinkled, velvety 2-inch rose-scented leaves and mauve to pink summer flowers. *P. citronellum* has lemon-scented 3½-inch-wide leaves with pointed lobes and pink summer flowers streaked purple on upright shrubs to 6 feet tall and half as wide. *P. crispum* (lemon geranium) has strongly lemon-scented, kidney-shaped ½-inch leaves and pink to lavender flowers in spring and summer on plants 2 feet tall and half as wide, whose leaves are traditionally used in finger bowls. *P. x fragrans* 'Variegatum' (nutmeg geranium) has small, downy gray-green leaves smelling of nutmeg and pine, and white spring to summer flowers lined with red on compact plants 12 to 16 inches tall and as wide. *P. graveolens* (rose geranium) has filigreed, rose-scented gray-green leaves and pale pink spring to summer flowers spotted purple on upright shrubs to 3 feet tall and as wide. *P. odoratissimum* (apple geranium) is a spreading plant 1 foot tall and twice as wide with small, kidney-shaped velvety, apple-scented leaves and red-veined white spring and summer flowers on trailing flower stalks. *P. tomentosum* (peppermint geranium) is a spreading plant to 3 feet tall and twice as wide with 4- to 5-inch peppermint-scented leaves and white spring to summer flowers.

SOAPWORT
Saponaria

Light: mostly sun	
Plant type: perennial	
Hardiness: Zones 3-8	
Height: 1 to 2 feet	
Soil and Moisture: well-drained, moist	
Interest: flowers, foliage	
Care: easy	

◀ Saponaria officinalis 'Rubra Plena'

Soapwort bears clusters of pale blush pink summer flowers scented with the aroma of raspberries and cloves atop clumps of erect stems. The flowers resemble ruffled funnels during the day, then open fully at night into casual, open bells. Toss flowers into salads or dry them for potpourri. Leaves, stems, and roots boiled in rainwater produce a soapy liquid prized for cleaning antique textiles. Soapwort once figured in herbal medicine but is now considered toxic.

Growing and care:

Sow soapwort in spring or fall, or divide mature plants in late fall or early spring. Avoid planting near ponds, as root secretions are toxic to fish. Plants self-sow invasively. Shear spent flowers to prevent seed formation and control spread. Shearing sometimes produces a second bloom. For liquid soap, boil sliced roots, stems, and leaves in lime-free water for 30 minutes and strain.

Selected species and varieties:

S. officinalis (bouncing Bet) has pointed oval leaves paired along sturdy stems and 1- to 1½-inch-wide pink flowers with single or double rows of petals; 'Rubra Plena' has double red petals that fade to pink.

SOCIETY GARLIC
Tulbaghia

Light: mostly sun	
Plant type: bulb	
Hardiness: Zones 9-10	
Height: 1 to 1½ feet	
Soil and Moisture: well-drained, fertile, moist	
Interest: flowers, foliage, fragrance	
Care: easy	

◀ Tulbaghia violacea

Society garlic is one of the most attractive plants in the herb garden, with large clusters of starry white, pink, or violet summer flowers on tall stalks above clumps of grassy evergreen leaves. Use society garlic's neat mound as a specimen in the perennial border, or grow the plant as an edging for garden beds or walkways. In cooler climates society garlic grows well as a potted plant and can be wintered on a sunny window sill. Use the flowers in fresh bouquets. The leaves, with an onion or garlic aroma and a mild taste that does not linger on the breath, can be chopped and used like garlic chives—as a garnish flavoring for salads, vegetables, and sauces.

Growing and care:
Propagate society garlic by removing and replanting the small bulblets growing alongside mature bulbs in spring or fall. Space plants 1 foot apart. For indoor culture, plant one bulb per 6- to 8-inch pot.

Selected species and varieties:
T. violacea has flat, grassy 8- to 12-inch leaves and ¾-inch white or violet flowers in clusters of eight to 16 blossoms on 1- to 2½-foot stalks; 'Silver Streak' has leaves striped cream and green.

SORREL
Rumex

Light: mostly sun	
Plant type: perennial	
Hardiness: Zones 3-8	
Height: 6 inches to 5 feet	
Soil and Moisture: well-drained, moist	
Interest: foliage, seed heads	
Care: easy	

◀ Rumex crispus

Sorrel is a very vigorous, persistent perennial that, once planted in the garden, often becomes a permanent resident. The slightly sour, lemony, arrowhead-shaped leaves add zest to salads and accent soups and sauces. Use fresh leaves sparingly, as the high oxalic acid content can aggravate conditions such as gout. Boil leaves for a spinachlike vegetable, changing the water once to reduce the acid content. Birds love the tiny seeds produced at the tips of the stalks.

Growing and care:
Sow sorrel indoors 6 to 8 weeks before the last frost, outdoors after the last frost, or divide mature plants and space 8 inches apart. Leaves become bitter in hot weather, but flavor returns with cooler temperatures. Pinch out flowering stalks to encourage leaf production and control invasive self-sowing. The plants self-sow prolifically and sometimes become more of a problem than a pleasure.

Selected species and varieties:
R. acetosa (garden sorrel, sour dock) bears narrow 5- to 8-inch leaves on clumps of 3-foot stems. *R. crispus* (curled dock) has extremely wavy, curly 12-inch leaves on plants 1 to 5 feet tall. *R. scutatus* (French sorrel) bears thick, broad shield-shaped leaves 1 to 2 inches long on trailing stems growing into mats 6 to 20 inches high and twice as wide.

SWEET FERN
Comptonia

Light:	mostly sun
Plant type:	shrub
Hardiness:	Zones 2-6
Height:	3 to 5 feet
Soil and Moisture:	well-drained, moist to dry
Interest:	foliage
Care:	easy

◀ Comptonia peregrina

In the morning and evening, sweet fern perfumes the air in the wildflower garden or perennial border with a warm, sweet fragrance unlike any other herb. The plants form neat, tidy mounds of deep green foliage and fit well into borders and herb gardens alike. Sweet fern's lacy deciduous leaves are lightly covered with rusty brown hairs and resemble the fronds of a fern. The leaves make a delightful tea that was used by Native Americans as a medicine.

Growing and care:
Sow ripe sweet fern seed in fall, and overwinter in cold frames to transplant in spring. Otherwise, remove and transplant rooted suckers in spring or layer branches to develop rooted cuttings. Sweet fern can be difficult to transplant; to disturb roots as little as possible, dig up a large rootball when moving suckers or layered cuttings. Sweet fern grows best in loose, open soils and tolerates dry conditions.

Selected species and varieties:
C. peregrina has fans of narrow 5-inch pointed leaves with red-brown dangling male catkins and smaller round female flowers in summer followed by shiny conical brown nutlets in fall.

SWEET FLAG
Acorus

Light:	mostly sun
Plant type:	perennial
Hardiness:	Zones 3-10
Height:	1 to 5 feet
Soil and Moisture:	well-drained to heavy, wet
Interest:	foliage
Care:	easy

◀ Acorus gramineus
'Variegatus'

Sweet flag is an aromatic herb with tangerine-scented leaves and cinnamon-smelling rhizomes. The plants thrive in wet soils along stream banks or in aquatic gardens and are easy to grow once established. Once used in herbal medicine, sweet flag is now considered hazardous. The spicy rhizomes are still gathered and used to scent potpourri.

Growing and care:
Sweet flag should be planted in soil that stays constantly wet, and thrives even when grown under 2 inches of water. It can be propagated from fresh seed sown soon after it is gathered or by division of the rhizomes in spring or fall. For potpourri collect rhizomes that are at least 2 to 3 years old in spring, wash well, slice, and dry; do not peel them, as much of their aromatic oil is in the outer layers.

Selected species and varieties:
A. calamus bears sword-shaped ¾-inch-wide leaves up to 5 feet tall and tiny yellow-green summer flowers. *A. gramineus* (Japanese sweet flag) has narrow leaves up to 20 inches long and a 2- to 3-inch spadix in summer; 'Ogon' has 12-inch leaves striped golden green and cream; 'Variegatus' has white-edged 1½-foot leaves only ¼ inch wide; Zones 7-10.

VALERIAN
Valeriana

Light: mostly sun	
Plant type: perennial	
Hardiness: Zones 3-9	
Height: 3 to 5 feet	
Soil and Moisture: well-drained, moist	
Interest: flowers, fragrance	
Care: easy	

◀ Valeriana officinalis

Valerian is an attractive plant that is as beautiful as it is useful. The tall, vigorous plants bear small flat-topped tufts of tiny fragrant flowers in summer above a rosette of lacy fernlike leaves. Both cats and butterflies find the plants irresistible. The flowers have the scent of vanilla and honey and add soft texture to fresh floral bouquets. While some gardeners find the odor of the dried roots agreeable and add them to potpourri, others compare it to dirty socks. The roots yield a sedative compound used in herbal medicine. Add the mineral-rich leaves to compost.

Growing and care:
Sow common valerian seed in spring, or divide the creeping roots in spring or fall. Space plants 2 feet apart and mulch to conserve moisture. The plants thrive in cool, shaded locations and are weakened by hot, humid weather. Valerian spreads quickly and will self-sow if the flower heads are not removed.

Selected species and varieties:
V. officinalis (common valerian) has erect hairy stems lined with light green ferny leaves and flower stalks to 5 feet with tubular white, pink, red, or lavender-blue flowers in clusters up to 4 inches wide.

WILD CELERY
Apium

Light: mostly sun	
Plant type: biennial grown as annual	
Height: 1 to 3 feet	
Soil and Moisture: well-drained, fertile, moist	
Interest: foliage	
Care: moderate	

◀ Apium graveolens

The ridged stems, parsleylike leaves, and tiny seeds of wild celery all share the scent of the cultivated vegetable beloved as an aromatic culinary staple. While the stems and leaves are a bit too bitter for use in salads, they are excellent tossed into the cooking pot as a seasoning. Use wild celery sparingly, as it is toxic in large amounts.

Growing and care:
Sow wild celery seed in sites sheltered from drying winds. Thin out the seedlings to stand 12 to 16 inches apart. Water regularly to keep soil moist. In warm regions mulch around plants to keep soil cool. Gather leaves as needed and dry in a single layer in a shady, well-ventilated area. To obtain seed, pick flower heads as they begin to brown and store in paper bags until they dry and release seeds.

Selected species and varieties:
A. graveolens (wild celery, smallage) has rosettes of flat fan-shaped leaflets with toothed edges the first year, followed by elongated, ridged, branching stems tipped with small clusters of greenish cream summer flowers.

CAROLINA JASMINE
Gelsemium

Light: mostly sun	
Plant type: woody vine	
Hardiness: Zones 6-9	
Height: 10 to 20 feet	
Soil and Moisture: well-drained, moist	
Interest: flowers, fragrance	
Care: easy	

◀ Gelsemium sempervirens

Carolina jasmine is a vigorous, twining evergreen vine with fragrant yellow funnel-shaped flowers in late winter to early spring. It is a favorite ornamental plant in the South. The tiered leaves provide fine texture to fences, trellises, or unsightly features, and the plant is also an excellent rambling ground cover. Planted at the base of a tree, it scrambles up the trunk. Tucked into the top of a retaining wall, it spills flowers and foliage over the side.

Growing and care:
Carolina jasmine grows best in soil well amended with rotted manure and compost but adapts to less fertile conditions. Best flowering occurs in mostly sunny locations. After a few years of growth the vines usually become top heavy and should be pruned back hard when dormant.

Selected species and varieties:
G. sempervirens (Carolina yellow jessamine, false jasmine, evening trumpet flower) is a vigorous grower with slender wiry stems bearing $1\frac{1}{2}$-inch-long flowers singly or in clusters in the axils of narrow lance-shaped dark green leaves 1 to $3\frac{1}{2}$ inches long that turn yellowish green or dull purplish in winter.

CHOKEBERRY
Aronia

Light: mostly sun	
Plant type: ground cover	
Hardiness: Zones 4-9	
Height: 2 to 10 feet	
Soil and Moisture: well-drained, moist to dry	
Interest: flowers, foliage, fruit	
Care: easy	

◀ Aronia arbutifolia 'Brilliantissima'

Chokeberry is a shrubby ground cover whose thick tangles of woody stems bear a profusion of tiny cherrylike blossoms in spring. The snow white flowers yield to abundant clusters of glossy red berries that persist from fall through winter. The plant's dark green oval leaves turn bright scarlet in fall. Chokeberry is a vigorous grower producing plentiful suckers and dense stands, making it very effective for slopes, meadows, or shrub borders.

Growing and care:
Plant chokeberries in well-worked soil amended with some organic matter. The plants should be watered regularly in the months after planting, but once established are very drought tolerant. Fertilize lightly after flowering is completed in spring. Propagate from seed, from cuttings, or by transplanting rooted suckers.

Selected species and varieties:
A. arbutifolia 'Brilliantissima' bears $\frac{1}{3}$-inch white spring-blooming flowers touched with red, followed by clusters of $\frac{1}{4}$-inch red berries on shrubs to 10 feet tall. *A. melanocarpa* (black chokeberry) is a very vigorous, fast-spreading shrub with dark green leaves turning bright red in fall, and white spring flowers followed by black berries.

CLEMATIS
Clematis

Light: mostly sun

Plant type: vine

Hardiness: Zones 3-9

Height: 6 to 25 feet

Soil and Moisture: well-drained, moist

Interest: flowers, foliage, seed heads, fragrance

Care: moderate

◀ Clematis x jackmanii 'Gypsy Queen'

Vigorous growth and large, spectacular flowers make clematis a favorite for growing on fences, trellises, or other structures. These hardy, leafy vines are covered with show-stopping fragrant flowers from late spring to fall, depending on the species. Masses of feathery seed heads add attractive accents after the flowers have faded.

Growing and care:
Plant clematis 2 to 3 inches deeper than it was growing in its container. Mulch in summer to keep roots cool, and again in late fall to protect from heaving in late winter. Propagate species from cuttings or seed, spacing plants 2 to 4 feet apart.

Selected species and varieties:
C. alpina (Alpine clematis) bears 1½- to 3-inch single lantern-shaped mauve or blue flowers in spring on 8-foot vines; Zones 3-7. *C. x jackmanii* (Jackman clematis) bears 4- to 7-inch deep violet flowers on 10-foot robust stems from late spring to frost; many cultivars are available, with flowers in shades of white, red, blue, and purple, some with single flowers, others with double; 'Gypsy Queen' has rich violet-red flowers; Zones 3-8. *C. paniculata* (sweet autumn clematis) bears 1- to 4-inch dainty white flowers on 25-foot vines in early fall. *C. texensis* (scarlet clematis) has leathery ¾-inch scarlet flowers in clusters from late spring until frost on 6- to 12-foot stems; Zones 6-9.

CLOCK VINE
Thunbergia

Light: mostly sun

Plant type: vine

Hardiness: Zone 10

Height: 3 to 6 feet

Soil and Moisture: well-drained, fertile, moist to dry

Interest: flowers

Care: easy

◀ Thunbergia alata

Clock vine is a perky climbing or trailing vine that produces masses of neat triangular leaves and cheerful-looking flowers throughout summer. Clock vine blossoms come in shades of deep yellow, gold, orange, and creamy white, each flower with a dark central eye. Plants are attractive in window boxes and hanging baskets, and are excellent as a fast-growing screen on a trellis or fence.

Growing and care:
Start seed indoors 6 to 8 weeks prior to the last frost, or sow directly outdoors after danger of frost has passed. Space plants 1 foot apart and provide support if you wish them to climb. Plants thrive where summer temperatures remain somewhat cool. Water during dry periods. If soil dries out the plants may stop flowering.

Selected species and varieties:
T. alata (black-eyed Susan vine) develops twining stems with 3-inch leaves with toothed margins and winged petioles. The solitary flowers are 1 to 2 inches across with five distinct rounded petal segments, usually surrounding a black or dark purple center; 'Susie' is a series with dark-centered flowers in three distinct shades of white, yellow, and orange.

CRIMSON STARGLORY
Mina

Light:	mostly sun
Plant type:	vine
Hardiness:	Zones 8-10
Height:	15 to 20 feet
Soil and Moisture:	well-drained, fertile, moist
Interest:	flowers
Care:	moderate

◀ Mina lobata

This vigorous, fast-growing vine is native to Mexico and brings tropical color and form to sunny gardens. The attractive plant climbs by twining its reddish stem around supports. Throughout summer numerous red buds open to reveal tubular flowers that turn from orange to white as they mature. Plants provide an elegant light-textured screen or background for other flowers when grown on a trellis or fence. They can also be grown in containers.

Growing and care:
Start seed indoors in individual peat pots 6 weeks prior to the last frost, or directly in the garden after danger of frost has passed. Keep plants well mulched and supplied with abundant water. Fertilize when the first flower buds appear. Plants are hardy from Zone 8 south, but in warmer areas will benefit from midday shade.

Selected species and varieties:
M. lobata produces attractive dark green, three-lobed leaves along self-twining stems. The 1-inch flowers appear in showy long-stalked clusters, beginning as red boat-shaped buds that open orange, change to yellow, and eventually turn creamy white. All colors are present on a single cluster.

FIG
Ficus

Light:	mostly sun
Plant type:	tender perennial vine
Hardiness:	Zones 9-10
Height:	20 to 60 feet
Soil and Moisture:	well-drained, moist
Interest:	foliage
Care:	moderate

◀ Ficus pumila

Related to the edible fig, this fig is grown for its rich green foliage rather than any fruit. Also known as creeping fig, this rambling vine rapidly covers walls or unsightly objects with a glossy mosaic of emerald-colored leaves. Particularly useful for covering masonry, fig's small, clinging roots, like those of English ivy, attach to brick, cement, or stucco. Young stems intertwine to create a dense network of branches. Creeping fig can also be grown in a container or as a houseplant.

Growing and care:
Creeping fig thrives with abundant water during the growing season. To promote bushiness pinch new shoots, and to maintain a neat, clinging habit remove the mature branches that extend away from the support. In late fall or early spring, thin plants to reduce density and maintain vigor. Although creeping fig is generally free of pests, woolly aphids can be a problem. Propagate by cuttings or layering.

Selected species and varieties:
F. pumila (creeping fig) produces numerous slender intertwined stems that crisscross to form a dense mat on a support, rapidly growing 20 to 60 feet, with 1-inch heart-shaped evergreen leaves; if allowed to develop, mature plants produce erect shoots with thickened 2- to 4-inch leaves and occasional 2-inch heart-shaped fruit; 'Variegata' bears white-mottled leaves.

GOTU KOLA
Centella

Light: mostly sun	
Plant type: perennial ground cover	
Hardiness: Zones 8-10	
Height: 6 to 20 inches	
Soil and Moisture: well-drained, moist to wet	
Interest: foliage	
Care: easy	

◀ Centella asiatica

Gotu kola is versatile ground cover that is as much at home in a hanging basket as it is in the garden. The dainty scalloped-edged leaves line slender, trailing reddish green stems forming mats of soft-textured foliage. Tiny white or pink flowers hide beneath the leaves. Allow gotu kola to ramble, or grow it in patio containers. Its colorful trailing stems make it an ideal plant for hanging baskets.

Growing and care:
Sow gotu kola seed in spring or fall in moist or wet soil. Plants grow best in mostly sunny places where moisture is abundant. The plant roots easily as it grows along the ground, and these natural layers can be transplanted anytime; space them 1 to 2 feet apart. Gotu kola is sometimes invasive where conditions are favorable for its growth.

Selected species and varieties:
C. asiatica [also classified as *Hydrocotyle asiatica*] (gotu kola, tiger grass) has kidney-shaped 1- to 2-inch bright green leaves with gently lobed edges and white to pink flowers in summer.

GRAPE
Vitis

Light: mostly sun	
Plant type: vine	
Hardiness: Zones 5-8	
Height: 20 to 50 feet	
Soil and Moisture: well-drained, moist	
Interest: foliage, fruit, bark	
Care: moderate	

◀ Vitis vinifera 'Purpurea'

Grapes are very vigorous, fast-growing vines that quickly cover arbors and trellises with a shady veil of green foliage. The plant's twining tendrils cling to just about any structure, providing nearly instant screens or canopies. The broad leaves, attractively lobed and incised, color brilliantly in fall. Older stems have shredding, peeling bark, while younger shoots carry clusters of blue-black fruit well into winter.

Growing and care:
Plant in deeply cultivated soil enriched with generous amounts of organic matter. Fertilize in spring a few weeks after flowering. When growing for shade or an arbor, cut canes back to a strong bud in winter to control spread. Propagate from cuttings.

Selected species and varieties:
V. amurensis (Amur grape) has 5- to 10-inch leaves that color crimson to purple in fall. *V. coignetiae* (crimson glory vine) is an extremely fast-growing vine—up to 50 feet per year—with 4- to 10-inch leaves turning scarlet in fall. *V. vinifera* 'Purpurea' (wine grape, common grape) bears 4- to 6-inch heart-shaped leaves that emerge reddish burgundy then mature to purple.

HONEYSUCKLE
Lonicera

Light: mostly sun	
Plant type: woody vine	
Hardiness: Zones 4-9	
Height: 15 to 30 feet	
Soil and Moisture: well-drained, fertile, moist to dry	
Interest: flowers, foliage, fragrance	
Care: easy	

◀ Lonicera sempervirens

The rich, sweetly scented flowers of honeysuckle add a unique ambiance to any garden. The distinctive tubular blossoms are produced in great abundance along the fast-growing twining stems and are a magnet to hummingbirds. These vines are easy to grow and some may even become invasive if their growth is left unchecked. In the garden, honeysuckle provides a long season of bloom and can be trained to climb a trellis or fence, or to grow over old shrubs, providing colorful boundaries to borders and plantings.

Growing and care:
Plant honeysuckle in soil with abundant organic matter. Fertilize when flower buds first appear in spring, and prune immediately after flowering to maintain desired size. Provide sturdy supports for twining stems. Do not allow honeysuckle to twine around young trees, because it can cause girdling. Propagate by seed or cuttings.

Selected species and varieties:
L. sempervirens (trumpet honeysuckle) bears dark blue-green leaves and spring-blooming flowers; 'Alabama Crimson' is a twining vine to 20 feet with showy clusters of small, trumpet-shaped crimson flowers with bright yellow stamens; 'Sulphurea' is a 20-foot twining vine with a dense habit, evergreen oval leaves, and yellow flowers followed by ¼-inch shiny red berries in late summer and fall.

MAZUS
Mazus

Light: mostly sun	
Plant type: ground cover	
Hardiness: Zones 6-9	
Height: 2 inches	
Soil and Moisture: well-drained, moist, fertile	
Interest: flowers, foliage	
Care: easy	

◀ Mazus reptans

A true ground hugger, mazus forms a dense, prostrate carpet with medium green oval leaves and one-sided clusters of charming rose to lavender flowers in late spring. The unusual blossoms have a white or yellow throat accented with polka dots. Mazus works well in rock gardens and borders, and since it tolerates occasional foot traffic, it makes an ideal plant for tucking between steppingstones.

Growing and care:
Set plants 12 to 15 inches apart in well-worked soil amended with rotted manure or peat moss. As mazus grows, roots develop along the stem, allowing it to compete well with weeds and grass. Propagate by dividing the plants in spring.

Selected species and varieties:
M. reptans has procumbent stems bearing inch-long coarsely toothed leaves that hold well into late fall or early winter, along with ½-inch-long flowers gathered into profuse lavender to purplish blue clusters, usually spotted with white or yellow in the center; 'Alba' has snowy white flowers.

ST.-JOHN'S-WORT
Hypericum

Light: mostly sun	
Plant type: ground cover	
Hardiness: Zones 5-8	
Height: 1 to 1½ feet	
Soil and Moisture: well-drained, moist to dry	
Interest: flowers	
Care: moderate	

◀ Hypericum calycinum

St.-John's-wort has long-lasting sunny yellow flowers accented by a pincushion clump of central stamens. In fall the old flower stems hold interesting winged fruit capsules that persist into winter. The plant makes a stunning ground cover for open, mostly sunny slopes, and is an excellent addition to rock gardens or wildflower plantings.

Growing and care:

Plant St.-John's-wort in gravelly well-drained soil rich in limestone. In acid soils add ground limestone a few weeks before planting in spring. Space plants 1 to 1½ feet apart. Propagate by division in spring or by softwood cuttings in early summer. Provide extra water during dry periods. The plants may be short lived and should be divided every 4 to 5 years to rejuvenate them.

Selected species and varieties:

H. calycinum (creeping St.-John's-wort) produces 2- to 3-inch vivid yellow flowers with bright red anthers from summer to early fall, and creeping stems with dark green semievergreen leaves that turn purplish in fall.

WINTER CREEPER
Euonymus

Light: mostly sun	
Plant type: ground cover	
Hardiness: Zones 4-8	
Height: 1 to 3 feet	
Soil and Moisture: well-drained, moist	
Interest: foliage	
Care: easy	

◀ Euonymus fortunei 'Emerald Charm'

Winter creeper is a versatile creeping shrub that is equally at home climbing a wall or spreading over the garden as a ground cover. The irregular mounds of glossy dark green leaves are perfect as an informal accent in the front of the shrub border, as a foundation planting, or in rock gardens. Winter creeper can also be trained as a climber on trellises or walls where the stout branches attract nesting birds.

Growing and care:

Plant winter creeper in loosened soil that has some organic matter. The plants grow well in full sun to full shade but prefer mostly sunny locations. Provide extra water during dry periods. Mulch in spring and fall to keep weeds down and conserve soil moisture.

Selected species and varieties:

E. fortunei is an evergreen ground cover with creeping stems covered with glossy, dark green leathery leaves; 'Dart's Blanket' is a salt-tolerant prostrate type growing 12 to 16 inches high with dark green leaves; 'Emerald Charm' grows to 3 feet with glossy green leaves; 'Gold Prince' grows in mounds 2 feet high with gold-tipped leaves that later turn all green.

BLUE OAT GRASS
Helictotrichon

Light: mostly sun

Plant type: ornamental grass

Hardiness: Zones 4-9

Height: 2 to 3 feet

Soil and Moisture: well-drained, moist to dry

Interest: foliage, flowers

Care: easy

◀ Helictotrichon sempervirens

Blue oat grass produces a dense clump of stiff, upright steel blue foliage and is a valuable addition to a rock garden or herbaceous border for both color and form. It contrasts well to perennials with green or silvery white leaves. The metallic blue color is also a lovely complement to the burgundy leaves of shrubs such as barberry 'Crimson Pygmy' or smokebush 'Royal Purple'. The flowers are buff colored and appear in graceful sprays above the leaves.

Growing and care:
Blue oat grass is easy to grow and develops its best color in dry, infertile soils. Space plants 1 to 1½ feet apart in an airy location with good air circulation. Cut back foliage to the ground in early spring before new growth begins. Propagate plants by division in early spring.

Selected species and varieties:
H. sempervirens forms a dense mound 2 to 3 feet high and equally wide, with light blue-gray leaves and flowers arrayed in drooping, one-sided 4- to 6-inch clusters on slender stems held above the foliage.

BRISTLE GRASS
Setaria

Light: mostly sun

Plant type: annual grass

Height: 2 to 5 feet

Soil and Moisture: well-drained, moist

Interest: foliage

Care: easy

◀ Setaria italica

Bristle grass is an ornamental grass from Asia with narrow linear leaves that have an agreeable though pungent odor when crushed. Cylindrical 1-foot-long seed heads appear in late summer to fall that gently bend among the arching leaves. Plants can be used as a background or summer hedge and are often cut for dried indoor arrangements.

Growing and care:
Bristle grass is a vigorous, easy-to-grow plant. Start seed indoors in individual peat pots 4 to 6 weeks prior to the last frost, or sow directly outdoors in early spring while soil is still cool. Transplant carefully, being sure not to disturb the roots and allowing 1 to 3 feet between plants. Water each week for a month to aid in rapid root growth. Once established, plants often self-seed and may become weedy.

Selected species and varieties:
S. italica (foxtail millet) produces rough-textured medium green leaves, each with a hairy basal sheath, and long-stemmed, dense flower spikes with green, purple, or brown bristles maturing into attractive seed heads in fall.

JAPANESE BLOOD GRASS
Imperata

Light: mostly sun

Plant type: ornamental grass

Hardiness: Zones 6-9

Height: 1 to 1 1/2 feet

Soil and Moisture: well-drained, moist

Interest: foliage

Care: easy

◀ Imperata cylindrica 'Red Baron'

Japanese blood grass is a show-stopping addition to any garden, with ember red erect leaves that resemble flames flicking skyward. The slender leaf blades emerge green in spring and turn vivid red as summer advances to fall. The erect clumps of straplike leaves are particularly striking massed in a border, especially when mixed with coneflower and golden yarrow.

Growing and care:

Japanese blood grass will grow in a variety of conditions but attains the best color in mostly sunny sites. Plant plugs 1 foot apart in spring while soil is still cool. Keep soil evenly moist throughout the growing season. Fertilize lightly in spring. Remove any parts of the plant that revert to the solid green color of the parent species as they appear. Cut back to ground level in late winter or early spring before new growth begins. Propagate by division of clumps in spring.

Selected species and varieties:

I. cylindrica 'Red Baron' produces nonflowering clumps of 1/4- to 1/2-inch-wide leaf blades that are green in spring and turn bright red in early summer through late fall.

LEMON GRASS
Cymbopogon

Light: mostly sun

Plant type: ornamental grass

Hardiness: Zones 9-10

Height: 2 to 6 feet

Soil and Moisture: well-drained, sandy, moist

Interest: foliage

Care: easy

◀ Cymbopogon citratus

Lemon grass is a clump-forming ornamental grass with abundant, flowing lemon-scented leaves. This easy-to-grow plant is as useful as it is ornamental, adding grace to borders and herb gardens as well as spicing up recipes. Steep fresh or dried leaves for a refreshing herbal tea. Lemon grass is also an excellent container plant for patios and decks, and is often grown on window sills in winter as part of a cold-season herb garden.

Growing and care:

Plant divisions of lemon grass in spring, spacing them 2 to 3 feet apart. Apply mulch both to conserve moisture in summer and to protect roots in winter. Where frost is a possibility, pot divisions in fall after cutting back to 3 inches and keep indoors over winter, watering only sparingly to prevent root rot. Provide moisture in extreme drought. Cut stems at ground level for fresh use, taking care when handling the leaf's sharp edges, and use the lower 3 to 4 inches for best flavor.

Selected species and varieties:

C. citratus (lemon grass, fever grass) has inch-wide aromatic evergreen leaves with sharp edges growing from bulbous stems in clumps to 6 feet tall and 3 feet wide.

MUHLY
Muhlenbergia

Light: mostly sun

Plant type: ornamental grass

Hardiness: Zones 6-10

Height: 1 to 4 feet

Soil and Moisture: well-drained, sandy, moist

Interest: flowers, foliage

Care: easy

◀ Muhlenbergia capillaris

The graceful foliage and airy flowers of these clump-forming perennial grasses make unforgettable mass plantings. In fall the softly colored seed heads complement the yellows and reds of the autumn garden. Plant muhly in mixed borders or rock gardens. The plants also look beautiful in meadows or on the upland shores of streams and ponds.

Growing and care:
Pink muhly adapts to moist or dry, sandy or clayey soil and tolerates occasional flooding or drought. Lindheimer muhly prefers moist, well-drained rocky soil, but it tolerates drought once established. Cut muhly grasses to the ground in early spring before new growth begins. Propagate by seed.

Selected species and varieties:
M. capillaris (pink muhly, hair grass) grows to 1½ to 3 feet with narrow, wiry, nearly evergreen leaves and 8- to 20-inch clusters of soft pink flowers on branching stems in early fall, followed by purplish seed heads; it is native to the eastern half of the United States. *M. lindheimeri* (Lindheimer muhly) produces clumps of narrow blue-green leaves 1½ feet long and purplish flower spikes on stalks up to 4 feet tall in fall, followed by silvery seed heads; Texas native; Zones 7-9.

SEDGE
Carex

Light: mostly sun

Plant type: ornamental grass

Hardiness: Zones 5-9

Height: 1 to 3 feet

Soil and Moisture: well-drained, fertile, moist

Interest: foliage

Care: easy

◀ Carex morrowii 'Variegata'

Sedge is a tough, very beautiful grasslike plant that thrives in a wide variety of gardening conditions. The neat mounds of gracefully arching narrow leaves make sedge useful in the foreground of edgings and rock gardens as well as sprinkled throughout mixed borders. It is also effective massed in large groups, where its soft texture and fluidity lend an airy, delicate touch to sunny landscapes.

Growing and care:
Plant sedge in moist, fertile soil that has been generously amended with organic matter. Space plants 12 to 15 inches apart. Sedge needs little care once established. Prune out any damaged leaves as they appear.

Selected species and varieties:
C. buchananii (leatherleaf sedge, fox-red sedge) has dense clumps of very narrow, reddish bronze leaves to 20 inches high; Zones 7-9. *C. morrowii* 'Variegata' (variegated Japanese sedge) has gracefully swirling 1- to 1½-foot-tall moplike mounds with leathery evergreen cream and green leaves ¼ to ½ inch wide; Zones 6-9. *C. pendula* (drooping sedge, giant sedge, sedge grass) produces mounds 2 to 3 feet high with bright green, furrowed, usually evergreen leaves ¾ inch wide and 1½ feet long.

SWEET GRASS
Hierochloë

Light: mostly sun

Plant type: ornamental grass

Hardiness: Zones 4-9

Height: 10 to 24 inches

Soil and Moisture: well-drained, moist

Interest: foliage, fragrance

Care: easy

◄ Hierochloë odorata

Sweet grass has delicate, gracefully arching leaves that have a soft lemon-vanilla smell. The dense tufts of bright green foliage gradually spread into wide mats, making a unique aromatic ground cover. In spring, tall flowering stalks bear loose clusters of brown spikelets above the leaves. Use sweet grass as an informal edging or allow tufts to spread in a meadow garden. Its creeping runners form mats of roots that help hold soil in steep or difficult locations. The leaves are often dried for use in potpourri, bundled into closet sachets, or woven into baskets and mats.

Growing and care:
Plant plugs or divisions of sweet grass in spring or fall, spacing them 15 to 24 inches apart. Fertilize lightly in spring. Sweet grass is a vigorous grower but can be restrained by planting in containers. Cut leaves at ground level and dry in bundles in a sunny location. For craftwork, boil the harvested green grass 10 minutes, then dry it in the sun for up to 1 week.

Selected species and varieties:
H. odorata (sweet grass, vanilla grass, holy grass, zubrovka) has thin, flat ¼-inch-wide leaves 10 to 20 inches long and pyramidal seed clusters on stalks to 2 feet.

WILD OATS
Chasmanthium

Light: mostly sun

Plant type: ornamental grass

Hardiness: Zones 5-10

Height: 2 to 4 feet

Soil and Moisture: well-drained, moist

Interest: flowers, foliage

Care: easy

◄ Chasmanthium latifolium

Wild oats is a versatile plant that offers easy-care four-season beauty to any garden. In spring bright green foliage appears, followed in summer by drooping panicles of green flowers. In autumn the plants ignite the garden with bright yellow-gold leaves. The panicles turn bronze and persist throughout winter, providing color and graceful movement. Wild oats is useful throughout the garden and is effective in mixed borders, specialty gardens, beside pools and streams, or massed in large groups.

Growing and care:
Unlike most ornamental grasses, *Chasmanthium* adapts well to mostly sunny spots, where the foliage attains its deepest colors. Plant in spring, spacing plants about 2 feet apart. Cut back to ground level before growth begins early in the following spring. Propagate by division or seed. It may self-sow.

Selected species and varieties:
C. latifolium (northern sea oats) is a clump-forming perennial grass from the eastern and central United States 2 to 4 feet in height with blue-green bamboolike leaves; its fall foliage is most intense in full sun. It bears oatlike spikelets of flowers on slender, arching stems in summer.

ABELIA
Abelia

Light: mostly sun	
Plant type: shrub	
Hardiness: Zones 6-10	
Height: 3 to 6 feet	
Soil and Moisture: well-drained, moist	
Interest: flowers, foliage	
Care: easy	

◀ Abelia x 'Edward Goucher'

Abelia's fountainlike sprays of glimmering foliage lend airy grace and fine texture to borders and hedges. Tiny bell-shaped or tubular flowers bloom from early summer to frost. The small, pointed, richly green leaves are bronze when young and, after turning green through summer, often become bronze or bronzy purple again in fall. In the northern parts of its range abelia is semievergreen while in the South the foliage remains all year long.

Growing and care:

For best growth and flower production plant abelia in a location that gets a little afternoon shade. The plants thrive in loosened soil that has had some organic matter added to it. Water regularly from early spring to fall. Prune in late winter or early spring, removing wood more than 4 years old and trimming to shape.

Selected species and varieties:

A. x *grandiflora* (glossy abelia) is a rounded shrub 3 to 6 feet high (to 8 feet in the South) and equally wide, with small pinkish white flowers in summer. *A.* x 'Edward Goucher', the result of a cross between *A.* x *grandiflora* and *A. schumannii,* forms a 4- to 5-foot-tall shrub with equal spread bearing pinkish lavender flowers in summer. *A. schumannii* bears mauve-pink flowers amid downy, blunt-pointed leaves; Zones 7-10.

'ALBA SEMI-PLENA' ROSE
Rosa

Light: mostly sun	
Plant type: shrub	
Hardiness: Zones 3-7	
Height: 6 feet	
Soil and Moisture: well-drained, moist	
Interest: flowers, fragrance	
Care: easy to moderate	

◀ Rosa 'Alba Semi-Plena'

Known also as White Rose of York, 'Alba Semi-Plena' is a very old variety. Its pure white semidouble flowers are 2½ inches across with a center of prominent golden stamens. The very fragrant blossoms appear in early summer with no repeat in fall. Elongated orange-red hips appear in late summer and fall. The foliage is gray-green. With sturdy, arching canes that develop a vase-shaped form, 'Alba Semi-Plena' can be grown as a freestanding shrub for a specimen or for use in borders, or it can be trained as a climber on a wall, a trellis, or a fence.

Growing and care:

Plant in well-worked soil to which organic matter has been added. Mulch in spring and again in fall around its root zone. Prune to desired shape after flowering is completed. 'Alba Semi-Plena' is very hardy and resistant to pests and disease.

Selected species and varieties:

R. 'Maxima' is a sport of 'Alba Semi-Plena' with even larger, very fragrant snow white blossoms; 'Suaveolens' is a near relative with pure white, intensely fragrant semi-double flowers in summer on canes reaching 6 feet.

ARBORVITAE
Thuja

Light: mostly sun	
Plant type: shrub, tree	
Hardiness: Zones 3-9	
Height: 3 to 30 feet	
Soil and Moisture: well-drained, moist	
Interest: foliage	
Care: easy	

◀ Thuja occidentalis 'Hetz Midget'

Arborvitae's fine-textured evergreen foliage develops along dense pyramids of branches in shades of green, yellow-green, and blue-green. These versatile plants fit well in just about any part of the landscape or garden. They are especially useful as specimens, grouped in the shrub border, or massed into hedges or screens. Planted around ponds or streams arborvitae adds cool ambiance and color.

Growing and care:
Plants can be transplanted year round from containers or in balled-and-burlapped form. Set plants in well-worked soil amended with abundant amounts of peat or other organic matter. *T. orientalis* is less cold tolerant than American arborvitae. Propagate from cuttings.

Selected species and varieties:
T. occidentalis (American or eastern arborvitae, white cedar) has shiny green needles that turn brown in winter; 'Hetz Midget' is a dense 3- to 4-foot globe; 'Lutea' forms a golden yellow pyramid to 30 feet; 'Nigra' has dark green foliage on trees 20 feet high and 4 feet wide; 'Rheingold' has deep gold foliage on oval shrubs to 5 feet; Zones 3-7. *T. orientalis* [also called *Platycladus orientalis*] (Oriental arborvitae) has bright green or yellow-green young foliage maturing to dark green and holding its color through winter; Zones 6-9.

ASH
Fraxinus

Light: mostly sun	
Plant type: tree	
Hardiness: Zones 2-9	
Height: 45 to 80 feet	
Soil and Moisture: well-drained, moist to dry	
Interest: foliage	
Care: easy	

◀ Fraxinus pennsylvanica

Ashes are fast-growing shade trees with attractive green foliage that turns yellow or plum violet in fall. When the leaves drop they often crumble into tiny pieces requiring little raking. Small greenish yellow flowers are borne on separate male and female trees in spring. Paddle-shaped winged seeds on female trees hang from the branches in conspicuous clusters. The seeds germinate easily and may become a weedy nuisance in gardens. Select a male clone or a seedless variety for least maintenance.

Growing and care:
Though ashes prefer moist, well-drained soil, white ash tolerates moderately dry and slightly alkaline soils, and green ash adapts to wet soils and high salt. Plant in a location that allows this large tree to develop unimpeded.

Selected species and varieties:
F. americana (white ash) grows to 80 feet tall with an open, rounded crown and compound leaves, dark green above and pale below, that turn a rich yellow, then maroon to purple in fall; hardy to Zone 3; 'Champaign County' reaches 45 feet, with a dense canopy of leaves. *F. pennsylvanica* (red ash, green ash) grows 50 to 60 feet tall with an irregular crown half as wide, bearing shiny green leaves that may turn yellow in fall; Zone 3; 'Patmore', a seedless form, grows 45 feet tall, with a symmetrical, upright-branching crown; Zone 2.

BEAUTYBERRY
Callicarpa

Light: mostly sun	
Plant type: shrub	
Hardiness: Zones 5-10	
Height: 3 to 8 feet	
Soil and Moisture: well-drained, moist	
Interest: fruit	
Care: moderate	

◀ Callicarpa americana

Beautyberry is an excellent description of this decorative, very ornamental shrub. Clusters of colorful ⅛-inch berries are gathered along beautyberry's arching stems for several weeks after the leaves have fallen in autumn. The oval, pointed leaves, arranged like ladders on either side of the stems, turn yellowish, sometimes pinkish, before dropping. Beautyberry is often used as a specimen, intermingled in the shrub border, or massed into an informal hedge.

Growing and care:
Prune to within 4 to 6 inches of the ground in early spring to create new shoots; only these produce flowers and fruit. Beautyberry is easy to grow from softwood cuttings or seed and is easily transplanted.

Selected species and varieties:
C. americana (American beautyberry) bears inconspicuous lavender summer flowers followed by magenta fruit clusters encircling stem tips; var. *lactea* produces white berries; Zones 7-10. *C. japonica* has violet to metallic purple berries; 'Leucocarpa' grows white berries after inconspicuous pink or white summer flowers; Zones 5-8.

BEECH
Fagus

Light: mostly sun	
Plant type: tree	
Hardiness: Zones 3-9	
Height: 50 to 70 feet	
Soil and Moisture: well-drained, moist, slightly acidic	
Interest: foliage, bark	
Care: easy	

◀ Fagus sylvatica 'Atropunicea'

Beeches are long-lived trees with massive trunks and branches clad in smooth gray bark. In spring, as inconspicuous flowers form, silky green leaves unfurl, turning bronze or ochre in the fall. Nuts are small but edible and are enclosed in a small, spiny husk. Beeches have long horizontal branches that often sweep the ground and offer the landscape a classic form that is both bold and graceful.

Growing and care:
Plant beeches in soil that has been generously amended with organic matter. Water regularly until trees are established and during dry periods.

Selected species and varieties:
F. grandifolia (American beech) grows 50 to 70 feet tall and almost as wide, with light gray bark and toothy leaves 2 to 5 inches long, dark green above and light green below. *F. sylvatica* (common beech, European beech, red beech) is usually 50 to 60 feet tall and 35 to 45 feet wide, with elephant-hide bark, branching close to the ground; Zones 4-7; 'Atropunicea' ['Atropurpurea'] (purple beech, copper beech) has black-red new leaves that turn purple-green; 'Aurea Pendula' is a weeping form with yellow new leaves aging to yellow-green; 'Dawyck Purple' grows in a narrow column with deep purple leaves.

BIRCH
Betula

Light: mostly sun

Plant type: tree

Hardiness: Zones 2-9

Height: 40 to 70 feet

Soil and Moisture: well-drained to heavy, moist to wet

Interest: foliage, bark

Care: moderate

◀ Betula nigra

Birches are graceful trees with pliant, flowing branches, pendent flower catkins, and decorative bark. Their airy canopies are composed of medium to dark green finely toothed leaves that flutter in the slightest breeze and turn a warm yellow in fall. In spring the flowers, called catkins, hang like slender ornaments from the tips of the branches. Birches create a light dappled shade and are lovely in groups or singly as specimens.

Growing and care:
Although river birches can thrive in periodic flooding, most species need good drainage and grow best in loose, rich, acid loams. Paper birch and European white birch tolerate neutral soils, but river birch must have acid soil. Amend soil with peat moss, leaf mold, or finished compost. Add sand as well if the soil is heavy. Mulch to retain moisture and to protect from lawn-mower damage. All birches bleed heavily in late winter or early spring and pruning should only be done in summer or fall. Bottom branches on paper birch can easily be removed to create a high-branched specimen tree. Although river birch and paper birch are resistant to the bronze birch borer, European white birch is quite susceptible. Most birches live about 50 years.

Selected species and varieties:
B. nigra (river birch, red birch) reaches 40 to 70 feet with a spread almost equal to its height, usually multitrunked, with cinnamon brown bark, peeling when young and becoming deeply furrowed into irregular plates with age, and nearly triangular leaves to 3½ inches long that often show brief fall color; Zones 4-9. *B. papyrifera* (paper birch, white birch, canoe birch) is a low-branched tree with reddish brown bark when young aging to creamy white and peeling thinly to reveal reddish orange tissue beneath, growing 50 to 70 feet tall by 25 to 45 feet in spread, and bearing 2- to 4-inch roundish, wedge-shaped leaves turning a lovely yellow in fall; Zones 2-7. *B. pendula* [also listed as *B. alba*] (European white birch, warty birch, common birch) produces graceful, slightly pendent branches on a 40- to 50-foot-tall by 20- to 35-foot-wide tree with the bark on the trunk and main limbs changing slowly from whitish to mostly black on white with age; golden brown twigs; and slender branches bearing serrated, almost diamond-shaped leaves 1 to 3 inches long that hold later in fall than do the other species but often show little fall color; Zones 2-7; 'Dalecarlica' (cutleaf weeping birch, Swedish birch) has weeping, pliant branches that often sweep the ground and dangling, deeply lobed and sharply toothed leaves.

BUCKEYE
Aesculus

◄ Aesculus glabra

Light:	mostly sun
Plant type:	tree
Hardiness:	Zones 3-7
Height:	20 to 40 feet
Soil and Moisture:	well-drained, moist
Interest:	flowers, foliage
Care:	easy

The buckeye is one of the harbingers of spring, coming into leaf before most other trees have broken bud. This low-branched, round-topped tree has deep green, very distinctive five-fingered compound leaves that turn a vibrant orange in fall. Its large greenish yellow spring flowers are held on long panicles and are sometimes difficult to see amid the foliage. The fruit is a brown seed capsule with a prickly cover, considered by some to be a good-luck charm. Buckeyes cast deep shade, discouraging most types of grass from growing beneath them. Plant them in a naturalized area or a mulched bed where leaf, flower, and fruit litter will not be a nuisance. The seeds are poisonous.

Growing and care:
A native to rich bottom lands and riverbanks, the Ohio buckeye prefers deep loam. Before planting, mix compost or leaf mold into the soil removed from the planting hole. Mulch well to conserve moisture and water regularly to avoid leaf scorch. Prune as needed in early spring.

Selected species and varieties:
A. glabra (Ohio buckeye, fetid buckeye) grows 20 to 40 feet tall with an equal spread, bearing medium to dark green leaflets 3 to 6 inches long that open bright green, followed by flower panicles up to 7 inches long, and later 1- to 2-inch oval fruit.

CEDAR
Cedrus

◄ Cedrus deodara

Light:	mostly sun
Plant type:	tree
Hardiness:	Zones 6-9
Height:	100 to 150 feet
Soil and Moisture:	well-drained, moist
Interest:	foliage
Care:	easy

Cedars are magnificent specimen trees with massive sweeping branches smothered with soft blue-green foliage. Their beauty is magnified by their towering height, which can easily surpass 100 feet. Cedars are best used as specimen plants for large properties with enough room for the great trees to grow.

Growing and care:
Cedars need ample room to develop and should have a site protected from strong winds. Atlas cedar grows best in moist, deep loam but will tolerate other soils as long as they are well drained. A moderately dry site is best for deodar cedar.

Selected species and varieties:
C. atlantica (Atlas cedar) is a slow-growing tree eventually reaching 100 feet tall with an open and spindly form when young but maturing into a stately flat-topped shape with bluish green or sometimes green to silvery blue inch-long needles and 3-inch-long cones that take 2 years to mature; 'Glauca' (blue Atlas cedar) has rich, steel blue needles. *C. deodara* (deodar cedar) has a pyramidal form and is more attractive when young than Atlas cedar, becoming flat topped and broad with age, growing 40 to 70 feet tall with a nearly equal spread but sometimes reaching 150 feet, with light blue to grayish green needles up to 1½ inches long, a gracefully drooping habit, and 3- to 4-inch cones; Zones 7-8.

'CELESTIAL' ROSE
Rosa

Light:	mostly sun
Plant type:	shrub
Hardiness:	Zones 3-8
Height:	5 feet
Soil and Moisture:	well-drained, fertile, moist
Interest:	flowers, fragrance
Care:	easy

◄ Rosa 'Celestial'

In late spring 'Celestial' blooms with blush pink, sweetly fragrant semidouble blossoms wrapped around a center of yellow stamens. The fast-growing plants reach 5 feet in height with the pliant, arching canes well covered in blue-green foliage. 'Celestial' is excellent as an informal hedge, planted in large groups for a mass display in meadows or on hillsides, or as a specimen.

Growing and care:
Plant 'Celestial' in a location with a little bright shade in loosened soil amended with some organic matter. Water well after planting and during dry periods. Mulch in spring and again in fall to keep roots cool and conserve soil moisture. Prune as needed to shape. 'Celestial' is virtually pest- and disease-free and once established requires little care.

Selected species and varieties:
R. 'Great Maiden's Blush' bears large 2- to 3-inch pink, very fragrant double blossoms in late spring to early summer that fade to a whitish blush on arching 5-foot canes with abundant blue-green foliage; Zones 4-10.

CHERRY
Prunus

Light:	mostly sun
Plant type:	shrub, tree
Hardiness:	Zones 4-10
Height:	3 to 50 feet
Soil and Moisture:	well-drained, moist
Interest:	flowers, foliage, fruit
Care:	moderate

◄ Prunus subhirtella var. pendula

This huge genus contains some of the most decorative flowering trees and shrubs. The plants are used for everything from specimens to screens, foundation plants, and hedges, but are most prized for their fragrant, blush pink to white blossoms that produce a blizzard of color in spring.

Growing and care:
Plant these flowering trees in well-worked loam that has had abundant organic matter mixed in. Prune cherries only when necessary, removing crossed or ungainly branches. In warmer climates, provide afternoon shade for Carolina cherry laurel, even in winter. Common cherry laurel is tolerant of wind and salt spray. Laurels take pruning well. Water regularly until established, fertilizing lightly in spring as growth begins.

Selected species and varieties:
P. caroliniana (Carolina cherry laurel) is an evergreen oval-pyramidal shrub or tree, 20 to 30 feet high and 15 to 25 feet wide, with lustrous dark green, sharply tapered, sometimes spiny leaves 2 to 3 inches long and 1 inch wide hiding black fruits, and heavily scented white flower clusters to 3 inches long in early spring; Zones 7-10; 'Bright 'n' Tight' has smooth-edged leaves smaller than the species on a tightly branched pyramid growing to 20 feet tall. *P. laurocerasus* (common cherry laurel, English laurel) has lustrous, medium to dark green leaves

(continued)

2 to 6 inches long and a third as wide, slightly toothed and borne on green stems tightly branched on a broad 10- to 18-foot-tall evergreen shrub that produces heavily fragrant flowers in racemes 2 to 5 inches long, and purple to black fruit masked by the leaves; Zones 6-8; 'Otto Luyken' is a compact form 3 to 4 feet tall and 6 to 8 feet wide that blooms profusely and has dark green leaves 4 inches long and 1 inch wide; 'Schipkaensis' has shorter, slightly narrower smooth-edged leaves, to 5 feet high; Zones 5-8. *P. lusitanica* (Portuguese cherry laurel, Portugal laurel) has fragrant white clusters 6 to 10 inches long in late spring, and dark purple cone-shaped fruits on a bushy shrub or tree 10 to 20 feet high with evergreen leaves 2½ to 5 inches long; Zones 7-9. *P. mume* (Japanese flowering apricot) has pale rose flowers in winter, after which shiny green leaves and yellowish fruit appear on a tree to 20 feet; Zones 6-9 (to Zone 10 in California). *P. subhirtella* var. *pendula* (weeping Higan cherry) has pink single flowers that appear before the leaves on graceful, weeping branches on a 20- to 40-foot tree, followed by black fruit; Zones 4-9. *P.* x *yedoensis* (Yoshino cherry, Japanese flowering cherry) is a 40- to 50-foot tree that bears pink or white flowers in spring before or as the leaves appear, and black fruit; Zones 5-8; 'Akebono' has pink double flowers on a tree 25 feet high and wide.

CINQUEFOIL
Potentilla

Light:	mostly sun
Plant type:	shrub
Hardiness:	Zones 2-7
Height:	1 to 4 feet
Soil and Moisture:	well-drained, moist to dry
Interest:	flowers, foliage
Care:	easy

◀ Potentilla fruticosa 'Abbotswood'

Cinquefoil's open five-petaled flowers resemble wild roses, and are held above spreading mounds of palmately compound silvery green leaves in summer. The plants are easy to grow and are effectively mixed into the shrub or perennial border. Cinquefoil is also useful massed onto hillsides or sprinkled in wildflower meadows, where its flowers sparkle like stars.

Growing and care:
Plant smaller cinquefoils 1 foot apart, larger types 2 feet apart. They flower best in mostly sunny places and with a not-too-rich soil. The plants generally need little care once established. Water during dry periods. Propagate by seed or division.

Selected species and varieties:
P. fruticosa (bush cinquefoil) grows 1 to 4 feet tall, 2 to 4 feet wide, with leaves that emerge gray-green then turn dark green, and 1-inch flowers from early summer to late fall; 'Abbotswood' grows to 2 feet with white flowers; 'Primrose Beauty' produces primrose flowers with deeper centers on 3-foot plants; 'Tangerine' grows 2 to 4 feet tall with yellow flowers flushed with orange and copper tones.

COTONEASTER
Cotoneaster

Light: mostly sun	
Plant type: shrub	
Hardiness: Zones 5-8	
Height: 1 to 15 feet	
Soil and Moisture: well-drained, moist	
Interest: foliage, fruit	
Care: easy	

◀ Cotoneaster
microphyllus

Cotoneasters are hardworking decorative shrubs with glossy evergreen foliage and brilliant red, hollylike berries from fall through winter. White or pink flowers, often quite small, appear in spring sprinkled along the stiff branches. Most cotoneasters spread at least as wide as their height, and are used as fast-growing ground covers that are ideal for slopes, rock gardens, and walls. Other species make interesting specimen plants for shrub borders.

Growing and care:
Bearberry cotoneaster is tolerant of most well-drained soils and is easily grown. Willowleaf and parney cotoneasters need moist, well-drained, acid to nearly neutral soil. Mature plants will tolerate drought, seashore conditions, and wind; dry or poor soil often produces the best fruiting. Cotoneaster is susceptible to fire blight, a blackened die-off of branch tips that, if not treated, is fatal to the plant; littleleaf cotoneaster may be more susceptible in the South. Other pests are borers, red spiders, and lace bugs. Prune only to control the plant's shape.

Selected species and varieties:
C. dammeri (bearberry cotoneaster) has a prostrate form 1 to 1½ feet high, and is an excellent ground cover because it roots wherever its branches touch soil. It spreads quickly to 6 feet wide, with white flowers up to ½ inch wide, a light crop of red berries, and narrow, 1-inch-long, lustrous dark green leaves that may become tinged with red-purple in winter; 'Skogholm' grows vigorously to 1½ to 3 feet high, spreading several feet each year. *C. lacteus* (red cluster-berry, parney cotoneaster) is a 6- to 10-foot shrub with a handsome fruit display persisting through winter and 2- to 3-inch-wide white flower clusters in spring, sometimes partly hidden by the foliage; Zones 6-8. *C. microphyllus* (littleleaf cotoneaster, rockspray cotoneaster) is a nearly prostrate shrub, usually 2 feet high or smaller, spreading up to 10 feet wide with ¼- to ½-inch-long glossy leaves, tiny white flowers, and red fruit; Zones 5-8. *C. salicifolius* (willowleaf cotoneaster) is a shrub with an arching habit, growing 10 to 15 feet tall with a smaller spread and producing narrow, willowlike leaves 1½ to 3½ inches long that are lustrous dark green in summer, becoming plum purple in winter. It bears flat 2-inch-wide white flower heads often masked by the foliage, and tiny, long-lasting bright red fruit; Zones 6-8; 'Autumn Fire' forms a 2- to 3-foot-high ground cover with 1½- to 2-inch very glossy leaves that turn reddish purple in winter, and scarlet fruit; 'Repens' has lustrous 1-inch leaves on a prostrate ground cover to 1 foot tall.

DOGWOOD
Cornus

Light: mostly sun	
Plant type: shrub, tree	
Hardiness: Zones 3-9	
Height: 15 to 30 feet	
Soil and Moisture: well-drained, wet to moderately dry	
Interest: flowers, foliage, bark	
Care: moderate	

◄ Cornus florida

Dogwoods can turn the spring landscape into a fairyland of foliage and flowers, and transform fall into a bounty of leafy color and brilliant fruit. These classic, versatile plants offer four-season interest and are excellent additions to formal and informal plantings including wildlife gardens, where the trees attract songbirds throughout the year.

Growing and care:
Give flowering and pagoda dogwoods a moist, acid soil enriched with leaf mold, peat moss, or compost. Mulch to keep soil cool and moist. Kousa dogwood prefers loose, sandy, acid soil rich with organic matter. It is more drought tolerant and disease resistant than flowering dogwood. Although adaptable to a wide range of soil types, cornelian cherry prefers moist, rich sites and is probably the best performer of the dogwoods for the Midwest. Susceptible to the usually fatal anthracnose, which has killed many dogwoods on the East Coast, flowering dogwood has a better chance of staying healthy if stress is reduced by providing optimal growing conditions. The other dogwoods listed here appear not to be affected. For colder climates, the best bud hardiness in flowering dogwoods occurs in trees grown in those regions.

Selected species and varieties:
C. alternifolia (pagoda dogwood, green osier) bears strongly fragrant yellowish white flowers borne in flat clusters 1½ to 2½ inches wide on a horizontally branched tree growing 15 to 25 feet tall with a greater spread and tierlike habit, also bearing fruit that matures from green to red to blue-black; Zones 3-7. *C. florida* (flowering dogwood) is a small tree with a broad, artistically shaped crown, usually 20 to 30 feet tall with an equal or greater spread, producing white flowerlike bracts lasting 10 to 14 days in spring before the leaves emerge, followed in fall by small, glossy red fruits borne in clusters of at least three to four; Zones 5-9. *C. kousa* (kousa dogwood) is a multistemmed small tree 20 to 30 feet tall and wide with exfoliating gray, tan, and brown bark and attractive tiered branches, flowering in late spring after the leaves appear and lasting for up to 6 weeks, followed by pink to red roundish fruit up to 1 inch wide in late summer to fall, when the leaves turn reddish purple or scarlet; Zones 5-8; var. *chinensis* (Chinese dogwood) grows to 30 feet and has larger bracts than the species. *C. mas* (cornelian cherry, sorbet) is a multistemmed shrub or small, oval to round tree 20 to 25 feet tall and 15 to 20 feet wide, branching nearly to the ground, with attractive exfoliating gray to brown bark, bearing small clusters of yellow flowers for 3 weeks in early spring and bright red fruit in midsummer that is partly hidden by the lustrous dark green leaves, 2 to 4 inches long, that usually show little fall color; Zones 4-8.

ELM
Ulmus

Light: mostly sun	
Plant type: tree	
Hardiness: Zones 4-9	
Height: 40 to 70 feet	
Soil and Moisture: well-drained, moist	
Interest: foliage, bark	
Care: moderate	

◀ Ulmus parvifolia

Exfoliating, mottled gray, green, orange, or brown bark is this graceful, durable shade tree's most outstanding feature. Lacebark elm has a spreading, rounded crown of medium fine, lustrous dark green foliage that holds late into fall, when it turns yellow to reddish purple. The trees make excellent specimens and add elegance when planted along long driveways.

Growing and care:
Lacebark elm grows best in moist, well-drained loams but adapts well to poor, dry soils, both acid and alkaline. Soil should be deep to accommodate the extensive root system. Growth averages 1½ feet per year. Prune to remove weak, narrow crotches as they appear. Although it is not immune to Dutch elm disease, it shows considerable resistance.

Selected species and varieties:
U. parvifolia (lacebark elm, Chinese elm, evergreen elm) grows 40 to 50 feet high and wide in most situations, usually with a forked trunk and drooping branches, bearing leathery, saw-toothed elliptical leaves ¾ to 2½ inches long and inconspicuous flower clusters hidden by the foliage in late summer to early fall, followed by ⅓-inch-wide winged fruits.

ENKIANTHUS
Enkianthus

Light: mostly sun	
Plant type: shrub, tree	
Hardiness: Zones 4-7	
Height: 6 to 30 feet	
Soil and Moisture: well-drained, moist	
Interest: flowers, foliage	
Care: easy	

◀ Enkianthus campanulatus

Enkianthus is an easy-to-grow, very attractive shrub or small tree that offers up pendulous clusters of dainty flowers in spring and then delights with brilliant fall foliage. The plant is excellent as a specimen and is quite charming when tucked in the midst of a border of rhododendrons and azaleas.

Growing and care:
Plant enkianthus in spring or fall in well-worked soil that has been amended with peat moss. Water regularly until established. Mulch with pine needles in spring and again in fall.

Selected species and varieties:
E. campanulatus (redvein enkianthus), with a narrow, upright habit, grows to 6 to 8 feet tall in cold areas, to 30 feet in warmer climates, and has layered branches bearing at their tips tufts of 1- to 3-inch-long medium green leaves that turn bright red to orange and yellow in fall, and producing long-stalked clusters of pale yellow or light orange bell-shaped flowers with red veins in late spring as the leaves develop, the blooms sometimes persisting for several weeks; hardy to parts of Zone 4. *E. perulatus* (white enkianthus) grows 6 feet high and wide, with white urn-shaped flower clusters in midspring before the foliage appears, the bright green 1- to 2-inch-long leaves turning scarlet in fall; hardy to Zone 5.

EUONYMUS
Euonymus

Light:	mostly sun
Plant type:	shrub
Hardiness:	Zones 4-8
Height:	4 inches to 70 feet
Soil and Moisture:	well-drained, moist
Interest:	foliage
Care:	easy to moderate

◀ Euonymus alata 'Compacta'

Euonymus is one of the most popular shrubs for yards and gardens. The full, rounded bushes are covered with medium green leaves in summer that turn fiery red in fall. Inconspicuous flowers form in spring, and pink to red fruit capsules split to expose orange seeds in fall, which attract birds. The plants are ideal for mixed borders, specimens, hedges, specialty gardens, and woodland plantings.

Growing and care:
Plant euonymus in spring or fall in lightly worked soil amended with some organic matter. The plants grow well in conditions from sun to shade but achieve their best color and form in sunny and mostly sunny locations. Water regularly until plants are established. Prune out damaged or diseased wood as it appears.

Selected species and varieties:
E. alata [also listed as *E. alatus*] (winged euonymus, burning bush) is a slow-growing, wide-spreading, flat-topped shrub of variable height, usually 15 to 20 feet tall and wide, with soft green leaves 1 to 3 inches long that turn brilliant red in fall, yellow-green flowers in spring, and small red fruits borne under the leaves; Zones 4-8; 'Compacta' [also listed as 'Compactus'] (dwarf burning bush) grows 10 feet tall, its slender branches exhibiting less prominent corky ridges and forming a denser, more rounded outline; Zones 5-8.

FOTHERGILLA
Fothergilla

Light:	mostly sun
Plant type:	shrub
Hardiness:	Zones 4-9
Height:	3 to 10 feet
Soil and Moisture:	well-drained, sandy, moist
Interest:	flowers, foliage
Care:	easy

◀ Fothergilla major

This beautiful flowering shrub combines glossy, dark green foliage with delicate sprays of bottlebrush blossoms. The fragrant white flowers appear in spring and the blue-green leaves turn a brilliant yellow, orange, and scarlet in fall. Fothergilla works well massed, in borders, and in foundation plantings.

Growing and care:
Fothergilla thrives in most soil types but does not tolerate limy soils. The plants are virtually pest-free and require little care.

Selected species and varieties:
F. gardenii (witch alder, dwarf fothergilla) forms a dense mound 3 feet tall and 4 feet wide with zigzag spreading branches bearing 1-inch-long white spikes before the appearance of 1- to 2-inch-long wedge-shaped leaves that are dark green above and bluish white below; 'Blue Mist' has a feathery, mounded habit with glaucous, bluish leaves and subdued fall colors; 'Jane Platt' has narrow leaves and longer flower clusters than in the species; 'Mount Airy' has an upright habit, with profuse flowers and excellent fall color. *F. major* [also classified as *F. monticola*] (large fothergilla) has an upright growth 6 to 10 feet high with 2- to 4-inch white flower spikes tinged with pink, appearing with oval to roundish dark green leaves that show brilliant fall colors; Zones 4-8.

GARDENIA
Gardenia

Light: mostly sun	
Plant type: shrub	
Hardiness: Zones 8-10	
Height: 1 to 6 feet	
Soil and Moisture: well-drained, fertile, moist	
Interest: flowers, foliage, fragrance	
Care: moderate to difficult	

◀ Gardenia augusta

Gardenias are classic warm-weather shrubs with rich evergreen leaves and linen white camellia-like summer flowers so intensely fragrant just one will perfume an entire room. While hardy only to Zone 8, this shrub is worth the effort to grow wherever conditions allow. Where it is not hardy it can be grown as a container plant.

Growing and care:
Plant gardenias in acid soil enriched with plenty of organic matter. They thrive in hot weather, and require monthly fertilizing during the growing season. Mulch to keep soil moist and protect the gardenia's shallow roots. Propagate by cuttings. Plants do poorly in overly wet or dry conditions.

Selected species and varieties:
G. augusta [formerly *G. jasminoides*] is an evergreen shrub 3 to 6 feet tall and wide with a dense, rounded habit, with 3- to 4-inch glossy oval leaves and double blooms up to 5 inches across; 'August Beauty' grows 4 to 6 feet tall with abundant 4- to 5-inch blooms; 'Radicans' grows to 1 foot tall and 3 feet wide with smaller foliage and flowers than the species.

HEBE
Hebe

Light: mostly sun	
Plant type: shrub	
Hardiness: Zones 8-10	
Height: 2 to 5 feet	
Soil and Moisture: well-drained, moist	
Interest: flowers, foliage	
Care: easy	

◀ Hebe buxifolia 'Patty's Purple'

Native to New Zealand, hebes are rounded, leathery-leaved evergreen shrubs that produce spikes of lovely white, pink, red, lavender, or purple flowers 2 to 4 inches long at the ends of the branches from midsummer to fall. Their small glossy leaves, densely arranged on stems, make these fine-textured spreading shrubs good candidates for shrub borders, hedges, edgings, rock gardens, and perennial beds.

Growing and care:
Plant hebes in well-worked soil amended with organic matter. Mulch each spring and fall to conserve moisture and keep soil cool. Hebes thrive in cool coastal gardens, and need partial shade where summers are hot. Prune after flowering to avoid legginess.

Selected species and varieties:
H. 'Autumn Glory' is a mounding shrub 2 to 3 feet high and 2 feet wide with glossy dark green leaves 1½ inches long tinged with red when young, and dark lavender-blue flower spikes 2 inches long and sometimes branched, blooming profusely from midsummer through fall. *H. buxifolia* 'Patty's Purple' (boxleaf veronica) has 1-inch-long purple clusters and leaves scarcely ½ inch long, growing to 3 feet.

HYDRANGEA
Hydrangea

Light:	mostly sun
Plant type:	shrub
Hardiness:	Zones 3-9
Height:	3 to 20 feet
Soil and Moisture:	well-drained, fertile, moist
Interest:	flowers, foliage
Care:	easy to moderate

◀ Hydrangea macrophylla

Hydrangeas are longtime favorite garden plants that range from small to large, showy shrubs. The large, coarse-textured leaves combine with the bold flower clusters to add color and form to the shrub border. Many species have persistent flower clusters or attractive bark that keep them interesting throughout the seasons.

Growing and care:

Plant hydrangeas in well-worked, fertile soil that has been generously amended with organic matter. Mulch in spring and again in fall. Water well after planting and provide extra water during dry periods. The plants grow well in conditions ranging from full sun to full shade, but do best in mostly sunny places that offer midday shade. Prune *H. macrophylla* after flowering, and other species in late winter.

Selected species and varieties:

H. macrophylla (bigleaf hydrangea) grows 3 to 6 feet tall with 8-inch leaves and globular 5-inch flower heads in summer; Zones 6-9. *H. paniculata* 'Grandiflora' (peegee hydrangea) is a large shrub or small tree 10 to 25 feet tall with 1- to 1½-foot white to russet flower clusters in summer above dark green leaves; Zones 3-8.

'KÖNIGIN VON DÄNEMARK' ROSE
Rosa

Light:	mostly sun
Plant type:	shrub
Hardiness:	Zones 3-8
Height:	4 feet
Soil and Moisture:	well-drained, fertile, moist
Interest:	flowers, fragrance
Care:	easy

◀ Rosa 'Königin von Dänemark'

Aristocratic in appearance, 'Königin von Dänemark' (or 'Queen of Denmark') is a classic rose. Short, deep pink buds open to 2½- to 3½-inch light pink double flowers with slightly lighter pink petals toward the edges. The flowers are borne singly or in small clusters of three to five and are richly fragrant. The upright canes have abundant thorns and are covered with attractive blue-green foliage. The mature canes form an open, spreading shrub that is excellent as a hedge, screen, mass planting, or specimen. 'Königin von Dänemark' is also stunning as a background for the perennial border.

Growing and care:

Plant this easy-to-grow rose in well-worked soil amended with organic matter. Mulch around its root zone in spring and fall. In mass plantings or hedges set plants about 3 to 4 feet apart. Prune out older canes as needed. 'Königin von Dänemark' is a hardy, tough rose that is pest and disease resistant.

Selected species and varieties:

R. 'Madame Legras De St. Germain' bears very large, very fragrant, fully double white flowers in early summer on robust 7-foot canes with dark green foliage.

'MADAME PLANTIER' ROSE
Rosa

Light: mostly sun	
Plant type: shrub	
Hardiness: Zones 4-8	
Height: 5 feet	
Soil and Moisture: well-drained, fertile, moist	
Interest: flowers, fragrance	
Care: easy	

◀ Rosa 'Madame Plantier'

A classic antique rose, 'Madame Plantier' has large, very double white flowers with a hint of cream at the edges of the petals. Borne in large clusters, the very fragrant 2½- to 3-inch flowers completely cover the plant in early to midseason. The vigorous, erect, nearly thornless canes reach to 5 feet tall with plentiful gray-green foliage. 'Madame Plantier' is charming trained against a wall or arbor and its free-flowing shape makes it attractive in mass plantings or informal hedges.

Growing and care:
Plant 'Madame Plantier' in well-worked soil well amended with rotted manure or compost. Mulch in spring and again in fall. Fertilize lightly in early spring as new growth appears. Prune to shape as needed and remove older canes periodically to ensure continued vigor. 'Madame Plantier' is a tough, good-looking plant that is virtually disease- and pest-free.

Selected species and varieties:
R. 'Blush Hip' has light pink double flowers on 5- to 6-foot smooth canes and gray-green foliage.

MAGNOLIA
Magnolia

Light: mostly sun	
Plant type: shrub, tree	
Hardiness: Zones 4-9	
Height: 15 to 80 feet	
Soil and Moisture: well-drained, moist	
Interest: flowers, foliage	
Care: easy to moderate	

◀ Magnolia liliiflora

Magnolias are renowned for their masses of showy, often fragrant flowers that turn these graceful trees into living bouquets. In spring or summer the plants produce broad, cup- or star-shaped pure white to deep purple blooms that often ripen into ornamental conelike fruit with red seeds. Magnolias are either evergreen or deciduous, and make excellent specimen plants.

Growing and care:
Plant in spring or fall in soil amended with peat moss or compost. Fertilize in spring and mulch around the base of the trunk. Many species are susceptible to leaf spot, which defaces the leaves in late summer but does not damage the health of the plants. Water during hot, dry periods. Propagate by collecting fresh seed in fall and chilling for 4 months. Sow in spring.

Selected species and varieties:
M. liliiflora (lily magnolia) is a 15-foot multistemmed deciduous tree with medium green 6-inch elliptical leaves and narrow-petaled, lilylike, fragrant reddish purple spring flowers; Zones 5-8. *M.* x *soulangiana* (saucer magnolia) is a 30-foot deciduous tree with 6-inch dark green oval leaves, and large cup-shaped flowers in spring; Zones 5-9 *M. stellata* (star magnolia) is a deciduous shrub or tree to 20 feet tall with fragrant 4-inch white late-spring flowers tinged with pink; Zones 5-9.

MAPLE
Acer

Light: mostly sun	
Plant type: tree	
Hardiness: Zones 2-9	
Height: 6 to 75 feet	
Soil and Moisture: well-drained, moist	
Interest: foliage, flowers, bark	
Care: easy	

◀ Acer griseum

The maples are a diverse group of deciduous plants ranging from towering shade trees with brilliant fall foliage to small, picturesque specimens ideal as centerpieces for ornamental beds. Between the large and small maples are types well suited for specimen plantings around patios and decks. These lovely trees combine stately beauty with overall easy care, making them an invaluable part of any landscape or garden.

Growing and care:

Most maples can withstand occasional drought but turn color earlier in fall in dry conditions. Red maples thrive in wet, moist, or dry soil. Sugar and red maples prefer slight acidity but tolerate other soil types. *A. rubrum* 'Autumn Blaze' is said to be slightly more drought tolerant than true red maple cultivars. Paperbark maples tolerate a wide range of acid and alkaline soils. Japanese maples need highly organic loam, and the soil should be amended with peat moss or leaf mold before planting. Threadleaf maples should be planted in a sheltered location away from strong breezes, and provided with even moisture to avoid leaf scorch. Large maples have extensive, shallow root systems that crowd the soil's surface in search of water and nutrients, making it difficult to sustain significant plantings beneath them. All maples benefit from fertilizing in spring.

Selected species and varieties:

A. griseum (paperbark maple) is an oval- to round-crowned tree 20 to 30 feet tall with up to an equal spread, clad in very attractive exfoliating cinnamon brown bark and producing dark green to blue-green leaves with three leaflets that may turn red in fall; Zones 4-8. *A. palmatum* (Japanese maple) is a diverse group of small, slow-growing trees 15 to 25 feet tall with deeply cut leaves having five, seven, or nine lobes, and young stems that are reddish purple to green and become gray with age; Zones 5-8; 'Bloodgood' grows upright to 15 to 20 feet with maroon or reddish purple leaves that turn scarlet in fall, blackish red bark, and attractive red fruit; 'Dissectum' (threadleaf Japanese maple) is a small, pendulous, lacy shrub usually 6 to 8 feet tall, with drooping green-barked branches that bear very finely divided pale green leaves with up to 11 lobes that turn yellow in fall; 'Dissectum Atropurpureum' has lacy purple-red new leaves that fade to green or purple-green and turn crimson or burnt orange in fall, as well as tortuous branching that is most apparent in winter. *A. rubrum* (red maple, scarlet maple, Canadian maple) is a medium-fast-growing tree to 60 feet tall with ascending branches forming an irregular, oval to rounded crown and lobed green leaves yielding a dazzling fall color that is unreliable in the species but consistent among cultivars; 'Autumn Blaze' (*A. x freemanii*) is a fast-growing cultivar reaching 50 feet tall exhibiting superb orange-red fall color on its dense, oval to rounded crown; hardy to Zone 4; 'October Glory' has a round crown and vivid bright orange to red foliage in midfall, holding late into the season. *A. saccharum* (sugar maple, rock maple) is a truly stunning large shade tree reaching 60 to 75 feet tall with a spread about two-thirds that height in a symmetrical crown bearing greenish yellow flowers in spring and three- to five-lobed medium to dark green leaves that turn yellow, burnt orange, or scarlet red in fall; Zones 3-8.

MINT TREE
Agonis

Light: mostly sun

Plant type: tree

Hardiness: Zone 10

Height: 25 to 35 feet

Soil and Moisture: well-drained, moist to dry

Interest: flowers, foliage, fragrance

Care: easy

◀ Agonis flexuosa

The mint tree is a fast-growing, gracefully attractive evergreen for warm climates. Its leaves are long and willowlike, appearing in billowy masses along the strong branches. The foliage has a strong, minty aroma when crushed. In early summer small, white, pleasingly fragrant flowers appear. Mint tree is a versatile plant well suited for streetside use as well as specimen planting. In more northern zones it also makes a fine container plant.

Growing and care:
The mint tree requires a warm, nearly frost-free location and prefers a loose soil to which some organic matter has been added. Once the plants are established they are quite drought tolerant.

Selected species and varieties:
A. flexuosa grows to 35 feet, with an equal spread of deep 3- to 6-inch-long evergreen leaves that have a minty fragrance when crushed; small white, lightly scented flowers appear in early summer, followed by decorative woody seed capsules; attractive reddish brown, vertically fissured bark accents the foliage.

MOCK ORANGE
Philadelphus

Light: mostly sun

Plant type: shrub

Hardiness: Zones 4-9

Height: 4 to 12 feet

Soil and Moisture: well-drained, fertile, moist

Interest: flowers, foliage

Care: easy to moderate

◀ Philadelphus coronarius

Mock orange is an old-fashioned, highly decorative shrub that produces delightfully fragrant blooms in early summer that look and smell like orange blossoms. The plant has a rounded habit, forming thick clumps after many years. It is best planted in combination with other flowering plants in a mixed-shrub border or used as an informal barrier hedge.

Growing and care:
Mock orange is easily transplanted, fast growing, and not too particular about site. It will perform best in soil supplemented with abundant organic matter prior to planting. Once established it is tolerant of dry soils. Prune immediately after flowering to control size. Cut back stems that have borne flowers to encourage branching. To rejuvenate an old or overgrown specimen, cut back to the ground.

Selected species and varieties:
P. coronarius (sweet mock orange) is a large, very vigorous rounded shrub with ascending, arching branches, growing 10 to 12 feet tall and equally wide, often becoming leggy with age, exposing exfoliating orange-brown bark. It produces extremely fragrant white single flowers; 'Aureus' produces leaves that emerge bright yellow in spring and gradually turn yellow-green by midsummer, and may be useful as a border accent.

NEW ZEALAND TEA TREE
Leptospermum

Light: mostly sun	
Plant type: shrub	
Hardiness: Zones 9-10	
Height: 6 to 10 feet	
Soil and Moisture: well-drained, fertile, moist	
Interest: flowers, foliage	
Care: moderate	

◀ Leptospermum
scoparium

The New Zealand tea tree is a fine-textured shrub with attractive evergreen leaves and small white, pink, or red flowers in winter, spring, or summer that put on a spectacular floral display. The plants are excellent for the shrub border, or informal hedges, or as specimen plants, where their show-stopping flowers and long, plentiful, twisting branches highlight the garden.

Growing and care:
The New Zealand tea tree is easy to grow in mild climates in a well-drained acid to neutral soil. It prefers some light shade, especially in areas with hot, dry summers. Warm temperatures combined with high humidity seem to weaken the plants and root rot often develops in poorly drained soils. Though it is somewhat drought tolerant, supplemental water should be supplied during dry periods or where the climate is hot. Prune as needed in early spring.

Selected species and varieties:
L. scoparium grows 6 to 10 feet high, slightly smaller in spread, with a rounded compact form. Leaves are dark gray-green and aromatic, profuse white flowers are ½ inch across; 'Compactum' has a dense, mounding habit reaching just 3 feet high.

OAK
Quercus

Light: mostly sun	
Plant type: tree	
Hardiness: Zones 2-9	
Height: 40 to more than 100 feet	
Soil and Moisture: well-drained to heavy, wet to dry	
Interest: foliage	
Care: easy	

◀ Quercus ilex

Oaks are large deciduous or evergreen trees with massive trunks and branches that can provide the dominant structure and framework for any landscape. The plants have a strong main trunk and usually stout horizontal branches supporting a broad canopy of dark green foliage. The leaves of deciduous forms often remain into winter. Small flowers form in spring, followed by acorns in late summer to fall that are sought out by many forms of wildlife. The acorns of red oaks require two years to mature.

Growing and care:
Oaks grow best in moist, deep soil, but most species fare well in a wide range of soil types. Holly oak can withstand inland drought and salt spray, but may become shrubby in exposed, seaside locations. Shumard red oak tolerates either wet or dry sites. A good oak for desert conditions, cork oak needs well-drained soil and is drought resistant once established; its leaves yellow in alkaline soil. Do not compact or change the elevation of soil within the oak's root zone, which usually extends far beyond the canopy's reach.

OAK
(continued)

Selected species and varieties:

Q. ilex (holly oak, holm oak, evergreen oak) reaches 40 to 70 feet high and wide, with leathery evergreen leaves, sometimes toothed and usually 1½ to 3 inches long, deep green above and yellowish to gray below; hardy to Zone 5. *Q. macrocarpa* (bur oak, mossy-cup oak) has a spreading crown of heavy branches and is usually 70 to 80 feet tall and at least as wide but has been known to top 100 feet. It bears 4- to 10-inch-long leaves, lobed near the stem, dark green above and whitish below, showing greenish yellow to yellow-brown fall color, and acorns, usually fringed, up to 1½ inches long; Zones 2-8. *Q. phellos* (willow oak) has narrow, slightly wavy willowlike leaves up to 5½ inches long, turning yellow, yellow-brown, and reddish in fall, on an oval crown 40 to 60 feet high and two-thirds as wide; Zones 5-9. *Q. robur* (English oak, truffle oak, common oak, pedunculate oak) has a short trunk that leads to a broad, fairly open crown, 40 to 60 feet tall with an equal spread under average landscape conditions (but it can reach 100 feet tall). It produces 2- to 5-inch-long rounded-lobed leaves that are dark green above and pale blue-green below, showing no fall color, and oblong acorns; Zones 4-8. *Q. shumardii* (Shumard's oak, Shumard red oak) grows 40 to 60 feet tall and wide, and is pyramidal when young but matures to a spreading crown, with russet-red to red fall color on deeply lobed and sharply pointed leaves 4 to 6 inches long and 3 to 4 inches wide; Zones 5-9. *Q. suber* (cork oak) is an evergreen tree 60 feet high and equally wide, with its trunk and main limbs clad in thick, corky bark, bearing coarsely toothed 3-inch lobeless leaves that are dark green above, fuzzy gray below; Zones 7-9.

OLEANDER
Nerium

◀ Nerium oleander

Light: mostly sun	
Plant type: shrub	
Hardiness: Zones 8-10	
Height: 6 to 20 feet	
Soil and Moisture: well-drained, moist	
Interest: flowers, foliage	
Care: easy	

Oleander is a tough, easy-to-grow evergreen for warm climates that softens the summer months with sprays of long-lasting, beautiful flowers. The plants are closely branched with long, lance-shaped, willowy leaves that serve as a wonderful background for the fragrant, vividly colored blossoms. Oleander makes an excellent hedge, screen, or border and is very effective when used in mass plantings. It makes an easy-to-grow container plant that gives a tropical ambiance to patios and decks all summer long. All parts of the oleander are poisonous.

Growing and care:

Oleanders prefer a moist, well-drained soil but adapt to drier conditions. They tolerate drought, wind, salt spray, and air pollution. Prune in early spring to desired height and shape and to maintain dense habit.

Selected species and varieties:

N. oleander is usually 6 to 12 feet tall with an equal spread but may reach 20 feet, with upright stems, a bushy, rounded form, and 3- to 5-inch-long leathery leaves that remain dark green throughout the year. Fragrant flowers that form in terminal clusters are pink, white, or red and very showy, with a long blooming season; 'Casablanca' grows 3 to 4 feet tall with single white flowers; 'Little Red' has red flowers; 'Mrs. Roeddling' grows to 6 feet; its smaller leaves result in a finer texture; flowers are double and salmon-pink.

POMEGRANATE
Punica

Light:	mostly sun
Plant type:	shrub, tree
Hardiness:	Zones 8-10
Height:	12 to 20 feet
Soil and Moisture:	well-drained, moist
Interest:	flowers, fruit
Care:	easy

◀ Punica granatum

Pomegranates produce small, carnation-like flowers with crumpled petals in red, orange, pink, white, or yellow from early summer and sometimes into fall. The juicy yellow edible fruits up to 3 inches across that follow the floral display make these plants a worthwhile addition to any garden. Use pomegranates in shrub borders and groups, or grow in containers for a handsome small patio specimen.

Growing and care:
Easily cultivated, pomegranate makes its best growth in rich, moist loam but is adaptable to a range of other soils as long as they are well drained. Water well on planting and regularly for first growing season. Fertilize lightly when growth begins in spring and again after flowers fade. Prune after flowering is complete.

Selected species and varieties:
P. granatum grows 12 to 20 feet high, with an equal or lesser spread, bearing lustrous dark green leaves 1 to 3 inches long and 1 inch or less wide that unfurl bronzy and turn yellow in fall, and producing red flowers 1 inch wide; 'Legrellei' has double flowers with salmon-pink petals variegated with white.

PRIVET
Ligustrum

Light:	mostly sun
Plant type:	shrub
Hardiness:	Zones 6-10
Height:	6 to 15 feet
Soil and Moisture:	well-drained, moist to dry
Interest:	foliage
Care:	easy

◀ Ligustrum japonicum

Privet's glossy green leaves and dense, abundant branches have made it one of the most popular plants for all types of hedges. The plants adapt well to heavy shearing and are easy to grow, making them useful for hedges, screens, foundation plants, and even topiary specimens. White flowers, often considered malodorous, bloom in late spring or early summer, followed by black or blue-black berries.

Growing and care:
Privet is easy to grow and is virtually pest- and disease-free. Plant in spring or fall in soil that has had some organic matter added to it. Water regularly until plants are established. Prune or shear as desired for shape.

Selected species and varieties:
L. japonicum (Japanese privet, waxleaf privet, waxleaf ligustrum) is an upright, dense evergreen shrub 6 to 12 feet tall and up to 8 feet wide with 2- to 6-inch-high pyramidal flower clusters offsetting very dark green leaves 1½ to 4 inches long; Zones 7-10. *L. ovalifolium* 'Aureum' (California privet) has yellow leaves with a green spot in the center when planted in sun, heavily scented flower clusters 2 to 4 inches wide in summer, and shiny black berries on 10- to 15-foot densely arranged upright stems. It is semievergreen to evergreen in warmer climates.

REDBUD
Cercis

Light: mostly sun	
Plant type: tree	
Hardiness: Zones 4-9	
Height: 8 to 30 feet	
Soil and Moisture: well-drained, moist	
Interest: flowers, fruit	
Care: easy	

◀ Cercis canadensis
'Forest Pansy'

Redbud is a small tree that graces the garden with four seasons of interest. In early spring the open branches are covered with white, pink, rose, or lavender flowers. Throughout summer the heart-shaped leaves are a lovely background to borders, and in fall attractive green seedpods turn brown and persist into winter.

Growing and care:
Eastern redbud needs some sun in late winter and early spring for the best flower production. In Zones 4 to 7, plant in spring; farther south, plant at anytime from fall to spring.

Selected species and varieties:
C. canadensis (eastern redbud) is a small tree with a spreading crown 20 to 30 feet tall, bearing 5-inch-wide leaves that turn a subdued yellow in fall; Zones 4-9; 'Alba' has white flowers; 'Forest Pansy' has red-purple leaves and pink-lavender flowers; Zones 7-9. *C. chinensis* (Chinese redbud) is a multitrunked tree 8 to 12 feet tall with upright growth and rose-purple flowers; Zones 6-9; 'Avondale' grows to 9 feet, with deep rose-purple flowers that bloom profusely. *C. reniformis* is usually 15 to 20 feet tall with glossy dark green leaves 2 to 4 inches wide and pale pink flowers; 'Oklahoma' has glossy leaves and wine red flowers; Zones 7-9.

REDLEAVED ROSE
Rosa

Light: mostly sun	
Plant type: shrub	
Hardiness: Zones 2-8	
Height: 5 feet	
Soil and Moisture: well-drained, moist	
Interest: flowers, foliage, fragrance, fruit	
Care: easy to moderate	

◀ Rosa glauca

Redleaved rose is a charming, very hardy rose that adds four-season interest to any garden. This graceful, arching shrub has pliant, nearly thornless reddish purple canes covered with attractive blue-green leaves tinged with burgundy. In late spring the plant is smothered with clusters of small single pink blossoms with white bases surrounding a cluster of airy yellow stamens. In late summer the bush is decorated with small, dull red hips that persist into winter. Redleaved rose has a relaxed, rounded, arching habit and is a valuable addition to the perennial border or used as a specimen.

Growing and care:
Plant in a sheltered, cool location in soil amended with organic matter. Mulch in spring and fall and water regularly. Redleaved rose likes some high-afternoon shade, especially in warmer regions.

Selected species and varieties:
R. 'Carmenetta' is very similar to redleaved rose but is more tolerant of hot summers. The plants have large blue-green leaves and pink single flowers on canes reaching to 7 feet.

SLENDER DEUTZIA
Deutzia

Light: mostly sun	
Plant type: shrub	
Hardiness: Zones 4-8	
Height: 2 to 5 feet	
Soil and Moisture: well-drained, moist	
Interest: flowers	
Care: easy to moderate	

◀ Deutzia gracilis

Slender deutzia has been prized by generations of gardeners for its long, graceful branches bearing pure white flowers in midspring. Like forsythia, it has a relatively short season of interest but is easy to grow and adaptable to most sites. Deutzia can be effectively used as a hedge, as a background for perennials, or in a mixed-shrub border. The plants are excellent for mass displays on slopes or woodland gardens.

Growing and care:
Plant in spring in moist, well-worked soil. Mulch around plantings in spring and again in fall. Provide extra water during dry periods. Prune out thick, older growth after flowering to keep plants vigorous. Plants can be propagated from softwood cuttings or by seed sown as soon as it ripens in late summer or fall.

Selected species and varieties:
D. gracilis grows to 5 feet tall and an equal width, with slender arching stems in a broad mounding habit, serrated leaves 1 to 3 inches long, and white flowers in erect clusters in spring that are effective for 2 weeks; 'Nikko' is a compact cultivar 2 feet tall and 5 feet wide with leaves that turn burgundy in fall.

SMOKEBUSH
Cotinus

Light: mostly sun	
Plant type: shrub	
Hardiness: Zones 5-8	
Height: 10 to 15 feet	
Soil and Moisture: well-drained, moist	
Interest: flowers, foliage	
Care: easy	

◀ Cotinus coggygria 'Velvet Cloak'

An eye-catching accent plant, smokebush has glossy plum-colored fall foliage and abundant misty plumes of translucent flower heads from summer to fall. It is a wonderful specimen plant and adds soft texture to the shrub border. Smokebush is not only attractive, but is also easy to grow and pest and disease resistant.

Growing and care:
Plant smokebush in spring or fall in well-worked soil. Fertilize lightly in spring as leaves emerge and provide extra water during dry periods. Overfertilizing and overwatering encourage soft, leafy growth with few flowers and poor autumn leaf color.

Selected species and varieties:
C. coggygria (common smokebush, smoke plant, Venetian sumac, wig tree) is a loose and open multistemmed deciduous shrub 10 to 15 feet wide, bearing 1½- to 3-inch-long leaves that unfurl pink-bronze in midspring, mature to medium blue-green, and sometimes show yellow, red, and purple fall color and branched puffs changing to gray; 'Royal Purple' has purplish maroon leaves with scarlet margins, eventually turning scarlet all over; 'Velvet Cloak' has purple plumes and velvety dark purple leaves throughout the summer before changing to reddish purple in fall.

SNOWBELL
Styrax

Light:	mostly sun
Plant type:	tree
Hardiness:	Zones 5-8
Height:	20 to 30 feet
Soil and Moisture:	well-drained, moist, fertile
Interest:	flowers, bark
Care:	easy

◄ Styrax japonicus

The delicate white bell-like flowers that dangle from the snowbell's wide-spreading branches are most visible from below, making this deciduous tree an ideal candidate to shade a patio or garden bench or to plant on slopes above walkways. The smooth, dark gray bark with interwoven orange colored fissures is attractive in winter.

Growing and care:

Plant in spring or fall in soil that has been generously amended with organic matter. Water well after planting and during dry periods. In northern areas do not plant in windy locations. Prune in winter if needed. Japanese snowbell is a remarkably pest-free plant.

Selected species and varieties:

S. japonicus (Japanese snowbell) is a dainty, low-branched tree whose crown is broader than its height, bearing medium to dark green pointed oval leaves 1 to 3½ inches long along the upper part of the branches; loose pendulous clusters of three to six slightly fragrant ¾-inch white flowers with prominent yellow stamens below the branches in late spring to early summer; and foliage that remains in place long enough to be killed by frost.

SOAPBERRY
Sapindus

Light:	mostly sun
Plant type:	tree
Hardiness:	Zones 6-9
Height:	25 to 50 feet
Soil and Moisture:	well-drained, moist to dry
Interest:	flowers, foliage, fruit, bark
Care:	easy

◄ Sapindus drummondii

Soapberry is a versatile, very attractive tree with panicles of yellowish white flowers in late spring on graceful branches. The strong branches form a rounded crown of medium green compound leaves that turn gold in fall. Small yellow-orange berries, used by Native Americans to make soap, emerge in fall and persist through winter, finally turning black. The scaly orange-brown bark adds an interesting element to the garden in winter.

Growing and care:

Soapberry is tolerant of most soils but is especially at home in the poor, dry soils of its native Southwest. It is also tolerant of urban pollution and is insect and disease resistant. Easy to cultivate, soapberry needs little attention. Water well after planting.

Selected species and varieties:

S. drummondii (western soapberry, wild China tree) is either single stemmed or low branched, 25 to 50 feet tall with an equal spread, producing eight to 18 tapered, slightly curved leaflets, each 1½ to 3½ inches long, per 10- to 15-inch leaf, glossy above and fuzzy below. It sometimes produces abundant crops of ½-inch berries.

SOURWOOD
Oxydendrum

Light: mostly sun

Plant type: tree

Hardiness: Zones 5-9

Height: 15 to 30 feet

Soil and Moisture: well-drained, moist

Interest: flowers, foliage, fragrance, seeds

Care: easy

◀ Oxydendrum arboreum

Sourwood is a spectacular medium-size tree that provides four seasons of interest to the garden. Its young spring leaves are tinted bronze, turn glossy green in summer, then brilliant red in fall. Clusters of pendent, fragrant summer flowers cover the tree in a veil of perfumed petals, followed by feathery fans of narrow, pointed seed capsules that persist through winter. Honeybees make a delicious honey from the blossoms.

Growing and care:
Plant sourwood in soil that is rich in organic matter. Water well until plants are well established. Mulch to protect shallow roots and fertilize lightly in spring before flowers appear. Propagate from seed.

Selected species and varieties:
O. arboreum (sourwood, lily-of-the-valley tree, titi) is a pyramidal tree to 30 feet tall and about half as wide, with lustrous, pointed oval leaves 5 to 8 inches long and drooping 10-inch clusters of small, creamy white flower bells in summer. In fall the leaves turn into a fireball of reds, yellows, and oranges.

SPIREA
Spiraea

Light: mostly sun

Plant type: shrub

Hardiness: Zones 3-8

Height: 2 ½ to 8 feet

Soil and Moisture: well-drained, moist

Interest: flowers, foliage

Care: easy

◀ Spiraea x vanhouttei

Spireas are deciduous shrubs with abundant clusters of tiny, roselike flowers in tight panicles along the entire length of their stems in spring, or at the tips of their branches in summer. Each of the small pink or white flowers has five petals and a spray of stamens, often with colored anthers, at the center. Spireas are easy to care for and can be used as specimen shrubs, in shrub borders, or in beds.

Growing and care:
Spireas are vigorous plants well adapted to the mostly sunny garden. They grow well in all but the driest soil and benefit from added moisture during the growing season. Prune summer bloomers in late winter and spring-blooming varieties immediately after they flower.

Selected species and varieties:
S. japonica (Japanese spirea) is rounded, 5 to 6 feet tall, with 1- to 3-inch toothed, pointed leaves and 5- to 8-inch clusters of pink flowers in late spring and early summer; 'Little Princess' has deep pink flowers and blue-green leaves tinted red in fall on 2½-foot stems; Zones 4-8. *S. nipponica* (Nippon spirea) is compact, 3 to 5 feet tall, with 1-inch oval, blue-green leaves and an abundance of white flower clusters in midspring. *S. x vanhouttei* (bridal-wreath) grows 6 to 8 feet tall, spreading in vase or fountain fashion to a width of 10 to 12 feet with 1- to 2-inch white flower clusters in spring; Zones 4-8.

SPRUCE
Picea

Light: mostly sun	
Plant type: shrub, tree	
Hardiness: Zones 2-7	
Height: 3 to 60 feet	
Soil and Moisture: well-drained, moist, acidic	
Interest: foliage	
Care: easy to moderate	

◀ Picea abies 'Nidiformis'

Spruces are a large group of very ornamental trees ranging from small shrubby forms to expansive giants. These needled, pyramidal evergreens are useful as windbreaks, screens, or single specimens. Smaller forms are good as accents in rock gardens or shrub borders.

Growing and care:
Plant spruce in well-worked soil that has been generously amended with peat moss or other organic matter. Water well at planting and during dry periods. Prune away brown galls that may appear at tips of branches. Shear to shape anytime when foliage is wet.

Selected species and varieties:
P. abies (Norway spruce) forms a fast-growing pyramid with drooping branches, 40 to 60 feet tall (it can reach 150 feet) and 25 to 30 feet wide. Its medium green foliage matures to dark green, bearing 4- to 6-inch cylindrical cones and often losing its form in old age; 'Nidiformis' (bird's-nest spruce) is a 3- to 6-foot-tall spreading mound. *P. glauca* (white spruce) is a tree that ages to a narrow, dense spire 40 to 60 feet tall by 10 to 20 feet wide, with ascending branches; Zones 2-6; 'Conica' (dwarf Alberta spruce) is a neat, very slow-growing (to 10 feet in 25 years) cone-shaped plant with light green foliage.

STEWARTIA
Stewartia

Light: mostly sun	
Plant type: shrub, tree	
Hardiness: Zones 5-9	
Height: 10 to 45 feet	
Soil and Moisture: well-drained, fertile, moist	
Interest: flowers, foliage, bark	
Care: moderate	

◀ Stewartia pseudocamellia

Stewartias add year-round charm and grace to the landscape, not only with their camellia-like flowers that bloom from mid- to late summer, but also with their colorful fall foliage and beautiful exfoliating bark. These stunning plants should be given a place of prominence in the landscape. The smaller types combine well with other flowering shrubs in mixed borders while the larger forms are best used as specimens.

Growing and care:
Stewartias are difficult to transplant and, once planted, should not be disturbed. Dig a large hole and add copious amounts of compost and peat moss to maintain an acid, organic soil. Stewartias require protection from drying winter winds and scorching summer sun. Provide extra moisture during dry spells. Once established, stewartias rarely need pruning.

Selected species and varieties:
S. koreana (Korean stewartia) is a pyramidal tree 35 to 45 feet tall with dark green foliage turning sunset red in fall, and 2- to 3-inch wavy-edged, creamy white flowers in late summer. *S. pseudocamellia* (Japanese stewartia) is an oval tree 20 to 40 feet tall with showy exfoliating bark, bearing 2- to 2½-inch white flowers with white filaments and orange anthers in summer, and 1½- to 3½-inch leaves that turn vibrant yellow, red, and purple in fall; Zones 5-7.

STRAWBERRY TREE
Arbutus

Light: mostly sun

Plant type: shrub, tree

Hardiness: Zones 7-9

Height: 8 to 12 feet

Soil and Moisture: well-drained, moist

Interest: flowers, foliage, bark, fruit

Care: easy

◀ Arbutus unedo

The strawberry tree is an excellent plant for the warm areas of the Southwest, providing garden interest throughout the year. The leaves are evergreen, the exfoliating bark is deep reddish brown, and the branches become attractively gnarled with age. Small urn-shaped flowers appear in 2-inch clusters in fall, and the orange-red berrylike fruit ripens the following season. Strawberry tree can be used as a hedge or a specimen, or to add variety to the shrub border.

Growing and care:
The strawberry tree tolerates a wide range of soil conditions as long as drainage is good. It requires watering only during periods of drought and is also tolerant of seaside conditions. Plant in a sheltered location away from drying winds.

Selected species and varieties:
A. unedo 'Compacta' is a slow-growing dwarf variety that eventually reaches 8 to 12 feet in height, producing dark green leaves, and bearing flowers and fruit almost continuously.

SUMAC
Rhus

Light: mostly sun

Plant type: shrub, tree

Hardiness: Zones 3-9

Height: 2 to 30 feet

Soil and Moisture: well-drained, moist to dry

Interest: foliage, fruit

Care: easy

◀ Rhus typhina 'Laciniata'

Sumacs are versatile, hardworking, easy-to-grow shrubs that add a tropical ambiance to landscapes and gardens. The plants spread rapidly to form dense thickets on steep banks and along walkways or roadsides, where they help stabilize the soil. Low-growing types are especially useful as ground covers or for fronting taller shrubs in a mixed border. Taller types should be limited to large-scale plantings. They are outstanding for their colorful fall foliage and bright red fruit, which is effective for many weeks.

Growing and care:
Sumacs prefer acid soil and do not tolerate poorly drained sites. They transplant easily and require minimal care, developing suckers and spreading rapidly to form colonies. Sumacs are virtually pest- and disease-free.

Selected species and varieties:
R. aromatica (fragrant sumac) grows from 3 to 6 feet tall, with glossy green trifoliate leaves turning red to reddish purple in fall; 'Gro-Low' reaches only 2 to 4 feet in height and is useful for the front of shrub borders, spreading to 8 feet wide with reliable orange-red fall color. *R. typhina* (staghorn sumac) is a 15- to 30-foot-tall tree with pinnately compound leaves that turn orange to scarlet in fall on velvety stems; 'Laciniata' (cut-leaf staghorn sumac) produces deeply dissected leaves that have a fine-textured appearance.

SWEET SHRUB
Calycanthus

Light: mostly sun

Plant type: shrub

Hardiness: Zones 4-10

Height: 6 to 12 feet

Soil and Moisture: well-drained, moist

Interest: flowers, fragrance

Care: easy

◀ Calycanthus occidentalis

Native to the United States and China, these delightfully unusual shrubs have distinctive segmented flowers with long, ribbonlike petals that have a pleasant fragrance reminiscent of tropical fruit. They are enjoyable additions to outdoor living areas or to foundation plantings, where the sweet fragrance of the flowers can drift through open windows. Sweet shrubs are medium size, with slightly rough dark green leaves and maroon-red flowers from midspring to summer.

Growing and care:
Sweet shrub should be planted in spring or fall. Prune as needed after flowering in summer. Propagate by dividing and transplanting suckers at the base of stems in fall. Fertilize lightly in spring as growth begins.

Selected species and varieties:
C. fertilis (Pale sweet shrub) grows 6 to 10 feet tall with 6-inch silvery green leaves and magnolia-like dark brown fragrant, flowers. *C. floridus* (sweet shrub, Carolina allspice) grows 6 to 9 feet tall and up to 12 feet wide with aromatic 2- to 5-inch leaves that turn bronzy yellow in fall, and 2-inch flowers with straplike petals that are usually burgundy-brown; 'Athens' has yellow flowers; 'Urbana' has an exceptionally sweet fragrance. *C. occidentalis* reaches 8 to 12 feet with slightly hairy 8-inch lance-shaped leaves and fragrant cinnamon-rose, narrow-petaled flowers; Zones 6-10.

VIBURNUM
Viburnum

Light: mostly sun

Plant type: shrub

Hardiness: Zones 4-9

Height: 3 to 12 feet

Soil and Moisture: well-drained, moist

Interest: flowers, foliage, fragrance

Care: easy

◀ Viburnum carlesii

Viburnums are easy-to-grow, extraordinarily attractive plants that add four-season interest to landscapes and gardens. These versatile plants offer snowy clouds of often intensely fragrant flowers in spring, beautiful summer and fall foliage, and colorful berries from autumn into winter. Viburnums are used as centerpieces for shrub borders, as screens, or as foundation plantings.

Growing and care:
Plant viburnums in loose, slightly acid loam soil amended with some organic matter. Fertilize in spring as growth begins and water regularly. Add a layer of mulch in spring and again in fall. Viburnums are remarkably pest- and disease-free and need little or no pruning.

Selected species and varieties:
V. carlesii (Koreanspice viburnum) has pink buds that open to white, domelike, enchantingly fragrant flower clusters 2 to 3 inches wide on a rounded, dense shrub 4 to 8 feet tall and wide, followed by ineffective black fruit in late summer; Zones 4-8. *V. plicatum* var. *tomentosum* (doublefile viburnum) has layered, tierlike horizontal branches on plants 8 to 10 feet tall and wide, with flat, pure white flower clusters; Zones 5-8; 'Shasta' grows 6 feet tall and 10 to 12 feet wide, with 4- to 6-inch, wide-spreading flower clusters so dense they obscure the dark green leaves.

WINTER HAZEL
Corylopsis

Light: mostly sun	
Plant type: shrub	
Hardiness: Zones 5-8	
Height: 4 to 15 feet	
Soil and Moisture: well-drained, moist	
Interest: flowers, fragrance, foliage	
Care: easy to moderate	

◀ Corylopsis pauciflora

Winter hazel is one of the first shrubs to flower in spring, with abundant drooping panicles of sweetly fragrant flowers. Through summer the branches are thick with attractive green foliage. Winter hazel is excellent in the shrub border, set against a wall or structure, or planted in a woodland garden.

Growing and care:
Winter hazels grow best in a location with some spring sunshine for best flower formation. Protect from winter winds, sudden temperature dips, and spring frosts, which can easily kill flower buds. Work leaf mold, peat moss, or compost liberally into the soil before planting. There is usually no need to fertilize.

Selected species and varieties:
C. glabrescens (fragrant winter hazel) grows 8 to 15 feet tall with a similar spread, followed by toothy, pointed oval leaves 2 to 4 inches long and yellow flowers; Zones 5-8. *C. pauciflora* (buttercup winter hazel) grows 4 to 6 feet tall, with flowers in clusters of only two or three and leaves 1½ to 3 inches long; Zones 6-8. *C. sinensis* (Chinese winter hazel) is usually 5 to 8 feet tall but may grow to 15 feet, bearing blue-green downy leaves 2 to 5 inches long and flowers in 2-inch drooping clusters.

YEW
Taxus

Light: mostly sun	
Plant type: shrub, tree	
Hardiness: Zones 4-7	
Height: 2 to 60 feet	
Soil and Moisture: well-drained, moist	
Interest: foliage	
Care: easy	

◀ Taxus x media 'Hicksii'

Yew is the ubiquitous evergreen plant seen in nearly every yard. With dense, very dark green needled foliage, the plants are easy to grow and provide a reliable, good-looking anchor to the landscape. Smaller forms make superb foundation plants or entrance shrubs. The plants can be left unpruned for an informal look or sheared into hedges and topiaries.

Growing and care:
Plant yews in soil lightly amended with organic matter. Water weekly until plants are established. Fertilize in spring when new growth appears. Prune or shear as needed to shape.

Selected species and varieties:
T. baccata (English yew, common yew) is a dense shrub or tree 30 to 60 feet high and 15 to 25 feet wide with a variable habit, often used as a screen or hedge; Zones 6-7. *T. cuspidata* (Japanese yew) grows from 10 to 40 feet tall with irregular, upright branches and abundant dark green needles; 'Densiformis' reaches 3 feet tall and 6 feet wide with very dark green foliage. *T.* x *media* is a cross between the English and Japanese yew with an extremely variable form, either a pyramidal tree or a spreading shrub 3 to 20 feet high, often with a central trunk; Zones 4-7; 'Hicksii' develops a columnar form to 20 feet tall in 15 to 20 years, narrow when young and becoming broader with age.

3

Plants for Mostly
Shady Places

The plants that grow in mostly shady places live most of their lives in the shadow of other things. Towering trees or structures block the sun most of the day, yet these shade-loving plants thrive just the same. These plants of the shadows are a diverse group, with some preferring the less intense sun of early morning or late afternoon and shade for the remainder of the day, and others thriving in day-long dappled light or alternating hours of shade and sun. To grow plants in mostly shade, plan gardens that include plants of different heights, so the tiers of overlapping foliage can most efficiently use the light that is present. Enrich the soil with compost or rotted manure to increase fertility and moisture retention. And mulch the plantings in spring and fall to minimize the competition of weeds and to keep the soil cool.

COLEUS
Coleus

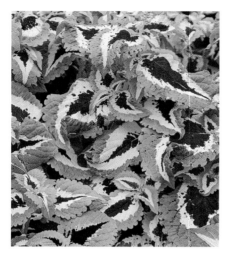

Light: mostly shade

Plant type: tender perennial grown as annual

Height: 9 inches to 2 feet

Soil and Moisture: well-drained, moist

Interest: foliage

Care: easy

◀ Coleus x hybridus 'Wizard Rose'

The vibrantly colored, heart-shaped opposite leaves of coleus grow on square stems and provide a long season of interest to borders in partially shaded sites. Leaves sport a wide variety of attractive patterns in colors that include chartreuse, green, orange, red, pink, bronze, and white.

Growing and care:

Start seed indoors or grow from leaf-stem cuttings overwintered indoors. Transplant outdoors after soil has warmed, allowing 8 to 12 inches between plants. Coleus are most colorful and grow best in partial shade, though some tolerate full sun if adequate water is supplied. Coleus is usually grown as an annual, but can be lifted from the garden in fall and repotted to be enjoyed as a houseplant through winter.

Selected species and varieties:

C. x *hybridus* has scalloped-edged leaves, usually 3 to 8 inches long, and upright pale blue flower spikes that are often removed to encourage growth; 'Fiji' series has fringed leaf margins in bright colors; 'Wizard' series grows to 10 inches in red, pink, and apricot shades with cream or green edges, and resists flowering.

COLLINSIA
Collinsia

Light: mostly shade

Plant type: annual

Height: 8 inches to 2 feet

Soil and Moisture: well-drained, moist to dry

Interest: flowers

Care: easy

◀ Collinsia heterophylla

Collinsia, also called Chinese houses, is a delicate annual wildflower of the western United States. The plants have very slender stalks topped with small clusters of snapdragon-shaped white, pink, blue, or purple flowers in spring. They are suited to rock gardens, woodland gardens, meadows, and borders, and are also easy to grow in containers.

Growing and care:

Sow seed directly in the garden in early spring while the soil is cool, in soil well amended with organic matter. Thin seedlings to stand 6 to 12 inches apart. Collinsia prefers areas with cool summers and partial shade. Once established the plants are moderately drought tolerant. Hot weather inhibits flowering. To extend flowering, remove faded blooms before seed can set. Propagate collinsias by seed; they often self-sow.

Selected species and varieties:

C. grandiflora (blue lips) grows 8 to 15 inches tall, bearing ¾-inch two-lipped flowers singly or in clusters in the leaf axils from mid- to late spring; the upper lip is white or purple and the lower lip is blue or violet. *C. heterophylla* (Chinese houses) grows 2 feet tall with blossoms arranged in tiers, and bright green foliage; the upper lip of the flower is lilac or white and the lower lip is rose-purple or violet.

FORGET-ME-NOT
Myosotis

Light: mostly shade	
Plant type: annual, biennial	
Height: 6 to 10 inches	
Soil and Moisture: well-drained, moist	
Interest: flowers, foliage	
Care: easy	

◀ Myosotis sylvatica 'Ultramarine'

Airy clusters of dainty flowers with prominent eyes open above the forget-me-not's low mounds of delicate foliage. Forget-me-nots provide a soft filler or a delicate border edging. They are particularly attractive in combination with spring-flowering bulbs such as tulips.

Growing and care:
Start seed outdoors in late summer to early fall for flowers the following spring. Enrich the soil with organic matter. Allow 6 to 12 inches between plants, and water during dry periods. Once established, forget-me-nots self-seed readily, performing like a perennial. Forget-me-nots do best in partial shade but thrive in mostly sun if plentiful moisture is available.

Selected species and varieties:
M. sylvatica (woodland forget-me-not, garden forget-me-not) produces 8- to 10-inch stems in clumps almost as wide, lined with soft, elongated leaves and tipped with loose clusters of ¼-inch yellow-centered blue flowers from spring through early summer; 'Ultramarine' is a dwarf, growing to 6 inches, with dark blue flowers; 'Victoria Blue' grows 6 to 8 inches, forming neat mounds and producing early flowers of gentian blue.

IMPATIENS
Impatiens

Light: mostly shade	
Plant type: annual or tender perennial grown as annual	
Height: 6 inches to 8 feet	
Soil and Moisture: well-drained, moist	
Interest: flowers, foliage	
Care: easy	

◀ Impatiens wallerana 'Super Elfin'

Massed as edgings or ground covers, impatiens brightens a shady garden with flowers in jeweled hues from summer through frost. These easy-to-grow plants are ideal when grouped beneath trees. Low-growing types are ideal for planters and hanging baskets.

Growing and care:
Plant *I. glandulifera* seed outdoors in fall. Start impatiens indoors 3 to 4 months prior to the last frost, or purchase bedding plants to transplant to the garden after all danger of frost has passed. Space *I. glandulifera* 2 feet apart, others 1 to 1½ feet apart. Impatiens grows best in partial to full shade, though some recently released varieties grow well in mostly sunny spots.

Selected species and varieties:
I. balsamina (garden balsam, rose balsam) grows to 3 feet, producing 1- to 2-inch flowers in mixed colors. *I. glandulifera* (Himalayan jewelweed) grows to 8 feet with 2-inch purple, pink, or white flowers in mid- to late summer. *I.* New Guinea hybrids (New Guinea impatiens) prefers more sun than other species and grows to 2 feet with showy, often variegated leaves, and flowers up to 3 inches across. *I. wallerana* (busy Lizzie) grows 6 to 18 inches tall with a compact, mounded habit and 1- to 2-inch flat-faced flowers available in many colors; 'Super Elfin' series bears flowers in assorted colors on wide-spreading plants.

MONKEY FLOWER
Mimulus

Light:	mostly shade
Plant type:	annual
Height:	10 to 14 inches
Soil and Moisture:	well-drained, moist, fertile
Interest:	flowers, foliage
Care:	easy

◀ Mimulus x hybridus

Blooming from midsummer to fall, this native of both North and South America provides bright color to shady beds and borders. It fits well alongside a garden pond or stream and also makes an attractive container plant. Funnel-shaped two-lipped flowers are thought to resemble monkeys' faces.

Growing and care:
Start seed indoors 10 to 12 weeks prior to the last frost for transplanting to the garden after all danger of frost has passed. Space plants 6 inches apart. Plants benefit from the addition of organic matter to the soil. They require partial shade and ample moisture to thrive. In fall, plants can be dug and potted to continue flowering indoors over winter.

Selected species and varieties:
M. x *hybridus* has a mounded habit with glossy 2- to 2½-inch leaves and 2-inch tubular flowers in shades of red, yellow, orange, rose, and brown, usually with brown or maroon spotting or mottling.

PANSY
Viola

Light:	mostly shade
Plant type:	annual, perennial grown as annual
Height:	3 to 12 inches
Soil and Moisture:	well-drained, moist
Interest:	flowers
Care:	easy

◀ Viola tricolor

Although many pansies are technically short-lived perennials, they are considered annuals because they bloom their first year from seed and their flowers decline in quality afterward, regardless of region. They may also be treated as biennials, sown in late summer for bloom early the following spring. Their vividly colored and interestingly marked flowers are borne over a long season, often beginning with the first signs of spring and lasting until the summer heat causes them to fade, although a bit of shade and water may encourage the blossoms to continue throughout most of the summer. The rounded flower petals overlap, and their patterns often resemble a face. Pansies are a good choice for planting with bulbs, combining well with the flower forms and providing cover for fading foliage. They are attractive when massed in beds, and useful as edgings or combined with other annuals in patio planters or window boxes.

Growing and care:
Sow seed outdoors in late summer for earliest spring blooms, or purchase transplants. Pansies started in late summer should be protected over winter in a cold frame or by covering plants with a light mulch or branches after the first hard frost. They can also be started indoors in midwinter to transplant to the garden in midspring. Germination can be enhanced by moistening and chilling the

(continued)

seed (between 40° and 45°F) for 1 week prior to planting. Space plants about 4 inches apart. Pansies prefer cool air and soil temperatures. In spring pansies can be grown in mostly sunny places if given ample water, and in shaded areas during summer. Remove faded blooms and keep plants well watered to extend flowering.

Selected species and varieties:

V. rafinesquii (field pansy) is a true annual that is native to much of the United States and grows 3 to 12 inches tall. Its ½-inch flowers are pale blue to cream, often with purple veins and a yellow throat. *V. tricolor* (Johnny-jump-up, miniature pansy) is a European native that has naturalized in much of the United States. It typically grows to 8 inches with a low, mounded habit and small, colorful flowers that have been favorites in the garden since Elizabethan times. The 1-inch flowers are fragrant, edible, and often used as a garnish. Colors include deep violet, blue, lavender, mauve, yellow, cream, white, and bicolors; 'Bowles' Black' bears blue-black flowers. *V.* x *wittrockiana* (common pansy) grows 4 to 8 inches tall and spreads to 1 foot. The 1- to 2-inch flowers are usually three toned in shades of purple, blue, dark red, rose, pink, brown, yellow, and white. Many varieties are available; 'Melody Purple and White' bears flowers with white and purple petals marked with deep violet-blue.

WISHBONE FLOWER
Torenia

◄ Torenia fournieri

Light:	mostly shade
Plant type:	annual
Height:	6 to 12 inches
Soil and Moisture:	well-drained, moist
Interest:	flowers
Care:	easy

The blossoms of wishbone flower, also called blue-wings, have upper- and lower-lobed lips and are borne above a mound of foliage from midsummer to early fall. Because it thrives in shady locations, it is the perfect choice for a woodland bed or shady border. The plants are also well suited to hanging baskets and patio planters.

Growing and care:

Start seed indoors 10 to 12 weeks prior to the last frost; in Zone 9 and warmer, seed can be sown directly outdoors in early spring. Space seedlings 6 to 8 inches apart. Plants thrive in humid areas, and grow best in partial shade. In regions with cool summers the plants can be grown in mostly sunny locations.

Selected species and varieties:

T. fournieri (bluewings) has a rounded compact habit with neat oval leaves 1½ to 2 inches long. The 1-inch flowers appear in stalked clusters; each bloom displays a pale violet tube with a yellow blotch and flaring lower petal edges marked with deep purple-blue. The two fused yellow stamens resemble a poultry wishbone, hence the common name.

ARROWHEAD
Sagittaria

Light: mostly shade	
Plant type: perennial	
Hardiness: Zones 3-10	
Height: 3 to 4 feet	
Soil and Moisture: wet	
Interest: flowers, foliage	
Care: easy	

◀ Sagittaria latifolia

Arrowhead, a perennial found throughout the United States and southern Canada in wet meadows, marshes, and ponds, has whorled clusters of showy flowers set off by large leathery leaves. The plants are easy-to-grow, reliable additions to water gardens, bogs, and marshes, and look especially nice planted along the shores of ponds and slow streams. Arrowhead produces edible tubers relished by ducks.

Growing and care:
Arrowhead grows best when its roots are submerged in shallow water, but it can also be grown in the wet soil of a bog garden. The plants are adaptable to a wide range of light conditions, from full sun to mostly shade. For a garden pool, plant arrowhead in containers, cover the soil with 2 inches of gravel, and submerge the containers. Propagate by seed or division in fall.

Selected species and varieties:
S. latifolia (wapatoo, duck potato) grows up to 4 feet tall with small, snow white flowers on leafless 1- to 3-foot stems from mid- to late summer. The arrow-shaped leaves are glossy green, dark and up to 16 inches long.

ASTILBE
Astilbe

Light: mostly shade	
Plant type: perennial	
Hardiness: Zones 3-9	
Height: 8 inches to 4 feet	
Soil and Moisture: well-drained, moist, fertile	
Interest: flowers, foliage	
Care: easy to moderate	

◀ Astilbe x arendsii 'Rheinland'

The feathery plumes held above mounds of graceful, deep green to bronze fernlike foliage make astilbe an ideal filler in shady borders, or for use as a background accent or woodland edging, or near water elements in the landscape. The 8-inch to 4-foot stalks bear thousands of tiny five-petaled flowers that resemble white, pink, lavender, or red clouds when massed in the garden.

Growing and care:
Plant astilbes 1½ to 2 feet apart in moist soil, preferably in a cool, shady location. Water well and mulch if in full sun or average soil. Propagate by division every 3 to 4 years in spring or early summer. Feed plants each spring with a high-phosphorus fertilizer, and provide extra water during hot, dry periods.

Selected species and varieties:
A. x arendsii (false spirea) grows 2 to 4 feet tall with loose panicles of pink, white, red, or lavender flowers in summer; 'Fanal' combines rich bronze foliage with deep red flowers; 'Rheinland' has clear pink flowers on sturdy 2-foot stems; Zones 4-9. *A. chinensis* (Chinese astilbe) grows 8 inches to 4 feet with white, rose-tinged, or purple flowers; 'Pumila' has a dwarf habit with spires of mauve-pink flowers in late summer on 8-inch stems; Zones 3-8. *A. x rosea* (rose astilbe) 'Peach Blossom' has a compact form with sturdy 2-foot stems and feathery foliage beneath pale blush summer flowers.

BEARDTONGUE
Penstemon

Light: mostly shade

Plant type: perennial

Hardiness: Zones 3-8

Height: 1 to 3 feet

Soil and Moisture: well-drained, moist to dry, sandy

Interest: flowers, foliage

Care: easy to moderate

◀ Penstemon digitalis

Beardtongues are reliable soft-textured perennials with showy terminal clusters of brightly colored two-lipped summer flowers. Most species are native to the open woodlands and prairies of the Midwest. The plants are easy to grow if planted in a well-drained, sandy soil. Beardtongues are excellent for adding an airy, upright element to borders.

Growing and care:

Plant in spring after last frost in a well-worked soil that has been amended with sand and organic matter. Space plants 1 to 1½ feet apart. Water regularly while plants are actively growing. Mulch in regions with hot summers. When grown in full sun beardtongues produce the most flowers but are short lived. Plantings will last much longer when grown in a spot with mostly shade. Propagate from seed after stratification.

Selected species and varieties:

P. barbatus bears 1-inch slightly nodding red flowers on stems 1 to 2 feet high; 'Rose Elf' has stems to about 20 inches tall and plentiful clear rose blossoms in early summer; Zones 3-7. *P. digitalis* 'Husker Red Strain' [also listed under *P. smolliix*] has masses of bronzy red foliage and pearl white flowers on 3-foot stems; Zones 3-8. *P.* 'Evelyn' has upright 1½- to 2-foot stems and abundant shell pink flowers in summer; Zones 6-8.

BELLFLOWER
Campanula

Light: mostly shade

Plant type: perennial

Hardiness: Zones 3-8

Height: 1 to 2 feet

Soil and Moisture: well-drained, moist to dry

Interest: flowers

Care: easy

◀ Campanula portenschlagiana 'Resholdt's Variety'

Bellflowers are some of the most popular perennials and have long been stalwarts of beds, borders, and rock gardens. Their growth forms range from low cushions to tall, upright clumps. The color palette of the tubular or flaring flowers ranges from violet to blue to white. Flowers are borne in clusters or spikes from late spring through summer, with some species lightly reblooming in fall.

Growing and care:

In cool-summer regions bellflowers grow best in mostly sun, but still flower well in mostly shade. In regions with hot summers the plants should be given mostly shade. Space low-growing bellflowers 1 to 1½ feet apart, larger ones 2 feet apart. Propagate by seed or division; divide every 3 to 4 years to maintain vigor.

Selected species and varieties:

C. persicifolia (peachleaf bellflower) bears nodding 1-inch deep blue to white flowers on pliant 2-foot stems in summer and reblooms in fall; 'Grandiflora Alba' has large, pure white flowers; 'Summer Skies' has double white flowers accented with pastel blue. *C. portenschlagiana* (Dalmatian bellflower) has loose panicles of purple-blue star-shaped flowers in late spring and early summer above 4- to 8-inch mounds of coarse kidney-shaped leaves; 'Resholdt's Variety' has large, deep purple flowers on 6-inch stems; Zones 5-7.

BERGENIA
Bergenia

Light: mostly shade

Plant type: perennial

Hardiness: Zones 3-9

Height: 1 to 1 1/2 feet

Soil and Moisture: well-drained, moist

Interest: flowers, foliage

Care: easy

◀ Bergenia cordifolia

Bergenias are noted for their large, showy rosettes of bold leathery leaves and 3- to 6-inch spikes of white, pink, or lavender-rose flowers in spring. In warmer climates the leaves are evergreen, while in the North they turn a dusky burgundy or bronze in the fall. Use bergenias in rock gardens, in beds and borders, as edging, or as a ground cover.

Growing and care:
Bergenias are very tolerant of cold, heat, and moist soil. A site that remains wet in winter may cause the roots to rot. Space plants 1 foot apart. They will spread quickly by rhizomes to form a thick ground cover. The plants are quite adaptable and thrive in fertile or poor soil and mostly sunny to mostly shady spots. Divide every 3 to 4 years to promote vigorous growth and flowering.

Selected species and varieties:
B. cordifolia [formerly listed as *Saxifraga cordifolia*] (heart-leaf bergenia, pig squeak) has clumps of 8- to 10-inch leaves with wavy edges and heart-lobed bases, and clusters of 1-inch pink flowers atop 10- to 18-inch stalks in early spring; 'Alba' has white flowers; 'Purpurea' has purple flowers. *B. crassifolia* (leather bergenia) has rounded leaves and lavender-pink flowers held high above bright green foliage. *B. stracheyi* (Strachey bergenia) has unwavy leaves edged with hairs, and white flowers in late winter or early spring; Zones 6-9.

BLEEDING HEART
Dicentra

Light: mostly shade

Plant type: perennial

Hardiness: Zones 3-8

Height: 4 inches to 3 feet

Soil and Moisture: well-drained, moist

Interest: flowers, foliage

Care: easy

◀ Dicentra spectabilis

Bleeding hearts have long panicles of ornate symmetrical flowers that dangle on arching stems above layers of soft, lacy foliage. The many Asian and North American species produce attractive flowers in spring and summer. In summer the gray-green foliage of most species fades as the plants become dormant. Bleeding hearts make excellent additions to woodland borders and mostly shady wildflower gardens.

Growing and care:
Bleeding hearts thrive in the dappled shade beneath tall trees. Plant *D. spectabilis* 2 to 3 feet apart and other species 1 to 2 feet apart. They will spread slowly by small tubers, self-sowing, or offsets. Propagate by division when plants are dormant.

Selected species and varieties:
D. canadensis (squirrel corn) reaches 6 to 10 inches with blue-gray leaves, and heart-shaped 1/2-inch white flowers in spring; Zones 3-7. *D. cucullaria* (Dutchman's-breeches) reaches 4 to 10 inches with yellow-tipped, double-spurred 1/2-inch fragrant white flowers in spring; Zones 3-7. *D. spectabilis* bears 1- to 1 1/2-inch pink and white or all-white flowers from spring to midsummer on 2- to 3-foot stalks above feathery foliage; Zones 4-8.

BLUESTAR
Amsonia

Light: mostly shade

Plant type: perennial

Hardiness: Zones 3-9

Height: 2 to 3 feet

Soil and Moisture: well-drained, moist

Interest: flowers

Care: easy

◀ Amsonia tabernaemontana

Bluestar produces pale blue star-shaped blossoms that hang above the green foliage like clusters of shooting stars. Blooming in late spring and early summer, it is particularly effective combined with more brightly colored flowers. Its densely mounded willowlike leaves remain attractive throughout the growing season, providing a lovely foil for later-blooming perennials.

Growing and care:
Bluestars grow best in mostly shady places but thrive in mostly to fully sunny places as well. In poor to moderately fertile soil they rarely need staking; avoid highly fertile soil, which produces rank, floppy growth. The plants prefer to be undisturbed once established but should be divided every 3 to 4 years in spring or fall to keep them vigorous. Prune lightly to keep plants tidy. Provide extra water during dry periods.

Selected species and varieties:
A. tabernaemontana produces steel blue flowers in terminal clusters on stiff 2- to 3-foot-tall erect stems with densely occurring leaves 3 to 6 inches long that turn yellow in fall; var. *salicifolia* has longer and thinner leaves and blooms slightly later than the species.

BOWMAN'S ROOT
Gillenia

Light: mostly shade

Plant type: perennial

Hardiness: Zones 4-8

Height: 2 to 4 feet

Soil and Moisture: well-drained, moist

Interest: flowers

Care: easy

◀ Gillenia trifoliata

Bowman's root is a tall, delicate perennial with white star-shaped flowers often blushed with pink. The attractive dark green foliage accents the flowers, which emerge from wine-colored sepals in spring to summer and remain ornamental long after the petals drop. The plants are a useful addition to borders and are excellent when naturalized with flowering shrubs in meadows or woodland plantings.

Growing and care:
Plant in fall in soil that contains some organic matter. Space plants 2 to 3 feet apart and water regularly until plants are established and during hot dry periods. The plants thrive in mostly shady situations but also grow well in mostly sunny locations. Mulch well in spring and fall to keep roots cool and retain soil moisture. Cut back stems after flowering is completed. Plants often require staking. Propagate from seed, which is often quite difficult, or by divsion in spring or fall.

Selected species and varieties:
G. trifoliata [formerly *Porteranthus trifoliata*] bears five-petaled flowers 1 inch wide, in loose, airy clusters on wiry branching stems 2 to 4 feet tall above lacy leaves with toothed edges.

BUGBANE
Cimicifuga

Light:	mostly shade
Plant type:	perennial
Hardiness:	Zones 3-8
Height:	3 to 7 feet
Soil and Moisture:	well-drained, moist, fertile
Interest:	flowers, foliage
Care:	moderate

◄ Cimicifuga ramosa
'Brunette'

Bugbane is a distinctive perennial wildflower with airy columns of lacy leaflets topped by long wands of tiny, icy white frilled flowers in late summer to fall. These tall, graceful plants are excellent as accent specimens, naturalized in a woodland garden, or massed at the edge of a stream or pond.

Growing and care:
Plant bugbane in shady to mostly shady areas of the garden in soil enriched with organic matter. Fertilize lightly in spring and provide extra water during dry periods. Mulch to keep roots cool. Disturb established plantings as little as possible. Propagate by division in spring.

Selected species and varieties:
C. americana (American bugbane) has dense spikes of creamy blossoms on branched 2- to 6-foot-tall flower stalks in late summer to fall. *C. ramosa* (branched bugbane) bears 3-foot wands of fragrant white flowers on reddish stalks in fall; 'Atropurpurea' grows to 7 feet with bronzy purple leaves; 'Brunette' has purplish black foliage and pink-tinged flowers on 3- to 4-foot stalks. *C. simplex* 'White Pearl' has 2-foot wands of white flowers on branching, arched 3- to 4-foot flower stalks followed by round, lime green fruits.

COLUMBINE
Aquilegia

Light:	mostly shade
Plant type:	perennial
Hardiness:	Zones 3-9
Height:	8 inches to 3 feet
Soil and Moisture:	well-drained, moist to dry
Interest:	flowers
Care:	easy to moderate

◄ Aquilegia canadensis

Columbines are unique, very colorful flowers bearing complex erect or nodding blossoms with long spurs at the base of brightly colored petals. Their rounded, lacy blue-green foliage adds a soft accent to the garden. They are excellent additions to the wildflower garden, naturalized in meadows, or used in beds, borders, and rock gardens.

Growing and care:
Columbines thrive in organic-rich soil with even moisture and in a range of conditions, from full sun to full shade. All columbines self-sow, some prolifically. Propagate native columbines by sowing the small seed indoors in late winter. Do not cover seed, as light is needed to germinate properly. Leaf miners sometimes do cosmetic damage to the foliage.

Selected species and varieties:
A. canadensis (wild columbine) has graceful 2-foot stems bearing dainty, nodding crimson and yellow blossoms from spring to midsummer. *A. x hybrida* (hybrid columbine) bears large 3-inch spring-blooming flowers on 3-foot stems; 'Crimson Star' has 1½-inch flowers with red spurs, white central petal tips, and a projecting shower of elegant golden stamens; 'Dragonfly Hybrids' are 1 foot tall and range in color from red, yellow, or blue to various bicolors; 'McKana Giants' have oversize flowers borne on 2½-foot stems.

CORYDALIS
Corydalis

Light:	mostly shade
Plant type:	perennial
Hardiness:	Zones 5-8
Height:	8 to 15 inches
Soil and Moisture:	well-drained, moist
Interest:	flowers
Care:	moderate

◀ Corydalis flexuosa 'Blue Panda'

Corydalis are delicate woodland wildflowers bearing spikes of small, tubular flowers that hang from slender stems from midspring to summer. The fernlike foliage is similar to that of bleeding heart and remains attractive throughout the growing season. The plants are useful for edgings, rock gardens, and perennial beds.

Growing and care:

Corydalis grows best in light or dappled shade but tolerates deep shade well. For increased vigor, work organic matter such as compost, leaf mold, or peat moss into the soil before planting. Good drainage and even moisture are essential. If soil dries out in summer the plants may cease flowering. Apply an all-purpose fertilizer in spring. After 2 to 3 years, divide plants in early spring. Propagate from seed or by stem cuttings. Yellow corydalis self-seeds freely.

Selected species and varieties:

C. flexuosa 'Blue Panda' forms 8- to 12-inch-tall mounds of blue-green foliage accented with dense sprays of porcelain blue flowers from late spring until frost. *C. lutea* (yellow corydalis, yellow bleeding heart) is a bushy multi-stemmed plant 12 to 15 inches tall with slender spikes of ¾-inch-long yellow flowers held high above the blue-green foliage.

EPIMEDIUM
Epimedium

Light:	mostly shade
Plant type:	perennial
Hardiness:	Zones 4-8
Height:	3 to 12 inches
Soil and Moisture:	well-drained, moist, fertile
Interest:	flowers, foliage
Care:	easy

◀ Epimedium grandiflorum

Epimediums have sprays of waxy bicolored flowers with downward-curving spurs that appear in midspring before the small heart-shaped leaves emerge. New leaves are pale green or red as they unfurl, turn medium green in summer and bronze in fall, and remain throughout winter in warmer regions. Epimediums are popular plants for shady rock gardens. Planted in large groups, they can be used as a creeping ground cover for shady areas.

Growing and care:

Epimediums prefer moist, peaty loam, but tolerate drier soils once established. The plants grow best in mostly shady locations. Add compost or peat moss before planting 8 to 10 inches apart. Remove dead foliage in early spring before new growth starts. Propagate by division of rhizomes in late summer.

Selected species and varieties:

E. alpinum (red Alpine epimedium) produces 1-foot masses of reddish green leaves and slipper-shaped yellow and red flowers. *E. grandiflorum* (longspur epimedium, bishop's hat) grows 1 foot tall with 1- to 2-inch red-, pink-, lavender-, or white-spurred flowers with red sepals and 2- to 3-inch leaves; 'Nanum' is 3 inches tall; 'Rose Queen' has large, deep pink flowers and foliage that emerges reddish and turns dark green as it matures; 'White Queen' has white flowers.

FALSE SOLOMON'S-SEAL
Smilacina

Light:	mostly shade
Plant type:	perennial
Hardiness:	Zones 3-7
Height:	2 to 3 feet
Soil and Moisture:	well-drained, moist, fertile
Interest:	flowers, foliage
Care:	easy

◀ Smilacina racemosa

A member of the lily family, false Solomon's-seal bears pyramidal flower panicles in spring on gracefully arching stems with oval leaves that have prominent parallel veins. Colorful red berries that are a favorite of wildlife follow in late summer to fall. Native to moist woodlands, false Solomon's-seal is best used for wildflower gardens and for naturalizing.

Growing and care:
False Solomon's-seal thrives best in deep soil in cool, moist, shady to mostly shady locations, such as along a stream or pond or along woodland paths. Amend the soil with compost, leaf mold, or peat moss. Propagate by dividing the rhizomes in fall, allowing at least one bud per segment. Replant with the bud facing up. Mulch with leaf litter to overwinter.

Selected species and varieties:
S. racemosa bears 6-inch-long creamy white flower clusters in mid- to late spring on arching stems 2 to 3 feet tall. It produces pointed, oval to lance-shaped leaves to 9 inches long, and small, pea-size green berries that turn red in fall.

FOAMFLOWER
Tiarella

Light:	mostly shade
Plant type:	perennial
Hardiness:	Zones 3-9
Height:	6 to 12 inches
Soil and Moisture:	well-drained, moist
Interest:	flowers, foliage
Care:	easy

◀ Tiarella cordifolia

Foamflowers have spikes of white frothy flowers that bloom in midspring, and are native to moist woodlands and stream banks in eastern North America. These plants produce stalks that rise out of low-growing mounds of attractive, sharp-lobed, fuzzy heart-shaped leaves that are medium green in summer and reddish bronze or dark purple in fall, and remain visible over winter. They make an exceptional ground cover, edging, or rock garden plant for shady spots, and are especially effective when massed.

Growing and care:
Foamflowers require additional water during dry spells. They grow best in slightly acid soil with a high organic content. Space plants 1 to 1½ feet apart; they will spread quickly by runners. Propagate by digging and replanting runners in spring or fall, or by sowing fresh seed in the garden in fall.

Selected species and varieties:
T. cordifolia (Allegheny foamflower) has compact clusters of tiny ¼-inch-wide star-shaped, five-petaled white flowers with long white stamens on 6- to 12-inch-tall stalks above neat mounds of lobed leaves from midspring to early summer; 'Major' bears salmon-red or wine-colored blossoms; 'Marmorata' has maroon flowers and bronze leaves that become marbled with purple in winter; 'Purpurea' has purple flowers.

FOXGLOVE
Digitalis

Light: mostly shade

Plant type: perennial, biennial

Hardiness: Zones 3-9

Height: 2 to 4 feet

Soil and Moisture: well-drained, moist

Interest: flowers

Care: easy to moderate

◀ Digitalis x mertonensis

Foxgloves produce 2- to 3-inch spotted tubular flowers that crowd along a stiff stalk from late spring to early summer. These short-lived perennials or biennials overwinter as a clump of attractive light green leaves. Evocative of English cottage gardens, foxgloves provide strong vertical accents for beds and borders. They are most effective when planted in clumps. They grow well in coastal gardens and make excellent cut flowers if picked when partially open.

Growing and care:

Foxgloves tolerate mostly sunny to shady locations but prefer mostly shady spots in soil amended with some organic matter. Space established plants 1 to 1½ feet apart. Propagate by seed sown ¼ inch deep in late summer, by division in fall, or by transplanted self-sown seedlings in early spring.

Selected species and varieties:

D. ferruginea (rusty foxglove) produces a basal clump of narrow, deeply veined dark green leaves, each up to 9 inches long. A leafy 3- to 4-foot flower stalk rises from the clump, bearing dense clusters of small yellowish blooms that open from mid- to late summer. Each flower is ½ to 1¼ inches long, yellow-brown, and netted with a rusty red. Tiny hairs fringe the flower lip. *D. grandiflora* (yellow foxglove) is a perennial with brown-spotted yellow flowers on 3-foot stalks that needs partial shade; 'Temple Bells' has large flowers. *D. x mertonensis* (strawberry foxglove) is a perennial with dark strawberry pink flowers neatly layered on 4-foot stems that is grown as a cool-season annual in the Southeast. *D. purpurea* (common foxglove) produces a broad clump of large, rough-textured woolly leaves from which an erect flower stem with smaller leaves emerges in early summer. The flower stalks range in size from 2 to 5 feet. The 2- to 3-inch pendulous flowers are borne in a one-sided cluster up to 2 feet long. Their colors include purple, pink, white, rust, or yellow, and their throats are often spotted; 'Alba' grows to 4 feet with white flowers; 'Apricot' grows to 3½ feet with flowers ranging from pale pink to bold apricot; 'Excelsior' grows to 4 feet with blooms borne all around the stem rather than on one side, in shades of purple, pink, white, cream, and yellow; 'Foxy' grows 2½ to 3 feet, with flowers in pastel shades from rose pink to white appearing the first year from seed; 'Giant Shirley' grows 5 feet or more, producing strong stems with large mottled blooms in shades of pink.

GAY-FEATHER
Liatris

Light:	mostly shade
Plant type:	perennial
Hardiness:	Zones 3-10
Height:	1 1/2 to 5 feet
Soil and Moisture:	well-drained, moist
Interest:	flowers
Care:	easy

◀ Liatris spicata

Gay-feathers are bold yet elegant plants with upright slender stalks topped with soft spikes of feathery flowers over clumps of grassy leaves. The 6- to 15-inch flower clusters open from top to bottom. They give a strong vertical accent to borders. Gay-feathers are superb for naturalizing in meadow gardens.

Growing and care:
Plant corms 3 to 4 inches deep in spring or fall in a well-worked soil amended with some organic matter. Space plants 1 to 2 feet apart in a sunny to mostly shady location. Propagate by separating and planting the tiny cormels that develop around mature corms.

Selected species and varieties:
L. ligulistylis has tufts of 3- to 5-foot stems with 1 1/2-inch clusters of rosy purple flowers from summer to fall and deep green, narrow leaves. *L. spicata* (spike gay-feather, button snakewort) has clumps 2 to 5 feet tall and 2 feet wide with very narrow 3- to 5-inch tapering leaves on erect, stout stems, and purple or rose flowers from mid- to late summer; 'Alba' is pure white; 'Kobold' is a 1 1/2- to 2-foot dwarf with dense heads of purple flowers tinged with burgundy.

GENTIAN
Gentiana

Light:	mostly shade
Plant type:	perennial
Hardiness:	Zones 3-8
Height:	2 inches to 3 feet
Soil and Moisture:	well-drained, moist to wet
Interest:	flowers
Care:	moderate to difficult

◀ Gentiana septemfida var. lagodechiana

Gentians are noted for their unique blossoms, which range from flaring bell-shaped forms of brilliant sapphire blue to more modest blue flowers that resemble unopened buds. The variability of this genus provides the gardener with plants that thrive in rock gardens, borders, or slightly alkaline fields.

Growing and care:
Gentians thrive in sunny to mostly shady locations in soil with abundant organic matter. Plant larger species 1 to 1 1/2 feet apart and smaller ones 4 to 12 inches apart. Propagate plants by mixing the fresh seed with dry, fine sand and spreading the mixture on the surface of the garden in spring. The seeds need light to germinate, so do not cover with soil. Divide clumps in early spring.

Selected species and varieties:
G. acaulis (stemless gentian) bears 2-inch bell-shaped sky blue flowers spotted with yellow in spring above thick rosettes of 2-inch leaves and 4-inch stems; Zones 4-8. *G. andrewsii* (closed gentian, bottle gentian) has clusters of closed blue flowers in late summer and fall that become purplish with age; forma *albiflora* has white flowers; Zones 5-8. *G. septemfida* (crested gentian) has small terminal clusters of pleated 2-inch bell-shaped blue flowers from mid- to late summer on 8- to 12-inch stems with erect or arching clumps; var. *lagodechiana* has deep blue flowers on 6- to 8-inch stems.

GERANIUM
Geranium

Light: mostly shade	
Plant type: perennial	
Hardiness: Zones 3-10	
Height: 9 inches to 2 feet	
Soil and Moisture: well-drained, moist to dry	
Interest: flowers, foliage, fragrance	
Care: easy to moderate	

◀ Geranium sanguineum

Geraniums have long been garden favorites for their bright five-petaled flowers in spring and summer and their spreading mounds of foliage. All have palmately lobed leaves, and some, such as *G. macrorrhizum*, which is the source of geranium oil, have strongly aromatic foliage. Geraniums are a versatile group of plants used in rock gardens and borders, as ground covers, or naturalized in meadows or woodland gardens. They sometimes are called hardy geraniums to distinguish them from the genus *Pelargonium,* also known as zonal geraniums.

Growing and care:
Plant geraniums in spring or fall, spacing them 1½ to 2 feet apart. Mulch after planting and fertilize lightly in spring. The plants flower best in mostly sunny locations but retain the best flower color in mostly shady spots. In regions with hot summers the plants need afternoon shade and supplemental water. Propagate geraniums by dividing clumps in spring every 3 to 4 years.

Selected species and varieties:
G. endressii 'Wargrave Pink' has 1- to 1½-inch bluish pink flowers with ragged 2- to 4-inch leaves divided into five segments and blossoming from spring to fall where summers are hot; Zones 4-8. *G. ibericum* (Iberian cranesbill) has 1- to 2-inch purple flowers from spring through summer on 1- to 1½-foot hairy stems clad with deeply lobed leaves; 'Album' has white flowers; Zones 5-8. *G.* x 'Johnson's Blue' has 15- to 18-inch leafy mounds with 1½- to 2-inch lavender-blue flowers traced with darker blue veins from spring to summer; Zones 5-8. *G. macrorrhizum* (bigroot geranium) produces 10- to 12-inch creeping stems bearing magenta flowers from late spring to early summer with very aromatic maple-shaped leaves that turn bright red in fall; 'Album' has white flowers; 'Bevan's Variety' has deep magenta flowers; Zones 3-8. *G. maculatum* (wild geranium, wild cranesbill, spotted cranesbill) has grayish maplelike leaves on 1- to 2-foot openly branched stems with 1-inch rose-purple to pale lilac flowers in late spring or early summer; Zones 3-7. *G.* x *oxonianum* grows 2 to 3 feet tall with slightly wrinkled, toothed leaves and pink summer flowers accented with darker-colored veins; 'A. T. Johnson' has pink flowers with a light silver cast; 'Rose Clair' has porcelain pink flowers in July on 1- to 2-foot stems; Zones 5-7. *G. psilostemon* (Armenian cranesbill) grows 1 to 2 feet tall with mounds of deeply toothed green leaves peppered in summer with bold magenta flowers marked with a prominent black eye; 'Bressingham Flair' has pink flowers on 1- to 3-foot stems; Zones 5-7. *G. sanguineum* (bloody cranesbill, blood-red cranesbill) bears solitary 1½-inch crimson flowers in spring and summer on 2-foot-wide mounds of gray-green leaves that turn red in fall; 'Album' has pure white flowers on 8- to 10-inch stems; 'Alpenglow' has dark green leaves and bright rose red flowers; 'Glenluce' bears clear pink blossoms on dense mounds of medium green leaves; var. *striatum* is a dwarf with soft pink flowers and purple veins; 'Splendens' is a vigorous grower with pearl-pink flowers accented with purple-red veins; Zones 4-9. *G. sylvaticum* (wood cranesbill) has crowded clusters of 1- to 1½-inch pinkish purple, violet-blue, or white flowers atop 1½- to 2-foot stems in late spring and summer; 'May-flower' has rich violet-blue flowers with white zones in the center; 'Nanum' has a low-growing habit and red flowers.

GOATSBEARD
Aruncus

Light: mostly shade

Plant type: perennial

Hardiness: Zones 3-7

Height: 1 to 6 feet

Soil and Moisture: well-drained, moist, fertile

Interest: flowers, foliage

Care: easy

◀ Aruncus dioicus

Goatsbeards bear dramatic 6- to 10-inch plumes of minute cream-colored flowers on 1- to 6-foot stems from midspring to early summer. After the flowers fade the tall mounds of deep green compound leaves provide a stately background for later-blooming plants. Goatsbeards are native to deciduous woodlands of the eastern and central United States and western Europe. The dwarf varieties often are mistaken for astilbes.

Growing and care:
Goatsbeards benefit from yearly additions of compost. The plants grow best in moist, fertile soil in light conditions ranging from mostly sun to mostly shade. Space plants 4 to 5 feet apart, and propagate by seed or from early-spring division of young plants.

Selected species and varieties:
A. dioicus (also listed as *A. sylvester*) has pinnately compound leaves bearing 20 or more 1- to 2½-inch dark green doubly toothed oval leaflets, and stems forming mounds up to 6 feet high with 4- to 16-inch-wide flower clusters borne at the tips of shoots and branches; 'Kneiffii' grows to about 3 feet high and has more finely divided foliage, giving it a more delicate appearance. *A. sinensis* is similar to *A. dioicus* but blooms a few weeks later and has more coarsely toothed leaves that are deep green overlain with light brown.

GOLDENROD
Solidago

Light: mostly shade

Plant type: perennial

Hardiness: Zones 3-9

Height: 3 to 4 feet

Soil and Moisture: well-drained, moist to dry

Interest: flowers, fragrance

Care: easy

◀ Solidago odora

Sweet goldenrod is an easy-to-grow perennial that artfully combines versatility with outstanding fall beauty. From summer into autumn, the tall, pliant stems are graced with delicate plumes of cheery yellow flowers and scores of smooth, lance-shaped green leaves that emit an anise fragrance when bruised. The blossoms add an airy touch to fresh or dried arrangements and have long been used to make a stunning yellow-colored dye for cloth. The leaves are used fresh or dried to make a soothing, anise flavored tea. Goldenrod is excellent in sunny to mostly shady wildflower meadows, herb gardens and rock gardens.

Growing and care:
Sow sweet goldenrod seeds or divide mature plants in early spring, spacing seedlings or divisions 12 to 15 inches apart. Goldenrod spreads rapidly and can be restrained easily by planting in large containers or surrounded with garden edging sunk into the soil. Shear plants to the ground in late winter or early spring before new growth begins.

Selected species and varieties:
S. odora (sweet goldenrod) bears slender single stems lined with glossy, narrow 2- to 4-inch smooth-edged leaves and tipped with one-sided 8- to 12-inch plumes of ¼-inch yellow flowers.

GOLDENSTAR
Chrysogonum

Light: mostly shade

Plant type: perennial

Hardiness: Zones 5-9

Height: 4 to 9 inches

Soil and Moisture: well-drained, moist

Interest: flowers, foliage

Care: moderate

◀ Chrysogonum virginianum var. virginianum

The deep green foliage of goldenstar provides a lush background for its bright yellow star-shaped flowers, which appear from late spring through summer. Its low-growing spreading habit makes it useful as a ground cover, for edging at the front of a border, or as an accent in a mostly shady rock garden.

Growing and care:

Goldenstar grows well in most soils with average fertility and produces more compact growth in poor soils. Mulch in spring and fall to retain moisture and keep soil cool. Flowering may stop during hot weather even if supplemental water is applied. For use as a ground cover, space plants 1 foot apart. Propagate by dividing the plants in spring in northern areas and in fall in warmer zones.

Selected species and varieties:

C. virginianum var. *virginianum* reaches 6 to 9 inches, with dark green leaves that are bluntly serrated along upright spreading stems, and flowers 1½ inches across that bloom throughout spring in warm areas, well into summer in cooler zones; var. *australe* is similar to var. *virginianum* but more prostrate.

HELLEBORE
Helleborus

Light: mostly shade

Plant type: perennial

Hardiness: Zones 4-9

Height: 2 inches to 1½ feet

Soil and Moisture: well-drained, moist

Interest: flowers, foliage

Care: moderate

◀ Helleborus orientalis

Hellebores have 2- to 3-inch cup-shaped flowers in subtle hues of creamy white, pink, and deep maroon nestled around attractive, deeply lobed evergreen leaves. They are valued for their late-winter or early-spring flowers, which appear when little else is in bloom. Hellebores are excellent for borders and paths and can be massed as a ground cover. The solitary blossoms make long-lasting cut flowers.

Growing and care:

Plant hellebores in spring in the North and in fall in the South, in full or partial shade, spacing them 1 to 2 feet apart. Mulch lightly in spring and again in fall. Give extra water during hot, dry periods. Propagate by seed or division in early summer, being careful not to damage the fragile roots. Plants also self-sow.

Selected species and varieties:

H. niger (Christmas rose) is 12 to 15 inches tall with nodding, creamy white flowers tinged with pink around prominent yellow stamens in late fall in the South and early spring in the North; 'Louis Cobbett' has white flowers stained with pink; Zones 5-8. *H. orientalis* (Lenten rose) is 15 to 18 inches tall with nodding clusters of two to six 2-inch cream, pink, maroon, or plum flowers from early to midspring; 'Queen of the Night' has blossoms with velvety deep red petals and a shower of bright yellow stamens.

HOSTA
Hosta

Light: mostly shade	
Plant type: perennial	
Hardiness: Zones 3-9	
Height: 15 inches to 4 feet	
Soil and Moisture: well-drained, moist	
Interest: flowers, foliage	
Care: easy	

◀ Hosta 'Gold Standard'

Hostas are prized mainly for their spreading clumps of attractive foliage, which make them ideal for textural and color accents in perennial beds and borders. The plants bear trumpet-shaped flowers along strong stalks in summer in colors ranging from white to lavender. Hosta is excellent in borders or as a ground cover in mostly to fully shady places.

Growing and care:
Good drainage is essential, especially in winter. Although most hostas thrive in deep shade, variegated and blue forms need bright shade to hold their color. *H.* 'Francee' tolerates some sun. Remove flowers to improve foliage and prevent crossbreeding. Propagate by division in fall or early spring. Deer love to nibble hosta and plantings should be protected.

Selected species and varieties:
H. 'Francee' has dark green heart-shaped leaves with white margins, growing to 1½ feet tall, with lavender flowers on 2-foot stems; 'Gold Standard' grows to 2½ feet tall and has veined yellow leaves with green margins, and violet flowers; 'Krossa Regal' is 4 feet tall, with veined blue leaves up to 8 inches long and 5 inches wide, and lilac flowers atop 5-foot stalks. *H. sieboldiana* 'Frances Williams' grows to 3 feet tall, bearing foot-long crinkled leaves with yellow margins, and lilac flowers amid the leaves.

JOE-PYE WEED
Eupatorium

Light: mostly shade	
Plant type: perennial	
Hardiness: Zones 3-9	
Height: 2 to 6 feet	
Soil and Moisture: well-drained, wet to moist	
Interest: flowers	
Care: easy	

◀ Eupatorium maculatum 'Atropurpureum'

These stately, robust natives to eastern North American wetlands display rounded clusters of small, misty, purplish pink or white flowers that attract honeybees, butterflies, and hummingbirds in late summer. Joe-Pye weed is ideal for planting near water elements or in bog gardens, or for naturalizing in wet meadows.

Growing and care:
Plant Joe-Pye weed in spring or fall in moist to wet soil in full sun to mostly shade. Space plants 2 to 3 feet apart. Divide clumps every 3 years in spring. Joe-Pye weed does not need mulching or fertilizing and is virtually pest-free.

Selected species and varieties:
E. maculatum (spotted Joe-Pye weed) bears flat-topped clusters of pink or purple late-summer flowers on 4- to 6-foot stems spotted with purple; 'Atropurpureum' has wine red flowers; Zones 3-6. *E. perfoliatum* (boneset) has loose clusters of antique white flowers from late summer to fall on 2- to 5-foot hairy stems piercing the base of the paired, stemless bright green leaves. *E. purpureum* (Joe-Pye weed) produces dome-topped clusters of pale pink to rose-purple flowers from late summer to fall on 3- to 6-foot green and purple stems above whorls of vanilla-scented leaves; Zones 4-9. *E. rugosum* (white snakeroot) grows to 5 feet with drooping terminal clusters of tiny white flowers from midsummer to early fall.

LADY'S-MANTLE
Alchemilla

Light:	mostly shade
Plant type:	perennial
Hardiness:	Zones 3-8
Height:	4 inches to 1 1/2 feet
Soil and Moisture:	well-drained, moist, fertile
Interest:	flowers, foliage
Care:	easy

◀ Alchemilla mollis

Lady's-mantle carpets the ground with large cupped leaves that reveal silvery undersides when tipped by a breeze. Use the frothy clusters of tiny greenish flowers that rise above the semievergreen foliage in summer as fillers in fresh or dried arrangements. Young leaves are sometimes tossed with salads or added to tea; they also yield a green dye. Lady's-mantle was traditionally used in herbal remedies.

Growing and care:
Sow seed in spring; transplant divisions or the freely self-sown seedlings in spring or fall. Cut plants back hard to keep them compact; they recover readily. Plants can tolerate full sun in cool, moist northern areas. To dry, cut flowers just as they open and hang in bunches in a well-ventilated area.

Selected species and varieties:
A. alpina (Alpine lady's mantle) has broad leaves composed of pointed, lobed leaflets arranged like fingers on a hand and clusters of green flowers on creeping plants 4 to 8 inches tall, ideal for informal edgings. *A. mollis* [also called *A. vulgaris*] (lady's mantle) has scalloped fan-shaped leaves up to 6 inches across and yellow-green flowers on plants to 1 1/2 feet tall.

LEADWORT
Plumbago

Light:	mostly shade
Plant type:	perennial
Hardiness:	Zones 9-10
Height:	6 to 8 feet
Soil and Moisture:	well-drained, moist
Interest:	flowers
Care:	easy to moderate

◀ Plumbago auriculata

Leadwort is a reliable large evergreen shrub that develops a mounded habit with long vinelike branches. Flowers are azure blue or white, and under ideal conditions they will appear year round.

Growing and care:
Leadwort is a mounding shrub and can be maintained through pruning as a dense, low hedge or foundation plant. If trained it will climb a trellis or wall, and it is also well suited as a tall ground cover for large, well-drained slopes. Leadwort thrives in full sun but tolerates light shade in hot areas; it tolerates coastal conditions as well but is sensitive to frost. Prune the oldest canes to the ground each year in early spring, and pinch new growth to encourage branching.

Selected species and varieties:
P. auriculata (Cape leadwort, Cape plumbago) grows 6 to 8 feet tall, spreading 8 to 12 feet or more. Leaves are 1 to 2 inches long, medium to light green, evergreen; flowers are 1 inch across in 3- to 4-inch clusters, blue or white. The main blooming season is from early spring through fall.

LEWISIA
Lewisia

Light: mostly shade	
Plant type: perennial	
Hardiness: Zones 3-8	
Height: 4 to 12 inches	
Soil and Moisture: well-drained, dry	
Interest: flowers	
Care: difficult	

◀ Lewisia cotyledon

Lewisias are low-growing perennials that inhabit rocky slopes and open woods of the western United States. They are excellent choices for rock gardens.

Growing and care:

Most lewisias prefer partial shade to thrive, yet *L. rediva* does well in mostly sunny locations. All species must have soil with excellent drainage. A mulch of gravel or stone chips 1 to 2 inches deep helps control crown rot. Keep soil moist but avoid wetting the foliage when watering. Starting plants from seed is often difficult and seedlings should grow for at least 1 year in containers before planting out.

Selected species and varieties:

L. columbiana (bitterroot) produces an evergreen rosette of flat, dark green leaves with branched clusters of pink-veined white or pink flowers on 4- to 12-inch stalks in spring; Zones 4-8. *L. cotyledon* (broadleaf lewisia) has neat rosettes of spoon-shaped leaves and loose clusters of white- or pink-striped flowers on 1-foot stalks in early summer; Zones 6-8. *L. rediviva* (bitterroot) has a rosette of cylindrical leaves that appears in late summer and remains green over winter. In early spring showy rose-colored flowers up to 2 inches across are borne on short stems. After flowering the plant goes dormant; Zones 4-8.

LOBELIA
Lobelia

Light: mostly shade	
Plant type: perennial	
Hardiness: Zones 4-8	
Height: 2 to 4 feet	
Soil and Moisture: well-drained, moist, fertile	
Interest: flowers, foliage	
Care: easy	

◀ Lobelia siphilitica

Lobelias are stunning perennials with strong, upright habits and bold flowers. The stout stems are covered with dark green leaves and topped with spikes of tubular flowers ranging from pastel blues to shocking scarlet. Lobelias are easy to grow and provide dynamic color to shady borders or woodland gardens.

Growing and care:

Plant lobelia in the garden in spring when soil is cool. Space plants 1 to 1½ feet apart in soil well amended with organic matter. Mulch around plants to keep roots cool and retain soil moisture. Provide extra water during dry periods. Propagate by sowing seeds in fall or by division in spring in northern areas and in fall in southern regions.

Selected species and varieties:

L. cardinalis (cardinal flower) is a strong-growing perennial usually 2 to 4 feet tall, but may reach 6 feet, with upright stalks of scarlet flowers in summer or fall; 'Compliment Scarlet' has vivid scarlet flowers on strong 3- to 4-foot stems in midsummer; Zones 5-8. *L.* x *gerardii* 'Verrariensis' has deep violet flowers along upright 3-foot stalks from mid- to late summer. *L. siphilitica* (great blue lobelia) is a perennial with blue tubular flowers on erect 2- to 3-foot leafy stems from late summer to early fall; Zones 4-7.

MARSH MARIGOLD
Caltha

Light: mostly shade	
Plant type: perennial	
Hardiness: Zones 3-8	
Height: 10 inches to 2 feet	
Soil and Moisture: moist to wet	
Interest: flowers, foliage	
Care: easy	

◀ Caltha palustris

As its common name implies, the marsh marigold is an appropriate perennial for wet soils, where its clusters of brightly hued 2-inch yellow flowers provide an impressive display in spring. The flowers form on long stems that are held above the clump of lush dark green foliage. In addition to providing the perfect background for its flowers and subsequent seedpods, the mound of leaves remains attractive well into summer. It makes a good choice for edging a pond or water garden, or in a bog garden, where it can be kept constantly moist.

Growing and care:

While marsh marigold will grow in moist soil, it performs best in a wet location especially in the spring. Unlike many bog plants, it does not become invasive. Plants go dormant in late summer, after which some drying out of the soil can be tolerated. Propagate marsh marigold by division in early spring.

Selected species and varieties:

C. palustris (marsh marigold, kingcup) produces a 1- to 1½-foot mound of 3- to 4-inch-wide dark green leaves, and round green buds that open in midspring to 2-inch buttercup yellow flowers with five showy sepals borne on upright stems; 'Alba' bears single white flowers with bold yellow stamens; 'Flore Pleno' bears abundant double flowers that are showier than those of the species.

MASTERWORT
Astrantia

Light: mostly shade	
Plant type: perennial	
Hardiness: Zones 4-8	
Height: 2 to 3 feet	
Soil and Moisture: well-drained, moist, fertile	
Interest: flowers	
Care: easy	

◀ Astrantia major

Masterwort is a charming, distinctive plant with long-blooming clover-shaped blossoms framed with a starry collar of bracts. The pink, violet, yellow, or white flowers appear in spring through summer and are held on strong stems well above the dark green deeply lobed foliage. Masterwort is a nice addition to cottage gardens or at the back of perennial borders. The plants make excellent cut flowers for fresh floral arrangements.

Growing and care:

Plant masterwort in well-worked soil that has some organic matter. Space plants 1½ feet apart. Provide extra moisture during periods of hot, dry weather. In warm, dry regions mulch plants in spring and fall. Propagate from seed sown in early spring or by division in spring or fall. Seed should not be covered, as it requires light to germinate. Of the two methods, division is usually preferred, as the seed can take up to 2 months to germinate.

Selected species and varieties:

A. major (great masterwort) bears unusual creamy white 2- to 3-inch blossoms tinged pink by the collar of purple bracts below the petals; 'Rosea' has rosy pink blooms suitable for drying and pressing; 'Sunningdale Variegated' has stripes of cream and yellow on lobed green leaves.

MEADOW RUE
Thalictrum

Light: mostly shade	
Plant type: perennial	
Hardiness: Zones 5-9	
Height: 2 to 7 feet	
Soil and Moisture: well-drained, moist	
Interest: flowers, foliage	
Care: moderate	

◀ Thalictrum delavayi

These graceful plants are grown both for their clusters of airy, fluffy blossoms displayed over several weeks, and for their deeply cut, lacy foliage, which adds a soft accent to the garden the rest of the growing season. Plant either species of meadow rue listed below for a longer season of flowering in borders, rock gardens, and wildflower informal gardens. They also make good cut flowers.

Growing and care:
Meadow rues prefer morning sun and soil that never dries out. Space *T. aquilegifolium* 1 foot apart and *T. delavayi* 2 feet apart. Plants benefit from staking, especially if subjected to wind. Propagate by fresh seed sown in fall, or by division in spring.

Selected species and varieties:
T. aquilegifolium (columbine meadow rue) grows 2 to 3 feet tall with delicate, rounded dark green leaves and large clusters of creamy flowers with mauve centers in late spring and early summer; 'White Cloud' is slightly taller than the species, with dense foliage and clouds of white flowers. *T. delavayi* [also listed as *T. dipterocarpum*] (Yunnan meadow rue) is clump forming, growing 4 to 7 feet tall with showy clusters of lavender-blue or rose-purple flowers accented with bright yellow stamens in late summer and early fall; 'Hewitt's Double' has multipetaled flowers.

MERRY-BELLS
Uvularia

Light: mostly shade	
Plant type: perennial	
Hardiness: Zones 3-8	
Height: 10 inches to 2 feet	
Soil and Moisture: well-drained, moist, fertile	
Interest: flowers	
Care: moderate	

◀ Uvularia grandiflora

Merry-bells are robust woodland perennials with drooping, medium green leaves and elegant yellow or cream-colored flowers in spring. These hardy wildflowers are native to the moist forests of eastern North America, where they grow equally well in well-drained uplands and along streams and marshes. The plants spread quickly once established and are beautiful additions to wildflower gardens, especially when intermingled with plantings of spring beauty.

Growing and care:
Grow merry-bells in moist, shaded locations and incorporate organic matter into the soil prior to planting. Mulch with leaves in winter. Propagate by seed sown immediately after ripening or by division in fall—although the plants grow best if left undisturbed.

Selected species and varieties:
U. grandiflora (big merry-bells) have arching stems 1½ to 2 feet tall with lemon yellow flowers 1½ inches long. The petals are slightly twisted; Zones 3-8. *U. sessilifolia* (little merry-bells, wild oats) grows 10 to 15 inches tall with cream-colored inch-long flowers; Zones 4-8.

MONKSHOOD
Aconitum

Light: mostly shade

Plant type: perennial

Hardiness: Zones 3-8

Height: 2 to 4 feet

Soil and Moisture: well-drained, moist, fertile

Interest: flowers

Care: moderate

◀ Aconitum x bicolor 'Spark'

The vivid to somber hues of monkshoods and their glossy dark green deeply cut leaves make striking additions to any perennial border or naturalized area. Blooming in summer to fall when there are few other blue flowers in the garden, the tall spikes of flowers also make excellent cuttings. Caution: All parts of the plant are poisonous.

Growing and care:

Though monkshoods prefer shade as a rule, they especially need it during hot summer afternoons. They tolerate full sun only in constantly moist soil in cool climates. Add peat moss, compost, or leaf mold to soil before planting, and space plants 1½ feet apart. Taller varieties need staking. Divide clumps in spring or fall.

Selected species and varieties:

A. anthora has clusters of yellow flowers on 2-foot stems. *A.* x *bicolor* 'Spark' bears violet-blue flowers on 4-foot stems in mid- to late summer. *A.* x *cammarum* 'Bicolor' grows 2 to 4 feet tall with blue and white flowers. *A. carmichaelii* 'Arendsii' (azure monkshood) has large blue flowers on 3- to 4-foot stems. *A. napellus* (common monkshood, Turk's-cap) grows 4 feet tall with indigo blue flowers; 'Carneum' has pink flowers.

OBEDIENT PLANT
Physostegia

Light: mostly shade

Plant type: perennial

Hardiness: Zones 4-10

Height: 1½ to 4 feet

Soil and Moisture: well-drained, moist to dry

Interest: flowers

Care: easy

◀ Physostegia virginiana 'Vivid'

The wandlike stems of obedient plants, topped with conical spikes of delicate pink, lavender, or white flowers, grow in spreading clumps. The flower spikes have four vertical rows of tubular flowers that look like miniature snapdragons. *Physostegia* is called obedient plant because its flowers stay put when moved laterally, rather than springing back to their original positions. Obedient plants make excellent cut flowers, and are used as a filler in beds and borders or for naturalizing in wildflower meadows.

Growing and care:

Obedient plants tolerate most growing conditions but can be invasive when grown in sunny, moist borders because of their vigorously spreading stolons. They are best behaved in mostly shady locations or in meadows. Space plants 1½ to 2 feet apart. Propagate by seed or division in early spring or late fall.

Selected species and varieties:

P. virginiana (obedience) grows 2 to 4 feet tall with dense clusters of 8- to 12-inch two-lipped white, deep pink, or lavender-pink summer flowers and dark green, wavy-edged narrowly lance-shaped leaves; 'Bouquet Rose' has light pink flowers; 'Summer Snow' has pure white flowers in early summer; 'Summer Spire' produces deep pink flowers; 'Vivid' has dark green leaves beneath spires of bright pink flowers.

PATRINIA
Patrinia

Light:	mostly shade
Plant type:	perennial
Hardiness:	Zones 5-9
Height:	2 to 6 feet
Soil and Moisture:	well-drained, moist
Interest:	flowers, seedpods
Care:	easy

◀ Patrinia scabiosifolia

Patrinia produces large, airy sprays of sun yellow flowers late in summer and fall, followed by bright yellow seedpods on orange stems. This very ornamental plant is well suited to the middle or rear of a perennial border or a natural garden, where it combines particularly well with ornamental grasses. Patrinia flowers can be cut for long-lasting indoor arrangements.

Growing and care:
Plant patrinias in moist, well-drained soil in light shade. Taller types often require staking. Once established, patrinias are long-lived perennials that frequently self-sow. Deadhead spent flowers to limit seed production if desired. Seedlings can be transplanted to other areas of the garden in spring.

Selected species and varieties:
P. scabiosifolia is 3 to 6 feet tall, with ruffled, pinnately divided 6- to 10-inch leaves that form a large basal mound, and yellow flowers that form 2-inch clusters held well above foliage in late summer and fall; 'Nagoya' grows 2 to 3 feet with a compact habit and flowers that are almost fluorescent yellow.

PINK
Dianthus

Light:	mostly shade
Plant type:	perennial
Hardiness:	Zones 4-8
Height:	3 to 24 inches
Soil and Moisture:	well-drained, moist
Interest:	flowers, fragrance
Care:	easy

◀ D. gratianopolitanus 'Karlik'

Pinks are old-fashioned perennials whose fragrant, clove-scented flowers have been grown in gardens for generations. The cheerful blossoms come in a range of pastel shades above attractive, grassy blue-green foliage that is evergreen in mild climates. Pinks are reliable, easy-to-grow plants that are excellent in rock gardens, edgings, borders, or when massed in group plantings.

Growing and care:
Plant in well-worked soil that has had some organic matter added. Space pinks 1 to 1½ feet apart. Keep soil moderately moist but not wet. Cut stems back after bloom and shear mat-forming types in the fall to promote dense growth. Maintain vigor by division every 2 to 3 years. Propagate from seed, from cuttings taken in early summer, or by division in spring.

Selected species and varieties:
D. x *allwoodii* (Allwood pink) has single or double flowers in a wide range of colors that grow for 2 months above gray-green leaves in compact mounds 1 to 2 feet tall; 'Aqua' grows white double blooms atop 1-foot stems. *D. alpinus* (Alpine pink) is a dwarf variety of Allwood pink; 'Doris' grows very fragrant salmon-colored double flowers with darker pink centers on 1-foot stems; 'Robin' has coral red flowers. *D. barbatus* (sweet William) is a biennial species that self-seeds so reliably that it performs like a perennial; unlike other pinks, it

(continued)

produces flowers in flat clusters and without fragrance; 'Harlequin' grows pink and white flowers; 'Indian Carpet' has single flowers in a mix of colors on 10-inch stems. *D. deltoides* (maiden pink) bears ¾-inch red or pink flowers on 1-foot stems above 6- to 12-inch-high mats of small bright green leaves; 'Brilliant' has scarlet flowers; 'Flashing Light' ('Leuchtfunk') has ruby red flowers. *D. gratianopolitanus* (cheddar pink) has 1-inch-wide flowers in shades of pink and rose on compact mounds of blue-green foliage 9 to 12 inches high; 'Karlik' has fragrant deep pink fringed flowers; 'Tiny Rubies' has dark pink double blooms on plants just 4 inches tall. *D. plumarius* (cottage pink) has fragrant single or semi-double flowers 1½ inches across in shades of pink and white or bicolors above 1- to 1½-foot-high mats of evergreen leaves; 'Essex Witch' produces fragrant salmon, pink, or white flowers.

RODGERSIA
Rodgersia

◀ Rodgersia pinnata

Light: mostly shade	
Plant type: perennial	
Hardiness: Zones 5-7	
Height: 2 to 6 feet	
Soil and Moisture: well-drained, moist to wet	
Interest: flowers, foliage	
Care: easy to moderate	

Rodgersia is a coarse-textured perennial with tiers of dark green compound leaves, pliant stems, and billowy plumes of creamy white flowers. The feathery blossoms and rough-looking foliage add interest to the back of the shady border and look stunning when planted near water gardens, streams, and ponds.

Growing and care:
Space rodgersia 3 feet apart in soil that is very moist or constantly wet, such as at the edge of streams and ponds. In colder climates, provide winter protection by mulching. Propagate by division in early spring, leaving the soil intact around each section.

Selected species and varieties:
R. aesculifolia (fingerleaf rodgersia) has bronzy green coarsely toothed horse-chestnut-like leaves that are arranged like fingers on a hand and arise from 3- to 6-foot stems topped with creamy white or pink flower plumes; Zones 5-6. *R. pinnata* (featherleaf rodgersia) produces plumes of buff pink flowers that emerge from late spring to midsummer above bronze-tinted dark green leaves with finely serrated margins on 3- to 4-foot stems; 'Superba' has very large red flowers. *R. podophylla* (bronzeleaf rodgersia) has finger-shaped leaves that are green at first before turning to metallic bronze in summer, borne on 3- to 5-foot stems with yellowish white 1-foot plumes; Zones 5-6.

RUELLIA
Ruellia

Light: mostly shade	
Plant type: perennial	
Hardiness: Zones 4-9	
Height: 1 to 3 feet	
Soil and Moisture: well-drained, sandy, dry	
Interest: flowers	
Care: easy	

◀ Ruellia caroliniensis

Ruellias are perennials found growing wild in open woods in the eastern United States. The plants produce decorative, deep green leaves and loose clusters of funnel-shaped flowers in shades of lavender, violet, or red. The plants blossom for a few weeks in summer and sporadically until fall. Ruellias add a delicate touch to wildflower meadows, herbaceous borders, and woodland edges.

Growing and care:
Plant in spring after soil has warmed. Ruellia prefers mostly sun to mostly shade while wild pertunia thrives in full sun to mostly shady spots. Space plants about 1½ to 2 feet apart. Water thoroughly, allowing soil to dry out between waterings. Ruellias prefer dry soils that are sandy or rocky but will adapt to other types of soils as long as they are not too moist. Propagate by cuttings taken in summer or by division in fall.

Selected species and varieties:
R. caroliniensis (ruellia) has clusters of two to four light purple flowers near the tops of unbranched stems 2 to 3 feet tall throughout summer; Zones 6-9. *R. humilis* (wild petunia) bears showy 2-inch lavender to purple flowers throughout summer and fall on compact bushy plants 1 to 2 feet tall.

SHOOTING-STAR
Dodecatheon

Light: mostly shade	
Plant type: perennial	
Hardiness: Zones 4-8	
Height: 4 to 20 inches	
Soil and Moisture: well-drained, moist to dry	
Interest: flowers	
Care: easy to moderate	

◀ Dodecatheon meadia

Shooting-stars are elegant, dainty wildflowers that grow in moist, open woods, on prairies, and on rocky slopes. These perennials have a basal rosette of rich green leaves and leafless stalks bearing an array of showy flowers with sharply backswept petals. Shooting-stars are a nice addition to the woodland wildflower garden or the shady border.

Growing and care:
Shooting-stars are easy to grow if they are given the proper conditions. Give *D. dentatum* a moist, mostly shady site. *D. meadia* prefers light, sandy soil with abundant moisture while in bloom, in mid- to late spring and drier conditions in fall and winter. Grow *D. amethystinum* in moist, well-drained alkaline soil in partial shade. Mulch plants in spring and keep soil moist while plants are actively growing. Propagation by seed is quite difficult and new plants can most easily be obtained by division in fall.

Selected species and varieties:
D. amethystinum [also called *D. pulchellum*] (amethyst shooting-star) bears rose-crimson flowers on 8- to 16-inch stalks in late spring; Zones 4-7. *D. dentatum* (dwarf shooting-star) has white flowers with a purple spot at the base of the petals on 4- to 14-inch stalks above crinkled, toothed leaves. *D. meadia* (shooting-star) has white to deep pink flowers on stalks up to 20 inches; Zones 5-8.

SPIDERWORT
Tradescantia

Light: mostly shade

Plant type: perennial

Hardiness: Zones 3-10

Height: 10 inches to 3 feet

Soil and Moisture: well-drained, moist, fertile

Interest: flowers, foliage

Care: easy to moderate

◀ Tradescantia ohiensis

Found in open woods and on prairies, spiderworts are upright or trailing perennials whose flowers have three wide petals and showy stamens. The flowers can be blue, pink, or white and have three petals nestled among a cluster of buds atop a slender stem. The glossy green leaves provide a soft backdrop to other plants after the flowers have faded.

Growing and care:

Plant spiderworts in a shady spot in well-drained humus-rich soil. Space plants 1 to 1½ feet apart. Propagate by seed, stem cuttings taken at anytime, or division. Spiderworts are easy to grow, reliable, and virtually pest-free.

Selected species and varieties:

T. bracteata (bracted spiderwort) has clusters of blue-violet flowers surrounded by leaflike bracts on erect 10- to 16-inch stems with grasslike foliage in late spring to early summer; Zones 3-8. *T. ohiensis* (Ohio spiderwort) has blue flowers clustered at the tops of erect branching stems 2 to 3 feet tall from spring to summer in warm climates and summer in cooler zones; Zones 4-10. *T. virginiana* (Virginia spiderwort) bears blue to blue-violet flowers 1½ to 3 inches wide from spring to summer on a dense clump of branching stems up to 3 feet tall with narrow bright green leaves 1 foot long; Zones 4-10.

TOAD LILY
Tricyrtis

Light: mostly shade

Plant type: perennial

Hardiness: Zones 5-9

Height: 2 to 3 feet

Soil and Moisture: well-drained, moist, fertile

Interest: flowers, foliage

Care: moderate

◀ Tricyrtis hirta

Unusually shaped toad lily flowers point upward from the leaf base in white or pinkish sprays that arch above clumps of dark green leaves. The bullet-shaped flower buds open in summer or fall to reveal six thin, flaring, spotted petals that are joined at the base. The blooming season is relatively long, lasting up to 6 weeks. Toad lilies are a good choice for shady perennial borders, and woodland or shady rock gardens.

Growing and care:

Space rhizome pieces 1 to 1½ feet apart in humus-rich loam. Remove dead leaves in late fall. In Zone 7 and colder regions, mulch plants after the ground freezes to protect from heaving. Propagate by division in spring or fall.

Selected species and varieties:

T. formosana (Formosa toad lily) grows 1 to 2 feet tall with shiny 5-inch deep green leaves and clusters of 1-inch white to light pink flowers with yellow throats and dark purple spots at their tips; Zones 6-9. *T. hirta* (hairy toad lily) is hairy, growing 2 to 3 feet tall with 6-inch lance-shaped leaves and waxy 1-inch bell-shaped creamy white flowers spotted with red or purple; 'Alba' has pure white flowers; 'Variegata' produces dark green leaves with white veins.

TURTLEHEAD
Chelone

Light:	mostly shade
Plant type:	perennial
Hardiness:	Zones 3-9
Height:	1 to 5 feet
Soil and Moisture:	well-drained, wet to moist, fertile
Interest:	flowers
Care:	moderate

◀ Chelone lyonii

The unique, tubular white, pink, or rose flowers of *Chelone* resemble turtles' heads and have a puckered upper lip and a bearded lower lip. They are borne in a raceme atop straight, smooth 3- to 5-foot stems with dark green lance-shaped leaves. Turtleheads are native to marshes, stream banks, and moist woodlands of the eastern, southeastern, and western United States. They are ideally suited to bog gardens and wet spots in wildflower gardens and meadows.

Growing and care:
Turtleheads can be grown in ordinary garden soil enriched with compost or peat moss. Space plants 8 inches apart and add a layer of mulch in late spring. *C. glabra* benefits from staking or being planted with other tall species that it can use for support. *C. lyonii* is a native to the Southeast and tolerates drier conditions better than other species. Propagate turtleheads by spring division, summer cuttings, or seed planted in fall.

Selected species and varieties:
C. glabra (white turtlehead) grows 3 to 5 feet tall with clusters of 1½-inch white to pale pink late summer flowers and 6-inch lance-shaped leaves; Zones 3-8. *C. lyonii* (pink turtlehead) grows 1 to 3 feet tall with 4- to 7-inch dark green oval leaves and 1-inch rose-violet flowers from summer to fall.

VIOLET
Viola

Light:	mostly shade
Plant type:	perennial
Hardiness:	Zones 3-9
Height:	2 to 10 inches
Soil and Moisture:	well-drained, moist
Interest:	flowers, fragrance
Care:	easy

◀ Viola tricolor

Violets have dainty five-petaled flowers borne on thin stems. The flowers always have a prominent nectar-filled spur projecting back from the lower petal. These versatile plants often have attractive heart-shaped leaves that form low mounds. Their rainbow of colors and long season of bloom make them perfect for edgings or borders, and for growing in containers.

Growing and care:
Sow seed indoors 3 months before planting in the garden. Plant in spring or fall in soil rich in organic matter. Space plants 6 to 12 inches apart. Fertilize once a month from late spring to summer. Provide plants with full shade in areas with hot summers, and partial shade in cooler regions.

Selected species and varieties:
V. cornuta (horned violet, tufted pansy) grows 5 to 10 inches tall, bearing pale to deep violet-purple pansylike flowers in spring and early summer, and oval, toothed evergreen leaves; 'Alba' has white flowers; 'Atropurpurea' bears dark purple blooms with small yellow centers; 'Chantreyland' has pale apricot-orange flowers; 'Cuty' bears prolific bouquets of flowers in combinations of purple, white, and lavender; Zones 5-8. *V. tricolor* (Johnny-jump-up) grows 2 to 8 inches tall with ½-inch violet, blue, and yellow flat-faced flowers from spring through early summer.

AMAZON LILY
Eucharis

Light: mostly shade	
Plant type: bulb	
Hardiness: Zones 9-10	
Height: 1 to 2 feet	
Soil and Moisture: well-drained, moist	
Interest: flowers, fragrance	
Care: moderate	

◄ Eucharis grandiflora

Amazon lilies are stunning, bold additions to any garden, with clusters of highly fragrant flowers that resemble daffodils. The blossoms rise from clumps of attractive, broad evergreen leaves with wavy edges. Amazon lilies thrive in regions with hot, humid summers where they are perfect for beds and borders. In northern regions the plants can be potted in containers and grown indoors.

Growing and care:

Outdoors, set bulbs with their necks at the soil line, spacing the bulbs 8 to 10 inches apart in a mostly shady location. The plants need high humidity and temperatures above 60°F to thrive, and they bloom best when crowded or potbound. Indoors, space bulbs 3 inches apart in pots, allowing three or four bulbs to each pot. To force, maintain bulbs at 80°F or higher for 4 weeks, then lower temperatures 10°F for another 12 weeks. Raise temperatures again to induce blooming. Propagate by removing and planting the bulb offsets.

Selected species and varieties:

E. grandiflora (Eucharist lily) bears clusters of large, drooping white flowers up to 5 inches across above leaves a foot long and 6 inches wide.

ARUM
Arum

Light: mostly shade	
Plant type: bulb	
Hardiness: Zones 5-9	
Height: 1 to 1½ feet	
Soil and Moisture: well-drained, moist, fertile	
Interest: flowers, foliage	
Care: easy	

◄ Arum italicum 'Pictum'

Arum makes a good specimen plant for perennial borders and woodland areas. Because of its clumping habit it also makes a fine container plant. The broad arrow-shaped leaves emerge in fall and, in milder zones, remain all winter. Callalike flowers in shades of cream, green, or purple atop erect 1½-foot leafless stalks in spring or early summer and precede upright clusters of colorful berries. Caution: All parts of the plant are poisonous.

Growing and care:

Arum is easy to grow in mostly sun to mostly shady locations and thrives in well-worked soil amended with some rotted manure or compost. Set tubers about 3 inches deep and 8 to 12 inches apart. Once established the plants spread quickly. Top-dress lightly with compost in fall. To propagate divide large clumps in spring or fall.

Selected species and varieties:

A. italicum (Italian arum) bears creamy to yellow flowers in late spring followed by upright clusters of orange-red berries in summer on a 1- to 1½-foot-high clump of foot-long glossy green leaves with pale veins; 'Marmoratum' has very large leaves marbled in yellow-green; 'Pictum' (painted arum) has whitish green flowers with purple spots and red-orange fruit that appears after the dark green leaves, which are marbled with gray and cream, have faded away.

BLUEBELL
Hyacinthoides

Light: mostly shade	
Plant type: bulb	
Hardiness: Zones 5-10	
Height: 15 to 20 inches	
Soil and Moisture: well-drained, moist, fertile	
Interest: flowers, foliage	
Care: easy	

◀ Hyacinthoides
hispanica

The dainty bell-shaped flowers of bluebells are one of the joys of spring. The plants produce stout, strong stems from clumps of shiny green foliage topped with clusters of white, pink, or violet flowers. Excellent for naturalizing beneath trees, in mass plantings, and in borders with other bulbs, bluebells also make good container plants and are useful as cut flowers.

Growing and care:

Set plants in a mostly shady location that receives some early-morning or late-day sun. Amend soil with organic matter and plant 3 to 4 inches deep in the fall. Water regularly during dry periods, except in summer. Bluebells can be naturalized as far north as Zone 5. In colder areas, mulch heavily in winter, or dig the bulbs and replant in spring. Bluebells are vigorous growers and thrive even among the roots of trees. Bluebells spread quickly by self-seeding and can often become weedy. Propagate by division.

Selected species and varieties:

H. hispanica [also classified as *Scilla campanulata* or *Endymion hispanicus*] (Spanish bluebell) has 20-inch stems, each producing up to 15 flowers ranging from white to pink to violet above leaf straps that are 1 inch wide; hardy to Zone 5; 'Rose Queen' produces rose-colored flowers; 'White Triumphator' has white flowers.

DAFFODIL
Narcissus

Light: mostly shade	
Plant type: bulb	
Hardiness: Zones 3-10	
Height: 6 to 20 inches	
Soil and Moisture: well-drained, moist	
Interest: flowers, fragrance	
Care: easy	

◀ Narcissus 'Carleton'

Daffodil is a huge group of spring-blooming bulbs that vary greatly in size, shape, and color. Each bloom has an outer ring of six petals called the perianth and a raised center called a corona, which may be a small cup, a large cup of medium length, or, when it is very long, a trumpet. Hybrids number in the thousands, and the genus is grouped into 12 divisions. There are miniature cultivars within almost every division. Used in rock gardens or borders or naturalized, daffodils give years of care-free early color.

Growing and care:

Plant large bulbs 6 to 8 inches deep, small ones 3 to 4 inches deep in well-prepared soil in fall, allowing time for the roots to become established before the ground freezes. Work peat moss or compost in for best results. After bloom, let foliage die down so the plant can build up nutrients for the next year's bloom. Propagate by dividing after foliage has died down. The chief pests are snails and slugs.

Selected species and varieties:

Division 1, Trumpet daffodils: 10 to 18 inches tall with one flower per stem with a trumpet-shaped corona; 'Beersheba' has white flowers on 15-inch stems; 'Lunar Sea' grows 18 to 20 inches tall with a yellow perianth and a white trumpet; 'Rijnveld's Early Sensation' has

(continued)

yellow winter blooms on 13-inch stems. *Division 2, Large-cupped daffodils*: Solitary flowers with the corona more than one-third but less than the full length of the petals; 'Carbineer' is bright yellow with an orange-red corona on 16-inch stems; 'Carleton' is fragrant, soft yellow with a frilled corona and broad perianth, 18 to 20 inches tall; 'Ice Follies' grows 17 inches tall with white petals and a corona that turns from yellow to white. *Division 4, Double daffodils*: One or more flowers on each 12- to 16-inch stem, with the petals, corona, or both doubled; 'Cheerfulness' is fragrant white with a corona flecked with yellow; 'Flower Drift' has ivory white petals and a yellow-orange corona; 'Yellow Cheerfulness' is fragrant yellow on yellow. *Division 6, Cyclamineus daffodils*: 8 to 14 inches tall with solitary yellow, white, or bicolored flowers having a long, wavy-rimmed corona and backward-flaring petals; hardy to Zone 4; 'February Gold', late-winter blooms with deep yellow petals and a yellow corona; 'Peeping Tom', all yellow, good for naturalizing; 'Tête-à-Tête', a miniature 6 to 8 inches tall, lemon yellow with a deeper yellow or orange corona; hardy to Zone 4. *Division 7, Jonquilla daffodils:* Delightfully fragrant flowers, as many as six to each 1-foot-tall stem; 'Pipit' has a fragrant white corona and pale yellow petals, to 15 inches; 'Sweetness' is 13 inches tall, very fragrant, all yellow; 'Trevithian', 17 inches with two or three very fragrant, deep yellow flowers per stem.

GIANT LILY
Cardiocrinum

Light:	mostly shade
Plant type:	bulb
Hardiness:	Zones 7-9
Height:	8 to 12 feet
Soil and Moisture:	well-drained, fertile, acidic
Interest:	flowers, fragrance
Care:	moderate

◀ Cardiocrinum giganteum

Giant lilies are massive plants with bold clusters of very large fragrant flowers as much as 6 inches long atop stout, thick stems. The long, narrow buds open into drooping flared funnels in tiers all around each stem. Glossy heart-shaped leaves up to 1½ feet long form a basal rosette and sparsely line each stem. Giant lilies grow best in filtered shade at the edges of moist woodlands and provide a dynamic presence when grown in borders and wildflower gardens.

Growing and care:
Plant giant lily bulbs in spring or fall with their tops just at the soil line, spaced 1½ feet apart. Giant lilies produce nonflowering shoots for several years before blossoming. The bulbs then die, leaving small bulblets, which will grow to flowering size in 3 to 4 years. Plant bulbs of different sizes to ensure blooms each year. Propagate by lifting and replanting bulblets after the main bulb flowers.

Selected species and varieties:
C. giganteum (heart lily) produces up to 20 nodding creamy white flowers suffused with green on the outside and striped maroon inside stout stems to 12 feet tall.

GRAPE HYACINTH
Muscari

Light:	mostly shade
Plant type:	bulb
Hardiness:	Zones 4-8
Height:	6 to 12 inches
Soil and Moisture:	well-drained, moist
Interest:	flowers
Care:	easy

◀ Muscari armeniacum 'Blue Spike'

Among the earliest of spring bulbs to brighten the garden, low-growing grape hyacinths rapidly spread into carpets of color. Their tiny flowers, less than ½ inch long, cluster in pyramidal tiers at the tips of slender stems above narrow grasslike leaves. The flowers are usually tubular, with their lips turned inward so that clusters resemble small bunches of grapes, or flipped outward like those of hyacinths. The fragrant blossoms are often attractively rimmed in contrasting color. Usually nodding, the flowers are occasionally so tightly crowded that lower blossoms hold upper ones facing out or up, giving the flowers a distinctive texture. Use grape hyacinths as edging plants, in beds or borders, or in wildflower or rock gardens, where they will naturalize quickly. They can also be forced for indoor bloom or used as cut flowers.

Growing and care:
Plant grape hyacinths from late summer to fall, setting bulbs 2 to 3 inches deep and 3 to 4 inches apart. The plants thrive in mostly shady locations but tolerate conditions ranging from mostly sunny to full shade. For indoor forcing, set bulbs 1 inch deep, allowing 10 to 12 bulbs per 6-inch pot. Grape hyacinths self-sow freely. Propagate by removing bulblets that grow around mature bulbs or from seed.

Selected species and varieties:
M. armeniacum (Armenian grape hyacinth) has dense clusters of 20 to 30 spring-blooming blue flowers with flipped white-rimmed edges nodding in overlapping tiers on 8- to 10-inch stems; 'Blue Spike' produces double-petaled long-lasting flowers; 'Cantab' has pale blue flowers blooming later than the species; 'Christmas Pearl', violet blooms; 'Fantasy Creation', soft blue double flowers; 'Saphir', long-lasting deep blue flowers rimmed with white. *M. aucheri* 'Tubergenianium' is a 6-inch dwarf with dense spikes of clear light blue blossoms at the top, shading to deep blue rimmed in white at the bottom. *M. azureum* [also called *Pseudomuscari azurea*] produces 20 to 40 cylindrical, open blue bells facing out and up on 8-inch stems; 'Album' is white. *M. botryoides* (common grape hyacinth, starch hyacinth) has overlapping tiers of nodding white, pink, violet, or blue flowers with white rims on 1-foot stems; 'Album' (Italian grape hyacinth) is a slightly shorter white cultivar. *M. comosum* [also called *Leopoldia comosa*] 'Plumosum' (feather hyacinth, tassel hyacinth) has dense clusters of light blue, violet, or fuchsia flowers with frilled threadlike petals on 4- to 6-inch stems. *M. latifolium* bears loose clusters of 10 to 20 flowers with flipped petals in spikes shading from light to dark blue on 1-foot stems. *M. neglectum* has dense clusters of 30 to 40 flowers with frilled white rims in spires shading from light to dark blue on 6-inch stems; 'Dark Eyes' is very dark blue; 'White Beauty' is white tinged pink.

NATAL LILY
Clivia

Light:	mostly shade
Plant type:	bulb
Hardiness:	Zones 9-10
Height:	1 to 1½ feet
Soil and Moisture:	well-drained, moist
Interest:	flowers, foliage
Care:	moderate

◀ Clivia miniata

A popular houseplant in Victorian times, the natal lily bears domed clusters of up to 20 trumpet-shaped 3-inch flowers in dramatic hues atop a single thick stalk flanked by pairs of broad, straplike evergreen leaves up to 1½ feet long. Bulbs may produce their long-lasting flowers twice a year under ideal conditions, and inch-long red berries follow the blossoms. *Clivia* can be grown outdoors in warm zones but bloom best as root-bound houseplants.

Growing and care:

Plant natal lilies outdoors in fall, in a location that receives mostly sun to mostly shade. Set the tops of the bulbous roots at the soil line, spacing them 1½ to 2 feet apart. Indoors, plant roots in 9-inch pots and leave undisturbed. Propagate from seed or by dividing the fleshy rootstocks after flowering.

Selected species and varieties:

C. x *cyrtanthiflora* (Kaffir lily) produces deep salmon-pink blooms. *C. miniata* (Kaffir lily) has scarlet blossoms with yellow-splashed throats; 'Aurea' grows golden yellow; 'Flame' is deep red-orange; 'Grandiflora' produces larger scarlet flowers.

RAIN LILY
Zephyranthes

Light:	mostly shade
Plant type:	bulb
Hardiness:	Zones 7-10
Height:	8 to 15 inches
Soil and Moisture:	well-drained, fertile, moist
Interest:	flowers
Care:	easy

◀ Zephyranthes atamasco

R ain lily is a bulbous perennial wildflower native to the damp woods and bottom lands of the southeastern United States. The plants form colonies of thin, grasslike leaves decorated in spring with delicate funnel-shaped white or pink flowers. The plants are easy to grow and naturalize rapidly in rock gardens and lawns, or along paths.

Growing and care:

Sow seed in spring directly in the garden in rich, well-worked soil well amended with organic matter. Plant bulbs 3 inches deep in fall. The plants thrive in a range of light conditions, from full sun to mostly shade. Thin or space 3 to 6 inches apart. Plants grown from seed will flower in 3 to 4 years. Fertilize lightly in spring with a complete organic fertilizer. Provide extra water during dry periods. In northern areas bulbs can be lifted in fall and replanted in spring.

Selected species and varieties:

Z. atamasco (atamasco lily, rain lily) has showy funnel-shaped white flowers 3 inches long on leafless stalks about 1 foot tall in mid- to late spring. The flowers are sometimes tinged with purple and turn pink as they age. The thick, shiny, grasslike leaves form a clump 8 to 15 inches tall.

SNOWDROP
Galanthus

Light: mostly shade	
Plant type: bulb	
Hardiness: Zones 3-8	
Height: 4 to 12 inches	
Soil and Moisture: well-drained, moist	
Interest: flowers, foliage	
Care: easy	

◀ Galanthus nivalis

Among the earliest of spring-flowering bulbs, snowdrops often bloom while their leaves and flowers are still dusted with late-winter snow. The solitary pendent flowers have three outer petal-like segments that hang over a shorter green-tipped tube. The leaves are glossy green and straplike. Plant snowdrops in rock gardens, along pathways, or at foundations, or naturalize in lawns or under deciduous trees and shrubs.

Growing and care:

In late summer or fall, work peat moss or compost into the soil and plant bulbs 3 inches deep and 3 inches apart and mark their locations. The plants tolerate mostly sunny locations but do best in mostly shady spots beneath deciduous trees and shrubs. Snowdrop bulbs multiply quickly and can be divided every 3 to 4 years. Divide clumps of bulbs in late spring after the leaves have yellowed. To force snowdrops, plant four to six bulbs 1 inch deep in a 4-inch pot in late fall. Chill in the refrigerator for 6 to 8 weeks. Once returned to a warm spot, the bulbs will bloom in a few weeks.

Selected species and varieties:

G. nivalis bears nodding 1-inch single white flowers on 4- to 6-inch stems with narrow leaves; 'Flore Pleno' (double snowdrops) has glossy green, narrow foliage and 4- to 6-inch stems topped with double white nodding blossoms in early spring.

SNOWFLAKE
Leucojum

Light: mostly shade	
Plant type: bulb	
Hardiness: Zones 4-9	
Height: 6 inches to 1 1/2 feet	
Soil and Moisture: well-drained, moist	
Interest: flowers, foliage	
Care: easy	

◀ Leucojum vernum

Snowflake is a perky little bulb with thin sprays of deep green leaves and nodding clusters of fragrant white flowers in spring. A native to woodlands, it thrives in the dappled light beneath forest trees and is perfect for wooded paths and wildflower gardens. Planted in masses snowflake quickly naturalizes, providing reliable annual displays. Once established the plants are best left undisturbed.

Growing and care:

Although they grow in average garden soil, snowflakes prefer sandy loam to which leaf mold, peat moss, or dried compost has been added. Plant bulbs 4 inches deep. Bloom may not occur the first year. Propagate by dividing, but keep bulbs moist while moving.

Selected species and varieties:

L. aestivum (summer snowflake, Loddon lily) grows 1 to 1 1/2 feet tall with three to seven 3/4-inch-long nodding flowers on each 1- to 1 1/2-foot stalk, blooming in spring and early summer in the East but in late fall and winter in warm areas of the West; prefers mostly shade; 'Gravetye' [also known as 'Gravetye Giant'] produces 1 1/2-inch flowers on 1 1/2-foot stems. *L. vernum* (spring snowflake) is 10 inches tall with glossy green leaves and fragrant white flowers borne singly or in pairs on 4- to 6-inch stems in late winter or spring; prefers mostly shade; Zones 4-8.

SQUILL
Scilla

Light: mostly shade	
Plant type: bulb	
Hardiness: Zones 3-10	
Height: 6 inches to 2 feet	
Soil and Moisture: well-drained, moist, fertile	
Interest: flowers, foliage	
Care: easy	

◀ Scilla peruviana

Squill is one of spring's classic bulbs, carpeting the ground beneath taller bulb plants and shrubbery with a haze of tiny bells that open into dainty stars. Sometimes facing upward, sometimes dangling, the blossoms appear in clusters on slender stems clasped at the base by a few narrow ribbonlike leaves. Mass squill at the edge of borders, in rockeries, or in woodland gardens, where it will naturalize rapidly. Squill can also be forced for indoor bloom.

Growing and care:

Select squills from reputable breeders who propagate their own bulbs, as collection has endangered many species in the wild. Plant tender species outdoors in spring, setting bulbs with their necks at the soil line 8 to 10 inches apart. North of Zone 9, grow them as container plants, starting bulbs indoors in late winter for summer bloom. Plant all other squills outdoors in fall, setting bulbs 2 to 3 inches deep and 3 to 6 inches apart. Siberian squill even succeeds under evergreens, where other bulbs fail. The plants prefer mostly shady spots but grow well in conditions ranging from mostly sunny to full shade. Squills, particularly Siberian squill, self-sow easily. They can be propagated from seed to reach blooming-size bulbs in 3 years or by dividing small bulblets produced by mature bulbs in fall. The plants often naturalize in lawns and open woods.

Selected species and varieties:

S. bifolia (twinleaf squill) has loose upright clusters of up to eight tiny ½-inch pale blue flowers on 6-inch stems above two or three leaves in early spring; 'Rosea' is rosy pink; Zones 4-8. *S. litardierei* (meadow squill) has up to 30 tiny ³⁄₁₆-inch blue flowers in a dense tuft on 8-inch stems in spring; Zones 5-8. *S. mischtschenkoana* [formerly *S. tubergeniana*] (Persian bluebell) has multiple 4- to 5-inch stems with sparse clusters of upturned 1½-inch pale blue flowers striped darker blue, blooming late winter to early spring; Zones 5-8. *S. peruviana* (Peruvian lily, Peruvian jacinth, Cuban lily) has dense, domed 6-inch clusters of deep violet ½-inch flowers above evergreen leaves on 1½-foot stems in summer; Zones 9-10. *S. scilloides* (Chinese squill, Japanese jacinth) has 1- to 1½-foot leafless stems with clusters of up to 60 deep pink blossoms in summer followed by leaves in fall, sometimes persisting into spring; Zones 5-8. *S. siberica* (Siberian squill) bears sparse clusters of nodding ½-inch gentian blue flowers on 4- to 6-inch stems in early spring; 'Alba' is white; 'Spring Beauty' has large, deep blue flower stars; Zones 3-8.

BLOODROOT
Sanguinaria

Light: mostly shade	
Plant type: perennial	
Hardiness: Zones 3-9	
Height: 3 to 8 inches	
Soil and Moisture: well-drained, moist, fertile	
Interest: flowers	
Care: easy	

◀ Sanguinaria canadensis

Bloodroot's very early-spring flowers emerge tightly clasped within kidney-shaped leaves. The waxy leaves, with deep lobes and scalloped edges, slowly unfurl to reveal a single flower resembling a tiny water lily. Allow the creeping rhizomes to spread slowly in woodland and rock gardens or under the shade of shrubs. The red-orange juice flowing in stems and roots was once used in herbal medicine and is now an ingredient in plaque-fighting toothpastes.

Growing and care:

Bloodroot grows best in shady locations beneath deciduous trees and shrubs but tolerates mostly sunny spots if ample moisture is available. Sow seed of the species in spring or fall or divide roots immediately after flowering. Set plants in soil well amended with organic matter, spacing plants 6 to 8 inches apart. *S. canadensis* 'Flore Pleno' must be grown from divisions, as it does not come true from seed.

Selected species and varieties:

S. canadensis (bloodroot) has grayish green leaves up to 6 inches across marked with radiating veins and 1½- to 2-inch flowers composed of a whorl of waxy, pointed white petals raised above leaves on 8-inch red stalks; 'Flore Pleno' [also called 'Multiplex'] has double whorls of petals.

SWEET CICELY
Myrrhis

Light: mostly shade	
Plant type: perennial	
Hardiness: Zones 3-8	
Height: 2 to 3 feet	
Soil and Moisture: well-drained, fertile, moist	
Interest: flowers, foliage, fragrance, seeds	
Care: moderate	

◀ Myrrhis odorata

Sweet cicely is a handsome herb with tall stalks of finely cut leaves that perfume the garden with the aroma of anise and celery from spring to fall. As flavorful as they are fragrant, the fresh leaves can be used as a sugar substitute for tart fruits or to flavor salads, omelets, and soups. The soft white spring-blooming flowers are followed by tasty seeds that can be added either green or ripe to fruit dishes, salads, baked goods, and other dishes. The anise-scented taproot can be chopped into salads, served raw with dressing, or steamed as a vegetable.

Growing and care:

Because sweet cicely seed germinates erratically, the most reliable way to grow it is to divide mature plants in fall and plant the divisions. Set plants in well-worked soil that has been generously amended with compost or rotted manure. Space plants 2 feet apart. The plants do well in a range of conditions from sun to shade, though mostly shady spots are preferred. Harvest fresh leaves anytime, seeds either green or ripe. Dry leaves lose their taste but can be used for crafts. Dig roots for culinary use in fall.

Selected species and varieties:

M. odorata has fernlike leaflets along arching stems to 3 feet and flat clusters of tiny white flowers followed by ¾-inch upright, oblong, ridged green seeds ripening to brown-black.

ARDISIA
Ardisia

Light: mostly shade

Plant type: ground cover

Hardiness: Zones 7-10

Height: $^2/_3$ to 6 feet

Soil and Moisture: well-drained, moist, fertile

Interest: flowers, foliage, fruit

Care: moderate

◀ Ardisia crenata

Ardisia is a lovely low evergreen ground cover for shady areas with glossy dark green serrated leaves that are tapered at both ends and clustered at the ends of stems. Small star-shaped flowers are borne in racemes in summer, followed by bright red berries that persist into winter. Ardisia is a nice addition to wooded plantings, where the flowers, foliage, and fruit contribute four-season interest.

Growing and care:
Plant in a shady location in slightly acid soils. Amend soil with leaf mold, peat moss, or compost. Provide protection from harsh winter winds. Variegated forms are less cold hardy than the green ones.

Selected species and varieties:
A. crenata (Christmas berry) grows from 4 to 6 feet with lustrous foliage and bright red berries. *A. japonica* (marlberry) is a mat-forming ground cover 8 to 12 inches tall with lustrous 1½- to 3½-inch-long dark green toothed leaves that are pink when new. It bears white flowers in summer and red berries in the fall; variably hardy to Zone 7 but best in Zones 8-10; 'Hakuokan' is one of the largest cultivars and has broad, white leaf margins; 'Ito Fukurin' has light silvery green leaves thinly edged in white; 'Nishiki' has rosy pink leaf margins that turn yellow with age.

BAMBOO
Sasa

Light: mostly shade

Plant type: ground cover

Hardiness: Zones 7-9

Height: 2 to 8 feet

Soil and Moisture: well-drained, moist, fertile

Interest: foliage

Care: easy

◀ Sasa veitchii

Bamboo is a vigorous, easy-to-grow ground cover plant that displays long green leaves that jut out from tall cylindrical canes. A woody grass that develops rhizomes, bamboo can spread rapidly, functioning both as a ground cover and, for the taller species, as a screen. It is evergreen except in the coldest climates.

Growing and care:
Bamboo that is healthy and vigorous can quickly take over an area and restraints on its growth are essential. If foliage looks unkempt at the end of winter, prune plants to the ground. Propagate by division. The plants grow well in a range of conditions from sun to mostly shade.

Selected species and varieties:
S. palmata (palm-leaf bamboo, palmate bamboo) has leaves up to 15 inches long and 4 inches wide, medium green above and bluish green beneath, arising from narrow canes up to 8 feet tall and slightly more than ¼ inch in diameter; Zones 7-9. *S. veitchii* (Kuma bamboo grass, Kuma zasa) has purplish canes 2 to 4 feet tall, bearing leaves up to 8 inches long and 2 inches wide that are dark green above and bluish gray below, developing straw-colored, dry leaf margins in fall; Zones 8-9.

CHOCOLATE VINE
Akebia

Light:	mostly shade
Plant type:	vine
Hardiness:	Zones 4-8
Height:	20 to 40 feet
Soil and Moisture:	well-drained, moist to dry
Interest:	flowers, fruit
Care:	easy

◄ Akebia quinata

Chocolate vine is equally good at covering ground or walls, quickly twining around anything close at hand. With its semievergreen foliage, it offers multiseason interest to the landscape. Fruit pods, usually a bright, rich purple, dangle abundantly from the plant in fall; in spring, small fragrant flowers peep out from the new foliage. A good choice for a trellis or pergola, *Akebia* can also provide a cover for an eyesore in the landscape.

Growing and care:

A tough, vigorous plant, *Akebia* tolerates nearly any growing conditions, from sun to shade and moist soil to dry. Its growth is so robust it can easily choke out other plants, sometimes to the point of becoming invasive. Pruning is required to keep it under control.

Selected species and varieties:

A. quinata (five-leaf akebia) has attractive dark blue-green compound leaves with five leaflets, each to 3 inches long, nearly masking dark purple fragrant flower racemes that are hard to see from a distance. The flowers are followed by purple fruit pods up to 4 inches long that ripen in late summer; the leaves usually hold their color until the first hard freeze.

CLIMBING HYDRANGEA
Hydrangea

Light:	mostly shade
Plant type:	vine
Hardiness:	Zones 4-7
Height:	60 to 80 feet
Soil and Moisture:	well-drained, fertile, moist
Interest:	foliage, flowers, bark
Care:	easy

◄ Hydrangea anomala ssp. petiolaris

Climbing hydrangea is regarded by many plant experts as being the best vine, bar none. The plants are vigorous with very ornamental cinnamon-red bark, tiers of dark green leaves, and abundant clusters of linen white flowers from late spring to early summer. Climbing hydrangea is stunning when grown against buildings or along arbors, and songbirds find the ample branches excellent places to build nests.

Growing and care:

Climbing hydrangea thrives in a range of light conditions, from sun to shade but does best when grown in partial shade. To reduce the chance of transplant injury, purchase only container-grown plants. Plant in well-worked soil that has been generously amended with compost or other organic matter. Climbs easily up most supports and does best with east or northern exposures. Fertilize lightly in spring as growth begins.

Selected species and varieties:

H. anomala ssp. *petiolaris* (climbing hydrangea) climbs by root-like holdfasts to 80 feet with 6- to 10-inch-wide clusters of white flowers in late spring to early summer and broad, oval dark green leaves that cover the reddish brown, exfoliating bark.

DEAD NETTLE
Lamium

Light: mostly shade

Plant type: ground cover

Hardiness: Zones 4-8

Height: $^2/_3$ to 2 feet

Soil and Moisture: well-drained, moist

Interest: flowers, foliage

Care: easy

◀ Lamium maculatum 'White Nancy'

Dead nettle, so called because it does not sting like other nettles, is a vigorous, colorful ground cover with silvery foliage and flowers that bloom from late spring to summer. Several cultivars have been bred to be less weedy than the genus.

Growing and care:
Set plants 1 foot apart in moist, well-worked soil in spring or fall. Shear plants in midsummer to encourage a second flush of leafy growth. *L. galeobdolon* tolerates deep to bright shade. *L. maculatum* needs bright to partial shade. Once established the plants need little care and often self-sow.

Selected species and varieties:
L. galeobdolon [also listed as *Lamiastrum galeobdolon*] (yellow archangel) grows to 2 feet tall with coarse-toothed 3-inch-long leaves and bright yellow blooms with brown marks; 'Herman's Pride' is 1 foot tall with green and silver leaves and yellow flowers; 'Variegata' has variegated green and silver leaves and yellow flowers. *L. maculatum* (spotted dead nettle) is a spreading ground cover to 1½ feet high bearing small crinkled leaves; 'Beacon Silver' has greenish silver leaves with green margins and pink flowers; 'Chequers' is a heat-tolerant cultivar with dark green leaves bearing a silver center stripe and violet flowers; 'White Nancy' has greenish silver leaves and white flowers.

DUTCHMAN'S-PIPE
Aristolochia

Light: mostly shade

Plant type: vine

Hardiness: Zones 4-8

Height: 25 to 30 feet

Soil and Moisture: well-drained, moist

Interest: flowers, foliage

Care: easy to moderate

◀ Aristolochia macrophylla

Dutchman's-pipe is a vigorous twining vine with glossy dark green heart-shaped deciduous leaves up to 10 inches long. Hidden in the overlapping foliage are dark flowers that look like small pipes with fluted edges. Valued for its fast growth, *Aristolochia* is perfect for shading a porch, covering a trellis for privacy, or concealing an unsightly wall. The plant grows so quickly that it can cover a large trellis, arbor, or pergola in a single season.

Growing and care:
Aristolochia does well in bright to medium or partial shade. It tolerates any average garden soil but performs with more vigor if planted in a mostly shady spot with compost applied to its base in spring. Provide extra water during extended periods of dry weather. New plants need training during the first year. Propagate by division in fall.

Selected species and varieties:
A. macrophylla [also classified as *A. durior*] (pipe vine) has 4- to 10-inch heart- or kidney-shaped dark green leaves masking pairs of purplish brown, yellow-throated flowers in midspring to early summer and 2- to 3-inch-long ribbed capsules in fall.

DWARF MONDO GRASS
Ophiopogon

Light: mostly shade	
Plant type: ground cover	
Hardiness: Zones 6-10	
Height: 2 to 14 inches	
Soil and Moisture: well-drained, moist	
Interest: flowers, foliage, fruit	
Care: easy to moderate	

◀ O. japonicus 'Nana'

Dwarf mondo grass forms moppy tufts of arching grasslike leaves that spread to create a ground cover in any kind of shade, from bright to dense. In appearance the plants resemble lilyturf, except dwarf mondo grass has flowers nestled within the shaggy foliage rather than above it. Clusters of small blue or black berries follow. Evergreen in the South, *Ophiopogon* is useful beneath trees and in borders and edgings.

Growing and care:
Although dwarf mondo grass tolerates average garden soil, it grows best when peat moss or leaf mold has been added. In colder climates the foliage tends to become shabby in appearance. Shear in early spring to promote new growth. Propagate by dividing in early spring.

Selected species and varieties:
O. japonicus (dwarf mondo grass) grows 6 to 14 inches tall with dark green leaves ⅛ inch wide or less and up to several bluish violet flowers per stalk; 'Kyoto Dwarf' is only 2 inches tall with narrow dark green leaves; 'Nana' is roughly half as tall as the species; Zones 7-9. *O. planiscapus* 'Nigrescens' (black dragon) has purplish black foliage 6 inches tall with pink or lilac flowers and black berries.

LILYTURF
Liriope

Light: mostly shade	
Plant type: ground cover	
Hardiness: Zones 4-10	
Height: 8 to 18 inches	
Soil and Moisture: well-drained, moist, fertile	
Interest: flowers, foliage, fruit	
Care: easy	

◀ L. muscari 'Variegata'

The grasslike blades of lilyturf start out in tufts, gradually spreading until large clumps form. Ideal for use in edgings and rock gardens or as a ground cover, it also comes in variegated forms that provide textural accents. Flower spikes in purple or white bloom in late summer above the semievergreen foliage, followed by shiny black berries. In colder climates, the leaves look messy in late winter.

Growing and care:
Amend the soil with organic matter. Once established, lilyturf grows well in a wide range of conditions from sun to full shade but usually does best in mostly shady locations. Shear or mow the old leaves before new growth begins in spring. Propagate by division in spring.

Selected species and varieties:
L. muscari (big blue lilyturf) has tufts of straplike leaves 1½ feet tall and violet flowers; Zones 6-9; 'Gold Banded' is a compact form with wide yellow-edged leaf blades; 'Monroe's White' grows 15 to 18 inches tall with narrower leaf blades than the species and white flowers; 'Variegata' is 1 foot tall with creamy yellow leaf margins and lilac flowers; hardy to Zone 6. *L. spicata* (creeping lilyturf) grows 8 to 18 inches tall with leaves only ¼ inch wide and purplish white flowers.

MANDEVILLA
Mandevilla

Light: mostly shade

Plant type: vine

Hardiness: Zones 8-10

Height: 10 to 20 feet

Soil and Moisture: well-drained, moist, fertile

Interest: flowers, foliage, fragrance

Care: moderate

◀ Mandevilla x amabilis

Mandevilla is one of the most beautiful climbing vines, with abundant dark green leaves and prominet clusters of fragrant white, pink, rose, or salmon flowers. While hardy only in warm climates, mandevilla can be grown farther north as an annual or as a potted plant kept indoors over winter. The twining vine can be trained to climb a trellis, post, or arbor, where its trumpet-shaped flowers produce an elegant summer display set off by lush foliage. Some selections bear flowers that are extremely fragrant.

Growing and care:
Plant in soil with abundant organic matter. The plants do best in light shade but tolerate some early- or late-day sun. Keep plants evenly moist throughout the growing season. Pinch shoots to encourage bushiness, and remove faded flowers.

Selected species and varieties:
M. x *amabilis* [also listed as *Dipladenia* x *amabilis*] is a vigorous twining vine with evergreen leaves and abundant summer flowers opening pale blush pink and maturing to deep rose; 'Alice du Pont' has dark oval evergreen leaves and 4-inch-wide coral pink flowers in clusters throughout summer; Zone 10. *M. laxa* [also listed as *M. suaveolens*] (Chilean jasmine) has twining stems 15 to 20 feet long with oval deciduous to semievergreen leaves and 2-inch fragrant white flowers in summer.

MOSS PHLOX
Phlox

Light: mostly shade

Plant type: ground cover

Hardiness: Zones 3-9

Height: 3 to 6 inches

Soil and Moisture: well-drained, fertile, moist to dry

Interest: flowers

Care: easy

◀ Phlox subulata

Moss phlox is an easy-to-grow, hardy ground cover that produces vivid carpets of spring flowers. The plants produce dense clumps of needlelike semi-evergreen foliage that effectively choke out most weeds. From mid- to late spring, abundant white, pink, blue, lavender, or red flowers appear. Moss phlox makes an ideal planting for rock gardens and is especially attractive when allowed to cascade over stones or walls.

Growing and care:
Plant moss phlox in spring in well-drained soil that has some organic matter. Space plants about 12 inches apart. The plants do well in a wide range of light conditions from full sun to mostly shade and are maintenance-free once established. Moss phlox is easily propagated by layering or by division after blooming in late spring.

Selected species and varieties:
P. subulata (moss phlox, moss pink) has white, pink, blue, lavender, or red flowers above dense carpets of semievergreen foliage 3 to 6 inches tall and 2 feet wide; 'Emerald Cushion' grows to 3 inches tall with dark green foliage and pink spring flowers; 'Sky Blue' has deep green leaves and blue flowers in spring.

PACHYSANDRA
Pachysandra

Light: mostly shade

Plant type: ground cover

Hardiness: Zones 4-9

Height: 4 to 12 inches

Soil and Moisture: well-drained, moist, fertile

Interest: foliage

Care: easy

◀ Pachysandra terminalis

Pachysandra forms an attractive, vigorous ground cover that thrives in shady areas where other plants may not. Japanese pachysandra tolerates dense shade and competes well with shallow-rooted trees.

Growing and care:
Set the plants 1 foot apart in soil enriched with leaf mold or peat moss. Keep soil mulched until plants start to spread. Pachysandra thrives in fully to mostly shady locations and tolerates dense shade.

Selected species and varieties:
P. procumbens (Allegheny spurge) has flat gray-green or blue-green scalloped-edged deciduous to evergreen leaves, 2 to 4 inches long and 2 to 3 inches wide, sometimes mottled with brownish purple, that turn bronze in fall, and fragrant white or pinkish early-spring flower spikes 2 to 4 inches long. *P. terminalis* (Japanese pachysandra) has lustrous green, toothed evergreen leaves, 2 to 4 inches long and 1 inch wide, in clusters at the end of unbranched stems 6 to 10 inches high, with 1- to 2-inch spikes of white flowers in spring and insignificant white berries in fall; Zones 4-8; 'Green Carpet' has small, waxy green leaves and, at 4 inches, hugs the ground; 'Silver Edge' has green leaves edged with white.

VINCA
Vinca

Light: mostly shade

Plant type: ground cover

Hardiness: Zones 4-9

Height: 6 to 12 inches

Soil and Moisture: well-drained, moist

Interest: flowers, foliage

Care: easy

◀ Vinca major 'Variegata'

A workhorse for difficult shady areas, vinca provides mats of dark green evergreen foliage on interlaced vines that bear blue, lilac, or white five-petaled flowers 1 inch across in spring and periodically throughout summer. Vincas are useful as ground covers for shady banks and other areas, and as trailing additions to window boxes and planters.

Growing and care:
Vincas spread quickly in soil amended with organic matter. They tolerate poor soil, but will grow more slowly. In warmer climates they perform better in light to full shade. Plant them in spring or fall, spacing plants 6 to 12 inches apart. Mulch to conserve moisture. Vincas are easily propagated by division in spring, or by cuttings taken at anytime.

Selected species and varieties:
V. major has creeping or trailing stems with 1- to 3-inch-long leathery oval leaves and blue spring flowers; 'Variegata' has light green leaves with creamy white edges and is highly favored as an accent plant in baskets or containers; Zones 7-9. *V. minor* has glossy leaves to 1½ inches long on stems that form a mat 6 to 8 inches thick, and spring flowers in shades of blue or white; 'Alba' bears white flowers; 'Albo-Variegata' produces gold and green leaves and white flowers; 'Flore Pleno' has dark green leaves and purple-blue double flowers; Zones 4-8.

WINTERGREEN
Gaultheria

Light: mostly shade

Plant type: ground cover

Hardiness: Zones 3-10

Height: 4 to 6 inches

Soil and Moisture: well-drained, moist

Interest: flowers, foliage, fragrance

Care: moderate

◀ G. procumbens

Wintergreen slowly creeps along to form low mats of glossy aromatic evergreen foliage ideal as a ground cover and for use in rock gardens and wildflower gardens. Waxy summer flower bells dangle below the leaves, followed by fleshy red berries that remain on plants through winter. Brew freshly chopped leaves or berries for a refreshing wintergreen-flavored tea. Add a few berries to jams. Both leaves and berries yield an oil, now replaced by a synthetic formula, that was once used as a food flavoring and was applied externally to soothe sore muscles.

Growing and care:
Wintergreen thrives in mostly to fully shady places, though flowering is sometimes reduced in deep shade. Propagate wintergreen by divisions in spring or fall, or from cuttings taken in summer, spacing plants 1 foot apart. Mulch with pine needles or compost to conserve moisture. Harvest leaves anytime, berries when ripe.

Selected species and varieties:
G. procumbens (wintergreen, checkerberry, teaberry, ivry-leaves) has leathery 2-inch oval leaves on short erect stalks along trailing stems and ¼-inch white to pink flowers followed by edible red berries.

WOODBINE
Parthenocissus

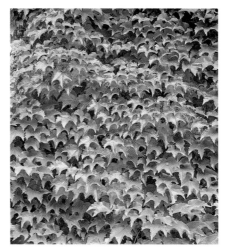

Light: mostly shade

Plant type: vine

Hardiness: Zones 3-9

Height: 50 feet or more

Soil and Moisture: well-drained, moist to dry

Interest: foliage

Care: easy

◀ Parthenocissus tricuspidata

A tough, extremely fast climber that can easily scale 10 feet and more in a season, woodbine can make short work of covering walls, trellises, and slopes. Fastening itself to a structure with tendrils, it needs no support. Its dark green compound leaves turn purplish red to crimson in fall.

Growing and care:
Set plants 2 feet apart in spring in loosened soil amended with some organic matter. Once established woodbine can quickly become invasive and should be planted where it can spread freely. The plants do best in a wide range of conditions from sun to mostly shade and are tolerant of urban and seaside conditions.

Selected species and varieties:
P. henryana (silver-vein creeper) produces leaves with five leaflets up to 2½ inches long that are bluish green veined with white when young, with purple undersides, and turn red to reddish purple in fall; Zones 7-8. *P. quinquefolia* (Virginia creeper, American ivy, five-leaved ivy) has five leaflets up to 4 inches long, opening reddish bronze then turning dark green, then purplish to crimson in fall, with greenish white early-summer flowers and small blue-black berries on bright red pedicles that are visible after the leaves have fallen. *P. tricuspidata* (Japanese creeper, Boston ivy) bears lustrous three-lobed simple leaves; Zones 4-8.

BAMBOO
Fargesia

Light:	mostly shade
Plant type:	grass
Hardiness:	Zones 5-9
Height:	10 to 15 feet
Soil and Moisture:	well-drained, moist to dry
Interest:	foliage
Care:	easy

◀ Fargesia murielae

Bamboo is a vigorous fast-growing plant with distinctive tapered dark green leaves that flutter from purplish sheaths on slender reddish gray canes, which arch as they mature and spread to form mounded clumps. The plants provide dramatic color and vertical accent in ornamental beds, lending the garden a soft texture. Cut canes make good garden stakes.

Growing and care:
Plant in soil that has been loosened and amended with some organic matter. As clumps begin to develop above soil level, divide and replant. Clump bamboo is less invasive than umbrella bamboo.

Selected species and varieties:
F. murielae [also classified as *Thamnocalamus spathaceus*] (umbrella bamboo) has slender bright green canes to 12 feet tall, aging to yellow, and bending at the top under the weight of rich green leaves 3 to 5 inches long that turn yellow in fall before dropping; Zones 6-9. *F. nitida* [also classified as *Sinarundinaria nitida*] (clump bamboo, hardy blue bamboo, fountain bamboo) has hollow dark purple canes 1/2 inch in diameter and 10 to 15 feet tall (reaching 20 feet under optimal conditions) coated with a bluish white powder when young. After the first year the canes produce leaves to 7 inches long with bristly margins on one side.

CHAIN FERN
Woodwardia

Light:	mostly shade
Plant type:	fern
Hardiness:	Zones 3-10
Height:	1 to 9 feet
Soil and Moisture:	moist to wet, fertile
Interest:	foliage
Care:	easy

◀ Woodwardia fimbriata

Chain ferns come in distinctly different forms, each recalling the primitive grace that ferns in general are famous for. The netted chain fern spreads vigorously on branching rhizomes to form a spreading, lacy ground cover. Arising in a clump, the giant chain fern's spray of large arching fronds makes a dramatic statement in the shady garden.

Growing and care:
One of the easiest ferns to grow, the netted chain fern does best in soil that mimics its native habitat, the bogs and marshes of the East, although it can tolerate drier conditions. The giant chain fern prefers consistently moist, shady settings.

Selected species and varieties:
W. areolata (netted chain fern) has erect, deciduous fronds rising 1 to 2 feet high from creeping rhizomes. The sterile fronds are reddish green when new, turning glossy dark green with maturity and bearing netted veins; Zones 3-9. *W. fimbriata* (giant chain fern) has arching, evergreen fronds to 9 feet high arising upright in clumps from woody rhizomes; Zones 8-10.

CUP FERN
Dennstaedtia

Light: mostly shade

Plant type: fern

Hardiness: Zones 3-8

Height: 1 to 3 feet

Soil and Moisture: well-drained, dry to moist

Interest: foliage

Care: easy

◀ Dennstaedtia punctilobula

Cup fern is an easy-to-grow, low-maintenance plant that forms wide-ranging, dense mats of finely textured light green fronds. The delicate foliage smells like fresh-mown hay when crushed. A moderately fast-growing ground cover, it is particularly useful for slopes and rocky areas.

Growing and care:

Although cup fern grows best in slightly acid, loamy soils, it tolerates a wide range of soil conditions and, once it is established, can withstand summer drought. Give the plants plenty of room, setting them 2 feet apart. It requires little care but enjoys a springtime application of bone meal to the soil surface at the rate of 1 ounce per square yard. It spreads by slender, underground rhizomes; divide by separating the rhizomatous mats in spring.

Selected species and varieties:

D. punctilobula (hay-scented fern, boulder fern) has curved, pyramidal, very lacy fronds up to 3 feet long and 3 to 6 inches wide, covered with gland-tipped whitish hairs from which the scent emerges; the foliage turns yellow to brown in fall.

CYRTOMIUM
Cyrtomium

Light: mostly shade

Plant type: fern

Hardiness: Zones 7-10

Height: 1 to 2 feet

Soil and Moisture: well-drained, moist, fertile

Interest: foliage

Care: easy to moderate

◀ Cyrtomium falcatum

Cyrtomium is a medium-height, spreading fern with toothy, hollylike semievergreen fronds arranged in a circle and arching outward. Scattered amid rhododendrons or other evergreens in a shady location, the medium-fine, leathery glossy foliage adds textural interest to the shady landscape. In the North, it is often grown as a houseplant.

Growing and care:

Good drainage is particularly important in winter, when the cyrtomium can be subject to rot. Work leaf mold, peat moss, or compost into the soil when planting. In marginal zones, provide a site that is sheltered from winter winds and hard frost, and mulch heavily.

Selected species and varieties:

C. falcatum (Japanese holly fern) grows 1 to 2 feet tall, with leathery, dark green coarsely serrated fronds having four to 10 pairs of pinnae about 3 inches long. *C. fortunei* has erect fronds to 2 feet high and up to 10 inches wide with 12 to 26 pairs of pinnae that taper sharply and are a paler green and less lustrous than those of Japanese holly fern and not as serrated.

FLOWERING FERN
Osmunda

Light:	mostly shade
Plant type:	fern
Hardiness:	Zones 2-10
Height:	2 to 6 feet
Soil and Moisture:	well-drained, moist, fertile
Interest:	foliage
Care:	easy

◀ Osmunda
cinnamomea

These stately deciduous ferns grow wild mostly in marshes and wet open forests, where they reach even greater heights, but they also adapt to the home garden. Spreading slowly on rhizomes, they make excellent background plantings in borders and rock gardens or against a wall. Cinnamon fern can be used to hide leggy shrubs. The plants prefer a partially shady location that receives some morning or late-afternoon sun.

Growing and care:
Flowering ferns thrive in soil consisting of 1 part loam, 1 part sand, and 2 parts leaf mold or peat moss. The interrupted fern needs fertile loam and slightly acidic conditions. Cinnamon and royal ferns can tolerate part sun if the soil remains wet, as by a stream or pond, but thrive in mostly shade elsewhere.

Selected species and varieties:
O. cinnamomea (cinnamon fern, fiddleheads, buckhorn) produces a 2- to 4-foot-tall fertile frond that looks like a cinnamon stick rising above light green foliage changing to gold in late summer before finally turning brown; Zones 3-9. *O. claytoniana* (interrupted fern) is 2 to 4 feet tall with tierlike new spring growth; Zones 2-8. *O. regalis* (royal fern) has 3- to 6-foot-tall fronds opening wine red then turning green, with 2- to 3-inch-long feathery leaflets that turn bright yellow in fall.

HAKONECHLOA
Hakonechloa

Light:	mostly shade
Plant type:	grass
Hardiness:	Zones 5-9
Height:	1 to 1½ feet
Soil and Moisture:	well-drained, moist, fertile
Interest:	foliage
Care:	easy

◀ Hakonechloa macra
'Aureola'

Hakonechloa is an easy-to-grow ornamental grass with warm-colored tapered blades that add a dynamic touch to walkways, borders, and rock gardens. This slow-spreading deciduous grass is stunning when planted in large groups on shady slopes or near water elements. Breezes rustling through the foliage produce soft textural effects. Hakonechloa is so adaptable it even grows well in containers, providing beauty to patios and decks throughout the summer.

Growing and care:
Plant in well-worked soil amended with some organic matter. Space plants 12 to 15 inches apart. Water regularly until plants are established and during extended dry periods. Hakonechloa thrives in partially shady locations with early-morning and late-afternoon sun, and should not be planted in locations that are excessively windy.

Selected species and varieties:
H. macra 'Aureola' (golden variegated hakonechloa) has a 1- to 1½-foot-high rhizomatous clump with an arching habit, consisting of bamboolike stems that display tapering 8-inch-long cream-colored leaves with bronzy green edges that usually spill over in the same direction and become buff colored in fall, as well as inconspicuous open panicles of yellowish green flowers that appear in late summer or early fall.

HOLLY FERN
Polystichum

Light:	mostly shade
Plant type:	fern
Hardiness:	Zones 3-9
Height:	1 to 4 feet
Soil and Moisture:	well-drained, moist, fertile
Interest:	foliage
Care:	moderate

◀ Polystichum munitum

The lustrous foliage of the holly fern provides evergreen beauty to rock gardens, borders, and edgings. These easy-to-grow plants thrive in the cool shade beneath deciduous trees.

Growing and care:
Holly ferns grow well in cool, rich, moist soil, although Christmas fern is tolerant of dry periods. Crown rot can be a problem; take special care to make sure the soil is well drained. Propagate by dividing in spring.

Selected species and varieties:
P. acrostichoides (Christmas fern, canker brake) is 1½ to 2 feet tall with dark green once-divided arching fronds that are widest at the base, developing multiple crowns. *P. braunii* (shield fern, tassel fern) has dark green twice-divided fronds to 2 feet long, tapering to the base and arranged in a vaselike circle; Zones 3-8. *P. munitum* (western sword fern, giant holly fern) is 2 to 3½ feet tall with long, narrow once-divided fronds; Zones 6-9. *P. setiferum* (soft shield fern, hedge fern, English hedge fern) has glossy semievergreen 1½- to 4-foot-long twice-divided fronds that are a rich medium green and soft to the touch; 'Divisilobum' has a very lacy habit with thrice-divided leaves; Zones 5-8.

OSTRICH FERN
Matteuccia

Light:	mostly shade
Plant type:	fern
Hardiness:	Zones 4-7
Height:	2 to 6 feet
Soil and Moisture:	well-drained, moist, fertile
Interest:	foliage
Care:	easy

◀ Matteuccia struthiopteris

Under average garden conditions, these magnificently feathery, medium green deciduous ferns easily tower to 3 feet—and even more in moist soil—making them excellent background plants. Vase shaped, they spread vigorously by way of stolons and can soon cover large areas. Fertile fronds are useful in dried flower arrangements.

Growing and care:
Ostrich ferns appreciate consistently moist locations and thrive in the partial shade of tall decidous trees, though they will tolerate mostly sunny locations if given ample moisture. They do best in moisture-retentive soil in cool climates and are not recommended for areas with hot summers. Easy to maintain and very vigorous, they can become invasive. Divide by cutting the stolons and digging up the new plants.

Selected species and varieties:
M. struthiopteris (ostrich fern) has upright plumelike, 3- foot-tall vegetative fronds with 30 to 50 pairs of feathery leaflets surrounding 1- to 2-foot-tall fertile fronds, which are olive green at first then change to light brown.

ALEXANDRIAN LAUREL
Danae

Light: mostly shade	
Plant type: shrub	
Hardiness: Zones 8-9	
Height: 2 to 4 feet	
Soil and Moisture: well-drained, moist	
Interest: foliage, fruit	
Care: moderate	

◀ Danae racemosa

The lustrous rich green leaves of Alexandrian laurel and its gracefully arching habit lend elegance and texture throughout the seasons to formal as well as more casual gardens. Related to butcher's-broom, this laurel has bamboolike sheaves of rich emerald green stems and leaves. Small, easily overlooked flowers are followed by delightfully ornamental orange-red berries that appear in fall. The branches are often cut for use in holiday decorations and long-lasting indoor arrangements.

Growing and care:
Alexandrian laurel prefers light, open shade in a well-worked soil generously amended with rotted manure or compost. Winter sun can discolor the leaves. The plants are resistant to most pests and diseases and once established require little care. Propagate by dividing.

Selected species and varieties:
D. racemosa grows 2 to 4 feet high and equally wide, with long, pointed, rich green "leaves" that are actually flattened stems 1½ to 4 inches long and ¼ to 1½ inches wide. Inconspicuous greenish yellow flowers are followed by orange-red showy berries that are ¼ to ⅜ inch in diameter.

AZALEA
Rhododendron

Light: mostly shade	
Plant type: shrub	
Hardiness: Zones 3-8	
Height: 2 to 12 feet	
Soil and Moisture: well-drained, fertile, moist	
Interest: flowers, fragrance, foliage	
Care: easy to moderate	

◀ Rhododendron occidentale

Azaleas are dramatic, elegant shrubs prized for their showy flowers and classic form. Azalea is one of the most popular blooming shrubs for shade and offers a range of colors, sizes, and hardiness to fit almost any garden. The plants are excellent as specimens, tucked into the shrub border, or naturalized into woodland or wildflower gardens. Mass plantings of azaleas are spectacular whether in a woodland setting or on the shore of a stream or pond.

Growing and care:
Plant azaleas in a sheltered site with morning and late-afternoon sun. Amend the soil with peat moss or other acidic organic matter. Keep soil moist and water deeply in dry periods and before the onset of winter. Azaleas are shallow-rooted plants and benefit from mulching in spring and fall. Prune in early spring, if needed, after blooming is completed.

Selected species and varieties:
Deciduous: Exbury and Knap Hill azaleas have an upright habit 8 to 12 feet tall and nearly as wide, with medium green leaves that turn yellow, orange, or red in fall, and flowers in pink, yellow, orange, rose, red, cream, and off-white; Zones 5-7; 'Gibraltar' has extra-large, brilliant orange ruffled flowers and orangy fall foliage; Zones 4-8. *Ghent azaleas* have a shrubby habit 6 to 10 feet tall with single or double flowers in yellow, white, pink,

(continued)

orange, red, and combination colors; generally hardy to Zone 5; 'Daviesi' has fragrant white flowers with yellow centers on a wide-growing multistemmed plant; 'Narcissiflora' has fragrant double yellow hose-in-hose blooms. *R. atlanticum* (coast azalea, dwarf azalea) is 3 to 6 feet high and wide, producing pinkish white flowers opening with or before blue-green leaves; hardy to Zone 6. *R. austrinum* [also known as *R. prinophyllum*] (rose-shell azalea, early azalea) is 2 to 8 feet tall with a densely branched spreading habit, bright green foliage that turns bronze in fall, and bright pink flowers that smell like cloves. *R. calendulaceum* (flame azalea, yellow azalea) has an open habit, 4 to 8 feet tall and wide, with flowers in a multitude of yellows, pinks, oranges, peach, and red, and medium green leaves changing to a quiet yellow or red in fall; Zones 5-7. *R. occidentale* (western azalea) is a native of the West Coast, with white or pinkish flowers, 1½ to 2 inches wide, in late spring and red or yellow fall foliage; Zones 6-7. *R. schlippenbachii* (royal azalea) grows 6 feet tall with an equal spread in a rounded upright habit, bearing large, fragrant, light to rose pink flowers that open with bronze foliage that turns yellow, orange, or red in fall; Zones 4-7. *R. vaseyi* (pink-shell azalea) has an upright form to 8 feet with rose-colored bell-shaped flowers appearing before medium green summer foliage that turns red in fall; Zones 5-8. *Evergreen: Gable Hybrids* grow 2 to 4 feet high and wide with glossy dark green 1-inch-long leaves and flowers in pink, red, lavender, and other colors; Zone 5; 'Rosebud' grows 4 feet high with double flowers similar to miniature roses in silvery deep pink.

BOXWOOD
Buxus

Light:	mostly shade
Plant type:	shrub
Hardiness:	Zones 4-9
Height:	2 to 20 feet
Soil and Moisture:	well-drained, moist
Interest:	foliage
Care:	easy to moderate

◀ *Buxus microphylla* 'Wintergreen'

Boxwoods are elegant evergreens with dense glossy green foliage that is perfect for shearing into hedges or topiaries. The plants are one of the most popular shrubs for formal gardens, and the branches are often used in holiday decorations.

Growing and care:
Plant in wind-protected areas and mulch to keep roots cool and moist. The plants grow well in a wide range of conditions, from sun to shade, with those grown in mostly shade being less subject to leaf scorch in winter. Plants grown in sun should be shaded until established.

Selected species and varieties:
B. microphylla (littleleaf boxwood) forms a very slow-growing mound 3 to 4 feet tall with an equal spread, producing medium green ⅓- to 1-inch-long leaves in summer that become yellowish to green-brown in winter; Zones 6-9; 'Tide Hill' grows slowly to 2 feet tall and 5 feet wide with foliage that stays green all winter; 'Wintergreen' has small, light green leaves. *B. sempervirens* (common boxwood) produces leaves ½ to 1 inch long on a slow-growing shrub 15 to 20 feet in height with an equal or greater spread; Zones 5-8; 'Suffruticosa' is very slow growing, dense, and compact, reaching 4 to 5 feet, with fragrant leaves; 'Vardar Valley' has a flat-topped habit, growing 2 to 3 feet tall with a 4- to 5-foot spread and dark blue-green foliage; Zones 4-8.

CAMELLIA
Camellia

Light: mostly shade	
Plant type: shrub, tree	
Hardiness: Zones 6-9	
Height: 6 to 25 feet	
Soil and Moisture: well-drained, fertile, moist	
Interest: flowers, foliage	
Care: moderate	

◀ Camellia sasanqua 'Yuletide'

Camellia is one of the most beautiful of shrubs, with large, stunning red, white, or pink flowers resembling peonies set against deep glossy green leaves. Camellia is lovely as a specimen plant set where the magnificent blossoms can be viewed easily.

Growing and care:
Camellias do best in a location with some early- and late-day sun and a good deal of cooling shade. Plant in spring to allow cold hardiness to become established. Shallow-rooted camellias benefit from an application of mulch. Prune plants after flowering.

Selected species and varieties:
C. japonica (common camellia, Japanese camellia) forms a 15- to 25-foot-tall pyramid having 3- to 5-inch-wide flowers in midfall for some varieties, winter or early spring for others; Zones 7-9; 'Adolph Adusson' has red semidouble flowers 4 inches wide in late fall or early winter; 'Berenice Boddy' has light pink semidouble flowers with dark pink undersides in winter. *C. oleifera* and *C. sasanqua* Ackerman selections bear midfall flowers on a more cold-hardy plant 6 to 10 feet high; Zones 6-8; 'Snow Flurry' has white double blooms; 'Winter's Interlude' bears lavender-pink anemone-like flowers. *C. sasanqua* 'Yuletide' grows 6 to 10 feet tall, bearing 2- to 3-inch single red flowers with yellow stamens from fall to early winter.

DAPHNE
Daphne

Light: mostly shade	
Plant type: shrub	
Hardiness: Zones 4-9	
Height: 3 to 5 feet	
Soil and Moisture: well-drained, sandy, moist	
Interest: flowers, fragrance, foliage	
Care: difficult	

◀ Daphne x burkwoodii 'Carol Mackie'

Daphnes are temperamental plants, but their intensely fragrant late-winter or early-spring flowers make them worthwhile to grow. They can be either deciduous or evergreen. Birds love the red berries that appear in summer. Daphne is a lovely plant for the shrub border or planted alone as a specimen. Caution: All parts of the plant are poisonous to humans.

Growing and care:
Plant daphne in spring or fall in a deep well-worked sandy soil that has had copious amounts of rotted manure or compost added. Once planted do not move. The plants do best in shady locations with some early- or late-day sun. Despite the best care, however, daphnes may suddenly die for unknown reasons.

Selected species and varieties:
D. x *burkwoodii* (Burkwood daphne) is 3 to 4 feet high with an equal spread, producing clusters of fragrant, creamy white to pinkish spring flowers and semievergreen foliage; Zones 4-8; 'Carol Mackie' has leaves with creamy margins. *D. mezereum* (February daphne) is 3 to 5 feet high and wide with lavender to rosy purple flowers that emerge in late winter to early spring before the semievergreen to deciduous leaves; Zones 4-8. *D. odora* (winter daphne) is 3 feet high, densely branched, and evergreen, growing extremely fragrant rosy purple flowers in late winter to early spring; Zones 7-9.

DEVILWOOD
Osmanthus

Light:	mostly shade
Plant type:	shrub, tree
Hardiness:	Zones 7-10
Height:	8 to 30 feet
Soil and Moisture:	well-drained, fertile, moist
Interest:	fragrance, foliage
Care:	easy

◀ Osmanthus fragrans

Devilwood's clusters of tiny white four-petaled fall flowers may be mostly hidden by its foliage, but the fragrance is spectacular. Some species have hollylike leaves with spines that are gradually lost as the plant ages. Because of their density, these shrubs make good barrier plants. Others are useful as foundation plants, in borders, and as screens, but are especially valuable near walkways.

Growing and care:
Devilwood transplants easily into well-worked soil amended with some organic matter. The plants can be heavily pruned with no ill effect. Devilwood is easy to grow and is tolerant of urban conditions. The plants thrive in mostly shady locations and tolerate mostly sunny sites, though the foliage may become discolored.

Selected species and varieties:
O. x *fortunei* (Fortune's osmanthus) has an oval habit 15 to 20 feet tall with white flowers in fall; Zones 8-10. *O. fragrans* (fragrant olive) is the most fragrant form, a 15- to 30-foot shrub or tree that sometimes produces a spring bloom as well, with lustrous dark green spineless leaves; reliably hardy only in Zones 9-10. *O. heterophyllus* 'Gulftide' (holly olive, Chinese holly) has an dense upright form 8 to 15 feet high with glossy green leaves and prominent spines; 'Variegatus' slowly grows to 8 feet or so, with white margins on the leaves; Zones 7-9.

DROOPING LEUCOTHOE
Leucothoe

Light:	mostly shade
Plant type:	shrub
Hardiness:	Zones 4-9
Height:	2 to 6 feet
Soil and Moisture:	well-drained, moist, fertile
Interest:	flowers, foliage
Care:	moderate

◀ Leucothoe fontanesiana 'Rainbow'

With its clusters of creamy urn-shaped flowers, lustrous green leaves, arching branches, and spreading broad-mounded habit, *Leucothoe* looks stunning in the garden either as a specimen plant or planted in masses. The low forms make elegant ground covers.

Growing and care:
Plant *Leucothoe* in spring in a sheltered spot away from persistent winds. Add peat moss, leaf mold, or dried compost liberally to soil when planting, and mulch to keep roots cool. The plants grow best in mostly to fully shady locations but will tolerate mostly sun if kept well watered. Prune after flowering is completed.

Selected species and varieties:
L. davisiae (Sierra laurel) grows to 5 feet high with nodding upright panicles of flowers up to 6 inches long, borne above 1- to 3-inch leaves in late spring or early summer. *L. fontanesiana* (dog-hobble, drooping leucothoe) is 3 to 6 feet high and wide with arching branches of dark green 2- to 5-inch-long pointed leaves that turn red-bronze for fall and winter, and fragrant 2- to 3-inch flower clusters protruding from beneath the foliage in spring; 'Nana' is a dwarf 2 feet tall spreading to 6 feet; Zones 4-6; 'Rainbow' [also called 'Girard's Rainbow'] has leaves variegated in pink, yellow, cream, and green.

FIVE-LEAF ARALIA
Acanthopanax

Light:	mostly shade
Plant type:	shrub
Hardiness:	Zones 4-8
Height:	6 to 10 feet
Soil and Moisture:	well-drained, moist to dry
Interest:	foliage
Care:	easy

◀ Acanthopanax
sieboldianus
'Variegatus'

Five-leaf aralia is an excellent plant for difficult sites. The arching wide-spreading stems form the plant into a broad rounded shrub, but it can be sheared to produce a dense hedge. Its bright green compound leaves appear in early spring and persist late into fall. Slender prickles along the stems make *Acanthopanax* an effective barrier.

Growing and care:
Acanthopanax is easy to transplant and adapts well to all light conditions, from full sun to deep shade. It tolerates a wide range of soil types, from acid to alkaline and from sandy to clay, and it stands up well to air pollution and drought. As a hedge it can be heavily pruned or sheared to encourage compact growth and maintain the desired height. In an informal mixed planting, little pruning is necessary.

Selected species and varieties:
A. sieboldianus is an erect shrub with arching branches, five to seven leaflets per leaf, and light brown stems with slender prickles; 'Variegatus' stands 6 to 8 feet tall and has leaves with creamy white margins.

FUCHSIA
Fuchsia

Light:	mostly shade
Plant type:	shrub
Hardiness:	Zones 9-10
Height:	1½ to 3 feet
Soil and Moisture:	well-drained, moist
Interest:	flowers
Care:	easy

◀ Fuchsia x hybrida

The colorful pendulous blooms of fuchsia resemble brightly colored earrings, and dangle from stems that may reach 3 to 5 feet in length. It is grown most often in a hanging basket or container that can take advantage of its trailing habit. Fuchsia makes an effective standard when trained and pruned to develop an upright stem with a rounded crown of foliage and flowers.

Growing and care:
Plant fuchsia in a well-drained moisture-retentive potting medium and water regularly. Plants thrive in mostly to full shade. Fuchsia is subject to infestations of mites, whiteflies, mealybugs, aphids, and Japanese beetles. To overwinter plants, bring the container into a cool (40°F) area prior to the first hard frost, and water sparingly. In very early spring, cut back stems and increase watering. Plants can be moved outdoors after danger of frost has passed. Propagate by cuttings taken in spring or autumn.

Selected species and varieties:
F. x *hybrida* grows 1½ to 3 feet tall with a rounded to trailing habit, 2- to 5-inch-long pointed leaves, and pendent flowers, each with a 2- to 3-inch-long calyx tube and four sepals, and ½-inch-long petals, often in a contrasting shade, surrounding protruding stamens and styles; 'Crusader' bears flowers with a double violet corolla, white sepals, and a red tube; 'Pink Chiffon' bears double pink blooms.

HEAVENLY BAMBOO
Nandina

Light: mostly shade

Plant type: shrub

Hardiness: Zones 6-9

Height: 2 to 8 feet

Soil and Moisture: well-drained, fertile, moist

Interest: flowers, foliage, fruit

Care: easy to moderate

◀ Nandina domestica

Heavenly bamboo is an excellent plant for the four-season garden, with attractive flowers, foliage, and fruit. In spring the emerging leaves have a coppery hue and, as they are turning their summer color of blue-green, panicles of creamy flowers appear. In late summer and fall spectacular clusters of red berries appear that persist through winter. *Nandina* is excellent for foundations or borders, in masses, or as a specimen.

Growing and care:
Although *Nandina* grows best in acid loam, it tolerates a wide range of other soils and withstands drought. Winter sun helps redden foliage, and the plants thrive in full sun to full shade. Plant in groups to improve berrying. If left unpruned it becomes leggy; remove old canes or cut canes to various lengths to create a dense plant. Canes cannot be forced to branch.

Selected species and varieties:
N. domestica (heavenly bamboo, sacred bamboo) has an erect habit 6 to 8 feet tall with compound leaves having sharply tapered leaflets, each $1\frac{1}{2}$ to 4 inches long and half as wide, 8- to 15-inch-long clusters of tiny white flowers with yellow anthers, and heavy panicles of $\frac{1}{3}$-inch berries; 'Harbour Dwarf' grows to 2 to 3 feet, forming a graceful mound.

HEMLOCK
Tsuga

Light: mostly shade

Plant type: tree

Hardiness: Zones 3-8

Height: 40 to 70 feet

Soil and Moisture: well-drained, moist

Interest: foliage

Care: easy to moderate

◀ Tsuga canadensis

Hemlocks are softly pyramidal evergreens whose graceful drooping branches and small needles lend a fine texture to the shade garden. The plants can be allowed to grow into towering specimens or sheared into formal hedges and screens. They are excellent when massed along the shore of a pond or stream.

Growing and care:
Hemlocks thrive in a wide range of light conditions, from full sun to deep shade, but grow best in mostly shaded locations that are sheltered from strong winds. Plant in deep soil amended with organic matter. Mulch to keep soil moist and cool. Sunscald occurs at 95°F and above. Canadian hemlocks can be kept at 3 to 5 feet with shearing. Host to a number of pests, the hemlock has been besieged in parts of the East by the woolly adelgid.

Selected species and varieties:
T. canadensis (Canadian hemlock, eastern hemlock) has a tapering trunk 65 feet or taller, bearing medium green needles $\frac{1}{4}$ to $\frac{2}{3}$ inch long and oval $\frac{1}{2}$- to 1-inch cones on slender, pliant branches. *T. caroliniana* (Carolina hemlock) grows 45 to 60 feet tall, is more tolerant of urban conditions, and has darker green needles than those of Canadian hemlock and a stiffer form.

HOLLY
Ilex

Light: mostly shade	
Plant type: shrub, tree	
Hardiness: Zones 3-9	
Height: 4 to 50 feet	
Soil and Moisture: well-drained, moist, moderately acidic to neutral	
Interest: foliage, fruit	
Care: moderate	

◄ Ilex 'Sparkleberry'

Evergreen hollies have lustrous broad-leaved foliage and often showy berries; deciduous hollies are attractive in winter, when they produce red fruits. Female hollies of both types produce red, black, and sometimes yellow berries if a male is nearby. The smaller hollies are useful for edgings and rock gardens, the medium-size varieties for foundation plantings and shrub borders, and the largest ones for screens and specimen trees.

Growing and care:
Evergreen hollies suffer when exposed to harsh sun, severe winter winds, and drought, and some hollies languish in heat and humidity. The plants prefer a sheltered, mostly shady site. If soil is either heavy or sandy, amend with organic matter such as leaf mold or peat moss. Water young hollies regularly. Female plants must have a male nearby for berries to form.

Selected species and varieties:
I. 'Apollo' grows 10 to 12 feet high and wide with reddish foliage aging to dark green. *I. crenata* (Japanese holly) has a dense rounded habit resembling boxwood, with dark green spineless leaves ½ to 1 inch long and black berries that are usually hidden under the leaves; Zones 5-8; 'Compacta' grows 5 to 6 feet tall and globular with leaves ¾ inch long; 'Convexa' is vase shaped and dense, to 9 feet tall and broader than its height, with ½-inch leaves; one of the hardiest of the species; 'Dwarf Pagoda' has tiny leaves ¼ inch wide and up to ½ inch long; 'Helleri' is a dwarf mound growing very slowly to 4 feet tall by 5 feet wide with small fine-toothed leaves; 'Hetzii' grows 6 to 8 feet tall and round with ½- to 1-inch leaves. *I. glabra* (inkberry, winterberry) is a multistemmed species 6 to 8 feet tall by 8 to 10 feet wide becoming loose and open with age, with ¾- to 2-inch-long spineless, spatula-shaped leaves and black fruit; 'Compacta' grows 4 to 6 feet high with denser branching than the species; Zones 4-9. *I. opaca* (American holly) grows 15 to 30 feet high, conical when young but later spreading, with dark green spiny evergreen leaves 1½ to 4 inches long and showy red or yellow fruit; 'Amy' has large lustrous leaves and large red berries; 'Cardinal', small light red berries and small, dark green leaves; 'Goldie', yellow berries and nonglossy leaves; 'Jersey Knight' (male) has a dense upright habit and dark green leaves; 'Old Heavy Berry' produces heavy yields of large red berries against large dark green leaves; Zones 5-9. *I. pedunculosa* (long-stalked holly) is a large shrub or small tree 15 to 25 feet high with wavy, shiny, smooth-margined leaves and berries on long stalks; Zones 5-7. *I.* 'Sparkleberry' has small red berries and nearly black bark. *I. verticillata* 'Winter Red' (winterberry, black alder) is a deciduous plant 6 to 10 feet tall and wide with 1½- to 3-inch spineless leaves and a profusion of red fruit on bare branches in early winter.

JAPANESE FATSIA
Fatsia

Light: mostly shade	
Plant type: shrub	
Hardiness: Zones 8-10	
Height: 6 to 10 feet	
Soil and Moisture: well-drained, moist	
Interest: flowers, foliage	
Care: moderate	

◄ Fatsia japonica

A bold, dramatic plant with a tropical effect, Japanese fatsia creates a rounded mound of deeply lobed dark green leaves up to 14 inches wide. In midautumn, round clusters of tiny white flowers form on long stalks, followed by round black fruit that persists through winter.

Growing and care:

Although *Fatsia* tolerates clay and sandy soils, it prefers light soils high in organic matter. The plants grow best in sheltered, mostly shady locations with some early- or late-day sun but also do well in full shade. Prune to control legginess. Fertilize in spring and after flowering.

Selected species and varieties:

F. japonica (Japanese fatsia, Formosa rice tree, paper plant, glossy-leaved paper plant) is a moderate to fast grower 6 to 10 feet high and wide, usually with an open, sparsely branched habit displaying lustrous evergreen leaves with seven to nine prominent lobes on 4- to 12-inch-long stalks, and flowers clustered in 1½-inch-wide spheres on white stalks, several spheres forming a showy, branched cluster. x *Fatshedera lizei* is an intergeneric hybrid between *F. japonica* 'Moseri' and *Hedera helix* 'Hibernica' with large, glossy, dark green leaves and slender stems that can be trained to a support.

JAPANESE ROSE
Kerria

Light: mostly shade	
Plant type: shrub	
Hardiness: Zones 4-9	
Height: 3 to 8 feet	
Soil and Moisture: well-drained, moist	
Interest: flowers, foliage	
Care: easy to moderate	

◄ Kerria japonica

Japanese rose sports abundant medium green leaves that serve as an excellent background for the vivid yellow springtime flowers. The foliage turns yellow in autumn and drops, revealing bare green stems that hold their color all winter. *Kerria* is excellent used in borders or massed at the edge of meadows.

Growing and care:

Kerria tolerates most soils and urban conditions but enjoys soil amended with organic matter. Excessive fertility produces reduced bloom. The plants grow best, and the yellow color of the flowers lasts longest, in mostly shady spots, though they also tolerate full shade. Remove winter-killed branches in early spring; other pruning should be done just after flowering. On 'Picta', remove any green shoots that emerge. Cut off old stems at the base every few years to maintain vigor.

Selected species and varieties:

K. japonica grows 3 to 6 feet tall with a greater spread of arching branches that bear glossy heavily veined coarse-toothed leaves 1½ to 4 inches long; 'Picta' [also known as 'Variegata'] is a dwarf clone growing to 3 feet tall with white-edged gray-green leaves and single yellow flowers; 'Pleniflora' [also known as 'Flora Pleno'] (globeflower kerria) grows semierectly 5 to 8 feet tall with very double pompom-like flowers 1 to 2 inches wide, more open in habit than the species.

LACE SHRUB
Stephanandra

Light:	mostly shade
Plant type:	shrub
Hardiness:	Zones 3-8
Height:	1½ to 3 feet
Soil and Moisture:	well-drained, moist
Interest:	foliage
Care:	moderate

◀ Stephanandra incisa 'Crispa'

Lace shrub, also called cutleaf stephanandra, is a tidy plant with a gracefully mounding habit of dense branches and plentiful attractive foliage. It may be grown on banks to prevent erosion or may be used as a low hedge or tall ground cover. Its thick foliage and low habit make it well suited to growing under low windows or among tall leggy shrubs in a mixed border.

Growing and care:
Plant lace shrub in moist, acid soil in a lightly shaded location. Add generous amounts of organic matter to the soil prior to planting to help retain moisture. Protect from breezy areas where drying winds can cause winter-kill of twig tips. Prune damaged or dead branches in spring as growth begins. The plant is easily propagated by simple layering of stems.

Selected species and varieties:
S. incisa 'Crispa' grows 1½ to 3 feet tall and 4 feet wide, and spreads by arching branches rooting readily when they touch the ground. Deeply lobed 1- to 2-inch-long bright green leaves turn reddish purple or red-orange in fall; inconspicuous pale yellow flowers appear in early summer.

MOUNTAIN LAUREL
Kalmia

Light:	mostly shade
Plant type:	shrub
Hardiness:	Zones 4-9
Height:	2 to 15 feet
Soil and Moisture:	well-drained, moist, fertile
Interest:	flowers, foliage
Care:	easy

◀ Kalmia latifolia 'Ostbo Red'

With its lustrous foliage and sometimes star-shaped flowers, mountain laurel is an exquisite plant for shady areas. The white, pink, or red blossoms appear in clusters in late spring, opening like little parasols. The flowers create a stunning display when the plants are massed along the shores of ponds or along paths.

Growing and care:
Although mountain laurel adapts to deep shade, it flowers best in mostly shady locations with some direct sunlight. Plants grown in sunny locations are more susceptible to leaf scorch in late winter and early spring. They do best in loose loam; add organic matter liberally to the soil when planting, and mulch to keep cool and preserve moisture. Remove flowers after they fade.

Selected species and varieties:
K. latifolia has a round habit, growing 5 to 15 feet high with 2- to 5-inch-long oval leaves. It flowers in clusters 4 to 6 inches wide in late spring to early summer; 'Bullseye' has deep purplish buds that open to creamy white flowers with a purple band; 'Ostbo Red', bright red buds that open to deep pink flowers; 'Raspberry Glow', wine red buds opening to raspberry pink blooms; 'Richard Jaynes', red buds opening to pink blooms that are silvery white inside; 'Silver Dollar', pink buds and large white flowers; 'Tiddlywinks' is a slow-growing dwarf 2 to 5 feet high with pink buds and lighter pink flowers.

OREGON GRAPE
Mahonia

Light: mostly shade

Plant type: shrub

Hardiness: Zones 5-10

Height: 10 inches to 12 feet

Soil and Moisture: well-drained, moist, fertile

Interest: flowers, fragrance, fruit

Care: moderate

◀ Mahonia bealei

Oregon grape's lemon yellow flowers in earliest spring can perfume a shady garden. The grapelike berries, maturing in summer, are covered with a blue bloom and are relished by birds. Stiff and formal in habit, *Mahonia* has leathery hollylike compound leaves that are blue-green in summer and purplish in winter.

Growing and care:

Plant *Mahonia* in spring in well-worked, acid soil that has been amended with abundant organic matter. The plants grow best in sheltered locations in mostly shade, though they will tolerate deep shade. Dry soils or too much sun will yellow leaves. Add a layer of mulch in spring and again in fall to retain soil moisture and provide extra water during dry periods.

Selected species and varieties:

M. aquifolium (mountain grape, holly barberry) has slightly fragrant flowers borne in terminal clusters 2 to 3 inches long and wide on upright stems on a 3- to 9-foot-tall shrub; Zones 5-8. *M. bealei* (leatherleaf mahonia) bears very fragrant flowers 6 to 12 inches wide and 3 to 6 inches long from late winter to early spring, and berries that turn from robin's-egg blue to blue-black on a 10- to 12-foot-tall shrub; hardy to Zone 7. *M. repens* (creeping mahonia) forms a spreading mat of stiff stems to 10 inches high with deep yellow flowers in 1- to 3-inch-long racemes.

PIERIS
Pieris

Light: mostly shade

Plant type: shrub

Hardiness: Zones 5-8

Height: 6 to 12 feet

Soil and Moisture: well-drained, moist, fertile

Interest: flowers, foliage

Care: easy

◀ Pieris japonica 'Variegata'

The ivory-colored clusters of pieris perfume the early-spring air with a subtle but unforgettable fragrance. New foliage, tinged with reddish bronze, unfurls and retains that hue for weeks before turning a lustrous dark green. Japanese pieris makes a beautiful four-season specimen, and also works well in foundations and borders.

Growing and care:

Japanese pieris grows best in well-drained soil well supplemented with leaf mold or peat moss. Mulch around plants with pine needles in spring and fall. Plant in a sheltered spot away from strong winds. Plants grown on northern exposures are less prone to winter leaf scald.

Selected species and varieties:

P. japonica (Japanese pieris, lily-of-the-valley bush) is an upright shrub 6 to 8 feet wide with spreading branches bearing rosettes of shiny leaves and slightly fragrant 3- to 6-inch-long flower clusters; 'Compacta' grows densely to a height of 6 feet with small leaves and prolific bloom; 'Crispa' has wavy leaves; 'Variegata' has leaves with creamy to silver margins.

PITTOSPORUM
Pittosporum

Light:	mostly shade
Plant type:	shrub
Hardiness:	Zones 8-10
Height:	10 to 12 feet
Soil and Moisture:	well-drained, moist
Interest:	flowers, foliage, fragrance
Care:	easy

◄ Pittosporum tobira

A dense, impenetrable evergreen shrub whose flowers carry the scent of orange blossoms, pittosporum is used in foundation beds, drifts, barriers, hedges, and windbreaks. The round-tipped leaves are borne in rosettes at the ends of branches, lending a soft, clean appearance to the slow-growing symmetrical mound. A variegated form works well as a bright accent. Pittosporums may be left unsheared or pruned into formal shapes.

Growing and care:
Pittosporums tolerate soil from dry and sandy to moist clay, requiring only that the soil be well drained. They withstand salt spray and thrive in hot, humid climates and exposed locations.

Selected species and varieties:
P. tobira (Japanese pittosporum, mock orange) grows 10 to 12 feet high and nearly twice as wide, with leathery dark green leaves 1½ to 4 inches long and up to 1½ inches wide, and tiny five-petaled creamy white flowers in 2- to 3-inch clusters in spring, turning yellow with age and eventually becoming green to brown pods that split to expose orange seeds in fall.

RHODODENDRON
Rhododendron

Light:	mostly shade
Plant type:	shrub
Hardiness:	Zones 4-8
Height:	2 to 12 feet
Soil and Moisture:	well-drained, fertile, moist
Interest:	flowers, foliage
Care:	easy to moderate

◄ Rhododendron 'P. J. M.'

R hododendrons are the backbone of many shrub borders, with bold, mostly evergreen glossy foliage accented with striking clusters of elegant late-spring flowers. The plants are excellent in beds and borders, or allowed to naturalize in woodland and wildflower plantings, while dwarf forms add interest to rock gardens. Rhododendrons are stunning when planted in masses near ponds, allowing the beauty of the flowers to be reflected in the water.

Growing and care:
Rhododendrons need well-drained soil with plenty of peat moss or leaf mold. Set plant so that the top of the rootball is an inch or two above the surface of the soil. Mulch to conserve moisture and to keep roots cool. Water deeply in dry periods, particularly before the onset of winter. Evergreen types should be protected from hot afternoon sun and winter winds. Morning sun enhances bloom without stressing the plant. Foundation plantings run the risk of failing, because lime leaching from structural cement sweetens the soil; in these cases, increase soil acidity with aluminum sulfate. Unlike other members of this genus, royal azalea does well in near-neutral soil.

Selected species and varieties:
R. catawbiense (Catawba rhododendron, mountain rosebay, purple laurel) bears lilac-purple, sometimes purplish

(continued)

rose flowers in midspring, growing 6 to 10 feet tall and not as wide. *R.* hybrids: 'Blue Diamond' grows to 3 feet with lavender-blue flowers; hardy to Zone 7; 'Bow Bells' has bright pink flowers, rounded leaves, and bronzy new growth to 4 feet; hardy to Zone 6; 'Cilpinense' grows to 2½ feet with light pink flowers fading to white, its buds reliably hardy only in Zone 8; 'Moonstone' grows to 2 feet with pale pink flowers turning creamy yellow, reliably hardy to Zone 7; 'Ramapo' has blue-green new foliage and violet-blue flowers, 2 to 4 feet tall; Zone 5; 'Scarlet Wonder' grows 2 feet tall with bright red flowers and shiny quilted foliage; Zone 6. *R. mucronulatum* (Korean rhododendron) is a deciduous shrub with a rounded open habit, 4 to 8 feet tall and wide, with rosy purple flowers in late winter followed by 1- to 4-inch-long medium green leaves that are aromatic when crushed and turn yellow to bronzy red in fall. *R.* 'P. J. M.' grows 3 to 6 feet tall and wide with lavender-pink flowers borne profusely in early to midspring and dark green evergreen leaves 1 to 2½ inches long that turn plum in fall and winter.

SILVER-BELL
Halesia

◀ Halesia monticola

Light:	mostly shade
Plant type:	tree
Hardiness:	Zones 4-8
Height:	25 to 80 feet
Soil and Moisture:	well-drained, fertile, moist
Interest:	flowers, fruit
Care:	easy

Silver-bell is a handsome tree with strong upright branches smothered in spring with snow white dangling clusters of bell-shaped flowers. The attractive green leaves turn shades of yellow in fall. Green to brown four-winged fruits remain after the leaves have fallen. The furrowed and plated bark is gray, brown, and black. Silver-bell serves well as an understory tree but can also be used to create shade for other plants.

Growing and care:
Silver-bells do best in moist soil amended with organic matter. They are easy to grow and tolerate urban conditions well. The plants are pest- and disease-free.

Selected species and varieties:
H. monticola (mountain silver-bell) grows 60 to 80 feet tall with a usually conical habit displaying 1-inch-long flowers in two- to five-flowered clusters as the 3- to 6½-inch-long leaves begin to develop; 'Rosea' has pale rose-colored flowers. *H. tetraptera* [also classified as *H. carolina*] (Carolina silver-bell, opossumwood) is a smaller low-branched version of mountain silver-bell 25 to 40 feet tall with a rounded crown 20 to 35 feet wide consisting of ascending branches with 2- to 4-inch leaves, flowers ½ to ¾ inch long, and fruits 1½ inches long.

SKIMMIA
Skimmia

Light: mostly shade

Plant type: shrub

Hardiness: Zones 7-9

Height: 3 to 4 feet

Soil and Moisture: well-drained, moist

Interest: flowers, foliage, fruit

Care: easy

◄ Skimmia japonica

Skimmia forms a low mound of leathery leaves decorated in spring with clusters of flowers and in fall with bright berries that remain into the next spring. In order for a female bush to produce berries, a male bush, which produces larger flowers that are also fragrant, has to be located within 100 feet. Skimmia is beautiful in foundation plantings and in masses.

Growing and care:
Japanese skimmia may be planted in Zone 9 on the West Coast and north to Zone 7 on the East Coast if given a protected location. In hot climates, site it out of afternoon sun. Foliage may discolor in winter sun. Add 1 part peat moss or leaf mold to every 2 parts of soil to improve drainage. Fertilizing and pruning are not usually necessary.

Selected species and varieties:
S. japonica (Japanese skimmia) has a rounded densely branched habit, slowly growing to 3 to 4 feet tall and slightly wider, bearing bright green leaves 2½ to 5 inches long that are tightly spaced at the ends of branches, and producing 2- to 3-inch clusters of red buds that open to creamy white flowers on reddish purple stems.

SUMMER-SWEET
Clethra

Light: mostly shade

Plant type: shrub, tree

Hardiness: Zones 3-10

Height: 3 to 25 feet

Soil and Moisture: well-drained, moist to wet

Interest: flowers, fragrance

Care: easy

◄ Clethra alnifolia

Summer-sweet's fragrant 4- to 6-inch-long clusters of sweetly fragrant white or pink flowers appear in late summer. It is found throughout North America, with the most ornamental species native to swamps and wet woodlands of the eastern United States. Summer-sweet is often used as a specimen plant in mixed-shrub borders, or naturalized in moist woodland gardens.

Growing and care:
Plant summer-sweets in spring in well-worked soil amended with peat moss or compost. Mulch to keep roots cool and to retain moisture. Propagate in spring by transplanting offshoots that appear near the base of the stem.

Selected species and varieties:
C. alnifolia (summer-sweet, sweet pepperbush) grows 3 to 8 feet tall and 4 to 6 feet wide with 4-inch spikes of heavily scented snowy white flowers in summer and lustrous green leaves that turn gold in fall; 'Pink Spires' has rosy red buds opening to pastel pink flowers; Zones 3-9. *C. arborea* (lily-of-the-valley tree) is 20 to 25 feet tall with 3- to 4-inch elliptical evergreen leaves and 6-inch softly drooping clusters of fragrant white flowers in late summer and early fall; Zones 9-10.

SWAMP ROSE
Rosa

Light:	mostly shade
Plant type:	shrub
Hardiness:	Zones 3-7
Height:	4 to 5 feet
Soil and Moisture:	well-drained to heavy, wet to dry
Interest:	flowers, fragrance, fruit
Care:	easy

◀ Rosa palustris

Swamp rose produces its fragrant dark rose pink single blooms intermittently throughout summer, providing a longer flowering season than most other species roses. Flowers are 2 inches across and are followed by oval orange-red hips in late summer through fall. Foliage is medium to dark green in summer, turning deep burgundy red in fall. The branches are long and graceful, forming a mounding shrub well suited for hedges and mass plantings.

Growing and care:
Plant swamp rose in a shaded location in soil that has some organic matter. The plants adapt to a wide range of conditions, and are at home in wet, marshy places as well as in drier ones. Prune out older canes to keep plants vigorous. Overgrown plants can be cut to ground level in fall or spring.

Selected species and varieties:
R. palustris var. *nuttalliana* has large flowers that appear from summer to fall. *R. palustris* var. *plena* is a variety of swamp rose with double rose pink flowers on canes about 5 feet high.

SWEETSPIRE
Itea

Light:	mostly shade
Plant type:	shrub
Hardiness:	Zones 5-9
Height:	2 to 5 feet
Soil and Moisture:	well-drained, fertile, moist to dry
Interest:	flowers, foliage, fragrance
Care:	moderate

◀ Itea virginica

Sweetspire is a handsome shrub with creamy white, lightly fragrant summertime flowers and a colorful fall foliage display that is second to none. The blossoms are packed along cylindrical racemes that appear at the ends of slender twigs. The leaves are medium green in summer, turning brilliant shades of violet, red, and scarlet for weeks in fall. The plants thrive in the moist, fertile soils of wet meadows, of marshes, and along streams and ponds, making them perfect for naturalizing. They are also very drought tolerant and can be used effectively in the shrub border as well as dry woodlands.

Growing and care:
Plant sweetspire in moist to dry soil that has been liberally amended with organic matter. In dry locations keep soil moist until plants are established. Sweetspire can be propagated by division or sowing seed as soon as it ripens in fall.

Selected species and varieties:
I. japonica 'Beppu' is 2 to 5 feet tall with a spreading moundlike habit, spreading by suckers, with leaves that are rich green in summer and red in fall, and fragrant white flowers; useful as a ground cover. *I. virginica* 'Henry's Garnet' grows 3 to 4 feet tall and 4 to 6 feet wide, with green leaves that turn purple-red in fall, and fragrant white flowers in clusters up to 6 inches long; an excellent addition to mixed-shrub borders.

4

Plants for Places with Full Shade

The plants that grow in the dim light of shady places do not have to face the desiccating rays of the sun each day. Instead they have different obstacles to overcome. Shady places warm up more slowly in the spring and stay wet longer than sunny spots. For many shady places, trees or shrubs are already present and their spreading canopies block out the sun while their roots absorb moisture and nutrients. Very few plants thrive in full shade compared to the number of plants that prefer sun; but those that do well in full shade can give the garden years of beauty. To grow the best plants in shady places make sure the soil is well drained and amended with plenty of organic matter. Allow each plant an area free of competing roots, and your shady plantings can achieve their full potential.

Very few plants thrive in full shade, with no direct light to spur their growth. This is particularly so for annuals, which as a group need direct sunlight to fuel their rapid growth and short life cycle. Full shade conditions vary depending on the intensity of light. Full shade beneath a stand of mature pine trees is much darker than the full shade under honey locusts, willows, or apple trees. With this range of shade in mind, consider the conditions in your garden as you establish your full shade plantings.

Plants in this book have been classified according to their preferred site and conditions. Because annuals do best with at least some sun they have been grouped in the other three chapters in this book. Yet even though full shade is not the best condition for annuals, there are some that do grow and blossom well there. These include: coleus, whose vibrant-colored leaves retain their brilliance longer when grown in shade; forget-me-not, which grows best in full sun to mostly shade but still flowers well when grown in very shady places; and impatiens, which ignites shade gardens with its vivid flowers from summer to fall.

BLUEBELLS
Mertensia

Light: full shade

Plant type: perennial

Hardiness: Zones 3-8

Height: 1 to 3 feet

Soil and Moisture: well-drained, moist to wet

Interest: flowers, foliage

Care: easy

◀ Mertensia virginica

These North American natives have long been grown in gardens for their springtime displays of pale blue trumpet-shaped flowers. Their leaves emerge in spring with a distinctive purplish sheen, and mature to pale blue-green. The flower shoots bear nodding clusters of pink buds that open to powder blue and fade to lilac. Bluebells enter dormancy shortly after flowering, and should be planted with companions such as ferns to fill in the vacant spaces. These plants are effective grown in large clumps in shady borders and rock gardens, or naturalized in deciduous woodlands or alongside streams.

Growing and care:
Propagate by sowing fresh seed in early summer, or by dividing the root mass immediately after flowers fade. It may be difficult to locate the dormant roots, so mark their locations to avoid damaging them later. Replant divisions 1½ feet apart, setting the plants so the crowns are even with the surface of the soil.

Selected species and varieties:
M. ciliata (mountain bluebells, Rocky Mountain bluebells) grows 1 to 3 feet high with a clumping habit, producing persistent smooth, succulent leaves and slightly fragrant ¾-inch flowers in late spring and summer; *M. virginica* (Virginia bluebells, Virginia cowslip) has 1½- to 2-foot shoots bearing thick elliptical leaves and clusters of 1-inch flowers in midspring; 'Alba' has white flowers.

DIPHYLLEIA
Diphylleia

Light: full shade

Plant type: perennial

Hardiness: Zones 6-8

Height: 2 to 3 feet

Soil and Moisture: well-drained, moist, fertile

Interest: flowers, foliage

Care: easy

◀ Diphylleia cymosa

Diphylleia is a decorative plant native to the eastern Appalachian Mountains. This easy-to-grow wildflower is useful for naturalizing in drifts under trees and large shrubs. Mammoth rounded, cleft leaves form the background for the cymes of white flowers with yellow stamens that appear in late spring or early summer. A month later, small powdery blue berries appear.

Growing and care:
Diphylleia is easily grown in settings that duplicate its native woodlands and does best beneath groves of tall deciduous trees. Work leaf mold, peat moss, or compost into the soil before planting. Mulch after planting with leaf mold to conserve soil moisture. Propagate by division in spring or by sowing seed at harvest.

Selected species and varieties:
D. cymosa (umbrella leaf) has 2- to 3-foot-tall stalks, and foliage that emerges copper colored before turning light green, consisting of only two leaves, each with a cleft dividing the leaf in half, each half with five to seven lobes. Flowers form above the foliage in flat-topped clusters, and berries appear later.

GOLDEN-RAY
Ligularia

Light: full shade	
Plant type: perennial	
Hardiness: Zones 4-10	
Height: 2 to 6 feet	
Soil and Moisture: fertile, moist to wet	
Interest: flowers, foliage	
Care: moderate	

◀ Ligularia stenocephala 'The Rocket'

Largely overlooked by many gardeners, golden-ray can be a valuable addition to shady gardens. The plants have large, boldly shaped leaves that accent the upright spikes of vivid yellow or orange flowers in summer. Golden-ray grows equally well in full or partial shade and in moist or wet soil. The plants form a coarse-textured ground cover that serves as a backdrop for the vivid flowers that seem to ignite shady areas.

Growing and care:
Because its enormous leaves lose large amounts of water, golden-ray does best in a cool spot where a continuous supply of moisture is assured. Propagate by division in spring or fall.

Selected species and varieties:
L. dentata (bigleaf golden-ray) has 20-inch-wide saucer-like leaves and daisylike flowers; 'Desdemona' has reddish leaves with purple beneath that turn bronze by summer on plants to 4 feet with reddish orange flowers; 'Othello' grows 3 feet tall with red-purple leaves and yellow-orange blooms; Zones 4-8. *L. stenocephala* [also listed as *L. przewalskii*] 'The Rocket' has clumps 4 to 6 feet tall with deeply cut leaves 8 to 12 inches wide and bright yellow flower spikes on black stems that emerge in summer and last longer than the species; Zones 5-8.

HARDY BEGONIA
Begonia

Light: full shade	
Plant type: perennial	
Hardiness: Zones 6-10	
Height: 2 to 3 feet	
Soil and Moisture: well-drained, moist, fertile	
Interest: flowers, foliage	
Care: easy	

◀ Begonia grandis ssp. evansiana

Hardy begonia is a delightful addition to shady gardens. The plants produce masses of medium green to reddish bronze leaves shaped like small elephant ears. Slender stems rise above the foliage, each displaying loose, drooping clusters of pale pink blossoms in summer. Hardy begonias are excellent for shaded borders, for rock gardens, or as an edging along wooded paths. They can also be grown in pots or window boxes to add color to patios and decks.

Growing and care:
Plant hardy begonias in a shaded location in soil well amended with compost or other organic matter. For container growing plant in a soil mix made of equal parts potting mix and peat moss. Mulch around plants in spring and provide extra water during dry periods. North of Zone 8 cover with a layer of winter mulch.

Selected species and varieties:
B. grandis [sometimes classified *B. grandis* ssp. *evansiana*] (hardy begonia, Evans's begonia) has 2- to 3-foot branching stems with clusters of pale pink blooms in summer and large toothy leaves that are green with red veins above and red below.

LILY-OF-THE-VALLEY
Convallaria

Light: full shade	
Plant type: perennial	
Hardiness: Zones 2-8	
Height: 9 to 12 inches	
Soil and Moisture: well-drained, moist, fertile	
Interest: flowers, foliage, fragrance	
Care: easy	

◀ Convallaria majalis 'Albistriata'

Lily-of-the-valley's fragrant white flower bells are a welcome sight in spring. The tiny blossoms that line arching square stems clasped by a pair of broad green leaves add fragrance to nosegays or small bouquets. Lily-of-the-valley can be forced for indoor enjoyment. Caution: The plant is poisonous.

Growing and care:

Plant lily-of-the-valley pips in late fall, setting them 1 inch deep and 6 to 12 inches apart. In subsequent years, mulch with compost or aged manure in fall. The white variegated foliage of *C. majalis* 'Albistriata' tends to lose its color in deep shade. To force lily-of-the-valley, buy prechilled pips or hold pips in the refrigerator in a plastic bag for 8 weeks or more; pot with tips just below the surface and bring into a warm room to grow and flower. Propagate lily-of-the-valley by division in fall.

Selected species and varieties:

C. majalis has deeply veined 9- to 12-inch-long deep green leaves up to 4 inches across and five to 13 small, very fragrant flower bells followed by orange to red fall berries; 'Albistriata' [also called 'Striata'] has white, fragrant flowers above leaves accented with white veins.

MAY APPLE
Podophyllum

Light: full shade	
Plant type: perennial	
Hardiness: Zones 3-9	
Height: 1 to 1½ feet	
Soil and Moisture: well-drained, wet, fertile	
Interest: flowers, foliage, fruit	
Care: moderate	

◀ Podophyllum peltatum

This woodland wildflower bears large deeply lobed leaves up to 1 foot wide, and nodding six- to nine-petaled 2-inch-wide white flowers that arise in spring at the joint between two leaves. Flowers mature into 1- to 2-inch berries. The common May apple quickly spreads to form large colonies that may be invasive. The foliage dies down in summer. The seeds, stem, and root are poisonous, but the fruits are edible and used as food in parts of the southern United States.

Growing and care:

Often found in boggy, low-lying areas near woodland streams, May apple thrives in constantly moist soil to which leaf mold has been added. Propagate by dividing rhizomes in late summer or fall. Mulch with leaf litter in winter.

Selected species and varieties:

P. hexandrum (Himalayan May apple) has clumped stems 1 to 1½ feet tall, with six-petaled white to pink flowers that bloom before the three- to five-lobed 10-inch leaves unfurl. *P. peltatum* (common May apple, wild mandrake, raccoon berry) develops leaves before the flowers, which are often hidden by the foliage and are followed by yellow fruit.

PHLOX
Phlox

Light: full shade

Plant type: perennial

Hardiness: Zones 3-9

Height: 5 to 14 inches

Soil and Moisture: well-drained, fertile, moist

Interest: flowers

Care: easy

◀ Phlox divaricata
'Fuller's White'

Phlox is best known as a plant for sunny gardens, yet many prefer the soft light of shady borders and yards. The plants have attractive, five-petaled flowers in a variety of colors to brighten up woodland plantings or other shady places. Phlox is generally easy to grow and forms large clumps that slowly spread into colonies. Creeping phlox is especially suited for rock gardens or places where it can cascade over walls and stones.

Growing and care:

Plant phlox in well-worked soil generously amended with compost or other organic matter. Fertilize in spring as growth begins, and lightly after flowering is complete. Set plants 1 to 1½ feet apart. Provide extra water during dry periods.

Selected species and varieties:

P. 'Chattahoochee' has 1-inch-wide, deep violet flowers with purple eyes on a spreading tuft of stems to 1 foot tall; Zones 4-9. *P. divaricata* (wild sweet William) has semievergreen oval leaves beneath 1-foot-tall scapes topped with blue, purple, or white flowers; 'Dirigo Ice' reaches 14 inches with fragrant pale lavender flowers; 'Fuller's White' has white flowers. *P. stolonifera* (creeping phlox) has creeping 5- to 10-inch stems with evergreen leaves forming a mat with blue, pink, or white flowers; Zones 3-8; 'Blue Ridge' has pale blue flowers and lustrous foliage; 'Pink Ridge', pink flowers.

PRIMROSE
Primula

Light: full shade

Plant type: perennial

Hardiness: Zones 3-8

Height: 2 to 24 inches

Soil and Moisture: well-drained, moist, fertile

Interest: flowers, fragrance

Care: moderate

◀ Primula japonica
'Postford White'

Neat, colorful primroses produce clusters of five-petaled blossoms on leafless stems above rosettes of tongue-shaped leaves, which are evergreen in milder climates. More than 400 species of primroses in nearly every color of the rainbow offer the gardener a multitude of choices in height and hardiness for borders or shady woodland gardens.

Growing and care:

Space primroses 1 foot apart in moisture-retentive soil. Water deeply during dry periods. Japanese primroses require a boglike soil. Other species tolerate drier conditions. Polyanthus primroses are short lived and often treated as annuals. Japanese star primroses go dormant after flowering. Propagate primroses from seed or by division every 3 years in spring.

Selected species and varieties:

P. japonica (Japanese primrose) has whorls of white, red, pink, or purple flowers on 2-foot stalks; 'Miller's Crimson' has deep red blossoms; 'Postford White' has white flowers; Zones 3-6. *P.* x *polyantha* (polyanthus primrose) bears flowers singly or in clusters on 6- to 12-inch stems in a wide choice of colors; Zones 3-4. *P. sieboldii* (Japanese star primrose) has nodding heads of pink, purple, or white flowers on 1-foot stalks. *P. vulgaris* (English primrose) produces fragrant single flowers in yellow and other colors on 6- to 9-inch stems.

SAXIFRAGE
Saxifraga

Light: full shade	
Plant type: perennial	
Hardiness: Zones 7-9	
Height: 4 inches to 2 feet	
Soil and Moisture: well-drained, moist, fertile	
Interest: flowers, foliage	
Care: moderate	

◀ Saxifraga umbrosa

An ideal plant for rock gardens, saxifrage's rosettes of leaves form a mat from which runners or stolons spread. The red threadlike runners of strawberry geranium, which is also grown as a houseplant, produce baby plants. Delicate flowers rise above foliage in spring.

Growing and care:
Saxifrages grow best in neutral, rocky soil but will tolerate other soils as long as they are very well drained but evenly moist. Generously enrich the soil with leaf mold or peat moss. Plant 8 to 10 inches apart in spring, and mulch lightly to overwinter. Apply an all-purpose fertilizer in spring. Strawberry geranium will tolerate some early- or late-day sun, while London-pride prefers full shade. Propagate by dividing after flowering.

Selected species and varieties:
S. stolonifera (strawberry geranium, beefsteak geranium) has 1½- to 2-foot branched stems bearing 1-inch-wide white flowers above 4-inch-tall clumps of round hairy leaves with white veins and red undersides, up to 4 inches wide. *S. umbrosa* (London-pride) has 1½-foot-high clumps of 2-inch-long oval leaves, pea green above and red beneath, with white, pink, rose, or bicolored flower sprays on 6-inch stems from late spring to early summer.

SOLOMON'S-SEAL
Polygonatum

Light: full shade	
Plant type: perennial	
Hardiness: Zones 4-8	
Height: 10 to 36 inches	
Soil and Moisture: well-drained, moist, fertile	
Interest: flowers, foliage, fruit	
Care: easy	

◀ P. odoratum 'Variegatum'

Arching stems arise from rootstocks to bear 1½-inch-long greenish white bell-shaped flowers that dangle from the axils of parallel-veined green leaves in late spring. Black or blue fruits mature in fall. The plant spreads slowly by rhizomes to form a good ground cover for shade.

Growing and care:
Supplement soil with leaf mold, peat moss, or compost before planting. Propagate by division.

Selected species and varieties:
P. biflorum (small Solomon's-seal) grows to 3 feet tall or taller, bearing greenish white flowers with greenish lobes that usually hang in pairs below the stem in late spring to early summer, followed by blue berries. *P. commutatum* (Great Solomon's-seal) grows up to 6 feet tall with large, very coarse green leaves and clusters of yellow flowers in spring. *P. multiflorum* is 3 feet tall, bearing white flowers with greenish apexes, in clusters of two to six usually on the bottom half of the stem, and blue-black berries. *P. odoratum* 'Variegatum' (variegated Solomon's-seal) has 1- to 3-foot-tall stems bearing leaves with white margins and tips, with fragrant white flowers that have green spots in the throat along pliant, arching stems, followed by blue-black berries.

TOOTHWORT
Dentaria

Light: full shade	
Plant type: perennial	
Hardiness: Zones 4-9	
Height: 6 to 16 inches	
Soil and Moisture: well-drained, moist, fertile	
Interest: flowers	
Care: easy	

◀ Dentaria diphylla

Toothworts are low-growing perennial wildflowers native to rich woods and bottom lands in the eastern and central United States. They grow from rhizomes, producing loose clusters of small bell-shaped flowers in spring. After flowering the plant goes dormant and the leaves disappear.

Growing and care:
Toothworts do not tolerate much direct sun and thrive in the soft light of mostly shady woodlands. Plant in soil well amended with organic matter. Mulch lightly with shredded leaves in winter. Propagate by seed sown immediately after it ripens in fall, or by division in early spring or after the plant goes dormant in summer.

Selected species and varieties:
D. diphylla (toothwort, crinkleroot) grows 8 to 16 inches tall with deeply dissected leaves and loose clusters of white or pale pink four-petaled flowers from early to late spring; Zones 4-7. *D. laciniata* (cut-leaved toothwort) grows 6 to 12 inches tall with a whorl of deeply divided and coarsely toothed leaves halfway up each stem, and clusters of pink or white flowers above the foliage in spring.

TRILLIUM
Trillium

Light: full shade	
Plant type: perennial	
Hardiness: Zones 2-9	
Height: 6 inches to 1½ feet	
Soil and Moisture: well-drained, moist, fertile	
Interest: flowers, foliage	
Care: difficult	

◀ Trillium grandiflorum

Trilliums are elegant woodland perennials whose solitary, usually nodding flowers consist of three broad petals and three greenish sepals. Below each flower is a broad whorl of three leaves. The plants thrive in the rich soils and shade of open forests and make enchanting additions to woodland pathways and gardens.

Growing and care:
Plant container-grown trilliums in spring or early fall in rich soil well amended with organic matter. Add a layer of leaf mold mulch each fall and keep plants well watered throughout the growing season. Trilliums transplant poorly and established plantings should not be disturbed. Purchase only nursery-grown plants and avoid those collected from the wild.

Selected species and varieties:
T. cernuum (nodding trillium) is 1 to 1½ feet tall with nodding white flowers 1½ inches across with deep rose anthers; Zones 3-7. *T. erectum* (purple trillium) grows to 1½ feet tall with nodding or upward-facing maroon flowers 2½ inches across that have a musky scent; Zones 2-6. *T. grandiflorum* (large-flowered trillium) grows up to 15 inches tall with upward-facing long-lasting white flowers 3 to 4 inches across that turn red with age; Zones 3-8. *T. sessile* (red trillium, toadshade) grows to 1 foot tall with maroon, brown, purple, or yellow flowers whose petals point upward; Zones 4-9.

WILD SARSAPARILLA
Aralia

Light: full shade

Plant type: perennial

Hardiness: Zones 3-10

Height: 1 to 6 feet

Soil and Moisture: well-drained, moist, fertile

Interest: foliage

Care: easy

◀ Aralia racemosa

Wild sarsaparilla is a perennial that grows in open woods over much of the United States. Its large compound leaves partially obscure the fluffy flowers that appear in spring and impart a lush appearance to the shady garden. In late summer and fall the ripening berries attract birds to the garden. Wild sarsaparilla makes a good woodland ground cover.

Growing and care:

Plant *Aralias* in well-worked soil amended with generous amounts of rotted manure or compost. The plants require little care once they have become established. Wild sarsaparilla grows well in dryish upland soil or moist soil, while spikenard prefers a moist, fertile one. Mulch around plants in fall for winter protection and to conserve moisture. Propagate by seed or division in fall.

Selected species and varieties:

A. nudicaulis (wild sarsaparilla) reaches up to 1 foot in height with 6-inch doubly compound leaves, greenish white flowers from late spring to early summer, and purplish fall berries; Zones 3-7. *A. racemosa* (spikenard) grows 6 feet tall with leaves up to 2½ feet long and large clusters of tiny white flowers tinged with yellow or green in early to midsummer followed by purple berries; Zones 4-10.

YELLOW WAXBELLS
Kirengeshoma

Light: full shade

Plant type: perennial

Hardiness: Zones 5-8

Height: 3 to 4 feet

Soil and Moisture: well-drained, moist, fertile

Interest: flowers, foliage

Care: moderate

◀ Kirengeshoma palmata

Yellow waxbells is an unusual but charming late-blooming perennial that thrives in shady gardens. The plants produce large, maple-shaped leaves and loose clusters of nodding, funnel-shaped flowers that range from cream to apricot colors in summer and fall. The soft-colored flowers combine with the bold leaves to provide an eye-catching accent to woodland or shady meadow gardens. The plants are also useful in informal borders and shady rock gardens.

Growing and care:

Yellow waxbells need soil that has been liberally supplemented with compost, leaf mold, or peat moss, and that is cool and moist and slightly acidic. Water during dry spells, and mulch to retain moisture. Propagate by dividing every 3 to 4 years in spring or fall, though plants grow best if left undisturbed.

Selected species and varieties:

K. palmata produces nearly round, toothed leaves, each with up to 10 lobes, that arise from opposite sides of the stems and have an almost platelike appearance beneath clusters of 1½-inch-long cream to apricot bell-shaped flowers whose buds last for months before opening.

ARISAEMA
Arisaema

Light: full shade	
Plant type: bulb	
Hardiness: Zones 4-9	
Height: 1 to 3 feet	
Soil and Moisture: well-drained, moist	
Interest: flowers, foliage	
Care: moderate	

◄ Arisaema triphyllum

Arisaemas produce a fleshy spike called a spadix nestled within an outer leaflike spathe that folds over the spadix like a hood. Glossy three-lobed leaves taller than the flower cluster persist throughout summer. The female flowers ripen to a cluster of attractive red fruit in fall. Use arisaemas in wildflower or woodland gardens or along stream banks, where they will slowly spread out and naturalize.

Growing and care:
Plant arisaema in fall, setting tubers 4 inches deep and 1 foot apart in soil that is constantly moist but not soggy. The plants do best in mostly shady locations but tolerate a range of conditions from mostly sunny to full shade. Cover with a light layer of mulch, such as leaf mold. Arisaemas can change sex from year to year, and a plant that bore fruit one year may not the next. Propagate by division in early fall.

Selected species and varieties:
A. dracontium (green-dragon) has a green spathe enfolding a 4- to 10-inch green or yellowish green spadix on a 1-foot stem. *A. sikokianum* bears an ivory spadix within a spathe that is deep maroon banded in green on the outside and ivory at its base on the inside, on a 1-foot stem. *A. triphyllum* (jack-in-the-pulpit, Indian turnip) has a green to purple spadix within a green to purple spathe striped purple, green, white, or maroon inside on a 1- to 2-foot stem.

BEAD LILY
Clintonia

Light: full shade	
Plant type: bulb	
Hardiness: Zones 2-9	
Height: 4 to 20 inches	
Soil and Moisture: well-drained, moist, fertile	
Interest: flowers, foliage, fruit	
Care: easy	

◄ Clintonia andrewsiana

Bead lilies are woodland wildflowers with attractive flowers, foliage, and fruit to grace the garden from spring to fall. The plants have a basal rosette of very shiny emerald green leaves and thin but strong leafless stalks topped by a cluster of small lilylike flowers in spring. The pale yellow, white, or rose-colored spring blossoms yield to round, marble-size berries of indigo or blue from summer to fall. Bead lilies naturalize easily and are perfect for woodland gardens and paths and look charming planted near streams and ponds.

Growing and care:
Plant in mostly to full deciduous shade in well-worked fertile soil that has abundant organic matter. Bead lilies require cool, damp, shady locations, where they make excellent ground covers. Mulch in fall or early winter.

Selected species and varieties:
C. andrewsiana has 10- to 20-inch stalks of deep rose bell-shaped flowers followed by blue berries; Zones 8-9. *C. borealis* (blue bead lily) has greenish yellow flowers on 8- to 15-inch stalks followed by bright blue berries; Zones 2-7. *C. umbellulata* (speckled wood lily, white bead lily) bears white flowers with green and purple specks on 6- to 20-inch stalks followed by black berries. *C. uniflora* (bride's bonnet) grows 4 to 8 inches tall with white flowers and amethyst blue berries; Zones 4-8.

BLETILLA
Bletilla

Light:	full shade
Plant type:	bulb
Hardiness:	Zones 5-8
Height:	8 to 20 inches
Soil and Moisture:	well-drained, moist, fertile
Interest:	flowers, foliage
Care:	moderate

◀ Bletilla striata

One of the few orchids that can be grown outdoors, bletilla produces sprays of light rosy purple flowers in late spring or early summer just above broad, pointed, papery leaves that have prominent parallel veins. Bletilla is useful as a specimen, in group plantings, or as a container plant.

Growing and care:
Bletilla thrives in full, bright shade and rich moist loam in a loaction sheltered from strong winds. Work peat moss or compost into the soil, and plant no more than 2 inches deep. Water during dry periods; drought can result in diminished or no bloom the following spring. Propagate by dividing the pseudobulbs.

Selected species and varieties:
B. striata (Chinese orchid, Chinese ground orchid, hyacinth orchid, hardy orchid) grows 8 to 20 inches tall with nodding deep pink or rosy purple flowers up to 1½ inches across borne in terminal racemes of six to 10 above dark green pleated leaves; 'Alba' has creamy white flowers; 'Albostriata' has leaves bearing longitudinal white stripes that stay attractive throughout the season, and purple to rosy purple flowers.

CALADIUM
Caladium

Light:	full shade
Plant type:	bulb
Hardiness:	Zone 10
Height:	1 to 2 feet
Soil and Moisture:	well-drained, moist
Interest:	foliage
Care:	easy

◀ Caladium bicolor 'Aaron'

Exotic caladiums form clumps of intricately patterned translucent leaves that eclipse their insignificant flowers. The arrow-shaped leaves, rising continuously throughout summer, are vividly marbled, shaded, slashed, veined, and flecked in contrasting colors to brighten shady borders or decorate indoor gardens.

Growing and care:
Caladiums do best in full, bright shade but also grow well in mostly shady locations. Plant in spring when night temperatures remain above 60°F, setting the tubers 2 inches deep and 8 to 12 inches apart. North of Zone 10, lift and dry tubers in fall to replant the next spring. Provide high humidity and temperatures of 60°F or more. Propagate by division in spring.

Selected species and varieties:
C. bicolor [formerly *C.* x *hortulanum*] has foot-long arrow- or heart-shaped leaves; 'Aaron' has green edges feathering into creamy centers; 'Candidum' is white with green veining; 'Fannie Munson', pink-veined red edged in green; 'Festiva', rose-veined green; 'Irene Dank', light green edged in deeper green; 'June Bride', greenish white edged in deep green; 'Pink Beauty' is a pink dwarf spattered with green; 'White Christmas' is white with green veining.

FAWN LILY
Erythronium

Light: full shade	
Plant type: bulb	
Hardiness: Zones 3-9	
Height: 4 inches to 2 feet	
Soil and Moisture: well-drained, moist, fertile	
Interest: flowers, foliage	
Care: moderate	

◀ Erythronium 'Kondo'

Native woodland wildflowers, fawn lilies produce delicate, nodding lilylike blooms with petals curved back to reveal prominent stamens and anthers either singly or in small clusters. The flowers rise from pairs of pointed oval leaves that are often marbled or mottled in gray, brown, or bronze. Mass fawn lilies in woodland gardens or as a spring ground cover beneath deciduous shrubs, where they will naturalize into colonies.

Growing and care:
Plant fawn lilies in summer or fall, placing the corms 2 to 3 inches deep and 4 to 6 inches apart in a location that receives deciduous shade. Fawn lilies often take a year to become established before blooming. Provide adequate moisture in summer after flowers and foliage fade. Propagate from seed to bloom in 3 to 4 years or by removing and immediately replanting the small cormels that develop at the base of mature corms in late summer or fall.

Selected species and varieties:
E. citrinum has clusters of 1½-inch white or cream flowers with pale lemon throats on 10- to 12-inch stems; Zones 6-8. *E. dens-canis* (dogtooth fawn lily, European dogtooth violet) bears white to pink or purple single flowers 2 inches across with blue or purple anthers on 6- to 12-inch stems above leaves marbled brown and bluish green; 'Charmer' produces pure white flowers touched with brown at their base above leaves mottled with brown; 'Frans Hals' has royal purple blooms with a green throat; 'Lilac Wonder' is soft lilac with a brownish base; 'Pink Perfection', bright pink; 'Purple King', reddish purple with a white throat above brown-spotted leaves; 'Rose Queen', rosy pink; 'Snowflake', pure white; var. *japonicum* is a miniature only 4 to 6 inches tall with violet flowers tinged purple at the base; var. *niveus* is pale pink; Zones 3-8. *E. grandiflorum* (glacier lily, avalanche lily) has golden yellow flowers with red anthers in clusters on 1- to 2-foot stems. *E. revolutum* (mahogany fawn lily, coast fawn lily) bears 1½-inch white to pale lavender flowers aging to purple on 16-inch stems; 'White Beauty' is a dwarf producing 2- to 3-inch white flowers with yellow throats on 7-inch stems above leaves veined in white; Zones 3-8. *E. tuolumnense* (Tuolumne fawn lily) has 1¼-inch yellow flowers touched with green at the base on 1-foot stems above bright green 1-foot leaves; Zones 3-8. *E.* hybrids: 'Citronella' yields lemon yellow flowers on 10-inch stems; 'Jeannine', sulfur yellow blooms; 'Kondo', greenish yellow blossoms touched with brown at the base; 'Pagoda', pale yellow flowers with a deeper yellow throat on 10-inch stems.

ORCHID PANSY
Achimenes

Light: full shade

Plant type: bulb

Hardiness: Zone 10

Height: 1 to 2 feet

Soil and Moisture: well-drained, moist

Interest: flowers

Care: moderate

◀ Achimenes longiflora

Orchid pansy is a beautiful flower with the elegance of orchids and the cheerfulness of pansies. The large, 2-inch flowers have long, tubular necks and bloom amid fleshy, downy leaves on slender arching or trailing stems. Blossom throats are often splashed or veined in a contrasting color. Excellent as houseplants, orchid pansies can also be used outdoors in containers and hanging baskets on shady patios in locations with mild temperatures.

Growing and care:
Plant orchid pansy in spring, setting tubers 1 inch deep and 3 to 4 inches apart. Flowers appear 12 to 14 weeks after planting. Keep soil moist but not soggy, and fertilize while the plants are blooming. Gradually withhold water after flowering ceases. Store potted tubers over winter in dry soil, or lift and dry tubers in fall for replanting in spring. Propagate by dividing dormant tubers into ½-inch pieces just before repotting in spring.

Selected species and varieties:
A. longiflora has white, pink, red, lavender, or violet flowers, sometimes with contrasting throats, in midsummer amid whorls of hairy leaves on stems to 1 foot; 'Ambroise Verschaffelt' is white with a deep purple throat; 'Paul Arnold' has blue-violet blossoms.

SPRING-BEAUTY
Claytonia

Light: full shade

Plant type: bulb

Hardiness: Zones 4-9

Height: 4 to 12 inches

Soil and Moisture: well-drained, moist, fertile

Interest: flowers

Care: easy

◀ Claytonia virginica

Spring-beauties are low-growing perennials found in rich woodlands throughout much of the eastern and central United States. Their dainty flowers are pink or white with darker pink stripes on the petals and dark pink stamens. They are lovely planted in large drifts or scattered among other woodland flowers. The plants disappear shortly after flowering.

Growing and care:
Only purchase nursery-grown plants and refuse any collected from the wild. Spring-beauties thrive and spread rapidly in a moist soil with high-humus content in locations beneath deciduous trees. Incorporate generous amounts of organic matter into the soil prior to planting. They do well when planted among merry-bells and blue bead lilies. Propagate by corms or seed.

Selected species and varieties:
C. caroliniana (broad-leaved spring-beauty) grows from corms to produce two oval leaves, each 2 inches long. Throughout spring dainty pinkish flowers are borne in loose clusters along the upper portion of the 4- to 12-inch stems. *C. virginica* (narrow-leaved spring-beauty) is similar to the above species except that its leaves are slender and grasslike.

TUBEROUS BEGONIA
Begonia

Light: full shade	
Plant type: bulb	
Hardiness: Zone 10	
Height: ²/₃ to 1¹/₂ feet	
Soil and Moisture: well-drained, moist	
Interest: flowers, fragrance	
Care: moderate	

◀ Begonia Picotee Group

Tuberous begonias produce an abundance of large flowers over a long season of bloom with soft, waxy petals in vivid tones of red, orange, apricot, rose, pink, yellow, cream, or white, sometimes bicolored, on fleshy upright or trailing stems. Blossoms open in succession amid pointed, crenelated green to bronze foliage that is deeply veined, sometimes in contrasting colors. Their diverse flower forms have plain, frilled, or fringed petals that mimic the blossoms of roses, camellias, carnations, and other garden favorites. Thousands of hybrids offer almost limitless combinations of forms and colors for varying purposes. Upright tuberous begonias are striking when massed as bedding plants or grown as specimens in patio containers, whereas cascading forms are appealing when allowed to trail gracefully from hanging baskets.

Growing and care:
Plant tuberous begonias outdoors in spring for summer bloom, setting tubers 1 to 2 inches deep with their concave side up, 12 to 15 inches apart. The plants do best in filtered full shade, such as beneath deciduous trees. For potted plants, space three or four tubers evenly in each pot or hanging basket, with the top of the tuber at the soil line. For earliest flowering, start tuberous begonias indoors 6 to 12 weeks before planting outside. Keep soil constantly moist but not soggy. Prune small tubers to a single stem, larger ones to three or four stems, and pinch early buds to encourage more prolific flowering.

Provide support for upright forms. Fertilize while blooming with a dilute balanced houseplant fertilizer. North of Zone 10, lift tubers in fall after the first light frost, allow them to dry, and store them for replanting in spring. Propagate tuberous begonias from stem cuttings taken in spring; by dividing tubers, making sure to maintain at least one growth bud in each section; or from seed sown indoors in January to bloom in June.

Selected species and varieties:
B. x *tuberhybrida* flowers to 4 inches or more across, with hundreds of hybrids classified in 12 groups according to flower form and color. *Single Group*: Broad, flat-faced flowers composed of four enormous petals surrounding a central cluster of prominent stamens. *Crispa or Frilled Group*: Flat-faced flowers with large petals whose edges are ruffled or fringed, surrounding a colorful cluster of stamens. *Cristata or Crested Group*: Raised, frilled crests punctuating the center of each of several large sepals. *Narcissiflora or Daffodil-Flowered Group*: Double rows of petals in an arrangement that resembles a flat-faced narcissus. *Camellia or Camelliiflora Group*: Smooth petals of a single color arranged in overlapping layers like camellia flowers on upright plants. *Ruffled Camellia Group*: Overlapping layers of ruffled petals that conceal the stamens. *Rosiflora or Rosebud Group*: Center petals tightly furled like a pointed, unopened rosebud. *Fimbriata Plena or Carnation Group*: Finely fringed petals overlapping in double rows. *Picotee Group*: Double rows of overlapping petals edged in a narrow or broad band of a deeper shade of the main petal color. *Marginata Group*: Double rows of petals edged in a narrow or broad band of a contrasting color. *Marmorata Group*: Double rows of pink or rose petals dappled with white. *Pendula or Hanging-Basket Group*: A profusion of single- or double-petaled blossoms on trailing stems. *Multiflora Group*: Small single- or double-petaled blossoms on bushy plants with compact stems.

BEARBERRY
Arctostaphylos

Light: full shade

Plant type: ground cover

Hardiness: Zones 2-6

Height: 6 to 12 inches

Soil and Moisture: well-drained, fertile, moist

Interest: flowers, foliage, fruit

Care: easy

◀ A. uva-ursi

Bearberry is a multifaceted plant with ornamental evergreen foliage that also has antibacterial properties, dainty spring flowers, and attractive red berries from fall to winter. The plants quickly spread into leafy mats that make an ideal ground cover to control erosion on difficult rocky or sandy banks. Dangling flower clusters lining the stems in spring are followed by bright red oval berries in fall. The berries attract various species of birds to the garden in fall and winter.

Growing and care:
Bearberry requires a sandy soil well amended with organic matter for best growth. The plants grow well in conditions ranging from full sun to full shade. Sow bearberry seed or set out rooted cuttings in spring, spacing plants 1 to 2 feet apart. Once established bearberry will tolerate dry conditions as long as it receives periodic deep watering. Propagate from seed, from stem cuttings, or by transplanting layered stems.

Selected species and varieties:
A. uva-ursi (common bearberry, hog cranberry, bear's grape, mealberry, kinnikinnick, sandberry, mountain box, creashak, trailing manzanita) has slender arching stems to 5 feet long, and produces ¼-inch urn-shaped red-tinged white flowers in spring, and clusters of red berries in fall through winter.

GINSENG
Panax

Light: full shade

Plant type: perennial

Hardiness: Zones 3-8

Height: 6 inches to 3 feet

Soil and Moisture: well-drained, moist, fertile

Interest: foliage, fruit

Care: difficult

◀ Panax quinquefolius

Ginseng's thick roots send up a single thin stalk with leaves composed of several pointed leaflets arranged like the fingers on a hand. In late spring or summer, a short flower stalk carries a cluster of tiny yellow-green flowers above the foliage, followed by red berries. In woodland gardens, ginseng slowly spreads into a lacy ground cover. Ginseng's Greek name means "all ills," reflecting its root's fame as an herbal tonic in Oriental medicine. Roots are also used in herbal teas.

Growing and care:
Ginseng grows best in full shade and is often planted with goldenseal in shady woods. You can sow ginseng seed in spring or fall, but division and replanting of roots in spring is often more successful, as the seeds take a year to germinate. Provide organic mulch annually. When roots are at least 6 years old, dig them up in fall to use fresh or dried for teas.

Selected species and varieties:
P. pseudoginseng [also classified as *P. ginseng*] has 2- to 3-foot-tall stems with two to six leaves composed of toothed leaflets growing from a carrotlike root. *P. quinquefolius* (American ginseng) has stems 6 to 20 inches tall with leaves composed of 6-inch leaflets growing from a cigar-shaped root.

GOLDENSEAL
Hydrastis

Light:	full shade
Plant type:	perennial
Hardiness:	Zones 3-8
Height:	6 to 12 inches
Soil and Moisture:	well-drained, fertile, moist
Interest:	foliage, flowers
Care:	difficult

◀ Hydrastis canadensis

Goldenseal sends up solitary stems, each with a few broad, coarse leaves, and very slowly spreads into mats in woodland gardens. Tiny spring flowers develop into inedible fruits resembling raspberries in fall. Native Americans used goldenseal for body paint, as an insect repellent, and in various herbal medicines. Modern herbalists now consider it toxic, especially in large doses. In the past, inflated claims as to its medicinal powers led to overcollecting in the wild, and goldenseal is now endangered in many places.

Growing and care:
Grow goldenseal from pieces of rhizomes with leaf buds collected in spring or fall. Set pieces ½ inch deep and space them 8 inches apart. Protect with a winter mulch. Propagation from seed is difficult, as seed needs 18 months to germinate.

Selected species and varieties:
H. canadensis (goldenseal, turmeric) has deeply lobed, hand-shaped leaves up to 8 inches across, a single leaf at the base of each stem, and one or two at the top. It grows from thick, yellow-fleshed rhizomes with a licorice odor and petal-less ½-inch green-white flowers with fluffy stamens.

LUNGWORT
Pulmonaria

Light:	full shade
Plant type:	perennial
Hardiness:	Zones 3-8
Height:	6 inches to 1½ feet
Soil and Moisture:	well-drained to heavy, moist
Interest:	flowers, foliage
Care:	easy

◀ Pulmonaria saccharata 'Dora Bieleveld'

While grown primarily for their clumps of broadly oval hairy leaves mottled with silvery white spots, lungworts also bear clusters of blue or white trumpet-shaped flowers that nod from the tops of arching stems in spring. Lungworts are effective as coarse, slowly spreading ground covers. Their foliage emerges in early spring and remains green until fall. They can also be used as accents in shady borders and beds.

Growing and care:
Lungwort thrives in full shade and is tolerant of locations with some early-morning or late-afternoon sun. Set plants in soil well amended with organic matter and provide extra water during dry periods. Space plants 1 to 1½ feet apart. Cut flowering stems back as blossoms fade to promote vigorous growth. Propagate by seed or division in fall.

Selected species and varieties:
P. angustifolia has lance-shaped green leaves beneath sapphire blue flowers; 'Azurea' has pinkish blue buds that open to flowers of bright blue; 'Johnson's Blue' is a dwarf with sky blue flowers. *P. saccharata* (Bethlehem sage) has pink flowers opening to blue or white on 6- to 18-inch stems above mottled green and white leaves; 'Dora Bieleveld' has rosy pink flowers; 'Sissinghurst White' has early-flowering white blossoms and well-spotted leaves.

SPICEBUSH
Lindera

Light: full shade

Plant type: shrub

Hardiness: Zones 4-9

Height: 6 to 15 feet

Soil and Moisture: moist to wet

Interest: flowers, foliage, fruit

Care: easy

◀ Lindera benzoin

A dense, informal deciduous shrub with erect branches, spicebush offers three-season interest, fragrance, and flavor as a specimen or in a shrub border. Flowers bloom along bare branches of both male and female plants in early spring, followed by spicy-scented leaves. On female plants, leaves color and drop in fall to reveal small, bright scarlet fruits. Steep young twigs and fresh or dried leaves and berries for herbal tea. Add dried leaves and berries to woodsy potpourris, or grind dried berries as a substitute for allspice.

Growing and care:

Sow ripe spicebush seed in fall before it dries out, or hold at least 4 months in the refrigerator and sow in spring. Otherwise, start new shrubs from softwood cuttings taken in summer. Spicebush grows best in shady spots beneath deciduous trees but tolerates sun if grown in consistently moist soil. Collect twigs in spring, leaves throughout the growing season, and berries in fall, and use either fresh or dried.

Selected species and varieties:

L. benzoin (spicebush, Benjamin bush) bears fragrant, tiny yellow-green flowers in clusters that emerge before the 2- to 5-inch pointed oval leaves, which turn deep gold in fall, and ½-inch oval red fruits.

WILD GINGER
Asarum

Light: full shade

Plant type: perennial

Hardiness: Zones 3-8

Height: 6 to 12 inches

Soil and Moisture: well-drained, moist

Interest: foliage, flowers

Care: easy

◀ Asarum canadense

P airs of deciduous heart-shaped leaves on thin arching stems hide wild ginger's bell-shaped, maroon spring flowers growing at ground level. The attractive foliage, resembling that of cyclamen, grows along creeping rhizomes that develop into ground-covering carpets. While the edible roots are seldom used, they can substitute for fresh or dried ground ginger. Young leaves add flavor to salads, though they may cause dermatitis. Wild ginger figures in traditional herbal medicine.

Growing and care:

Wild ginger grows best in deep woodland shade but tolerates some dappled light. Sow wild ginger seed in spring, or plant divisions in spring or fall, cutting sections of rhizome with at least one pair of leaves. Set sections 1 inch deep in beds prepared with abundant leaf mold, compost, or other organic amendments, and space plants 1 foot apart. Wild ginger does especially well in sheltered areas in soil above limestone or marble bedrock. Keep new beds evenly moist. Once established, wild ginger becomes a low-maintenance weed-suppressing ground cover.

Selected species and varieties:

A. canadense (Canadian wild ginger) has broad, hairy dark green leaves up to 7 inches across on 6-inch-tall stems with inch-wide brown to purple flowers.

BUNCHBERRY
Cornus

Light: full shade	
Plant type: ground cover	
Hardiness: Zones 2-6	
Height: 4 to 8 inches	
Soil and Moisture: well-drained, moist	
Interest: flowers, foliage, fruit	
Care: moderate	

◀ Cornus canadensis

Bunchberry is one of the most charming native ground covers, with small, white to pinkish blossoms resembling flowering dogwood amid a sea of tidy bright green foliage. The flowers appear in spring and yield to a cluster of bright red berries in late summer. In fall the green leaves turn a vivid scarlet. Bunchberry thrives in shady, cool forests and carpets the ground beneath evergreens and deciduous trees alike. The plants make excellent ground covers for woodland gardens or a shady rock garden. They naturalize readily and grow well next to partridgeberry and wood sorrel.

Growing and care:
Plant in spring or fall in well-worked soil that has abundant organic matter. The plants do best in mountain areas or in cool, shady locations that stay evenly moist. Mulch with pine needles in fall. Bunchberry is easy to grow if its requirements are met and needs little attention once established.

Selected species and varieties:
C. canadensis is a beautiful ground cover with 4- to 8-inch creeping woody stems and four showy white bracts in late spring. In late summer and fall bright red berries and scarlet foliage appear.

IVY
Hedera

Light: full shade	
Plant type: vine	
Hardiness: Zones 5-10	
Height: 6 inches to 100 feet	
Soil and Moisture: well-drained, moist	
Interest: foliage	
Care: easy	

◀ Hedera helix

Ivies are perfect for carpeting shady banks and borders and, with their aerial roots, for climbing fences and posts. After climbing ceases at maturity, they produce yellowish green flowers 1½ to 2½ inches wide, and poisonous black berries.

Growing and care:
Though ivy tolerates a wide variety of soil types, it benefits from a good start: Enrich the soil with organic matter and keep the plants moist until they are established. Plant ivy in spring or fall, setting plants about 2 feet apart. Propagate by simple stem layering.

Selected species and varieties:
H. canariensis (Algerian ivy, canary ivy, Madeira ivy) has three- to seven-lobed dark green leathery leaves on dark red petioles; Zones 9-10; 'Variegata' has showy yellow or pale green streaks. *H. colchica* 'Dentata' (colchis ivy, fragrant ivy, Persian ivy) is a fast climber with slightly toothed leaves from 5 to 10 inches wide; hardy to Zone 6; 'Dentata-Variegata' has creamy yellow margins. *H. helix* 'Cavendishii' (English ivy) has three- to five-lobed leaves 2 to 4 inches wide with creamy white margins; 'Gold Heart' has triangular leaves with a gold center; 'Needlepoint' is a very dense slow grower with dark green leaves ¼ to 1 inch wide.

PARTRIDGEBERRY
Mitchella

Light: full shade	
Plant type: ground cover	
Hardiness: Zones 3-9	
Height: 2 to 4 inches	
Soil and Moisture: well-drained, moist, fertile	
Interest: flowers, foliage, fruit	
Care: easy	

◀ Mitchella repens

Partridgeberry is a dainty low-growing evergreen native to woodlands and stream banks of the eastern and central United States. The small, dark green leaves often form glossy carpets that accent the pairs of pinkish white late spring flowers and scarlet fall fruit. It provides a fine-textured year-round ground cover for shaded areas and is a lovely addition to a rock garden. The plants naturalize easily and slowly spread into large colonies.

Growing and care:

Partridgeberry thrives in cool, moist, humus-rich soil in partial to full shade and is one of the few plants to thrive in the deep shade beneath conifers. Where snow cover is sparse mulch lightly with pine needles in winter. The easiest way to propagate partridgeberry is to take 6-inch stem cuttings in early spring; keep plants evenly moist in well-drained soil.

Selected species and varieties:

M. repens (partridgeberry, twinberry) has pairs of ¾-inch white to pinkish white flowers in late spring and bright red berries in fall. It has small, rounded, shiny dark green leaves with white veins on trailing stems up to 1 foot long that root as they creep over the ground.

SWEET WOODRUFF
Galium

Light: full shade	
Plant type: ground cover	
Hardiness: Zones 4-8	
Height: 6 to 36 inches	
Soil and Moisture: well-drained, moist	
Interest: flowers, foliage, fragrance	
Care: easy	

◀ Galium odoratum

Sweet woodruff spreads into ground-covering mats with small clusters of white spring flowers above ruffs of leaves that become vanilla scented as they dry. Yellow bedstraw bears plumes of honey-scented yellow flowers from summer to fall. Weave fresh sweet woodruff stems into wreaths to dry or add dried leaves to potpourri. Use the dried flowers of yellow bedstraw to stuff herbal pillows.

Growing and care:

Sow woodruff seed in late summer or divide roots after flowering, setting plants 6 to 9 inches apart in a shady, moist location enriched with organic matter. Sow bedstraw seed or divide roots in spring, setting plants 9 to 12 inches apart. The plants do best in full shade but tolerate early- or late-day sun. To control these robust plants, set a container with the bottom removed in the soil; plant the seed or divisions in the can.

Selected species and varieties:

G. odoratum (sweet woodruff) bears open clusters of ¼-inch flowers and shiny 1½-inch leaves on 6- to 8-inch stems. *G. verum* (yellow bedstraw, Our-Lady's bedstraw) has elongated clusters of ¼-inch flowers and needlelike leaves on 1- to 3-foot stems.

ATHYRIUM
Athyrium

Light: full shade	
Plant type: fern	
Hardiness: Zones 4-7	
Height: 1 to 3 feet	
Soil and Moisture: well-drained, moist	
Interest: foliage	
Care: easy	

◄ Athyrium nipponicum 'Pictum'

Athyriums are deciduous woodland ferns that thrive in a variety of light conditions, from mostly sun to full shade. Arising in clumps, the light green fronds are finely divided and grow upright or gracefully arched. These delicately textured plants work well as accents, space fillers, or background plants, or beside water. By late summer the foliage tends to look worn; it dies back in fall.

Growing and care:
Although lady ferns perform best in the slightly acid, rich loam of their native woodland settings, they accept a wide range of soil types and are among the easiest of all ferns to grow. Locate them out of windy areas, as the fronds are easily broken. The Japanese painted fern does well in partial to full shade, while lady fern prefers mostly sun to light shade.

Selected species and varieties:
A. filix-femina (lady fern) grows 2 to 3 feet tall with reddish, brownish, or tan stalks and erect, twice-pinnate fronds 6 to 9 inches wide and often wider. *A. nipponicum* 'Pictum' [also classified as *A. goeringianum*] (Japanese painted fern) is 1 to 1½ feet tall with divided fronds and gray-green foliage flushed with maroon on only the upper half of maroon stems.

MAIDENHAIR FERN
Adiantum

Light: full shade	
Plant type: fern	
Hardiness: Zones 2-10	
Height: 8 inches to 3 feet	
Soil and Moisture: well-drained, moist, fertile	
Interest: foliage	
Care: moderate	

◄ Adiantum pedatum

Maidenhair ferns add airiness and texture to rock gardens and naturalized areas. Black or sometimes chestnut stripes accent the delicately etched green fronds. Slowly creeping on rhizomes, these mostly deciduous ferns form colonies.

Growing and care:
Maidenhair ferns do best in sites that mimic the moisture and shade of their native woodland settings. They thrive along woodland paths or in moist soils along the north side of buildings. Amend soil with leaf mold or peat moss before planting, and top-dress with bone meal every year. Propagate by dividing rhizomes in spring.

Selected species and varieties:
A. capillus-veneris (common maidenhair, duddergrass) has 1- to 2-foot-tall arching fronds; Zones 7-10. *A. hispidulum* (rosy maidenhair, Australian maidenhair) bears erect finely textured fronds, rosy as they unfurl, growing to 1 foot tall with hairy stripes; Zones 8-10. *A. pedatum* (northern maidenhair, five-fingered maidenhair) has slightly arching 10- to 18-inch-tall branched fan-shaped fronds, with chestnut brown stripes, spreading slowly; Zones 2-8. *A. venustum* (evergreen maidenhair) has medium green graceful, lacy arching fronds 8 to 12 inches long; Zones 5-8.

AUCUBA
Aucuba

Light: full shade

Plant type: shrub

Hardiness: Zones 7-10

Height: 6 to 10 feet

Soil and Moisture: well-drained, moist, fertile

Interest: foliage, fruit

Care: easy

◀ Aucuba japonica 'Variegata'

A rounded upright shrub with large leathery leaves that are often marked with flecks of gold or yellow, aucuba brightens shady areas. An excellent transition plant between woodland and garden, it is also useful for hedges and borders. If a male plant is nearby, female aucubas produce scarlet berries that last all winter but are often hidden by the foliage. Leaf color remains unchanged throughout the seasons.

Growing and care:
Aucuba prefers slightly acid loam but will tolerate other soils. Once established it withstands moderate drought. Full shade is best to maintain leaf color; direct sun, particularly in warmer climates, tends to blacken the foliage. Prune to control height and maintain shape.

Selected species and varieties:
A. japonica (Japanese aucuba, Japanese laurel, spotted laurel) has lustrous medium to dark green leaves 3 to 8 inches long and up to 3 inches wide that dominate tiny purple flowers borne in erect panicles in early spring, and ½-inch-wide bright red berries; 'Variegata' (gold-dust plant) is female and has deep green leaves heavily sprinkled with yellow.

HORNBEAM
Carpinus

Light: full shade

Plant type: tree

Hardiness: Zones 3-9

Height: 30 to 60 feet

Soil and Moisture: well-drained, moist to dry

Interest: foliage, bark

Care: easy

◀ Carpinus betulus 'Fastigiata'

A deciduous tree with crisp summer foliage, smooth gray bark, and a well-contoured winter silhouette, hornbeam (also called ironwood) makes a handsome specimen tree. Because it has dense foliage that takes well to pruning, however, it is often used as a hedge or screen. The dark green leaves may turn yellow or brown in fall. Hornbeam has extremely hard wood that was once used to make ox yokes.

Growing and care:
A highly adaptable and trouble-free plant, hornbeam tolerates a wide range of soil conditions. Plant in spring and keep well watered until established. European hornbeam prefers mostly sunny locations, while American hornbeam does best in full shade.

Selected species and varieties:
C. betulus (European hornbeam, common hornbeam) is pyramidal when young, maturing to a rounded crown, growing 40 to 60 feet tall under average conditions with a spread of 30 to 40 feet, bearing sharply toothed leaves 2½ to 5 inches long and 1 to 2 inches wide that remain unusually pest-free; 'Columnaris' has a densely branched steeple-shaped outline; 'Fastigiata' grows 30 to 40 feet tall with an oval to vaselike shape, and a forked trunk; Zones 4-8. *C. caroliniana* (American hornbeam) grows from 20 to 30 feet tall with a spreading canopy of toothed, roughly oblong leaves and smooth, gray bark.

SWEET BOX
Sarcococca

Light: full shade	
Plant type: shrub	
Hardiness: Zones 5-8	
Height: 1½ to 5 feet	
Soil and Moisture: well-drained, moist, fertile	
Interest: foliage, fragrance, fruit	
Care: moderate	

◀ Sarcococca hookerana var. humilis

A handsome plant with year-round ornamental value, sweet box has shiny narrow leaves on its roundly mounded shape. In late winter to early spring, inconspicuous but fragrant white flowers bloom, to be replaced by shiny black or red berries that linger into fall. *Sarcococca* spreads slowly by suckers; the low form makes a good ground cover.

Growing and care:
Best grown in Zone 8 in the South and along the Pacific Coast, *S. confusa* and *S. ruscifolia* need shelter in Zone 7. Protect from winter winds. Add leaf mold or peat moss to the soil to improve drainage. Mulch to conserve moisture.

Selected species and varieties:
S. confusa has leaves to 2 inches long and ¾ inch wide on a densely branched shrub growing 3 to 5 feet tall and wide; Zones 7-8. *S. hookerana* var. *humilis* (Himalayan sarcococca) is 1½ to 2 feet tall and wide, blooming in early spring under 2- to 3½-inch-long and ½-inch-wide leaves. *S. ruscifolia* (fragrant sarcococca, fragrant sweet box) bears very fragrant flowers and red fruits on a 3-foot-high mound with an equal spread; Zones 7-8.

TERNSTROEMIA
Ternstroemia

Light: full shade	
Plant type: shrub	
Hardiness: Zones 7-10	
Height: 6 to 15 feet	
Soil and Moisture: well-drained, moist, fertile	
Interest: flowers, foliage, fragrance	
Care: easy	

◀ Ternstroemia gymnanthera

Leathery leaves that open brownish red and mature to rich, glossy green clothe the gracefully arching branches of ternstroemia. In early summer small clusters of fragrant creamy white flowers put on a modest display. Small red berries turn black and last through winter. Primarily grown for its foliage, ternstroemia works well as a foundation plant or hedge; it can also be trained into a small tree.

Growing and care:
Although Japanese ternstroemia grows best in rich, slightly acid soil that stays moist, it tolerates occasional drought. Good drainage is essential. Given suitable conditions, the species is usually problem-free. Prune after flowering. Propagate by stem cuttings.

Selected species and varieties:
T. gymnanthera [sometimes confused with *Cleyera japonica*] (Japanese ternstroemia) grows 10 to 15 feet tall and wide with elliptical to oblong 2- to 6-inch-long leaves often arranged in whorls on the ends of branches and ½-inch flowers produced in clusters on the previous year's growth. Bloom and berries occur only on mature plants.

WITCH HAZEL
Hamamelis

Light: full shade	
Plant type: shrub, tree	
Hardiness: Zones 3-8	
Height: 6 to 20 feet	
Soil and Moisture: well-drained, moist	
Interest: flowers, foliage, fragrance	
Care: easy	

◀ Hamamelis japonica 'Zuccariniana'

Witch hazels brighten the fall and winter landscape with heavily fragrant yellow to red flowers on angular branches, sometimes appearing long after their colorful foliage has fallen. The two-valved dry fruit capsules explode, propelling the black seeds many feet away.

Growing and care:

Common and American witch hazels can tolerate heavy, poorly drained clay but grow best in well-drained, rich forest loams. Give Chinese and Japanese witch hazels well-drained acid soil to which organic matter has been added. Prune *H.* x *intermedia* to encourage dense branching.

Selected species and varieties:

H. x *intermedia* 'Arnold Promise' grows to 20 feet tall and wide with 1½-inch primrose yellow flowers in winter to early spring and gray-green foliage that becomes yellow, orange, or red in fall; hardy to Zone 5; 'Diane' grows 14 to 20 feet tall, bearing slightly fragrant orange-red flowers with purple-red calyxes and yellow-orange to red autumn foliage; 'Jelena' (sometimes called 'Copper Beauty') has copper-colored flowers and orange-red fall foliage; 'Primavera' has very fragrant prolific clear yellow flowers borne later than the species; 'Ruby Glow' bears coppery red to reddish brown flowers and orange-red fall foliage. *H. japonica* 'Sulphurea' (Japanense witch hazel) grows 10 to 15 feet high and wide with an open flat-topped habit, producing yellow flowers with red calyx cups in late winter and lustrous green leaves that turn yellow, red, and purplish in fall; hardy to Zone 5; 'Zuccariniana' has rich yellow flowers with a hint of green inside the calyx. *H. mollis* 'Goldcrest' (Chinese witch hazel) is an oval, broadly open large shrub or small tree 10 to 15 feet tall and wide with medium green leaves in summer that turn a vivid yellow to yellow-orange in fall and fragrant yellow flowers with red-brown calyx cups blooming for a long period in winter; reliably hardy to Zone 6; 'Pallida' has a spreading habit and lustrous leaves, with yellow flowers suffused with a blush of chartreuse in late winter; hardy to Zone 5. *H. vernalis* (American witch hazel) has a broad multistemmed rounded outline 6 to 10 feet tall with a greater spread, producing very fragrant yellow to red flowers from late winter to early spring and medium to dark green foliage in summer that turns golden yellow in fall; hardy to Zone 4; 'Carnea' has richly colored flowers with a red calyx and petals that are red at the base blending to orange at the tip. *H. virginiana* (common witch hazel) is a large shrub to small tree 20 feet tall and equally wide with angular spreading branches and fragrant yellow flowers that emerge in mid- to late fall, sometimes just as its 4- to 6-inch leaves have turned yellow.

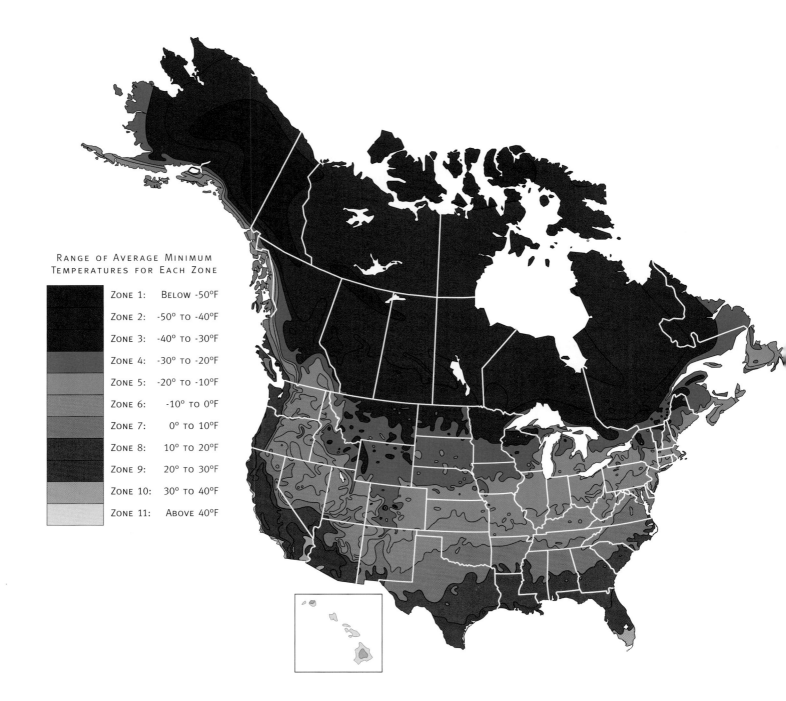

RANGE OF AVERAGE MINIMUM
TEMPERATURES FOR EACH ZONE

ZONE 1:   BELOW -50°F

ZONE 2:   -50° TO -40°F

ZONE 3:   -40° TO -30°F

ZONE 4:   -30° TO -20°F

ZONE 5:   -20° TO -10°F

ZONE 6:   -10° TO 0°F

ZONE 7:   0° TO 10°F

ZONE 8:   10° TO 20°F

ZONE 9:   20° TO 30°F

ZONE 10:   30° TO 40°F

ZONE 11:   ABOVE 40°F

A ZONE MAP OF THE UNITED STATES AND CANADA

A plant's winter hardiness is critical in deciding whether it is suitable for your garden. The map above divides the United States and Canada into 11 climatic zones based on average minimum temperatures, as compiled by the U.S. Department of Agriculture. Find your zone and check the zone information in the plant encyclopedia chapters to help you choose the plants most likely to flourish in your climate.

The editors wish to thank Henry W. Art, Williamstown, MA, and Donna Smallin, Troy, NY, for their valuable assistance in the preparation of this volume.

The sources for the illustrations that appear in this book are listed below. Credits from left to right are separated by semicolons; credits from top to bottom are separated by dashes.

Cover: Jerry Pavia. Back cover insets: Joanne Pavia—Carole Ottesen—Jerry Pavia—Jerry Pavia. End papers: Jerry Pavia/designed by Louise G. Smith. 1: Jerry Pavia. 2, 3: © Allan Mandell, Garden Photographer, Inc. 6, 7: Jerry Pavia. 9: Jerry Pavia. 11: Jerry Pavia. 13: Jerry Pavia. 15: © Pam Spaulding/Positive Images. 17: © Patricia J. Bruno/Positive Images. 19: © Pam Spaulding/Positive Images. 21: © Patricia J. Bruno/Positive Images. 23: © Pam Spaulding/Positive Images. 25: © Harry Haralambou/Positive Images. 26, 27: © Patricia J. Bruno/Positive Images. 28: Jerry Pavia. 29: Jerry Pavia; © Walter Chandoha. 30: Jerry Pavia; Cynthia Woodyard. 31: Joanne Pavia; Thomas E. Eltzroth. 32: Jerry Pavia. 33: Jerry Pavia; Richard Shiell. 34: Peter Loewer; Jerry Pavia. 35: Joanne Pavia. 36: Jerry Pavia; Richard Shiell. 37: Jerry Pavia; Thomas E. Eltzroth. 38: Jerry Pavia; Thomas E. Eltzroth. 39: Jerry Pavia. 40: Jerry Pavia; Charles Mann. 41: Jerry Pavia; Thomas E. Eltzroth. 42: Thomas E. Eltzroth; Jerry Pavia. 43: Joanne Pavia; Mark Turner. 44: Jerry Pavia. 45: © Walter Chandoha. 46: Jerry Pavia. 47: Jerry Pavia; © Crandall & Crandall. 48: M. W. Carlton/National Wildflower Research Center; Steven Still. 49: Jerry Pavia. 50: R. Todd Davis Photography; Thomas E. Eltzroth. 51: Jerry Pavia. 52: Jerry Pavia; Steven Still. 53: Cynthia Woodyard; Jerry Pavia. 54: Michael Dirr; Steven Still. 55: Joanne Pavia; Joseph G. Strauch, Jr. 56: C. Colston Burrell; Richard Shiell. 57: Jerry Pavia; Joanne Pavia. 58: Richard Shiell; Steven Still. 59: Jerry Pavia; Richard Shiell. 60: Joanne Pavia; C. Colston Burrell. 61: Michael Dirr; Richard Shiell. 62: R. Todd Davis Photography; Joanne Pavia. 63: Jerry Pavia; Thomas Eltzroth.

64: Joanne Pavia; Richard Shiell. 65: C. Colston Burrell; John A. Lynch. 66: Joanne Pavia; Holly H. Shimizu. 67: Joseph G. Strauch, Jr.; Jerry Pavia. 68: Jerry Pavia. 69: © Roger Foley/design by Sheela Lampietti; Jerry Pavia. 70: Joseph G. Strauch, Jr. 71: Steven Still; C. Colston Burrell. 72: Mark Turner; Joanne Pavia. 73: David Cavagnaro; Steven Still. 74: Bill Johnson; David Cavagnaro. 75: Michael Dirr; Steven Still. 76: Virginia R. Weiler; Jerry Pavia. 77: Charles Mann; Joanne Pavia. 78: Joanne Pavia; Joseph G. Strauch, Jr. 79: Joanne Pavia; André Viette. 80: Joanne Pavia; Bill Johnson. 81: Joanne Pavia; Jerry Pavia. 82: Jerry Pavia. 83: Jerry Pavia; Brent Heath. 84: Thomas E. Eltzroth; © Saxon Holt. 85: Robert E. Lyons; Eric Crichton Photos, Blanford Forum, Dorset. 86: © Saxon Holt; Jerry Pavia. 87: Jerry Pavia. 88: David Cavagnaro; Joanne Pavia. 89: Richard L. Doutt; © Michael S. Thompson. 90: Jerry Pavia. 91: Photos Horticultural, Ipswich, Suffolk; C. Colston Burrell. 92: Joanne Pavia. 93: Jerry Pavia. 94: J. S. Sira/Garden Picture Library, London; Richard Shiell. 95: © Michael S. Thompson; Photos Horticultural, Ipswich, Suffolk. 96: Jerry Pavia. 97: David Cavagnaro. 98: Brent Heath; judywhite. 99: Brent Heath; Thomas E. Eltzroth. 100: Andrew Lawson, Charlbury, Oxfordshire; Richard Shiell. 101: Richard Shiell; Jerry Pavia. 102: Jerry Pavia; Photos Horticultural, Ipswich, Suffolk. 103: Brent Heath; C. Colston Burrell. 104: Photos Horticultural, Ipswich, Suffolk; Brent Heath. 105: Brent Heath; Bill Johnson. 106: Dency Kane; Steven Foster. 107: Holly H. Shimizu; Dency Kane. 108, 109: Jerry Pavia. 110: Holly H. Shimizu; Thomas E. Eltzroth. 111: Holly H. Shimizu; Jerry Pavia. 112: Jerry Pavia; Dency Kane. 113: Joanne Pavia; Thomas E. Eltzroth. 114: Thomas E. Eltzroth. 115: Rita Buchanan; Richard Shiell. 116: Holly H. Shimizu. 117: Jerry Pavia; Joanne Pavia. 118: Dency Kane; Joanne Pavia. 119: Catriona Tudor Erler; Jerry Pavia. 120: Holly H. Shimizu; Jerry Pavia. 121: Jerry Pavia. 122: William H. Allen, Jr.; Jerry Pavia. 123: Richard Shiell. 124: Thomas E. Eltzroth; Holly H. Shimizu. 125: Richard Shiell. 126: Holly H. Shimizu; Jerry Pavia. 127: Joseph G. Strauch, Jr.; Photos Horticul-

tural, Ipswich, Suffolk. 128: © Roger Foley; Thomas E. Eltzroth. 129: Thomas E. Eltzroth; Dency Kane. 130: Jerry Pavia. 131: Thomas E. Eltzroth; Jerry Pavia. 132: Deni Bown/Oxford Scientific Films, Long Hanborough, Oxfordshire. 133: Dency Kane; Jerry Pavia. 134: Jerry Pavia; Richard Shiell. 135: Richard Day/Daybreak Imagery; Carole Ottesen. 136: Jerry Pavia; Dency Kane. 137: C. Colston Burrell; Richard Day/Daybreak Imagery. 138: Michael Dirr; © Michael S. Thompson. 139: Jerry Pavia. 140: Thomas E. Eltzroth; Jerry Pavia. 141: Jerry Pavia; Peter Haring. 142: Jerry Pavia. 143: Peter Haring; Jerry Pavia. 144: © Crandall & Crandall; Anita Sabarese. 145: Charles Mann; © Crandall & Crandall. 146: Peter Haring; Jerry Pavia. 147: R. Todd Davis Photography; Joseph G. Strauch, Jr. 148: R. Todd Davis Photography; Thomas E. Eltzroth. 149: Richard Shiell; Peter Haring. 150: Michael Dirr; Dency Kane. 151: Jerry Pavia. 152: Richard Shiell; Jerry Pavia. 153: Jerry Pavia; Michael Dirr. 154: Jerry Pavia. 155: Peter Haring; Jerry Pavia. 156: Jerry Pavia; Bill Johnson. 157: Richard Shiell; Jerry Pavia. 158: Jerry Pavia; Richard Shiell. 159, 160: Jerry Pavia. 161: Richard Shiell. 162: Mike Shoup; Peter Haring. 163: David Cavagnaro; Peter Haring. 164: Richard Shiell; Jerry Pavia. 165: R. Todd Davis Photography. 166: Peter Haring; Thomas E. Eltzroth. 167: Lefever/Grushow/Grant Heilman Photography, Inc.; © Runk/Schoenberger/Grant Heilman Photography, Inc. 168, 169: Jerry Pavia. 170: Jerry Pavia; Cynthia Woodyard. 171: Jerry Pavia. 172: Thomas E. Eltzroth; Jerry Pavia. 173: Jerry Pavia. 174: Thomas E. Eltzroth; David Cavagnaro. 175: Jerry Pavia; Bill Johnson. 176: Jerry Pavia; Thomas E. Eltzroth. 177: Jerry Pavia; Joanne Pavia. 178: Jerry Pavia. 179: Thomas E. Eltzroth; Jerry Pavia. 180: Jerry Pavia. 181: Peter Loewer; Photos Horticultural, Ipswich, Suffolk. 182: Thomas E. Eltzroth; Jerry Pavia. 183-185: Jerry Pavia. 186: Joanne Pavia. 187: Jerry Pavia. 188: Jerry Pavia; Cynthia Woodyard. 189: Jerry Pavia; Thomas E. Eltzroth. 190,191: Joanne Pavia. 192: Jerry Pavia. 193: Bill Johnson; Jerry Pavia. 194: Joseph G. Strauch, Jr.; Richard Shiell. 195: Richard Shiell;

Steven Still. 196: Thomas E. Eltzroth; Joseph G. Strauch, Jr. 197: Bill Johnson; © Saxon Holt. 198: Richard Shiell; Jerry Pavia. 199: Jerry Pavia; Richard Shiell. 200: Jerry Pavia; Joanne Pavia. 201: Jerry Pavia. 202: W. D. Bransford/National Wildflower Research Center; Jerry Pavia. 203: Jerry Pavia; R. Todd Davis Photography. 204: Jerry Pavia; Carole Ottesen. 205: Jerry Pavia; Carole Ottesen. 206: Jerry Pavia; Steven Still. 207: Jerry Pavia. 208: Joanne Pavia; Carole Ottesen. 209: John A. Lynch; Virginia R. Weiler. 210: David Cavagnaro; Jerry Pavia. 211: Jerry Pavia. 212: Carole Ottesen; Thomas E. Eltzroth. 213: Joanne Pavia; Jerry Pavia. 214: Joseph G. Strauch, Jr.; Jerry Pavia. 215: Joseph G. Strauch, Jr.; Jerry Pavia. 216: Steven Still; Jerry Pavia. 217: John A. Lynch; Andy Wasowski. 218: Photos Horticultural, Ipswich, Suffolk; Bill Johnson. 219: Charles Mann; Jerry Pavia. 220: Brent Heath; Joanne Pavia. 221: Brent Heath; © Michael S. Thompson. 222: Robert E. Lyons. 223: © Michael S. Thompson. 224: Joanne Pavia; Jerry Pavia. 225: Joseph G. Strauch, Jr. 226: Brent Heath. 227: Leonard G. Phillips; Robert E. Lyons. 228: Jerry Pavia; Andy Wasowski. 229: PhotoSynthesis™; W. D. Bransford/National Wildflower Research Center. 230: Holly H. Shimizu; Jerry Pavia. 231: Jerry Pavia; Dency Kane. 232: Holly H. Shimizu; Joanne Pavia. 233: Richard Shiell; Jerry Pavia. 234, 235: Jerry Pavia. 236: Dency Kane; Holly H. Shimizu. 237: Jerry Pavia. 238: Jerry Pavia; Joanne Pavia. 239, 240: Jerry Pavia. 241: Rita Buchanan; Jerry Pavia. 242: Catriona Tudor Erler; Dency Kane. 243: Jerry Pavia. 244: Jerry Pavia; Joanne Pavia. 245: Jerry Pavia. 246: Harry Smith Horticultural Photographic Collection, Wickford, Essex; Jerry Pavia. 247: Jerry Pavia; Michael Dirr. 248: Charles Mann; © Walter Chandoha. 249: Richard Shiell; Jerry Pavia. 250: Catriona Tudor Erler; Mark Lovejoy. 251: Jerry Pavia; © Michael S. Thompson. 252: Robert E. Lyons; R. Todd Davis Photography. 253: Steven Still; © Michael S. Thompson. 254: Jerry Pavia; Richard Shiell. 255: Carole Ottesen; Jerry Pavia. 256: Dency Kane; Jerry Pavia. 257: Richard Shiell; Peter Haring. 258: Jerry Pavia; Michael Dirr. 259: Michael Dirr; Jerry Pavia. 260: © 1997 Alan & Linda Detrick. 261:

Richard Shiell; Jerry Pavia. 262: Peter Haring; Jerry Pavia. 263: Joseph G. Strauch, Jr. 264, 265: Jerry Pavia. 266: Thomas E. Eltzroth; Jerry Pavia. 267: Richard Shiell; Jerry Pavia. 268: Derek Fell; Richard Shiell. 269: R. Todd Davis Photography; © 1997 Alan & Linda Detrick. 270: Peter Haring; Joanne Pavia. 271: Jerry Pavia. 272: Thomas E. Eltzroth; Jerry Pavia. 273: Thomas E. Eltzroth; Jerry Pavia. 274: Michael Dirr. 275: Richard Shiell; Jerry Pavia. 276: Joanne Pavia; © 1997 Alan & Linda Detrick. 277: Jerry Pavia. 278: C. Colston Burrell; Michael Dirr. 279: Joanne Pavia; Charles Mann. 280: Jerry Pavia; Joseph G. Strauch, Jr. 281: Michael Dirr; Richard Shiell. 282: Thomas E. Eltzroth; Jerry Pavia. 283: Jerry Pavia. 284, 285: Allan Mandell, Garden Photographer, Inc. 286: Jerry Pavia; Photos Horticultural, Ipswich, Suffolk. 287-289: Jerry Pavia. 290: Sally Kurtz; Thomas E. Eltzroth. 291: Jerry Pavia; David Cavagnaro. 292: © Crandall & Crandall; judywhite. 293: Jerry Pavia. 294: Steven Still; © 1997 Alan & Linda Detrick. 295: © Michael S. Thompson; Joseph G. Strauch, Jr. 296: Jerry Pavia; Joseph G. Strauch, Jr. 297: Joseph G. Strauch, Jr. 298: Charles Mann; Thomas E. Eltzroth. 299: Richard Shiell. 300: Jerry Pavia. 301: Jerry Pavia; Joseph G. Strauch, Jr. 302: Jerry Pavia; Bill Johnson. 303: Joanne Pavia; Richard Shiell. 304: Joanne Pavia; Jerry Pavia. 305: Jerry Pavia; Steven Still. 306: Bill Johnson; Carole Ottesen. 307: © Michael S. Thompson; © Crandall & Crandall. 308: Robert S. Hebb; Jerry Pavia. 309: R. Todd Davis Photography. 310: Virginia R. Weiler; John A. Lynch. 311: Jerry Pavia; Bill Johnson. 312: Richard Shiell; Jerry Pavia. 313: Eric Crichton Photos, Blanford Forum, Dorset; R. Todd Davis Photography. 314: C. Colston Burrell; Thomas E. Eltzroth. 315, 316: © Michael S. Thompson. 317: Rosalind Creasy; Carole Ottesen. 318: judywhite; Richard Shiell. 319: © Michael S. Thompson. 320: Joanne Pavia. 321: Jerry Pavia; © Michael S. Thompson. 322: © Michael S. Thompson; Jerry Pavia. 323: Jerry Pavia; Richard Shiell. 324: Richard Shiell; Jerry Pavia. 325: Richard Shiell; Jerry Pavia. 326: Jerry Pavia; Mark Turner. 327: Jerry Pavia. 328: Michael Dirr;

© Michael S. Thompson. 329: Jerry Pavia. 330: Jerry Pavia; Robert E. Lyons. 331: Joanne Pavia; Jerry Pavia. 332: Michael Dirr; Jerry Pavia. 333: Jerry Pavia. 334: Richard Shiell; Jerry Pavia. 335: Jerry Pavia. 336: Michael Dirr; Jerry Pavia. 337, 338: Jerry Pavia. 339: Jerry Pavia; judywhite. 340: Steven Still; Jerry Pavia. 341: Jerry Pavia; Richard Shiell. 342: Richard Shiell; Jerry Pavia. 343: Robert E. Lyons. 344: Jerry Pavia; Joseph G. Strauch, Jr. 345: Mike Shoup; R. Todd Davis Photography. 346, 347: R. Todd Davis Photography. 349: David Cavagnaro; Michael Dirr. 350: judywhite; Jerry Pavia. 351: Deni Bown/Oxford Scientific Films, Long Hanborough, Oxfordshire; Carole Ottesen. 352: Joanne Pavia; Jerry Pavia. 353: Jerry Pavia. 354: Joanne Pavia; C. Colston Burrell. 355: C. Colston Burrell; Jerry Pavia. 356: Joanne Pavia; Jerry Pavia. 357: R. Todd Davis Photography; Jerry Pavia. 358: Joanne Pavia. 359: Brent Heath; Richard Day/Daybreak Imagery. 360: Robert E. Lyons. 361: Joanne Pavia; Tom Ulrich/Oxford Scientific Films, Long Hanborough, Oxfordshire. 362: Rita Buchanan; Joseph G. Strauch, Jr. 363: © Walter Chandoha; Jerry Pavia. 364: Mark Turner; Jerry Pavia. 365, 366: Jerry Pavia. 367: Jerry Pavia; Thomas E. Eltzroth. 368: Jerry Pavia; Thomas E. Eltzroth. 369: © Michael S. Thompson. 370: Map by John Drummond, Time-Life Books, Inc.

TIME® LIFE BOOKS

Time-Life Books is a division of Time Life Inc.

TIME LIFE INC.
President and CEO: Jim Nelson

TIME-LIFE TRADE PUBLISHING
Vice President and Publisher: Neil Levin
Senior Director of Acquisitions and Editorial Resources:
  Jennifer Pearce
Director of New Product Development: Carolyn Clark
Director of Trade Sales: Dana Coleman
Director of Marketing: Inger Forland
Director of New Product Development: Teresa Graham
Director of Custom Publishing: John Lalor
Director of Special Markets: Robert Lombardi
Director of Design: Kate L. McConnell

PICK THE RIGHT PLANT
Managing Editor: Donia Ann Steele
Project Management: Kathleen Mallow
Picture Coordination: David Cheatham
Production Manager: Carolyn Clark
Technical Specialist (spiral): Monika Lynde
Project Coordinator (spiral): Jennifer L. Ward
Production Manager (spiral): Vanessa Hunnibell
Quality Assurance: James D. King, Stacy L. Eddy

**Produced by Storey Communications, Inc.,
Pownal, Vermont**
President: M. John Storey
Executive Vice President: Martha M. Storey
Custom Director: Amanda R. Haar
Custom Acquisitions Director: Deirdre Lynch
Custom Managing Editor: Catherine Gee Graney
Project Managers: Robert Pini and Andrea Reynolds
Book Design: Jonathan Nix/Verso Design
Production Assistance: Eileen Clawson, Jennifer Jepson,
  Betty Kodela, Erin Lincourt, Leslie Noyes, Stephanie Saunders
Editor: Charles W. G. Smith

Adapted from **The TIME-LIFE Complete Gardener** series.

©1998 Time Life Inc. All rights reserved.
No part of this book may be reproduced in any form or by any electronic or mechanical means, including information storage and retrieval devices or systems, without prior written permission from the publisher, except that brief passages may be quoted for reviews.

Pre-Press Services, Time-Life Imaging Center
Printed in U.S.A.
10 9 8 7 6 5 4 3 2 1

TIME-LIFE is a trademark of Time Warner Inc.,
and affiliated companies.

Library of Congress Cataloging-in-Publication Data
Pick the right plant: a sun and shade guide to successful plant
  selection / by the editors of Time-Life Books
    p. cm.
  Includes index.
  ISBN 0-7835-5293-9 (hardcover)
  ISBN 0-7370-0621-8 (deluxe spiral binding)
  1. Plants, Ornamental. 2. Plants, Ornamental—Selection.
3. Plants, Ornamental—United States. 4. Plants, Ornamental—Canada. I. Time-Life Books.
SB407.P48   1998   97-44631
635.9'54—dc21   CIP

Books produced by Time-Life Trade Publishing are available at a special bulk discount for promotional and premium use. Custom adaptations can also be created to meet your specific marketing goals. Call 1-800-323-5255.